Gender in Society Reader

Gender in Society Reader

Edited by **Amy Kaler**

OXFORD

UNIVERSITY PRESS

OXFORD
UNIVERSITY PRESS

Oxford University Press is a department of the University of Oxford.
It furthers the University's objective of excellence in research, scholarship,
and education by publishing worldwide. Oxford is a registered trade mark of
Oxford University Press in the UK and in certain other countries.

Published in Canada by
Oxford University Press
8 Sampson Mews, Suite 204,
Don Mills, Ontario M3C 0H5 Canada

www.oupcanada.com

Library and Archives Canada Cataloguing in Publication
Title: Gender in society reader / edited by Amy Kaler.
Names: Kaler, Amy, editor.
Description: Includes bibliographical references.
Identifiers: Canadiana (print) 20210228458 | Canadiana (ebook) 20210228539 | ISBN 9780195401431
(softcover) | ISBN 9780195401448 (spiral bound) | ISBN 9780190165451 (EPUB)
Subjects: LCSH: Sex role—Canada—Textbooks. | LCSH: Sex differences (Psychology)—Canada—Textbooks. |
LCSH: Gender identity—Canada—Textbooks. | LCSH: Sex discrimination—Canada—Textbooks. | LCSH:
Equality—Canada—Textbooks. | LCGFT: Textbooks.
Classification: LCC HQ1075.5.C3 G46 2021 | DDC 305.30971—dc23

Cover image: © iam2mai/Shutterstock
Cover and Interior design: Sherril Chapman

Oxford University Press is committed to our environment. Wherever possible,
our books are printed on paper which comes from responsible sources.

Printed in Canada by Marquis Book Printing

Contents

IV • Gendered Sexualities 131

V • Gendered Families 177

VI • The Gendered Classroom   217

VII • The Gendered Workplace   255

VIII • Gender and Media   297

IX • Gender and Violence   333

X • Gendered Activism   361

Preface

My work as an editor took place on Treaty 6 land, the traditional meeting ground of Métis, Dene, Cree, Blackfoot, Dene, Saulteaux, and Nakoda Sioux, as well as settlers from other nations.

Editing a collection like this is a pleasure and a challenge. The pleasure was in the chance to read widely and to familiarize myself with the liveliness and curiosity that characterizes the best gender research in Canada today. The challenge lay in the difficulty of choosing among the lively and invigorating array of research and scholarship on gender. For every article that you're going to read in this book, many others could just as easily have been chosen, which reflects the range of intellectual activity in this field.

If I were writing this introduction 20 years ago, or even 10 years ago, I'd probably start by saying something about how gender is one of the primary axes of differentiation in Canadian society, and how the social construction of masculinity and femininity shapes everyone's lives. All of that is still true, but gender is about much more than just sorting people and experiences into male and female, pink and blue. Thanks to the revolution in queer theory and nonbinary scholarship, we know that gender can't be reduced to two exclusive and exhaustive categories into which we're placed at birth. Transgender, third-gender, intragender, and agender lives are visible today as never before, and that makes the study of gender even more important and exciting than just the study of male/female binaries.

At the same time as the nonbinary revolution has been taking place, the revolution in intersectional thinking and scholarship has demonstrated that although gender is important everywhere, nowhere is it the *only* thing that's important. People make gender through social construction, and people also make race and sexuality and indigeneity and many other forms of social identification and collective experience. When we're talking about gender, we're never talking *only*

about gender. It's impossible to split off some parts of people's lives and say "Okay, that's gender happening there," while ignoring all the other things that are going on.

For this reader, I used several criteria in choosing texts to include. The most obvious criterion was that the texts had to be Canadian; they had to deal with the lives and experiences of Canadians, and ideally also be written by Canadian authors. I focused on the nationality of the texts not because I wanted to fill some arbitrary quota for Canadian content, but because I wanted to enable Canadian students to take a critical, analytical look at the country in which their own gendered identities are being formed. I wanted to avoid the problem my own students often complain about: the tendency to universalize American experiences and to treat the United States as the norm for the entire world.

My concern with Canadian specificity is consistent with the broader feminist imperative to question all universalizing tendencies and to de-centre the experiences of the powerful in our writing, thinking, and teaching. There is no question that Canada and the United States are similar in many ways when it comes to the workings of gender, but it's important not to just assume that if it's happening there, it's happening here too.

For similar reasons, I have prioritized qualitative accounts of lived experience over heavily quantitative texts. I don't think that qualitative research is somehow better or truer than quantitative studies, but I do think that qualitative work offers undergraduates a way, at least partially, to get inside the lifeworlds of gendered subjects, including those who are gendered differently from the students themselves. Qualitative work also enables readers to get a sense of the complex intersections of gender and other social categories, such as race, socio-economic class, sexuality, and bodily status, all of which shape the experience of being gendered in subtle but powerful ways. For students who are not deeply immersed in a social science discipline, qualitative accounts also offer a good way in to studying gender. I also wanted to retain sense of hope and possibility for the transformation of gender, creating a better, more humane world for everyone, no matter what gender they identify as.

I was lucky to have an excellent team at Oxford University Press Canada. Many thanks to Mariah Fleetham and Ian Nussbaum for all their work on behalf of this book. I'd also like to acknowledge the students in my Sociology of Gender classes at the University of Alberta. I hope this book intrigues, entertains, and possibly enlightens its readers.

Introduction

Amy Kaler

Twenty-first century Canada is a very interesting time to be a student of gender. In our daily lives, we're operating with two very different stories about gender.

On the one hand, we hear that males and females are fundamentally different, and this difference is so important that it must be acknowledged at every possible opportunity, starting with "gender reveal" parties before we're even born and continuing through pink and blue Legos and Disney princesses before we even reach the age when we might be reading this book.

On the other hand, we learn that gender is not really a thing anymore—girls can do anything boys can do, and the very idea that everybody fits into either the pink box or the blue box is being challenged by gender neutrality and the increasing number of people who identify as transgender or genderqueer.

Which of these stories is right? The story about how different men and women are, or the story about how the male/female binary is old-school? Well, both.

The gender binary is being deconstructed with a speed that would have amazed earlier generations of feminists and gender activists. The idea that maleness and femaleness are the foundational building blocks of personal identity and collective experience is no longer credible in a world in which people can identify as transgender, agender, demigender, cisgender, and more.

Media and popular culture have been leading the way in producing new representations of gender and new ways to think about it, with political activism flourishing both on and off the screen. Not everyone is on board with the proliferation of gendered identities in the twenty-first century, and some people are nostalgic for a world in which boys grew up to be manly men and girls became sweet and pretty women and no other kinds of people existed. But the multiplication of gender identities in Canada can't be turned back.

Nonetheless, the male/female, masculine/feminine division remains important. Although individual experiences of gender are diverse, there are two near-universal phenomena that define gender in almost every culture we have ever known. First, *virtually every single society differentiates people on the basis of gender.* Why are women and men perceived as different in every known society? What are the differences that are perceived? Why is gender such an important way of differentiating who does what work, under what conditions, and gets what rewards (also known as the division of labour)? Second, *virtually every known society is based on male domination.* Why are social, political, ideological, material, and economic resources divided unequally between men and others? Why do men end up with more money, leisure time, prestige, and possessions than others do, time and time again?

As long as the male/female binary is the template for dividing up power and responsibility among people, the relationship between that group of people called *men* and that group of people called *women* will be a powerful force in social life. Even if we don't personally identify as male or female (or if we do identify as male or female but don't accept the cultural baggage that goes along with those designations), we can't help but be affected by the state of gender relations in the society in which we live. Gender remains a powerful organizing force, even as the gender categories we've inherited from the people who came before us are being reworked and reimagined. Understanding how the masculine/feminine divide shapes our experiences in families, schools, workplaces, and pretty much any other public or private setting helps us understand our own lives.

In the past three decades, the pioneering work of feminist scholars, both in traditional disciplines and in women's and gender studies, has made us very aware of how gender affects individual life experiences and how individuals collectively create gender. We know that gender is changeable, that some experiences are more strongly gendered than others, and that gender interacts with other forms of categorization, such as race, class, sexuality, and religion, to influence individual identities. Today, people are probably more conscious of gender as a social force and of gender inequality than at any other time in history.

It's important to note that we are talking about broad social trends here. Not every individual man has more power than every individual woman. Other social categories, such as race, class, and religion, also influence the distribution of the good things in life. Nonetheless, when looking at societies at the collective level, men, as a group, almost always hold more power and resources, on average, than do women as a group.

Of course, there are dramatic differences across societies regarding the ways in which men and women are thought to be different, the levels of gender inequality, and the amount of power (including violence) that is used to maintain systems of difference and domination. But the basic fact remains: *Virtually every society known to us is founded on assumptions of gender difference, which produces gender inequality, and these assumptions are based on the belief that there are two physically distinct types of people.* How is this possible? Since human beings everywhere are the same in their biological attributes, is it true that gender inequality is just written on our bodies?

Gender, masculine and feminine, is often assumed to be based on biology. Human anatomy—physical sex—sets the stage on which the dramas of gender are enacted. But this biological explanation falls very short. Although anatomy varies very little from society to society, experiences of gender vary enormously. And it has been the task of the social and behavioural sciences to explore the variations in gender. Biological universalism can't explain this diversity. This is the point at which the social and behavioural sciences—anthropology, history, psychology, sociology—have all had an important role to play in our understanding of gender.

What they tell us is that what it means to be a man or a woman varies in four significant ways. First, the *meanings* of gender differences vary from one society to another. What it means to be a man or a woman differs—whether in nineteenth-century Alberta, among Indigenous Peoples in the Australian outback today, in rural Norway a decade ago, or in medieval Japan. It has been the task of anthropologists to specify some of those differences, to explore the different meanings that gender has in different cultures. Some cultures, like our own, encourage men to be stoic and to prove their masculinity, and men in other cultures seem even more preoccupied with demonstrating sexual prowess than North American men seem to be. Other cultures prescribe a more relaxed definition of masculinity, based on civic participation, emotional responsiveness, and the collective provision for the community's needs. Some cultures encourage women to be decisive and competitive; others insist that women are naturally passive, helpless, and dependent.

Second, the experiences of being masculine or feminine vary within any one culture *over time*. The experience of being a man or a woman in seventeenth-century Quebec is probably very different from what it might mean there today. Your grandparents' experience of gender relations is not going to be the same as the experience of people who are born today in your grandparents' hometown. Gender is often intertwined with tradition and heritage, but it's never simply passed down from one generation to the next.

Third, gender is never simply gender, all by itself. Our experiences as gendered people are shaped by our experiences with other forms of social categorization, such as race, religion, or class. Since the 1970s, social scientists have come to realize that it is impossible to isolate gender and study it in a vacuum, detached from other forms of identity. Early sociologists who did so fell into the error of assuming that the experiences of certain gendered people with high visibility and social power—in North America, typically white, middle-class anglophones—can be generalized to all men or women.

Feminist scholars of colour have provided a strong corrective to the tendency to simply extrapolate from the experiences of the white middle class—tendencies that unfortunately have not disappeared from the social sciences. These scholars have argued that gender should be seen as "intersectional," in the words of Kimberlé Crenshaw. Intersectionality means that gender is one of many ways in which people categorize and come to understand themselves and others, and that these different ways of understanding influence one another. Activists in broad-based social movements have called the same phenomenon "unbreakapartability" (Crew, 2009), recognizing that all forms of inequality and oppression are connected, so that we cannot study inequalities of gender, for instance, without taking into consideration the effects of race or sexual orientation or economic class.

What does intersectionality mean for individuals? In everyday life, this means that being a young, white, Canadian man (for example) is both similar to and different from being a man of colour, or an immigrant man, or an older man. All these men share an identification with masculinity, but the ways in which they "do" masculinity, and the ways in which others interact with them, may be very different. It also means that when we look at stratification or hierarchy through a gender lens, we see more than simply men and women as two distinct groups. For instance, while men still out-earn women in Canada, when we look at average salaries for full-time, full-year work the gender picture becomes more nuanced when we broaden our lens to include racial categories. White women, on average, out-earn men of colour, while men (and women) of different racial categories are distributed unevenly across the Canadian workforce. We are never purely or simply just men or just women.

Fourth, the meaning of masculinity and femininity will change *over the life course* as any individual person grows. Growing up and growing older brings new challenges and new opportunities for individuals to experience life as gendered beings, from early childhood through adolescence, adulthood, midlife, and the senior years. Accepting the idea that individuals face different developmental tasks as they grow and develop, psychologists have examined the ways in which the meanings of masculinity and femininity change over the course of a person's life. The issues confronting a man about proving himself and feeling successful and the social institutions in which he will attempt to enact those experiences will change, as will the meanings of femininity for prepubescent women, women in childbearing years, and post-menopausal women, or for women entering the labour market or those retiring from it.

Finally, the meanings of gender will vary *among* different groups of women and men within any particular culture at any particular time. Simply put, not all Canadian men and women are the same. Our experiences are also structured by class, race, ethnicity, age, sexuality, and region of the country. Each of these axes modifies the others. When we focus on gender in this book, we don't assume that it is consistent in the face of all these other kinds of differences. Imagine, for example, an older, black, gay man in Montreal and a young, white, heterosexual male farmer in southern Saskatchewan. Wouldn't they have different definitions of masculinity? Or imagine a 22-year-old lesbian Somali Canadian in Toronto and a wealthy, white, Irish Catholic widow in Newfoundland. Wouldn't their experiences of being female be very different? One of the important elements of a sociological approach is to explore the differences *among* men and *among* women since, as it turns out, these are often more decisive than the differences between women and men.

If gender varies across cultures, over historical time, over the life course, and among men and women within any one culture, this means we really cannot speak of masculinity or femininity as though they were constant, universal essences that are common to all women and to all men. Rather, gender is an ever-changing assemblage of meanings, behaviours, opportunities, and resources. It's more appropriate (and more realistic) to think of *masculinities* and *femininities* rather than *masculinity* and *femininity* as though these words meant the same thing everywhere and all the time.

At the same time, we can't forget that all masculinities and femininities are not created equal. Some expressions of masculinity and femininity are more powerful and persuasive than others. In North American society, almost everyone can point to models of idealized femininity and masculinity, standards to which individuals learn to compare themselves (and almost always find themselves wanting).

We also learn what is considered *unfeminine* or *unmasculine*. In fact, some sociologists and psychologists would argue that North Americans are less preoccupied with emulating the models of their own gender than they are with avoiding excessive resemblance to the other gender. Think of the horror with which small boys recoil from being called a "sissy." And while many women admire the androgynous style and range of gender expression available to women at the beginning of the twenty-first century, fewer actually embrace the label "mannish." Men in particular are often under pressure to make it clear—eternally, compulsively, decidedly—that they are not like women.

In this book, we begin with some of the most important tools for thinking about gender in Part I,

which is on "ways of knowing" what we think we know about gender. You'll probably find yourself returning to these articles again and again as you make your way through the rest of the book.

Part II shows that gender is not *only* about gender but intersects with other social categories such as race. Here we emphasize racism and racialization because these processes are about the distribution of power rather than just about differences among groups of people.

Part III begins our discussion of the most basic unit of social life, the body itself. Our human bodies are never just human bodies—they bear the marks of gender in what we do with our bodies and how our bodies are "read" by others, like texts about our gendered identities. Through our bodies, we express some of the most intimate and important relationships in our lives, and Part IV explores these gendered intimacies.

The next three sections focus on gendered institutions. By institutions I mean not buildings of stone or concrete, but recurrent patterns of interactions connected through shared strategies and goals, even when these goals may not be explicit or obvious. In this way, a baby shower can be considered a social institution (and a very gendered one at that!) and so can the United Nations, the café where you get your morning coffee, or a AAA hockey team. Some institutions are extremely gendered, by which we mean that men's and women's experiences in these institutions are very different—just think about a traditional white wedding—and that they strongly reinforce ideas about gender. Other institutions may be less gendered—think about an organic chemistry class, for instance—in that gender is not a prominent feature of the institution, although gender may be present in subtle, unexpected ways.

For most people, the primary social institution through which we learn gender is the family. In Part V, we examine families as institutions that are both gendered *and* gendering, from which individuals go forth to engage with bigger, broader institutions. For most people, school provides the first encounter with the world beyond the family, and the process of learning (both the formal classroom subjects and the "hidden curriculum" of the playgrounds, halls, and cafeterias) is often deeply gendered. This gendering is explored in Part VI, where we investigate educational institutions.

After, or often during, formal education, most individuals work, whether for money in the paid workforce or without pay in the tasks of raising children and running households. Part VII examines both the work*place* and the work*force* as institutions structured by gender.

Family, school, and work—is that all there is in a gendered life? Most people would quickly point out the pervasive, even saturating, influence of media. Thanks to new technologies, words and images of gender, carrying explicit and implicit messages, are inescapable, and Part VIII on media explores some of these representations of gender.

In Part IX, we examine the most poisonous manifestation of gender inequalities—gender violence. This type of violence is perpetrated by people who believe that some aspect of their gender (usually, but not always, some aspect of masculinity) legitimates their use of violence against others who appear to threaten their rigid notions about gender. Gender-based violence, particularly when it intersects with racism or other forms of marginalization, may also be excused, trivialized, or even encouraged. In the future, the real measure of gender transformation will be the extent to which gender violence is eradicated so an individual's

gender no longer determines their likelihood of perpetrating or experiencing violence.

Fortunately, movements for the transformation of gender are thriving. Despite the pervasive gendering influences of all these institutions, human beings are not passive recipients of ideas about gender who create and re-create inegalitarian social structures without thinking. Part X on gendered social movements explores some of the ways in which people have rethought and reworked gender, with varying degrees of success and with not a little controversy.

I hope you come away from this book with the sense that you're living in the most interesting time possible to be reading about gender. This is because, paradoxically, when we study gender we see plenty of other forces at work too. Gender is never just gender by itself—other social formations like race, class, ability, religion, and so forth are always present in gendered lives. Old certainties about gender—including the idea that there are only two genders—are giving way to new ideas. At the same time, the gender inequalities that have accorded the lion's share of power, authority, and resources to men haven't faded away. When you finish this book, I hope you see the world just a bit differently, and that you're able to see gender at work both in yourself and in the institutions that shape your social life.

Reference

Crew, L. A. (2009, January/February). "Ideas in Action: An
    LA Story." *Left Turn* (31), p. 54.

Part I
Gendered Ways of Knowing

Before we can think about the ways that gender manifests itself in social life, we have to think about gender itself. What do we know about gender? More to the point, how do we know what we think we know about gender? We open with one of the classic statements on gender and culture. Candace West and Don Zimmerman's foundational article on gender as something that is enacted in everyday life clarifies and develops the concept of "doing gender." From this perspective, gender is not a way of dividing the human species into two groups, nor is it a quality possessed by individuals, objects, or situations. Instead, gender exists as interpersonal actions; an infinite set of interpersonal encounters through patterns, and variations emerge related to the gender of the actor.

Susan Bordo's reflections on the relationship between bodies and gender is also a classic (and is still hotly debated). Bordo claims that bodies are not the foundation of gender (male/female, man/woman) but the grounds on which gender is played out. Using anorexia and "hysteria" to make her point, she claims that our physical selves are also always gendered selves.

Although much gender scholarship has focused on women, gender isn't just something that women have, and that's where Carrigan and his co-authors come in. They not only think about what masculinity is, they also provide a short history of the "ways of knowing" about gender that have predominated in the social sciences, demonstrating that knowledge is always situated.

Collins and Bilge, major figures in the intersectionality revolution in social sciences of the past couple of decades, provide grounded examples of how we come to know about gender—and show that what we know about gender is never just about gender: It's also about race, class, and many other social categories.

Questions for Critical Thought

1. Is it possible to live in the world without "doing gender"? Or perhaps more accurately, is it possible to live in the world without being interpreted by others as a gendered person?

2. West and Zimmerman contend that most of our "doing gender" is done unconsciously—that is, men and women are not constantly trying to conform to an idealized idea of gender norms, but rather have internalized concepts of what is appropriate for members of their sex category and deploy these concepts unconsciously. Can you recall times in which you have been conscious of "doing gender"—where you have deliberately shaped your behaviour, appearance, or interactions to be consistent with generally accepted norms for your sex category?

3. Imagine that you woke up one morning to discover that your best friend had changed their gender. How do you think they might be different? How might they be the same?

4. Some transgender people choose to "pass" as a member of a particular gender, while others choose to disrupt the assumption of a two-gender social system. What does a transgender person have to do to pass in a society that is based on the assumption that there are two and only two genders? How might transgender people disrupt the two-gender system through the choice not to pass?

5. Could you successfully pass as a member of a different gender if you wanted to do so?

6. What did you learn about gender in secondary school?

7. Have you ever had an experience like the ones Collins and Bilge describe, where you're in a situation that makes you extremely conscious of gender, or of race or class or ability as they intersect with gender?

8. Many scholars following West and Zimmerman have argued that the social censure men face for not doing gender in an approved way—for "acting like a girl" or "being a sissy"—is much stronger than the social censure women face for not doing femininity in conventional ways. Has this been true in your experience? If so, why do you think this asymmetry exists?

Chapter 1

Overview

By now you will have become familiar with the idea that sex and gender are not the same thing—that our physical bodies do not always determine what course our lives as gendered individuals will take. So if gender is not sex, what is gender? This classic essay written in 1987 is an early attempt by prominent sociologists to grapple with that question. They define gender as an "accomplishment"—something that is done or achieved, not a trait or personality characteristic, or a label stuck on people with particular types of bodies. We "do gender" through our gender displays, which are visible and (usually) intelligible to others.

Using the experience of Agnes, a transgender woman, West and Zimmerman differentiate between sex (our biological hardware), sex category (the social systems for classifying bodies based on that hardware, or on the presumption that individuals possess that hardware), and gender: the "ongoing task" of being a woman or man and fitting one's actions to social expectations about how members of particular sex categories will behave in given situations. West and Zimmerman emphasize that doing gender is always improvisational—there is no set "gender script" that dictates how a man or woman ought to act, so we are continually reinventing gender as we go, through our interactions with others. How exactly we do this is still unclear, so West and Zimmerman lay out a research agenda for understanding how humans become competent gender actors.

By focusing on the improvisational quality of gender and by emphasizing that it is accomplished through interactions with, and in response to, the actions of our fellow gendered humans, West and Zimmerman moved beyond the confines of gender-as-role, which had dominated much sociological and psychological thinking in the twentieth century, and paved the way for the emergence of postmodern and post-structural ways of thinking about gender.

Doing Gender

Candace West and Don H. Zimmerman

In the beginning, there was sex and there was gender. Those of us who taught courses in the area in the late 1960s and early 1970s were careful to distinguish one from the other. Sex, we told students, was what was ascribed by biology: anatomy, hormones, and physiology. Gender, we said, was an achieved status: that which is constructed through psychological, cultural, and social means. To introduce the difference between the two, we drew on singular case studies of hermaphrodites and anthropological investigations of "strange and exotic tribes."

West, Candace, and Don H. Zimmerman. "Doing Gender," *Gender & Society* (Vol. 1, No. 2), pp. 125–51, copyright 1987 by Sociologists for Women in Society. Reprinted by Permission of SAGE Publications.

Inevitably (and understandably), in the ensuing weeks of each term, our students became confused. Sex hardly seemed a "given" in the context of research that illustrated the sometimes ambiguous and often conflicting criteria for its ascription. And gender seemed much less an "achievement" in the context of the anthropological, psychological, and social imperatives we studied—the division of labour, the formation of gender identities, and the social subordination of women by men. Moreover, the received doctrine of gender socialization theories conveyed the strong message that while gender may be "achieved," by about age five, it was certainly fixed, unvarying, and static— much like sex.

Since about 1975, the confusion has intensified and spread far beyond our individual classrooms. For one thing, we learned that the relationship between biological and cultural processes was far more complex—and reflexive—than we previously had supposed. . . .

Our purpose in this article is to propose an ethnomethodologically informed, and therefore distinctively sociological, understanding of gender as a routine, methodical, and recurring accomplishment. We contend that the "doing" of gender is undertaken by women and men whose competence as members of society is hostage to its production. Doing gender involves a complex of socially guided perceptual, interactional, and micropolitical activities that cast particular pursuits as expressions of masculine and feminine "natures."

When we view gender as an accomplishment, an achieved property of situated conduct, our attention shifts from matters internal to the individual and focuses on interactional and, ultimately, institutional arenas. In one sense, of course, it is individuals who "do" gender. But it is a situated doing, carried out in the virtual or real presence of others who are presumed to be oriented to its production. Rather than as a property of individuals, we conceive of gender as an emergent feature of social situations: both as an outcome of and a rationale for various social arrangements and as a means of legitimating one of the most fundamental divisions of society. . . .

To elaborate our proposal, we suggest that important but often overlooked distinctions be observed among *sex, sex category*, and *gender*. *Sex* is a determination made through the application of socially agreed upon biological criteria for classifying persons as females or males. The criteria for classification can be genitalia at birth or chromosomal typing before birth, and they do not necessarily agree with one another. Placement in a *sex category* is achieved through application of the sex criteria, but in everyday life, categorization is established and sustained by the socially required identificatory displays that proclaim one's membership in one or the other category. In this sense, one's sex category presumes one's sex and stands as proxy for it in many situations, but sex and sex category can vary independently; that is, it is possible to claim membership in a sex category even when the sex criteria are lacking. *Gender*, in contrast, is the activity of managing situated conduct in light of normative conceptions of attitudes and activities appropriate for one's sex category. Gender activities emerge from and bolster claims to membership in a sex category. . . .

We begin with an assessment of the received meaning of gender, particularly in relation to the roots of this notion in presumed biological differences between women and men.

Perspectives on Sex and Gender

In Western societies, the accepted cultural perspective on gender views women and men as naturally and unequivocally defined categories of being, with distinctive psychological and behavioural propensities that can be predicted from their reproductive functions. Competent adult members of these societies see differences between the two as fundamental and enduring—differences seemingly supported by the division of labour into women's and men's work and an often elaborate differentiation of feminine and masculine attitudes and behaviours that are prominent features of social organization. Things are the way they are by virtue of the fact that men are men and women are women—a division perceived to be natural and rooted in biology, producing, in turn, profound psychological, behavioural, and social consequences. The structural arrangements of a society are presumed to be responsive to these differences. . . .

Taking a different tack, role theory has attended to the social construction of gender categories, called "sex roles" or, more recently, "gender roles" and has analyzed how these are learned and enacted. . . . Role theory has emphasized the social and dynamic aspect of role construction and enactment. But at the level of face-to-face interaction, the application of role theory to gender poses problems of its own. Roles are *situated* identities—assumed and relinquished as the situation demands—rather than *master identities*, such as the sex category, that cut across situations.

Unlike most roles, such as "nurse," "doctor," and "patient," or "professor" and "student," gender has no specific site or organizational context.

Moreover, many roles are already gender marked, so that special qualifiers—such as "female doctor" or "male nurse"—must be added to exceptions to the rule. Thorne (1980) observes that conceptualizing gender as a role makes it difficult to assess its influence on other roles and reduces its explanatory usefulness in discussions of power and inequality. Drawing on Rubin (1975), Thorne calls for a reconceptualization of women and men as distinct social groups, constituted in "concrete, historically changing—and generally unequal—social relationships" (Thorne, 1980: 11).

We argue that gender is not a set of traits, nor a variable, nor a role, but the product of social doings of some sort. What then is the social doing of gender? It is more than the continuous creation of the meaning of gender through human actions. We claim that gender itself is constituted through interaction. . . .

Sex, Sex Category, and Gender

Garfinkel's (1967) case study of Agnes, a transsexual raised as a boy who adopted a female identity at age 17 and underwent a sex reassignment operation several years later, demonstrates how gender is created through interaction and, at the same time, structures interaction. Agnes, whom Garfinkel characterized as a "practical methodologist," developed a number of procedures for passing as a "normal, natural female" both prior to and after her surgery. She had the practical task of managing the fact that she possessed male genitalia and that she lacked the social resources a girl's biography would presumably provide in everyday interaction. In short, she needed to display herself as a woman, simultaneously learning what it was to be a woman. Of necessity, this full-time pursuit took place at a time when most people's gender would be well-accredited and routinized. Agnes had to consciously contrive what the vast majority of women do without thinking. She was not "faking" what "real" women do

naturally. She was obliged to analyze and figure out how to act within socially structured circumstances and conceptions of femininity that women born with appropriate biological credentials come to take for granted early on. As in the case of others who must "pass" . . . , Agnes's case makes visible what culture has made invisible—the accomplishment of gender. . . .

Sex

Agnes did not possess the socially agreed-upon biological criteria for classification as a member of the female sex. Still, Agnes regarded herself as a female, albeit a female with a penis, which a woman ought not to possess. The penis, she insisted, was a "mistake" in need of remedy (Garfinkel, 1967). Like other competent members of our culture, Agnes honoured the notion that there are "essential" biological criteria that unequivocally distinguish females from males. However, if we move away from the common-sense viewpoint, we discover that the reliability of these criteria is not beyond question. Moreover, other cultures have acknowledged the existence of "cross-genders" and the possibility of more than two sexes.

More central to our argument is Kessler and McKenna's (1978) point that genitalia are conventionally hidden from public inspection in everyday life; yet we continue, through our social rounds, to "observe" a world of two naturally, normally sexed persons. It is the *presumption* that essential criteria exist, and would or should be there if looked for, that provides the basis for sex categorization. Drawing on Garfinkel, Kessler and McKenna argue that "female" and "male" are cultural events—products of what they term the "gender attribution process"—rather than some collection of traits, behaviours, or even physical attributes. Illustratively, they cite the child who, viewing a picture of someone clad in a suit and a tie, contends, "It's a man, because he has a pee-pee" (Kessler and McKenna, 1978: 154). Translation: "He must have a pee-pee [an essential characteristic] because I see the *insignia* of a suit and tie." . . . Kessler and McKenna note [that] we operate with a moral certainty of a world of two sexes. We do not think, "Most persons with penises are men, but some may not be" or "Most persons who dress as men have penises." Rather, we take it for granted that sex and sex category are congruent—that knowing the latter, we can deduce the rest.

Sex Categorization

Agnes's claim to the categorical status of female, which she sustained by appropriate identificatory displays and other characteristics, could be *discredited* before her transsexual operation, if her possession of a penis became known, and after by her surgically constructed genitalia. In this regard, Agnes had to be continually alert to actual or potential threats to the security of her sex category. Her problem was not so much about living up to some prototype of essential femininity but preserving her categorization as female. This task was made easy for her by a very powerful resource, namely, the process of commonsense categorization in everyday life.

The categorization of members of society into indigenous categories such as "girl" or "boy," or "woman" or "man," operates in a distinctively social way. The act of categorization does not involve a positive test, in the sense of a well-defined set of criteria that must be explicitly satisfied prior to making an identification. Rather, the application of membership categories relies on an "if–can" test in everyday interaction. This test stipulates that if people *can be seen* as members of relevant categories, *then categorize them that way*. That is, use the category that seems appropriate, except in the presence of discrepant information or obvious features that would rule out its use. This procedure is quite in keeping with the attitude of everyday life, which has us take appearances at face value unless we have special reason to doubt. . . .

Agnes's initial resource was the predisposition of those she encountered to take her appearance (her figure, clothing, hair style, and so on) as the undoubted appearance of a normal female. Her further resource was our cultural perspective on the properties of "natural, normally sexed persons." Garfinkel (1967) notes that in everyday life, we live in a world of two—and only two—sexes.

This arrangement has a moral status, in that we include ourselves and others in it as "essentially, originally, in the first place, always have been, always will be, once and for all, in the final analysis, either 'male' or 'female'" (Garfinkel, 1967: 122). Consider the following case:

> This issue reminds me of a visit I made to a computer store a couple of years ago. The person who answered my questions was truly a *salesperson*. I could not categorize him/her as a woman or a man. What did I look for? (1) Facial hair: She/he was smooth skinned, but some men have little or no facial hair. (This varies by race; Native Americans and Blacks often have none.) (2) Breasts: She/he was wearing a loose shirt that hung from his/her shoulders. And, as many women who suffered through a 1950s adolescence know to their shame, women are often flat-chested. (3) Shoulders: His/hers were small and round for a man, broad for a woman. (4) Hands: Long and slender fingers, knuckles a bit large for a woman, small for a man. (5) Voice: Middle range, unexpressive for a woman, not at all the exaggerated tones some gay males affect. (6) His/her treatment of me: Gave off no signs that would let me know if I were of the same or different sex as this person. There were not even any signs that he/she knew his/her sex would be difficult to categorize and I wondered about that even as I did my best to hide these questions so I would not embarrass him/her while we talked of computer paper. I left still not knowing the sex of my salesperson, and was disturbed by that unanswered question (child of my culture that I am). (Diane Margolis, personal communication)

What can this case tell us about situations such as Agnes's or the process of sex categorization in general? First, we infer from this description that the computer salesperson's identificatory display was ambiguous, since she or he was not dressed or adorned in an unequivocally female or male fashion. It is when such a display *fails* to provide grounds for categorization that factors such as facial hair or tone of voice are assessed to determine membership in a sex category. Second, beyond the fact that this incident could be recalled after "a couple of years," the customer was not only "disturbed" by the ambiguity of the salesperson's category but also assumed that to acknowledge this ambiguity would be embarrassing to the salesclerk. Not only do we want to know the sex category of those around us (to see it at a glance, perhaps), but we also presume that others are displaying it for us, in as decisive a fashion as they can.

Gender

Agnes attempted to be "120 per cent female" (Garfinkel, 1967: 129)—that is, unquestionably in all ways and at all times feminine. She thought she could protect herself from disclosure before and after surgical intervention by comporting herself in a feminine manner, but she also could have given herself away by overdoing her performance. . . . Her problem was to produce configurations of behaviour that would be seen by others as normative gender behaviour.

Agnes's strategy of "secret apprenticeship," through which she learned expected feminine decorum by carefully attending to her fiancé's criticisms of other women, was one means of masking incompetencies and simultaneously acquiring the needed skills (Garfinkel, 1967). It was through her fiancé that Agnes learned that sunbathing on the lawn in front of her apartment was "offensive" (because it put her on display to other men). She also learned from his critiques of other women that she should not insist on having things her way and that she should not offer her opinions or claim equality with men (Garfinkel, 1967: 147–8). (Like other women in our society, Agnes learned something about power in the course of her "education.")

Popular culture abounds with books and magazines that compile idealized depictions of relations between women and men. Those focused on the etiquette of dating or prevailing standards of feminine comportment are meant to be of practical help in these matters. However, the use of any such source *as a manual of procedure* requires the assumption that doing gender merely involves making use of discrete, well-defined bundles of behaviour that can simply be plugged into interactional situations to produce recognizable enactments of masculinity and femininity. The man "does" being masculine by, for example, taking the woman's arm to guide her across a street, and she "does" being feminine by consenting to be guided and not initiating such behaviour with a man.

. . . To be successful, marking or displaying gender must be finely fitted to situations and modified or transformed as the occasion demands. Doing gender consists of managing such occasions so that, whatever the particulars, the outcome is seen and seeable in context as gender-appropriate or, as the case may be, gender-*in*appropriate—that is, *accountable*.

Gender and Accountability

As Heritage (1984: 136–7) notes, members of society regularly engage in "descriptive accountings of states of affairs to one another," and such accounts are both serious and consequential. . . .

. . . [S]ocietal members orient to the fact that their activities are subject to comment. Actions are often designed with an eye to their accountability—that is, how they might look and how they might be characterized. The notion of accountability also encompasses those actions undertaken so that they are specifically unremarkable and thus not worthy of more than a passing remark, because they are seen to be in accord with culturally approved standards.

Heritage observes that the process of rendering something accountable is interactional in character:

> [This] permits actors to design their actions in relation to their circumstances so as to permit others, by methodically taking account of circumstances, to recognize the action for what it is. (1984: 179)

The key word here is *circumstances*. One circumstance that attends virtually all actions is the sex category of the actor. As Garfinkel comments:

[T]he work and socially structured occasions of sexual passing were obstinately unyielding to [Agnes's] attempts to routinize the grounds of daily activities. This obstinacy points to the *omnirelevance* of sexual status to affairs of daily life as an invariant but unnoticed background in the texture of relevances that compose the changing actual scenes of everyday life. (1967: 118, emphasis added)

If sex category is omnirelevant (or even approaches being so), then a person engaged in virtually any activity may be held accountable for performance of that activity as a *woman* or a *man*, and their incumbency in one or the other sex category can be used to legitimate or discredit their other activities. Accordingly, virtually any activity can be assessed as to its womanly or manly nature. And note, to "do" gender is not always to live up to normative conceptions of femininity or masculinity; it is to engage in behaviour *at the risk of gender assessment*. While it is individuals who do gender, the enterprise is fundamentally interactional and institutional in character, for accountability is a feature of social relationships and its idiom is drawn from the institutional arena in which those relationships are enacted. If this be the case, can we ever *not* do gender? Insofar as a society is partitioned by "essential" differences between women and men and placement in a sex category is both relevant and enforced, doing gender is unavoidable.

Resources for Doing Gender

Doing gender means creating differences between girls and boys and women and men, differences that are not natural, essential, or biological. Once the differences have been constructed, they are used to reinforce the "essentialness" of gender. In a delightful account of the "arrangement between the sexes," Goffman (1977) observes the creation of a variety of institutionalized frameworks through which our "natural, normal sexedness" can be enacted. The physical features of social setting provide one obvious resource for the expression of our "essential" differences. For

example, the sex segregation of North American public bathrooms distinguishes "ladies" from "gentlemen" in matters held to be fundamentally biological, even though both "are somewhat similar in the question of waste products and their elimination" (Goffman, 1977: 315). These settings are furnished with dimorphic equipment (such as urinals for men or elaborate grooming facilities for women), even though both sexes may achieve the same ends through the same means (and apparently do so in the privacy of their own homes). To be stressed here is the fact that:

The *functioning* of sex-differentiated organs is involved, but there is nothing in this functioning that biologically recommends segregation; that arrangement is a totally cultural matter. . . . [T]oilet segregation is presented as a natural consequence of the difference between the sex-classes when in fact it is a means of honoring, if not producing, this difference. (Goffman, 1977: 316)

Standardized social occasions also provide stages for evocations of the "essential female and male natures." Goffman cites organized sports as one such institutionalized framework for the expression of manliness. There, those qualities that ought "properly" to be associated with masculinity, such as endurance, strength, and competitive spirit, are celebrated by all parties concerned—participants, who may be seen to demonstrate such traits, and spectators, who applaud their demonstrations from the safety of the sidelines (1977: 322).

Assortative mating practices among heterosexual couples afford still further means to create and maintain differences between women and men. For example, even though size, strength, and age tend to be normally distributed among females and males (with considerable overlap between them), selective pairing ensures couples in which boys and men are visibly bigger, stronger, and older (if not "wiser") than the girls and women with whom they are paired. So, should situations emerge in which greater size, strength, or experience is called for, boys and men will be ever ready to display it and girls and women, to appreciate its display. . . .

Many situations are not clearly sex categorized to begin with, nor is what transpires within them obviously gender relevant. Yet any social encounter can be pressed into service in the interests of doing gender. Thus, Fishman's (1978) research on casual conversations found an asymmetrical "division of labour" in talk between heterosexual intimates. Women had to ask more questions, fill more silences, and use more attention-getting beginnings in order to be heard. Her conclusions are particularly pertinent here:

> Since interactional work is related to what constitutes being a woman, with what a woman is, the idea that it is work is obscured. The work is not seen as what women do, but as part of what they are. (Fishman, 1978: 405)

We would argue that it is precisely such labour that helps to constitute the essential nature of women as women in interactional contexts.

Individuals have many social identities that may be donned or shed, muted or made more salient, depending on the situation. One may be a friend, spouse, professional, citizen, and many other things to many different people—or, to the same person at different times. But we are always women or men—unless we shift into another sex category. What this means is that our identificatory displays will provide an ever-available resource for doing gender under an infinitely diverse set of circumstances.

Some occasions are organized to routinely display and celebrate behaviours that are conventionally linked to one or the other sex category. On such occasions, everyone knows his or her place in the interactional scheme of things. If an individual identified as a member of one sex category engages in behaviour usually associated with the other category, this routinization is challenged. Hughes (1945: 356) provides an illustration of such a dilemma:

> [A] young woman . . . became part of that virile profession, engineering. The designer of

an airplane is expected to go up on the maiden flight of the first plane built according to the design. He [sic] then gives a dinner to the engineers and workmen who worked on the new plane. The dinner is naturally a stag party. The young woman in question designed a plane. Her co-workers urged her not to take the risk—for which, presumably, men only are fit—of the maiden voyage. They were, in effect, asking her to be a lady instead of an engineer. She chose to be an engineer. She then gave the party and paid for it like a man. After food and the first round of toasts, she left like a lady.

On this occasion, parties reached an accommodation that allowed a woman to engage in presumptively masculine behaviours. However, we note that in the end, this compromise permitted demonstration of her "essential" femininity, through accountably "ladylike" behaviour.

Hughes (1945: 357) suggests that such contradictions may be countered by managing interactions on a very narrow basis—for example, "keeping the relationship formal and specific." But the heart of the matter is that even—perhaps, especially—if the relationship is a formal one, gender is still something one is accountable for. Thus a woman physician (notice the special qualifier in her case) may be accorded respect for her skill and even addressed by an appropriate title. Nonetheless, she is subject to evaluation in terms of normative conceptions of appropriate attitudes and activities for her sex category and under pressure to prove that she is an "essentially" feminine being, despite appearances to the contrary. Her sex category is used to discredit her participation in important clinical activities, while her involvement in medicine is used to discredit her commitment to her responsibilities as a wife and mother. Simultaneously, her exclusion from the physician colleague community is maintained and her accountability *as a woman* is ensured.

In this context, "role conflict" can be viewed as a dynamic aspect of our current "arrangement between the sexes" (Goffman, 1977), an arrangement that provides for occasions on which persons of a particular sex category can "see" quite clearly that they are out of place and that if they were not there, their current troubles would not exist. What is at stake is, from the standpoint of interaction, the management of our "essential" natures, and from the standpoint of the individual, the continuing accomplishment of gender. If, as we have argued, sex category is omnirelevant, then any occasion, conflicted or not, offers the resources for doing gender.

We have sought to show that sex category and gender are managed properties of conduct that are contrived with respect to the fact that others will judge and respond to us in particular ways. We have claimed that a person's gender is not simply an aspect of what one is, but, more fundamentally, it is something that one *does*, and does recurrently, in interaction with others.

What are the consequences of this theoretical formulation? If, for example, individuals strive to achieve gender in encounters with others, how does a culture instill the need to achieve it? What is the relationship between the production of gender at the level of interaction and such institutional arrangements as the division of labour in society? And, perhaps most important, how does doing gender contribute to the subordination of women by men?

Research Agendas

To bring the social production of gender under empirical scrutiny, we might begin at the beginning, with a reconsideration of the process through which societal members acquire the requisite categorical apparatus and other skills to become gendered human beings.

Recruitment to Gender Identities

. . . Cahill (1982, 1986a, 1986b) analyzes the experiences of preschool children using a social model of recruitment into normally gendered identities. Cahill argues that categorization practices are fundamental to learning and

displaying feminine and masculine behaviour. Initially, he observes, children are primarily concerned with distinguishing between themselves and others on the basis of social competence. Categorically, their concern resolves itself into the opposition of "girl/boy" classification versus "baby" classification (the latter designating children whose social behaviour is problematic and who must be closely supervised). It is children's concern with being seen as socially competent that evokes their initial claims to gender identities:

> During the exploratory stage of children's socialization . . . they learn that only two social identities are routinely available to them, the identity of "baby," or, depending on the configuration of their external genitalia, either "big boy" or "big girl." Moreover, others subtly inform them that the identity of "baby" is a discrediting one. When, for example, children engage in disapproved behaviour, they are often told "You're a baby" or "Be a big boy." In effect, these typical verbal responses to young children's behaviour convey to them that they must behaviourally choose between the discrediting identity of "baby" and their anatomically determined sex identity. (Cahill, 1986a: 175)

Subsequently, little boys appropriate the gender ideal of "efficaciousness"—that is, being able to affect the physical and social environment through the exercise of physical strength or appropriate skills. In contrast, little girls learn to value "appearance"—that is, managing themselves as ornamental objects. Both classes of children learn that the recognition and use of sex categorization in interaction is not optional, but mandatory.

Being a "girl" or a "boy" then, is not only being more competent than a "baby," but also being competently female or male—that is, learning to produce behavioural displays of one's "essential" female or male identity. In this respect, the task of four- to five-year-old children is very similar to Agnes's:

For example, the following interaction occurred on a preschool playground. A 55-month-old boy (D) was attempting to unfasten the clasp of a necklace when a preschool aide walked over to him.

A: Do you want to put that on?

D: No. It's for girls.

A: You don't have to be a girl to wear things around your neck. Kings wear things around their neck. You could pretend that you're a king.

D: I'm not a king. I'm a boy. (Cahill, 1986a: 176)

As Cahill notes in this example, although D may have been unclear as to the sex status of a king's identity, he was obviously aware that necklaces are used to announce the identity "girl." Having claimed the identity "boy" and having developed a behavioural commitment to it, he was leery of any display that might furnish grounds for questioning his claim.

In this way, new members of society come to be involved in a *self-regulating process* as they begin to monitor their own and others' conduct with regard to its gender implications. The "recruitment" process involves not only the appropriation of gender ideals (by the valuation of those ideals as proper ways of being and behaving) but also *gender identities* that are important to individuals and that they strive to maintain. Thus gender differences, or the sociocultural shaping of "essential female and male natures," achieve the status of objective facts. They are rendered normal, natural features of persons and provide the tacit rationale for differing fates of women and men within the social order.

Additional studies of children's play activities as routine occasions for the expression of gender-appropriate behaviour can yield new insights into how our "essential natures" are constructed. In particular, the transition from what Cahill (1986a) terms "apprentice participation" in the sex-segregated worlds that are common among elementary school children to "bona fide participation" in the heterosocial world so frightening to adolescents is likely to be a keystone in our understanding of the recruitment process.

Gender and the Division of Labour

Whenever people face issues of *allocation*—who is to do what, get what, plan or execute action, direct or be directed, incumbency in significant social categories such as "female" and "male" seems to become pointedly relevant. How such issues are resolved conditions the exhibition, dramatization, or celebration of one's "essential nature" as a woman or man.

Berk (1985) offers elegant demonstration of this point in her investigation of the allocation of household labour and the attitudes of married couples toward the division of household tasks. Berk found little variation in either the actual distribution of tasks or perceptions of equity in regard to that distribution. Wives, even when employed outside the home, do the vast majority of household and childcare tasks. Moreover, both wives and husbands tend to perceive this as a "fair" arrangement. Noting the failure of conventional sociological and economic theories to explain this seeming contradiction, Berk contends that something more complex is involved than rational arrangements for the production of household goods and services:

> Hardly a question simply of who has more time, or whose time is worth more, who has more skill or more power, it is clear that a complicated relationship between the structure of work imperatives and the structure of normative expectations attached to work as *gendered* determines the ultimate allocation of members' time to work and home. (Berk, 1985: 195–6)

She notes, for example, that the most important factor influencing wives' contribution of labour is the total amount of work demanded or expected by the household; such demands had no bearing on husbands' contributions. Wives reported various rationales (their own and their husbands') that justified their level of contribution and, as a general matter, underscored the presumption that wives are essentially responsible for household production.

Berk contends that it is difficult to see how people "could rationally establish the arrangements that they do solely for the production of household goods and services" (1985: 201)—much less, how people could consider them "fair." She argues that our current arrangements for the domestic division of labour support *two* production processes: household goods and services (meals, clean children, and so on) and, at the same time, gender. As she puts it:

> Simultaneously, members "do" gender, as they "do" housework and child care, and what [has] been called the division of labor provides for the joint production of household labor and gender; it is the mechanism by which both the material and symbolic products of the household are realized. (1985: 201)

It is not simply that household labour is designated as "women's work," but that for a woman to engage in it and a man not to engage in it is to draw on and exhibit the "essential nature" of each. What is produced and reproduced is not merely the activity and artifact of domestic life, but the material embodiment of wifely and husbandly roles, and derivatively, of womanly and manly conduct. What are also frequently produced and reproduced are the dominant and subordinate statuses of the sex categories.

How does gender get done in work settings outside the home, where dominance and subordination are themes of overarching importance? Hochschild's (1983) analysis of the work of flight attendants offers some promising insights. She found that the occupation of flight attendant consisted of something altogether different for women than for men:

> As the company's main shock absorbers against "mishandled" passengers, their own feelings are more frequently subjected to rough treatment. In addition, a day's exposure to people who resist authority in a woman is a different experience than it is for a man. . . . In this respect, it is a disadvantage

to be a woman. And in this case, they are not simply women in the biological sense. They are also a highly visible distillation of middle-class American notions of femininity. They symbolize Woman. Insofar as the category "female" is mentally associated with having less status and authority, female flight attendants are more readily classified as "really" females than other females are. (1983: 175)

In performing what Hochschild terms the "emotional labor" necessary to maintain airline profits, women flight attendants simultaneously produce enactments of their "essential" femininity.

Sex and Sexuality

What is the relationship between doing gender and a culture's prescription of "obligatory heterosexuality"? As Frye (1983: 22) observes, the monitoring of sexual feelings in relation to other appropriately sexed persons requires the ready recognition of such persons "before one can allow one's heart to beat or one's blood to flow in erotic enjoyment of that person." The appearance of heterosexuality is produced through emphatic and unambiguous indicators of one's sex, layered on in ever more conclusive fashion (Frye, 1983: 24). Thus, lesbians and gay men concerned with passing as heterosexuals can rely on these indicators for camouflage; in contrast, those who would avoid the assumption of heterosexuality may foster ambiguous indicators of their categorical status through their dress, behaviours, and style. But "ambiguous" sex indicators are sex indicators nonetheless. If one wishes to be recognized as a lesbian (or heterosexual woman), one must first establish a categorical status as female. Even as popular images portray lesbians as "females who are not feminine" (Frye, 1983: 129), the accountability of persons for their "normal, natural sexedness" is preserved.

Nor is accountability threatened by the existence of "sex-change operations"—presumably, the most radical challenge to our cultural perspective on sex and gender. Although no one coerces transsexuals into hormone therapy, electrolysis, or surgery, the alternatives available to them are undeniably constrained:

> When the transsexual experts maintain that they use transsexual procedures only with people who ask for them, and who prove that they can "pass," they obscure the social reality. Given patriarchy's prescription that one must be *either* masculine or feminine, free choice is conditioned. (Raymond, 1979: 135, emphasis added)

The physical reconstruction of sex criteria pays ultimate tribute to the "essentialness" of our sexual natures—as women *or* as men.

Gender, Power, and Social Change

Let us return to the question: Can we avoid doing gender? Earlier, we proposed that insofar as sex category is used as a fundamental criterion for differentiation, doing gender is unavoidable. It is unavoidable because of the social consequences of sex category membership: the allocation of power and resources not only in the domestic, economic, and political domains but also in the broad arena of interpersonal relations. In virtually any situation, one's sex category can be relevant, and one's performance as an incumbent of that category (i.e., gender) can be subjected to evaluation. Maintaining such pervasive and faithful assignment of lifetime status requires legitimation.

But doing gender also renders the social arrangements based on sex category accountable as normal and natural—that is, legitimate—ways of organizing social life. Differences between women and men that are created by this process can then be portrayed as fundamental and enduring dispositions. In this light, the institutional arrangements of a society can be seen as responsive to the differences—the social order being merely an accommodation to the natural order. Thus if, in doing gender, men are also doing dominance and women are doing deference, the resultant social order, which supposedly reflects "natural differences," is a powerful reinforcer and legitimator of hierarchical arrangements. Frye observes:

> For efficient subordination, what's wanted is that the structure not appear to be a cultural artifact kept in place by human decision or custom, but that it appear *natural*—that it appear to be quite a direct consequence of facts about the beast which are beyond the scope of human manipulation. . . . That we are trained to behave so differently as women and men, and to behave so differently toward women and men, itself contributes mightily to the appearance of extreme dimorphism, but also, the *ways* we act as women and men, and the *ways* we act toward women and men, mold our bodies and our minds to the shape of subordination and dominance. We do become what we practice being. (Frye, 1983: 34)

If we do gender appropriately, we simultaneously sustain, reproduce, and render legitimate the institutional arrangements that are based on sex category. If we fail to do gender appropriately, we as individuals—not the institutional arrangements—may be called to account (for our character, motives, and predispositions).

Social movements such as feminism can provide the ideology and impetus to question existing arrangements, and the social support for individuals to explore alternatives to them. . . . To be sure, equality under the law does not guarantee equality in other arenas. As Lorber (1986: 577) points out, assurance of "scrupulous equality of categories of people considered essentially different needs constant monitoring." What such proposed changes can do is provide the warrant for asking why, if we wish to treat women and men as equals, there needs to be two sex categories at all. . . .

Gender is a powerful ideological device, which produces, reproduces, and legitimates the choices and limits that are predicated on sex category. An understanding of how gender is produced in social situations will afford clarification of the interactional scaffolding of social structure and the social control processes that sustain it.

References

Berk, S.F. 1985. *The Gender Factory: The Apportionment of Work in American Households*. New York: Plenum.

Cahill, S.E. 1982. "*Becoming Boys and Girls*." PhD dissertation, Department of Sociology, University of California, Santa Barbara.

Cahill, S.E. 1986a. "Childhood Socialization as Recruitment Process: Some Lessons from the Study of Gender Development," in P. Adler and P. Adler, eds., *Sociological Studies of Child Development*, pp. 163–86. Greenwich, Conn: JAI Press.

Cahill, S.E. 1986b. "Language Practices and Self-Definition: The Case of Gender Identity Acquisition," *The Sociological Quarterly* 27: 295–311.

Fishman, P. 1978. "Interaction: The Work Women Do," *Social Problems* 25: 397–406.

Frye, M. 1983. *The Politics of Reality: Essays in Feminist Theory*. Trumansburg, NY: The Crossing Press.

Garfinkel, H. 1967. *Studies in Ethnomethodology*. Englewood Cliffs, NJ: Prentice-Hall.

Goffman, E. 1977. "The Arrangement between the Sexes," *Theory and Society* 4: 301–31.

Heritage, J. 1984. *Garfinkel and Ethnomethodology*. Cambridge, UK: Polity Press.

Hochschild, A.R. 1983. *The Managed Heart. Commercialization of Human Feeling*. Berkeley: University of California Press.

Hughes, E.C. 1945. "Dilemmas and Contradictions of Status," *American Journal of Sociology* 50: 353–59.

Kessler, S.J., and W. McKenna. 1978. *Gender: An Ethnomethodological Approach*. New York: Wiley.

Lorber, J. 1986. "Dismantling Noah's Ark," *Sex Roles* 14: 567–80.

Raymond, J.G. 1979. *The Transsexual Empire*. Boston: Beacon.

Rubin, G. 1975. "The Traffic in Women: Notes on the 'Political Economy' of Sex," in R. Reiter, ed., *Toward an Anthropology of Women*, pp. 157–210. New York: Monthly Review Press.

Thorne, B. 1980. "Gender . . . How Is It Best Conceptualized?" Unpublished manuscript.

Chapter 2

Overview

"The Body and the Reproduction of Femininity" is Susan Bordo's classic and not uncontroversial take on the relationship between physical bodies and the social worlds through which they move. Bordo focuses on the situation of middle-class white women in the nineteenth and twentieth centuries who, she argues, embodied their distress at the constraints of their gender in different ways. She provides a history of psychosomatic illness from hysteria in the nineteenth century through agoraphobia in the early twentieth century to anorexia near the end of the twentieth century. She "diagnoses" these conditions not just as medical or psychiatric afflictions but as symptoms of gender power relations that pressure women to remain subdued, voiceless, and childlike. Retreating into a private indoor space or starving oneself may seem like an excessive form of conformity to these pressures, but Bordo argues that the agoraphobic or anorexic woman is also using her body as a form of protest, drawing attention to the destructive impact of patriarchy, whether she deliberately intends to do so or not. Bordo is also critical of some aspects of twentieth-century feminism, in which an emphasis on personal control and individual power gets turned against women's bodies, diverting their energies and attentions into an impossible quest for a "perfect" physique. Her argument sees bodies not just as physiology but as social texts on which the dominant narratives of gender are written and rewritten.

The Body and the Reproduction of Femininity

Susan Bordo[1]

Reconstructing Feminist Discourse on the Body

The body—what we eat, how we dress, and the daily rituals to which we attend—is a medium of culture. The body, as anthropologist Mary Douglas has argued, is a powerful symbolic form, a surface on which the central rules, hierarchies, and even metaphysical commitments of a culture are inscribed and thus reinforced through the concrete language of the body (Douglas, 1966, 1982). The body may also operate as a metaphor for culture. From quarters as diverse as Plato and Hobbes to French feminist Luce Irigaray, an imagination of body morphology has provided a blueprint for diagnosis and/or vision of social and political life.

The body is not only a text of culture. It is also, as anthropologist Pierre Bourdieu and philosopher Michel Foucault (among others) have argued, a practical, direct locus of social control. Banally, through table manners and toilet habits, through seemingly trivial routines, rules, and practices, culture is "made body," as Bourdieu puts it—converted into automatic, habitual activity. As such, it is put "beyond the grasp of consciousness . . . [untouchable] by voluntary, deliberate transformations" (Bourdieu, 1977: 94). Our conscious politics, social commitments, and strivings for change may be undermined and betrayed by the life of our bodies—not the craving, instinctual body imagined by Plato, Augustine, and Freud, but what Foucault calls the "docile body," regulated by the norms of cultural life.[2]

Throughout his later "genealogical" works (*Discipline and Punish, The History of Sexuality*), Foucault constantly reminds us of the primacy of practice over belief. Not chiefly through ideology, but through the organization and regulation of the time, space, and movements of our daily lives, our bodies are trained, shaped, and impressed with the stamp of prevailing historical forms of selfhood, desire, masculinity, and femininity. Such an emphasis casts a dark and disquieting shadow across the contemporary scene. Women, as study after study shows, are spending more time on the management and discipline of our bodies than we have in a long, long time. In a decade marked by a reopening of the public arena to women, the intensification of such regimens appears diversionary and subverting. Through the pursuit of an ever-changing, homogenizing, elusive ideal of femininity—a pursuit without a terminus, requiring that women constantly attend to minute and often whimsical changes in fashion—female bodies become docile bodies—bodies whose forces and energies are habituated to external regulation, subjection, transformation, and "improvement." Through the exacting and normalizing disciplines of diet, makeup, and dress—central organizing principles of time and space in the day of many women—we are rendered less socially oriented and more centripetally focused on self-modification. Through these disciplines, we continue to memorize on our bodies, the feel and conviction of lack, of insufficiency, of never being good enough. At the farthest extremes, the practices of femininity may lead us to utter demoralization, debilitation, and death.

Viewed historically, the discipline and normalization of the female body—perhaps the only gender oppression that exercises itself, although to different degrees and in different forms, across age, race, class, and sexual orientation—has to be acknowledged as an amazingly durable and flexible strategy of social control. In our own era, it is difficult to avoid the recognition that the contemporary preoccupation with appearance, which still affects women far more powerfully than men, even in our narcissistic and visually oriented culture, may function as a backlash phenomenon, reasserting existing gender configurations against any attempts to shift or transform power relations.[3] . . .

This essay will focus on the analysis of one particular arena where the interplay of these dynamics is striking and perhaps exemplary. It is a limited and unusual arena—that of a group of gender-related and historically localized disorders: hysteria, agoraphobia, and anorexia nervosa.[4] I recognize that these disorders have also historically been class- and race-biased, largely (although not exclusively) occurring among white middle- and upper-middle-class women. Nonetheless, anorexia, hysteria, and agoraphobia may provide a paradigm of one way in which potential resistance is not merely undercut but *utilized* in the maintenance and reproduction of existing power relations.[5]

The central mechanism I will describe involves a transformation (or, if you wish, duality) of meaning, through which conditions that are objectively (and, on one level, experientially) constraining, enslaving, and even murderous, come to be experienced as liberating, transforming, and life-giving. I offer this analysis, although limited to a specific domain, as an example of how various contemporary critical discourses may be joined to yield an understanding of the subtle and often unwitting role played by our bodies in the symbolization and reproduction of gender.

The Body as a Text of Femininity

The continuum between female disorder and "normal" feminine practice is sharply revealed through a close reading of those disorders to which women have been particularly vulnerable. These, of course, have varied historically: neurasthenia and hysteria in the second half of the nineteenth century; agoraphobia and, most dramatically, anorexia nervosa and bulimia in the second half of the twentieth century. This is not to say that anorectics did not exist in the nineteenth century—many cases were described, usually in the context of diagnoses of hysteria (Showalter, 1985: 128–9)—or that women no longer suffer from classical hysterical symptoms in the twentieth century. But the taking up of eating disorders on a mass scale is as unique to the culture of the 1980s as the epidemic of hysteria was to the Victorian era.[6]

The symptomatology of these disorders reveals itself as textuality. Loss of mobility, loss of voice, inability to leave the home, feeding others while starving oneself, taking up space, and whittling down the space one's body takes up—all have symbolic meaning, all have political meaning under the varying rules governing the historical construction of gender. Working within this framework, we see that whether we look at hysteria, agoraphobia, or anorexia, we find the body of the sufferer deeply inscribed with an ideological construction of femininity emblematic of the period in question. The construction, of course, is always homogenizing and normalizing, erasing racial, class, and other differences and insisting that all women aspire to a coercive, standardized ideal. Strikingly, in these disorders, the construction of femininity is written in disturbingly concrete, hyperbolic terms: exaggerated, extremely literal, at times virtually caricatured presentations of the ruling feminine mystique. The bodies of disordered women in this way offer themselves as an aggressively graphic text for the interpreter—a text that insists, actually demands, that it be read as a cultural statement, a statement about gender.

Both nineteenth-century male physicians and twentieth-century feminist critics have seen, in the symptoms of neurasthenia and hysteria (syndromes that became increasingly less differentiated as the century wore on), an exaggeration of stereotypically feminine traits. The nineteenth-century "lady" was idealized in terms of delicacy and dreaminess, sexual passivity, and a charmingly labile and capricious emotionality (Vicinus, 1972, x–xi). Such notions were formalized and scientized in the work of male theorists from Acton and Krafft-Ebing to Freud, who described "normal," mature femininity in such terms.[7] In this context, the dissociations, the drifting and fogging of perception, the nervous tremors and faints, the anesthesias, and the extreme mutability of symptomatology associated with nineteenth-century female disorders can be seen to be concretizations of the feminine mystique of the period, produced according to rules that governed the prevailing construction of femininity. Doctors described what came to be known as the hysterical personality as "impressionable, suggestible, and narcissistic; highly labile, their moods changing suddenly, dramatically, and seemingly for inconsequential reasons . . . egocentric in the extreme . . . essentially asexual and not uncommonly frigid" (Smith-Rosenberg, 1985: 203)—all characteristics normative of femininity in this era. As Elaine Showalter points out, the term hysterical itself became almost interchangeable with the term *feminine* in the literature of the period (Showalter, 1985: 129).

The hysteric's embodiment of the feminine mystique of her era, however, seems subtle and ineffable compared to the ingenious literalism of agoraphobia and anorexia. In the context of our culture this literalism makes sense. With the advent of movies and television, the rules for femininity have come to be culturally transmitted more and more through standardized visual images. As a result, femininity itself has come to be largely a matter of constructing, in the manner described by Erving Goffman, the appropriate surface presentation of the self (Goffman, 1959). We are no longer given verbal descriptions or exemplars of what a lady is or of what femininity consists. Rather, we learn the rules directly through bodily discourse: through images that tell us what clothes, body shape, facial expression, movements, and behaviour are required.

In agoraphobia and, even more dramatically, in anorexia, the disorder presents itself as a virtual, though tragic, parody of twentieth-century constructions of femininity. The 1950s and early 1960s, when agoraphobia first began to escalate among women, was a period of reassertion of domesticity and dependency as the feminine ideal. Career woman became a dirty word, much more so than it had been during the war, when the economy depended on women's willingness to do "men's work." The reigning ideology of femininity, so well described by Betty Friedan and perfectly captured in the movies and television shows of the era, was childlike, non-assertive, helpless without a man, "content in a world of bedroom and kitchen, sex, babies and home" (Friedan, 1962: 36).[8] The housebound agoraphobic lives this construction of femininity literally. "You want me in this home? You'll have me in this home—with a vengeance!"

The point, upon which many therapists have commented, does not need belabouring. Agoraphobia, as I.G. Fodor has put it, seems "the logical—albeit extreme—extension of the cultural sex-role stereotype for women" in this era (Fodor, 1974: 119; see also Brehony, 1983).

The emaciated body of the anorectic, of course, immediately presents itself as a caricature of the contemporary ideal of hyper-slenderness for women, an ideal that, despite the game resistance of racial and ethnic difference, has become the norm for women today. But slenderness is only the tip of the iceberg, for slenderness itself requires interpretation. "*C'est le sens qui fait vendre,*" said Barthes, speaking of clothing styles—it is meaning that makes the sale (Culler, 1983: 74). So, too, it is meaning that makes the body admirable. To the degree that anorexia may be said to be "about" slenderness, it is about slenderness as a citadel of contemporary and historical meaning, not as an empty fashion ideal. As such, the interpretation of slenderness yields multiple readings, some related to gender, some not. For the purposes of this essay I will offer an abbreviated, gender-focused reading. But I must stress that this reading illuminates only partially, and that many other currents not discussed here— economic, psychosocial, and historical, as well as ethnic and class dimensions—figure prominently.[9]

We begin with the painfully literal inscription, on the anorectic's body, of the rules governing the construction of contemporary femininity. That construction is a double bind that legislates contradictory ideals and directives. On the one hand, our culture still widely advertises domestic conceptions of femininity, the ideological moorings for a rigorously dualistic sexual division of labour that casts woman as chief emotional and physical nurturer. The rules for this construction of femininity (and I speak here in a language both symbolic and literal) require that women learn to feed others, not the self, and to construe any desires for self-nurturance and self-feeding as greedy and excessive.[10] Thus, women must develop a totally other-oriented emotional economy. In this economy, the control of female appetite for food is merely the most concrete expression of the general rule governing the construction of femininity: that female hunger—for public power,

Figure 2.1

Figure 2.2

for independence, for sexual gratification—be contained, and the public space that women be allowed to take up be circumscribed, limited. Figure 2.1, which appeared in a women's magazine fashion spread, dramatically illustrates the degree to which slenderness, set off against the resurgent muscularity and bulk of the current male body-ideal, carries connotations of fragility and lack of power in the face of a decisive male occupation of social space. On the body of the anorexic woman such rules are grimly and deeply etched.

On the other hand, even as young women today continue to be taught traditionally "feminine" virtues, to the degree that the professional arena is open to them, they must also learn to embody the "masculine" language and values of that arena—self-control, determination, cool, emotional discipline, mastery, and so on. Female bodies now speak symbolically of this necessity in their slender spare shape and the currently fashionable men's-wear look. (A contemporary clothing line's

clever mirror-image logo, shown in Figure 2.2, offers women's fashions for the "New Man," with the model posed to suggest phallic confidence combined with female allure.) Our bodies, too, as we trudge to the gym every day and fiercely resist both our hungers and our desire to soothe ourselves, are becoming more and more practised at the "male" virtues of control and self-mastery. Figure 2.3 illustrates this contemporary equation of physical discipline with becoming the "captain" of one's soul. The anorectic pursues these virtues with single-minded, unswerving dedication. "Energy, discipline, my own power will keep me going," says ex-anorectic Aimee Liu, re-creating her anorexic days. "I need nothing and no one else. . . . I will be master of my own body, if nothing else, I vow" (Liu, 1979: 123). . . .

In the pursuit of slenderness and the denial of appetite, the traditional construction of femininity intersects with the new requirement for women to embody the "masculine" values of the public arena. The anorectic, as I have argued, embodies this

Figure 2.3

intersection, this double bind, in a particularly painful and graphic way.[11] I mean *double bind* quite literally here. "Masculinity" and "femininity," at least since the nineteenth century and arguably before, have been constructed through a process of mutual exclusion. One cannot simply add the historically feminine virtues to the historically masculine ones to yield a New Woman, a New Man, a new ethics, or a new culture. . . . Explored as a possibility for the self, the "androgynous" ideal ultimately exposes its internal contradiction and becomes a war that tears the subject in two—a war explicitly thematized, by many anorectics, as a battle between male and female sides of the self.

Protest and Retreat in the Same Gesture

In hysteria, agoraphobia, and anorexia, then, the woman's body may be viewed as a surface on which conventional constructions of femininity are exposed starkly to view, through their inscription in extreme or hyperliteral form. They are written, of course, in languages of horrible suffering. It is as though these bodies are speaking to us of the pathology and violence that lurks just around the corner, waiting at the horizon of "normal" femininity. It is no wonder that a steady motif in the feminist literature on female disorder is that of pathology as embodied *protest*—unconscious, inchoate, and counterproductive protest without an effective language, voice, or politics, but protest nonetheless. . . .

Robert Seidenberg and Karen DeCrow, for example, describe agoraphobia as a "strike" against "the renunciations usually demanded of women" and the expectations of housewifely functions such as shopping, driving the children to school, accompanying their husband to social events (1983: 31). Carroll Smith-Rosenberg presents a similar analysis of hysteria, arguing that by preventing the woman from functioning in the wifely role of caretaker of others, of "ministering angel" to husband and children, hysteria "became one way in which conventional women could express—in most cases unconsciously—dissatisfaction with one or several aspects of their lives" (1985: 208). A number of feminist writers, among whom Susie Orbach is the most articulate and forceful, have interpreted anorexia as a species of unconscious feminist protest. The anorectic is engaged in a "hunger strike," as Orbach calls it, stressing that this is a political discourse, in which the action of food refusal and dramatic transformation of body size "expresses with [the] body what [the anorectic] is unable to tell us with words"—her indictment of a culture that disdains and suppresses female hunger, makes women ashamed of their appetites and needs, and demands that women constantly work on the transformation of their body (Orbach, 1985).[12]

The anorectic, of course, is unaware that she is making a political statement. She may, indeed, be hostile to feminism and any other critical perspectives that she views as disputing her own autonomy and control or questioning the cultural ideals around which her life is organized. Through embodied rather than deliberate demonstration she exposes and indicts those ideals, precisely by pursuing them to the point at which their destructive potential is revealed for all to see.

The same gesture that expresses protest, moreover, can also signal retreat; this, indeed, may be part of the symptom's attraction. Kim Chernin, for example, argues that the debilitating anorexic fixation, by halting or mitigating personal development, assuages this generation's guilt and separation anxiety over the prospect of surpassing our mothers, of living less circumscribed, freer lives (Chernin, 1985). Agoraphobia, too, which often develops shortly after marriage, clearly functions in many cases as a way to cement dependency and attachment in the face of unacceptable stirrings of dissatisfaction and restlessness.

Although we may talk meaningfully of protest, then, I want to emphasize the counterproductive, tragically self-defeating (indeed, self-deconstructing) nature of that protest. Functionally, the symptoms of these disorders isolate, weaken, and undermine the sufferers; at the same time they turn the life of the body into an all-absorbing fetish, beside which all other objects of attention pale into unreality. On the symbolic level, too, the protest collapses into its opposite and proclaims the utter capitulation of the subject to the contracted female world. The muteness of hysterics and their return to the level of pure, primary bodily expressivity have been interpreted, as we have seen, as rejecting the symbolic order of the patriarchy and recovering a lost world of semiotic, maternal value. But at the same time, of course, muteness is the condition of the silent, uncomplaining woman—an ideal of patriarchal culture. Protesting the stifling of the female voice through one's own voicelessness—that is, employing the language of femininity to protest the conditions of the female world—will always involve ambiguities of this sort. Perhaps this is why symptoms crystallized from the language of femininity are so perfectly suited to express the dilemmas of middle-class and upper-middle-class women living in periods poised on the edge of gender change, women who have the social and material resources to carry the traditional construction of femininity to symbolic excess but who also confront the anxieties of new possibilities. The late nineteenth century, the post–Second World War period, and the late twentieth century are all periods in which gender becomes an issue to be discussed and in which discourse proliferates about "the Woman Question," "the New Woman," "What Women Want," "What Femininity Is."

Collusion, Resistance, and the Body

The pathologies of female protest function, paradoxically, as if in collusion with the cultural conditions that produce them, reproducing rather than transforming precisely that which is being protested. In this connection, the fact that hysteria and anorexia have peaked during historical periods of cultural backlash against attempts at reorganization and redefinition of male and female roles is significant. Female pathology reveals itself here as an extremely interesting social formation through which one source of potential for resistance and rebellion is pressed into the service of maintaining the established order. . . .

Here, examining the context in which the anorexic syndrome is produced may be illuminating. Anorexia will erupt, typically, in the course of what begins as a fairly moderate diet regime, undertaken because someone—often the father—has made a casual critical remark. Anorexia *begins in*, emerges out of, what is, in our time, conventional feminine practice. In the course of that practice, for any number of individual reasons, the practice is pushed a little beyond the parameters of moderate dieting. The young woman discovers what it feels like to crave and want and need and yet, through the exercise of her own will, to triumph over that need. In the process, a new realm of meanings is discovered, a range of values and possibilities that Western culture has traditionally coded as "male" and rarely made available to women: an ethic and aesthetic of self-mastery and self-transcendence, expertise, and power over others through the example of superior will and control. The experience is intoxicating and habit-forming.

At school the anorectic discovers that her steadily shrinking body is admired, not so much as an aesthetic or sexual object, but for the strength of will and self-control it projects. At home she discovers, in the inevitable battles her parents fight to get her to eat, that her actions have enormous power over the lives of those around her. As her body begins to lose its traditional feminine curves, its breasts and hips and rounded stomach, it begins to feel and look more like a spare, lanky male body, and she begins to feel untouchable, out of reach of hurt, "invulnerable, clean and hard as the bones etched into my silhouette," as one student described it in her journal. She despises, in particular, all those parts of her body that continue to mark her as female. "If only I could eliminate [my breasts]," says Liu, "cut them off if need be" (1979: 99). For her, as for many anorectics, the breasts represent a bovine, unconscious, vulnerable side of the self. Liu's body symbolism is thoroughly continuous with dominant cultural associations. Brett Silverstein's studies on the "Possible Causes of the Thin Standard of Bodily Attractiveness for Women" (1986) testify empirically to what is obvious from every comedy routine involving a dramatically shapely woman: namely, our cultural association of curvaceousness with incompetence. The anorectic is also quite aware, of course, of the social and sexual vulnerability involved in having a female body; many, in fact, were sexually abused as children.

Through her anorexia, by contrast, she has unexpectedly discovered an entry into the privileged male world, a way to become what is valued in our culture, a way to become safe, to rise above it all—for her, they are the same thing. She has discovered this, paradoxically, by pursuing conventional feminine behaviour—in this case, the discipline of perfecting the body as an object—to excess. At this point of excess, the conventionally feminine deconstructs, we might say, into its opposite and opens onto those values our culture has coded as male. No wonder anorexia is experienced as liberating and that the anorectic will fight family, friends, and therapists in an effort to hold onto it—fight them to the death, if need be. The anorectic's experience of power is, of course, deeply and dangerously illusory. To reshape one's body into a male body is not to put on male power and privilege. To *feel* autonomous and free while harnessing body and soul to an obsessive body-practice is to serve, not transform, a social order that limits female possibilities. And, of course, for the female to become male is only for her to locate herself on the other side of a disfiguring opposition. The new "power look" of female bodybuilding, which encourages women to develop the same hulk-like, triangular shape that has been the norm for male body-builders, is no less determined by a hierarchical, dualistic construction of gender than was the conventionally "feminine" norm that tyrannized female body-builders such as Bev Francis for years.

Although the specific cultural practices and meanings are different, similar mechanisms, I suspect, are at work in hysteria and agoraphobia. In these cases too, the language of femininity, when pushed to excess—when shouted and asserted, when disruptive and demanding—deconstructs into its opposite and makes available to the woman an illusory experience of power previously forbidden to her by virtue of her gender. In the case of nineteenth-century femininity, the forbidden experience may have been the bursting of fetters—particularly moral and emotional fetters. John Conolly, the asylum reformer, recommended institutionalization for women who "want that restraint over the passions without which the female character is lost" (Showalter, 1985: 48). Hysterics often infuriated male doctors by their lack of precisely this quality. S. Weir Mitchell described these patients as "the despair of physicians," whose "despotic selfishness wrecks the constitution of nurses and devoted relatives, and in unconscious or half-conscious self-indulgence destroys the comfort of everyone around them" (Smith-Rosenberg, 1985: 207). It must have given the Victorian patient some illicit pleasure to be viewed as capable of such disruption of the staid nineteenth-century household. A similar form of power, I believe, is part of the experience of agoraphobia.

This does not mean that the primary reality of these disorders is not one of pain and entrapment. Anorexia, too, clearly contains a dimension of physical addiction to the biochemical effects of starvation. But whatever the physiology involved, the ways in which the subject understands and thematizes her experience cannot be reduced to a mechanical process. The anorectic's ability to live with minimal food intake allows her to feel powerful and worthy of admiration in a "world," as Susie Orbach describes it, "from which at the most profound level [she] feels excluded" and unvalued (1985: 103). The literature on both anorexia and hysteria is strewn with battles of will between the sufferer and those trying to "cure" her; the latter, as Orbach points out, very rarely understand that the psychic values she is fighting for are often more important to the woman than life itself.

Textuality, Praxis, and the Body

The "solutions" offered by anorexia, hysteria, and agoraphobia, I have suggested, develop out of the practice of femininity itself, the pursuit of which is still presented as the chief route to acceptance and success for women in our culture. Too aggressively pursued, that practice leads to its own undoing, in one sense. For if femininity is, as Susan Brownmiller has said, at its core a "tradition of imposed limitations" (1984: 14), then an unwillingness to limit oneself, even in the pursuit of femininity, breaks the rules. But, of course, in another sense the rules remain fully in place. The sufferer becomes wedded to an obsessive practice, unable to make any effective change in her life. She remains, as Toril Moi has put it, "gagged and chained to [the] feminine role," a reproducer of the docile body of femininity (1985: 192).

This tension between the psychological meaning of a disorder, which may enact fantasies of rebellion and embody a language of protest, and the practical life of the disordered body, which may utterly defeat rebellion and subvert protest, may be obscured by too exclusive a focus on the symbolic dimension and insufficient attention to praxis. As we have seen in the case of some Lacanian feminist readings of hysteria, the result of this can be a one-sided interpretation that romanticizes the hysteric's symbolic subversion of the phallocentric order while confined to her bed. This is not to say that confinement in bed has a transparent, univocal meaning—in powerlessness, debilitation, dependency, and so forth. The "practical" body is no brute biological or material entity. It, too, is a culturally mediated form; its activities are subject to interpretation and description. The shift to the practical dimension is not a turn to biology or nature, but to another "register," as Foucault puts it, of the cultural body, the register of the "useful body" rather than the "intelligible body" (Foucault, 1979: 136). The distinction can prove useful, I believe, to feminist discourse.

The intelligible body includes our scientific, philosophic, and aesthetic representations of the body—our cultural *conceptions* of the body, norms of beauty, models of health, and so forth. But the same representations may also be seen as forming a set of practical rules and regulations through which the living body is "trained, shaped, obeys, responds," becoming, in short, a socially adapted and "useful body" (Foucault, 1979: 136). Consider this particularly clear and appropriate example: the nineteenth-century hourglass figure, emphasizing breasts and hips against a wasp waist, was an intelligible *symbolic* form, representing a domestic, sexualized ideal of femininity. The sharp cultural contrast between the female and the male form, made possible by the use of corsets and bustles, reflected, in symbolic terms, the dualistic division of social and economic life into clearly defined male and female spheres. At the same time, to achieve the specified look, a particular feminine *praxis* was required—straitlacing, minimal eating, and reduced mobility—rendering the female body unfit to perform activities outside its designated sphere. This, in Foucauldian terms, would be the "useful body" corresponding to the aesthetic norm.

The intelligible body and the useful body are two arenas of the same discourse; they often mirror and support each other, as in the above illustration. Another example can be found in the seventeenth-century philosophic conception of the body as a machine, mirroring an increasingly more automated productive machinery of labour. But the two bodies may also contradict and mock each other. A range of contemporary representations and images, as noted earlier, have coded the transcendence of female appetite and its public display in the slenderness ideal in terms of power, will, mastery, and the possibilities of success in the professional arena. These associations are carried visually by the slender superwomen of prime-time television and popular movies and promoted explicitly in advertisements and articles appearing routinely in women's fashion magazines, diet books, and weight-training publications. Yet the thousands of slender girls and women who strive to embody these images and who in that service suffer from eating disorders, exercise compulsions, and continual self-scrutiny and self-castigation are anything *but* the "masters" of their lives. . . .

This is not to deny the benefits of diet, exercise, and other forms of body management. Rather, I view our bodies as a site of struggle, where we must work to keep our daily practices in the service of resistance to gender domination, not in the service of docility and gender normalization. This work requires, I believe, a determinedly skeptical attitude toward the routes of seeming liberation and pleasure offered by our culture. It also demands an awareness of the often contradictory relations between image and practice, between rhetoric and reality. Popular representations, as we have seen, may forcefully employ the rhetoric and symbolism of empowerment, personal freedom, "having it all." Yet female bodies, pursuing these ideals, may find themselves as distracted, depressed, and physically ill as female bodies in the nineteenth century were made when pursuing a feminine ideal of dependency, domesticity, and delicacy. The recognition and analysis of such contradictions, and of all the other collusions, subversions, and enticements through which culture enjoins the aid of our bodies in the reproduction of gender, require that we restore a concern for female praxis to its formerly central place in feminist politics.

Notes

1. Early versions of this essay, under various titles, were delivered at the philosophy department of the State University of New York at Stony Brook, the University of Massachusetts conference on Histories of Sexuality, and the twenty-first annual conference for the Society of Phenomenology and Existential Philosophy. I thank all those who commented and provided encouragement on those occasions. The essay was revised and originally published in Alison Jaggar and Susan Bordo, eds., *Gender/Body/Knowledge: Feminist Reconstructions of Being and Knowing* (New Brunswick: Rutgers University Press, 1989).

2. On docility, see Michel Foucault, *Discipline and Punish* (New York: Vintage, 1979), 135–69. For a Foucauldian analysis of feminine practice, see Sandra Bartky, "Foucault, Femininity, and the Modernization of Patriarchal Power," in her *Femininity and Domination* (New York: Routledge, 1990); see also Susan Brownmiller, *Femininity* (New York: Ballantine, 1984).

3. During the late 1970s and 1980s, male concern over appearance undeniably increased. Study after study confirms, however, that there is still a large gender gap in this area. Research conducted at the University of Pennsylvania in 1985 found men to be generally satisfied with their appearance, often, in fact, "distorting their perceptions [of themselves] in a positive, self-aggrandizing way" ("Dislike of Own Bodies Found Common Among Women," *New York Times*, 19 March 1985: C1). Women, however, were found to exhibit extreme negative assessments and distortions of body perception. Other studies have suggested that women are judged more harshly than men when they deviate from dominant social standards of attractiveness. Thomas Cash et al., in "The Great American Shape-Up," *Psychology Today* (April 1986): 34, report that although the situation for men has changed, the situation for women has more than proportionally worsened. Citing results from 30,000 responses to a 1985 survey of perceptions of body image and comparing similar responses to a 1972 questionnaire, they report that the 1985 respondents were considerably more dissatisfied with their bodies than the 1972 respondents, and they note a marked intensification of concern among men. Among the 1985 group, the group most dissatisfied of all with their appearance, however, were teenage women. Women today constitute by far the largest number of consumers of diet products, attenders of spas and diet centres, and subjects of intestinal by-pass and other fat-reduction operations.

4. On the gendered and historical nature of these disorders: the number of female to male hysterics has been estimated at anywhere from 2:1 to 4:1, and as many as 80 per cent of all agoraphobics are female (Annette Brodsky and Rachel Hare-Mustin, *Women and Psychotherapy* [New York: Guilford Press, 1980], 116, 122). Although more cases of male eating disorders have been reported in the late eighties and early nineties, it is estimated that close to 90 per cent of all anorectics are female (Paul Garfinkel and David Garner, *Anorexia Nervosa: A Multidimensional Perspective* [New York: Brunner/Mazel, 1982], 112–13). For a sophisticated account of female psychopathology, with particular attention to nineteenth-century disorders but, unfortunately, little mention of agoraphobia or eating disorders, see Elaine Showalter, *The Female Malady: Women, Madness and English Culture, 1830–1980* (New York: Pantheon, 1985). For a discussion of social and gender issues in agoraphobia, see Robert Seidenberg and Karen DeCrow, *Women Who Marry Houses: Panic and Protest in Agoraphobia* (New York: McGraw-Hill, 1983). On the history of anorexia nervosa, see Joan Jacobs Brumberg, *Fasting Girls: The Emergence of Anorexia Nervosa as a Modern Disease* (Cambridge: Harvard University Press, 1988).

5. In constructing such a paradigm I do not pretend to do justice to any of these disorders in its individual

complexity. My aim is to chart some points of intersection, to describe some similar patterns, as they emerge through a particular reading of the phenomenon—a political reading, if you will.

6. On the epidemic of hysteria and neurasthenia, see Showalter, *The Female Malady;* Carroll Smith-Rosenberg, "The Hysterical Woman: Sex Roles and Role Conflict in Nineteenth-Century America," in her *Disorderly Conduct: Visions of Gender in Victorian America* (Oxford: Oxford University Press, 1985).

7. See Carol Nadelson and Malkah Notman, *The Female Patient* (New York: Plenum, 1982), 5; E.M. Sigsworth and T.J. Wyke, "A Study of Victorian Prostitution and Venereal Disease," in Vicinus, *Suffer and Be Still*, 82. For more general discussions, see Peter Gay, *The Bourgeois Experience: Victoria to Freud.* Vol. 1: *Education of the Senses* (New York: Oxford University Press, 1984), esp. 109–68; Showalter, *The Female Malady*, esp. 121–44. The delicate lady, an ideal that had very strong class connotations (as does slenderness today), is not the only conception of femininity to be found in Victorian cultures. But it was arguably the single most powerful ideological representation of femininity in that era, affecting women of all classes, including those without the material means to realize the ideal fully. See Helena Mitchie, *The Flesh Made Word* (New York: Oxford, 1987), for discussions of the control of female appetite and Victorian constructions of femininity.

8. Betty Friedan, *The Feminine Mystique* (New York: Dell, 1962), 36. The theme song of one such show ran, in part, "I married Joan . . . What a girl . . . what a whirl . . . what a life! I married Joan . . . What a mind . . . love is blind . . . what a wife!"

9. For other interpretive perspectives on the slenderness ideal, see "Reading the Slender Body" in [*Unbearable Weight: Feminism, Western Culture, and the Body*]; Kim Chernin, *The Obsession: Reflections on the Tyranny of Slenderness* (New York: Harper and Row, 1981); Susie Orbach, *Hunger Strike: The Anorectic's Struggle as a Metaphor for Our Age* (New York: W.W. Norton, 1985).

10. See "Hunger as Ideology," in [*Unbearable Weight: Feminism, Western Culture, and the Body*], for a discussion of how this construction of femininity is reproduced in contemporary commercials and advertisements concerning food, eating, and cooking.

11. Striking, in connection with this, is Catherine Steiner-Adair's 1984 study of high-school women, which reveals a dramatic association between problems with food and body image and emulation of the cool, professionally "together," and gorgeous superwoman. On the basis of a series of interviews, the high schoolers were classified into two groups: one expressed skepticism over the superwoman ideal, the other thoroughly aspired to it. Later administrations of diagnostic tests revealed that 94 per cent of the pro-superwoman group fell into the eating-disordered range of the scale. Of the other group, 100 per cent fell into the non-eating-disordered range. Media images notwithstanding, young women today appear to sense, either consciously or through their bodies, the impossibility of simultaneously meeting the demands of two spheres whose values have been historically defined in utter opposition to each other.

12. When we look into the many autobiographies and case studies of hysterics, anorectics, and agoraphobics, we find that these are indeed the sorts of women one might expect to be frustrated by the constraints of a specified female role. Sigmund Freud and Joseph Breuer, in *Studies on Hysteria* (New York: Avon, 1966), and Freud, in the later *Dora: An Analysis of a Case of Hysteria* (New York: Macmillan, 1963), constantly remark on the ambitiousness, independence, intellectual ability, and creative strivings of their patients. We know, moreover, that many women who later became leading social activists and feminists of the nineteenth century were among those who fell ill with hysteria and neurasthenia. It has become a virtual cliché that the typical anorectic is a perfectionist, driven to excel in all areas of her life. Though less prominently, a similar theme runs throughout the literature on agoraphobia. One must keep in mind that in drawing on case studies, one is relying on the perceptions of other acculturated individuals. One suspects, for example, that the popular portrait of the anorectic as a relentless over-achiever may be coloured by the lingering or perhaps resurgent Victorianism of our culture's attitudes toward ambitious women. One does not escape this hermeneutic problem by turning to autobiography. But in autobiography one is at least dealing with social constructions and attitudes that animate the subject's own psychic reality. In this regard the autobiographical literature on anorexia, drawn on in a variety of places in [*Unbearable Weight: Feminism, Western Culture, and the Body*], is strikingly full of anxiety about the domestic world and other themes that suggest deep rebellion against traditional notions of femininity.

References

Bourdieu, P. 1977. *Outline of a Theory of Practice.* Cambridge: Cambridge University Press.

Brehony, K. 1983. "Women and Agoraphobia," in V. Franks and E. Rothblum, eds., *The Stereotyping of Women.* New York: Springer.

Brownmiller, S. 1984. *Femininity.* New York: Ballantine.

Chernin, K. 1985. *The Hungry Self: Women, Eating, and Identity.* New York: Harper and Row.

Culler, J. 1983. *Roland Barthes.* New York: Oxford University Press.

Douglas, M. 1966. *Purity and Danger*. London: Routledge and Kegan Paul.

Douglas, M. 1982. *Natural Symbols*. New York: Pantheon.

Fodor, I.G. 1974. "The Phobic Syndrome in Women," in V. Franks and V. Burtle, eds., *Women in Therapy*. New York: Brunner/Mazel.

Foucault, M. 1979. *Discipline and Punish*. New York: Vintage.

Friedan, B. 1962. *The Feminine Mystique*. New York: Dell.

Goffman, E. 1959. *The Presentation of the Self in Everyday Life*. Garden City, NJ: Anchor Doubleday.

Liu, A. 1979. *Solitaire*. New York: Harper and Row.

Moi, T. 1985. "Representations of Patriarchy: Sex and Epistemology in Freud's Dora," in C. Bernheimer and C. Kahane, eds., *In Dora's Case: Freud—Hysteria—Feminism*. New York: Columbia University Press.

Orbach, S. 1985. *Hunger Strike: The Anorectic's Struggle as a Metaphor for Our Age*. New York: W.W. Norton.

Showalter, E. 1985. *The Female Malady: Women, Madness and English Culture, 1830–1980*. New York: Pantheon.

Siedenberg, R., and K. DeCrow. 1983. *Women Who Marry Houses: Panic and Protest in Agoraphobia*. New York: McGraw-Hill.

Silverstein, B. 1986. "Possible Causes of the Thin Standard of Bodily Attractiveness for Women," *International Journal of Eating Disorders* 5: 907–16.

Smith-Rosenberg, C. 1985. "The Hysterical Woman: Sex Roles and Role Conflict in Nineteenth-Century America," in C. Smith-Rosenberg, *Disorderly Conduct: Visions of Gender in Victorian America*. Oxford: Oxford University Press.

Vicinus, M. 1972. "Introduction: The Perfect Victorian Lady," in M. Vicinus, *Suffer and Be Still: Women in the Victorian Age*, pp. x–xi. Bloomington: Indiana University Press.

Chapter 3

Overview

How did gender theory become theory about gendered people, not just about women? In this classic piece from 1985, three sociologists excavate the beginnings of the sociological study of masculinity. They argue that relations between men and women have always involved domination or oppression—a statement that some people might take issue with—but it leads the authors to a place where they can consider the various meanings of being a man within these gender relations. They dispose of earlier sociological approaches to gender difference by pointing out the limitations of a purely biological approach to men and women, and the constraints of the popular "sex role" framework of the mid-twentieth century, which was born out of sociologists' urge to justify the gender hierarchies of conservative post-war societies.

When feminist sociologists came along to disrupt the assumption that being a man or a woman was simply a matter of fulfilling the appropriate "sex role," they produced a revolution in the way sociologists understood women, but the study of men lagged behind. Early feminist sociology found that traditional masculinity led to sexism and the domination of women, and an early "Men's Liberation Movement" attempted to challenge these expectations. Carrigan and his colleagues expand their definition of masculinity beyond simple "not being women" to consider how men treat other men, developing the idea that masculinity is something that is created among men, not just an expression of a binary gender system. They also introduce the notion of "hegemonic masculinity," a way of being a man that has immense social power and value, even though very few real live men can (or want to) actually live that way.

Toward a New Sociology of Masculinity

Tim Carrigan, Bob Connell, and John Lee

The upheaval in sexual politics of the last twenty years has mainly been discussed as a change in the social position of women. Yet change in one term of a relationship signals change in the other. . . .

The political meaning of writing about masculinity turns mainly on its treatment of power. Our touchstone is the essential feminist insight that the overall relationship between men and women is one involving domination or oppression. This is a fact about the social world that must have profound consequences for the character of men. . . .

There are, however, some accounts of masculinity that have faced the issue of social power, and it is here that we find the bases of an adequate theory of masculinity. But they too face a characteristic danger in trying to hold to feminist insights about men. For a powerful current in feminism, focusing on sexual exploitation and violence, sees masculinity as more or less unrelieved villainy and all men as agents of the patriarchy in more or less the same degree. Accepting such a view leads to a highly schematic view of gender relations, and leads men in particular into a paralyzing politics of guilt. . . .

We hope for a realist sociology of masculinity, built on actual social practices rather than discussion of rhetoric and attitudes. And we hope for a realistic politics of masculinity, neither fatuously optimistic nor defeatist. . . .

Origins

The Early Sociology of Gender and the "Sex Role" Framework

"The problem of women" was a question taken up by science generally in the second half of the nineteenth century, at first in a mainly biological frame work. This was not simply part of the widening scope of scientific inquiry. It was clearly also a response to the enormous changes that had overtaken women's lives with the growth of industrial capitalism. And, towards the end of the century, it was a response to the direct challenge of the women's emancipation movement.

The relationship of the emerging social sciences to this nineteenth- and early twentieth-century discourse on women was profound. In a useful sociology of knowledge investigation of the growth of the discourse, Viola *Klein* observed that

> There is a peculiar affinity between the fate of women and the origins of social science, and it is no mere co-incidence that the emancipation of women should be started at the same time as the birth of sociology.[1]

The political stakes were particularly evident in psychological research. The area usually referred to today as "sex difference research" has been a major component in the development of social science work on gender. In the view of one prominent observer of the field, this work was originally

> motivated by the desire to demonstrate that females are inherently inferior to males. . . . But from 1900 on, the findings of the psychologists gave strong support to the arguments of the feminists.[2]

. . .

By the mid-century functionalist sex-role theory dominated the western sociological discourse on women. The key figure in this development was Talcott Parsons, who in the early 1950s wrote the classic formulation of American sex role theory, giving it an intellectual breadth and rigor it had never had before. The notion of "role" as a basic structural concept of the social sciences had crystallized in the 1930s, and it was immediately applied to questions of gender. Two of Parsons's own

Carrigan, Tim, Bob Connell, and John Lee. "Toward a New Sociology of Masculinity." *Theory and Society*, September 1985, 14, pp. 55–604. Reprinted by permission from Springer Nature.

papers of the early 1940s talked "freely of sex roles." In the course of his argument he offered an interesting account of several options that had recently emerged within the female role. There was, however, little sense of a power relation between men and women; and the argument embedded the issue of sex and gender firmly in the context of the family.[3] . . .

This version of the role framework fitted comfortably with the intense social conservatism of the American intelligentsia in the 1950s, and with the lack of any direct political challenge from women. For functionalist sociology "the problem of women" was no longer how to explain their social subordination. It was how to understand the dysfunctions and strains involved in women's roles, primarily in relation to the middle-class family. Given the normative emphasis on the family, the sociological focus was strongly on "social problems": the conflicts faced by working wives, "maternal deprivation," divorce rates and juvenile delinquency, and intergenerational family conflict. The sense of conflict is strong in the work of Mirra Komarovsky who, after Parsons, made the most impressive application of the functionalist framework to sex roles in the 1940s. She developed a general argument about modernization producing a clash between a feminine "homemaker" ideal and a "career girl" ideal. The implications remained vague, but there was much more sense of complexity within sex roles than in Parsons's grand theorizing.[4]

Through the 1950s and I 960s the focus of sex role research remained on women in the family. And the field of sex role research remained a distinctly minor one within the overall concerns of sociology. This changed dramatically with the impact of second-wave feminism. . . .

It was not only a matter of establishment social science registering the issues raised by the new feminism. . . .

Towards Redefinition

Sex Roles Revisited

We have shown the massive influence of "sex role" notions in both formal social science and the informal literature associated with the "men's movement" of the 1970s. We have offered reasons to be dissatisfied with particular formulations, and now turn to the general critique of the "sex role" framework.

Broadly, the "role" framework has been used to analyze what the difference is between the social positions of women and men, to explain how they are shaped for those positions, and to describe the changes and conflicts that have occurred in and about those positions. At the simplest level, it is clear that the sex role framework accepts that sexual differentiation is a social phenomenon: sex roles are learnt, acquired, or "internalized." But the precise meaning of the sociality proposed by the framework is not nearly as simple as its proponents assume.

The very idea of a "role" implies a recognizable and accepted standard, and sex role theorists posit just such a norm to explain sexual differentiation. Society is organized around a pervasive differentiation between men's and women's roles, and these roles are internalized by all individuals. There is an obvious commonsense appeal to this approach. But the first objection to be made is that it does not actually describe the concrete reality of people's lives. Not all men are "responsible" fathers, nor "successful" in their occupations, and so on. Most men's lives reveal some departure from what the "male sex role" is supposed to prescribe.

The problem here is that the sex role literature does not consistently distinguish between the expectations that are made of people and what they in fact do. The framework often sees variations from the presumed norms of male behavior in terms of "deviance," as a "failure" in socialization. This is particularly evident in the functionalist version of sex role theory, where "deviance" becomes an unexplained, residual, and essentially non-social category. . . .

As social theory, the sex role framework is fundamentally static. This is not to say that it cannot recognize social change. Quite the contrary: change has been a leading theme in the discussion of men's sex roles by authors such as Pleck and Brannon.[5] The problem is that they cannot grasp it as history, as the interplay of praxis and structure. Change is always something that happens to sex roles, that impinges on them—whether from the direction of the society at large (as in discussions of how technological and economic change demands a shift to a "modern" male sex role), or from the direction of the asocial "real self" inside the person, demanding more room to breathe. Sex role theory cannot grasp change as a dialectic arising within gender relations themselves.

This is quite simply inherent in the procedure by which any account of "sex roles" is constructed: generalizing about sexual norms, and then applying this frozen description to men's and women's lives. . . .

The role framework, then, is neither a conceptually stable nor a practically and empirically adequate basis for the analysis of masculinity. Let us be blunt about it. The "male sex role" does not exist. It is impossible to isolate a "role" that constructs masculinity (or another that constructs femininity). Because there is no area of social life that is not the arena of sexual differentiation and gender relations, the notion of a sex role necessarily simplifies and abstracts to an impossible degree. . . .

Outline of a Social Analysis of Masculinity

Men in the Framework of Gender Relations

The starting point for any understanding of masculinity that is not simply biologistic or subjective must be men's involvement in the social relations that constitute the gender order. In a classic article Rubin has defined the domain of the argument as "the sex/gender system," a patterning of social relations connected with reproduction and gender division that is found in all societies, though in varying shapes.[6] This system is historical, in the fullest sense; its elements and relationships are constructed in history and are all subject to historical change.[7] It is also internally differentiated, as Mitchell argued more than a decade ago.[8] Two aspects of its organization have been the foci of research in the past decade: the division of labor and the structure of power. (The latter is what Millett originally called "sexual politics,"[9] and is the more precise referent of the concept "patriarchy.") To these we must add the structure of cathexis, the social organization of

sexuality and attraction—which as the history of homosexuality demonstrates is fully as social as the structures of work and power.

The central fact about this structure in the contemporary capitalist world (like most other social orders, though not all) is the subordination of women. This fact is massively documented, and has enormous ramifications—physical, mental, interpersonal, cultural—whose effects on the lives of women have been the major concerns of feminism. One of the central facts about masculinity, then, is that men in general are advantaged through the subordination of women.

To say "men in general" is already to point to an important complication in power relations. The global subordination of women is consistent with many particular situations in which women hold power over men, or are at least equal. Close-up research on families shows a good many households where wives hold authority in practice.[10] The fact of mothers' authority over young sons has been noted in most discussions of the psychodynamics of masculinity. The intersections of gender relations with class and race relations yield many other situations where rich white heterosexual women, for instance, are employers of working-class men, patrons of homosexual men, or politically dominant over black men.

To cite such examples and claim that women are therefore not subordinated in general would be crass. The point is, rather, that contradictions between local situations and the global relationships are endemic. They are likely to be a fruitful source of turmoil and change in the structure as a whole.

The overall relation between men and women, further, is not a confrontation between homogeneous, undifferentiated blocs. Our argument has perhaps established this sufficiently by now; even some role theorists, notably Hacker,[11] recognized a range of masculinities. We would suggest, in fact, that the fissuring of the categories of "men" and "women" is one of the central facts about patriarchal power and the way it works. In the case of men, the crucial division is between hegemonic masculinity and various subordinated masculinities.

Even this, however, is too simple a phrasing, as it suggests a masculinity differentiated only by power relations. . . .

The differentiation of masculinities is psychological—it bears on the kind of people that men are and become—but it is not only psychological. In an equally important sense it is institutional, an aspect of collective practice. In a notable recent study of British printing workers, Cynthia Cockburn has shown how a definition of compositors' work as hypermasculine has been sustained despite enormous changes in technology.[12] The key was a highly organized practice that drove women out of the trade, marginalized related labor processes in which they remained, and sustained a strongly-marked masculine "culture" in the workplace. What was going on here, as many details of her study show, was the collective definition of a hegemonic masculinity that not only manned the barricades against women but at the same time marginalized or subordinated other men in the industry (e.g., young men, unskilled workers, and those unable or unwilling to join the rituals). Though the details vary, there is every reason to think such processes are very general. Accordingly we see social definitions of masculinity as being embedded in the dynamics of institutions—the working of the state, of corporations, of unions, of families—quite as much as in the personality of individuals.

Forms of Masculinity and Their Interrelationships

. . .

The ability to impose a particular definition on other kinds of masculinity is part of what we mean by "hegemony." Hegemonic masculinity is far more complex than the accounts of essences in the masculinity books would suggest. It is not a "syndrome" of the kind produced when sexologists like Money reify human behavior into a "condition,"[13] or when clinicians reify homosexuality into a pathology. It is, rather, a question of how particular groups of men inhabit positions of power and wealth, and how they legitimate and reproduce the social relationships that generate their dominance.

An immediate consequence of this is that the culturally exalted form of masculinity, the hegemonic model so to speak, may only correspond to the actual characters of a small number of men. On this point at least the "men's liberation" literature had a sound insight. There is a distance, and a tension, between collective ideal and actual lives. Most men do not really act like the screen image of John Wayne or Humphrey Bogart; and when they try to, it is likely to be thought comic (as in the Woody Allen movie *Play It Again, Sam)* or horrific (as in shoot-outs and "sieges"). Yet very large numbers of men are complicit in sustaining the hegemonic model. There are various reasons: gratification through fantasy, compensation through displaced aggression (e.g. poofter-bashing by police and working-class youths), etc. But the overwhelmingly important reason is that most men benefit from the subordination of women, and hegemonic masculinity is centrally connected with the institutionalization of men's dominance over women. It would hardly be an exaggeration to say that hegemonic masculinity is hegemonic so far as it embodies a successful strategy in relation to women. . . .

[. . .]

The most important feature of this masculinity, alongside its connection with dominance, is that it is heterosexual. Though most literature on the family and masculinity takes this entirely for granted, it should not be. Psychoanalytic evidence goes far to show that conventional adult heterosexuality is constructed, in the individual life, as one among a number of possible paths through the emotional forest of childhood and adolescence. It is now clear that this is also true at the collective level, that the pattern of exclusive adult heterosexuality is a historically-constructed one. Its dominance is by no means universal. For this to become the hegemonic form of masculine sexuality required a historic redefinition of sexuality itself, in which undifferentiated "lust" was turned into specific types of "perversion"—the process that is documented, from the under side, by the historians of homosexuality already mentioned. A passion for beautiful boys was compatible with hegemonic masculinity in renaissance Europe, emphatically not so at the end of the nineteenth century. In this historical shift, men's sexual desire was to be focused more closely on women—a fact with complex consequences for them—while groups of men who were visibly not following the hegemonic pattern were more specifically labelled and attacked.

So powerful was this shift that even men of the ruling classes found wealth and reputation no protection. It is interesting to contrast the experiences of the Chevalier d'Eon, who managed an active career in diplomacy while dressed as a woman (in a later era he would have been labelled a "transvestite"), with that of Oscar Wilde a hundred years later.

"Hegemony," then, always refers to a historical situation, a set of circumstances in which power is won and held. The construction of hegemony is not a matter of pushing and pulling between ready-formed groupings, but is partly a matter of the *formation* of those groupings. To understand the different kinds of masculinity demands, above all, an examination of the practices in which hegemony is constituted and contested—in short, the political techniques of the patriarchal social order. . . .

Acknowledgements

We are grateful for the help of Cynthia Hamilton, Helen Easson, Margaret Clarke and other secretarial staff of the School of Behavioural Sciences at Macquarie University; and for technical assistance from the staff of the Kuring-gai College of Advanced Education Resources Centre. The work was funded by a grant, "Theory of Class and Patriarchy," from the Australian Research Grants Scheme.

Notes

1. V. Klein, *The Feminine Character: History of an Ideology* (London: Routledge and Kegan Paul, 1971 (1946)), 17.
2. L. Tyler, *The Psychology of Human Differences* (New York: Appleton Century Crofts, 1965), 240
3. T. Parsons, "Age and Sex in the Social Structure of the United States," in *Essays in Sociological Theory* (New York: The Free Press, 1964): 89–103; and, in the same volume, "The Kinship System of the Contemporary United States": 177–196.
4. M. Komarovsky, "Cultural Contradictions and Sex Roles," *American Journal of Sociology* 52 (November 1946): 184–189; and Komarovsky, "Functional Analysis of Sex Roles," *American Sociological Review* 15 (August 1950): 508–516.
5. J. H. Pleck, "The Male Sex Role: Definitions, Problems and Sources of Change," *Journal of Social Issues* 32 (1976): 155–164.
6. G. Rubin, "The Traffic in Women: Notes on the 'Political Economy' of Sex," in R. Reiter, ed., *Toward an Anthropology of Women* (New York: Monthly Review Press, 1975), 157–210.
7. R. W. Connell, "Theorising Gender," *Sociology* 19 (May 1985): 260–272.
8. J. Mitchell, *Woman's Estate* (Harmondsworth: Penguin, 1971).
9. K. Millett, *Sexual Politics* (New York: Doubleday, 1970).
10. Dowsett, "Gender Relations in Secondary Schooling," *Sociology of Education* 58 (January 1985): 34–48.
11. H. M. Hacker, "The New Burdens of Masculinity," *Marriage and Family Living* 19 (August 1957): 229.
12. C. Cockburn, *Brothers: Male Dominance and Technological Change* (London: Pluto Press, 1983).
13. J. Money, "Sexual Dimorphism and Homosexual Gender Identity," *Psychological Bulletin* 74, (1970): 425–440.

Chapter 4

Overview

Intersectionality is one of the most important ideas in gender studies today, often invoked to describe the ways in which multiple social categories, such as gender, race, class, or disability, interact to produce experiences that cannot simply be reduced to one category plus another category plus another, and so forth. The whole, in other words, is greater than the sum of its parts. Collins and Bilge describe how the concept emerged (from the experiences of black women, who found themselves experiencing racism and sexism simultaneously) and provide a practical application of intersectionality to something that may at first seem far removed from the study of gender—the 2014 FIFA World Cup in Brazil. They show how different forms of power were exercised in the lead up to and the playing of the World Cup, which affected different people in different ways. Around the same time as the World Cup was played, the Latinidades festival of Brazilian feminism was held in Brasília. These two very different events provide the material for two very different intersectional experiences by the people who participated in them. Watching the World Cup or attending a feminist festival of ideas and arts may be different experiences, but an intersectional approach shows what both events have in common. Collins and Bilge say that intersectionality incorporates six qualities, which are expressed and analyzed in the chapters that follow.

What Is Intersectionality?

Patricia Hill Collins and Sirma Bilge

In the early twenty-first century, the term "intersectionality" has been widely taken up by scholars, policy advocates, practitioners, and activists in many places and locations. College students and faculty in interdisciplinary fields such as women's studies, ethnic studies, cultural studies, American studies, and media studies, as well as those within sociology, political science, and history and other traditional disciplines, encounter intersectionality in courses, books, and scholarly articles. Human rights activists and government officials have also made intersectionality part of ongoing global public policy discussions. Grassroots organizers look to varying dimensions of intersectionality to inform their work on reproductive rights, antiviolence initiatives, workers' rights, and similar social issues. Bloggers use digital and social media to debate hot topics. Teachers, social workers, high-school students, parents, university support staff, and school personnel have taken up the ideas of intersectionality with an eye toward transforming schools of all sorts. Across these different venues, people increasingly claim and use the term "intersectionality" for their diverse intellectual and political projects.

If we were to ask them, "What is intersectionality?" we would get varied and sometimes contradictory answers. Most, however, would probably accept the following general description:

> Intersectionality is a way of understanding and analyzing the complexity in the world, in people, and in human experiences. The events and conditions of social and political life and the self can seldom be understood as shaped by one factor. They are generally shaped by many factors in diverse and mutually influencing ways. When it comes to social inequality, people's lives and the organization of power in a given society are better understood as being shaped not by a single axis of social division, be it race or gender or class, but by many axes that work together and influence each other. Intersectionality as an analytic tool gives people better access to the complexity of the world and of themselves.

. . . Despite debates about the meaning of this term, or even whether it is the right term to use at all, intersectionality is the term that has stuck. It is the term that is increasingly used by stakeholders who put their understandings of intersectionality to a variety of uses. Despite these differences, this general description points toward a general consensus about how people understand intersectionality.

Collins, Patricia Hill, and Sirma Bilge. "What is intersectionality?" Chapter 1 from *Intersectionality*. John Wiley & Sons, 2016.

Using Intersectionality as an Analytic Tool

People generally use intersectionality as an analytic tool to solve problems that they or others around them face. Most US colleges and universities, for example, face the challenge of building more inclusive and fair campus communities. The social divisions of class, race, gender, ethnicity, citizenship, sexuality, and ability are especially evident within higher education. Colleges and universities now include more college students who formerly had no way to pay for college (class), or students who historically faced discriminatory barriers to enrollment (race, gender, ethnicity or citizenship status, religion), or students who experience distinctive barriers and discrimination (sexuality and ability) on college campuses. Colleges and universities find themselves confronted with students who want fairness, yet who bring very different experiences and needs to campus. Initially, colleges recruited and served groups one at a time, offering, for example, special programs for African Americans, Latinos, women, gays and lesbians, veterans, returning students, and persons with disabilities. As the list grew, it became clearer that this one-at-a-time approach not only was slow, but that most students fit into more than one category. First-generation college students could include Latinos, women, poor whites, returning veterans, grandparents, and transgender individuals. In this context, intersectionality can be a useful analytic tool for thinking about and developing strategies to achieve campus equity.

Ordinary people can draw upon intersectionality as an analytic tool when they recognize that they need better frameworks to grapple with the complex discriminations that they face. In the 1960s and 1970s, African-American women activists confronted the puzzle of how their needs simply fell through the cracks of anti-racist social movements, feminism, and unions organizing for workers' rights. Each of these social movements elevated one category of analysis and action above others, for example, race within the civil rights movement, or gender within feminism or class within the union movement. Because African-American women were simultaneously black and female and workers, these single-focus lenses on social inequality left little space to address the complex social problems that they face. Black women's specific issues remained subordinated within each movement because no social movement by itself would, nor could, address the entirety of discriminations they faced. Black women's use of intersectionality as an analytic tool emerged in response to these challenges.

Intersectionality as an analytic tool is neither confined to nations of North America and Europe nor is it a new phenomenon. People in the Global South have used intersectionality as an analytic tool, often without naming it as such. Consider an unexpected example from nineteenth-century colonial India in the work of Savitribai Phule (1831–1897), regarded as an important first-generation modern Indian feminist. In an online article titled "Six Reasons Every Indian Feminist Must Remember Savitribai Phule," published in January 2015, Deepika Sarma suggests:

> Here's why you should know more about her. She got intersectionality. Savitribai along with her husband Jyotirao was a staunch advocate of anti-caste ideology and women's rights. The Phules' vision of social equality included fighting against the subjugation of women, and they also stood for Adivasis and Muslims. She organized a barbers' strike against shaving the heads of Hindu widows, fought for widow remarriage and in 1853, started a shelter for pregnant widows. Other welfare programmes she was involved with alongside Jyotirao include opening schools for workers and rural people, and providing famine relief through 52 food centers that also operated as boarding schools. She also cared for those affected by famine and plague, and died in 1897 after contracting plague from her patients. (Sarma 2015)

Phule confronted several axes of social division, namely caste, gender, religion, and economic disadvantage or class. Her political activism encompassed intersecting categories of social division—she didn't just pick one.

These examples suggest that people use intersectionality as an analytic tool in many different ways to address a range of issues and social problems. They find intersectionality's core insight to be useful: namely, that major axes of social divisions in a given society at a given time, for example, race, class, gender, sexuality, dis/ability, and age operate not as discrete and mutually exclusive entities, but build on each other and work together. Many people typically use intersectionality as a heuristic, a problem-solving or analytic tool, much in the way that students on college campuses developed a shared interest in diversity, or African-American women used it to address their status within social movement politics, or Savitribai Phule advanced women's rights. Even though those who use intersectional frameworks all seem to be situated under the same big umbrella, using intersectionality as a heuristic device means that intersectionality can assume many different forms.

. . . In the remainder of this section, we demonstrate three uses of intersectionality as an analytic tool that were inspired by important global events that took place in 2014.

Power Plays: The FIFA World Cup

Brazil's international reputation as a football (soccer) powerhouse raised high hopes for its winning the 2014 FIFA World Cup. As one of the most successful national teams in the history of the World Cup, Brazil was the only country whose teams had qualified for and attended every World Cup tournament. Brazil had also produced some of the greatest players in the history of world football. The legendary Pelé remains Brazil's highest goal-scorer of all time. Italy, Germany, and Argentina are all football powerhouses, yet, in terms of star power and status, they were no match for Brazil.

Because the 2014 tournament was held in Brazil, the stakes were especially high. The potential payoff for a winning Brazilian team in

Brazil could be huge. Hosting the FIFA World Cup would enable Brazil to shed vestiges of its troubled history of being ruled by a military dictatorship (1964–1985), as well as signal its arrival as a major economic player. Brazil's victory, both on the field and via its hosting, would attract global attention. The World Cup was the most widely watched and followed sporting event in the world, exceeding even the Olympic Games. From the perspective of Brazil's policy makers and financiers, the possibilities of reaching a massive global market were endless. For example, the cumulative audience for all matches during the 2006 World Cup was estimated to be 26.29 billion people, with an estimated 715.1 million people watching the final match in Berlin, an astonishing one-ninth of the entire population of the planet.

So how did the 2014 FIFA World Cup games go? The challenges associated with hosting the games began well before the athletes arrived on the playing fields. Brazil estimated a figure of US$11.3 billion in public works-spending for the event. The initial plan presented to the public emphasized that the majority of the spending on infrastructure for the World Cup would highlight general transportation, security, and communications. Less than 25% of total spending would go toward the twelve new or refurbished stadiums. Yet, as the games grew nearer, cost overruns increased stadium costs by at least 75%, with public resources reallocated from general infrastructure projects. The FIFA cost overruns aggravated ongoing public demonstrations in several Brazilian cities against the increase in public transportation fares and political corruption. For example, on June 20, 2013, one and a half million people demonstrated in São Paulo, Brazil's largest metropolitan area with a population of 18 million people. In this context, the exorbitant cost of stadiums, the displacement of urban dwellers for construction, and the embezzlement of public funds became a new theme at the forefront of public protests (Castells 2015: 232). As the countdown to the kickoff began, Brazilians took to the streets with banners against the World Cup. "FIFA go home!" and "We want hospitals up to FIFA's standards!" were common slogans in protests throughout more than a hundred cities. "The World Cup steals money from healthcare, education and the poor. The homeless are being forced from the streets. This is not for Brazil, it's for the tourists," reported a *Guardian* article (Watts 2014).

The games began as this social unrest intensified. Of the thirty-two teams that qualified for the World Cup, Brazil was one of four that reached the semifinals, facing an undefeated Germany. The match wasn't even close. Germany led 5–0 at half time, scoring an unheard of four goals in a span of six minutes, and went on to win the World Cup. For its stunned fans in the stadium, as well as for the massive global audience, Brazil's loss was shocking. The media depicted the match as a national disgrace, with Brazilian newspapers carrying headlines such as "The Biggest Shame in History," "A Historical Humiliation!," and "Brazil is Slain." Global media joined in with headlines that described the defeat as the "ultimate embarrassment" and the "most humiliating World Cup host nation defeat of all time."

On the surface, intersectionality seems far removed from Brazil's 2014 FIFA World Cup experience. Because many people enjoy sporting events or play sports themselves, sports seem distant from intersectionality's concern with social inequality. Yet using intersectionality as an analytic tool to examine the FIFA World Cup sheds light on the organization of power. Intersectionality as an analytic tool examines how power relations are intertwined and mutually constructing. Race, class, gender, sexuality, dis/ability, ethnicity, nation, religion, and age are categories of analysis, terms that reference important social divisions. But they are also categories that gain meaning from power relations of racism, sexism, heterosexism, and class exploitation.

One way of describing the organization of power identifies four distinctive yet interconnected domains of power: interpersonal, disciplinary, cultural, and structural. These four dimensions of the organization of power provide opportunities for using intersectionality as an analytic tool to better understand the 2014 FIFA World Cup.

The Interpersonal Domain of Power

First, power relations are about people's lives, how people relate to one another, and who is advantaged or disadvantaged within social interactions. Without the athletes, there would be no World Cup. The athletes are individuals and, whether famous or not, their actions shape power relations just as much as the policy makers who bid on the games, the media that covered the Brazilian national team's defeat, or the activists who took to the street to protest cost overruns.

As a people's sport, football can be played almost anywhere by almost anyone. Each team is composed of a constellation of individuals who, on some level, love football and have chosen to play. One does not need expensive lessons, or a carefully manicured playing field, or even shoes. It requires no special equipment or training, only a ball and enough players to field two teams. Compared with ice skating, tennis, skiing, or American football, soccer has far fewer barriers between athletic talent and the means to develop that talent. Across the globe, there is no way of knowing exactly how many people play football. Yet FIFA's surveys provide a good guess: an estimated 270 million people are involved in football as professional soccer players, recreational players, registered players both over and under age 18, futsal and beach football players, referees, and officials. This is a vast pool of potential elite athletes and a massive audience reaching across categories of social class, age, gender, ethnicity, and nation. When one adds the children and youth who play football but who are not involved in any kind of organized activity detectable by FIFA, the number swells greatly.

The fanfare granted to the World Cup is a small tip of the iceberg of the everyday social interactions that shape people's relationships with one another in regard to football. From elite athletes to poor kids, football players want to play on a fair playing field. It doesn't matter how you got to the field: all that matters once you are on the field is what you do on the field. The sports metaphor of a level playing field speaks to the desire for fairness. Whether winners or losers, this team sport rewards individual talent yet also highlights the collective team nature of achievement. When played well and unimpeded by suspect officiating, football rewards individual talent. In a world that is characterized by so much unfairness, competitive sports such as football become important venues for seeing how things should be. The backgrounds of the players should not matter when they hit the playing field. What matters is how well they play. The cries of anguish from the losing 2014 Brazil team may have made the news, but few people questioned the outcome of the game. Fair play ruled.

Football is a people's sport, but not all people get to play. One important rule of football, and of most sports for that matter, is that men and women do not compete directly against one another. The rules of fair play may apply within gender categories, yet how fair are those categories? Sports generally, and professional sports in particular, routinely provide opportunities for men that are denied to women. By this rule of gender segregation, the 2014 World Cup showed that the kind of football that counts for FIFA and fans alike is played by men.

Using intersectionality as an analytic lens highlights the multiple nature of individual identities and how varying combinations of class, gender, race, sexuality, and citizenship categories differentially position each individual. Regardless of the love of soccer, these axes of social division work together and influence one another to shape each individual biography.

The Disciplinary Domain of Power

When it comes to the organization of power, different people find themselves encountering different treatment regarding which rules apply to them and how those rules will be implemented. Within football's disciplinary domain, some people are told they lack talent and are discouraged from playing, whereas others may receive extra coaching to cultivate the talent they have. Many are simply told that they are out of luck because they are the wrong gender or age to play at all. In essence, power operates by disciplining people in ways that put people's lives on paths that make some options seem viable and others out of reach.

For example, South Africa's 2010 hosting of the World Cup helped highlight the disciplinary practices that African boys faced who wanted to play football in Europe. European football clubs offer salaries on a par with those offered within US professional football, basketball, and baseball to play for teams in the United Kingdom, France, Italy, and Spain. The surge in the number of Africans playing at big European clubs reflects the dreams of young African football players to make it big. Yet these practices also makes them vulnerable to exploitation by unscrupulous recruiters. Filmmaker Mariana van Zeller's 2010 documentary *Football's Lost Boys* details how thousands of young players are lured away from their homelands, with their families giving up their savings to predatory agents, and how they are often left abandoned, broke, and alone. Some refer to the treatment of young African players as human trafficking.

The increasing racial/ethnic diversity on elite European teams who recruit African players, other players of color from poorer nations, and racialized immigrant minorities may help teams to win. But this racial/ethnic/national diversity of elite football teams has also highlighted the problem of racism in European football. The visible diversity among team players upends long-standing assumptions about race, ethnicity, and national identity. When the national team of France won the 1998 World Cup, defeating Brazil 3–0, some fans saw the team as nonrepresentative of France because most of the players weren't white. Moreover, white European fans may love their teams, yet many feel free to engage in racist behavior, such as calling African players monkeys, chanting racial slurs, and carrying signs with racially derogatory language. In one case, Polish fans threw bananas at a Nigerian football player. The fans aren't the only problem—racial slurs among players are also an issue. For example, at the 2006 World Cup, France's Zinedine Zidane, a three-time winner of FIFA's world player of the year violated a rule of fair play by headbutting Italy's Marco Materazzi in the chest. Zidane, the son of Algerian immigrants, said he was goaded by Materazzi's racist and sexist slurs against his mother and sister. Materazzi was kept in play while Zidane was ejected from what was to be his last ever World Cup match.

The Cultural Domain of Power

When it comes to the organization of power, ideas matter in providing explanations for social inequality and fair play. Televised across the globe, the World Cup sends out important ideas about competition and fair play. Sports contests send an influential message: not everyone can win. On the surface, this makes sense. But why do some people win and other people lose? More importantly, why do some people consistently win and others consistently lose? FIFA football has ready-made answers. Winners have talent, discipline, and luck, and losers suffer from lack of talent, inferior self-discipline, and/or bad luck. This view suggests that fair competition produces just results. Armed with this worldview concerning winners and losers, it's a small step to using this frame to explain social inequality itself.

What conditions are needed for this frame to remain plausible? This is where the idea of a level or flat playing field becomes crucial. Imagine a tilted football field that was installed on the side of a gently sloped hill with the red team's goal on top of the hill and the blue team's goal in the valley. The red team has a clear advantage: when they try to score, gravity propels the ball toward their opponent's goal. No matter how gifted, their team players need not work as hard to score. In contrast, the blue team has an uphill battle to score a goal. The blue team members may need to be especially gifted to continue playing the game. They may have talent and self-discipline but they have the bad luck of playing on a tilted playing field.

Football fans would be outraged if the actual playing field were tilted in this way. Yet this is what social divisions of class, gender, and race do—we all think we are playing on a level playing field when we are not. The cultural domain of power helps manufacture messages that playing fields are level, that all competitions are fair, and that any resulting patterns of winners and losers have been fairly accomplished.

With the advent of new communications technologies, mass media has increased in significance for the cultural domain of power. Via contests between nations, cities, regions, and all sorts of things, mass media stages entertainment that reinforces the myth of a level playing field where one doesn't actually exist. For FIFA, 195 or so nation-states theoretically can compete in the World Cup as long as they play by the rules and their teams are good enough. This is the myth of equal opportunity to compete. When national teams compete, nations themselves compete. Yet because rich nations have far more resources than poor ones, few nation-states can field teams.

The message of mass-media spectacles goes beyond any one event. The competitive and repetitive nature of contests—such as the World Cup and the Olympics—reflects intersecting power relations of capitalism and nationalism. Competing mass-media spectacles reiterate the belief that unequal outcomes of winners and losers are normal outcomes of marketplace competition. In other words, social inequalities that are fairly produced are socially just. The repetitive nature of sporting events, beauty pageants, reality television, and the like provide a useful interpretive context for viewing the marketplace relations of capitalism as being similarly organized. These mass media spectacles and associated events also present important scripts of gender, race, and nation that work together and influence one another. The bravery of male athletes on national teams makes them akin to war heroes on battlefields, while the beauty, grace, and virtue of national beauty pageants are thought to represent the beauty, grace, and virtue of the nation. Mass-media spectacles may appear to be mere entertainment, yet they serve political ends.

The Structural Domain of Power

Fair play on a level playing field may be the ethos of football, yet how much of this fair play characterizes the organization of FIFA football itself? The structural domain of power here refers to how FIFA itself is organized or structured. Because intersectionality embraces complexity, it questions how intersecting power relations of class, gender, race, and nation shape the institutionalization and organization of the World Cup. As a global industry, FIFA has organized the populist sensibility of football into a highly profitable global network. With an executive committee of 25 businessmen, FIFA's headquarters are located in Switzerland, where the government provides it legal protection as an international NGO. Its legal status has allowed FIFA to control billions of euros without substantial government oversight. As big business, FIFA has managed to organize football into a global industry with tremendous reach and considerable influence with governments. For example, in 2012 FIFA succeeded in having the Brazilian parliament adopt a General World Cup Law that imposed bank holidays on host cities on the days of the Brazilian team's matches, cut the number of places in the stadiums, and increased prices for ordinary spectators. The law also allowed alcoholic drinks to be taken into the stadiums, a change in the law which was of special benefit to Anheuser-Busch, the makers of Budweiser beer and one of FIFA's main sponsors. The bill also exempted companies working for FIFA from taxes and fiscal charges, banned the sale of any goods in official competition spaces, their immediate surroundings and their principal access routes, and penalized bars who tried to schedule showings of the matches or promote certain brands. Finally, the bill defined any attack on the image of FIFA or its sponsors as a federal crime.

Given FIFA's global reach and largely unchecked powers, it should come as no surprise that, because FIFA is unregulated, it has for years come under suspicion of corruption. In June 2015, the US Department of Justice issued indictments against top FIFA officials and others involved in FIFA, bringing FIFA's corruption allegations into public purview. At the request of the United States, Interpol issued six alerts for two former senior FIFA officials and four corporate executives. They were a former FIFA vice-president from Trinidad and Tobago who was accused of accepting bribes in connection with the awarding of the 2010 World Cup to South Africa; a Paraguayan citizen and former FIFA executive committee member; three business persons who control two sports-marketing business based in Argentina; and a Brazilian citizen who owns broadcasting businesses. Accused of rigging the bidding process for awarding the games, the indictments traced financial payoffs to key FIFA figures in exchange for FIFA's endorsements. At the heart of the corruption were charges of "pay to play," rather than fair play.[1] . . .

Latinidades: The Black Women's Movement in Brazil

Two weeks after the raucous fans departed from Brazil's 2014 World Cup spectacle, more than a thousand women of African descent, their friends, family members, colleagues, and allies travelled to Brasilia, the national capital. They arrived at the iconic National Museum of the Republic, several blocks away from the refurbished but now empty World Cup stadium, to attend the seventh meeting of Latinidades, the Afro-Latin and Afro-Caribbean women's festival. As the largest festival for black women in Latin America, the event was scheduled to coincide with the annual International Day of Black Latin American and Caribbean Women. Latinidades's seasoned event organizers had recruited an impressive list of main sponsors: the State Secretary of Culture, the Office of Racial Equality, the Funarte Palmares Cultural Foundation and Petrobras, Brazil's multinational energy corporation. Unlike the goals of FIFA, Latinidades's success would not be judged by corporate profits or the success of mass-media spectacle. Unlike the hefty ticket prices for the World Cup, the six-day Latinidades festival was free and housed in public space.

Latinidades was no ordinary festival: its expressed purpose lay in promoting "racial equality and tackling racism and sexism." The festival drew mostly women of African descent but also many men and members of diverse racial/ethnic groups from all areas of Brazil's states and regions, as well as from Costa Rica, Ecuador, and other Latin American and Caribbean nations. This geographic heterogeneity reflected the many different ways participants were connected to promoting racial equality and tackling how racism and sexism affected Afro-Latin women. Community organizers, professors, graduate students, parents, artists, schoolteachers, high-school students, representatives of samba schools, government officials, and music lovers, among others, made the journey to Brasilia to attend Latinidades.

The festival's programming was inclusive, with something for all attendees, even the youngest ones. Latinidades had elements of an academic symposium, a political organizing event, an African cultural heritage event, and a mass-music festival rolled into one. Latinidades's academic component resembled a standard academic conference, complete with plenary sessions and an array of panels on issues as varied as health, psychology, literature from the African diaspora, and a session devoted to new books by and about black women. Important Afro-Brazilian feminist intellectuals attended. Some sessions examined community-organizing initiatives in favelas (low-income urban communities), as well as forms of wisdom associated with land, sustainability, and the environment.

The festival's strong activist orientation permeated both its sessions and its special events. For example, Angela Davis's keynote address got the audience on its feet, many with fists raised in the Black Power salute. The festival also set aside time for a planning meeting to educate attendees about the upcoming Black Women's March for a National Day of Denouncing Racism. Community organizers rubbed shoulders with academics, as did young people with revered elders. . . .

Not only was Latinidades a success, its very existence constituted one highly visible moment of an Afro-Brazilian women's movement that took several decades to build. Holding a festival that was devoted to the issues and needs of black women in Brazil specifically, as well as Afro-Latin and Afro-Caribbean women more generally, would have been impossible several decades earlier. Since the 1930s, when Brazil adopted an ideology of racial democracy, Brazil officially claimed not to have "races." The Brazilian government collected no racial statistics and, without racial categories, Brazil officially had neither race nor black people. Within this social context, women of African descent may have constituted a visible and sizable segment of Brazilian society, yet in a

Brazil that ostensibly lacked race, the category of black women did not exist as an officially recognized population.

How might using intersectionality as an analytic tool shed light on Latinidades's commitment to challenging racism and sexism against a group that officially did not exist? For one, black women challenged Brazil's national identity narrative concerning racial democracy. They saw the historical interconnections between ideas about race and Brazil's nation-building project as setting the stage for the erasure of Afro-Brazilian women. Brazil's cultivated image of national identity posited that racism did not exist and that color lacks meaning, other than celebrating it as a dimension of national pride. This national identity neither came about by accident nor meant that people of African descent believed it. By erasing the political category of race, Brazil's national discourse of racial democracy effectively eliminated language that might describe the racial inequalities that affected black Brazilian people's lives. This erasure of "blackness" as a political category allowed discriminatory practices to occur against people of visible African descent in education and employment because there were neither officially recognized terms for describing racial discrimination nor official remedies for it (Twine 1998). Brazil's military government (1964–1985) upheld this national ideology of racial democracy and also suppressed social protest in general. The end of the dictatorship in 1985 created new opportunities for seeing the connections between racism and Brazilian nationalism, as well as for social movements.

Second, using intersectionality as an analytic tool also sheds light on how women of African descent or Afro-Brazilian women are situated within gendered and sexualized understandings of Brazilian history and national identity. Brazil's specific history of slavery, colonialism, predictatorship democracy, dictatorship and post-dictatorship democracy framed distinctive patterns of intersecting power relations of gender and sexuality. Sexual engagements, both consensual and forced, among African-, indigenous- and European-descended populations created a

Brazilian population with varying hair textures, skin colors, body shapes, and eye colors, as well as a complex and historically shifting series of terms to describe them. Claims of Brazil's racial democracy notwithstanding, Brazil, like other Latin American countries, developed a carefully calibrated lexicon of ethnoracial classification. Skin color, hair texture, facial features, and other aspects of appearance became de facto racial markers for distributing education, jobs, and other social goods. As Caldwell points out, "popular images of Brazil as a carnivalesque, tropical paradise have played a central role in contemporary constructions of mulata women's social identities. Brazil's international reputation as a racial democracy is closely tied to the sexual objectification of women of mixed racial ancestry as the essence of Brazilianness" (Caldwell 2007: 58). For Afro-Brazilian women, those of mixed ancestry or with more European physical features are typically considered to be more attractive. Moreover, women of visible African ancestry are typically constructed as non-sexualized, and often as asexual laborers or conversely as prostitutes (Caldwell 2007: 51). Appearance not only carries differential weight for women and men, but different stereotypes of black women rest on beliefs about their sexuality. These ideas feed back into notions of national identity, using race, gender, sexuality, and color as intersecting phenomena.

A third dimension of using intersectionality as an analytic tool concerns how intersectionality's framework of mutually constructing identity categories enabled Afro-Brazilian women to develop a collective identity politics. In this case, they cultivated a political black feminist identity at the intersections of racism, sexism, class exploitation, national history, and sexuality. The political space created by reinstalling democracy in the late 1980s benefited both women and blacks. Yet there was one significant difference between the two groups. In a climate where women's rights encompassed only the needs of white women and where blacks were not politically recognized, Afro-Brazilian women were differentially treated within both the feminist movement and the Black Movement. Clearly, women and men had

different experiences within Brazilian society—there was no need to advocate for the integrity of the categories themselves. Yet the framing of the women's movement, even around such a firm subject as "woman," was inflected through other categories. Because upper-class and middle-class women were central to the movement, their status as marked by class yet unmarked by race (most were white) shaped political demands. Brazil's success in electing women to political office reflected alliances among women across categories of social class. With the noteworthy exception of Benedita da Silva, the first black woman to serve in the Brazilian Congress in 1986 and the Senate in 1994, feminism raised issues of gender and sexuality, but did so in ways that did not engage issues of anti-black racism that were so important to Afro-Brazilian women.

Unlike white Brazilian women, black Brazilians of all sexes and genders had to create the collective political identity of "black" in order to build an anti-racist social movement that highlighted the effects of anti-black racism. Brazil's history with transatlantic slavery left it with a large population of African descent—by some estimates, 50% of the Brazilian population. Claiming an identity as "black" seemed to contradict the national identity of racial democracy, and thus ran the risk of being accused of disloyalty and not being fully Brazilian. In this sense, the Black Movement that emerged in the 1990s did not call for equal treatment within the democratic state for an already recognized group. Rather, recognition meant both naming a sizable segment of the population and acknowledging that it experienced anti-black racial discrimination (Hanchard 1994).

Neither Brazilian feminism led by women who were primarily well off and white, nor a Black Movement that was actively engaged in claiming a collective black identity that identified racism as a social force could by itself adequately address Afro-Brazilian women's issues. Black women who participated in the Black Movement found willing allies when it came to anti-racist black activism but much less understanding of how the issues faced by black people took gender-specific forms.

Indeed, they found little recognition of the special issues of living lives as black women in Brazil at the intersections of areas of racism, sexism, class exploitation, second-class citizenship, and heterosexism. Brazil's history of class analysis that saw capitalism and workers' rights as major forces in shaping inequality made space for exceptional individuals such as Benedita da Silva. Yet when it came to race, class politics asked them to see both gender and race as secondary. Black women faced similar pressures to subordinate their special concerns under the banner of class solidarity. These separate social movements of feminism, antiracism, and workers' movements were important, and many black women continued to participate in them. Yet because no one social movement alone could adequately address Afro-Brazilian women's issues, they formed their own. . . .

In brief, Latinidades thus marked the celebration of a long struggle to build a complex social movement that acknowledged race, gender, class, nation and sexuality as mutually constructing and multidimensional aspects of Afro-Brazilian women's lives. Women of African descent in Brazil knew on one level, through personal experience, that they were part of a group that shared certain collective experiences. They were disproportionately found in domestic work. Their images were maligned in popular culture. They were disproportionately targets of violence against women. They were mothers who lacked the means to care for their children as they would have liked, but had ties to the value placed on mothering across the African diaspora. Yet because they lacked a political identity and accompanying analysis to attach to these experiences, they couldn't articulate a collective identity politics to raise their concerns. None of their closest allies—black men in the Black Movement, or white women in the feminist movement, or socialists in organizations that advocated for workers' rights—would have their own best interests at heart as fervently as they did. Lacking a language that spoke directly to their experiences, black women such as Léila Gonzalez, Sueli Carneiro and a long list of activist/scholars painstakingly organized the various constituencies of black women that were needed to address black women's concerns (Carneiro 1995, 2014).

Core Ideas of Intersectional Frameworks

Intersectionality is a way of understanding and analyzing the complexity in the world, in people, and in human experience. The previous section showed three different uses of intersectionality as an analytic tool that sheds light on the complexity of people's lives within an equally complex social context. Each case illustrates how the events and conditions of social and political life at play were not shaped by any one factor. Rather, the dynamics in each case reflected many factors that worked together in diverse and mutually influencing ways.

The FIFA World Cup, and the black Brazilian feminist social movement also help clarify six core ideas that appear and reappear when people use intersectionality as an analytic tool: inequality, relationality, power, social context, complexity, and social justice. . . .

1. *Social inequality*: Both cases grapple with social inequality, albeit from very different vantage points. The case of social inequality within World Cup football juxtaposes the search for fairness on the playing field with the unfairness of FIFA's global organization. Latinidades illustrates how the Afro-Brazilian women's movement responded intellectually and politically to historical and contemporary forms of social inequality, especially the intersections of racism and sexism, in shaping social class differ within the particular history of the Brazilian nation-state.

    . . . Intersectionality exists because many people were deeply concerned by the forms of social inequality they either experienced themselves or saw around them. Intersectionality adds additional layers of complexity to understandings of social inequality, recognizing that social inequality is rarely caused by a single factor. Using intersectionality as an analytic tool encourages us to move beyond seeing social inequality through race-only or class-only lenses. Instead, intersectionality encourages understandings of social inequality based on interactions among various categories.

2. *Power*: Both cases highlight different dimensions of the organization of power relations. The case study of the World Cup examines the multi-faceted power relations of FIFA World Cup football. . . . In contrast, the Latinidades case shows how power relations operate within political projects and social movements. By examining how black women in Brazil organized to resist multiple forms of social inequality, the Latininades case illustrates political activism not only from top-down policy endeavors or global social movements, but rather from the space of community organizing and grassroots coalition politics.

   These cases raise two important points about power relations. First, intersectional frameworks understand power relations through a lens of mutual construction. In other words, people's lives and identities are generally shaped by many factors in diverse and mutually influencing ways. Moreover, race, class, gender, sexuality, age, disability, ethnicity, nation, and religion, among others, constitute interlocking, mutually constructing or intersecting systems of power. Within intersectional frameworks, there is no pure racism or sexism. Rather, power relations of racism and sexism gain meaning in relation to one another.

   Second, power relations are to be analyzed both via their intersections, for example, of racism and sexism, as well as across domains of power, namely structural, disciplinary, cultural, and interpersonal. The framework of domains of power provides a heuristic device or thinking tool for examining power relations. The World Cup case introduced this heuristic by analyzing each domain of power separately. It broke them down into the kinds of power relations that are solidified in social structures (e.g., organizations like FIFA and institutions like national governments) that are shared through ideas and media, or culture broadly speaking, that appear over and over again in the ways that informal social rewards and punishments get distributed in everyday interactions, and that play out in everyday interactions among people. These are the structural, cultural, disciplinary, and interpersonal domains of power, respectively. Looking at how power works in each domain can shed light on the dynamics of a larger social phenomenon, like the social unrest around the 2014 World Cup. Yet, in actual social practice, the domains overlap, and no one domain is any more important than another.

3. *Relationality*: The Latinidades case of the Afro-Brazilian women's movement illustrates a historical and contemporary commitment to develop coalitions or relationships across social divisions. Whether the relationality of multiple identities within the interpersonal domain of power or the relationality of analysis required to understand how class, race, and gender collectively shape global social inequality, this idea of connectedness or relationality is important.

   Relational thinking rejects either/or binary thinking, for example, opposing theory to practice, scholarship to activism, or blacks to whites. Instead, relationality embraces a both/and frame. The focus of relationality shifts from analyzing what distinguishes entities, for example, the differences between race and gender, to examining their interconnections. This shift in perspective opens up intellectual and political possibilities. The global inequality case illustrates how class-only arguments may be insufficient to explain global social inequality, and that intersectional arguments that examine the relationships between class, race, gender, and age might be more valuable. Relationality takes various forms within intersectionality and is found in terms such as "coalition," "dialog," "conversation," "interaction," and "transaction." Because this core idea of relationality traverses much intersectional inquiry and practice, it is also central to this book. Power is better conceptualized as a relationship, as in power relations, than as a static entity. Power is not a thing to be gained or lost as in the zero-sum conceptions of winners and losers on the football playing field. Rather, power constitutes a relationship.

4. *Social context*: [Both] cases also provide opportunities for examining intersecting power

relations in context. While both the World Cup and the black women's movement involve Brazil, the latter case highlights the significance of specific historical contexts in the production of intersectional knowledge and action, even in the absence of the term itself. The case of the black women's movement in Brazil shows how intellectual and political activism work by growing from a specific set of concerns in a specific social location, in this case the identity politics of Afro-Brazilian women.

. . . Contextualization is especially important for intersectional projects produced in the Global South because scholars and activists working in Brazil, South Africa, Trinidad, Bangladesh, India, Nigeria, and other nation-states of the Global South face specific sets of difficulties in reaching wider audiences. To understand increasing global social inequalities, relationality sheds light on how intersections of racism, class exploitation, sexism, nationalism, and heterosexism work together to shape social inequality. These systems operate relationally across structural, cultural, disciplinary, and interpersonal domains. Attending to social context grounds intersectional analysis.

5. *Complexity*: These core themes of social inequality, power, relationality, and social context are intertwined, introducing an element of complexity into intersectional analysis. Intersectionality itself is a way of understanding and analyzing the complexity in the world. Using intersectionality as an analytic tool is difficult, precisely because intersectionality itself is complex. This level of complexity is not easy for anyone to handle. It complicates things and can be a source of frustration for scholars, practitioners, and activists alike,

who are looking for a neat tool to apply: a tidy methodology for intersectional research (the dream of some students perhaps); or a crisp instruction manual for applying intersectionality to various fields of practice (how to make an intersectional social work intervention; how to make intersectional policy analysis; how to use intersectionality for fostering coalitions in social movement politics). These are perfectly legitimate and undoubtedly useful expectations that scholars, practitioners, and activists engaged in intersectionality all have to address seriously and collaboratively.

6. *Social justice*: These cases engage varying angles of vision on social justice. The World Cup case suggests that competition is not inherently bad. People accept the concept of winners and losers if the game itself is fair. Yet fairness is elusive in unequal societies where the rules may seem fair, yet differentially enforced through discriminatory practices. Fairness is also elusive where the rules themselves may appear to be equally applied to everyone yet still produce unequal and unfair outcomes: in democratic societies, everyone has the "right" to vote, but not everyone has equal access to do so. . . .

Social justice may be intersectionality's most contentious core idea, but it is one that expands the circle of intersectionality to include people who use intersectionality as an analytic tool for social justice. Working for social justice is not a requirement for intersectionality. Yet people who are engaged in using intersectionality as an analytic tool and people who see social justice as central rather than as peripheral to their lives are often one and the same. These people are typically critical of, rather than accepting of, the status quo.

Note

1. FIFA's legal troubles aside, the business of the World Cup goes far beyond the games themselves. Rather, as the scope of people who were indicted indicates, the World Cup is situated at the convergence of increasingly important global industries: sports and entertainment, global telecommunications and

tourism, and the globalized World Cup paraphernalia industry. For example, the FIFA-approved official ball of the 2014 World Cup, Adidas Brazuca, at a price tag of US$160, was manufactured in The Forward Sports factory at Sialkot (Pakistan) by Pakistani women

(90 percent of the workforce) who each made barely US$100 per month. After selling 13 million official World Cup match balls in 2010, Adidas made hundreds of millions of dollars. In 2014, it expected to sell more than 14 million of them.

References

Caldwell, Kia Lilly. 2007. *Negras in Brazil: Re-envisioning Black Women, Citizenship, and the Politics of Identity.* New Brunswick, NJ: Rutgers University Press.

Carneiro, Sueli. 1995. "Defining Black Feminism," in A. O. Pala (ed.), *Connecting Across Cultures and Continents: Black Women Speak Out on Identity, Race and Development.* New York: United Nations Development Fund for Women, pp. 11–18.

Carneiro, Sueli. 2014. *Leila Gonzalez: o feminismo negro no palco da historia [Leila Gonzalez: Black Feminism on the Stage of History].* Brasilia: Abravideo.

Castells, Manuel. 2015. *Networks of Outrage and Hope: Social Movements in the Internet Age*, 2nd edn. Cambridge: Polity Press.

Hanchard, Michael G. 1994. *Orpheus and Power: The Movimento Negro of Rio de Janeiro and Sao Paulo, Brazil, 1945–1988.* Princeton: Princeton University Press.

Sarma, Deepika. 2015. "Six Reasons Why Every Indian Feminist Should Remember Savitribai Phule." January 5. http://theladiesfinger.com/six-reasons-every-indian-feminist-shouldremember-savitribai-phule/

Watts, Jonathan. 2014. "Anti-World Cup Protests in Brazilian Cities Mark Countdown to Kickoff." *The Guardian.* June 12. http://www.theguardian.com/football/2014/jun/12/anti-worldcup-protests-brazilian-cities-sao-paulo-rio-de-janeiro

Part II
Gender, Racism, and Racialization

Picking up from Collins and Bilge's introduction to intersectionality, we now consider how gender is racialized (or how race is gendered, depending on which way you want to look at it). The authors in this section provide empirical examples of the interaction between the social construction of gender and racial identity across a range of communities.

They are all appropriately wary of reducing racialization to a mere acknowledgement of "cultural differences." Abji, Kortweg, and Williams examine how service providers in South Asian communities have to navigate the racist discourse that posits honour killings in these communities as just a manifestation of "bad cultural traditions" by racialized communities, rather than instances of gender-based violence against women. They work to create new ways of talking about gender and race that avoid falling into stereotypes.

Taking up the challenges faced by Abji, Kortweg, and Williams' participants, Aujla examines the literary productions of South Asian women. She demonstrates how the identity work these young women do in their writings does not merely refuse and refute gendered racial stereotypes, but also gives voice to new ways of representing gendered lives.

Karimi, Bucerius, and Thompson also focus on the experience of racialized youth in their work with young Somali immigrants in Edmonton. These young people, both men and women, have to negotiate expectations from the Somali community as well as negative stereotyping outside the community, which are shaped and differentiated by gender. Like Aujla's participants, these youth work to produce their own identities, which are simultaneously Somali, Muslim, and Canadian.

White privilege, in the form of obliviousness to racism and microaggressions, is the substance of Mohamed and Beagan's piece on Canadian universities, where we can explore higher education as a site of racism and other forms of prejudice. Racialized teachers and researchers describe what they experience as "strange faces" on predominantly white campuses, and the subtle as well as obvious ways in which racialization remains a presence in their working lives. It's probably safe to say that the microaggressions and devaluations they experience are not deliberate, in the sense that they're not motivated by conscious racism, but unconscious whiteness can be as harmful as the more overt expressions of gendered discrimination in the work of Abji and colleagues, Aujla, and Karimi and colleagues.

Finally, Nicoll explores a different kind of gendered identity construction in her personal essay—coming to know oneself as a gendered, racialized white settler. Her own whiteness, which was the taken-for-granted backdrop of her life growing up, becomes more obvious to her as she explores the ways in which white privilege is sustained through the ideas white people like to hold about themselves.

Questions for Critical Thought

1. Can you think of circumstances similar to the "strange faces" that Mohamed and Beagan describe? Perhaps these circumstances affected you yourself, or perhaps you observed the experiences of other people.

2. Cultural and ethnic "belonging" is important to the participants in several of these studies. How does gender shape the ways that one can "belong" to a community of origin?

3. Is there such a thing as a positive racial stereotype, or is all stereotyping always harmful?

4. Nicoll argues that white women have to "lose their innocence" when it comes to confronting and grappling with racism. What historical or social conditions produce this "innocence"?

5. The service providers interviewed by Abji, Kortweg, and Williams argue against overly cultural explanations for gender violence (i.e., the idea that people do these things because "it's part of their culture"). What does the term "culture" mean to you? Do you know of cultural practices that are beneficial as well as harmful?

6. Several authors prefer to speak in terms of "racialization" and "racialized" people rather than "race" or "people of colour." Why do you think they have this preference? What other terms or words could be used here?

Chapter 5

Overview

"Culture" is often invoked when talking about gender, used as an oversimplified generalization for explaining why people do what they do—"it's just part of their culture to do . . . ", or "in our culture, we . . . ". But "culture talk" can obscure complex dynamics of power that shape gender relations. In Canada in recent years, "culture talk" has been deployed in public in the context of violence against women, with certain cultural groups assumed to be more prone to violence than others. Abji, Korteweg, and Williams investigate how people use talk about culture and violence, focusing on 15 people who work in anti-violence activism in South Asian communities in the Greater Toronto Area. Their participants must work to carve out a discursive space for confronting violence against women without falling into mainstream discourse that positions South Asian communities as exceptionally sexist, but also without glossing over the harms suffered by South Asian women and girls. They find that their participants use a range of rhetorical strategies when talking about culture: They emphasize that violence against women is found everywhere, not just in South Asian cultures, and they point to diverse forms of oppression experienced by racialized people in Canada. They discern the factors within their communities that produce violent or dangerous situations for women and girls, and they make a strong case for the importance of anti-violence activism that develops organically from shared experiences. Their understanding of the intersection between gender and culture contrasts with the efforts by other Canadians to target specific groups as particularly prone to violence, as in the passage of the Zero Tolerance for Barbaric Cultural Practices Act of 2015.

Culture Talk and the Politics of the New Right

Navigating Gendered Racism in Attempts to Address Violence against Women in Immigrant Communities

Salina Abji, Anna C. Korteweg, and Lawrence H. Williams

. . . We analyze how service providers navigate the gendered, racialized production of a "culture and violence" nexus and how this nexus is implicated in the politics of the new Right. We examine how frontline workers and advocates in one major metropolitan area approached violence against women and grappled with the needs of their South Asian clients. Analyzing interviews conducted in 2011–12, when the notion of honor-based violence entered public consciousness in Canada, these frontline workers and advocates substituted "community" for "culture" as they tried to find ways of undermining the racialization engendered by talk of culture. . . .

[W]e see all violence as cultural: violence occurs in specific contexts and is both perceived and responded to according to situated understandings (Haraway 1988), and violence is interpreted through specific meaning-making

Abji, Salina, Anna C. Korteweg, and Lawrence H. Williams. "Culture Talk and the Politics of the New Right: Navigating Gendered Racism in Attempts to Address Violence against Women in Immigrant Communities." *Signs: Journal of Women in Culture and Society*, 2019, 44(3), 797–822. Reprinted by permission of University of Chicago Press—Journals.

processes that are open-ended in terms of alignment with a particular politics. However, when violence against women in South Asian communities is labeled "cultural" in essentializing ways that create structural inequalities, we describe these practices as culture *talk* (see also Razack 1994; Mamdani 2007). Culture-as-meaning-making can scale up to culture talk when it is used, through a process of racialization, to categorize people as belonging to communities that are made identifiable by particular gendered practices of violence.

While identifying the dangers of culture talk, our findings suggest a need for the continued application of a focus on culture-as-meaning-making to understand experiences of and responses to gendered violence across varied communities and social groupings. Importantly, culture-as-meaning-making centers rather than elides structural forces that shape experiences of violence. This allows us to embed feminism and gender analysis in the contexts within which they develop and are applied to processes of law making and the organizational work of states and societies.

Feminist Debates on Culture and Violence: Essentialism, Relativism, and the Politics of the New Right

Culture played a key role in feminist debates about difference in the 1980s and 1990s.[1] . . .

One outcome of these debates within feminist spaces of social service provision was an increased focus on the structural factors that shape experiences of violence across gender, race, class, and sexuality, among other lines (Barnoff 2001; Raj and Silverman 2002). Indeed, some feminists have been rightly preoccupied with the structural implications of criminal-justice responses to violence against women, particularly in the contexts of neoliberalism and the retrenchment of the welfare state.[2] . . . An emphasis on the structural factors underlying violence against women grew in prominence in the 1990s and beyond. However,

attention to cultural factors waned in relation, leaving the question of how to talk about culture at an impasse (Korteweg et al. 2013).

. . . Culture talk reinforces the idea that certain cultures are barbaric and in need of Western intervention . . . in its rendering of Western culture as superior to others. Culture talk has been used to explain acts of terrorism as the presence of Muslim minorities grows in the West and to justify the War on Terror. As a response to violence against women, culture talk positions Muslim, immigrant, and racialized men as more prone to violence (Amar 2011), rendering women from these communities as "imperiled" subjects (Razack 2004) in need of saving through state surveillance and punitive controls (Zine 2009; Haque 2010; Abu-Lughod 2011). Culture talk likewise positions gender equality as a defining characteristic of "more civilized" Western societies compared to "barbaric" immigrant others (Korteweg 2014, 2017). . . .

Racialized Gendered Violence in Canadian Politics: Immigration, Settler Colonialism, and the Violence-against-Women Sector

Canada's superdiverse population (Vertovec 2007) reflects a complex history of colonization and settler colonialism. Canada is an amalgamation of former British and French colonies and a contemporary member of the British Commonwealth. Immigration policies prior to 1967 privileged white Northern and Western Europeans, leading to a largely white population occupying Indigenous land. After changes in immigration law in 1967, increasing numbers of immigrants arrived from the global South: currently, the three main sources of immigration are India, China, and the Philippines. The latest census data shows that cities like Toronto have a population that is over 50 pecent foreign-born, compared to the Canadian average of 21.9 (Statistics Canada 2017). Across Canada, 22.3% of the population falls withinthe"visibleminority"category(whichexcludes Indigenous, Metis, and Inuit), while in major urban centers like Toronto that percentage sits at 51.5% (Ballingall 2017). . . .

[T]he sector of social service agencies addressing violence against women has struggled to develop approaches to gendered violence that take the increases in diversity over the past few decades into account. From the 1970s onward, a number of women's organizations adopted a strong second-wave-feminist approach to gendered violence, which highlighted the gender/patriarchy dimension of such violence, paying some attention to class but without interrogating how cultural whiteness permeated its analysis of violence (Dobrowolsky and Jenson 2004; Dustin and Phillips 2008). The 1980s and 1990s saw the emergence of an antiracist, antioppressive approach to social work practice, a dominant profession among advocates addressing violence against women. Led by immigrant women and women of color, this approach highlighted the structural and institutional conditions of racism and ethnocentrism as key elements in women's experiences of violence (Agnew 1998; Barnoff 2001). . . .

Analytical Framework: Culture-as-Meaning-Making versus Culture Talk

The problem of culture in feminist approaches to violence against women is that culture, which is enmeshed with lived experience, has multiple meanings that make it difficult to navigate both analytically and politically. Importantly, violence against women is always made legible through a process of categorization developed in interaction with our selves, other people, places, structures, histories, and so forth. . . . [C]ulture has become a narrative trope that has done great damage, evidenced by the harm done through the impulse to save brown women from brown men (Spivak 1988) and in the justification of wars to liberate women from inequality (e.g., the American invasion of Afghanistan) and so forth. In these cases, culture becomes a tool in the violation of diverse communities by suggesting that some cultures are inherently violent toward women. We suggest that this latter use of culture is best captured by "culture talk" (Razack 1994, Mamdani 2007). . . .

Drawing from feminist and sociological literatures, we use the concept of discursive repertoires to capture both the meaning-making practices and opportunity structures that render political claims legible and actionable (Steinberg 1998; Ferree 2003). . . .

Methods

[W]e conducted fifteen open-ended interviews with key stakeholders working in the violence-against-women sector, whose work and activism focused explicitly on the South Asian communities in the greater Toronto area (Korteweg et al. 2013).[3] The interviews lasted between one and three hours and focused on the aggregate experience of the interviewees rather than the professional positions they occupied at the time.

While our sample was by no means comprehensive, we tapped into a cluster of people recognized within this community of service providers as key actors in the field. Many of them were highly educated with advanced degrees in social work and other fields. Almost all had worked in the social service sector for over a decade, some three decades or longer. They occupied a range of positions in the field. Two of them worked for the police as educators or community liaisons, while the rest had long-standing engagements with a variety of social service agencies both as service providers and in activist roles. Fourteen of our interviewees identified as women, one as a man. All of them self-identified as members of one of the greater Toronto area's South Asian communities. . . .

When analyzing the data, we found that each interviewee would cycle through a series of claims that delineated a particular discursive repertoire (Steinberg 1998) to frame violence against women in South Asian communities. The following three discursive strategies highlight how our interviewees managed culture talk as they articulated the issues and needs they associated with violence against women.

Violence against Women as a Universal Practice

When we asked service providers how they defined violence against women in general as well as among South Asian groups in particular, they often responded by first challenging what they saw as our implicit distinction between mainstream and culturally specific forms of violence. This challenge often involved a quick performative move, where interviewees would preface their answers by first insisting that violence against women is a universal phenomenon, affecting all women regardless of ethnicity or culture. For example, Hansa, a service provider with over forty years of experience, explained to us that "I am not judging any form of violence because I think violence is violence and must be condemned in all forms." Indeed, the phrase "violence is violence" was a common refrain used by service providers as a strategy to counter perceived judgments of racialized communities as more prone to violence. Similarly, Diya, an advocate with policy-level and grassroots experience, exemplified this strategy when arguing that "a murder is a murder, right? Sexual assault is a sexual assault under the criminal code. . . . Is it any different in South Asian communities than it is in mainstream communities or in other communities? The notion of control and power in that context is still applicable." In this discursive strategy, interviewees rejected notions of culture as causing violence, instead framing violence as a universal practice that must be condemned in all cases, not only when it affects women in racialized communities. . . . By relating the experiences of South Asian women to women in "mainstream" communities, our interviewees prioritized gender over culture as a totalizing explanation across all cultures. Such arguments were often accompanied by an overt rejection of the term "culture" itself to describe any pattern of violence affecting South Asian families.

Structural Forces and Interlocking Systems of Oppression

While our interviewees used a "violence against women as universal" strategy to resist racializing culture talk, at other times they also expressed frustration with such universalizing explanations. This frustration was especially pronounced when we asked interviewees to comment on existing social service models for addressing violence against women. Zaina, a service provider with over fifteen years of experience, challenged the too narrow definition of violence against women used by more mainstream women's organizations, instead calling for a broad-based structural approach: "I look at poverty as violence, I look at immigration as violence, I look at the school system as violence, I look at racism as violence and that healing from that is just as important." We interpreted such critiques as a structural framing of violence against women that contrasted with the universalist framing our interviewees also deployed. . . .

The coexistence of both universal and structural frames in service providers' accounts signaled the strategic work that our interviewees were performing in trying to relay the complexities of violence, where they were caught between totalizing and relativizing narratives that they tried to negotiate almost in the same breath. Indeed, our interviewees expressed a consensus that service providers needed to see violence against women in South Asian communities as universal violence in an already violence-laden country *and* as having particular qualities, because people within these communities also experienced structural violence via immigration and racism.

Violence as a Community Issue

Structural explanations of violence against women were useful in capturing particularities of violence beyond universalist arguments. However, our interviewees still struggled to account for patterns of violence that we would identify as cultural, or shaped by situated practices of meaning making. This struggle was evident in the slippage we noticed in participants' articulations of violence, where they tended to substitute the term "community" for "culture" when describing patterns they witnessed in their work.

In moments where Zaina discussed so-called honor-based violence, for example, the structural explanations she tended to use could not fully convey the specificities of violence she observed:

"I don't want to use the term honor crimes. . . . I feel it's very much *exotifying* violence, and violence is contextual. . . . Not to disregard the fact that violence against women happens in very specific ways in specific communities: as a result of immigration status, as a result of criminalization of that community, as a result of the way that community is treated by the outside world. And also, there's things that—the *values and systems*—that come with specific individuals within those communities." Zaina's work in the field led her to problematize terms like "honor crimes" as culture talk, and instead she advocated for a structural analysis of intersecting oppressions like immigration and criminalization. In doing so, she emphasized both the universality and particularism of violence against women we show in the discursive strategies discussed above (Haraway 1988). . . .

These three discursive strategies of framing violence as universal, placing it in structural locations, and situating it in community did not occur in isolation. Rather, our interviewees intertwined these approaches as they attempted to negotiate racializing culture talk. In what follows, we show how advocates' resistance to culture talk carried over into their evaluations of potential solutions to violence against women, where culture-as-meaning-making was a central dimension of the situated approaches they emphasized.

Situated Understandings of Violence against Women and Culture-as-Meaning-Making: Integrating Universalism, Structural Violence, and Community in Service Provision and Advocacy

When we asked service providers about potential solutions to violence against women as experienced by the communities they worked with, they offered strong critiques of current approaches to culture in policy and service provision. . . . [M]any of our interviewees cautioned against totalizing tendencies or the combination of universalizing and cultural relativism underpinning the idea that one could be an "expert" in any particular culture—an assumption that they saw as deeply problematic in prevailing cultural-competency models of social work provision. As Jamila, an advocate with counseling and program development experience, explained: "I don't believe that anyone can ever be culturally competent. I think that this is a lifelong journey. . . . Even as service providers you are constantly needing to learn from others" experiences and their perspectives. And I think the day you say "I think we figured this out, this is what you need to do, and this is how you are culturally competent'—I think it is wrong. . . . This has to be an ongoing process and self-reflective process." . . .

The issue of safety planning offers a key example of a situated knowledge approach. In her conversations with survivors, Jamila took care not to impose her own assumptions of what safety from violence might look like. Instead, she recounted trying to support South Asian (and other) women in their own interpretations of a good outcome. Thus, Jamila learned that for some South Asian women, safety from violence does not always entail leaving their families or communities, which is a historically dominant approach to violence against women in social work provision. Rather, some women's coping strategies involved temporary respite in temples or other community spaces, where they could, as Jamila described, "have a sort of break . . . cooking with other women . . . stay there the night . . . recharge their batteries" in a way that would still be "acceptable by the family."

Jamila and other interviewees found that such approaches to safety were particularly salient for women who encountered intersecting forms of violence outside their families and communities, including racism, poverty, and precarious immigration status, which render the family or community simultaneously a space of safety and of violence. From this perspective, mainstream service providers can revictimize racialized and immigrant women by judging them for not wanting to leave situations of domestic or interpersonal violence and expressing a desire to educate "those" women. . . .

Isha, a violence-against-women counselor and scholar trained in social work, added to the conversation . . . as an advocate who is seen as a "cultural insider." In her account, we started seeing the ways in which "community" is only a limited tool to undermine culture talk. "Like for myself, I am an insider to the community. . . . So, I have to be so conscious of every single word that I say, so that I am not—because my worth will be taken up as—'she is from that community and she said that that's what's happening there, so it must be true.' . . . And so, so I think what ends up happening is that people like myself in this line of work get really defensive, and say 'actually *no*—it's not our men who are these barbaric beings who are hurting women!'" Isha pointed to how attempts to talk about the specificities of violence were problematically taken up as proof of the backwardness of minority communities in that community membership becomes racialized so that one's words get reproduced as culture talk. . . .

By acknowledging that violence against women always occurs in specific contexts, interviewees' narratives worked to support Narayan's (1998) . . . claims that both seemingly benign, relativistic interventions and more end-oriented, totalizing interventions share the same fault: assuming both a place of clear understanding of the issue of violence against women and clear, generalizable strategies for moving forward. Interviewees' narratives also supported the definition of culture-as-meaning-making through their emphasis on the simultaneously structural yet personal and community-situated experiences of violence against women. Across all interviewees, violence against women was seen as nearly impossible to discuss due to the difficulty of acknowledging violence as a problem in their already racialized communities. . . .

Discussion and Conclusions

This research has focused on strategies for addressing violence against women in contemporary contexts of superdiversity. . . . Culture played a critical role in these efforts: "culture talk"—or politicized uses of culture that scale up to produce social inequality—shaped the work of both social service provider advocates and politicians, with service providers and center/left politicians resisting and right-wing politicians embracing racializing uses of culture. At the same time, service providers in particular struggled to make claims for resources in a context where they needed targeted support but where claims for such targeted support too often seemed to reinforce culture talk. . . .

[O]ur findings pointed to the limits of avoiding talk of culture in favor of more structural explanations. This was particularly evident in the tendency of interviewees to use the term "community" as a substitute for what were in essence cultural specificities of violence against women. . . .

In the end, we argue that an active focus on culture-as-meaning-making rather than as uniformly shared values offers a potentially useful way forward, both for us as researchers and (more implicitly) for the people we interviewed. . . .

Such recognition of complexity echoes concerns long held by feminists studying violence against women in that, in order to be curtailed, the situated, structured, *and* cultural components of this type of violence all need to be simultaneously considered. Without doing so, attempts to address violence against women—such as speaking about it in terms of community rather than culture—may lead to the kind of alternations between totalizing community accounts and relativizing cultural accounts that circumvent the complexities of violence against women.

Notes

1. See Razack (1994), Agnew (1998), Code (1998), and Narayan (1998).
2. See Bumiller (2009), Bernstein (2012), Bhuyan (2012), Mohanty (2013), and Abraham and Tastsoglou (2016)
3. All but two of the interviews were conducted one-on-one by the first author, Abji, who is herself South Asian and an activist on these issues. These interviews had an assumption of familiarity and a feeling of ongoing conversation. This changed somewhat for the two interviews where two of the three authors, Abji and Korteweg, were present, Korteweg being of white immigrant background. In those cases, interviewees placed more emphasis on explanation to a presumed outsider.

References

Abraham, Margaret, and Evangelia Tastsoglou. 2016. "Addressing Domestic Violence in Canada and the United States: The Uneasy Co-habitation of Women and the State." *Current Sociology* 64(4):568–85.

Abu-Lughod, Lila. 2011. "Seductions of the 'Honor Crime.'" *differences* 22(1):17–63.

Agnew Vijay. 1998. *In Search of a Safe Place: Abused Women and Culturally Sensitive Services.* Toronto: University of Toronto Press.

Amar, Paul. 2011. "Turning the Gendered Politics of the Security State Inside Out? Charging the Police with Sexual Harassment in Egypt." *International Feminist Journal of Politics* 13(3):299–328.

Ballingall, Alex. 2017. "A Majority of Torontonians Now Identify Themselves as Visible Minorities." *The Star*, October 25. https://www.thestar.com/news/gta/2017/10/25/a-majority-of-torontonians-now-identify-themselves-as -visible-minorities-census-shows.html.

Barnoff, Lisa. 2001. "Moving beyond Words: Integrating Anti-oppression Practice into Feminist Social Service Organizations." *Canadian Social Work Review* 18(1):67–85.

Bernstein, Elizabeth. 2012. "Carceral Politics as Gender Justice? The 'Traffic in Women' and Neoliberal Circuits of Crime, Sex, and Rights." *Theory and Society* 41(3):233–59.

Bhuyan, Rupaleem. 2012. "Negotiating Citizenship on the Frontlines: How the Devolution of Canadian Immigration Policy Shapes Service Delivery to Women Fleeing Abuse." *Law and Policy* 34(2):211–36.

Bumiller, Kristin, 2009. *In an Abusive State: How Neoliberalism Appropriated the Feminist Movement against Sexual Violence.* Durham, NC: Duke University Press.

Code, Lorraine. 1998. "How to Think Globally: Stretching the Limits of Imagination." *Hypatia* 13(2):73–85.

Dobrowolsky, Alexandra, and Jane Jenson. 2004. "Shifting Representations of Citizenship: Canadian Politics of 'Women' and 'Children.'" *Social Politics* 11(2):154–80.

Dustin, Moira, and Anne Phillips. 2008. "Whose Agenda Is It? Abuses of Women and Abuses of Culture in Britain." *Ethnicities* 8(3):405–24.

Ferree, Myra Marx. 2003. "Resonance and Radicalism: Feminist Framing in the Abortion Debates of the United States and Germany." *American Journal of Sociology* 109(2):304–44.

Haque, Eve. 2010. "Homegrown, Muslim, and Other: Tolerance, Secularism, and the Limits of Multiculturalism." *Social Identities* 16(1):79–101.

Haraway, Donna. 1988. "Situated Knowledges: The Science Question in Feminism and the Privilege of Partial Perspective." *Feminist Studies* 14(3):575–99.

Korteweg, Anna C. 2014. "'Honour Killing' in the Immigration Context: Multiculturalism and the Racialization of Violence against Women." *Politikon* 41(2):183–208.

Korteweg, Anna C. 2017. "The 'What' and 'Who' of Co-optation: Gendered Racialized Migrations, Settler Nation-States, and Postcolonial Difference." *International Feminist Journal of Politics* 19(2):216–30.

Korteweg, Anna C., Salina Abji, Lisa Barnoff, and Deepa Mattoo. 2013. "Citizenship, Culture, and Violence against Women: Social Service Provision in the South Asian Communities of the GTA." CERIS Research Report. http://www.torontolip.com/Portals/0/Resources/General/Citizenship,%20Culture,%20and%20Violence%20Against%20Women%20_CERIS%20report.pdf?verp2016-04-05-032200-000.

Mamdani, Mahmood. 2007. "The Politics of Culture Talk in the Contemporary War on Terror." Hobhouse Memorial Public Lecture, London School of Economics, March 8.

Mohanty, Chandra Talpade. 2013. "Transnational Feminist Crossings: On Neoliberalism and Radical Critique." *Signs* 38(4):967–91.

Narayan, Uma. 1998. "Essence of Culture and a Sense of History: A Feminist Critique of Cultural Essentialism." *Hypatia* 13(2):86–106.

Raj, Anita, and Jay Silverman. 2002. "Violence against Immigrant Women: The Roles of Culture, Context, and Legal Immigrant Status on Intimate Partner Violence." *Violence against Women* 8(3):367–98.

Razack, Sherene H. 1994. "What Is to Be Gained by Looking White People in the Eye? Culture, Race, and Gender in Cases of Sexual Violence." *Signs* 19(4):894–923.

Razack, Sherene H. 2004. "Imperilled Muslim Women, Dangerous Muslim Men, and Civilised Europeans: Legal and Social Responses to Forced Marriages." *Feminist Legal Studies* 12(2):129–74.

Spivak, Gayatri Chakravorty. 1988. "Can the Subaltern Speak?" In *Can the Subaltern Speak? Reflections on the History of an Idea*, edited by Rosalind C. Morris, 21–78. New York: Columbia University Press.

Statistics Canada. 2017. "2016 Census Topic: Immigration and Ethnocultural Diversity." October 25. http://www12.statcan.gc.ca/census-recensement/2016/rt-td/imm-eng.cfm.

Steinberg, Marc W. 1998. "Tilting the Frame: Considerations on Collective Action Framing from a Discursive Turn." *Theory and Society* 27(6):845–72.

Vertovec, Steven. 2007. "Super-Diversity and Its Implications." *Ethnic and Racial Studies* 30(6):1024–54.

Zine, Jasmin. 2009. "Unsettling the Nation: Gender, Race, and Muslim Cultural Politics in Canada." *Studies in Ethnicity and Nationalism* 9(1):146–63.

Chapter 6

Overview

Where do you belong? The answer to that question often depends on the biases of the person asking. Angela Aujla surveys writings by Canadian women of South Asian descent to locate the origins of that question within Canada's own history of Asian exclusion. She argues that South Asian women have historically been treated as submissive, subservient, or overly sexualized, both within their own communities and by white Canadians, so that they are continually running against stereotypes that are strongly gendered. South Asians as a group, of whatever gender, have also been treated as threats to Canada, whether because they are presumed to harbour terrorists, in the twenty-first century, or because they threaten to "out-reproduce" white people, in the eugenic arguments of the nineteenth and twentieth centuries. To avoid this stereotyping, South Asian women feel pressured to assimilate and downplay markers of their difference, but still encounter distorted images of their gender and racial background in popular media and in the encounters of everyday racism. Nonetheless, as Aujla notes, South Asian Canadian women have found ways to speak up and speak back to these stereotypes, centering their own voices in the literature they produce.

Others in Their Own Land

Second Generation South Asian Canadian Women, Racism, and the Persistence of Colonial Discourse

Angela Aujla

"Go back to where you came from!"
"Where are you *actually* from?"
"*Paki!*"

Though born and raised in Canada, the national identity of multigenerational South Asian Canadian women is subject to incessant scrutiny and doubt, as reflected in the phrases above. They are othered by a dominant culture which categorizes them as "visible minorities," "ethnics," immigrants, and foreigners—categories considered incommensurable with being a "real" Canadian, despite the promises of multiculturalism. Never

quite Canadian enough, never quite white enough, these women remain "others" in their own land. Not only are they excluded from national belonging, they are haunted by a discourse which has historically constructed non-white women as a threat to the nation-state. Contemporary constructions of South Asian Canadian women are situated in a larger racist, sexist, and colonial discourse which cannot be buried under cries of "unity in diversity."

In this article, I focus on how the gendered racialization of multigenerational South Asian Canadian women excludes them from national belonging and pressures them to assimilate. The literary production of these women reflects the deep repercussions of this exclusion and provides a location where issues of identity, otherness, and racism

Aujla, Angela. "Others in Their Own Land: Second Generation Asian Canadian Women, Racism, and the Persistence of Colonial Discourse," *Canadian Woman Studies/Les Cahiers De La Femme*, Vol. 20, No. 2, Spring 2000, pp. 41–7. Reprinted by permission of the author.

may be articulated and resisted. I will look at poetry and personal narratives by multigenerational South Asian Canadian women as points of intervention into these issues. Beginning with a brief overview of racism against South Asians in Canada, I will discuss how racist and colonial discourses of the past continue to influence dominant discourses and perceptions of South Asian Canadian women today.

Unity against Diversity

Despite the many differences among multigenerational South Asian Canadian women, similar experiences can be identified. These include experiences of racism, feelings of being "other" and not belonging, colonialism, patriarchy, sexism, and living in a diasporic culture. I use the term "South Asian" because it challenges the geographical locatedness of cultures and identities through its wide scope of reference. Generally, the category "South Asian" refers to those who trace their ancestry to places including India, Pakistan, Sri Lanka, Bangladesh, Bhutan, Tanzania, Uganda, South Africa, and the Caribbean (Henry et al; Agnew). Terms such as "East Indian" and "Indo-Canadian" are problematic because of their narrow reference. Both refer directly to the Indian subcontinent, excluding other South Asian regions. They also refer to nation states and nationalities, implying the idea that ethnicity, identity, and "race" are neatly confined within the borders of homogenous states.

Much in the same spirit as colonial cartography, South Asians have been "mapped" and inscribed by the dominant culture through racialized discourse and state practices since they began immigrating to Canada in the late nineteenth century (Buchnigani and Indra). Surrounded by an imposed mythos of being deviant, threatening. Undesirable, and inferior to the white "race," South Asians were constructed as "other" to the dominant Canadian culture who could not even bear to sit beside them on trains (Henry et al.). This attitude is evident in the contemporary phenomena of "white flight" in certain BC municipalities where some white residents have chosen to move rather than live alongside the South Asians who are "ruining the neighbourhood." In the early 1900s, they were

not permitted to participate as full citizens, the Canadian state controlled where they could live, where they could work, and even what they could or could not wear. Though they were British subjects, they could not vote federally until 1947 (Henry et al.). Though in a less overt form, the traces of this mapping continue to effect South Asian bodies today. Dominant representations of South Asian Canadians are largely stereotypical and impose static notions of culture and identity on them, whether they are immigrants or multigenerational.

The history of media images of South Asians attests to this. In the early [twentieth] century, the South Asian presence in British Columbia was referred to as "a Hindu Invasion" by the news media; a proliferation of articles in BC newspapers stressed the importance of maintaining Anglo-Saxon superiority[1] (Henry et al.). Negative media portrayal of South Asians still persists. As Yasmin Jiwani states ". . . even contemporary representations cohere around an 'us' versus 'them' dichotomy that ideologically sediments a notion of national identity that is clearly exclusionary" (1998: 60).

Canadian Sikhs for example, have been depicted as over-emotional religious extremists predisposed to violence. Used repeatedly, these images reinforce prejudice against all South Asians, both male and female. The *Vancouver Sun* headlines "Close Watch on City Sikhs" and "Sikh Militancy Grows" have not strayed very far from the cry of "Hindu Invasion" in the early part of the twentieth century. Representations of South Asian Canadian women in the media portray them as the meek and pitiful victims of arranged marriages and abusive husbands or uses them as colourful, orientalized exotica to be fawned over (Jiwani, 1998). Such media images subtly exclude South Asian Canadians from national belonging. Their cultures are represented as barbaric and backwards, as "clashing" and "conflicting" with civilized and modern Canadian society. These portrayals imply that South Asians do not "fit in" here, and that they are certainly not "real" Canadians. Edward Said states,

> [The] imaginative geography of the "our land/ barbarian land" variety does not require that

the barbarians acknowledge the distinction. It is enough for "us" to set up these boundaries in our own minds; "they" become "they" accordingly, and both their territory and their mentality are designated as different from "ours." (54)

Said describes how the us–them boundary and its accompanying mythos about "others" mentalities has historically been constructed by the dominant culture and imposed onto "others" regardless of their consent. Though Said was referring to relations between colonizer and colonized, his idea remains just as relevant when applied to contemporary relations between South Asian Canadians and the dominant Canadian culture.

Feel-good, multicultural goals of unity in diversity and ending racism are simplistic and certain to fail because they do not acknowledge the deeply rooted racist, sexist, and colonial discourse that has constructed Canada and "Canadian identity." As Ann Laura Stoler argues, "the discourse of race was not on parallel track with the discourse of the nation but part of it" (93). Historically, Canadian identity has not been a First Nations identity, or even a French identity. It has been, and continues to be a white, British, Anglo-Saxon identity. As in other white-settler colonies, and in Britain, the civility and superiority of blood and nation was constructed against the "backwardness" and inferiority of the "darker races" (Stoler; Jiwani, 1998; Dua). For example, the modernity of the Canadian state was juxtaposed to the pre-modern South Asian woman, the blood of the superior Anglo Saxon race was juxtaposed to the degenerate blood of non-white races (Henry et al.). White, Anglo-Canadian unity was constructed in opposition to non-white "diversity." But now, with the introduction of multiculturalism, we are suddenly expected to make the very unrealistic leap from unity against "diversity," to unity *in* diversity.

The Persistence of Colonial Discourse

South Asian women have been both sexualized and racialized through colonial discourse as oppressed, subservient, tradition-bound, and

pre-modern (Dua). They are also constructed as seductive, exotic objects of desire. In another construction they are considered overly-fertile, undesirable, smelly, and oily-haired (Jiwani, 1992; Brah). The legacy of colonial discourse is evident in contemporary racialized and sexualized constructions of South Asian women. In a *Guardian* article published September 5, 1985, a 19-year-old South Asian woman in London recounts the sexualized racist comments she faces walking home from college:

> . . . if I'm on my own with other girls it's, "Here comes the Paki whore, come and fuck us Paki whores, we've heard you're really horny." Or maybe they'll put it the other way around, saying that I am dirty, that no one could possibly want to go to bed with a Paki (qtd. in Brah 79)

These co-existing sentiments of desire and revulsion can be seen as remnants of British colonial attitudes towards South Asian women. While their colonizers considered non-white women savage, and backwards, they were also thought to possess a "sensual, enticing and indulgent nature" (Smits 61). According to Yasmin Jiwani, in British imperialist fiction by authors including Rudyard Kipling, the Indian woman was characterized by her rampant sexuality and her abundant fertility (1992). As can be inferred from the comments yelled at the 19-year-old South Asian woman walking home from college, contemporary stereotypes of multigenerational South Asian women remain deeply rooted in the colonial tradition.

Race, blood, and nation have historically been deeply interconnected and overlapping concepts in the West. Historically, the immigration and presence of women of colour in Canada, and other Western countries was seen as a threat to the nation-state. They brought with them the danger of increasing the non-white population and the possibility of miscegenation—a danger all the more immanent given their "overly fecund" nature. Dua comments that "In Canada, as well as other settler colonies, racial purity was premised on the Asian peril—the danger of Anglo-Saxons being overrun by more fertile races" (252). Non-white women endangered Western "civility" and national identity; the proliferation of non-white babies was not just a threat to the racial purity of Western societies, but to their dominance and very existence. It was thought that miscegenation and too many non-white births could lead to the demise of the Anglo-Saxon race, and therefore, the demise of the nation state itself. As Dua writes,

> . . . the submissiveness of Hindu women was linked to a decline into pre-modern conditions. While white bourgeois women were racially gendered as mothers of the nation, colonized women were racially gendered as dangerous to the nation-state. (254)

Similarly, in everyday the racist/xenophobic discourse of this country, the "real" Canadians complain that immigrants are invading their neighbourhoods, cities, and the country itself. The *Globe and Mail* warns, "soon there will be more visible minorities than whites in Vancouver and Toronto," and that their number "is the highest in history." Feeding into fears of non-white women's limitless fertility, they also report that the number of visible minorities born in Canada is rising steadily and that they are younger than "the total Canadian population" (Mitchell). Such articles reflect the persistence of colonial discourse; while the white woman's regulated fecundity was supposed to ensure the reproduction of the social body, the non-white woman's "limitless fertility" was seen as endangering the reproduction of the social body. Non-white and "mixed race" bodies signalled a danger to the State.

I Am Canadian?

> "Are you Fijian by any chance?" the stranger asked.
> "No," I replied.
> "Are you from India?"
> "No."

During this brief encounter on Vancouver's Robson Street in 1997, various thoughts quickly ran through my head: do I reply with the answer that I know he wants to hear? Or do I explain that I'm Canadian only to be met with the standard reply of "Where are you really from?" or "But where are you from *originally*?" I walked away frustrated, glad I didn't give him the answer he expected, but upset that I didn't take the opportunity to challenge his preconceptions further by stating that not all brown people are immigrants, or saying "why do you ask?" taking the spotlight off me and hopefully inciting him to question the motivation behind his intrusive inquiry. Kamala Visweswaran states,

> Certainly the question "Where are you from?" is never an innocent one. Yet not all subjects have equal difficulty in replying. To pose a question of origin to a particular subject is to subtly pose a question of return, to challenge not only temporally, but geographically, one's place in the present. For someone who is neither fully Indian nor wholly American, it is a question that provokes a sudden failure of confidence, the fear of never replying adequately. (115)

Even in "multicultural" Canada, skin colour and ethnicity continue to act as markers of one's place of origin, markers which are used to ascertain traits and behaviours which are associated with certain "races." It is a question that left me with an acute sense of being out of place and being "other"—if I seemed out of place to the man who asked the question, I must appear so to the people around me. Underlying such (frequently asked) questions are racist assumptions about what a "real" Canadian looks like. In that brief encounter, the stranger automatically linked me to a far away land that I have never seen, a place where I would surely be considered an outsider, and certainly not be considered Indian. His question served as a reminder of my "visible minority" status—that I was not quite Canadian and could never be so.

The "other" does not necessarily have to be "other" in terms of exhibiting strange or "exotic" language and behaviour. Time and time again, the dominant culture reduces identity down to imaginary racial categories. The fact that multigenerational South Asian Canadians are treated as other, as not-quite Canadians, attests to this. At what point do multigenerational South Asian Canadians cease being seen as from somewhere else? As Himani Bannerji comments, "[t]he second generation grows up on cultural languages which are not foreign to them, though they are still designated as foreigners" (1993: 186). South Asian Canadian women are in a predicament of perpetual foreignness—constantly being asked where they are from and having stereotypical characteristics assigned to them despite their "Canadianness." Though they are in their country of origin, they are not *of* it.

Presentation of self is one way in which we demonstrate our personal identities and recognize those of others. This holds true if we encountered someone who had inscribed her body with tattoos, multiple body-piercings, and blue hair. However, it is quite a different situation when a South Asian Canadian woman tries to ground her personal identity in this way; regardless of whether her hair is covered by a *hijab* or is short and chic, regardless of whether she is wearing a *salwaar-kameez* or jeans, she is still subject to an otherization based on an imaginary "South Asian other" constructed through racist ideology. Her own body inscriptions are ignored, as the only signifier needed for recognition from the dominant culture seems to be phenotypical. These phenotypical characteristics stand, as they have in the past, though perhaps to a lesser extent, as signifiers of difference and inferiority.

In Farzana Doctor's poem "Banu," the narrator traces her changing responses and attitudes towards racism at different stages throughout her life. During childhood and as a young adult, assimilation is her response. Eventually she rejects assimilation in favour of resistance. In "Banu," the racist interpellation "Paki go home" (218) is directed at the little girl in the poem. According to the *Oxford English Dictionary*, "Paki" is an abbreviation for Pakistani, and is also described as a slang word. In "Banu," however, the common use of the term does not reflect its literal or etymological meaning. The term has become imbued with racist emotions and signifies detest, hatred, and intolerance towards all South Asians, regardless of their geographical place of origin.

A generically used term in places such as Canada, Great Britain, and the United States, "Paki" is a common racist insult directed toward those who appear to be of South Asian ancestry (Bannerji, 1993; Sheth and Handa). Unlike racist insults against South Asians that are based on food or dress such as "curry-eater" or "rag-head," the insult "Paki" is based simply on one's "foreign/other" appearance. The insult "Paki" does not simply express disgust at aspects of South Asian cultures as the previously mentioned insults do. Rather, it expresses disgust or hatred directly toward one's "race" or ethnic background. For a multigenerational South Asian Canadian to be told "Paki go home" is particularly disturbing because she is told that Canada is not her home, but a far away land which she may have never set foot on. Regardless of being Canadian by citizenship and birth, she remains, under racist eyes, simply a "Paki." When the South Asian *Canadian* girl in the poem is told to "go home," she is not only told that she does not belong in Canadian society, but is also told that she should leave. The man who uttered the slur obviously felt he was a "real" Canadian with the right to tell the "foreigner" what to do. The popularity of this term in racist discourse not only reflects an ignorance about South Asian cultures and their diversity, but also reinforces the opinion that Canada does not have room for non-white "others."

Others in Their Own Land

In looking at Canadian multiculturalism and its promotion of diversity and tolerance, one would not find any overt pressures promoting assimilation. If anything, it seems that assimilation is not an issue—they tell us that we can all co-exist harmoniously within our respective tile of the mosaic. Yet, unstated, implied, and subtle pressures to assimilate remain a powerful force. As Michel Foucault stated, "[t]here is no need for arms, physical violence, material constraints, just a gaze" (155). While official Canadian multiculturalism may promote the acceptance of diversity, the lived experience of multiculturalism is quite a different thing. For many South Asian Canadian women the strong desire to "fit in," as a result of being discriminated against, culminates in an internalization of the gendered racism they receive. Frantz Fanon argues that the consequence of racism from the dominant group to the minority group is guilt and inferiority. The inferiorized group attempts to escape these feelings by "proclaiming his [sic] total and unconditional adoption of the new cultural models, and on the other, by pronouncing an irreversible condemnation of his own cultural style" (38–9).

This is a process multigenerational South Asian Canadian women undergo in their attempts to reject South Asian culture and assimilate. Assimilation has often been used as a coping mechanism not only by South Asian Canadians, but by all visible minorities where the majority of the dominant culture is white. Obvious forms of assimilation include speaking English and wearing Western-style clothing. A less obvious form is the desire to change one's physical appearance (Bannerji, 1990; Sheth and Handa; James; Karumanchery-Luik). Based on personal experiences and literature by multigenerational South Asian Canadian women, the desire to be white or possess typically Western features is, unfortunately, quite common. The impact of this is compounded for multigenerational South Asian Canadian women who have been socialized into the Western beauty ideal.

Internalized racism is a theme common to much of the literature by multigenerational South Asian Canadian women. One manifestation of this is illustrated by the proliferation of ads for "Fair and Lovely" skin cream and skin bleaches aimed at South Asian women, and the desire expressed in matrimonial ads for light-skinned wives. Sheth comments that light skin is so desirable in India that "the cosmetics industry continually pitch skin-lightening products to women" (Sheth and Handa 86). Various cosmetic products promising to do this are also found in Vancouver and Surrey's South Asian shops.

The desire for whiteness is demonstrated in second generation South Asian Canadian activist and theatre artist Sheila James' personal narrative about how she unnaturally became a blond because "All the sex objects on TV, film and magazines were blond-haired and blue eyed. I figured I could adjust the colour in my head to fit the role" (137). Underlying the desire for "whiteness" is a racist ideology which interprets the world associated with the dark skin of Indian and African people with danger, savagery, primitiveness, intellectual inferiority, and the inability to progress beyond a childlike mentality. Meanwhile whiteness is equated with purity, virginity, beauty, and civility (Ashcroft et al.; Arora).

Assimilation pressures and internalized racism experienced by the second generation are captured quite forcefully in Himani Bannerji's short story "The Other Family" (1990: 140–145) in which the second-generation South Asian protagonist of the story draws what is supposed to be a picture of her family for a school project. The picture, however, bears very little resemblance to her own family. She draws her family as white with blond hair and blue eyes, and herself as having a button nose and freckles. The drawing can be interpreted as an illustration of the little girl's desire to belong and to be like the other children—to fit in at the cost of the negation of her own body, of her own physical appearance. An essay by a multigenerational South Asian Canadian woman, Nisha Karumanchery-Luik, reflects a similar theme:

> When I was younger, I hated my brown skin. I had wished that I was not so dark, that my skin would somehow magically lighten. When I was younger, I was ashamed and embarrassed of my Indian heritage and the "foreignness" that my skin betrayed. I developed creative strategies of denial and pretense to cope with and survive in a racist environment. (54)

Her choice of phrase that her skin "betrayed" her "foreignness" and Indian heritage is a significant one. It speaks to the circumstance that many multigenerational South Asian Canadian women and other multigenerational visible minorities are in—though they may act "Canadian" in the mainstream-white-Anglo-Saxon-Protestant sense of the word (language, clothes, behaviour), their skin colour and phenotypical characteristics, signifying them as "other," never fail to give them away. Being different from the mainstream is, of course, not a problem in and of itself. It becomes one as the resulting of the othering, gendered racism, and exclusion that multigenerational South Asian Canadian women are subject to. In the following excerpt of a poem by Reshmi J. Bissessar, she reveals the shame she felt over being Guyanese:

I was there last in '86
At age fourteen
Eleven years ago
When I would say
Thank you
If someone told me that I didn't look
Guyanese.
My, how loyalties change. (22)

Often, multigenerational South Asian Canadian women try to hide and mask what it is that singles them out for racist taunts and prying gazes. For example, in another poem, the parent of a young South Asian Canadian woman asks the daughter "why do you cringe when seen by white folks in your sari? / why are you embarrassed when speaking Gujurati in public?" (Shah 119). Thus the pressures to assimilate and "belong" result in denying aspects of South Asian culture—even to the point of internalizing the dominant ideology and seeing themselves as inferior. Thinking that their food "stinks," that their physical characteristics are less beautiful and undesirable according to Western standards, embarrassment over being seen in Indian clothing, or by the accents of their parents, are all aspects of their inferiorization.

At the Borders of National Belonging

Multigenerational South Asian Canadian women's efforts at masking their ethnicity are, of course, in vain. The closest they come is to be mistaken for a less marginalized ethnic group or to be bestowed with the status of "honorary white," through comments to the effect of "you're different . . . you're not like the *rest* of them." I was given this status when deciding where to go for dinner with a group of people. One white woman asked me if I ate meat, implying that I must have "strange" eating habits as a South Asian. Before I could answer, another white woman exclaimed, "Oh of course she does, she's *just like us!*" But despite the "acceptance" of being just like them, I was still othered by the initial curiosity of "do you eat meat?" If I was "just like them" why was I the only one to whom that question was posed? Thus, even the "honorary white" status given to some South Asians fails to appease a sense of not belonging. Suparana Bhaskaran outlines the limiting typology of the "assimilated South Asian" and the "authentic South Asian" which can be applied to the phenomena of the "honorary white" discussed above:

The logic of purity allows South Asians to be conceptually defined in only two ways: as authentic South Asians or assimilated South Asians. The "authentic South Asian" may range from being conservative, lazy and poor to being spiritual, brilliant, non-materialistic and religious. By this definition, the assimilated South Asian pursues the promise of the "post-cultural" full citizenship of Anglo life. (198)

Though some multigenerational South Asian Canadian women may, by the above typology, be considered "assimilated South Asians" and therefore subject to the discrimination faced by the "authentic South Asian," we see in the literature by South Asian Canadian women that seeking this identification and inclusion into "Anglo-life" is, for the most part, unattainable and continues to be fraught with othering and a sense of exclusion.

Being singled out as "other" and the consequent pressures to assimilate has a particularly strong effect on multigenerational South Asian Canadian women. They have been socialized in Canadian society from birth and have thus, unlike their parents, lived their entire lives as "ethnic/other," and different from the dominant culture. For the second generation, the assimilation process begins much earlier and in the more formative years. Therefore, racism and being othered by the dominant culture has a deeper, more detrimental impact on multigenerational South Asian Canadians than it does on their parents who did not grow up in Canada. Though the parents of second-generation South Asian Canadians may be more "othered" due to their accents, the fact that they wear Indian clothing, and from having been socialized in a non-Western culture, they have come to Canada with some pre-established sense of identity (though it changes through their experiences in their new country), which is not the case for their children.

It is likely that many Canadians would be quite content if South Asian Canadians and other "visible minorities" simply integrated into Anglo-Canadian society instead of making a fuss about racist immigration policies or their right to wear *hijab*s. Of course, assimilation can no longer be overtly legislated, although it continues to be suggested in more subtle ways, as reflected in the literature by South Asian women. Because of "subtle" pressures to assimilate, many South Asian Canadian women have interiorized the inspecting gaze of the dominant culture to the point that they are exercising surveillance over themselves. Foucault argues that physical violence and constraints are no longer needed to control a population once they have interiorized the inspecting gaze—"a gaze which each individual under its weight will end by interiorizing to the point that he is his own overseer, each individual thus exercising this surveillance over, and against himself" (155).

The inspecting gaze in this context, are the judgmental eyes of the dominant culture—state officials, journalists, neighbours, teachers, and peers. The pressure to assimilate is no longer over, it is embedded in everyday language and stereotypes used to describe and "other" South Asian Canadian women, in popular culture and media depictions, and in structures such as institutional racism. The content of the literature by multigenerational South Asians discussed earlier reveals that they have interiorized the inspecting gaze of

the dominant culture, though it is a gaze which many of them have come to reject. Over and over again, these writers express the desire they have or once had to belong, to be accepted, and to "fit" into the dominant culture.

Conclusion

Though I have concentrated on how multigenerational South Asian Canadians have been "raced" and gendered through the dominant ideology, it is important to note that those constructed as other are not merely the passive recipients of power. In many cases, they are remapping themselves by challenging dominant representations of "their kind" through subversive forms of literary production. I would argue that in the tension between imposed identities and those asserted by multigenerational South Asian Canadian women, spaces of resistance have formed in the anthologies and other venues in which they publish, and in the act of writing itself. These venues provide a forum for South Asian Canadian women to creatively express their insights, anger, pain, and reflections. It is a textual space created by and for multigenerational South Asian Canadian women in which their marginalization and repression is both articulated and resisted.

Multigenerational South Asian Canadian women's literature is considered a new, diasporic form of cultural production. It is new in that these women are writing as both insiders and outsiders to Canadian society. Their literature demonstrates an ongoing negotiation of two intertwined cultural contexts and influences. The positionality of these women allows for a unique vantage point from which to comment on Canadian racism, sexism, and other repressions. Their writing poses an important challenge to the idea that culture and identity arc fixed within certain national borders.

Note

1. The Daily Colonist wrote: "To prepare ourselves for the irrepressible conflict, Canada must remain a White Man's country. On this western frontier of the Empire will be the forefront to the coming struggle. . . . Therefore we ought to maintain this country for the Anglo-Saxon and those races which are able to assimilate themselves to them. If this is done, we believe that history will repeat itself and the supremacy of our race will continue" (Henry et al. 71).

References

Agnew, V. 1996. *Resisting Discrimination: Women from Asia, Africa, and the Caribbean and the Women's Movement in Canada.* Toronto: University of Toronto Press.

Arora, P. 1995. "Imperilling the Prestige of the White Woman: Colonial Anxiety and Film Censorship in India," *Visual Anthropology Review* 11(2): 36–49.

Ashcroft, B., G. Griffiths, and H. Tiffin. 1998. *Key Concepts in Post-Colonial Studies.* London: Routledge.

Bannerji, H. 1990 "The Other Family," in L. Hutcheon and M. Richmond, eds., *Other Solitudes: Canadian Multicultural Fictions.* Toronto: Oxford University Press.

Bannerji, H. 1993. "Popular Images of South Asian Women," in H. Bannerji, ed., *Returning the Gaze.* Toronto: Sister Vision Press.

Bhaskaran, S. 1993. "Physical Subjectivity and the Risk of Essentialism," in Women of South Asian Descent Collective, eds., *Our Feet Walk the Sky: Women of the South Asian Diaspora.* San Francisco: Aunt Lute Books.

Brah, A. 1996. *Cartographies of Diaspora: Contesting Identities.* London: Routledge.

Buchnigani, N., and D. Indra. 1985. *Continuous Journey: A Social History of South Asians in Canada.* Toronto: McClelland and Stewart.

Doctor, F. 1995. "Banu," in F. Rafiq, ed., *Aurat Durbar.* Toronto: Second Story Press.

Dua, E. 1999. "Beyond Diversity: Exploring the Ways In Which the Discourse of Race Has Shaped the Institution of the Nuclear Family," in E. Dua and A. Robertson, eds., *Scratching the Surface: Canadian Anti-Racist Feminist Thought.* Toronto: Women's Press.

Foucault, M. 1980. *Power/Knowledge.* New York: Pantheon.

Henry, F., C. Tator, W. Mattis, and T. Rees. 1995. *The Colour of Democracy.* Toronto: Harcourt, Brace and Co.

James, S. 1995. "From Promiscuity to Celibacy," in F. Rafiq, ed., *Aurat Durbar.* Toronto: Second Story Press.

Jiwani, Y. 1992. "The Exotic, Erotic, and the Dangerous: South Asian Women in Popular Film," *Canadian Woman Studies* 13(1): 42–46.

Jiwani, Y. 1998. "On the Outskirts of Empire: Race and Gender in Canadian TV News," in V. Strong-Boag et al., eds., *Painting the Maple: Essays on Race, Gender and the Construction of Canada.* Vancouver: University of British Columbia Press.

Karumanchery-Luik, N. 1997. "The Politics of Brown Skin," in S.K. Chatree, ed., *Shaktee Kee Awaaz: Voices of Strength.* Toronto: Shakti Kee Chatri.

Mitchell, A. 1998. "Face of Big Cities Changing," *Globe and Mail*, 18 February: A1, A3.

Said, E.W. 1994. *Orientalism.* New York: Vintage.

Shah, S. 1997. "The Interrogation," in S.K. Chatree, ed., *Shaktee Kee Awaaz: Voices of Strength.* Toronto: Shakti Kee Chatri.

Sheth, A., and A. Handa. 1993. "A Jewel in the Frown: Striking Accord between Indian Feminists," in H. Bannerji, ed., *Returning the Gaze.* Toronto: Sister Vision Press.

Smits, D. 1987. "Abominable Mixture," *The Virginia Magazine of History and Biography* 95(2): 227–61.

Stoler, A.L. 1995. *Race and the Education of Desire: Foucault's History of Sexuality and the Colonial Order of Things.* Durham: Duke University Press.

Visweswaran, K. 1994. *Fictions of Feminist Ethnography.* Minneapolis: University of Minnesota Press.

Chapter 7

Overview

Is religion—specifically Islam—incompatible with gender equity? Three criminologists set out to explore this question in conversation with young Somali immigrants in Edmonton. Their work grows out of scholarship on gender and migration, which finds that the migrant experience often produces profound changes in how individuals understand gendered norms and behaviours.

The authors investigate how young Somali Canadians interpret religious expectations and community norms as they construct their own gendered identities. In Canada—in a national context that is officially multicultural but often discriminatory in practice—identifying as Muslim is important to these participants, but they also derive personal meaning from being Canadian. Participants said that their gender-egalitarian ideas did not always line up with their parents' ideas about the differences between sons and daughters, but their affection and attachment to their parents' community and their religious institutions remained strong. They might not attend mosque as regularly as their parents would like, but they found their own ways to reconcile Islam, immigrant identity, and gender equality.

Gender Identity and Integration

Second-Generation Somali Immigrants Navigating Gender in Canada

Ahmad Karimi, Sandra M. Bucerius, and Sara Thompson

Introduction

Immigration scholars have long documented a difficult relationship in many countries between immigrant Muslim minorities and autochthonous populations. . . . In the wake of 11 September 2001, anti-Muslim sentiment increased in many Western states (Open Society Justice Initiative 2009) and has intensified since the onset of the global refugee crisis, which has left North American and many European countries with significant influxes of Muslim refugees (Tausch 2016). These and other global developments have recreated essentializing labels that rely on gender and sexuality to construct Westerners as democratic and feminist, versus what are often perceived to be "uncivilized Muslims" (Nusair 2008). . . .

Against this global backdrop of public and political discourse, we turn our attention to Canada. Widely recognized as a haven for immigrants, the country has seen its own discussions about the compatibility of Islam with Canadian society (Reitz, Phan, and Banerjee 2015). . . . Yet the popular portrayals of Islamic gender roles generally presuppose their fundamental incompatibility with those in the West. Our interviews with 256 young second-generation Somali-Canadians, however, suggest that gender-egalitarian identities are

achieved—they are constructed and deployed by our study participants to practice integration and express belonging in Canada. Our study, therefore, contributes to the emergent literature in migration studies that examines gender in relation to ethnic and national identities . . . (Crul and Schneider 2010; Scheible and Fleischmann 2013). . . . [W]e propose an understanding of gender as a form of cultural capital (Bourdieu 1986), and analyse modalities of "doing" gender and constructing gender identities (West and Zimmerman 1987) as potential strategies of accumulating capital in furthering successful integration.

. . . [W]e begin by defining and contextualizing gender within the field of migration studies. We next explain our conceptual understanding of gender and cultural capital. Third, we discuss the concepts of multiculturalism and integration. We then discuss the Canadian sociocultural context followed by a discussion of our participants' cultural and immigration backgrounds. [. . . W]e thematically present the results of our study and argue that egalitarian gender norms are an integral part of the identity formation of second-generation Somalis and this, as a form of capital, facilitates integration and belonging to Canada. Finally, we conclude that our participants understand their gender roles primarily in terms of family and societal membership, and not in rigid religious terms. Our findings emphasize that the host society's national context and immigrants' cultural

Karimi, Ahmed, Sandra M. Bucerius, and Sara Thompson. "Gender Identity and Integration: Second-Generation Somali Immigrants Navigating Gender on Canada." *Ethnic and Racial Studies*, 2019, 42(9), pp. 1534–1553. Reprinted by permission of Taylor & Francis Ltd. www.tandfonline.com

background may be simultaneously influential in the successful integration of second-generation immigrants (Crul and Schneider 2010).

Immigration and Gender

. . . Traditionally, questions around gender and migration mostly examined first-generation immigrants, especially with respect to their integration into labour markets (Hoang 2016; Tienda and Booth 1991) or households (Mahler 1995; Momsen 1999). . . .

In our study, we . . . examine transformations of gender identities among young, second-generation Somali-Canadians. . . . Here, we place gender as the focal point of consideration, to initiate discussion around further theorizing and operationalizing gender as a form of cultural capital (Dumais 2002; Laberge 1995) that regulates upward mobility and the successful integration of immigrants. . . .

Gender and Capital

The literature on second-generation immigrants has emphasized the role of family relations, kinship and ethnicity in contributing to immigrants' capital and driving social mobility (Nee and Sanders 2010; Portes and Rumbaut 2001; Portes and Zhou 1993; Zhou and Bankston 1994). To date, gender as a form of capital has been undertheorized. West and Zimmerman (1987, 126) define gender as a "social doing of sorts" that is "undertaken by women and men" and "involves a complex of socially guided perceptual, interactional, and micropolitical activities." Accordingly, gender becomes "an accomplishment, an achieved property of situated conduct" and "a means of legitimating" one's social position (West and Zimmerman 1987, 126). This understanding of gender as socially constructed individual activities that may become an accomplishment is in line with Bourdieu's theorization of cultural capital. Bourdieu (1986) defines capital as "accumulated labor (in its materialized form or its '*incorporated*,' *embodied form*) (my emphasis)," which may enable agents to acquire power and produce profit.

Bourdieu identified three forms of cultural capital and we argue that gender represents cultural capital in "the embodied state, i.e. in the form of long-lasting dispositions of the mind and body (emphasis in the original)". . . . This process is undertaken by individuals and, depending on social values and structures, functions as symbolic capital that, along with other forms of capital, renders individuals and groups as advantaged or disadvantaged. It is therefore important to explore the modalities of doing gender, i.e. accumulating and deploying cultural capital, in understanding certain groups' successful integration, or lack thereof.

Accordingly, we understand gender identities as outputs of the very processes of constructing "the personality traits of masculinity and femininity," and "attitudinal differences regarding the roles, rights, and responsibilities of women and men" (Fischer and Arnold 1994, 164). We argue that depending on immigrants' agency and contextual factors (Crul and Schneider 2010), certain gender identities, i.e. the embodied dispositions, may be socially interpreted as profitable cultural capital and facilitate integration or as less valuable and a barrier to integration. The outcome depends on the compatibility of gender identities with the socially sanctioned meanings of gender whether at national, community or family level. This means that doing gender and constructing gender identities according to certain sociocultural norms could be viewed as a form of cultural capital, comparable to language skills or educational attainment (Lamont and Lareau 1988; Nee and Sanders 2010).

. . . [W]e elaborate on the ways the decline in religious and community commitments have diminished the constraining aspects of social networks on participants' cultural attitudes and on accumulating cultural capital (Zontini 2010) while multicultural context, access to citizenship and education have contributed to the accumulation of capital in the form of more egalitarian gender identities that avail second-generation Somalis with integration (Röder 2014). These findings invite gender and feminist scholars and migration researchers to further explore the impact of doing gender identities as a form of capital. . . .

Multiculturalism, Canadian Context and Integration

... In Canada, dominant ... identities and institutions draw on denial of explicit racism and ethno-centrism and perceive immigrants as "good for the economy" (Reitz 2011). All agents involved in the management of the national rhetoric avoid explicit references to racial discrimination, anti-immigrant sentiment and/or job-market inequalities (Moodley 2010; Reitz 1988). ... As a consequence, immigrants tend to perceive Canada as immigrant-friendly and immigrant groups tend to express positive attitudes towards national policies and the Canadian national identity (Wenshya Lee and Hébert 2006). This open support is thought to render social inequality in Canada less visible, at least for a time, thereby facilitating the integration process for many immigrants.

According to the literature on immigrant youths' process of integration, individuals and groups develop accommodating changes in their customs, identities and socioeconomic and political life as a result of intercultural contact (Berry et al. 2006). These changes are thought to bridge their respective home and host cultures. Indeed, the second-generation Somali-Canadians in our sample appear to have adapted their gender identities by drawing upon various discourses informed by their ethnic culture, religion, class situation and Canadian national identity (Reitz, Phan, and Banerjee 2015). ...

Somali Culture and Immigration Background in Canada

Since the late 1970s, Somalia has experienced several conflicts resulting in famine, clan clashes, and civil war. During the 1990s, these events resulted in the collapse of the Somali government and forced emigration of Somalis to neighbouring countries. In addition, Western countries, including Canada, have welcomed Somali refugees through asylum procedures. When examining our participants' views on gender, it is important to keep in mind Somalia's history of war and trauma, which potentially influences their willingness to divorce from some of their cultural practices and traditions (Boyle and Ali 2009).

... [The] literature on Somali immigrants in the West shows that experiences of war and trauma, absence of a centralized government and a shared culture of mobility are reflected in the lack of organized intergenerational diasporic communities (Alitolppa-Niitamo 2002; Boyle and Ali 2009). This absence of extended community contacts—or, the absence of traditional forms of "social capital" (Boyle and Ali 2009)—has diminished the power of ethnic networks in perpetuating traditional gender norms and family ties (Zontini 2007). This has pushed many Somali families to open up to Western norms and become more autonomous with less direct cultural control over children. ... All of these changes are complemented and reinforced by acculturation through schools and the accumulation of cultural capital (Nee and Sanders 2010), as the Somali culture highly values education. Once in the West, "many Somali parents supported their children and placed high expectations on the children's school achievement" (Alitolppa-Niitamo 2002). At the same time, however, an international body of research has documented a trend among women in Somali diasporas towards heightened awareness of and involvement in cultural practices and religious activities (see, for example, Berns-McGown 1999, 2013; McMichael 2002; Tiilikainen 2003). However, this is not a simple process of retreating back to established cultural practices and norms in the face of immense social and cultural change. Rather, and harkening back to the aforementioned notion of integration requiring mutual change and some degree of convergence this activity becomes part of women's "daily agency" (Tiilikainen 2003) that aims to "transforms Islam" (Berns-McGown 1999), and to build it into the very fabric of the host country.

Methodology and Setting

We conducted 301 semi-structured, in-depth interviews with members of the Somali-Canadian diaspora in Edmonton between the ages of 16 and

30. The overwhelming majority (78 per cent) of our participants self-identified their family background as low income, with the remaining 22 per cent self-identifying as middle income. Two hundred and fifty six out of our 301 participants were born in Canada, i.e. second-generation immigrants.

. . . We designed our interview instrument in continuous consultation and collaboration with our Somali-Canadian research assistants to ensure that our questions were culturally appropriate and meaningful.

Our research team was diverse; some interviewers were of Somali-Canadian background with strong connections to their community, and others were undergraduate and graduate students of non-Somali background. Our team had both male and female research assistants. In keeping with Bucerius' (2013) argument that status traits such as gender, ethnicity and social orientation matter in the research process, we, too, found that the diversity of our research team greatly enriched our study. . . .

We approached our research from a critical realist perspective (Maxwell 2013), aiming to elicit and understand how our research participants construct their individual and shared meanings around our phenomena of interest. Essentially, we treated our participants' perceptions, intentions, experiences, and feelings as real—although unobserved—phenomena (Maxwell 2013). We digitally recorded all interviews. Once transcribed, we established a coding scheme that captured key themes and categories that emerged in the data.

Findings

Religious and Community Commitments

. . . All of our participants identified as Muslim, though not necessarily actively practising, and many insisted that religion played an important role in shaping their identities. . . .

In the interviews, Faduma, for example, a 21-year-old female, gave this response to the question What role does religion play in your life?[1]

Religion is the, it's basically who I am. It basically guides what I do. It's like a blueprint for me, it helps me, it gives me the morals, it tells me what sort of morals to possess, how to be a good person, how to live my life day to day.

Similarly, Sagal, a 23-year-old, refers to religion as a significant part of her life and her "spiritual guide." Uba, a 22-year-old, adds that her religion structures her daily life: "I pray five times a day, I fast in Ramadan. I would like to go to Hajj [pilgrimage], if I could." Focusing on the impact that religion has not only on individual community members, but on the Somali community as a whole, Ahmed, a 19-year-old male, clarifies: "It's big role in the Somali community, especially because our culture revolves around Islam, and so, like, anything we do, we have to think back to . . . our religion."

While almost all participants claimed Islam plays an important role in their lives, a small minority (17 of 256) expressed that they are moving away from self-identifying as a practising Muslim. Jibril, a 20-year-old male, explained, "I don't really go to the mosque, but my dad's Muslim and he lives in Somalia, but I don't really take that into, kind of, consideration." And Siman, a 21-year-old female, was careful to point out that being religious and identifying as Muslim may be two separate things: "My parents are Muslim, but I wouldn't say I'm that religious, but if anything, I'd say I'm Muslim." . . .

Huda describes how some relatives try to encourage her to participate in community events, but that she, like the great majority of our participants, is unsure how she would benefit from such involvement. She goes on to describe that her sister is the only person she can think of who is actively involved in community matters—which Huda admires, yet cannot relate to:

I have an uncle who is very involved in the community who's always telling me to come out to the events. But I feel like, I don't gain anything from these events. . . . My sister is very involved in the Somali community, I don't know how that happened; but I'd have to say out of the five of us she's the one who's really connected.

Lastly, reflecting on the low level of participation in intergenerational community events, Siman points out that some of the more traditional gender views may simply not stand a chance of being reinforced with the younger generation:

> We have our events, BBQs and stuff, but that's among the young people only. Almost no one goes to events with our parents and so we talk a lot about how we see life amongst us. And so, the more old-school people with views from back home and, so, they don't really get a chance to lecture us.

Our data suggest that religiosity among many of the young, second-generation Somali-Canadians in our sample has become a "symbolic" (Diehl, Koenig, and Ruckdeschel 2009) identity. This, coupled with a generalized and declining commitment to maintaining community ties, allows for looser control of traditions and social networks, resulting in the adoption and expression of more egalitarian gender identities. In what follows we describe the ways schooling and access to citizenship contribute to our participants' attitudes towards belonging and bridging cultural differences, including gender identities.

Multiculturalism, Citizenship and Education

. . . [Our] participants asserted that they mostly feel welcomed in Canadian society and schools. Except in rare cases, our participants had not experienced racism or harmful discrimination in schools and were optimistically aware of their higher-education options and their career goals in Canada. This is, for example, illustrated by the common desire to achieve high levels of education within our sample. . . .

When asking Anisa, a 22-year-old female, her general view on Canadian society, she responded, "[O]utside I haven't been, I haven't been discriminated, so I think it's good, actually." She goes on to talk about her ethnic identity: ". . . it's pretty big because it defines who I am,

you know, like, tells people where I'm from, you know, so I'm proud of being Somali. Like, I'm not going to hide it." Likewise, Uba points out that she varies between identifying as Somali or as Canadian: "Like my, like Somalian, um, important, yeah important, but I don't . . . tell, like, random people I'm Somalian, I'm Canadian." Ahmed's response to the question about his ethnic identity best reflects the sentiment of the great majority of our participants, who mostly identify as Somali-Canadian: "I guess there's not a lot of culture here, but like in Somali groups if you, like, look at them closely, like, we're basically all westernized I guess, like we're all turning to, like, we're going to this Canadian society . . . I say Somali Canadian."

. . . About a quarter of our participants claimed that they are not expected to help in any household chores or caregiving duties at all. Perhaps surprisingly, more female participants claimed they fall into this category than males. Bila, a 16-year-old female, explained how her parents actively steered her away from household chores and expected her to do well in school.

> I'm thinking of going into nursing and then upgrading to something even bigger, hopefully, but for now I'm just going to stick to nursing, yeah . . . currently I have no roles and since my parents are not letting me work, they're telling me to focus on school.

What Bila describes here is well documented in the North American immigration literature, commonly referred to as the "immigrant drive" (Portes and Rumbaut 2001). That is, many first-generation immigrants have a strong interest in the academic success of their children, which directly contributes to the accumulation of cultural capital and transformations in gender identities. . . .

Discussion

Our findings suggest that changing religiosity and the decline in community commitments have loosened the restrictive role of social networks on gender identities among the young

Somali-Canadians in our sample. At the same time, a widespread sense of belonging to Canadian multiculturalism and the simultaneous adoption of national and ethnic identities have fostered accumulation of capital in form of gender-egalitarian identities among the second-generation Somalis. . . .

Most of our participants observe the differences in their gender identity and ascribed roles and those of their parents' generation. However, they assert that they are not urged to abide by traditional gender arrangements, and do not necessarily perceive that there are, or should be, any fundamental differences based on their gender in terms of household chores, education or occupation. Many of our male participants state that they see much similarity between their gender identities and those of their Canadian-born counterparts since they have taken up duties that are traditionally considered feminine, such as taking care of siblings, cooking and cleaning. By contrast, female participants, claiming to belong to Canada and comparing their career aspirations with those of Canadian decent, showed interest in pursuing education in traditionally male-dominant majors such as engineering. Speaking to responsibilities and expectations for men and women within the Somali community, Bashir, a 17-year-old male, stated:

> I mean, obviously, in the Somali community they expect only males to work and females to stay at home with the kids . . . but, I mean, for kids that are born here and want to be part of this society, I guess it's kind of different, like more with the Canadian culture and what not. So, I guess same, same rights for males and females.

Bashir's account illustrates that our participants have been exposed to a different set of cultural norms in Canada, and notice a shift from the traditional gender views still held by their parents' generation (Diehl, Koenig, and Ruckdeschel 2009). However, Bashir goes on to report that second-generation Somali-Canadians appear to be moving towards an "equal rights" approach to gender, in order to avoid family conflict and labour market issues that their parents experienced

due to traditional gender expectations and arrangements (Boyle and Ali 2009; Fuglerud and Engebrigtsen 2006).

Similar to Bashir, Faduma explains how her own family, and specifically her father, has moved significantly away from traditional gender norms, raising his daughters to be independent women while she seizes this opportunity to be successful in Canada:

> I feel like the Canadian Somali community, the ideology that they used to follow back home, is quite different because they've realized that in Canada it's different . . . my dad raised us so that we can be independent, and be self-sufficient, self-reliant and I have learnt to be independent similar to my [Canadian] friends. . . .

When asked about critical examples of using gender-egalitarian identities to navigate life in Canada, Atisa, a 17-year-old female, reported that the younger generations of Somali immigrants are well of aware of the differences between host and ethnic cultures, but work towards balancing their empowered gender identities with their individual and family lives:

> . . . when they're here it's like land of opportunity so women tend to like get out of their shell and they experience new things and they feel like I don't have to be with this person for this and this reason I need to be my own person. They find themselves I feel like.

Atisa goes on to report that gender-egalitarianism is also apparent within the parental household and in intergenerational interactions:

> Like luckily my family is very . . . um . . . I think my mom is like a feminist at heart or whatever so she doesn't really like assign roles to like my brother and I, um sometimes my dad will look at me like this: "you need to do this because you're a girl," and like that, and to me it's like "no no no," like, you know, if I accept that then I will not be the same [Canadian] in society. . . .

Asad, 23-year-old male, described how the idea of gender-egalitarianism plays out in his family:

> I feel like as a guy you're expected to do a great deal more. You know, you're held in a certain, at a certain level and you're expected to you know, survive . . . for them [his sisters], they love to play the card that you know, "We're independent. We do our own thing." You know? That's one of the downsides to being in charge in the family.

He continued to point out that as a Somali-Canadian man he will eschew conservative gender roles, because he prefers the "Canadian" approach: "So when you come to a community where it's more of a socializing thing, where it's more a you know going out, companionship . . . being uh for love to be more than just duties upon each other but friendship. . . ."

Conclusion

In this study of second-generation Somali immigrants in Canada, we explored gender identities at the intersection of ethnic and national identities. . . . Our findings demonstrate that Islam, among second-generation Somalis, plays an important role in terms of defining their moral systems and ethnic identity, and does not go against their host country's social norms. Our participants seem incredibly apt at not only oscillating between both structures but actively merging established cultural and religious activities with Canadian norms and expectations, thereby carving out gender-specific Canadian-Somali identities. Our data show that our participants have accumulated a form of cultural capital drawn from ethnic and national values that appears to inform the ongoing process of constructing gender identities, and that enables them to successfully integrate into the host culture.

Furthermore, based on our findings, it is evident that our study participants have generally been able to reconcile Islam with Canadian egalitarian gender norms. This . . . brings into question the validity of claims made by right-wing politicians about the incompatibility of Muslim immigrants with Western values and the need to restrict immigration from Muslim countries.

Lastly, our theoretical intervention of analysing gender as a form of capital invites researchers to explore gender and gender identities not as mere sociocultural products, but as situated conducts and embodied states that put individuals at an advantage or disadvantage. . . .

Note

1. Unless otherwise indicated, we are using our most representative interview material to demonstrate our findings.

References

Alitolppa-Niitamo, Anne. 2002. "The Generation In-Between." *Intercultural Education* 13 (3): 275–290.

Berns-McGown, R. 1999. *Muslims in the Diaspora*. Toronto: University of Toronto Press.

Berns-McGown, R. 2013. "I am Canadian." *Institute for Research on Public Policy* 38.

Berry, John, Jean Phinney, David Sam, and Paul Vedder. 2006. "Immigrant Youth." *Applied Psychology: An International Review* 55 (3): 303–332.

Boyle, Elizabeth, and Ahmed Ali. 2009. "Culture, Structure, and the Refugee Experience in Somali Immigrant Family Transformation." *International Migration* 48 (1): 48–79.

Bourdieu, P. 1986. "The Forms of Capital." In *Handbook of Theory and Research for the Sociology of Education*, edited by J.G. Richardson, 241–258. Westport, CT: Greenwood Press.

Bucerius, Sandra. 2013. "Becoming a 'Trusted Outsider'." *Journal of Contemporary Ethnography* 42 (6): 690–721.

Crul, M., and J. Schneider. 2010. "Comparative Integration Context Theory." *Ethnic and Racial Studies* 33 (7): 1249–1268.

Diehl, C., M. Koenig, and K. Ruckdeschel. 2009. "Religiosity and Gender Equality." *Ethnic and Racial Studies* 32 (2): 278–301.

Dion, K. K., and K. L. Dion. 2004. "Gender, Immigrant Generation, and Ethnocultural Identity." *Sex Roles* 50 (5–6): 347–355.

Dumais, Susan. 2002. "Cultural Capital, Gender, and School Success." *Sociology of Education* 75 (1): 44–68.

Fischer, Eillen, and Stephen Arnold. 1994. "Sex, Gender Identity, Gender Role Attitudes, and Consumer Behavior." *Psychology & Marketing* 11 (2): 163–182.

Fuglerud, Oivind, and Ada Engebrigtsen. 2006. "Culture, Networks and Social Capital." *Ethnic and Racial Studies* 29 (6): 1118–1134.

Hoang, L. A. 2016. "Vietnamese Migrant Networks in Taiwan: The Curse and Boon of Social Capital." *Ethnic and Racial Studies* 39 (4): 690–707.

Kleist, N. 2010. "Negotiating Respectable Masculinity: Gender and Recognition in the Somali Diaspora." *African Diaspora* 3 (2): 185–206.

Laberge, Suzanne. 1995. "Toward an Integration of Gender into Bourdieu's Concept of Cultural Capital." *Sociology of Sport Journal* 12 (2): 132–146.

Lamont, Michele, and Annette Lareau. 1988. "Cultural Capital." *Sociological Theory* 6 (2): 153–168.

Mahler, Sarah. 1995. *American Dreaming*. Princeton, NJ: Princeton University Press.

Maxwell, Joseph. 2013. *Qualitative Research Design*. Washington: Sage.

McMichael, C. 2002. "'Everywhere is Allah's Place': Islam and the Everyday Life of Somali Women in Melbourne, Australia." *Journal of Refugee Studies* 15 (2): 171–188.

Moodley, Kogila. 2010. "Canadian Multiculturalism as Ideology." *Ethnic and Racial Studies* 6 (3): 320–331.

Momsen, Janet. 1999. *Gender, Migration and Domestic Service*. London: Routledge.

Nee, Victor, and Jimmy Sanders. 2010. "Understanding the Diversity of Immigrant Incorporation." *Ethnic and Racial Studies* 24 (3): 386–411.

Nusair, Isis. 2008. "Gendered, Racialized and Sexualized Torture at Abu-Ghraib." In *Feminism and War*, edited by Chandra T. Mohanty, Robin L. Riley, and Minnie B. Pratt, 179–193. London: Zed Books.

Open Society Justice Initiative. 2009. *Ethnic Profiling in the European Union: Pervasive, Ineffective, and Discriminatory*. New York: Open Society Foundations.

Portes, Alejandro, and Ruben Rumbaut. 2001. *Legacies*. Berkeley, CA: University of California Press.

Portes, Alejandro, and Min Zhou. 1993. "The New Second Generation." *ANNAS, AAPPS* 530 (1): 74–96.

Reitz, Jeffrey. 1988. "Less Racial Discrimination in Canada, or Simply Less Racial Conflict?" *Canadian Public Policy* 14 (4): 424–441.

Reitz, Jeffrey. 2011. "Pro-Immigration Canada." *IRPP Study*, 1–29.

Reitz, Jeffrey, Mai B. Phan, and Rupa Banerjee. 2015. "Gender Equity in Canada's Newly Growing Religious Minorities." *Ethnic and Racial Studies* 38 (5): 681–699.

Röder, A. 2014. "Explaining Religious Differences in Immigrants' Gender Role Attitudes." *Ethnic and Racial Studies* 37 (14): 2615–2635.

Scheible, Jana, and Fenella Fleischmann. 2013. "Gendering Islamic Religiosity in the Second Generation." *Gender & Society* 27 (3): 372–395.

Tausch, Arno. 2016. "Muslim Immigration Continues to Divide Europe." *Middle East Review of International Affairs* 20 (2): 37–50.

Tienda, Marta, and Karen Booth. 1991. "Gender, Migration, and Social Change." *International Sociology* 6 (1): 51–72.

Tiilikainen, M. 2003. "Somali Women and Daily Islam in the Diaspora." *Social Compass* 50 (1): 59–69.

Wenshya Lee, Jenifer, and Yvonne Hébert. 2006. "The Meaning of Being Canadian." *Canadian Journal of Education / Revue Canadienne de L'éducation* 29 (2): 497–520.

West, Candace, and Don Zimmerman. 1987. "Doing Gender." *Gender & Society* 1 (2): 125–151.

Zhou, M., and C. Bankston. 1994. "Social Capital and the Adaptation of the Second Generation." *International Migration Review* 28 (4): 821–845.

Zontini, E. 2010. "Enabling and Constraining Aspects of Social Capital in Migrant Families." *Ethnic and Racial Studies* 33 (5): 816–831.

Chapter 8

Overview

Are Canadian universities racist places? Mohamed and Beagan argue that while overt racism is not as obvious on campuses in the twenty-first century, racism and colonialism still constrain people of colour. Focusing on faculty members who may spend their entire adult careers in universities, the authors find that their participants experience racism and colonialism as a pervasive sense of being out of place or not belonging—"strange faces" in an environment optimized for white students and staff. They use the concept of everyday racism and microaggressions—brief reminders that people of colour are out of place, expressed through words or behavioural interactions—to characterize the experience of colonialism and racism in higher education from the perspective of faculty. Microaggressions may not have malicious intent, but when accumulated over months and years, they still result in psychological harm. Participants talk about having the focus of their teaching and research queried as not being academic enough, about being repeatedly asked to take on the work of serving on committees and task forces related to anti-racism or colonialism, and about working in an environment where white people's experiences were implicitly assumed to be universal, without ever being stated explicitly. Other participants shared experiences of being treated as different from and lesser than their white peers through the actions of their supervisors and people in authority. Everyday racism proves to be much harder to eradicate than the more obvious forms of discrimination.

"Strange Faces" in the Academy

Experiences of Racialized and Indigenous Faculty in Canadian Universities

Tameera Mohamed and Brenda L. Beagan

Introduction

Despite institutional commitments to equity in Canadian universities, racism and colonialism . . . have profound impacts on the daily work lives of racialized and Indigenous academics. . . .

Drawing on 13 interviews from a larger Canada-wide study exploring the experiences of "minority" faculty, this paper presents the everyday experiences of belonging and exclusion for racialized and Indigenous faculty members. All participants described everyday racism, including experiences of microaggressions—interactions generally not intended to be racist or colonialist, but which nonetheless convey subtle messages of not-quite-belonging (Wing-Sue 2010). Participants also described routine systems and academic cultural norms, including institutional and epistemological racism, which affected their experiences within the profession. Institutionalized whiteness, along with neoliberalism and an "audit culture" (Ahmed 2012), coalesce to entrench a toxic culture in which racism is subsumed into normalized practices and performance measures. These routinized expectations demand that racialized and Indigenous faculty do extra, invisible work in order to prove "legitimate" academics in both research and teaching, also in addition to meeting scholarly expectations. Instances of overt hostility were more common than might be expected, suggesting current equity policies are ineffective in addressing even explicit forms of racism in the academy.

Literature Review

Everyday Racism: Microaggressions and Impacts

Many scholars argue that racism has not so much diminished as changed form, with less overt processes dominating (Bonilla-Silva 2010; Essed 1991; Wing-Sue 2010). Philomena Essed (1991) coined

Mohamed, Tameera, and Brenda L. Beagan. "'Strange faces' in the academy: experiences of racialized and Indigenous faculty in Canadian universities." *Race Ethnicity and Education*, 2019, 22(3), pp. 338–354. Reprinted by permission of Taylor & Francis Ltd. www.tandfonline.com

the term "everyday racism" to describe the ways in which contemporary racism has been integrated "into everyday situations through practices ... that activate underlying power relations" (50). Everyday racism manifests in a multitude of subtle ways, including behaviours, humour, ways of speaking, and body language, leaving it often unnoticed and difficult to challenge. Everyday interactions between members of marginalized groups and dominant groups are micro-level instantiations of macro-level power relations, "practices that infiltrate everyday life and become part of what is seen as 'normal' by the dominant group" (288).

In psychology the term "microaggressions" has been advanced by scholars like Wing-Sue to define the "brief and commonplace daily verbal, behavioural, and environmental indignities, whether intentional or unintentional, that communicate hostile, derogatory, or negative ... slights to the target person or group" (2010, 7). What makes these experiences significant is that they are part of the everyday fabric of racism; while one microaggression seems insignificant, they are an everyday reality for racialized people with detrimental cumulative consequences. Some argue that these subtler forms of racism have a greater impact than overt racism, in which "no guesswork is involved" in deciphering the intention behind and meaning of an incident (Wing-Sue 2010, 23). Since racial microaggressions are repetitive, those on the receiving end are often especially attuned to their presence and "have a more accurate assessment" of their occurrence and meaning than dominant group members (Wing-Sue 2010, 47). The subtlety of microaggressions means that those on the receiving end may experience self-doubt in their analysis, relying on each other to "sanity-check" their interpretations (Wing-Sue 2010, 74–75).

Racism and Colonialism in the Academy

In higher education, everyday racism can occur not only in individual interactions, but also through the structure of the institution itself; the lack of administrators and tenured professors of colour tell students and faculty of colour that they do not belong and their likelihood of advancing in the academy is low (Huber and Solozano 2015; Wing-Sue 2010). ...

Despite increases in relative numbers of "minority" faculty, racialized and Indigenous faculty frequently report being the only such individuals in their department or university as a whole (Henry and Tator 2012; James 2012). Such "institutional isolation" (Smith and Calasanti 2005) may leave them feeling isolated and alienated, lacking important information networks without which they are less able to participate in decisions and policy-making (Ross and Edwards 2016). Tenure and promotion processes are particularly difficult when role models are lacking (Henry and Tator 2012).

The challenges of tenure and promotion review are exacerbated by the fact that academic norms are decidedly Eurocentric. When only certain types of knowledge are seen as legitimate, only certain types of research questions and methods "count", only certain journals are recognized, and only certain knowledges enter into curricula (Henry and Tator 2012; Ross and Edwards 2016), this constitutes epistemological racism, a form of racism that effectively renders the ways of knowing of some groups as lesser, unauthoritative. The kinds of research many racialized and Indigenous faculty engage in may be deemed less scholarly than "mainstream" research (Henry and Tator 2012; Ross and Edwards 2016). Moreover, they may need to publish in "lesser" journals that are more open to critical perspectives. These norms render racialized and Indigenous faculty as "illegitimate".

Hesitance to see racialized and Indigenous faculty as legitimate is also evident in student evaluations of teaching, wherein racialized faculty are rated less favourably than white colleagues (Ross and Edwards 2016). Proving themselves authoritative experts in the classroom expends untold energy (e.g. Mayuzumi 2015). At the same time, alongside their regular faculty duties, racialized and Indigenous faculty are disproportionately likely to be involved in equity and diversity initiatives and mentoring minority students, often experiencing futility in those endeavours (Henry and Tator 2012; Ross and Edwards 2016). They may be essentialized—invited to work on diversity concerns simply because of their race—even as their involvement in such work confirms stereotypes of narrow self-interest, resulting in potential career harm. As James (2012) reports, racialized faculty face negative repercussions whether they raise issues of equity or not.

The impacts of racism are significant: Henry and Tator (2012) found that racialized and Indigenous faculty report low self-esteem, physical and mental health impacts, and serious considerations of leaving academia, demonstrating that these "daily small events and incidents" have the potential to severely affect career trajectory and engagement (78–79). The current study builds on the recent work of Frances Henry and her colleagues (2017a, 2017b), exploring the experiences of racialized and Indigenous academics in Canadian universities. Here, we explicitly tease apart instances of everyday racism and instances of more overt hostility, the kind of thing typically understood as racism. We highlight the extra work demanded of racialized and Indigenous faculty in order to navigate the institutional whiteness of academia and examine how the culture of academia perpetuates racism in the lives of racialized and Indigenous faculty.

. . .

Results

Everyday Exclusion

Lack of Representation

Many participants described working in departments and faculties where they were among very few racialized faculty members; some were the only Indigenous professors at their universities. Robert had been the sole Indigenous faculty member at several universities, positioning him as the singular voice for Aboriginal issues on campus:

> Someone called me up and said, "I'm consulting with the Aboriginal community on campus, about how they're doing in their faculty and staff positions.". . . So, we had a nice conversation and then at the end I said, "Can you tell me who else at the university you've been talking to?" And he said, "You're it". So, I was the Aboriginal community at the time. . . . That's happened two or three times in my career.

Rachel was not only the sole racialized faculty member in her department, but remains the only one in her entire field in the country: "Still today, I'm the first and only Black professor [in my field] teaching at a Canadian university". As Henry et al. note, underrepresentation "underpins, loneliness, isolation, and tokenism. Everyday racism thrives in an atmosphere of nonrepresentation" (2017a, 127).

. . . [M]any participants were asked to participate in administrative or academic service work representing racialization or Indigeneity. While many enjoyed this work, it was also experienced as tokenizing, especially when the work was unconnected to academic expertise:

> From the time I was hired, people started asking me to talk about women and science or racialized minorities in science or under-represented groups in science, or bias in science. When I started, I knew nothing about any of that, other than my personal experience. So, the feeling that having been hired into this role, in addition to my day job, I have this other responsibility, to represent for my race, was kind of odious, really. (Marianna)

Participants often struggled to know whether they were asked to engage in service work for their abilities or their identity. Tokenism "goes to the heart of how racialized (and Indigenous) faculty are perceived and evaluated. Their presence is required not because of their special abilities, aptitude or knowledge, but because of their essential nature as members of particular groups" (Henry et al. 2017a, 125). Moreover, they felt invited to represent difference, disguising the fact that nothing at the university really changed.

Being often the only non-white person in the room may make explicit a sense of "not belonging". As Janet described, this increases with career advancement:

> I can't pretend to be surprised when I walk into a space and I'm the only person of colour. I sort of scan the room, "Are there any other people of colour here?" I'm not even going to think about are there any other Black people here. That's just not going to happen, there

aren't going to be any other Black people. Or that will be very rare. So now I'm looking for people of colour, or any of my Indigenous brothers and sisters. . . . And certainly, the further you go up, like, from pre-tenure to tenure, to then as a tenured faculty member in an administrative position, this gets more and more sort of rare.

. . .

Such experiences of not-fitting make apparent the institutionalized whiteness that is the norm in Canadian universities (Henry et al. 2017a). Racialized Others may be welcomed to the university, but they are invited to inhabit a preexisting whiteness, a taken-for-granted assumption that the bodies occupying that space are white bodies. As Ahmed states, "To inhabit whiteness as a nonwhite body can be uncomfortable" (2012, 40). Racialized and Indigenous faculty are present as unexpected guests, explicitly not in the position of hosts who already occupy the space.

. . .

Whiteness and the Culture of Academia

Many participants reflected on the Eurocentric culture of academia, describing intentional shifts and sacrifices they have made to "fit" within it, learning academic cultural norms and sometimes relinquishing elements of their own culture. For example, Rachel described academic culture as "ways of mainstream, coded Euro-Canadian engagement that are not universal, [but] that all the white people who might be your colleagues think are universal". She referred to the use of Robert's Rules in department meetings as one example of an intensely culture-bound system that professes universality and impartiality. . . .

Rachel described a version of whiteness inextricably bound up with academic elitism, conveyed through rejection of popular culture from a stance of superiority:

There's a certain type of white professor who has totally forsaken any pop culture. . . . I think that's racially specific. I don't find a lot of black professors who do that, or are that unplugged and detached from pop culture.

And so the kind of jokes and conversations you can have with people, their idea of assumed knowledge is not universal knowledge. And that really pisses me off. . . . "You guys are so in your own world of whatever you think is universal that you don't get that when you're citing this play and this [classical music], that not everybody knows what the hell you're talking about". But why do I know that I have to explain to you who Beyoncé is? . . . it's still a kind of white cultural supremacy, like a certain type of white culture too, that passes as universal and what you should know because you have a PhD.

This is precisely the way whiteness places "the interests and perspectives of white people at the centre of what is considered normal and everyday" (Gillborn 2015, 278). Ahmed describes the too-frequent experience of being the only person of colour in an academic setting as being like "walking into a sea of whiteness" (2012, 35). The presence of a few racialized and Indigenous faculty confirms the norm of whiteness. One of our participants described an "unpredictable" but profound sense of not-fitting in the context of whiteness: "Sometimes you'll be having a discussion in a faculty meeting and suddenly, in my head it feels like a chasm opens up between me and the rest of the faculty" (Marianna).

. . .

Not Belonging: "There's This Strange Face That Shouldn't Be in That Hallway"

Participants routinely described feeling that they did not belong in academia, most often as a result of micro-level interactions that positioned them as outsiders. Such instances of everyday racism (Essed 1991) frequently began in graduate school, where several participants had been discouraged from continuing their studies, regardless of excellent performance. Participants interpreted these experiences as reflecting an unacknowledged belief that racialized and Indigenous people do not belong in academia. The power of everyday racism lies in its repetition, the accumulation of messages of not belonging, which participants described as occurring consistently throughout their academic careers.

. . .

Rachel suggested it was more than being unfamiliar with Black people as professors, but actual discomfort with Black authority and expertise: "White students are uncomfortable with someone that they don't identify with being the purveyor of knowledge at the front of the class". The normative whiteness that attaches to the role of professor meant that some racialized and Indigenous faculty were mistaken for students, as Marianna described: "When I first started here, they would knock on the door and say 'Oh, is Professor [name] here?' They'd look over my shoulder (laugh)". Similarly, Janet described, "People thinking 'Well, you must be a student. You can't be a faculty member'". Both Marianna and Janet interpreted being misread as students as revealing an institutional given that a professor will/should be white. As Ahmed argues, "Being asked whether you are the professor is a way of being made into a stranger, of not being at home in a category that gives residence to others" (2012, 177).

The most explicit instance of "being made into a stranger" was described by Laurie. After completing multiple degrees and moving into a teaching position at the same university, she had spent many years on campus, in the same buildings. Yet, she was stopped one day by security and asked for ID, while three white colleagues (all new to campus) proceeded unquestioned:

> I thought "That's strange". And they didn't even notice. We were all chatting, all of us, chatting. And they continue chatting, and I'm stopped. . . . You begin to question yourself, when you get these things all the time. So I went home that evening and it was still bothering me. But I didn't want to overreact to it. And so the next day I asked my colleagues, Did you notice what happened? Did you see that I was stopped there? And they were like, "Oh yeah, yeah. I think you were". But they didn't really even make anything of it.

. . .

In a context of institutionalized whiteness, non-white bodies are rendered both invisible and hyper-visible: "Bodies stick out when they are out of place" (Ahmed 2012, 41). Laurie was seen in a way her white colleagues were not, yet unseen in that she remained unfamiliar. The ability of white bodies to move about institutional spaces with ease, not noticing who is or is not present, confirms the normative expectation of whiteness. Our participant Rachel suggested she is visible as a Black woman because she is in the position of professor—beyond her station:

> There's a certain kind of white person who . . . would be more comfortable with me as a janitor, because that's what I'm supposed to be doing. But as a professor, it's like, "No, you're supposed to be in your place", which is always already beneath me. So, there's a certain type of racism that's reserved for so called over-achieving blacks.

Experiences of everyday racism in academia—from being misread as a student to being treated as an interloper—send a message to racialized and Indigenous faculty that they do not fully belong, that they remain a "strange face" in the academy. Yet, each individual instantiation of power relations, each incident, is subtle and open to interpretation. As Laurie said, "you begin to question yourself". This uncertainty, this "guesswork" (Wing-Sue 2010, 23) attached to everyday racism takes its own emotional toll. Marianna described a powerful member on a committee ignoring everything she said. When two trusted colleagues later confirmed, "That guy didn't listen to anything you said!" she felt "vindicated": "'I'm not just imagining it. It's not just that I made weak points.' And that's the problem with all of it, is that it can just erode your confidence if you're not careful". . . . Thus, everyday racism may contribute to low self-esteem, low self-confidence, hopelessness, and poorer physical, emotional, and mental health (Henry et al. 2017a, 2017b).

Overt Racism: The "Illegitimate" Academic

Though universities may overtly commit to diversity and inclusion (Universities Canada 2017), and to challenging the existence of racism and colonialism in the institution (Ahmed 2012), the racialized and Indigenous faculty we interviewed reported numerous instances of overt racism, such as ignorant or hostile comments from colleagues and students. . . . Some instances of overt racism detrimentally affected tenure and promotion.

Racialized and Indigenous faculty described having course evaluations and positive feedback removed from their files, making this information unavailable during tenure and promotion considerations. For example, Rachel's department chair received a sudden influx of positive emails from community members about an event Rachel had organized; they later disappeared:

> She was actually upset with me. . . . She was getting all of these letters about how wonderful the event was and how I should be tenured immediately. And said if I had put these people up to this, it wasn't going to do me any good. So, that taught me a lesson in – You know, I was aware that if I failed, there would be repercussions, but *succeeding* could be punished as well. But when I went up for tenure then, a couple years later, I wrote to her and said "Can I get the letters? They're not in my file". And she claimed to not know that the letters existed. So, she destroyed them.

Similarly, Janine received almost-perfect evaluations for a course she taught, only to have the student comments "lost" by the department secretary:

> When they did the student evaluations at the end of the year, the secretary told me, "Oh yeah, you got really good marks in your [Indigenous content] course, but what's the point? They were all Indians in your class, weren't they?" "So, where are my comments?" "Oh, they got lost". And I had, like, a 4.8 out of 5.

In both cases, the assumption seemed to be that racialized and Indigenous faculty members could not possibly be performing well enough to receive legitimate positive feedback, and any such feedback is either coerced or evidence of intra-racial favouritism—a critique not typically levelled against white faculty who receive evaluations from majority white students.

. . .

Students commonly demonstrated overt racism, often in anonymous course evaluations—though a few people had experienced "outright, hostile, racist attacks in class". Course evaluations hold serious ramifications for faculty and are problematic for racialized and Indigenous professors (Henry et al. 2017a). As Rachel noted, "there is stuff that people will say, do, and put on women of colour faculty that I know they would never do to a white guy". Some participants received course evaluations attacking their qualifications, but equally common were comments about appearance and accent. For Laurie and Fathima, accents were repeatedly raised as shortcomings in course evaluations. Even though she adjusts her teaching to account for her accent, Azedeh reported, "Students seem to associate not doing well in a course with the accent of the professor, or any other shortcoming of the professor that they can find". Janine noted that Indigenous colleagues received evaluations asking why they "wear beads and feathers to class?" As Rachel said, there are "too many ways in which students who don't like your identity will attack you through an evaluation". Again, this may stem from racialized and Indigenous faculty being "unexpected occupants" of the professor position, presumed less competent, but also the target of hostility for having moved beyond their expected station in life.

. . .

Additional Work: "We Get Pulled Too Many Ways"

In addition to their regular teaching and research duties, many participants were involved in unusually high levels of service work, often involving equity and diversity initiatives. This meant hours of additional work each week that significantly detracted from their research. Eva pointed out that lack of representation of Indigenous faculty means "everybody wants us to be on their committees" with the weight of equity issues falling on very few shoulders. Marianna noted this means racialized faculty "get offered interesting service", but it also means they "get offered every bit of service that comes along". While Indigenous and racialized academics often agree to sit on committees where "diversity" is sought, this may be highly strategic, as noted by Laurie: "If you're not at the table, then where are you? Probably on the menu, where you'll be eaten up". Many people participated willingly, even eagerly, in equity-related work, finding passion and sense of value there.

At the same time, however, the burden is high. Some have called this a "race tax" or "cultural taxation" (Henry et al. 2017a), extra service work that contributes to exhaustion and burnout. Lauren described routinely "being asked to, or being told that you're going to sit on things because they need someone who's Aboriginal." . . .

Some of the extra work—particularly mentoring and supporting racialized and Indigenous students—felt meaningful and rewarding, even if it also felt like a duty and additional work. Laurie's experience as a student of "not seeing any Black professors you can go to and talk to" informs her own approach to mentoring students:

> Even when you have your own quota of students that you can supervise, you see a student, a Black student in my case, who is struggling and you want to be on their committee so you can help. That is an additional burden that you take on.

Similarly, when Janine was a graduate student, an Indigenous mentor was critical to her success: from guidance in applying to graduate schools, to sharing childcare, to seeking out spiritual healing ceremonies when needed. For Eva, mentoring Indigenous students—even on matters unrelated to their academic work—was a professional responsibility, a duty to her home community. As Henry et al. (2017a, 164) point out, "despite the difficulties, the exhaustion . . . racialized faculty will continue to put in the extra time because we feel that we cannot refuse", not only due to moral commitment to communities but also due to a (stated or unstated) sense that this is why they were hired.

Given the experiences of being cast as "illegitimate academics", it is not surprising that many participants perceived they needed to work harder than their white colleagues to be seen as equally good:

> If my colleagues were publishing two articles a year, I have to publish three. So at least I know when they're looking at my file, they're not going to find something that is not equal to what other people have. They should always find something that's more. (Laurie)

. . .

Part of that extra work entailed defending their scholarship. Community-engaged research was devalued, seen as not meeting "expectations in terms of what counts as scientific knowledge . . . the work that is valued" (Laurie). Several people found their research on issues concerning race or Indigeneity was dismissed as "biased" and lacking rigor. Janet said, "If you're a Black woman doing research on Black issues, there's something fishy about that . . . doing research that's not considered sort of the important research questions". Janine's research on an aspect of colonialism was dismissed: "People didn't really consider it a relevant topic". She went on to say, "[long pause] It wasn't really important. It wasn't. I mean, it was only important to me. Right? . . . I wanted to contribute something. And then it just ended up being trashed. . . . Maybe it was too personal. It was too [pause]—" This final "it was too—" is painful. It suggests the kind of low self-confidence, hopelessness, and internalized doubt that others have noted among racialized and Indigenous faculty (Henry et al. 2017b). It speaks of a distressing sense of "failure to fit" within the overwhelming whiteness of academia (Ahmed 2012). Janine said elsewhere in her interview, "I'm really, in terms of my professional development, a failure. Like, I have failed. I don't know why. I don't know how. I don't know if I'm not smart enough, if I'm not good enough, if—"

. . .

There is labour involved in being racialized and Indigenous faculty in institutions infused with whiteness. Racialized and Indigenous faculty are "unexpected bodies" in academia, requiring they work to ease the tensions of their presence: "The body that causes their discomfort (by not fulfilling an expectation of whiteness) is the one that must work hard to make others comfortable" (Ahmed 2012, 41). There is work in challenging—or deciding not to challenge—preconceptions. There is work in building connection across not belonging. There is work in being different enough to represent diversity yet not so much so as to embody the negative perceptions of your group. There is work in making space for others. There is work in deciding whether and how to respond to racism, and in the responding itself. As Ahmed (2012, 174) notes, only the continual "practical labour of 'coming up against' the institution" allows its whiteness to become apparent'. She describes this as going against the flow, akin to "the experience of going the wrong way in a crowd", requiring great effort (Ahmed 2012, 186).

Conclusion

Assumptions of whiteness have exacted an incalculable cost for many racialized and Indigenous scholars. They rob the academy and the broader society of a wealth of talent and the invaluable heterogeneity of people, their knowledge, and the perspectives that could make universities more equitable, diverse, and excellent (Henry et al. 2017b, 311).

. . .

Our participants were isolated, few in number with increasing scarcity as people moved up the hierarchy. This under-representation fuels both tokenism and the burden of extra service demands. Both informal conversations rife with culture-bound elitism, and the structure of meetings conveyed messages of not belonging. Faculty were undermined by students and sabotaged by colleagues and staff seemingly uncomfortable with racialized and Indigenous people in positions of authority. Contemporary universities are simultaneously neoliberal and archaic, emphasizing entrepreneurial innovation and productivity alongside conventional modes of hierarchy that stretch back centuries. This is a perfect context for competition, rivalry, distrust, isolation, superiority, and egoism, all of which exacerbate the power imbalances of racism while making them even harder to see. While all faculty are affected by power relationships with more senior colleagues and administrators, it is notable that racialized and Indigenous faculty are also vulnerable to power plays by students and staff. Moreover, the potential critiques of and challenges to business-as-usual are silenced when toxic power hierarchies leave them unsafe to speak out.

. . .

This study is limited by reliance on a small sample, which nonetheless included considerable heterogeneity. There is a risk of essentializing race when experiences across a wide range of racialized groups, including Indigenous scholars, are analysed together. While there is value in seeing the similarities across groups, nuances of different ways racism and colonialism play out may be lost. We have not here teased apart the differences among disciplines, nor the inevitable intersections of race and Indigeneity with other social identities, such as gender identity, sexuality, social class background, disability, or immigration history. Continued attention to such nuances is much needed in the Canadian context.

References

Ahmed, S. 2012. *On Being Included: Racism and Diversity in Institutional Life.* London: Duke University Press.

Bonilla-Silva, E. 2010. *Racism without Racists: Color-Blind Racism and the Persistence of Racial Inequality in the United States.* 3rd ed. Oxford: Rowman & Littlefield.

Essed, P. 1991. *Understanding Everyday Racism: An Interdisciplinary Theory*. California: Sage Publications.

Gillborn, D. 2012. "Race and Education." In *Banks Encyclopedia of Diversity in Education*, ed J. A. Banks, 1742–1747. Los Angeles: Sage Reference.

Henry, F., and C. Tator. 2012. "Interviews with Racialized Faculty Members in Canadian Universities." *Canadian Ethnic Studies* 44 (2): 75–99. doi:10.1353/ces.2012.0003.

Henry, F., C. E. Enakshi Dua, A. K. James, L. Peter, H. Ramos, and M. S. Smith. 2017a. *The Equity Myth: Racialization and Indigeneity at Canadian Universities*. Vancouver: UBC Press.

Henry, F., E. Dua, A. Kobayashi, C. James, P. Li, H. Ramos, and M. S. Smith. 2017b. "Race, Racialization and Indigeneity in Canadian Universities." *Race, Ethnicity and Education* 20 (3): 300–314. doi:10.1080/13613324.2016.1260226.

Huber, L., P. Huber, and D. G. Solozano. 2015. "Racial Microaggressions as a Tool for Critical Race Research." *Race Ethnicity and Education* 18 (3): 297–320. doi:10.1080/13613324.2014.994173.

James, C. E. 2012. "Strategies of Engagement: How Racialized Faculty Negotiate the University System."

Canadian Ethnic Studies 44 (2): 133–152. doi:10.1353/ces.2012.0007.

Mayuzumi, K. 2015. "Navigating Orientalism: Asian Women Faculty in the Canadian Academy." *Race, Ethnicity and Education* 18 (2): 277–296. doi:10.1080/13613324.2014.946495.

Ross, H. H., and W. J. Edwards. 2016. "African American Faculty Expressing Concerns: Breaking the Silence at Predominantly White Research Oriented Universities." *Race Ethnicity and Education* 19 (3): 461–479. doi:10.1080/13613324/2014/969227.

Smith, J. W., and T. Calasanti. 2005. "The Influences of Gender, Race and Ethnicity on Workplace Experiences of Institutional and Social Isolation: An Exploratory Study of University Faculty." *Sociological Spectrum* 25 (3): 307–334. doi:10.1080/027321790518735.

Universities Canada. 2017. "Universities Canada Principles on Equity, Diversity and Inclusion." https://www.univcan.ca/media-room=media-releases/universities-canada-principles-equitydiversity-inclusion/.

Wing-Sue, D. 2010. *Microaggressions in Everyday Life: Race, Gender, and Sexual Orientation*. Hoboken: Wiley.

Chapter 9

Overview

When Fiona Nicoll began inquiring into her own relationship to Indigenous self-assertion in Australia and Canada, she ran into a complex tangle of ideas connecting expressions of anti-racism with a gendered form of virtue. She found that many of her white female colleagues made statements supporting Indigenous claims because they saw themselves as nice, well-intentioned women—in other words, they were speaking from an individualistic perspective rather than from a perspective that took in the history of white domination. This tendency to conflate individual virtue with expressions of anti-racist solidarity became even more pronounced after the election of Donald Trump, when white women professed shock and horror over his overt bigotry. Nicoll argues that white people need to "lose their religion," by which she means the belief that they individually are good people, and that is all that needs to be done to meet their responsibilities to counter racism. She delves into her own family history with a Christian church to develop this metaphor. She argues that white women need to remember where they are located in the structures of racism and not rely so much on individual innocence or feminine virtue.

On (Not) Losing My Religion

Interrogating Gendered Forms of White Virtue in Pre-Possessed Countries

Fiona Nicoll

Introduction

This chapter explores how white women academics become virtuously oriented towards values such as "recognition", "inclusion", "diversity" and "reconciliation" as individuals? And it asks how this orientation might, paradoxically, prevent universities' stated aims and policies of equity and social justice from being realised? Calls to "decolonize the academy" and to "Indigenize the syllabus" raise related questions for non-Indigenous faculty. How do we avoid teaching to white ignorance? How do we avoid centring virtuous white subjectivity and its "fragilities"?[1] How are values such as "being right, knowing better and feeling good"[2] woven together as everyday racial practices of university life? And how does the presumed secularity of these values amplify their power? My hope is that, by addressing these questions, we can expand university spaces for coalitions of Indigenous and non-Indigenous staff and students to work together in a way that sustains our world against the possessive drives that Moreton-Robinson names as "patriarchal white sovereignty"[3].

I am a middle-class white woman from a white settler-colonial state (Australia) who is making a home and a career in another white settler-colonial state (Canada). I have moved from Jagera and Turrubul countries in Brisbane, Australia to occupy the pre-possessed countries of Treaty Six in Edmonton, which my university acknowledges as ". . . a traditional gathering place for diverse Indigenous peoples including the Cree, Blackfoot, Metis, Nakota Sioux,

Iroquois, Dene, Ojibway/Saulteaux/Anishinaabe, Inuit, and many others."[4] A common critique of such acknowledgements, made in universities and other government and non-government institutions, is that they are empty performances of benevolence at best, and mere tokenism at worst. This is a valid critique. Attributions of virtue to individual white people are a significant obstacle for anti-racist and decolonising projects and do not move us closer to the kind of research and activism needed to shift the prerogative of white occupation embedded in the neoliberal university. So, I hope the argument of this chapter is intrinsically, rather than virtuously, connected to these acknowledgements of country.

. . .

Problematizing Virtue

My first encounter with white virtue as a political and epistemological problem occurred when I began to engage Aileen Moreton-Robinson's sociological study of white feminists committed to anti-racist activism in and beyond the university titled *Talkin Up to the White Woman*. This work made me aware of the limits of the post-colonial and post-structuralist theoretical models through which I'd previously understood political relationships between Indigenous and non-Indigenous people in Australia. Her study found that, notwithstanding the commitment of white feminists to anti-racist research and teaching, they were often incapable of understanding the effects of their own racialized subject position as "middle-class white woman". . . .

Nicoll, F, "On (Not) Losing My Religion: Interrogating Gendered Forms of White Virtue in Pre-possessed Countries." *Resisting Neoliberalism in Higher Education*, 2019, Volume II, pp. 111–132. Reprinted by permission of Springer International Publishing.

Moreton-Robinson's work prompted me to consider how my subject position as a middle class white woman contributed to problems that my scholarship purported to address. This was not a call for me to feel guilty or morally paralysed as an individual. It was a call for me to see and to redress an ignorance that was shared with other white men and women of different class positions, educational achievements and sexual orientations. It was also a call to understand race and sovereignty in intersectional terms, to recognise that the way I took on white virtue as an academic woman was shaped by my gender and that my white male counterparts did not embody and enact it in the same way. I began to ask whether it was possible for me to queerly cast off the bonds of white heterosexual femininity when a colonial regime of power that Moreton-Robinson calls "patriarchal white sovereignty"[5] had a possessive claim on me two centuries before my birth.

. . .

Unholier than Thou? Rethinking White Virtue after Trump

I first encountered Donald Trump as a business celebrity while teaching a course on television and popular culture in Australia. *The Apprentice* was an example of cheap global television formats that became popular from the late 1990s. I examined how Trump's format was adapted by British and Australian producers, using local millionaires as presenters with more or less success. It was clear from watching many episodes of the show that Trump was a talented actor within the reality TV genre.

. . .

The 2016 US election race was followed closely by academics in universities in Canada, Australia and in the UK, where many were reeling from the Brexit referendum vote to separate from the European Union. Like many other left-leaning, white academics around the world, I watched the presidential nominations and the election race unfold with a mixture of fascination and horror. Along with many others, I was stunned and sickened when Trump won on a platform that promised to overturn political and human rights for women, immigrants, Muslims, Latino and African-Americans. Together, on social and mainstream media outlets, we devoured the post-mortem opinion pieces and polling analyses and, together, we both felt and fuelled a sense of moral outrage, despair, and defiance.

Our shared sense of incredulity was encapsulated in questions circulating after the election: "How could such an apparently unvirtuous character convert so many white Americans?"; "How could such a narcissistic buffoon come to occupy the nation's highest office?"; Or in a more pathologising and moralistic register: "Trump is either bad or mad. How could anyone in their right mind could vote for this man?" After a few days of this I began to feel irritated, both with myself and with my academic and other middle-class, professional, white peers.

. . .

The post-election period saw some scathing critiques of white social justice advocates and media commentators whose support for Clinton was qualified by resentment about her campaign's treatment of Bernie Sanders or whose critical analyses of neoliberalism caused them to focus on all of the ways the candidates were more similar than different. Days after the election, political scientist Jane Junn wrote about the 53% of white women who voted for Trump:

> The elephant in the room is white and female and she has been standing there since 1952. This result has been hiding in plain sight, disguised by a narrative that women are more democratic than men.[6]

She demonstrates that it was the increase in the participation of African American voters since the 1980s that had made the Democratic vote skew female. This stubborn illusion of a post-racial feminist sisterhood united in a virtuous commitment to social justice needs explanation.

African American philosopher George Yancy provides some useful thinking to guide us here.[7] The opacity of whiteness to those who inhabit it is captured in Yancy's invitation to imagine what might change if we understand ourselves as objects of a non-white gaze. He points to a common experience that painfully shatters the illusion that white people are racially unmarked subjects of universal forms of knowing and being in the world. This is when we find ourselves "ambushed by racism"; a racist joke or slur leaps from our lips before we are even aware of it. Following this kind of event, especially when it happens in public or is observed by others, there is often a reflex that Moreton-Robinson describes as attempting to "recuperate our virtue".[8] We didn't mean it. We have done *so* much for the communities who were the object of our offensive statement.

These events of being "ambushed by racism" unsettle us on an ontological level. And they highlight virtue as linked to a possessive relationship that white subjects have with the self—which we conceive as an autonomous individual in the first instance. Or to put it another way, they reveal the limitations of accounts of racism as something that individuals simply *have* and can discard as morally repugnant. This collective illusion, in part, underpinned the assumptions that women would support Hilary Clinton as a coherent, identity-based bloc. Subsequent election analyses showed that many married white women—in particular—voted *for* their husbands and families rather than *against* Trump.[9]

In everyday conversations following the election, white racism was often distanced from a middle class *us* who sought to rationalise the unexpected outcome. Transposed as a "class issue", Trump's victory was slated to the support of struggling white workers of de-industrialized rust belts, notwithstanding that people of colour make up the majority of working class and minimum wage workers in America. I was surprised to hear such rationalisations voiced by some white academic men and women whose writings and formal presentations displayed sophisticated understandings of the transnational (alleged Russian interference), economic (falling wages and unemployment) and socio-cultural (celebrity culture, the war on political correctness) factors that produced Trump's victory.

While I didn't buy into the "rust-belt" arguments, it is now clear that my refusal to take seriously the religious aspects of his appeal is connected to my sense of moral agency as a white academic feminist as being on the "right side of history".[10] Along with many of my academic peers, I assumed that the decline of white Evangelical Protestants as a demographic in the United States, where they now make up less than 20% of the population, was an irreversible trend and had not understood that the almost undivided supported of this group would be a major factor in the election of Trump.

On (Not) Losing My Religion

The notion that virtue can be simply claimed or dissociated from by individual white people is tied to an understanding of history that takes "secularity" as a modern condition against racial constructions of "traditional" or "tribal" societies relegated to humanity's past. A cherished personal narrative about losing my religion illustrates how the conceit of secular individualism can attach virtue to whiteness in our everyday lives. When I was fifteen years old, I was part of a youth group in my local church being prepared for "confirmation" into the Christian faith. I made a request of the church elders which they agreed to. For a period of two months, they came to talk to the group and provided arguments to persuade us about why we should accept the teaching of the church and to accept its embrace through the ritual of confirmation. After two months, it was time to make a decision. I was unconvinced by the arguments I had heard. With a clear head and a light heart, I declined confirmation and watched from my seat as the other members of the youth group went to the front of the church in a special communion service. As far as I was concerned, that was that. I had made a rational and principled decision as an individual.

When I came to work in universities I found myself mostly around kindred spirits. Young white people who identified as secular, progressive and relentlessly critical. Paradigms of critical analysis, Marxist, feminist, postcolonial, and concepts such as myth, hegemony and governmentality provided a theoretical grid within which to understand the irrational commitments and practices of others. Being secular was a good thing. We were making the world a better place. We were all good people. And if we were not, well that was a problem of hypocrisy—Marxist men behaving badly being a notorious example—not a problem of subjectivity.

The Trump election has made me increasingly aware that being white in a settler colonial society is not like a religion that I can cast aside in the interest of progressive social causes. Rather, as Vincent Lloyd suggests: "race and secularism are entwined. Put more starkly, whiteness is secular, and the secular is white. The unmarked racial category and the unmarked religious category jointly mark their others. . . ."[11] And William Hart explains: ". . . there are tropes associated with imperial/colonial modernity that tie specifically to religious and secular constructions of blackness".[12] In this context, it is important to acknowledge that the decision of my fifteen-year-old self to cast aside the faith of my parents in the Christian church in which I'd grown up was hardly an earth-shattering event.

It did not separate me from my grandmother's Islamophobia, or "the great Australian silence" about how Indigenous people supposedly "lost" their country. *As an individual,* I could disagree with and argue against these propositions. But I still remained related to these people and was unable to prevent their racist propositions from becoming bonds of love to a nation constructed as a white possession. As Ahmed reminds us, violent white nationalist subjects are not simply prisoners of negative affect; their love of those included within the brother and sisterhood equally moves their speech and acts.[13] *Make America Great Again.*

How does a self-conception as secular enable white academics to perpetuate the invisibility of white possession in everyday life? I've argued that a racial sense of virtue relates closely to our sense of individual self-possession. In this final part of this chapter I want to suggest how the virtue we perform as white individuals within our institutions of family, of work, of politics might participate in the racial logic that enabled Trump to attract the Presidency.

. . .

When we disparage the racial prejudices of our ancestors and our family members we performatively stake a claim to virtue against Indigenous demands to accept responsibility for genocidal realities here and now. In moments of serious reflection, most white academic feminists would reject the proposition that there was a racist and colonial time in our nation's past that ended happily with civil and human rights victories last century. And we would certainly dispute that "the pendulum has swung too far" and white men have become an endangered species. But what do we practically do with this knowledge? How can we engage more rigorously with the social and historical forces that have made us as activist subjects?

Familiarising White Virtue

Reflecting on my premonition that Trump would win the US election triggered strong memories of my grandfather who passed away when I was a teenager. This was around the time that I declined to be confirmed in the Christian faith. Grandpa was a protestant minister and he was momentarily connected with an iconic figure of evangelical Christianity in the US: Billy Graham. Graham toured Australia in 1959 and is an early example of the connection between celebrity culture and the politically organised white evangelicalism so effectively exploited in Trump's campaign.[14] The fact that "Grandpa shared a stage with Billy Graham" was a matter of pride in my extended family when I was growing up.

Two other stories about Grandpa that recently came to light. The first is the most recent. Grandpa converted to Christianity during the Great Depression. From a family of modest means, he had got into Melbourne University and topped his class in the Engineering faculty. There were very few jobs for engineers when he graduated. He was converted to evangelical Christianity, studied theology, was ordained and became a minister of religion.

The other family story came out sometime after national protests by Indigenous people against the celebrations of the bicentennial of white invasion in 1988. It was the story about how Grandpa nearly lost his job in one of his ministries in a large rural Victorian parish. The reason for this is that he "put David Unaipon in the pulpit". David Unaipon was a public intellectual and Ngarrindjeri man from the South Australian Raukkan mission.[15] In addition to being an author and a preacher, he was an inventor. As the Australian Dictionary of Biography relates:

> By 1909 Unaipon had developed and patented a modified handpiece for shearing. He was obsessed with discovering the secret of perpetual motion. In 1914 his repetition of predictions by others about the development of polarized light and helicopter flight were publicized, building his reputation as a "black genius" and "Australia's Leonardo".[16]

My mother, the oldest of four children, remembers Unaipon's visits to Grandpa well. In addition to their theological discussions, the two men bonded over a shared love of engineering and inventions.[17]

What am I to take from the fact that Grandpa shared the stage with Billy Graham and his own pulpit with David Unaipon? For one thing, this family story highlights my personal story of being a secular white feminist committed to social justice through anti-racist research and pedagogy as an extremely shallow one. The other point I take is that Grandpa not only risked his job and family to provide a platform for Unaipon to speak—though this is important. He also engaged with Unaipon as a knowledgeable Aboriginal man and this was a source of great enjoyment to him. My mother also relates that, during his visits, Unaipon always slept in a bedroom in an enclosed veranda, instead of the interior guest room used for visiting white missionaries. So, this is not a story of my Grandfather as a heroic individual. Neither is it a story of him as a captive of a form of institutional racism characterising a certain moment within Australian history. It is a story that underlines continuities between his moment and ours. And it makes me consider the relegation of Indigenous and critical race scholarship to the enclosed veranda of the house that is the neoliberal university as a corollary of our possessive claims to *virtue and virtuosity* as individuals.

. . .

I have drawn on critical studies of race and religion to probe the limits of my previous work on gendered forms of white virtue. I have used personal and family stories about (not) losing my religion to demonstrate racial links between the moral value of virtue and the epistemological premise of self-possession. Gendered attributions of virtue anchor white women to the problem of individuality in specific ways within the neoliberal academy. I cannot easily lose this religion. Refusing virtue and performing transgression—or race "traitorship"—will not buy me out of it. More profound changes are needed if white women are to "get nasty"[18] in a way that does not perpetuate intergenerational white racism and theft.[19] I've argued that an individual orientation to virtue makes it difficult to acknowledge our ties to the people who came before us and the ways they made Indigenous countries over as white nations at least partly through legitimating discourses supplied by Christianity. For this reason, we need to stop taking racism personally. Instead, we need to think about the ways in which *racism possesses us* rather than focussing on racism and religion as something that we or others possess and can discard at will.

. . .

Post-script

About a year after arriving in Canada to take up a new academic position, I was invited to a women's ceremony in a dedicated Indigenous space within my university. I found myself both unwilling and unable to refuse the religion being offered and the political and epistemological bond it created with the other Aboriginal, Metis and non-Aboriginal women who participated. This bond was created in part through a teaching of gratitude for the gifts of this country celebrated in ceremony. This teaching holds regardless of whether we are worthy or unworthy individuals and of whether we have an inherited sense of virtue or achieved the highest levels of virtuosity. It requires us to accept the gift and responsibility of being *here* at this time. And it invites us to meditate on the material possessions and dispossessions attendant to all of the specific *places* that the neo-liberal university has established itself. The gendered recuperation of white virtue in service of reproducing a secular academic subject detaches the university from specific places in the name of universal and global knowledge projects. In turn, this naturalises institutional participation in the ongoing occupation of sovereign Indigenous territories. Leaving our virtue and virtuosity at the door is essential if middle-class white academic women are to join those whose survival depends on the hard work of prising open the cracks of the neoliberal university, from both inside and out.

Notes

1. See Robin Di Angelo, "White Fragility" *The International Journal of Critical Pedagogy*, 3.3, (2011): 54–70.
2. See Barbara Applebaum, *Being white, being good: White complicity, white moral responsibility, and social justice pedagogy* (Lanham: Lexington Press, 2010)
3. Aileen Moreton-Robinson, "Writing Off Sovereignty: Security and the Discourse of Patriarchal White Sovereignty", in *The White Possessive: Property, Power and Indigenous Sovereignty* (University of Minnesota Press, 2015) 137–152.
4. University of Alberta, "Acknowledgement of Traditional Territory", accessed 31 October, 2017, http://www.toolkit.ualberta.ca/CommunicationsTools/AcknowledgmentOfTraditionalTerritory.aspxb.
5. Moreton-Robinson, "Writing Off Sovereignty", 137.
6. Jane Junn, "Hiding In Plain Sight: White Women Vote Republican", *Politics of Colour,* November 13, 2016. http://politicsofcolor.com/white-women-vote-republican/
7. This book of essays "Look a White!" inverts Franz Fanon's unforgettable example of racial subjectification through the eyes of a white child who exclaims to her parent "Look a negro!" George Yancy, *Look A White! Philosophical Essays on Whiteness*, (Philadelphia: Temple University Press, 2012).
8. Aileen Moreton-Robinson, "Virtuous Racial States", *The White Possessive: Property, Power, and Indigenous Sovereignty* (University of Minnesota Press, 2015), 180.
9. Christopher T. Stout, Kelsy Kretschmer, Leah Ruppanner, "Gender Linked Fate, Race/Ethnicity, and the Marriage Gap in American Politics", *Political Research Quarterly*, 70.3 (2017):509–522.
10. Daniel Cox and Robert P Jones, "America's Changing Religious Identity" *Public Religion Research Institute,* September 6, 2017, accessed October 31, https://www.prri.org/research/american-religious-landscape-christian-religiously-unaffiliated/
11. Vincent W Lloyd, "Introduction: Managing Race, Managing Religion", in *Race and Secularism in America*, edited by Johnathan S Khan and Vincent W Lloyd, (New York: Columbia University Press, 2016), 5.
12. William D Hart, "Secular Coloniality: The Afterlife of Religious and Racial Tropes", in *Race and Secularism in America*, edited by Johnathan S Khan and Vincent W Lloyd, (New York: Columbia University Press, 2016), 179.
13. Sara Ahmed, "Affective Economies", *Social Text*, 22.2, Summer (2004):117–139.
14. For an excellent account of the cultural impact of this visit see Ken Inglis, "Billy Graham in Australia", *Observing Australia, 159–1999,* edited by Craig Wilcox. (Parkville, Melbourne University Press, 1999), 22–60.
15. For more information about David Unaipon, see Stephen Muecke and Adam Shoemaker, editors, *David Unaipon: legendary tales of the Australian Aborigines* (Parkville: Melbourne University Press, 2001). The family history recounted above is from oral sources of my mother, who was the eldest child of 4 and remembers Unaipon's visits as well as learning from his book of illustrated traditional Aboriginal stories.
16. Philip Jones, Unaipon, David (1872–1967), *Australian Dictionary of Biography*. http://adb.anu.edu.au/biography/unaipon-david-8898 accessed November 4 2017.
17. Unaipon's role in Australia's public life has subsequently been recognised in state currency which features his portrait on the 50 Dollar note along with images of the first mechanical shears and the Church building at his hometown of Raukkan.
18. Donald Trump created a social media storm after calling Hilary Clinton a "nasty woman" in the final debate, an appellation that was quickly appropriated by feminist supporters of the candidate. Nicky Woolf, "'Nasty woman': Trump attacks Clinton during final debate", 20 October 2016. Accessed 1 November 2016. https://www.theguardian.com/us-news/2016/oct/20/nasty-woman-donald-trump-hillary-clinton
19. See Robert Nichols, "Theft Is Property! The Recursive Logic of Dispossession", *Political Theory* (first published April 2 (2017): 1–26.

Part III

Gendered Bodies

We all walk around in bodies. That's pretty obvious, isn't it? We use our bodies to do what we need to do in order to get from day to day, as well as for playing and enjoying life beyond just the necessities of survival. And our bodies are subjected to social pressures as well as individual desires to look (or not look) a certain way, to accomplish certain things, and to be perceived by others as a particular type of (gendered) person. Gendered norms of embodiment are the unspoken backdrop to our embodied lives, as our bodies are both formed and interpreted by gendered norms of physicality.

DiCarlo interviewed a group of women for whom these gendered norms are ever-present in their consciousness as female hockey players. They encountered the expectation that because they possess a certain kind of (female) body, other athletes assumed they would be more vulnerable, less aggressive, and more likely to be attracted to women than to men (none of which are necessary aspects of possessing a body identified as female). Sports, as a field of social life in which bodies are literally front and centre, is a fascinating area to study the relationships between body and gender.

Women, of course, are not the only people who grapple with the gendered challenges of living in gendered bodies. As Atkinson describes, men too may seek to modify their bodies through surgery, among other means. Men who use cosmetic surgery, however, need to navigate the apparent contradiction between cosmetic surgery and hegemonic forms of masculinity, which suggest that concern with one's appearance marks one as "feminine."

Racist, colonialist, or sexist institutions can be the sites of great harm to gendered bodies, as de Finney demonstrates in her exploration of the ways in which Canadian colonial institutions have harmed or neglected Indigenous girls. However, harm and obliteration are not the only stories that can be told about gendered Indigenous bodies. De Finney's work ends on a slightly more hopeful note, as she explores how embodied ritual practices and the resurgence of Indigenous teachings are producing new forms of resilience for women and girls that go beyond just physical safety.

Beyond the binary of male and female, Scheim and Bauer undertook one of the first large-scale Canadian surveys of what it's like to live in a trans body. They found that while many of their respondents thought of themselves as masculine or feminine, a significant minority did not and embodied alternatives to the gender binary. Such bodies don't fit neatly into the many institutions that are predicated on two sexes/two genders, meaning that trans people can face challenges in representing themselves and being seen for who they are, not who other people want them to be.

Questions for Critical Thought

1. How much do you depend on the appearances of bodies to shape your interactions with other people? Do you react differently to different kinds of bodies?

2. Do you think there is one dominant or hegemonic ideal of beauty for women today? What about for men?

3. As social interaction is increasingly mediated by technologies, such as Facebook or text messaging, as distinct from face-to-face encounters, do you think the significance of embodiment for gender identity has changed?

4. Is there such a thing as a "perfect" body? If so, what does it look like?

5. Why did the men in Atkinson's study seek cosmetic surgery? Are their reasons different from the reasons that women seek out these procedures?

6. What generational or age-related patterns do you see emerging from Scheim and Bauer's survey of trans people? Do you think their results might have been different if this study had been done 30 years ago, or 30 years in the future?

7. Do you play any sports? Has your gender or your body shaped which sports you play or how you play them?

8. How might people use their bodies to express resistance to dominant ideas about gender?

9. What are some of the challenges faced by people whose bodies and identities do not fit into two-sex, two-gender categories?

10. If you are cisgender, imagine waking up one morning and discovering that your physical appearance had changed and your body no longer gave any visual clues to your gender. How do you think your life would be different?

Chapter 10

Overview

Ice hockey is the quintessential Canadian sport. It has also historically been associated with qualities that make up hegemonic masculinity—competitiveness, physical toughness and speed, and the willingness to use aggression when needed to win. Female and nonbinary hockey players experience the ice differently from their normative male counterparts. Danielle DiCarlo interviewed seven female hockey players who had experience on non-professional teams of mixed genders and all women. She focuses on three forms of embodiment that the female players had to negotiate: the unstated assumption that female bodies were weaker than male bodies and therefore needed more protection; the belief that female bodies lacked the aggressive drive that men possessed; and the conflation of body size with sexuality, such that female players who were physically larger than other women were assumed to also be lesbians, unless they went out of their way to perform heterosexuality through behaviour such as flirting with men on the ice. Simply the fact of being a female hockey player in a male-dominated sport did not produce transformative understandings of gender, and DiCarlo's participants did not overtly question the gendered and heteronormative assumptions about women and sport.

Playing Like a Girl?

The Negotiation of Gender and Sexual Identity among Female Ice Hockey Athletes on Male Teams

Danielle DiCarlo

While no one can deny the rich history of girls and women in sport, they continue to face obstacles to their full participation and representation, specifically in the Canadian ice hockey system. For example, in March 2009, the Hockey Hall of Fame announced they would be re-writing their by-laws to allow female athletes to be considered for induction separately from their male counterparts (Cox 2009). The separation of male and female ice hockey inductees highlights the cultural ambivalence and ideological struggle around women's sport generally, and the legitimacy of women's ice hockey specifically. . . .

Indeed, the gendering of ice hockey space is not new; there have been numerous well-known cases of women playing on, or attempting to play on, male ice hockey teams.[1] Women have migrated into these sport spaces through the development of female teams and leagues, but also through their participation on male teams and leagues. Sport is often contentious for those female athletes who participate in sports traditionally played exclusively by men and, arguably, even more so for those women who participate on male teams (Theberge 1995, 2000). Apart from media portrayal of female athletes, our knowledge of the lived experience of non-celebrity girls and women is under-researched in the study of sex, gender and sexuality, especially in and around the subculture of ice hockey. The lived experiences of female ice hockey athletes playing on male

DiCarlo, Danielle. "Playing Like a Girl? The Negotiation of Gender and Sexual Identity Among Female Ice Hockey Athletes on Male Teams." Sport in Society, 2016, 19:8–9, pp. 1363–1373. Reprinted by permission of Taylor & Francis Ltd.

teams is important in revealing details about how females come to negotiate binaries of gender created through sport and how these negotiations shape their thoughts regarding the female athlete. To that end, we simply do not know enough about the lived experiences of girls and women who navigate these gendered sport spaces. . . . I begin with an attempt to frame the participants' experiences within the context of previous academic work around sport, gender and sexuality, connecting this work to current broader perspectives regarding women's ice hockey. Next, I discuss the results of this study paying attention to how these female athletes experience and negotiate their female sporting identities, with particular emphasis on the tensions and contradictions around gender and sexual identity.

Sport and the Construction of Sex, Gender and Sexuality

. . . While competitive sport is an arena where the production and expression of gender continues to be challenged, sport is a social institution where this gender logic is perhaps most apparent (Burke 2004). Historically speaking, in contrast to the empowerment of men through sport, women were often excluded from sport or admitted on restricted teams where events were changed in order to coincide to a view of women as fragile and weak (Kidd 1996). . . . The naturalization of women being "less able" than men has become status quo and remains, although at times subtle, evident today (Anderson 2005; Burke 2004; Ezzell 2009).

What Theberge (1997) has called the "myth of female frailty" has had a long-lasting effect on the history of women's restriction to sport and has perpetuated problematic gender binaries concerning athletic participation. . . . In fact, cultural conceptions of femininity and female beauty make women's sport participation quite problematic. As such, female athletes who participate in traditional male sports, considered outside the female domain, are reminded that they are challenging the outer ranges of "acceptable" feminine behaviour (Daniels 1992). Thus, sport has functioned as a male preserve, or an all-male domain, in which men not only play games together, but also demonstrate and affirm their manhood by dictating the gender appropriate behaviours of men and women (Sartore and Cunningham 2009).

In addition to sport being identified as an institution organized by hegemonic masculinity (Connell and Messerschmidt 2005) reinforcing a distinction between two genders, sport has also been organized around the notion of "compulsory heterosexuality" (Anderson 2008; Theberge 2000). The gender binary classification model followed today is based on the notion that heterosexuality is natural and normal and those who express feelings, actions and thoughts outside of the socially constructed categories of masculine and feminine are considered "deviant" or "out of bounds" when it comes to gender (Coakley and Donnelly 2009). A two-category model does not recognize nor provide space for those individuals who are neither heterosexual males nor heterosexual females. In the realm of sport, where heterosexuality is considered by most compulsory, this may have dire consequences for individuals who push the boundaries of what constitutes traditional masculinity and femininity. Given this, the historical social constructions of gender and sexuality has influenced and, at times, has resulted in problematic consequences concerning the development and organization of sport in Canada, in general, and in ice hockey in particular.

The Case of Women's Ice Hockey: Sporting Identities and Broader Perspectives

. . . [B]roader social tensions still exist in the sport of ice hockey and these tensions are rooted in the gender binary. For example, a common question within ice hockey culture is whether female athletes should play solely within female leagues to enhance their development or if this development should essentially transfer over into male ice hockey (Schneider 2000). There is a strong cultural and societal element which favours the argument for separate development. Individuals opposed to female athletes participating on male teams argue that girls and women should not imitate male sport, but instead should build different models of sport which are fundamentally more humane (or less violent than male ice hockey) and empowering for female athletes (Lenskyj 2003).

Despite the significance of all female ice hockey teams providing empowering group association for female athletes, as argued by Lenskyj, proponents of women participating on male ice hockey teams diverge from this claim. Supporters of women playing on male ice hockey teams have argued that women's presence in what is known as "male ice hockey culture" challenges the oppositional binary of what constitutes femininity (e.g. the female athlete as weak and less capable) and masculinity (e.g. the male athlete as aggressive and disciplined) in sport (McDonagh and Pappano 2009). Given these diverging perspectives, how might sex integration in the sport of ice hockey challenge and/or reaffirm hegemonic constructions of gender and sexuality in this unique sport space?

Methodology

. . .

Initially, participants for this study were recruited via the distribution of flyers posted in ice hockey arenas and university gyms and through snowball sampling. The decision where to distribute recruitment flyers was made based on insider familiarity of the female ice hockey community and knowledge of particular female teams' home arenas. In terms of snowball sampling, potential participants were initially approached through friends who knew of women who play(ed) ice hockey on male and female teams as well as through my own contacts. Further contacts were recruited based on referral from those initial participants. No explicit attempts were made to target groups on the basis of race, ethnicity, (dis)ability and/or sexual orientation. While participants were not asked about their sexual orientation, one participant did identify herself as homosexual. It is important to note, the sample population used for this study is limited to white, middle-class, (majority) heterosexual and able-bodied female ice hockey athletes. While a methodological goal of this research was to gather a more diverse group of participants by enlisting a broad range of female ice hockey athletes that crossed racial, ethnic, sexual, cultural, educational and class lines, the final participants for this study did not adequately reflect this intent. As such, the experiences of minority (individuals of colour, multiple sexualities) female ice hockey athletes who have played on both male and female teams remains understudied. The goal of future research should take into account the above social demographics in order to get a broader picture and deeper understanding of the experiences of Canadian female ice hockey athletes.

To that end, seven female ice hockey athletes who have experience participating on male and female teams in the past were recruited to participate in in-depth, semi-structured interviews. . . .

It is important to note, while I have not explicitly and purposefully employed an auto-ethnographic analysis, I have most certainly drawn on my own experiences as a female ice hockey athlete immersed in ice hockey culture. My status as a female athlete and an insider in this particular culture helped a great deal in the preparation of this research since the topic of study pertains to female ice hockey athletes, a group to which I belong. As a female athlete who has played on female ice hockey teams, I share similar experiences with my participants which, at times, influenced the interview process and the co-construction of data between interviewer and interviewee. . . .

Results

Gender Identity: The Conceptualization of Female Athletes as Weak

The view that female athletes are fragile was particularly problematic for the women interviewed in this study. Although none of the women in this study explicitly stated there was a belief among male players that the female athlete is inherently weaker than the male athlete, they expressed that not being treated the same as male athletes in terms of physical contact and aggression was a contentious issue. . . . According to the participants, these women were involved in situations where it was assumed by others (particularly by male coaches and male teammates) that they would get hurt and, as female athletes, they did not completely understand the reasoning behind this belief. As female athletes involved in a traditionally male sport and playing on all male teams, this view of female frailty had a lasting influence on these athletes' experiences. Despite the women discussing feeling angry by the fact that many of their male teammates would "hold back" from hitting them or as one participant says, "they'd be afraid to hit me", these women never voiced their opinion to their teammates regarding this volume while playing on male teams. In this way, they consented to the view of the female athlete as fragile by their male teammates. The social construction of being weak and, in some cases, infantilized, is part and parcel of the construction of idealized femininity (see Channon 2013). For example, some of the participants spoke of the treatment they received from their coaches and male teammates as childlike in nature:

> They [coaches] I don't know. They treated us like . . . I wouldn't say a baby, but if the guys made a mistake they'd get yelled at. But, if I made a mistake it was, "It's okay, you'll do fine next time". The coaches would always . . . kind of talk to us like we're stupid, explaining plays and stuff like we wouldn't understand it. I didn't really think of it at the time because I was still learning, but now it would be kind of insulting.

When asked how she was treated as a female athlete playing on a male team by her (male) coaches, another participant added, "They [male teammates and coaches] always stuck up for me. My coaches always stuck up for me. The coaches, they were sometimes a little easier on me than the guys". As these narratives illustrate, an essential part of the social construction of idealized femininity, particularly for the women interviewed for this study, centred on infantilization of the female athlete. Dominant gender meanings—in particular, the ideology that female athletes are inferior to male athletes especially with regard to strength—are somewhat reaffirmed by the women studied as these athletes did not challenge nor reject this "hierarchical" difference. Although the participants, by

very nature of being involved as female athletes in a traditionally male sport, challenged hegemonic constructions of femininity, they still embodied normative gender expectations. Furthermore, these women failed to connect their experiences as female athletes on male teams to greater struggles around equity in sport. . . .

The Female Athlete and Aggression

If female athletes playing on male teams are thought of and, at times, construct themselves as inherently fragile, what specifically does this mean for female athletes and their displays of aggressiveness in sport? Even though participants all possessed varying levels of aggressive on-ice behaviour themselves, they were particularly consistent in their descriptions of themselves as tomboys. One said:

> I'm the exception to the rule. I never fit inside this very traditional little square cube of what you would define a girl so I feel like a lot of my life things have been okay for me because that's always just been me. I think I was fortunate enough to come across a lot of my friends who accepted me for being that tomboy.

It is interesting to note that even though this participant recognized the problematic way in which gender is socially constructed, she still feels the need to classify herself. Although she spoke about not classifying herself as a "typical" female, she does, nonetheless, place herself in a category belonging to tomboys. By categorizing herself as a tomboy, she is reifying exactly what she argued against; not fitting the idealized and socially acceptable role of what being a female means. For these participants, they used the notion of being a tomboy to help with their negotiations in and around aggressiveness. By classifying themselves as tomboys, these women believed that although they are women and understood by coaches and male teammates as inherently weaker than or not naturally as tough as male athletes, because they grew up as tomboys they can be or are "allowed" to be aggressive. Also, identifying female athletes who play on male teams as tomboys, these women are reaffirming that they belong to the male sporting community (Helstein 2005). In a sense, being a tomboy provides these participants with an excuse to be aggressive.

This paradox between femininity and aggressiveness is clear regarding the discourse these women used when they spoke of body contact and aggression on the ice. It is interesting to note that the participants considered themselves aggressive because they had experience playing on all male teams, however, were conflicted in their discussions around aggressiveness and female athletes who do not have the experience of playing in a male dominant environment. As one participant explained:

> I wish I played still. Sometimes I miss it. But girls' hockey ruined it for me. Girls are *so* [emphasis in original] timid and they can't take criticism at all. In guy's (ice) hockey, you learn because your coaches they yell at you, they yell at guys. They're so much harder on guys. But the girls . . . I think it's female's nature to be that way and also (ice) hockey's more of a manly sport, you know? So maybe they [female athletes] feel they can't compete to that level in a way.

For this participant, there is a deeply embedded contradiction or tension surrounding the notion of female athletes and aggressiveness. Her reasoning behind female athletes not being aggressive on the ice, once again, reinforces the ideology that females are weak and thus not naturally aggressive. While playing ice hockey, these athletes were continuously involved in, at times consciously and at others subconsciously, a gendered performance (Butler 1990). Rather than putting on a gendered performance where they engaged in feminizing behaviours on the ice, they engaged in masculinized behaviour(s) (such as identifying themselves as tomboys) in order to legitimate their involvement in sport and a traditionally aggressive sport. In fact, this gendered behaviour was so influential for these participants that, throughout the interview, the discourse used was one describing female athletes on all female teams in highly feminized ways (e.g. catty, emotional, timid, etc.) when it came to aggression and physical contact on the ice. Their discourses closely parallel the reification of the ice hockey rink as male domain and questions women's ability to compete with men as well as one another powerfully, aggressively and successfully in ice hockey (Migliaccio and Berg 2007).

Identity and Sexuality

There seemed to be a common discourse used by participants throughout the interviews which compared their body ideal with non-heterosexual athletes. The female athletes interviewed constructed their identities as heterosexual ice hockey players in order to distinguish themselves from their homosexual female teammates. Some of the participants suggested that homosexual athletes were the "butch" or "manly" athletes who they described as the better players on an all female team:

> Well within girls' (ice) hockey I found that the better players were the ones who were more butch. They're more . . . they look like men. Their body image is more manly. I also found that there was more gay girls. A lot of female players who are good are gay. That's just something I found. And, when I think of a female athlete I just think built, like broad shoulders. I don't think very thin or skinny or feminine body. I see a more manly body with muscle. I see muscle.

Based on the response by this particular athlete, it is impossible to ignore the connection between the view of the female sporting body, masculine hegemony and the gender binary. The notion of the female sporting body, for this participant, does not challenge masculine hegemony nor the gender binary as female athletes who are considered the highly skilled players "look like men" and engage their bodies in socially constructed masculine ways. The female athlete, as representative of westernized femininity, is read against the "gender deviant other" sporting body as embodied by the homosexual female athlete (Davis-Delano, Pollock, and Ellsworth Vose 2009).

While women acknowledged the promotion of heteronormative sexuality within ice hockey culture, none of the women explicitly recognized that within their narratives around sexuality there was clearly a sexualized image of the female athlete. For example, as one participant described her experience playing on a male team:

> There'd always be flirting. I was okay. This was okay. I was a huge flirt, like, huge, ridiculous. Whether it was at high school or whether it was on the bench playing ice hockey with them it didn't really matter. I was flirting with them. So, yes, there was a lot of sexual tension on the bench because I created it by being there, by flirting and stuff. There was a lot of tension too because I'd flirt with the Refs.

This sexualized image of the female athlete was, at times, (re)produced by the female athletes themselves. In this sense, women collude with being sexy and attractive at the same time as being sportswomen. As the above narratives illustrate, these women's experiences assist in the maintenance of heterosexuality and heteronormativity. It is also interesting to acknowledge the silence around the negation of heterosexuality. The women interviewed spoke very little to sexual relations with teammates (male or female) and, at times, seemed to resist or struggle with questions relating to sexuality and sexual relations. Silence around the negation of heterosexuality was quite unexpected since the women interviewed were playing on female ice hockey teams at a time/age when sexual experimentation is perhaps most evident (Sharpe 2003).

Conclusion

Some of the women in this study accepted normative constructions of femininity and the female body. Despite engaging in new terrain through their participation on male ice hockey teams, many of these women (re)produced hegemonic ideas about sex, gender and sexuality.

Female athletes in this study exhibited neither a complete adherence to nor rejection of ideal femininity within their constructions of gender. Their definitions of femininity tended to fall within the traditional and reinforced gender differences as natural and inherent, which was evident in their discourse around gender identity. Contradiction and tension marked these women's experiences as

the women in this study negotiated a path of both acceptance of and resistance to the assumption of female frailty and lack of aggression and struggled over hegemonic masculinity and idealized femininity. For example, many of the participants were quite consistent in linking together female athlete and tomboy to help with their negotiations in and around aggression. Yet, none of the participants critiqued or explored the implications of assuming this gendered role—that is, no one questioned why a woman had to rationalize her athleticism via the use of the concept of tomboy (a pseudo-boy). . . . Furthermore, participants constructed their (heterosexual) identities through comparison of self with homosexual female teammates and their narratives around heteronormativity. Female athletes within this sample also spoke openly about the promotion of heteronormative sexuality within the sporting community and how this translated into an overt sexualized image of the female athlete. Narratives of their experiences assist in the maintenance of heterosexuality and heteronormativity in and around the sporting realm.

. . . By not politicizing their experiences, these women consented, to a degree, to the social constructions of the feminine ideal and heteronormativity. These women are still dealing with hegemonic notions of sex, gender and sexuality that often, but not always, conflict with their experiences as active and vibrant women in sport. Identity is a fluid and dynamic concept that struggles against seemingly rigid binaries of sex, gender and sexuality such that the participants—even though their actions resist hegemonic notions of idealized femininity—offer numerous examples of their adoption of cues, symbols and practices of idealized femininity and their acceptance (i.e. consent) of a gender binary. The women interviewed demonstrated that the sporting culture of ice hockey is a site—where these women were, at times, complicit in following—for reaffirming beliefs not only regarding the sex binary and gender logic, but also concerning the promotion of a hierarchical ranking of the sexes and the maintenance of heterosexuality. The ambiguous nature of the participants' responses on matters of gender identity and sexuality mirrors conceptions of binary categories and the contradictory nature of constructing gender and the sporting body.[2] Indeed, the reflections of these seven women raise important questions regarding the argument for separate development leagues and different sporting cultures. . . . Among the competing arguments for mixed/single sex sport spaces, it may be argued that the dominant interpretation, at least by the female athletes interviewed for this study, demonstrate the cultural precariousness and ideological struggle around women's sport generally, and the female athlete more specifically. These women's narratives demonstrate how difficult it is to challenge the technologies of femininity and the reification of the above-mentioned themes while at the same time illustrating critical issues in the social construction of sport (Theberge 1995). . . .

Acknowledgements

This research insight is based on findings from the author's master's thesis and was presented at the 31st Annual North American Society for the Sociology of Sport conference. I would like to thank Dr. Parissa Safai for her guidance and support in completing this research as well as the two anonymous reviewers for their helpful feedback.

Notes

1. Such female athletes include, but are not limited to, Abigail Hoffman, Justine Blainey, Manon Rhéaume and Hayley Wickenheiser.

2. Despite the contradictions and tensions lived by the participants, it would be inappropriate to suggest that there was no transformative potential in their experiences (see Young and White 1995).

References

Anderson, E. 2005. "Orthodox and Inclusive Masculinity: Competing Masculinities among Heterosexual Men in a Feminized Terrain." *Sociological Perspectives* 48 (3): 337–55.

Anderson, E. 2008. "'I Used to Think Women Were Weak': Orthodox Masculinity, Gender Segregation, and Sport." *Sociological Forum* 23 (2): 257–80. doi:10.1111/j.1573-7861.2008.00058.x.

Burke, M. 2004. "Radicalising Liberal Feminism by Playing the Games That Men Play." *Australian Feminist Studies* 19 (44): 169–84.

Butler, J. 1990. *Gender Trouble: Feminism and the Subversion of Identity*. New York: Routledge.

Channon, A. G. 2013. "Enter the Discourse: Exploring the Discursive Roots of Inclusivity in Mixed-sex Martial Arts." *Sport in Society* 16 (10): 1293–308. doi:10.1080/17430437.2013.790896.

Coakley, J., and P. Donnelly. 2009. *Sport and Society: Issues and Controversies*. McGraw-Hill Ryerson. http://www.primisonline.com.

Connell, R., and J. Messerschmidt. 2005. "Hegemonic Masculinity: Rethinking the Concept." *Gender and Society* 19 (6): 829–59. doi:10.1177/0891243205278639.

Cox, Damien. 2009. "Women to Be Admitted to Hockey Hall of Fame." *Toronto Star*, April 1.

Daniels, D. B. 1992. "Gender (Body) Verification (Building)." *Play and Culture* 5: 370–77.

Davis-Delano, L., A. Pollock, and J. Ellsworth Vose. 2009. "Apologetic Behavior among Female Athletes: A New Questionnaire and Initial Results." *International Review for the Sociology of Sport* 44: 131–50. doi:10.1177/1012690209335524.

Ezzell, M. 2009. "'Barbie Dolls' on the Pitch: Identity Work, Defensive Othering, and Inequality in Women's Rugby." *Social Problems* 56 (1): 111–31.

Helstein, M. T. 2005. "Rethinking Community: Introducing the Whatever Female Athlete." *Sociology of Sport Journal* 22 (1): 1–18.

Kidd, B. 1996. *The Struggle for Canadian Sport*. Toronto, ON: University of Toronto Press.

Lenskyj, H. 2003. "Good Sports? Feminists Organizing on Sport Issues." Chap. 4 in *Out on the Field: Gender, Sport and Sexualities*. Toronto, ON: Canadian Scholars' Press.

McDonagh, E., and L. Pappano. 2009. *Playing with the Boys: Why Separate Is Not Always Equal in Sports*. New York: Oxford University Press.

Migliaccio, T., and E. Berg. 2007. "Women's Participation in Tackle Football: An Exploration of Benefits and Constraints." *International Review for the Sociology of Sport* 42 (3): 271–87.

Sartore, M., and G. Cunningham. 2009. "Gender, Sexual Prejudice and Sport Participation: Implications for Sexual Minorities." *Sex Roles* 60: 100–13.

Schneider, A. 2000. "On the Definition of Woman in the 'Sport' Context." In *Philosophical Perspectives on Gender in Sport and Physical Activity*, edited by P. Davis and C. Weaving, 40–55. New York: Routledge.

Sharpe, T. 2003. "Adolescent Sexuality." *The Family Journal: Counseling and Therapy for Couples and Families* 11 (2): 210–15.

Theberge, N. 1995. "Playing with the Boys: Manon Rheaume, Women's Hockey and the Struggle for Legitimacy." *Canadian Woman Studies* 15 (4): 37–41.

Theberge, N. 1997. "It's Part of the Game: Physicality and the Production of Gender in Women's Hockey." *Gender and Society* 11 (1): 69–87.

Theberge, N. 2000. *Higher Goals: Women's Ice Hockey and the Politics of Gender.* New York: State University of New York Press.

Young, K., and P. White. 1995. "Sport, Physical Danger, and Injury: The Experiences of Elite Women Athletes." *Journal of Sport and Social Issues* 19: 45–61.

Chapter 11

Overview

When we read about cosmetic surgery in the media, the "patient" is often presumed to be a woman, seeking to look younger, sexier, or thinner. However, Michael Atkinson interviewed 44 men who opted to use their surgery to change their appearance. In some ways, this seems a counter-normative choice—aren't women supposed to be the ones who worry about looking old or unattractive? However, Atkinson suggests that men seek out these procedures to shore up their sense of masculinity—to acquire a bodily appearance that is visually congruent with gendered ideals of strength, confidence, and vigour. Atkinson situates these surgeries within the context of a "crisis" of masculinity, as he argues that men find it increasingly difficult to live up to what they believe they ought to be, do, or look like as men. He uses the conceptual tools of figurational sociology to present cosmetic surgery as a means through which men attempt to assert control over their bodies and their social lives, in a world in which the achievement of masculine ideals constantly threatens to elude them.

Exploring Male Femininity in the "Crisis"
Men and Cosmetic Surgery

Michael Atkinson

Cosmetic Surgery, Figurational Sociology

Since the year 2000, men's cosmetic surgery practices in Canada have mushroomed. Estimates suggest that over 10,000 Canadian men have received

Atkinson, Michael. "Exploring Male Femininity in the 'Crisis': Men and Cosmetic Surgery," Body & Society, March 2008, 14: 67, pp. 67–87. Reprinted by Permission of SAGE.

aesthetic surgery in the past 10 years, with participation rates rising sharply in the past three years alone—a 20 per cent increase in participation (Medicard, 2004). The collective willingness of men to experiment with surgical intervention in the pursuit of more youthful, vibrant, attractive, and healthy-looking bodies (especially around the face) perhaps signifies that these men's collective sensibilities, or habituses, are shifting; stated differently, it may symbolize how men are presently negotiating traditional parameters of "established" (Elias and Scotson, 1965) masculine identity performance to include cosmetic bodywork.

While there has been a reinvigorated interest in masculinity research (see Pronger, 2002), there is a paucity of extended, standpoint investigations of men's experiences with aesthetics and body modification that do not attempt to theoretically dissect the practice from either feminist or pro-feminist viewpoints—save, perhaps, for the literature on men and masculinity in the sociology of sport (Young, 2003), or within the burgeoning literature on gay/metro masculinities (Atkinson, 2003). The lack of theoretically innovative research symbolizes, as Connell (2005) suggests, a general tendency to view masculinity as a singularly constructed and unproblematic gender identity. Masculinity still tends to be framed by gender researchers along very narrow conceptual lines, as Grogan and Richards (2002) illustrate. Dominant constructions of masculinity are either interpreted as rigidly hegemonic/traditional (Garlick, 2004), or drastically alternative and deeply marginalized (Hise, 2004). Neither of these polar positions accurately captures how clusters of men often wrestle with and negotiate established constructions of masculinity in novel ways . . .

. . . There is a noticeable dearth of empirical investigations of men's experiences with aesthetic body modification (Davis, 2002). Few have studied, for instance, how "everyday" men engage bodywork in order to appear "regular," or have responded to broader cultural fluctuations in masculine hegemony with scripted body ritual. Fewer still have inspected how men play with innovative forms of aesthetic masculinity (i.e., beyond the context of "gym work," tattooing or other stereotypically masculine body projects) to bolster their *self-perceived* social power in a context of felt crisis.

To explore how selected men in Canada fashion cosmetic surgery as a technique of bodywork, Elias's (1978) figurational analysis of social power balances and control mechanisms serves as a departure point.

In *What Is Sociology?* (1978), Elias outlined three basic social controls that are interwoven into figurational power dynamics. For Elias (1978, 2002), members of social figurations enact power and control:

1. over nature through technological advancements
2. over groups of individuals through institutional processes
3. over drives and desires through learned mechanisms of self-restraint

Elias argues in *The Civilising Process* (2002) that the collective history of Western nations reveals a common tendency for complex groups of densely interdependent agents (what he referred to as *figurations*) to rely upon the third source of social control over the long term. That is, while court-centred monarchies and then nation-states relied upon the threat of force as a main tool of control over citizenries, the course of civilizing processes paved the way (although unintentionally) for the development of self-restraint as the dominant social control mechanism. Of course, as a full range of gender theorists point out, the social groups responsible for dominating others first by force and later via codes of mannered conduct have been, over time, controlled by men.

Figurational sociologists have argued that a central task in civilizing processes has been to "tame" masculinity (Dunning, 1999). Indeed, the history of social discipline and punishment illustrates how aggressiveness and psychological/affective orientations (typically described as "masculine" or attributed as essential characteristics of men) were transformed as complex social institutions took form. In such a theoretical meta-narrative, struggles for power and control in figurational life progress from hand-to-hand combat to symbolic power plays between men for knowledge, authority, and physical distinction enacted across institutional fields (Elias, 1978, 1996, 2002). Elias illustrates, for example, in *The Germans* (1996) that as physical violence becomes less pervasive in social life and inner restraint increases in importance as a means of revealing one's distinction (*qua* power) to others, the institutional control of productive forces and knowledge dissemination became more central. As Brinkgreve (2004) argues, these mechanisms of control tend to be dominated by men in Western figurations.

The emerging literature on contemporary masculine politics in Western nations like Canada suggests that the institutional sources of men's social control have been fractured, both materially and symbolically, by ongoing structural and cultural change (or what Elias, [2002] called "sociogenesis;" see also Mosse, 1996). Horrocks (1994) outlines how movements toward gender equality in families, educational sites, workplaces, religious institutions, and a full host of other institutional sites calls into question the very basis of masculine hegemony. As an extension of what Elias (2002) referred to as the "parliamentarisation of conflict," gender stratification and related power imbalances have been systematically disputed through highly institutionalized, formal, and rationalized rule systems. The splintering and redistribution of masculine control across institutional landscapes has spurred on a "crisis of masculinity," in that men are no longer certain about what constitutes men's roles and statuses, or how to enact properly gendered masculine identities (Whitehead, 2002). . . .

In sum, in this article I read the crisis of masculinity not as a cultural truth per se, but as a conceptual backdrop for interpreting why men may be selecting and inscribing aesthetic bodywork as an innovative technique of "male-feminine" biopower. Cosmetic surgery is configured by the men in this study as a tool for "re-establishing" a sense of empowered masculine identity in figurational settings that they perceive to be saturated by gender doubt, anxiety, and contest. In figurational terms, surgically altering the flesh is a return to a very basic technique of social control in a context of cultural uncertainty. Men, as de Certeau (1984) might predict, seize control over their bodies in order to "reframe" (White et al., 1995) their masculinity as revitalized and empowered. With diffuse ideological and material pressures to consume, commodify the body and perform scripted identity work through highly rationalized physical displays (Crewe, 2003; Featherstone, 2000), it is

understandable why, at this historical juncture, Canadian men are finding "collective solutions" to common "status problems" (Cohen, 1955) via cosmetic surgery. The empirical evidence presented in this study suggests a pervasive but tactically managed "cultural victim" mentality among the men, and also why their habituses (Elias, 1991, 1996, 2002) may be underpinned by a sense of doubt regarding the concept of established masculine dominance.

Method

Although there exists a rather full literature on women's experiences with cosmetic surgery in North America and elsewhere (Sarwer and Crerand, 2004), incredibly few body theorists have empirically addressed men's embodied interpretations of the cosmetic surgery process (Davis, 2002). My own involvement with cosmetically altered men commenced when I first encountered a surgery patient named "Les" in southern Ontario. Les exercised in a local health club I attended, and learned about my previous research on tattooing. During the middle of a workout one day, Les approached me and inquired as to whether I had studied cosmetic surgery. Following a brief conversation, he disclosed his experiences with three cosmetic procedures: Botox injections, liposuction, and an eye lift procedure. Over the course of time I pondered Les's confessional narrative to me, and considered the viability of a study of men and cosmetic surgery. By the autumn of 2004, I sought out additional patients in the southern Ontario area (e.g., Toronto, Hamilton, Mississauga, London, and Burlington) for interviews.

Through Les's sponsorship, I encountered and subsequently interviewed 44 cosmetic surgery patients in southern Ontario. I asked Les to provide the names of several other patients he knew personally. At the time of his interview, Les offered five names of fellow patients in the city of Hamilton alone. Rather surprisingly, all of the patients agreed to be interviewed for the study. Subsequently, each patient provided the names of, on average, 2–4 other male patients, and the sample expanded progressively. . . .

Interviews with the men were conducted in a variety of settings such as my office at the university, a coffee shop, a local park, or a restaurant. In all but a few instances, I used a tape-recorder during the interviews and field notes were taken both during and after the interviews. Notes were then (within several hours or, at maximum, one day) transcribed onto computer files and filled in considerably as I conceptually analyzed the texts in a constant comparison process. With further regard to data analysis, the interview texts were coded holistically as conceptual types of narratives about the experience of body modification, and then open-coded separately and comparatively around emergent themes related to masculinity and its embodied performance. It is important to note that theoretical lines of inquiry related to the crisis of masculinity were neither prefigured into the interview schedule, nor crudely fitted onto the emergent data. Rather, the theoretical reading of crises in the men's narratives reflected how men, themselves, told stories about and ascribed meaning to their cosmetic surgery experiences. The narrative theme of "crisis" I outline in the article is one of the most consistently present themes, but not the only one woven across the men's narratives. . . .

Most of the discussions started with a basic request: "So, tell me about your cosmetic surgery." I wanted the men to craft narratives from the interpretive standpoints they wished, and from starting points they found to be sensible. Over the course of time, I tactically discussed my own personal doubts, interpretations, and scepticisms about cosmetic surgery, as a means of encouraging participants to share the more intimate details of their personal narratives. As a "bad cop" technique of narrative elicitation (Hathaway and Atkinson, 2003), I challenged the basis of cosmetic surgery as "appropriate" masculine bodywork. Here, I wanted to inspect how practitioners justify and tell stories about cosmetic surgery to outsiders. By engaging such interactive techniques with respondents I wanted our conversations to probe motivations for cosmetic surgery, emotional accounts of its performance, and elements of patients' social biographies.

Men, Cosmetics, and the Triad of Social Controls

> I looked at my neck droop for so long before I mustered up enough courage to have it fixed. . . . I look like I'm 20 again; well, at least around my neck. At least no one calls me "turkey neck" anymore . . . you have no idea how many times I wore a turtleneck sweater to avoid derision. I can't buy enough low-collared shirts to show off my work. (Tom, facelift)

Tom is a 46-year-old advertisement executive living in Toronto. Although one may never glance at him and suspect his "work," he is proud of his body for the first time in his life and exudes comfort in his "new skin." Tom's cosmetic surgery narrative is a typical one: he tells a story about cosmetic surgery as a pathway toward body enhancement, as a vehicle for fitting in, and as a technique for building self-esteem. As part of his narrative, Tom expresses a clear understanding of his own interest in body enhancement; he simply wants to be present, recognized, and very "commonly" male.

Among the select few men who choose to tell stories about cosmetic surgery, a common narrative theme similar to Tom's underpins their accounts. For these men, transforming the body into something socially "common" (and therefore something to show off as "common") motivates their aesthetic projects. The act of cosmetic surgery becomes a process of gaining power over others' negative stares and comments. Cosmetic surgery is not sought out by the men I interviewed egomaniacally, nor is it intended to draw the social gaze to the surgically enhanced flesh. The intervention is intended to achieve the opposite: to allow the individual to fade into a crowd as a "regular guy." With few exceptions, such as a hair transplant, collagen/Botox injections, or muscle implants, the most common forms of surgery men undertake physically and symbolically "remove" unwanted, stigmatizing features from their bodies. A liposuction patient named Patrick (37) described:

There's a comfort every day in walking out of your house and knowing that people won't be looking at your gut when you pass by . . . when people ignore you, it's because you are the average person, the nondescript regular guy. I was a fat kid, and then a fat man, and all I ever wanted was to look regular. Yeah, when people ignore you, wow, what a great feeling.

Like many of the men interviewed in this research, Patrick's cosmetic surgery stories are replete with the idea of feeling "average," of looking "regular," and not being marginalized. The ability to do so, these patients articulate, is an act of biopower for them; a power to negotiate a portion of their public image through non-traditionally masculine work. As discussed below, however, the sense of being average deeply resonates with very traditional images and ideologies of established masculinity in Canada.

Physicality, Violence, and Masculine Bodies

In a poignant analysis of the gendering of power in Western figurations, Brinkgreve (2004) comments that men's social control has been challenged along a number of lines, especially men's ability to wield unfettered dominance as public practice. In adopting a figurational perspective, she argues that men's agency for expressing aggressive affect has been curtailed over the course of long-term civilizing processes, or showcased in contained manners in social forms like sport or theatre (see also Atkinson and Young, 2008). The massive cultural popularity among men of violent sports in Canada like ice hockey, lacrosse, football, and rugby, argue Atkinson and Young (forthcoming), is proportionately related to the degree to which aggression and violence are taboo in other social spheres. . . .

Yet some men, contends Godenzi (1999), interpret the ongoing and unfinished civilizing "attack" on aggression as a challenge to the very foundation of established masculinity. Labre (2002) examines how groups of men perceive the (external) restraint of men or male bodies as a critical condemnation of and attempt to control the very basis of the male psyche and/or the male social order. In perceiving masculinity as threatened through diffuse anti-authoritarian (read *anti-male*) social doctrines and politically correct "sensitivity policies," some Canadian men feel encouraged to reflexively engage in forms of bodywork to shore up their traditionally masculine images in socially "non-threatening" ways. The cosmetic surgery patient Allan (41) explains:

I'd never looked like a handsome guy until I underwent the hair transplantation, you know. . . . I'm like every other man who's lived with teasing about being bald so young. Women find the look totally unsexy and not very strong looking, but all the same attack me as a chauvinist, just because I am male. I hear that all the time at work. If I became angry about being teased for my baldness, I would be called hothead or the Alpha male trying to vent his anger. What a joke. I could never win then, and now the only way people leave you alone and accept you now [as a man], is if you look good without "acting out" as a guy.

As Allan and like-minded peers explain, men may find novel forms of social power by reclaiming their "threatened" bodies and repackaging them as aesthetically desirable (i.e., as emotionally pacified). They tactically align with "new" or "metrosexual" images of "male femininity" through cosmetic surgery as a technique for illustrating their consent to late modern social codes about men (Atkinson, 2006). By drawing on current cultural preferences in Canada for the fit, toned, groomed, and non-aggressive body (Niedzviecki, 2004), the men, at least from their interpretive standpoints, negotiate their way through the contemporary crisis of masculinity.

For many of the men I interviewed, exploring one or another form of cosmetic surgery displays a willingness to submit the body to others. The late modern Canadian man "gives" his body to a corporeal professional such as a surgeon to be re-worked in stereotypically feminine ways; in the process, he acknowledges a central deficiency with his body. It is both an admission of weakness (i.e., the failure to physically live up to masculine cultural expectations) and a moral gesture of the desire for self-improvement. Such a "confessional" practice finds grounding not only in one's desire to explore masculinity in novel but power-building ways, but also in a traditional Canadian middle-class aesthetic (see White et al., 1995) that targets bodies as sites of strict monitoring and disciplining. Byron (28) comments:

> I haven't spoken to a lot of people about the face peel, because I'm so young and the reaction would probably be seriously negative. But the women I've told react in a similar way; they congratulate me for my body care. Some say it makes me sound more gentle and sensitive, and into looking beautiful. . . . I should have done this years ago. At this point in my life, I have no problem admitting I need help to be as attractive as possible, especially if I get something [accolades] out of it . . . people, at least from my perspective, appreciate a body that is maintained and controlled. A "tight" body communicates that I care about myself, and probably take care of things in my life in general.

. . . Men's involvement in cosmetic surgery, especially invasive and painful forms, might be configured as an ironically self-aggressive response to cultural stereotypes linking masculinity and violence. Davis (2002) has argued that acts of cosmetic surgery are implicitly self-violent. Yet, as noted elsewhere (Atkinson, 2006), involvement in painful forms of body modification can be (re)interpreted by men as a process of masculine character-building (i.e., as part of one's ability to withstand painful body ordeals with a quiet resolve) and a hyperbolically masculine solution to problems of cultural doubt. Kevin (39) suggests:

> When the doctor stripped away the layers of fat from around my waist, he removed 30 years of anguish from my soul. I'd always been the fat outsider, the little boy who never quite made the cut for anything. Being inside a body that is a gelatinous prison kills a tiny piece of you every moment of your life. . . . When I woke up after the surgery and looked down, I felt strong and confident as a man

should. I could, never ever in my life, speak to anyone about how much being heavy hurt me emotionally, and now I don't have to. . . . Surgery is the best psychotherapy offered on the market. You have to go through hell and the pain [of surgery] to come out on top. Being beaten up through surgery is temporary, but being beaten up socially can last a lifetime.

Kevin's perspective teaches us that the current boom in Canadian men's cosmetic surgery might be, at least in part, viewed as an indicator of the cultural imperative for these men to engage in cosmetic, self-abusive forms of body work.

Institutional Control and Masculine Bodies

Although marked gaps continue to exist between the genders in relation to established-outsider power balances within most institutions, the men interviewed in this study believe their position as established authority figures has been dislodged by women's participation in the economic and political spheres. When telling stories about motivations underpinning cosmetic procedures, nearly three-quarters (74 per cent) of the men interviewed talked about feeling threatened at work by younger, smarter, and healthier women—especially in image-oriented business environments that equate outward appeal with intellectual competency and moral worth. It seems that as women have secured preliminary inroads to power sources in Western cultures like Canada, some men become rather fear-oriented in their disposition. For figurational sociologists, the sociogenic shifts in work patterns and relationships may impact men's habituses and corresponding body regimens. Peter (54) teaches us:

> Our company hired three new managers last year, and two of them didn't look any older than 25. What makes it worse is that they are well-spoken, bright, charming women who are gorgeous. So there is me, an ageing guy in a changing business environment who appears as if he's missed more nights of sleep

than he should have. The superficiality of that realisation kind of makes you sick . . . but these people won't want me around unless I adapt, unless I change.

Important is that Peter's fear-orientation encourages him to consider self-aggressive cosmetic bodywork as a rational solution to his incompetence anxieties. Peter's masculinity, partly anchored in his ability to physically appear as competent in the workplace, as Sennett (1998) might predict, is reconciled through physical intervention. The outward ability to "look good" supersedes concerns about his ability to perform intellectually as a business administrator.

For other men, their ascribed social positions as established workers within dense chains of interdependency are threatened by subtle implications that their bodies appear decisively non-masculine, and therefore socially impotent. As Connell and Wood (2005) document through the study of masculine business cultures, one's sense of masculinity is often validated by peers' positive comments (or at least lack of mockery) regarding one's body image and style while "on the job." Therefore, when a man experiences persistent teasing about his body as lacking masculinity (i.e., the fat, unhealthy, powerless body), the passive ridicule may eventually manifest into a fear that others view him as inadequate socially. A man adopting such an interpretive mindset associates his peers' lack of public acknowledgement of him as a business "expert" as an indicator of their collective interpretation of his deficient body image. Andrew (33) explains:

> With my job, I don't have time to work out two or three hours a day, and I have to eat most meals on the run . . . and most of it is not healthy. And, it's hard to lose weight, so the liposuction gave a little kick-start to the process. Now I'm not the office fat guy everyone pokes fun at and ignores. People listen to me and consider my opinions on practically everything. No one looks at a fat guy and says, there's a real go-getter . . . they say the opposite, he's lazy, unmotivated and someone worth firing.

Andrew's cosmetic surgery narrative is filled with self-effacing accounts of his "bigness" and correlated social inferiority. For him, cosmetic surgery is an act of masculine "re-establishment," and a self-directed technique of threat management. Andrew is not concerned with his body as a potential health risk to him, but as a social symbol of inferiority. For men like Andrew, surgery is a more rational and controlled response to body problems than the styles of self-starvation among young men described by Braun et al. (1999). Aesthetic surgery is, then, a civilized and self-restrained response to long-term emotional distress.

The men who describe risk or threat at work as a motivator for cosmetic surgery strategically employ classic techniques of neutralization (Sykes and Matza, 1956) to account for their body projects. When interviewed and challenged about the source of their concerns at work, and the perceived lack of control experienced in the workplace, men typically respond by arguing that cosmetic bodywork is neither morally problematic nor physically dangerous. Further still, they highlight how the degree to which they are willing to sacrifice their bodies to look masculine jibes with a sense of worth and personal dedication to succeed—once more, their clearly habituated middle-class aesthetic. Buttressing these accounts is a stereotypically Western, consumeristic, and present-centred mentality, in that the solution to their lack of work control must be immediate and discoverable in a commodity/service form. Derrick, a 52-year-old marketing expert who regularly receives Botox and microdermabrasion treatments, says:

> I can't wait another 20 years to take action. I need to be a man who walks into the room and no one says, "Damn, he looks tired." If that continues to happen, I'll be out the door. I could have experimented with herbal remedies, creams or lotions to erase the years from my face, but it might take years, if it even works. Why wait when I can have better results from a doctor in only one day?

For Derrick, any risk or potential long-term effects of the procedures is secondary to the immediate gains received from medical intervention.

The means–end, here-and-now mentality is directly reflective of the commodified and highly rationalized manner by which people come to approach bodies (and body problems) in "civilized" figurations (Elias, 2002). Any service that cures his problems of masculinity is thus justified as worthwhile, particularly when the service may be purchased from a qualified medical professional with celerity and precision.

What the above narratives underscore is the process by which men come to frame and reframe their bodies/identities as innovatively "male feminine" through surgical intervention. For the men in the current sample, actively responding to a perceived control threat through traditionally feminine bodywork is strategically interpreted as a very masculine endeavour: as a manoeuvre designed to make them appear culturally invested in new social constructions of masculinity. Surgery is, then, configured as a technique of biopower and control as it helps men respond to the fear of the masculinity crisis "head on" (Sargent, 2000) without resorting to "uncivilized" types of male aggression. Resonant with White et al.'s (1995) description of how male athletes reframe the injury process as a silent testing ground of masculine character-building, cosmetic surgery patients often tell stories about how their willingness to endure painfully invasive surgeries re-establishes their ability to meet social threats with "modern" masculine resolve.

Knowledge Production and Masculine Bodies

Compounding the threat some men perceive to exist regarding their masculinity in the workplace and across institutional settings is the type of work men are performing and the lack of spare-time exercise they undertake. With more men than ever in service or information-processing industries, the current generation of middle-class Canadian men are perhaps the most "stationary" workforce in the country's history. With decreasing amounts of spare-time, dietary habits revolving around high calorie fast-food choices, and leisure time dominated by consumption and inactivity, the

physical toll on their bodies is evident (Critser, 2002). The post-industrial economy and associated lifestyles, it seems, are not easily reconciled with traditional images of the powerful, performing, and dominant male (Faludi, 1999).

Men interviewed in the present study express a sense of frustration with the form and content of their work responsibilities. For these men, ritually performing disembodied or virtual work (i.e., computer-facilitated) every day encourages a mind–body separation and neglect (Potts, 2002). Roger's (45) words are emblematic of the disaffection some men experience with their work:

> Sitting at a desk for 10 hours a day, then a car for 2, on then on your couch for 3 more wears your body down. Not to mention that my skin barely ever sees the light of day. At times, I can feel my face literally sagging because of my posture. . . . Looking in the mirror when you're 40 and having a road map for a face shouldn't be surprising. That's not who I am, that's not the image of my inside I want to project.

Men like Roger refuse to link marginalized external bodies with inner selves. Roger's body is further objectified and instrumentalized in the cosmetic surgery process, as he views his physical form as a site of much-needed management. Such an interpretation of the body only exacerbates existing fears about men's bodies as socially non-masculine. Cosmetic surgery provides a fast, efficient and highly rational way of alleviating these psychological strains and social discomfort:

> From the time I was 15 years old, I gained weight. I watched my diet and tried to work out, but I kept packing on inches. By the time I graduated school and started office work [computer programmer], it only grew worse . . . literally. Liposuction saved me from my self-hatred and the ridicule I faced from others. It's like having the clock re-set, or like a magic wand being waved and your troubles are gone. (Ray, 43)

Narratives about the role of cosmetic surgery in eliminating the unfortunate side effects of sedentary lifestyles are equally filled with constructions of the "male-feminine" body as "victimized" by established cultural expectations that men must labour for long hours. For men like Leo (37), a graphics designer living in Sarnia, Ontario, his "need" for facial surgeries results from a social pressure to work in support of his extended family:

> It's not like I can quit my job, or be there for less than 12 hours a day if I want to earn a living. No one pays me for sitting on my ass and doing nothing, they pay me for sitting on my ass and designing! If I choose not to work, I'm choosing not to feed my family. . . . We come from a very traditional Italian background, and it's not questioned that I'm the sole provider. . . . There's an unspoken rule that a man who cannot provide [for his family] isn't really a man.

For nearly 10 years, Leo's work habits have, in his terms, "weathered" his body. The three facial surgeries he has received temporarily remove the unwanted "marks of masculinity" from his appearance. Like other men, Leo configures his surgical preferences as a symbol of his dedication to looking his best, even in the context of incredible social/work pressure. Surgery, for Leo, is a decisively calculated male-feminine response to the social problems of "men's work" inherent in everyday life. . . .

. . . Alan, a 50-year-old office manager, re-directs criticism about "problematic" body practices back to the source:

> Everyone who picks on me for having my skin re-surfaced I bet never thinks about the million ways they change their bodies every day by going to the gym or eating low-carb, kill-yourself diets. . . . Don't call me less of a man because I do something to improve my looks that you are too afraid to do yourself.

Ironically, while men like Alan frequently position themselves as victims of work structures and expectations, through their cosmetic surgery storytelling they vehemently deny losing agency or possessing an inferior masculine status by undergoing the cosmetic surgery process. Quite predictably, as Davis (2002) mentions, these men never pathologize invasive body interventions as self-victimizing. Instead, they reframe surgical intervention as masculine character building. The courage associated with undergoing cosmetic surgery is highlighted as a powerfully decisive response to their identity/body problems.

Discussion

The men's narratives included in this article provide a conceptual composite of what a selection of men in Canada consider to be the "re-established" male-feminine body. It is a body that is at once firm, fit, flexible and fat-free, and open to exploring non-traditional (feminized) forms of bodywork in order to appear as innovatively male. But most importantly, as Frank (2003) notes, it is a body that exudes a cultural awareness and acceptance, a form articulating a deep sensibility toward changing roles, statuses and identities of "new men." The male's cosmetically altered body is one that is economically invested in the established cultural brand of masculinity (Schmitt, 2001). At the same time, it is an aesthetically contoured body validated by "muted" social recognition and kudos from admiring others. In these ways and others, the cosmetically altered body is interdependent with shifting constructions of masculinity and derives social meaning from extended social interaction across social settings.

Upon first glance, one might interpret the recent turn to cosmetic surgery among men as a stark indicator of shifting habituses among men. Indeed, the participation in quintessentially feminine forms of bodywork might indicate a fracturing of traditional notions of masculine physical manipulation and display. However, while men may respond to sociogenic change and contemporary ideological currents with heretofore non-traditional forms of masculine modification (Benwell, 2003), the narratives discussed in this article illustrate how men may tactically reframe cosmetic surgery along established masculine lines of power and authority.

First, involvement in cosmetic surgery reaffirms how bodies are employed by men as texts of strength, authority and power. The cosmetically altered male is readable as a signifier of power at a time when traditionally masculine bodies are perceived to be under siege (Niva, 1998). The surgically tucked, sharpened, minimized, or masculinized body provides men with a restored or re-established sense of social control—especially when other forms of institutional control and knowledge production are fragmented.

Second, the implicit risk-taking and objectification of the body in order to affirm one's sense of masculinity equally suggests how cosmetic surgery is incorporated into a wide range of men's "self-aggressive" or "risk-oriented" body practices. As Elias (2002) suggested, cosmetic instances of body performance are encoded communicative gestures of masculine distinction and ability to endure pain, further demarcating one's sense of social power and achieved cultural worth. The willingness to engage in surgery as self-aggressive risk may be, nevertheless, a civilizing turn in men's habituses. The social battle over gender power and the "fragmentation of masculinity" is turned inward and then inscribed on the skin rather than cast outward through aggressive physicality or dominance of others. Akin to Elias and Dunning's (1986) description of sport in the civilizing process, cosmetic surgery is a form of social mimesis for some men, as aesthetic alterations to the body become proxy representations of a social battle between genders.

Third, the men in the study comment on how cosmetic surgery tends to be quietly managed and privately experienced. At present, the men interviewed in this study do not openly discuss their cosmetic body projects with "outsiders." Men typically express how cosmetic surgery is not mainstream masculine performance in Canada, and how an air of stigma still hovers around the practice. The men perceive themselves as, in Goffman's (1963) terms, "discreditable deviants" whose predilections for surgical enhancement might jeopardize their status as "real" masculine men. In response, the men refrain from expressing emotion about the cosmetic surgery process and prefer to suffer the physical pains of surgery in silence. They do, however, relish the positive comments received regarding their "fresh"-looking faces, newly toned bodies, or magically reinvigorated senses of self.

Fourth, the widening use of cosmetic surgery among men may be a clever technique of masculine power attainment via collective image work. In a beauty/image-saturated and obsessed culture, these men glean significant attention and social accolades for their secretly "improved" physical forms. The beautification of men's bodies through cosmetic surgery might be considered as the poaching of a traditionally feminine technique of power attainment through the body, inasmuch as men are colonizing a site of social power traditionally dominated by women. . . .

. . . Men's narratives about cosmetic surgery allude to how established masculinity is reframed in innovative ways to reproduce traditional results: social power and distinction for men across the Canadian social landscape. In this way, the proverbial "song remains the same" for men, masculinity and social control.

References

Atkinson, M. 2003. *Tattooed: The Sociogenesis of a Body Art.* Toronto: University of Toronto Press.

Atkinson, M. 2006. "Masks of Masculinity: Cosmetic Surgery and (Sur)passing Strategies," in P. Vanni and D. Waskul, eds., *Body/Embodiment: Symbolic Interaction and the Sociology of the Body*, pp. 247–61. London: Ashgate.

Atkinson, M., and K. Young. 2008. *Deviance and Social Control in Sport.* Champaign, Ill: Human Kinetics.

Benwell, B. 2003. *Masculinity and Men's Lifestyle Magazines.* Oxford: Blackwell.

Braun, D., S. Sunday, A. Huang, and K. Halmi. 1999. "More Males Seek Treatment for Eating Disorders," *International Journal of Eating Disorders* 25(4): 415–24.

Brinkgreve, C. 2004. "Elias in Gender Relations: The Changing Balance of Power Between the Sexes," in S. Loyal and S. Quilley, eds., *The Sociology of Norbert Elias*, pp. 67–88. Cambridge: Cambridge University Press.

Cohen. A. 1955. *Delinquent Boys: The Culture of the Gang.* New York: Free Press.

Connell, R. 2005. *Masculinities.* Berkeley, Calif: University of California Press.

Connell, R., and J. Wood. 2005. "Globalisation and Business Masculinities," *Men and Masculinities* 7(4): 347–64.

Crewe, B. 2003. *Representing Men: Cultural Production and Producers in the Men's Magazine Market.* Oxford: Berg.

Critser, G. 2002. *Fat Land: How Americans Became the Fattest People in the World*. New York: Houghton Mifflin.

Davis, K. 2002. *Dubious Equalities and Embodied Differences: Cultural Studies and Cosmetic Surgery*. New York: Rowman and Littlefield.

de Certeau, M. 1984. *The Practice of Everyday Life*. Berkeley, Calif: University of California Press.

Dunning, E. 1999. *Sport Matters: Sociological Studies of Sport, Violence, and Civilisation*. London: Routledge.

Elias, N. 1978. *What Is Sociology?* London: Hutchinson.

Elias, N. 1991. *The Society of Individuals*. Oxford: Basil Blackwell.

Elias, N. 1996. *The Germans: Studies of Power Struggles and the Development of Habitus in the Nineteenth and Twentieth Centuries*. Oxford: Polity Press.

Elias, N. 2002. *The Civilising Process*. Oxford: Blackwell.

Elias, N., and E. Dunning. 1986. *The Quest for Excitement: Sport and Leisure in the Civilising Process*. Oxford: Basil Blackwell.

Elias, N., and J. Scotson. 1965. *The Established and the Outsiders*. London: Sage.

Faludi, S. 1999. *Stiffed: The Betrayal of the American Man*. New York: William Morrow and Co.

Featherstone, M. 2000. *Body Modification*. London: Sage.

Frank, A. 2003. "Emily's Scars: Surgical Shapings, Technoluxe, and Bioethics," *Hastings Center Report* 34(2): 18–29.

Garlick, S. 2004. "What Is a Man? Heterosexuality and the Technology of Masculinity," *Men and Masculinities* 6(3): 156–72.

Godenzi, A. 1999. "Style or Substance: Men's Response to Feminist Challenge," *Men and Masculinities* 1(4): 385–92.

Goffman, E. 1963. *Stigma*. New York: Prentice Hall.

Grogan, S., and H. Richards. 2002. "Body Image: Focus Groups with Boys and Men," *Men and Masculinities* 4(3): 219–32.

Hathaway, A., and M. Atkinson. 2003. "Active Interview Tactics in Research on Public Deviance: Exploring the Two Cop Personas," *Field Methods* 15(2): 161–85.

Hise, R. 2004. *The War against Men*. Oakland, Calif: Elderberry Press.

Horrocks, R. 1994. *Masculinity in Crisis: Myths, Fantasies and Realities*. Basingstoke: St Martin's Press.

Labre, M. 2002. "Adolescent Boys and the Muscular Male Body Ideal," *Journal of Adolescent Health* 30(4): 233–42.

Medicard. 2004. *Report on Cosmetic Surgery in Canada*. Toronto.

Mosse, G. 1996. *The Image of Man: The Creation of Modern Masculinity*. Oxford: Oxford University Press.

Niedzviecki, H. 2004. *Hello, I'm Special*. New York: Penguin.

Niva, S. 1998. "Tough and Tender: New World Order Masculinity and the Gulf War," in M. Salewski and J. Parpart, eds., *The "Man" Question in International Relations*, pp. 109–28. Boulder, Colo: Westview Press.

Potts, A. 2002. "The Essence of the Hard-on: Hegemonic Masculinity and the Cultural Construction of 'Erectile Dysfunction,'" *Men and Masculinities* 3(1): 85–103.

Pronger, B. 2002. *Body Fascism: Salvation in the Technology of Physical Fitness*. Toronto: University of Toronto Press.

Sargent, P. 2000. "Real Men or Real Teachers? Contradictions in the Lives of Men Elementary Teachers," *Men and Masculinities* 2(4): 410–33.

Sarwer, D., and C. Crerand. 2004. "Body Image and Cosmetic Medical Treatments," *Body Image: An International Journal of Research* 1: 99–111.

Schmitt, R. 2001. "Proud to be a Man?," *Men and Masculinities* 3(3): 393–404.

Sennett, R. 1998. *The Corrosion of Character*. New York: W.W. Norton.

Sykes, G., and D. Matza. 1956. "Techniques of Neutralisation," *American Sociological Review* 22: 664–70.

White, P., K. Young, and J. Gillett. 1995. "Bodywork as a Moral Imperative: Some Critical Notes on Health and Fitness," *Loisir et Société* 18(1): 159–82.

Whitehead, S.M. 2002. *Men and Masculinities: Key Themes and New Directions*. Cambridge: Polity Press.

Young, K. 2003. *Sporting Bodies, Damaged Selves: Sociological Studies of Sports Related Injury*. London: Elsevier.

Chapter 12

Overview

Most people in Canada are aware of the enormous toll of racism and violence on Indigenous Peoples, but Indigenous resilience and resistance aren't as widely reported. Sandrina de Finney brings a gendered lens to the ways that Indigenous girls work to survive and thrive despite the barriers thrown up by the white-dominated society. She describes the ways in which settler colonialism has affected Indigenous girls in particular, contrasting the normalization of violence against girls with the Canadian government's outlays of money and resources for other less important ends, such as locating the Franklin expedition's ship. Nonetheless, she argues that young Indigenous women have powerful resources for building resilience and resistance through the healing practices of Indigenous communities, the strength of extended families, and the ideas and actions arising from Indigenous activists such as the flowering of two-spirit teachings and practices. These are not individual-level psychological attributes, as in some common definitions of resilience, but arise from shared experiences and reclamations of history. She makes the case that these forms of resilience amount to "sovereign girlhoods"—the possibility of living as a young Indigenous woman in a way that is not defined entirely by settler political institutions and cultural stigmas.

Indigenous Girls' Resilience in Settler States
Honouring Body and Land Sovereignty
Sandrina de Finney

Introduction

Canada enjoys a global reputation as a welcoming multicultural haven. . . . Despite living in one of the world's wealthiest countries, Indigenous peoples now live as "second-class citizens" in "fourth world conditions"[1] (Allan and Smylie, 2015; Amnesty International, n.d.).

Under British and French colonial rule, Indigenous girls and women in Canada have always been constructed as sexual objects. . . . Compared to other groups of Canadian girls and women, they experience the highest rates of sexual and racialized violence and exploitation, incarceration, murder, poverty, underhousing, homelessness, and underservicing in health and education (Anderson, 2011; S Hunt, "Tina Fontaine's death shows how little is being done for Indigenous women," The Globe and Mail, 20 August 2014[2]; Sikka, 2009). Having survived hundreds of years of active colonial rule in Canada, Indigenous girls are still seen as less worthy than white girls, and the violence and social inequities they experience do not generate appropriate public outrage or political and policy responses (de Finney and Saraceno, 2014).

. . . Informed by two decades of work as an Indigenous frontline worker, community-based researcher, educator, and advocate, I ask: How do we challenge the persistent construction of Indigenous girls as dispensable "damaged goods"? How do we develop understandings of resilience that foreground the political, historical, economic, and sociocultural forces that both produce and excuse sexualised violence against Indigenous girls? . . .

In considering these questions, I seek to understand resilience from an Indigenous perspective, beyond Euro-Western binaries of humans/nonhumans and society/nature. My theoretical exploration draws on Indigenous scholarship related to gender, Indigenous resurgence, and decolonisation to critique mainstream resilience frameworks. This analysis positions resilience as embedded in Indigenous body and land sovereignty, a perspective that honours girls as citizens of sovereign Indigenous nations who are intimately linked to their tribal and kinship networks, lands, and ancestors.

Indigeneity in Settler States: Defining Key Concepts

I use the terms Indigenous and First Peoples to refer to societies with ancestral ties to their territories that predate colonial occupation. . . .

Any feminist discussion of resilience should contend with the intimate link between colonial exploitation of both Indigenous lands and Indigenous bodies. This is particularly true for territories that remain actively colonised. Countries such as Canada, the United States (US), and Australia, as well as other territories under continued European rule, can be considered settler colonial states. In a settler state, the settler "never leaves" (Tuck and Yang, 2012:5). . . .

Colonised Girlhoods

Colonial systems have brutalised Indigenous children. Generation after generation of Indigenous children have been forcibly removed from their families and placed in residential schools and white foster and adoptive homes, where they were severed from their families, communities, and lands, beaten for speaking their language and practising their spiritual traditions, and often systematically abused—physically, spiritually, sexually, and emotionally. This situation is not improving: More Indigenous children are in government care today than ever before in Canadian history (Blackstock, 2016). According to the United Nations' *State of the World's Indigenous Peoples* (2009:25), 60% of Indigenous children live below the poverty line in Canadian cities, and over half of First Nations children "live in houses [that] are inadequate or substandard, manifested in deteriorated units [and] toxic mould." Yet Indigenous children receive the least state funding—between 22% and 40% less for social services and education than non-Indigenous children (First Nations Education Council, 2009). According to Canada's auditor general, "in a country as rich as Canada, this disparity is unacceptable" (Office of the Auditor General of Canada, 2011:1–2).

This story is all too familiar for Indigenous girls and young women in settler states, who experience poverty and gender violence—including sexual exploitation and trafficking—more than any other group of girls. Kingsley and Marks (2000:4) stress that in some communities, "commercial sexual exploitation of Aboriginal children and youth forms more than 90 per cent of the visible sex trade." Canada is facing endemic levels of gender-based violence against Indigenous girls and women. Hundreds have been kidnapped, disappeared, and murdered (Truth and Reconciliation Commission of Canada, 2015). . . . These statistics paint an inexcusable reality for Indigenous girls. In a wealthy Western state that champions girls' and women's rights internationally, how did we get here? In the next two sections, I seek to explore that question by interrogating colonial constructions of Indigenous

women and land and how resilience and well-being are intimately controlled by the settler state.

Colonial Constructions of Women and Land as Property

. . . Under colonial heteropatriarchy, "white settlers uprooted traditional spiritual and intellectual values accorded to Indigenous women and replaced them with notions of inferiority, hierarchy, and the paradigm of women as property" (Sikka, 2009:7). Discourses of Indigenous womanhood exemplified by the "dirty squaw" have constructed Indigenous women as lazy and sexually deviant. Sarah Deer (2009:150) writing on the need to decolonise rape law argues: "Rape and sexual violence are deeply embedded in the colonial mindset. Rape is more than a metaphor for colonization—it is part and parcel of colonization." For instance, government agents would often "withhold rations unless Aboriginal women were made available to them" (Razack, 2002:131). Leanne Simpson (2013:11) writes that under colonial logics, both Indigenous women and Indigenous lands were cast as colonial property, and both have been constructed as "rapeable":

> Colonialism and capitalism are based on extracting and assimilating. My land is seen as a resource. My relatives in the plant and animal worlds are seen as resources. My culture and knowledge is a resource. . . . Colonialism has always extracted the indigenous . . . indigenous knowledge, indigenous women, indigenous peoples.

. . .

(Un)grievable Lives: Who Matters in Colonial States—And Who Does Not?

For feminist theorist Judith Butler, grievability presupposes that a life matters:

> Without grievability, there is no life (. . .) Instead, "there is a life that will never have been

lived," sustained by no regard, no testimony, and ungrieved when lost (2009:14–15).

Thousands of Indigenous lives have been lost to colonial violence, and actively grieved, missed and remembered by their families and communities. However, Indigenous girls' traumas and deaths continue to be seen as normal and acceptable in the Canadian public realm (de Finney and Saraceno, 2014; Razack, 2002; Turpel-Lafond, 2014). In 2014, for example, a First Nations girl hanged herself two weeks before her 15th birthday (Turpel-Lafond, 2014). The girl's well-being had been severely compromised by neglect, bullying, and emotional, physical, and sexual abuse. Numerous chronically unexplored official reports stated she was at high risk for self-harm. In her final month, a concerned school counsellor predicted that the girl would commit suicide without immediate help. None was given. Sixteen days later, she hanged herself.

This story attracted scant attention. In sharp contrast, around the same time when a dog injured his snout while chasing a porcupine in a city park, pictures of his quill-riddled face were featured in heavy rotation on the daily news. We learned the dog's name, the parks he visits, and his favourite foods. In two days, over $10,000 was garnered on GoFundMe for his surgery (Canadian Broadcasting Corporation, "Dogs injured by porcupine quills get fundraising support of $10K," *CBC News*, 3 November 2015).[3]

In another example of incomprehensible priorities, two years ago the Canadian government spent millions digging a sunken colonial ship out of the Arctic ice. The ship "had to be" rescued because it was part of the 1845 Franklin expedition of European explorers (Canadian Broadcasting Corporation, "Franklin expedition ship found in Arctic ID'd as HMS Erebus," *CBC News*, 1 October 2014).[4] Prime Minister Stephen Harper said the ship was an invaluable artifact of our proud Canadian identity. Its rescue was celebrated with historical TV vignettes and lavish press conferences.

Around the same time, a 15-year-old Indigenous girl named Tina Fontaine was sexually assaulted, murdered, and dumped into a river in a body bag (S Hunt, "Tina Fontaine's death shows how little is being done or Indigenous women," *The Globe and Mail*, 20 August 2014).[5] Tina was in the child protection system (i.e., a ward of the state). She had been reported missing and was stopped by police several times in the days before her disappearance, including one evening when they found her in a car with an intoxicated older white man. Unbelievably, no one intervened to ensure her safety. No rescue plans were put into place. No press conference was called to declare her value. And, when asked about the thousand other missing and murdered Indigenous girls and women in Canada, Prime Minister Harper noted, "It's not really on our radar, to be honest" (T Kappo, "Stephen Harper's comments on missing, murdered Aboriginal women show 'lack of respect'," *CBC News*, 19 December 2014).[6]

What does it mean when a government spends millions of dollars to locate a missing 200-year-old ship but is unconcerned about missing and murdered Indigenous girls and women? What does it mean when Canadian society upholds a hierarchy in which resource extraction, effigies of colonial history, and domestic pets are all more valued than Indigenous girls?

Not only are ungrievable Indigenous girls targeted for sexualised violence, a normalised attitude prevails that blames them for their abuse while excusing the perpetrators (Razack, 2002). Indigenous girls do not fit the construction of victim that has been negotiated and sustained by the media and government discourses that inform anti-violence policies and funding (de Finney and Saraceno, 2014). And of course, despite their personal knowledge and contestations of the complex dynamics of sexualised violence, Indigenous girls are rarely included in research, policy, and programming debates (de Finney and Saraceno, 2014). Their voices are also largely invisible in research on trauma and resilience.

Resilience

. . .

Depsychologising Resilience: An Indigenous Analysis

In the face of evidence-based measures of Indigenous girls' complex traumas and high risk, an entire industry of resilience-promoting programmes, interventions, and specialists has been deployed (de Finney and di Tomasso, 2015; Reynolds, 2013; Richardson and Reynolds, 2012). Meanwhile, the colonial violence girls experience is reduced to psychometric measurements and assessments (e.g., complex trauma, non-compliance, post-traumatic stress disorder, attachment disorder, self-harm, depression, substance use, etc.). This psycho-pathologising, in turn, furthers a victim-blaming discourse. The lucky ones who survive and even thrive are called "resilient," and their stories of "exceptional" success (i.e., the disadvantaged Indigenous girl from a family of intergenerational survivors who surpassed all odds to complete college) are celebrated. Other girls come to be measured against the yardstick of exceptionality. Those who cannot "bounce back" from abuse and violence are pathologised as holding complex, intergenerational trauma; this diagnostic process is rooted in evidence-based measures that typically exclude Indigenous peoples (de Finney and di Tomasso, 2015; Reynolds, 2013). Western-centric diagnostic procedures in turn fuel the need for more Western-controlled services targeting "problem" Indigenous girls.

. . .

Resilience . . . is a meaningless concept unless we place it in a historical and political context. Focusing exclusively on girls' processes and functioning takes vital energy away from urgently needed political, policy, and economic responses to coloniality. Indigenous peoples have succeeded in (and in some cases died) protecting and passing on their languages, their relationships to land, their social and kinship systems, and their spiritual worldviews. This in itself is a testament to the most impressive and expansive kind of resilience. The fact that Indigenous nations continue to uphold their sovereignty demands expanded definitions of resilience as a political act. That girls may or may not demonstrate normative definitions of resilience is not a reflection of existing resources and capacities, but a measure of the overwhelming and pervasive impact of colonial violence.

. . .

The issues at stake in critically examining the existence of sexualised violence are threefold.

First, under settler violence, the level, diversity, and scope of violence imposed on Indigenous girls and their communities is so overwhelming and constitutive as to be incomparable to the levels of violence girls might experience otherwise. In this context, generations of Indigenous communities have experienced, and may be reproducing, violence. This means that sexual violence against girls can operate in any direction: horizontally, laterally, within families, in communities, with peers, across siblings, in the media, in private, in systems and by authorities, and in public. Second, much of the violence girls experience in their own communities, even when it is perpetrated by peers, family members, and community members, stems from colonial trauma. It is clearly documented by Canada's Truth and Reconciliation Commission (2015) that generations of children (who are now parents, grandparents, other adult relatives, and community members) suffered sexual violence and exploitation, creating an intergenerational cycle of abuse and shame. Analysing girls' resilience in isolation of this broader context further isolates girls while ignoring the root causes of the violence. Finally, the overwhelming systemic and transgenerational nature of this violence means that communities' and girls' capacity to respond to it—and to other kinds of violence—has been severely stressed. In this regard, culturally congruent practices that have always existed in communities to prevent and respond to violence have been compromised. By legitimate oral and historical accounts, Indigenous societies have always had, and continue to have, community-generated responses and interventions to address gender and sexual violence (Aboriginal Justice Implementation Commission, 1999; First Nations Health Authority, 2017). . . . Revitalizing these practices in a contemporary context is critical to reasserting the knowledge systems that upheld Indigenous girls' and women's well-being, leadership, and dignity prior to and since contact.

Resilience as Sovereignty

In a context of increased Indigenous advocacy for self-determination in matters related to health, well-being, education, and child and family services, how do we ensure that Indigenous girls have meaningful connections with their ancestral territories and kinship systems? How do we foster ways for girls to live with pride and dignity that do not include violence against their bodies and resource exploitation of their homelands? Finding a path forward through these complexities is challenging, not because of a lack of community-based knowledge about what is needed, but rather due to denial and unaccountability on the part of settler powers. Scott Clark, executive director of a prominent Indigenous social services agency in western Canada (cited in L Britten, "First Nation suicides: The view from Vancouver and Cowichan Valley," *CBC News*, 12 April 2016)[7], stresses that "we know why these issues are the way they are. Perhaps the biggest challenge we have is getting people in leadership to recognize [them]." Clark insists that:

> [t]he answers are going to be in the communities, with the young people, with the grandmas, with the grandpas, with the parents. That's where your strength lies . . . but that's not the model that's endorsed in this country, federally or provincially or municipally. Enough programs—you're programming Indians across this country to death!

With Clark's advocacy for community-controlled responses in mind, I look for productive frameworks by which to understand body and land sovereignty, wellness, and healing. . . . An important step in this process involves honouring and supporting the creative ways in which Indigenous and community members, for hundreds of years, have mobilised as activists, teachers, stewards, caregivers, healers, leaders, and advocates, pushed for legislative and policy change, initiated grassroots movements, organized international advocacy, created community-based services and alternative economies, and acted as community, spiritual and cultural leaders (see Anderson and Lawrence, 2003; Martin-Hill, 2003; Suzack et al, 2010).

Many of the girls I work with are aware of these tremendous legacies, and many participate in individual and collective resistances of all kinds that connect them with a most creative and spirited kind of resilience (de Finney, 2015). In advocating for justice and dignity for themselves, their friends, their families, and their communities, they recreate resilient circles of care and justice. One such example is a study I am currently involved in, entitled Sisters Rising: A Community-Based Research Project Honouring Indigenous Girls.[8] Rooted in building community-generated responses to historical sexualised violence, Sisters Rising is a community-engaged, arts-based research study with Indigenous girls and youth in western Canada. The project focuses on challenging the victim-blaming climate of racialized gender violence by recentring Indigenous values and teachings and focusing on linking body sovereignty to questions of decolonisation and land sovereignty.

Sovereign Girlhoods

Expanding our conceptualisation of resilience to encompass sovereignty requires conceptual shifts about how we understand gender and sexuality. First, to depsychologise sexualised and gender violence under settler regimes, we need expanded definitions of girlhood itself. The idea of a strict gender binary ensconced in unequal gender roles is a damaging tenet of colonialism (Filice, 2015). Indigenous girls are constrained by a Eurocentric definition of girlhood that creates "marginalized others whose lives, bodies, relationships, and selves do not conform" to white privileged norms (Aapola et al, 2005:3). Indigenous nations have always had their own diverse gender formations and roles.

A concept that has gained salience across Indigenous contexts is "two spirit," a translation of the Anishinaabeg term *niizh manidoowag* that refers to a person who embodies both a masculine and feminine spirit (Filice, 2015). Given that two spirit, gender fluid, gender nonconforming, trans, gay, lesbian, bisexual, and queer young people are at high risk for gender-based and sexualised violence (Hunt, 2015; Toomey et al, 2013), the concept of two spirit has quickly taken off. It has provided an Indigenous space to discuss gender and sexuality outside of colonial categories. However, its growing popularity has also raised concerns that its specific teachings have been appropriated and diluted into English terminology and a pan-Indigenous model. It is certainly important to safeguard the integrity of complex Indigenous teachings that are specific to particular histories and territories, and that do not have direct English translations. What is useful about the emerging relevance of two spirit teachings is that it has opened space for Indigenous communities to recentre their distinct teachings and concepts of gender and sexual wellbeing. Such a movement would reassert flexibility for Indigenous children and youth to live genders and sexualities outside of prescriptive, inequitable Euro-Western norms that prioritise a strict gender binary, cisgender privilege and heteronormativity, and the primacy of men over women. As examples, Indigenous-led projects such as Sisters Rising, 2spirits, and the Native Youth Sexual Health Network[9] are shifting conversations about gender and sexuality to a place of honouring Indigenous teachings about gender, bodies, relationships, and consent. At the heart of these initiatives is the importance of supporting young Indigenous people to self-identify and build community using whatever terminology and concepts best fit for them. Such work also highlights the importance of directly including Indigenous children and youth of all genders and sexualities in developing research, practice, and policy for antisexual violence and anti-settler violence initiatives.

Second, a focus on inclusive resilience highlights the vitality of kinship models that go beyond Eurocentric ideas of nuclear and extended families. Indigenous scholar Leroy Little Bear (2000) asserts that in many Indigenous worldviews, children, from birth, are objects of kindness and love from a large circle of kin and friends. He describes Indigenous notions of kinship as a "spider-web of relations" (Little Bear, 2000:79) that includes humans and the natural

world and necessitates complex arrangements of rights and obligations. Such a concept of kinship clearly exceeds the boundaries of Western notions of psycho-social resilience. Here, true connectedness represents a connection to "all relations," which Richard Wagamese ("'All my relations' about respect," *Kamloops Daily News*, 11 June 2013)[10] defines as:

> a recognition of the principles of harmony, unity and equality. It's a way of saying that you recognize your place in the universe and that you recognize the place of others and of other things in the realm of the real and the living . . . everything that you are kin to. Everyone. You also mean everything that relies on air, water, sunlight and the power of the Earth and the universe itself.

Indigenous communities hold significant holistic healing practices and processes that need to be amplified and centred in our discussions about sexualised violence. Restitching kinship networks is an essential step in this journey. As one leader of an Indigenous child and family agency (cited in Turpel-Lafond, 2016:33) expressed, we need to build on

> our cultural practices of supporting those who come forward instead of isolating them and simply moving them through this difficult time. Healing is a meaningless word if we don't have our culture and resources to blanket our children and youth. We need to wrap them in love and care and walk with them to see that the violence is exposed.

. . .

Conclusion

. . . [W]e need expanded definitions of girls' resilience that foreground the political, historical, economic, and sociocultural forces that structure colonial heteropatriarchy and sexualized violence. Without a focus on land sovereignty and "all relations," Eurocentric notions of resilience serve to pathologies Indigenous girls for living in a systematically violent colonial context.

. . . When they have been able to maintain their family kinship models, connections with land, and worldviews in the midst of hundreds of years of concerted state attempts to eliminate them, we can assert very clearly and proudly that Indigenous resilience supercedes mainstream systems and definitions. This is no simplistic romanticising of survival. I have taken great care to outline the continued structural violence that Indigenous communities live with and the

diverse approaches to self-determination, healing, dignity, and kinship that might unsettle the supremacy of Euro-Western concepts of socio-psychological well-being. With this objective in mind, we need to create spaces and projects for girls and youth of all genders to share this message with each other. This conceptual shift takes resilience out of its individualised definition and places it instead in a broader social-political context that accounts for transgenerational kinship networks, in relationship with ancestors, lands, and all our relations.

Notes

1. Fourth world describes how Indigenous peoples across the world "today are completely or partly deprived of the right to their own territories and [their] riches" (Manuel 1974, cited in Griggs, 1992:3).

2. Available at: http://www.theglobeandmail.com/opinion/tina-fontaines-death-shows-how-littleis-being-done-for-indigenous-women/article20138787/ (site accessed 22 March 2017).

3. Available at: http://www.cbc.ca/news/canada/saskatchewan/dogs-recovering-from-porcupinequills-1.3301295 (site accessed 5 March 2017).

4. Available at: http://www.cbc.ca/news/politics/franklin-expedition-ship-found-in-arctic-id-d-ashms-erebus-1.2784268 (site accessed 5 March2017).

5. Available at: http://www.theglobeandmail.com-opinion/tina-fontaines-death-shows-how-littleis-being-done-for-indigenous-women/article20138787/(site accessed 22 March 2017).

6. Available at: http://www.cbc.ca/news/indigenous/stephen-harper-s-comments-on-missing-murdered-aboriginal-women-show-lack-of-respect-1.2879154 (site accessed 5 March 2017).

7. Available at: http://www.cbc.ca/news/canada/british-columbia/first-nation-suicides-bc-1.3532929 (site accessed 22 March 2017).

8. For more information about Sisters Rising, visit www.sistersrising.uvic.ca. See also de Finney Set al (forthcoming) "Sisters rising: Shape shifting settler violence through art and land retellings" in C Mitchell & R Moletsane (eds) Young People Engaging with the Arts and Visual Practices to address Sexual Violence, Rotterdam: Sense Publishers.

9. See http://www.nativeyouthsexualhealth.com/index.html.

10. Available at: http://www.kamloopsnews.ca/opinion/columnists/wagamese-allmyrelations-about-respect-1.1237759 (site accessed 22 March 2017).

References

Aapola S, Gonick M & Harris A (2005) *Young Femininity: Girlhood, Power, and Social Change*, New York: Palgrave Macmillan.

Aboriginal Justice Implementation Commission (1999) "Chapter 13: Aboriginal Women", Report of the Aboriginal Justice Inquiry of Manitoba, available at: http://www.ajic.mb.ca/volumel/chapter13.html#4 (site accessed 22 March 2017).

Allan B & Smylie J (2015) *First Peoples, Second Class Treatment: The Role of Racism in the Health and Well-Being of Indigenous Peoples in Canada*, Toronto, ON: The Wellesley Institute.

Amnesty International (n.d.) "Indigenous Peoples: Overview", available at: https://www.amnesty.org/en/what-we-do/indigenous-peoples/ (site accessed 18 March 2017).

Anderson K (2011) "Native women, the body, land, and narratives of contact and arrival" in H Lessard, R Johnson & J Webber (eds) *Storied Communities: Narratives of Contact and Arrival in Constituting Political Community*, Vancouver: UBC Press.

Anderson K & Lawrence B (eds) (2003) *Strong Woman Stories: Native Vision and Community Survival*, Toronto, ON: Sumach Press.

Blackstock C (2016) "The long history of discrimination against First Nations children", *Policy Options*, 6 October, available at: http://policyoptions.irpp.org/magazines/october-2016/the-long-history-ofdiscrimination-against-first-nations-children/ (site accessed 9 May 2017).

Butler J (2009) *Frames of War: When Is Life Grievable?*, London: Verso.

de Finney S (2015) "'Playing Indian' and other settler stories: Disrupting western narratives of Indigenous girlhood", in *Continuum: Journal of Media and Cultural Studies*, 29, 2, 169–81.

de Finney S & Saraceno J (2014) "Warrior girl and the searching tribe: Indigenous girls' everyday negotiations of racialization under neocolonialism" in C Bradford & M Reimer (eds) *Girls, Texts, Cultures*, Waterloo, ON: Wilfrid Laurier Press.

de Finney S & di Tomasso L (2015) "Creating places of belonging: Expanding notions of permanency with indigenous youth in care", in *First Peoples Child and Family Review*, 10, 1, 63–85.

Deer S (2009) "Decolonizing rape law: A native feminist synthesis of safety and sovereignty", in *Wicazo Sa Review*, Fall, 149–67, available at: https://turtletalk.files .wordpress.com/2009/10/deer-decolonizing-rape-law .pdf (site accessed 17 March 2017).

Filice M (2015) "Two-spirit", *The Canadian Encyclopedia*, available at: http://www.thecanadianencyclopedia .ca/en/article/two-spirit/ (site accessed 22 March 2017).

First Nations Education Council (2009) *First Nations Education Funding: Current Trends*, Wendake, QC: First Nations Education Council.

First Nations Health Authority (2017) "Our history, our health", available at: http://www.fnha.ca/wellness/ our-history-our-health (site accessed 22 March 2017).

Griggs R (1992) "Background on the term 'fourth world': An excerpt from CWIS Occasional Paper #18, The meaning of 'nation' and 'state' in the fourth world", available at: http://cwis.org/GML/background/FourthWorld/ (site accessed 20 March 2017).

Hunt S (2015) "Representing colonial violence: Trafficking, sex work, and the violence of law", in *Atlantis*, 27, 2, 25–39.

Kingsley C & Marks M (2000) *Sacred Lives: Canadian Aboriginal Children and Youth Speak Out About Sexual Exploitation*, Ottawa, ON: Save the Children, available at: https://www.gov.mb.ca/fs/traciastrust/pubs/sacred_ lives.pdf (site accessed 21 March 2017).

Little Bear L (2000) "Jagged worlds colliding" in M Battiste (ed) *Reclaiming Indigenous Voice and Vision*, Vancouver: UBC Press.

Martin-Hill D (2003) "She No Speaks and other colonial constructs of 'the traditional woman'" in K Anderson & B Lawrence (eds) *Strong Woman Stories: Native Vision and Community Survival*, Toronto, ON: Sumach Press.

Office of the Auditor General of Canada (2011) Matters of Special Importance—2011, 2011 June Status Report of the Auditor General of Canada, available at: http://www.oag-bvg.gc.ca/internet/English/parl_ oag_201106_00_e_35368.html (site accessed 22 March 2017).

Razack S (2002) *Race, Space, and the Law: Unmapping a White Settler Society*, Toronto, ON: Between the Lines.

Reynolds V (2013) "The problem's oppression not depression" in M Hearn & the Purple Thistle Centre (eds) *Stay Solid!: A Radical Handbook for Youth*, Oakland, Calif: AK Press.

Richardson C & Reynolds V (2012) "'Here we are amazingly alive': Holding ourselves together with an ethic of social justice in community work", in *International Journal of Child, Youth, and Family Studies*, 1, 1–19.

Sikka A (2009) *Trafficking of Aboriginal Women and Girls in Canada, Aboriginal Policy Research Series*, Ottawa, ON: Institute on Governance.

Simpson L (2013) "Dancing the world into being: A conversation with Idle No More's Leanne Simpson", available at: http://www.yesmagazine.org/peace-justice/ dancing-the-world-into-being-a-conversation-with- idle-no-more-leanne-simpson (site accessed 20 March 2017).

Suzack C, Huhndorf S, Perrault J & Barman J (2010) *Indigenous Women and Feminism: Politics*, Activism, Culture, Vancouver: UBC Press.

Toomey RB, Ryan C, Diaz RM, Card NA & Russell ST (2013) "Gender-nonconforming lesbian, gay, bisexual, and transgender youth: School victimization and young adult psychosocial adjustment", in *Psychology of Sexual Orientation and Gender Diversity*, 1, S, 71–80. doi: 10.1037/2329-0382.1.S.71

Truth and Reconciliation Commission of Canada (2015) *Honouring the Truth, Reconciling for the Future* (final report), available at: http://www.trc.ca/websites/ trcinstitution/File/2015/Honouring_the_Truth_ Reconciling_for_the_Future_July_23_2015.pdf (site accessed 6 July 2017).

Tuck E & Yang KW (2012) "Decolonization is not a metaphor", in *Decolonization: Indigeneity, Education, and Society*, 1, 1, 1–40, available at: http:// decolonization/index.php/des/article/view/18630 (site accessed 5 March 2017).

Turpel-Lafond ME (2014) "Lost in the shadows: How a lack of help meant a loss of hope for one First Nations girl", available at: http://www.rcybc.ca/sites/default/files/ documents/pdf/reports_publications/rcy_lost-in-the- shadows_forweb_17feb.pdf (site accessed 21 March 2017).

Turpel-Lafond ME (2016) "Too many victims: Sexualized violence in the lives of children and youth in care". Victoria, BC: Representative for Children and Youth, available at: https://www.rcybc.ca/toomanyvictims (site accessed 22 March 2017).

United Nations (2009) *State of the World's Indigenous Peoples*, available at: http://www.un.org/esa/socdev/ unpfii/documents/SOWIP/en/SOWIP_web.pdf (site accessed 22 March 2017).

Chapter 13

Overview

One of the most important developments in the study of gender over the past decade has been the flourishing of theory and scholarship on the experiences of transgender or nonbinary people. Trans and nonbinary lives are a profound challenge to the long-held idea that there are two and only two biological sexes that map onto two and only two genders. Ayden Scheim and Greta Bauer dive into the data about trans lives in Ontario via a large quantitative research project on trans people's health (the Trans PULSE Project). They found that while most of their participants claimed either a masculine or a feminine gender identity, a sizable minority identified as gender-fluid or completely nonbinary. The authors speculate that people who were assigned male at birth but identified with femininity (trans-feminine) faced barriers of "transmisogyny," the combination of transphobia (fear or hatred of trans people) with misogyny (sexism or antagonism toward women). The complexity and diversity of the trans population, as well as the sheer number of people who are identifying as trans, has significant implications for health care as well as for any Canadian institution that is organized on the presumption of two fixed and distinct sex categories—male and female.

Sex and Gender Diversity among Transgender Persons in Ontario, Canada

Results from a Respondent-Driven Sampling Survey

Ayden I. Scheim and Greta R. Bauer

Health researchers increasingly recognize the need to understand, measure, and distinguish among the impacts of gender relations, gendered identity, and sex-linked biology in order to support the development of effective policy, programmatic, and clinical interventions (Johnson, Greaves, & Repta, 2009; Krieger, 2003). Similarly, sex researchers have been called on to more carefully consider both sociocultural and biological dimensions of gender, sex, and their interplay as they relate to sexuality (Tolman & Diamond, 2001). Trans (transgender, transsexual, and transitioned)

Scheim, Ayden I., and Greta R. Bauer. "Sex and Gender Diversity Among Transgender Persons in Ontario, Canada: Results From a Respondent-Driven Sampling Survey," *The Journal of Sex Research*, 2015, 52:1, pp. 1–14.

individuals represent a gender/sex-minority population that has been excluded from much population health and sexuality research (Bauer, 2012), though new evidence suggests that trans persons, broadly defined, may comprise 0.5% of the adult population (Conron, Scott, Stowell, & Landers, 2012). The field of trans health and sexuality research has burgeoned in the past two decades (Melendez, Bonem, & Sember, 2006). Yet we know little about how biological sex and social gender are understood, lived, and embodied within the broad trans population and the concrete practice and policy problems related to sex and gender diversity within trans communities.

We use the term *trans* to describe those who identify with a sex/gender other than that assigned at birth, and *cisgender* for individuals who identify with the sex/gender assigned at birth or raised in (Tate, Ledbetter, & Youssef, 2013). . . . *Trans* is used to encompass a wide range of gender-variant or nonconforming identities (Kuper, Nussbaum, & Mustanski, 2012)—from transsexuals, who identify with the opposite sex to that assigned at birth, to genderqueers, who identify outside of the male/female gender binary (Bauer et al., 2012).

Genderqueer people (variously referred to *as gender fluid, gender nonconforming, or nonbinary*) have gained visibility in recent years (Hansbury, 2005; Kuper et al., 2012). Although such individuals may seek medical transition, they are less likely to do so (Grant et al., 2011; Kuper et al., 2012), and they may not feel that the concept of transitioning across the categories of male and female is applicable to them. Of respondents to the U.S. National Transgender Discrimination Survey (NTDS), 13% reported a gender identity other than male, female, or part time in both roles; most of these individuals wrote in "genderqueer" (Harrison, Grant, & Herman, 2011). Emerging information regarding the unique demographic and health-related profile of this group highlights the importance of their inclusion in research and of comprehensive measures of gender identity and expression (Kuper et al., 2012; Tate et al., 2013).

. . .

Not all trans persons transition gender and/or sex. But for those who do, Bockting (2008) argued that transition is primarily a psychosocial process. Social transition can include disclosing one's gender identity to others; change in gender presentation through clothing, hairstyle, and methods of de-emphasizing sex characteristics (e.g., breast binding or padding); use of a new name and/or gender pronoun; and change of name and/or sex marker on government-issued identification (Coleman, Bockting, et al., 2011). The NTDS, the largest convenience sample of trans persons in the United States to date (n = 6,456), found that 55% lived full time in a gender different from that assigned at birth, 27% were not living full time but wanted to, and 18% did not want to live full time in a different gender (Grant et al., 2011). Trans people differ regarding the goals of social transition, with many not wanting to be perceived as cisgender (nontrans)men or women, or realizing that such

a goal may not be realistic (Bockting, 2008). Nevertheless, visibility as a trans person may increase exposure to discrimination and marginalization (Lombardi, 2009), while lack of visibility has been associated with depression among MTF-spectrum trans Ontarians (Rotondi et al., 2011). . . .

Attending to the multidimensionality of gender and sex, and the increasingly visible diverse subgroups of trans persons, the current study sought to describe sex, gender, and transition-related characteristics among trans Ontarians and to identify their implications for policy, practice, and research. . . .

. . . Specifically, we aimed to describe (1) trans Ontarians who had undertaken various degrees of social and/or medical transition, disaggregated by youth status and ethnoracial group; (2) assigned sex at birth, gender identity, and intersex status; (3) the frequency with which social, administrative, and medical transition options or treatments were taken; and (4) the timing of first awareness of trans status, social transition, and surgeries. Drawing on earlier theorizations that distinguished dimensions of sex and gender, our aim was to quantify this diversity in a trans population.

Method

Trans PULSE Project

The Trans PULSE Project is a community-based research study examining the impacts of social exclusion on the health of trans people in Ontario, Canada. The project began as a partnership between trans community members, community organizations, and academic researchers. Ethics approval was obtained from the University of Western Ontario and Wilfrid Laurier University.

Sampling

Respondent-driven sampling (RDS) was used to recruit participants (n = 433). RDS is a chain-referral sampling and analysis method developed for use with hidden populations (Heckathorn, 1997; Salganik & Heckathorn, 2004). . . .

. . . Individuals who indicated they were trans, following a broad definition, were eligible to participate; they were not required to have undertaken any social or medical transition, nor to have a desire to. In addition, they needed to be 16 years of age or older and live, work, or receive health care in Ontario.

Demographics

All measures were based on self-report. Demographic variables included gender spectrum, ethnoracial group, and youth status (age 16 to 24). Participants were asked to indicate their assigned sex at birth, and this information was used to categorize gender spectrum as MTF or FTM. Respondents did not necessarily identify as female or male, but could identify as genderqueer, bigender, or other fluid identities. Ethnoracial group was classified based on responses to multiple check-all-that-apply items. Those who indicated being First Nations, Inuit, or Métis (Canada's Aboriginal groups) or were of other Indigenous ethnicity were coded as Aboriginal, while those who reported only white background(s) were coded as non-Aboriginal whites. Participants were coded as non-Aboriginal racialized if they reported only non-white racialized ethnicities. . . . Those who reported both white and racialized ethnicities were categorized on a case-by-case basis, based on responses to these items and whether they indicated being perceived as persons of color.

Gender Identity

Participants selected gender identity labels from a prespecified list but could also select "Other" and write in their own terms. Those who endorsed only nonbinary gender identities (such as cross-dresser, bigender, genderqueer, or two-spirit) were coded as having a "fluid" gender identity. . . .

Social Transition and Gender Characteristics

Social gender variables included the frequency of daily living in one's felt gender, number of years living in one's felt gender, use of a new name or pronoun in daily life, completion of a legal name change, change of sex markers on government-issued identification, frequency perceived as trans by others, and desire to be perceived as trans by others. . . .

Medical Transition and Sex Characteristics

Medical transition and sex characteristics included having been diagnosed with a medically recognized intersex condition, self-described medical transition status (with respect to hormones and/or surgery), history of hormone use (whether or not prescribed them by a physician), and having undergone each specified transition-related surgery or medical procedure from a list provided (and, if so, the year in which the procedure took place).

Social and Medical Transition Status

Social gender and medical sex transition status (transition status) was classified as "'no transition," where participants were not using hormones and had not had surgery, and were either not living in their felt gender or were living part time but not using a new name or pronoun. Transition status was classified as "social only" if participants had not used hormones or had any surgical treatments but were living in their felt gender full time, or part time while using a new name and/or pronoun. Where participants indicated being in the process of medical transition and living in their felt gender full or part time, transition status was classified as "some social and some medical." Finally, those who self-reported a complete medical transition and who were living in their felt gender full time were classified as "complete" with respect to transition. . . .

Results

In total, 433 trans Ontarians participated in the study, including 205 male-to-female spectrum trans persons (MTFs) and 227 female-to-male spectrum trans persons (FTMs). Participants ranged in age from 16 to 77 years old. . . .

Social and Medical Transition Status

Information regarding the demographic characteristics of trans Ontarians has been published elsewhere (Bauer et al., 2012). Proportions of trans Ontarians who fell into each social and medical transition status group, disaggregated by youth status, gender spectrum, and ethnoracial group, are presented in Table 13.1. Overall, 30% (95% CI: 20–35) of trans Ontarians had not undertaken any gender/sex transition, and 23% (95% CI: 18–33) were living in their felt gender with no medical intervention. FTMs were 3.7 times (95% CI: 1.9–9.1) as likely as MTFs to have socially transitioned only, whereas MTFs were 1.7 times (95% CI: 1.1–3.1) as likely to have undergone some social and some medical transition. As compared to adults age 25 and older, youth (16–24 years) were 2.1 times (95% CI: 1.1–3.9) as likely to have socially transitioned only. There were no statistically significant differences in the proportions who indicated they had completed transition. There were no significant differences between ethnoracial groups with respect to social and medical transition status.

Gender Identity

Gender identity characteristics are described in Table 13.2. While most on the MTF spectrum identified as female or feminine, and most on the FTM spectrum as male or masculine, a sizable proportion (an estimated 27% of MTFs and 14% of FTMs, respectively) were fluid, meaning that they endorsed only nonbinary gender identities (e.g., genderqueer, bigender, two-spirit). In addition, a substantial minority of MTFs identified as cross-dressers (19%; 95% CI: 9–31), including 43% (95% CI: 21–66) of those who had not transitioned. Another 7% of trans Ontarians (95% CI: 4–10) indicated identifying with a gender other than those listed. Gender identities written in included androgyne, butch, human, post gender, work in progress, genderless and gender-creative. An estimated 63% of MTFs and 38% of FTMs had been aware that they were trans or gender incongruent for 20 years or more. The majority of both persons on both gender spectra first realized that they were trans before age 10.

Social Transition and Gender Characteristics

Table 13.3 includes social transition and gender characteristics. We estimated that approximately half of trans Ontarians were living full time in their felt gender. MTF-spectrum persons were 1.9 (95% CI: 1.0–4.6) times as likely to report not living in their felt gender, even part time, as compared to FTM-spectrum persons. While we did not collect information about plans to socially

transition, planning to medically transition likely implies plans to socially transition as well. Therefore, we note that a majority of nontransitioned FTMs, and a minority of nontransitioned MTFs, were planning to medically transition (75%, 95% CI: 58–95 versus 27%, 95% CI: 11–47). The majority . . . who were living in their felt gender had begun to do so within the past four years (59%, 95% CI: 50–69). However, approximately 10% had socially transitioned 15 years ago or more, and the number of years since social transition reported by participants ranged from 0 to 56 years.

Although most trans persons reported being perceived as trans by others occasionally, rarely, or never, MTFs were more likely to always or frequently be perceived as trans (18%, 95% CI: 11–28 versus 7%, 95% CI: 2–12). Gender spectrum differences with respect to the frequency with which trans persons were socially perceived as trans were especially notable among those who had begun medical transition. In this group, the variable can be interpreted as reflecting "passing" in their felt gender role. MTFs with some social and some medical transition were 7.0 times (95% CI: 1.9, upper limit not calculable) as likely to report always or very frequently being perceived as trans, as compared to FTMs of the same transition status. Similarly, those who had completed transition were about half as likely as completely transitioned FTMs to report never or very rarely being perceived as trans (RR = 0.52, 95% CI: 0.40–0.89). While 60% (95% CI: 50–73) of MTFs and 77% (95% CI: 66–87) of FTMs were using a new name and/or pronoun in daily life, only about one-third of trans persons had legally changed their names. An estimated 29% of MTFs and 24% of FTMs had changed the sex designation on at least one form of government-issued identity document.

Medical Transition and Sex Characteristics

Medical transition and sex characteristics are presented in Table 13.4. In all, 7% (95% CI: 2–13) of MTF-spectrum persons and 5% (95% CI: 1–10) of FTM-spectrum persons indicated having a medically recognized intersex condition. An estimated 46% (95% CI: 35–60) of MTFs

Table 13.1 Social Gender and Medical Sex Transition Status Among Trans[a] Ontarians

Transition Status	Total (n ¼ 433)		Gender Spectrum				Age				Ethnoracial Group					
			MTFs[b] (n ¼ 205)		FTMs[c] (n ¼ 227)		Adults (25 þ) (n ¼ 309)		Youth (16–24) (n ¼ 123)		Aboriginal (n ¼ 35)		Racialized[d] (n ¼ 62)		White[d] (n ¼ 333)	
	%	95% CI	%	95% CI	%	95% CI	%	95% CI	%	95% CI	%	95% CI	%	95% CI	%	95% CI
No transition	30	(20, 35)	37	(23, 46)	23	(12, 32)	33	(21, 40)	24	(12, 36)	23	(8, 48)	27	(6, 34)	31	(21, 38)
Social only	23	(18, 33)	10	(4, 18)[y]	35	(27, 50)[y]	18	(10, 28)	37	(25, 50)	11	(3, 23)	26	(12, 52)	22	(16, 32)
Some social, some medical	24	(18, 31)	31	(22, 43)[y]	18	(11, 23)[y]	24	(18, 32)	24	(12, 35)	54	(20, 74)	17	(7, 32)	24	(18, 32)
Complete[e]	23	(17, 31)	22	(14, 33)	24	(14, 34)	26	(18, 36)	15	(8, 28)	13	(3, 29)	30	(12, 53)	23	(16, 31)

[a]Transgender, transsexual, transitioned.
[b]Male-to-female or transfeminine spectrum.
[c]Female-to-male or transmasculine spectrum.
[d]Non-Aboriginal.
[e]Complete transition was self-defined and could include varying combinations of hormones and=or surgeries.
[y]Indicates statistically significant difference in proportions between MTFs and FTMs at the a ¼ .05 level.
Indicates statistically significant difference in proportions between youths and adults at the a ¼ .05 level.

Table 13.2.   Gender Identity Characteristics of Trans[a] Ontarians

Gender Characteristic	Male-to-Female Spectrum (MTF)										Female-to-Male Spectrum (FTM)									
	All MTFs (n = 205)		No Transition (n = 52)		Social Only (n = 22)		Some Social and Some Medical (n = 64)		Complete Social and Medical (n = 62)		All FTMs (n = 227)		No Transition (n = 27)		Social Only (n = 59)		Some Social and Some Medical (n = 55)		Complete Social and Medical (n = 84)	
	%	95% CI	%	95% CI	%	95% CI	%	95% CI	%	95% CI	%	95% CI	%	95% CI	%	95% CI	%	95% CI	%	95% CI
Gender identity																				
Female or feminine	73	(62, 84)	37	(19, 58)	67	(45, 90)	94	(86, 100)	100	(100, 100)	2	(0, 6)	9	(0, 22)	0	(0, 0)	0	(0, 0)	0	(0, 0)
Male or masculine	0	(0, 0)	—	—	—	—	—	—	—	—	84	(73, 92)	69	(59, 93)	71	(44, 91)	98	(95, 100)	99	(97, 100)
Fluid	27	(16, 38)	63	(42, 81)	33	(10, 55)	6	(0, 14)	0	(0, 0)	14	(7, 25)	22	(5, 34)	29	(9, 56)	1	(0, 5)	1	(0, 3)
Gender identity label																				
Girl or woman	41	(30, 52)[y]	7	(3, 12)	43	(10, 75)	59	(45, 81)	73	(56, 90)	7	(1, 13)[y]	18	(0, 21)	8	(0, 21)	0	(0, 0)	0	(0, 0)
Boy or man	8	(2, 14)[y]	20	(3, 34)	13	(0, 31)	2	(0, 7)	1	(—, —)	64	(54, 74)[y]	56	(30, 80)	58	(39, 80)	75	(56, 90)	67	(47, 82)
MTF or FTM	45	(36, 56)[y]	34	(16, 53)	32	(12, 63)	58	(35, 71)	51	(32, 76)	58	(47, 68)[y]	61	(32, 89)	47	(30, 67)	62	(40, 79)	64	(41, 81)
Trans girl=woman	37	(27, 48)[y]	18	(5, 32)	30	(9, 58)	52	(29, 68)	35	(20, 57)	0	(0, 0)[y]	—	—	—	—	—	—	—	—
Trans boy=man	0	(0, 0)[y]	—	—	—	—	—	—	—	—	52	(39, 61)[y]	28	(5, 54)	48	(25, 66)	73	(51, 86)	55	(32, 73)
T girl	16	(8, 24)[y]	13	(2, 25)	24	(5, 50)	28	(11, 43)	10	(2, 23)	0	(0, 0)[y]	—	—	—	—	—	—	—	—
Shemale	8	(2, 14)[y]	10	(0, 19)	0	(0, 0)	12	(2, 27)	4	(0, 12)	0	(0, 0)[y]	—	—	—	—	—	—	—	—
Feel like a girl sometimes	12	(6, 20)	22	(7, 37)	29	(2, 52)	11	(0, 20)	1	(0, 2)	7	(3, 14)	14	(0, 16)	5	(1, 10)	2	(0, 4)	3	(—, —)
Feel like a boy sometimes	2	(1, 5)	—	—	—	—	—	—	—	—	14	(8, 24)	18	(1, 29)	16	(5, 32)	5	(0, 16)	2	(0, 9)

Gender Characteristic	Male-to-Female Spectrum (MTF)										Female-to-Male Spectrum (FTM)									
	All MTFs (n = 205)		No Transition (n = 52)		Social Only (n = 22)		Some Social and Some Medical (n = 64)		Complete Social and Medical (n = 62)		All FTMs (n = 227)		No Transition (n = 27)		Social Only (n = 59)		Some Social and Some Medical (n = 55)		Complete Social and Medical (n = 84)	
	%	95% CI	%	95% CI	%	95% CI	%	95% CI	%	95% CI	%	95% CI	%	95% CI	%	95% CI	%	95% CI	%	95% CI
Cross-dresser	19	(9, 31)y	43	(21, 66)	16	(2, 33)	5	(0, 18)	0	(0,0)	5	(1, 9)y	—	—	—	—	—	—	—	—
Genderqueer	10	(5, 16)y	9	(2, 20)	28	(7, 56)	11	(1, 23)	9	(0, 22)	32	(22, 43)y	47	(23, 72)	41	(22, 63)	19	(6, 35)	8	(3, 16)
Two spirit	11	(4, 19)	18	(2, 34)	11	(2, 29)	11	(1, 22)	1	(0, 4)	5	(2, 10)	—	—	—	—	—	—	—	—
Bigender	7	(2, 13)	16	(3, 30)	22	(1, 50)	1	(0, 2)	0	(0, 0)	3	(1, 5)	—	—	—	—	—	—	—	—
Years since first aware of trans status																				
9 years ago or less	16	(8, 27)	20	(6, 42)	15	(0, 46)	16	(3, 31)	4	(0, 12)	24	(16, 36)	28	(8, 51)	35	(13, 56)	19	(3, 26)	11	(3, 23)
10–19 years ago	21	(12, 32)y	17	(4, 38)	5	(0, 28)	27	(12, 48)	10	(3, 27)	38	(26, 49)y	26	(5, 46)	38	(16, 58)	32	(18, 58)	35	(17, 57)
20–29 years ago	19	(13, 29)	4	(0, 11)	31	(12, 69)	20	(6, 42)	30	(11, 49)	15	(8, 23)	21	(13, 51)	11	(1, 30)	28	(8, 48)	22	(13, 44)
30 ½ years ago	44	(29, 55)y	59	(32, 77)	49	(5, 75)	38	(17, 53)	56	(31, 75)	23	(13, 34)y	25	(0, 32)	15	(4, 39)	21	(7, 43)	31	(7, 47)
Age first aware																				
9 years or under	60	(49, 70)	36	(15, 56)	52	(21, 85)	58	(41, 76)	88	(76, 95)	57	(44, 65)	55	(23, 79)	40	(20, 61)	61	(43, 79)	74	(59, 85)
10–14 years	23	(14, 32)	33	(13, 55)	11	(2, 33)	34	(17, 51)	7	(2, 15)	21	(14, 31)	17	(2, 39)	27	(11, 50)	23	(12, 48)	11	(5, 21)
15–19 years	10	(4, 18)	21	(3, 36)	5	(0, 18)	7	(0, 14)	3	(0, 10)	15	(9, 25)	19	(4, 50)	28	(9, 49)	9	(0, 16)	8	(2, 18)
20 years or older	7	(3, 14)	10	(2, 35)	33	(0, 63)	2	(0, 5)	2	(0, 8)	8	(3, 13)	9	(0, 23)	5	(0, 12)	7	(0, 8)	7	(0, 15)

Note. Proportions may not add up to 100% due to rounding and RDS estimation procedures for stratum-specific estimates. (—, —) confidence interval could not be calculated. Multiple response options were allowed; proportions will not add up to 100%.
a Transgender, transsexual, transitioned.
y Indicates statistically significant difference in proportions between MTFs and FTMs at the a = .05 level.

Table 13.3. Social Transition and Gender Characteristics of Trans[a] Ontarians

	Male-to-Female Spectrum (MTF)										Female-to-Male Spectrum (FTM)									
	All MTFs (n ¼ 205)		No Transition (n ¼ 52)		Social Only (n ¼ 22)		Some Social and Some Medical (n ¼ 64)		Complete Social and Medical (n ¼ 62)		All FTMs (n ¼ 227)		No Transition (n ¼ 27)		Social Only (n ¼ 59)		Some Social and Some Medical (n ¼ 55)		Complete Social and Medical (n ¼ 84)	
	%	95% CI	%	95% CI	%	95% CI	%	95% CI	%	95% CI	%	95% CI	%	95% CI	%	95% CI	%	95% CI	%	95% CI
Living in felt gender																				
Full time	46	(37, 59)	—	—	52	(29, 86)	64	(51, 87)	100	(—, —)	49	(38, 61)	—	—	42	(27, 64)	76	(56, 91)	100	(—, —)
Part time	24	(13, 30)	17	(5, 28)	48	(14, 71)	36	(13, 49)	—	—	35	(25, 47)	38	(11, 64)	58	(36, 73)	24	(9, 44)	—	—
Not at all	30	(21, 42)^y	83	(72, 95)	—	—	—	—	—	—	16	(7, 26)^y	62	(36, 89)	—	—	—	—	—	—
Years since social transition^b																				
1 year or less 2–	20	(8, 25)^y	—	—	43	(0, 72)	28	(8, 40)	7	(0, 15)	35	(25, 50)^y	—	—	60	(53, 85)	42	(18, 60)	4	(0, 10)
4 years	39	(27, 52)^y	—	—	17	(0, 49)	44	(29, 70)	36	(16, 52)	23	(16, 34)^y	—	—	11	(3, 22)	34	(21, 57)	32	(27, 62)
5–14 years 15	31	(20, 46)	—	—	30	(0, 59)	16	(5, 37)	52	(37, 73)	31	(20, 42)	—	—	18	(2, 28)	19	(3, 35)	54	(26, 63)
b years	10	(3, 26)	—	—	10	(0, 74)	13	(0, 33)	5	(2, 12)	12	(2, 16)	—	—	11	(1, 13)	5	(0, 13)	10	(0, 21)
Using new name and= or pronoun	60	(50, 73)^y	6	(1, 15)	89	(70, 100)	82	(67, 97)	100	(100, 100)	77	(66, 87)^y	14	(3, 32)	97	(93, 100)	99	(—, —)	99	(98, 100)
Perceived as trans																				
Always or very frequently	18	(11, 28)^y	6	(1, 17)	33	(0, 76)	28	(12, 48)	17	(5, 26)	7	(2, 12)^y	7	(0, 21)	7	(0, 19)	4	(0, 11)	3	(0, 7)

	Male-to-Female Spectrum (MTF)										Female-to-Male Spectrum (FTM)									
	All MTFs (n ¼ 205)		No Transition (n ¼ 52)		Social Only (n ¼ 22)		Some Social and Some Medical (n ¼ 64)		Complete Social and Medical (n ¼ 62)		All FTMs (n ¼ 227)		No Transition (n ¼ 27)		Social Only (n ¼ 59)		Some Social and Some Medical (n ¼ 55)		Complete Social and Medical (n ¼ 84)	
	%	95% CI	%	95% CI	%	95% CI	%	95% CI	%	95% CI	%	95% CI	%	95% CI	%	95% CI	%	95% CI	%	95% CI
Occasionally=rarely	41	(30, 51)	33	(16, 58)	49	(13, 80)	38	(20, 54)	45	(24, 68)	42	(33, 53)	18	(3, 32)	64	(49, 83)	62	(45, 82)	22	(13, 37)
Never or very rarely	42	(30, 52)	61	(34, 78)	8	(3, 46)	34	(17, 56)	39	(18, 63)	51	(40, 61)	75	(56, 94)	28	(12, 44)	34	(17, 51)	75	(59, 85)
Wants to be perceived as trans	18	(9, 26)	16	(3, 31)	12	(0, 22)	22	(5, 38)	1	(0, 2)	18	(10, 27)	27	(6, 56)	28	(12, 45)	12	(1, 27)	4	(1, 9)
Yes	54	(44, 66)	53	(25, 64)	52	(13, 85)	40	(28, 69)	79	(65, 92)	52	(41, 62)	30	(0, 47)	36	(19, 61)	48	(33, 71)	86	(76, 95)
No	29	(19, 40)	31	(22, 61)	36	(12, 76)	38	(13, 53)	21	(8, 34)	30	(21, 41)	44	(23, 77)	37	(15, 53)	40	(18, 55)	10	(2, 19)
Don't care	33	(23, 44)	0	(—, —)	5	(0, 15)	38	(21, 59)	86	(70, 98)	35	(25, 46)	4	(0, 14)	19	(7, 37)	56	(40, 80)	81	(59, 96)
Legal name change																				
Sex marker change																				
On all ID	11	(4, 19)	0	(0, 2)	0	(—, —)	2	(0, 5)	46	(15, 61)	10	(4, 17)	0	(—, —)	0	(0, 0)	9	(0, 34)	38	(20, 57)
On any ID	18	(10, 29)	0	(0,0)	34	(0, 73)	24	(8, 49)	33	(19, 62)	14	(8, 21)	0	(0, 0)	5	(0, 13)	18	(7, 34)	37	(18, 56)

Note. Proportions may not add up to 100% due to rounding and RDS estimation procedures for stratum-specific estimates; (—, —) confidence interval could not be calculated.

[a] Transgender, transsexual, transitioned.

[b] Among those who had begun to live in felt gender full or part time.

[c] Indicates statistically significant difference in proportions between MTFs and FTMs at the a ¼ .05 level.

Table 13.4. Medical Transition and Sex Characteristics of Trans[a] Ontarians

Medical Transition or Sex Characteristic	Male-to-Female Spectrum (MTF)										Female-to-Male Spectrum (FTM)									
	All MTFs (n = 205)		No Transition (n = 52)		Social Only (n = 22)		Some Social and Some Medical (n = 64)		Complete Social and Medical (n = 62)		All FTMs (n = 227)		No Transition (n = 27)		Social Only (n = 59)		Some Social and Some Medical (n = 55)		Complete Social and Medical (n = 84)	
	%	95% CI	%	95% CI	%	95% CI	%	95% CI	%	95% CI	%	95% CI	%	95% CI	%	95% CI	%	95% CI	%	95% CI
Medically recognized intersex condition[b]																				
Yes	7	(2, 13)	3	(0, 9)	9	(0, 31)	3	(0, 11)	18	(2, 31)	5	(1, 10)	9	(0, 32)	4	(0, 10)	10	(2, 19)	1	(0, 4)
Unsure	17	(10, 26)	4	(1, 9)	40	(3, 67)	37	(16, 57)	3	(0, 7)	14	(7, 21)	18	(4, 52)	12	(1, 26)	15	(0, 22)	7	(1, 18)
Self-described medical transition status[b]																				
Completed	25	(17, 39)	—	—	—	—	10	(—, —)	100	(—, —)	25	(15, 35)	—	—	—	—	9	(—, —)	100	(—, —)
In process	32	(24, 44)[y]	—	—	—	—	88	(76, 99)	—	—	16	(10, 22)[y]	—	—	—	—	92	(76, 100)	—	—
Planning but not begun	15	(7, 22)[y]	27	(11, 47)	58	(29, 86)	—	—	—	—	38	(28, 49)[y]	75	(58, 95)	59	(37, 78)	—	—	—	—
Not planning	3	(1, 5)	6	(2, 12)	20	(2, 46)	—	—	—	—	6	(1, 14)	12	(0, 29)	12	(1, 26)	—	—	—	—
Not sure	13	(5, 21)	33	(—, —)	21	(—, —)	—	—	—	—	6	(2, 15)	1	(—, —)	11	(—, —)	—	—	—	—

Medical Transition or Sex Characteristic	Male-to-Female Spectrum (MTF)										Female-to-Male Spectrum (FTM)									
	All MTFs (n ¼ 205)		No Transition (n ¼ 52)		Social Only (n ¼ 22)		Some Social and Some Medical (n ¼ 64)		Complete Social and Medical (n ¼ 62)		All FTMs (n ¼ 227)		No Transition (n ¼ 27)		Social Only (n ¼ 59)		Some Social and Some Medical (n ¼ 55)		Complete Social and Medical (n ¼ 84)	
	%	95% CI	%	95% CI	%	95% CI	%	95% CI	%	95% CI	%	95% CI	%	95% CI	%	95% CI	%	95% CI	%	95% CI
Concept does not apply	11	(3, 15)	28	(9, 46)	5	(0, 12)	—	—	—	—	9	(4, 14)	17	(2, 29)	16	(6, 24)	—	—	—	—
Hormone use																				
Current	46	(35, 60)	—	—	—	—	69	(49, 92)	95	(80, 100)	39	(28, 49)	—	—	—	—	84	(70, 98)	100	(98, 100)
Past	7	(3, 13)	—	—	—	—	3	(0, 9)	5	(0, 20)	1	(0, 3)y	—	—	—	—	6	(0, 15)	1	(0, 2)
Never	47	(34, 59)	—	—	—	—	28	(3, 48)	0	(0, 0)	60	(50, 72)	—	—	—	—	11	(1, 22)	0	(0, 0)

Note. Proportions may not add up to 100% due to rounding and RDS estimation procedures for stratum-specific estimates; (—, —) confidence interval could not be calculated.

aTransgender, transsexual, transitioned.

bHormonal and=or surgical treatments.

yIndicates statistically significant difference in proportions between MTFs and FTMs at the a ¼ .05 level.

and 39% (95% CI: 28–49) of FTMs were currently using hormones for medical transition.

Medical Treatments and Surgeries

Tables 13.5 and 13.6 report the proportions of MTF- and FTM-spectrum persons, respectively, who had undergone particular medical and surgical treatments for transition. Hair removal was the most common medical intervention for MTFs, reported by 56% (95% CI: 42–67) overall, including 18% (95% CI: 5–26) of those who had not otherwise begun social or medical transition and 38% (95% CI: 1–77) of those who had socially transitioned only (data not shown). About one-quarter of MTFs (24%, 95% CI: 14–35) and 30% of FTMs (95% CI: 21–40) had undergone any surgery. . . . However, not all had undergone genital surgeries or, in some cases, any surgery at all.

. . .

Discussion

Our findings demonstrate great heterogeneity of sex, gender, and transition status characteristics among trans Ontarians. This wide diversity belies the popular notion that a linear and rapid transition from one binary sex/gender to the other is the norm among trans persons (Serano, 2007). Only an estimated 23% of trans Ontarians had completed social and medical transition, and this did not necessarily include both hormones and surgery.

FTM-spectrum persons were more likely than MTF-spectrum persons, and youth (aged 16–24) were more likely than adults age 25 and over, to have socially transitioned without medical intervention. As FTMs had a younger age distribution than MTFs, gender-spectrum effects also represent age effects and vice versa. That FTMs were more likely to have socially transitioned without medical intervention reflects a cohort effect (60% of this group had begun to socially transition within the past year), and some of these FTMs may have since medically transitioned. However, FTMs were also more likely to identify as genderqueer (consistent with previous research; Factor and Rothblum, 2008; Kuper et al., 2012), and this group may include FTMs who have socially transitioned to a nonbinary gender and do not plan to medically transition.

That MTF-spectrum persons were less likely to be living in their felt gender, and were less likely to socially transition without medical intervention, may be shaped by the heightened levels of transphobia faced by MTFs (Marcellin, Scheim,

Table 13.5. Transition-Related Procedures: Male-to-Female Spectrum Trans[a] Ontarians

Procedure	All MTFs (*n* ¼ 205)		Some Social and Some Medical (*n* ¼ 64)		Complete Social and Medical (*n* ¼ 62)	
	%	95% CI	%	95% CI	%	95% CI
Hair removal	56	(42, 67)	75	(61, 93)	89	(75, 98)
Any surgery[b]	24	(14, 35)	13	(3, 26)[y]	72	(46, 86)
Vocal cord surgery	3	(0, 9)	0	(0, 0)	13	(0, 27)
Facial surgery	4	(1, 8)	3	(0, 10)	11	(1, 23)
Adam's apple shave	10	(2, 18)	2	(0, 0)	30	(4, 51)
Hair transplant	2	(0, 3)	1	(0, 4)	3	(0, 9)
Breast augmentation	12	(4, 22)	3	(0, 11)	43	(15, 62)
Orchiectomy	21	(11, 33)	10	(0, 27)	67	(41, 85)
Vaginoplasty	15	(7, 27)	0	(0, 0)	59	(32, 80)

[a]Transgender, transsexual, transitioned.
[b]Reported any transition-related surgical procedure (not including hair removal).
[y]Indicates statistically significant difference in proportions between MTFs and FTMs at the a ¼ .05 level.

Table 13.6. Transition-Related Procedures: Female-to-Male Spectrum Trans[a] Ontarians

Procedure	All FTMs (n ¼ 227)		Some Social and Some Medical (n ¼ 55)		Complete Social and Medical (n ¼ 84)	
	%	95% CI	%	95% CI	%	95% CI
Any surgery[b]	30	(21, 40)	38	(20, 60)[y]	88	(72, 96)
Breast reduction	5	(1, 8)	6	(1, 18)	5	(1, 12)
Mastectomy	25	(17, 36)	31	(14, 52)	83	(70, 94)
Hysterectomy	13	(6, 19)	20	(5, 40)	36	(17, 56)
Oophorectomy	12	(6, 19)	19	(3, 40)	35	(16, 55)
Metoidioplasty[c]	—	—	—	—	—	—
Phalloplasty	0.4	(0, 1)	0	(0, 0)	1	(0, 4)

[a]Transgender, transsexual, transitioned.
[b]Reported any transition-related surgical procedure.
[c]Unable to calculate due to high homophily: 1% of all FTM participants (unweighted) and 4% of FTM participants who had completed social and medical transition (unweighted) reported undergoing metoidioplasty.
[y]Indicates statistically significant difference in proportions between MTFs and FTMs at the a ¼ .05 level.

Bauer, & Redman, 2013). Transmisogyny, the interaction of transphobia with sexism (Serano, 2007), may make it more difficult for MTF-spectrum people to transition, particularly without hormones and/or surgery. In addition, variation in the need or desire to transition may contribute to the higher proportion of MTFs who had not transitioned, as we estimated that the majority (63%; 95% CI: 42–81) of nontransitioned MTFs had nonbinary gender identities (predominantly cross-dresser) and were less likely to report plans to transition. Care should be taken in interpreting these cross-sectional results; current gender identities and transition plans may represent lifelong identities and plans or an evolving stage in a trajectory of identity discovery, coming out, and transition. . . .

It is clear that diversity in sex characteristics among trans persons abounds, at all states of transition. . . . Some trans persons had begun to transition many years ago but still needed access to additional medical transition procedures: an estimated 13% of MTFs and 5% of FTMs who had undergone some social and some medical transition had begun their social transition 15 years ago or more. In addition, while current or past hormone use was universal among those who had completed medical transition, surgery was not. Contrary to the assumption that medical transition begins with hormones, some of those who had undergone some social and some medical transition had surgically but not hormonally transitioned.

Few trans Ontarians in 2009–2010 had undergone genital surgery. Such surgeries were particularly rare among FTM-spectrum trans people, consistent with findings from other regions (Grant et al., 2011; Newfield et al., 2006) and qualitative reports that many FTMs do not seek or desire genital surgery (Schilt & Waszkiewicz, 2006). These data primarily reflect the experiences of trans persons who transitioned, and had surgery, in a context where these procedures were not publicly funded; 78% of reported surgeries occurred during the decade where transition-related surgeries were not covered by the province's universal health plan, and some who planned to medically transition had undoubtedly not accessed surgeries they would otherwise have had during this time.

A total of 6% of trans Ontarians reported having a medically recognized intersex condition (Coleman, Bauer, et al., 2011), and a high proportion reported that they were unsure. The same proportion of NTDS respondents identified as intersex (Grant et al., 2011). Though the prevalence of gender variance among intersex persons is unknown, clinical data suggest that intersex persons are more likely than nonintersex persons to experience gender dysphoria and to transition, with much variation between intersex conditions (Meyer-Bahlburg, 2009; Yang, Baskin, & DiSandro, 2010). That such a high proportion of trans Ontarians reported having intersex conditions or were unsure may reflect increased incidence of gender transition among intersex persons. However, these results could also be attributed to increased scrutiny and screening for potential intersex conditions as part of the medical transition process, or to the belief of some trans people that trans status is a form of intersex (Spurgas, 2009). As most intersex individuals do not identify as trans or gender nonconforming, intersex advocates caution against conflation of intersex and trans issues (Feder, 2009). . . .

Our findings of great sex and gender heterogeneity within and across transition status groups underscore the need for more precise and valid measurement of sex and gender-related variables in health and sexuality research (Bauer, 2012). . . .

Approaches to clinical care of trans people in Canada and the United States are increasingly de-emphasizing the psychiatric diagnosis of gender identity disorder (now gender dysphoria; American Psychiatric Association, 2013), moving from a "disease-based" to an "identity-based" model of trans health (Bockting & Coleman, 2007), and recognizing a wider range of gender nonconformity and, consequently, of transition trajectories (Fee, Brown, & Laylor, 2003; Coleman, Bockting, et al., 2011). Our results provide empirical evidence of the diversity increasingly observed by clinicians. . . .

Social policies have been slow to respond to the heterogeneity within trans populations. In recent years, some countries have made great advances in adapting policies and practices to accommodate those who transition gender and/or sex. For instance, a requirement that one must have transition-related surgery in order to change one's sex designation on an Ontario birth certificate was eliminated in 2012. Similar restrictions have been lifted in Argentina, Australia, Taiwan, and the United Kingdom. However, less attention has been paid to the needs of nontransitioning, "partially" transitioning, and gender-nonconforming persons. In Ontario, to change the sex designation on identification, individuals must certify that they "are living full-time in that gender identity and intend to maintain it" (Ontario Ministry of Health and Long-Term Care, 2012). Trans persons with nonbinary identities, or who are in process of transition, or who are not perceived in their felt gender despite transitioning may be better served by policies that eliminate gender and sex markers, wherever possible. We question whether there is any need for sex/gender designation on Canadian identification, as sex/gender is rarely used for identity verification and serves no legal purpose since laws based on sex have been equalized (e.g., marriage, property, inheritance, voting). Similar issues arise with gender and sex fields in computerized record systems, which typically do not have simple mechanisms for changing gender and sex markers. This can lead to problems with health records, insurance, and billing; outing in professional and education settings; and denial of commercial services due to suspicion of fraud. These problems could be partially remedied through introduction of options to allow for changes to gender and sex markers in these systems, and by delinking other processes (e.g., ordering of medical tests or procedures) from gender fields (Deutsch et al., 2013). A more comprehensive solution would be to eliminate these markers wherever they are not necessary.

Requiring trans individuals to have taken hormones or undergone transition-related surgeries, or to have changed their sex designation, to access the gender-segregated institution or facility most appropriate to their felt gender will clearly exclude the majority of trans Ontarians. However, even more liberal policies that respect gender self-identification may not address the needs of the substantial proportion of trans persons who do not identify as primarily male or female, or who live part time in their felt gender role. Optional gender-neutral facilities, including mixed-gender and single room options, are crucial to ensure the safety and dignity of all trans persons.
. . .

References

American Psychiatric Association. (2013). *Diagnostic and statistical manual of mental disorders* (5th ed.). Arlington, Va: American Psychiatric Publishing.

Bauer, G. R. (2012). Making sure everyone counts: Considerations for inclusion, identification, and analysis of transgender and transsexual participants in health surveys. In Institute of Gender & Health Canadian Institutes of Health Research (Ed.), *What a difference sex and gender make* (pp. 59–67). Vancouver, Canada: Institute of Gender and Health, Canadian Institutes of Health Research.

Bauer, G. R., Travers, R., Scanlon, K., & Coleman, T. (2012). High heterogeneity of HIV-related sexual risk among transgender people in Ontario, Canada: A province-wide respondent-driven sampling survey. *BMC Public Health*, 12, 292. doi:10.1186/1471-2458-12-292

Bockting, W. O. (2008). Psychotherapy and the real-life experience: From gender dichotomy to gender diversity. *Sexologies*, 17, 211–24. doi:10.1016/j.sexol.2008.08.001

Bockting, W. O., & Coleman, E. (2007). Developmental stages of the transgender coming out process: Toward an integrated identity. In R. Ettner, S. Monstrey, & E. Eyler (Eds.), *Principles of transgender medicine and surgery* (pp. 185–208). Binghamton, NY: Haworth Press.

Coleman, E., Bockting, W., Botzer, M., Cohen-Kettenis, P., DeCuypere, G., Feldman, J., . . . Zucker, K. (2011). Standards of care for the health of transsexual, transgender, and gendernonconforming people, version 7. *International Journal of Transgenderism*, 13, 165–232. doi:10.1080/15532739.2011.700873

Coleman, T., Bauer, G. R., Scanlon, K., Travers, R., Kaay, M., & Francino, M. (2011, November 30). Challenging the binary: Gender characteristics of trans Ontarians. *Trans PULSE E-Bulletin*, 2(2). Retrieved from http://transpulseproject.ca/wp-content/uploads/2011/12/E4English.pdf

Conron, K. J., Scott, G., Stowell, G. S., & Landers, S. J. (2012). Transgender health in Massachusetts: Results from a household probability sample of adults. *American Journal of Public Health*, 102, 118–22. doi:10.2105/AJPH.2011.300315

Deutsch, M. B., Green, J., Keatley, J., Mayer, G., Hastings, J., & Hall, A. M. (2013). Electronic medical records and the transgender patient: Recommendations from the World Professional Association for Transgender Health EMR Working Group. *Journal of the American Medical Informatics Association*, 20, 700–703. doi:10.1136/amiajnl-2012-001472

Factor, R. J., & Rothblum, E. (2008). Exploring gender identity and community among three groups of transgender individuals in the United States: MTFs, FTMs, and genderqueers. *Health Sociology Review*, 17, 235–53. doi:10.5172/hesr.451.17.3.235

Feder, E. K. (2009). Imperatives of normality: From "intersex" to "disorders of sex development." *GLQ: A Journal of Lesbian and Gay Studies*, 15, 225–47. doi:10.1215/10642684-2008-135

Fee, E., Brown, T. M., & Laylor, J. (2003). One size does not fit all in the transgender community. *American Journal of Public Health*, 93, 899. doi:10.2105/AJPH.93.6.899

Grant, J. M., Mottet, L. A., Tanis, J., Harrison, J., Herman, J. L., & Keisling, M. (2011). *Injustice at every turn: A report of the National Transgender Discrimination Survey*. Washington, DC: National Center for Transgender Equality and National Gay and Lesbian Task Force.

Hansbury, G. (2005). The middle men: An introduction to the transmasculine identities. *Studies in Gender and Sexuality*, 6, 241–64. doi:10.1080/15240650609349276

Harrison, J., Grant, J. M., & Herman, J. L. (2011). A gender not listed here: Genderqueers, gender rebels, and otherwise in the National Transgender Discrimination Survey. *LGBTQ Policy Journal at the Harvard Kennedy School*, 2, 13–24.

Heckathorn, D. D. (1997). Respondent-driven sampling: A new approach to the study of hidden populations. *Social Problems*, 44, 174–99. doi:10.2307/3096941

Johnson, J. L., Greaves, L., & Repta, R. (2009). Better science with sex and gender: Facilitating the use of a sex and gender-based analysis in health research. *International Journal for Equity in Health*, 8, 14. doi:10.1186/1475-9276-8-14

Krieger, N. (2003). Genders, sexes, and health: What are the connections—And why does it matter? *International Journal of Epidemiology*, 32, 652–57. doi:10.1093/ije/dyg156

Kuper, L. E., Nussbaum, R., & Mustanski, B. (2012). Exploring the diversity of gender and sexual orientation identities in an online sample of transgender individuals. *Journal of Sex Research*, 49, 244–54. doi:10.1080/00224499.2011.596954

Lombardi, E. (2009). Varieties of transgender/transsexual lives and their relationship with transphobia. *Journal of Homosexuality*, 56, 977–92. doi:10.1080/00918360903275393

Marcellin, R. L., Scheim, A., Bauer, G., & Redman, N. (2013, March 7). Experiences of transphobia among trans Ontarians. *Trans PULSE E-Bulletin*, 3(2). Retrieved from http://transpulseproject.ca/wp-content/uploads/2013/03/Transphobia-E-Bulletin-6-vFinal-English.pdf

Melendez, R., Bonem, L., & Sember, R. (2006). On bodies and research: Transgender issues in health and HIV research articles. *Sexuality Research and Social Policy*, 3, 21–38. doi:10.1525/srsp.2006.3.4.21

Meyer-Bahlburg, H. F. L. (2009). Variants of gender differentiation in somatic disorders of sex development: Recommendations for Version 7 of the World Professional Association for Transgender Health's Standards of Care. *International Journal of Transgenderism*, 11, 226–37. doi:10.1080/15532730903439476

Newfield, E., Hart, S., Dibble, S., & Kohler, L. (2006). Female-to-male transgender quality of life. *Quality of Life Research*, 15, 1447–57. doi:10.1007/s11136-006-0002-3

Ontario Ministry of Health, & Long-Term Care. (2012). Ontario Health Insurance Plan questions and answers. Retrieved from http://www.health.gov.on.ca/en/public/programs/ohip/ohipfaq_mn.aspx

Rotondi, N. K., Bauer, G. R., Travers, R., Travers, A., Scanlon, K., & Kaay, M. (2011). Depression in male-to-female transgender Ontarians. *Canadian Journal of Community Mental Health*, 30, 113–33.

Salganik, M. J., & Heckathorn, D. D. (2004). Sampling and estimation in hidden populations using respondent-driven sampling. *Sociological Methodology*, 34, 193–240. doi:10.1111/j.0081-1750.2004.00152.x

Schilt, K., & Waszkiewicz, E. (2006, August). I feel so much more in my body: Challenging the significance of the penis in transsexual men's bodies. Paper presented at the annual meeting of the American Sociological Association, Montreal, Quebec, Canada.

Serano, J. (2007). *Whipping girl: A transsexual woman on sexism and the scapegoating of femininity*. Berkeley, Calif: Seal Press.

Spurgas, A. K. (2009). (Un)Queering identity: The biosocial production of intersex/DSD. In M. Holmes (Ed.), *Critical intersex* (pp. 97–122). Surrey, UK: Ashgate.

Tate, C. C., Ledbetter, J. N., & Youssef, C. P. (2013). A two-question method for assessing gender categories in the social and medical sciences. *Journal of Sex Research*, 50, 767–76. doi:10.1080/00224499.2012.690110

Tolman, D. L., & Diamond, L. M. (2001). Desegregating sexuality research: Cultural and biological perspectives on gender and desire. *Annual Review of Sex Research*, 12, 33–74. doi:10.1080/10532528.2001.10559793

Yang, J. H., Baskin, L. S., & DiSandro, M. (2010). Gender identity in disorders of sex development: Review article. *Urology*, 75, 153–59. doi:10.1016/j.urology.2009.07.1286

Part IV
Gendered Sexualities

Love and sex and marriage and dating and partnerships . . . living our intimate lives, including our sexual lives, can be a wonderfully positive experience or can be fraught with disaster. And gender is almost always at work here. Some of the oldest clichés about gender arise from love, romance, and dating—for example, the idea that "opposites attract" or that "men are from Mars, women are from Venus."

But gender is not necessarily destiny when it comes to intimacy. In heterosexual relationships, we find a mixed pattern of convergence and divergence between men and women in terms of the way they experience love and sex. As Tsui and Nicoladis demonstrate in their study of first intercourse experiences among Canadian university students, men and women have much more similar experiences of first intercourse than the men-are-from-Mars-women-are-from-Venus model of gender difference might lead us to expect.

Beres develops this theme further, suggesting that men and women use similar presumptions and discourses to shape their experience of heterosexual casual sex—although, as Beres argues, these discourses tend to position men as active sexual pursuers and women as more passive participants in sexual activities. Nonetheless, some women manage to find ways to meet their own sexual desires, even without overtly challenging dominant ways of thinking about sex.

The subjects of Chenier's research—lesbian couples of past decades—are also women who sought to carve out their own ways of partnering in a heterosexist era. Chenier examines the enduring appeal of the wedding—while some might see it as a manifestation of patriarchal beliefs about purity and women as property, Chenier shows that the symbolic meaning of a commitment ritual isn't just reducible to the reinforcement of gender binaries. The women she studied integrated lesbian weddings into their same-gender-focused lives for decades past.

Scheim and his co-authors also examine what happens when sexuality is de-linked from heterosexist attitudes about gender, and indeed de-linked from rigid gender binaries. They study the sexual histories of transgender men who seek sexual partners among other men and who have to come up with ways to present their gendered selves within the various "sexual fields" in which gay or bisexual men seek partners.

Finally, Roth and Sanders use the story of Jennifer Murphy as a cautionary tale about what can happen when gendered double standards about sexuality are allowed to dominate public discourse. They demonstrate, similar to Beres, that men and women are held to different sexual standards when it comes to having multiple partners or recreational sex, and shows how these double standards were used, in conjunction with stereotypes about class, to frame Murphy as a woman whose sexuality put her outside the protection of the law.

Questions for Critical Thought

1. Is it possible to have sexuality without gender? Can physical attraction or desire exist in the absence of gender?

2. Sexual relationships are intensely intimate, individualized, and personal, yet they exist within a gender-differentiated world. How does gender influence the ways that people experience sexual intimacy and closeness?

3. Why is virginity very important to some people and not so important to others? What are some of the different cultural and personal significances of virginity?

4. Beres identifies several gendered discourses that her participants invoked when they talked about their casual sex experiences. Have you seen these discourses or others presented elsewhere? Which ones appear in your experience to be most powerful?

5. In your experience, or in the experiences of people you know, are long-term, intimate relationships gendered differently than short-term, casual relationships?

6. Some theorists have criticized the idea of gender "scripts" as being too restrictive and standardized for the way that people actually act. This is why Beres uses the vocabulary of sexual "discourses" rather than roles or scripts, for instance. How "scripted" do you think sexuality is, in terms of gender?

7. What do you think should be covered in a "sex education" curriculum for young people who are not yet sexually active?

8. How does an individual's gender influence the way they express their sexuality?

Chapter 14

Overview

Lily Tsui and Elena Nicoladis provide a detailed empirical account of how virginity and sexual experience are gendered. When undergraduates in a psychology class are asked about their experiences of first intercourse, men's and women's accounts diverge in some respects and converge in others. Men and women appear to be similar in their accounts of their relationship status and the emotional impact of first intercourse. However, women were significantly more likely to report they believed they were in love with their partner at the time they had sex and that their male partner took the initiative leading up to sex. These accounts appear to hew quite closely to the old stereotypes of female sexuality—built on a foundation of romantic love and awakened by the actions of men.

Tsui and Nicoladis neither confirm nor reject the Mars-and-Venus way of looking at gender but suggest that what is emerging among younger generations in Canada is a mixed picture: When it comes to significant life experiences like having sex for the first time, men and women have some things in common, but other things remain different. Their sample is limited to heterosexual intercourse, raising the question of how men and women would report their sexual experiences if they were being asked about same-sex sexuality. How much of the gender differences we see here might be the result of interactions between men and women, which are intrinsic to heterosexuality, and how much might be apparent even if the people having sex were of the same gender?

Losing It

Similarities and Differences in First Intercourse Experiences of Men and Women

Lily Tsui and Elena Nicoladis[1]

Introduction

Historically, a woman's virginity was crucial to marriage in terms of both honour and value; women who were found not to be virgins on their wedding night (often determined by the presence of blood at first intercourse) were seen as worthless in many cultures. In contrast, "proof" of male virginity is unavailable physically and less important culturally. Such differences in how virginity has been perceived in society have created

an environment in which men and women may have different perceptions of first intercourse and its meanings.

Quantitative studies have demonstrated gender differences in both attitudes toward and actual experience of first intercourse. For example, Carpenter (2001) found that women were twice as likely as men to think of their virginity as a gift to a future partner (61 per cent versus 36 per cent), while men were three times more likely than women to view their virginity as a stigma (57 per cent versus 21 per cent). Darling, Davidson, and Passarello (1992) found that a greater percentage of men than women perceived their first intercourse to be physiologically satisfying (81 per cent

Tsui, Lily and Elena Nicoladis, "Losing It: Similarities and Differences in First Intercourse Experiences of Men and Women." Reprinted with permission from *The Canadian Journal of Human Sexuality*. Published by the Sex Information and Education Council of Canada.

versus 28 per cent) and psychologically satisfying (67 per cent versus 28 per cent).

Qualitative studies based on feminist analyses of power differences between men and women have suggested possible explanations for such findings. For example, young adults' accounts of first sexual intercourse reveal that men gain an affirmation of manhood through first intercourse. It is thus primarily a young man's moment that marks his "coming of age" or his entry into manhood (Holland, Ramazanoglu, Sharpe, and Thomson, 2000). However, the dependence on women for this validation of men has taken on multiple social meanings, many of which are viewed by feminist thinkers as embedded in a patriarchal culture.

Holland et al. (2000) found that young men's accounts of first intercourse were mostly concerned with their own performance, orgasm, and sense of having reached a landmark. Their partners' pleasure or orgasm was seen as "icing on the cake." The problem with young men having this construction of first intercourse is that it leaves young women to cope with first intercourse experiences that may fail to meet their own expectations to affirm feelings of love and romance (Holland et al., 2000). In this view, sex differences in first intercourse experiences have their basis in different perceptions of its meaning and in constructions of sexuality.

Burr (2001) argues that the contemporary construction of men's sexuality as "active, dynamic, powerful, and, potentially uncontrollable," also portrays women's sexuality as essentially passive. In this construction, sex for women is not about active participation but about something that is received (Darling et al., 1992). Women may thus be seen as dependent on men for introducing them to the physical pleasure aspects of sexual activities because conventional femininity demands that a woman appear to be sexually unknowing, to desire not just sex but a relationship, to let sex "happen" without requesting it, to trust, to love, and to make men happy (Holland et al., 2000). Traditional dating scenarios reinforced this perspective in that the woman was expected to wait for the man to ask her out and the man was expected to handle details of cost, transportation, and activity (Allgeir and Royster, 1991).

Social discourses around sexuality, and particularly female sexuality, reflect and influence personal and educational perspectives on first intercourse. Fine (1997) identifies three such discourses. The first discourse, sexuality as violence, instills fear of sex by focusing on abuse, incest, and other negative outcomes of sexual activity. The second discourse, sexuality as victimization, identifies females as subject to the pressuring tendencies of male sexuality and focuses attention on the risk of women "being used" or coerced and thus on ways to avoid the physical, social, and emotional risks of sexual intimacy. Messages related to unintended pregnancy and sexually transmitted infections (STIs) may reinforce notions of risk and are used by some to pressure for classroom priority on strategies to avoid sex, "saying no," and "abstinence only" approaches to sexuality education. In this context, Fine's third discourse, sexuality as individual morality, would value women's choice about sexuality as long as the choice is premarital abstinence. Such discourses, Fine suggests, lead to a construction of sexuality where the male is in search of desire and the female is in search of protection. Largely absent from public sexual education is a fourth discourse, sexuality as desire. Fine notes that

> The naming of desire, pleasure, or sexual entitlement, particularly for females, barely exists in the formal agenda of public schooling on sexuality. . . . A genuine discourse of desire would invite adolescents to explore what feels good and bad, desirable and undesirable, grounded in experiences, needs, and limits. (Fine, 1997)

The Present Study

Given the questions implicit in these background observations, the present study sought to identify university students' perspectives on various aspects of their first experience of consensual heterosexual sexual intercourse. The questionnaire designed for this purpose dealt with precursors to, experience of, and subsequent feelings about first intercourse. Students who had not had intercourse answered selected questions based on their expectations.

Apart from the anticipation arising from the literature review that men's and women's experiences would differ and that men's would be more positive, we refrained from making more specific hypotheses. This reticence was due to our perception that the literature had given a clearer picture of what to ask than what to expect. We consider the study to be a descriptive and exploratory step in determining if and how women's and men's experiences of first intercourse differ and to what extent the findings reflect the various constructions of sexuality portrayed in the literature.

Method

Questionnaire

Respondents who had experienced first intercourse answered questions about the context of their first intercourse, preparations prior to intercourse, actual circumstances of first intercourse, and feelings afterward. Those who had not experienced consensual first intercourse were asked about their expectations of first intercourse including preparation, anticipation of pain, orgasm, etc. The questionnaire is presented in Appendix A.

Definitions

This study defined first intercourse as the first time the person had consensual heterosexual intercourse. The four participants whose first experience of sexual intercourse happened in the context of a sexual assault therefore did not provide answers about their first intercourse based on this experience but rather on their first consensual experience, if that had occurred. If they had not had consensual intercourse, their responses were based on their expectations regarding first intercourse, as were those of others who had not had consensual intercourse.

Participants

Among the 358 introductory psychology undergraduate students who participated (114 men,

244 women), the mean age was 19.4 years (SD = 2.32, range 17–38). Participants who had not had intercourse were slightly but significantly younger on average than those who had (19.0 versus 19.73 years respectively) $t(356) = 2.99$; $p =.002$. Most participants were born in Canada (79 per cent). Grouping of free-response items on cultural background yielded six categories: "Canadian" (30 per cent); "European" (39 per cent); "Asian" (18 per cent); "Middle Eastern" (4 per cent); and "Other" (10 per cent). Religious affiliation grouped into five categories: "Christian (not Catholic)" (33 per cent); "Catholic" (31 per cent); "Hindu/Sikh/Muslim" (9 per cent); "Buddhist /Taoist" (3 per cent); and "No religious affiliation" (25 per cent).

Based on the definition of first intercourse as the first experience of consensual sexual intercourse, 55.6 per cent ($n = 199$) of the sample had experienced first intercourse and 44.4 per cent ($n = 159$) had not. Men and women did not differ in this respect (44.7 per cent of men and 44.3 per cent of women had not had first intercourse).

Results

Contextual Variables of First Intercourse

Age at First Intercourse

All but one participant could recall their age at first intercourse. Mean age for first intercourse was 17.13 years (SD = 1.65; range 13–28) with no significant difference between the sexes (17.04 for women and 17.31 for men).

Partner's Age at Participant's First Intercourse

On average, women had first intercourse with partners who were significantly older than they were (mean of 17.04 years for women and 18.41 years for their partners) ($t(132) = -6.01$, $p <.001$, $d = -1.38$) whereas mean age at first intercourse for men (17.31 years) did not differ from that of their partners (17.6 years).

Relationship to Partner at Time of First Intercourse

The great majority of both women and men (84 per cent overall) said they were in a couple/romantic relationship with their first intercourse partner while 16 per cent were not in a romantic relationship. There was no significant sex difference in relationship status at first intercourse.

Duration of Relationship with Partner prior to First Intercourse

Among the 84 per cent of participants who were in a relationship at the time of first intercourse, mean relationship duration was 7.4 months (SD = 7.29 months, range = less than one month to 36 months) with men approaching a significantly greater likelihood of having shorter duration than women (5.74 months for men, 8.14 months for women) ($t(163) = 1.97$, $p =.051$, $d = -2.40$). On average, all participants had known their partner for 31 months (SD = 39.5; range was less than one month to 2 years) with no significant difference between the sexes in this respect.

Intercourse Experience of Participant's First Partner

Just over half of the participants reported that they were the first person with whom their partner had intercourse (52.3 per cent). The sexes did not differ in this respect.

Perceptions of Being in Love at First Intercourse and in Hindsight

Women were significantly more likely than men to report that they were in love with their partner at the time of first intercourse (63 per cent and 43 per cent respectively) ($\chi^2(2, N = 199) = 7.78$, $p =.02$). This difference was not present in hindsight (47 per cent and 41 per cent respectively) with men appearing to move from "unsure" to "no" and women from "yes" to "no."

Decision to Have Intercourse

Participants were asked whether the decision to have first intercourse was mutual or whether one partner took the lead. While 57 per cent of men and 61 per cent of women said the decision was mutual, Chi-squared analysis showed a significant effect of gender on the decision to have first intercourse. In cases where women did not report a mutual decision, 79 per cent assigned the initiative to their partner and 21 per cent to themselves; for men, 42 per cent assigned the initiative to their partners, and 42 per cent to themselves. Since these students were not reporting on first intercourse with other respondents, it is not possible to determine whether these sex differences in perception of who initiated would also be seen within couples.

Discussions prior to First Intercourse

Among the six pre-intercourse discussion items listed in Table 14.1, participants were most likely to have discussed having sexual intercourse and condom use (63–73 per cent), somewhat less likely to have discussed other methods of birth control (48–58 per cent), and most unlikely to have discussed sexually transmitted infections, possible outcomes of pregnancy, and emotional implications of intercourse for them (32–40 per cent). The sexes did not differ significantly on any of these items (see Table 14.1).

Circumstances Associated with First Intercourse

Nine items in Table 14.1 assessed different aspects of the participants' actual first intercourse experience. Although less than half of respondents indicated that first intercourse had occurred when they expected it to (41 per cent of males, 46 per cent of females), condom use at first intercourse was common (75–80 per cent). Alcohol use by self or partner was less common (14–21 per cent), and drug use by self or partner was rare (0–2 per cent). The sexes did not differ on any of these items (see Table 14.1).

Women were much more likely than men to report pain at first intercourse (52 per cent versus 5 per cent), much less likely than men to report orgasm at first intercourse (12 per cent versus 76 per cent), and more likely to report partner orgasm than were men (73 per cent versus 32 per cent). Each of these differences was statistically significant (see Table 14.1). We did not ask about prior orgasm history of women in our sample but note that our female participants appear less likely to have had orgasm at first intercourse (12 per cent) than

Table 14.1 Participants' "Yes" Responses to Questions about Prior Discussion, Circumstances of, and Follow-Up to First Intercourse (%)

	Men (n = 63)	Women (n = 136)	$\chi^2(1, 199)$
Pre-Intercourse Discussion			
Having intercourse	76	74	ns
Condom use	63	73	ns
Other methods of birth control	58	48	ns
Sexually transmitted infection	33	32	ns
Outcomes if pregnancy were to occur	33	37	ns
Emotional implications	33	40	ns
Circumstances Associated with First Intercourse			
Did intercourse occur when expected?	41	46	ns
Was a condom used?	75	80	ns
Were you drinking?	19	21	ns
Was your partner drinking?	14	18	ns
Were you using any drugs?	0	0	ns
Was your partner using any drugs?	2	2	ns
Was first intercourse painful?	5	52	41.49*
Did you have an orgasm?	76	12	81.91*
Did your partner have an orgasm?	32	73	30.18*
Feelings/Outcomes Subsequent to First Intercourse			
Physical satisfaction	62	35	12.39*
Emotional satisfaction	56	54	ns
Sex again with same partner?	87	89	ns
Stayed a couple or became a couple after?	83	86	ns
Pregnancy occur?	0	0	—

*p <.001
ns indicates not significant

was reported by our male respondents of their first intercourse partners (32 per cent; see Table 14.1).

Feelings and Outcomes after First Intercourse

Men were significantly more likely than women to report feeling physically satisfied after first intercourse (62 per cent versus 35 per cent). However, the sexes did not differ on reports of emotional satisfaction (56 per cent and 54 per cent), having

had sex again with the same partner (87 per cent and 89 per cent), or staying as or becoming a couple after first intercourse (83 per cent and 86 per cent). None of the respondents reported pregnancy as a consequence of first intercourse. Men and women were similar in the extent to which they reported no regrets about first intercourse (76 per cent and 72 per cent) and in their perception that they had first intercourse at "the right age" (63 per cent and 65 per cent; see Table 14.1).

Overall Assessment of First Intercourse Experience

Participants were asked to give an overall "rating" of their first intercourse experience based on six options. There was no statistically significant sex difference in these overall assessments with 72 per cent of men and 61 per cent of women rating the experience as either perfect, very good, or good in contrast to the 11 per cent and 13 per cent respectively who recalled their first intercourse as either "bad" or "very bad."

Slightly less than one quarter of all respondents chose the "neither good nor bad" option.

Expectations of First Intercourse among Participants Who Had Not Had Intercourse

Participants who had not had intercourse ($n = 159$) answered 9 items from Table 14.1 based on their expectations of first intercourse. Students who had not had intercourse did not generally consider it important that their first intercourse partner would also have not had intercourse (36 per cent of men and 29 per cent of women said yes). We did not ask about current relationship status and thus cannot determine how many students in this subsample might, at the time of the study, have been in a relationship with an eventual first intercourse partner.

With respect to their expectations of discussion of particular topics prior to first intercourse, the sexes in this non-intercourse group differed significantly in their expectations about discussing methods of birth control other than condoms $\chi^2(2, n = 156) = 10.65, p = .005$. Women were more likely than men to expect such discussion (77 per cent versus 53 per cent respectively) and men more often unsure (41 per cent versus 17 per cent respectively). Men and women who had not had intercourse also differed significantly in their expectations about prior discussion of STIs, $\chi^2(2, n = 157) = 8.17, p = .017$ (57 per cent of women expected such discussion versus 36 per cent of men; 36 per cent of women and 46 per cent of men were unsure or did not know).

The sexes also differed in their expectation of pain at first intercourse, $\chi^2(2, n = 157) = 69.01, p < .001$, with a smaller percentage of men (4 per cent) than women (34 per cent) expecting to experience pain. Men and women also differed in expectations about their own and their future partner's

likelihood of having orgasm at first intercourse, $\chi^2(2, n = 156) = 39.44, p < .001$, and $\chi^2(2, n = 156) = 7.80, p = .020$ respectively.

Comparison of Expectations of Participants Who Had Not Had Intercourse with Actual Experiences of Those Who Had First Intercourse

[This study] also provides an opportunity to compare the first intercourse expectations of the participants who had not had intercourse with the first intercourse experiences of those who had. A comparison of the experiences of the latter with the expectations of the former invites speculation about the extent to which expectations may or may not match experience. For example, women who had not had intercourse appeared more likely to expect pre-intercourse discussion of birth control methods other than condoms (77 per cent) than was actually experienced by women who had first intercourse (48 per cent). The expected sex difference on this item experienced by those who had intercourse was in the reverse direction to that expected by those who had not. In the relation to the pre-intercourse discussion items as a whole, the trend appears to be for women who have not had intercourse to have higher expectations for such discussion than occurred in practice for those who had. Women's expectation of their own orgasm at first intercourse (11 per cent) matched that of women who had intercourse (12 per cent) but women's expectation of their partner's orgasm (28 per cent) was lower than that reported about their partners by women who had had intercourse (73 per cent).

Discussion

In contrast to other studies that highlighted differences between the sexes in their experience of first intercourse (Darling et al., 1992; Cohen and Shotland, 1996; Guggino and Ponzetti, 1997; Holland et al., 2000; Carpenter, 2001), the present findings indicate that, with some exceptions, women's and men's reports of the experience were quite similar. The average age at first intercourse was the same for both sexes. Men and women were equally likely to have had first intercourse within the context of a romantic relationship, to have known their first intercourse partner for the same average length of time, and to have had a first partner who had previous intercourse experience. Women were as likely as men to report activities indicating that they had discussed preparations for and other aspects of first intercourse. In a majority of cases, the decision to have first intercourse was a mutual one. On average, men and women gave similar responses to questions about condom use (usually), alcohol use (seldom), drug use (almost never), and whether first intercourse was expected. The finding that 75 per cent of men and 80 per cent of women reported condom use at first intercourse is consistent with the relatively high levels of protection against unintended pregnancy and STI at first intercourse reported in other recent Canadian studies of young adults (e.g., Hampton, Smith, Jeffrey, and McWatters, 2001). In addition, the sexes did not differ significantly in their evaluation of their feelings and follow-up to first intercourse in relation to emotional satisfaction, subsequent intercourse with first partner, regret, timing, and overall rating.

The women and men in our study who had not had intercourse were also similar to each other on such items as whether it was important that their first partner had also not previously had intercourse (about one-third said yes) and on their expectation of discussion in advance of condom use (high) and possible outcomes if unintended pregnancy were to occur (slightly over half).

The degree of gender similarity in this sample of university students may not represent accurately what is going on in the general population. However, it is also possible that this sample reflects a shift in the sexual practice of young people towards more equally balanced engagement in discussions and decisions related to sexual activity in general and first intercourse in particular. Since the limited research that has been done on first intercourse experience is from the United States, it has been tempting to assume that the Canadian population is similar. However, strongly conservative political and religious influences in the US may reflect an environment that has been more hostile than Canada to premarital sexual activity and hence to the education that would support more informed, and perhaps egalitarian, decision making and experiences surrounding first intercourse.

Some of our findings do suggest gender differences in which men appear to have greater influence on sexual interactions in heterosexual relationships, at least when it comes to first intercourse. The greater age differences between women and their first intercourse partners could result in men having more power and control in the sexual relationship. On the other hand this could simply be a reflection of our society's tendency for younger women to be drawn to older partners and vice versa. The fact that men had known their first intercourse partners for a shorter period of time than women is consistent with Cohen and Shotland's (1996) report that men consider sexual intercourse acceptable earlier in a dating relationship than do women. Among the approximately 40 per cent of women and men in our study who said first intercourse had not been a "mutual decision," women were significantly more likely to say that their partner had suggested intercourse than were men. This fits with the traditional dating scenario in which men are more likely to take initiative with the sexual aspects of romantic relationships. However, our questions did not explore what these students meant by their partner "taking the initiative" nor did they explore other aspects of relationship dynamics.

On average, women were more likely than men to believe that they were in love at first intercourse (men were more likely to be unsure). These views converged, in retrospect, with both sexes being equally likely to believe that they were not in love. The greater tendency for women to believe they were in love at first intercourse may reflect greater internalization by women than men of the feeling that sex is about love. There may be a parallel here in the finding of Quackenbush, Strassberg, and Turner (1995) that the inclusion of romance in erotica can serve as a relationship buffer that make erotic material more acceptable to women. Similarly, the belief that they are "in love" might be viewed as the relationship buffer necessary for some women to justify first intercourse.

We think these findings have important implications for sexual health education although we are also aware that the study has a number of limitations that invite cautious interpretation of the results. The study was conducted on a convenience sample of introductory psychology students and cannot be generalized to other populations, including students who did not go to university or who left school early. The questionnaire was designed for this study and has not been validated. Participants were only asked about consensual first intercourse and not about other sexual activities such as oral sex. Thus, the study cannot shed light on participants' prior sexual behaviour or on the attitudes that may have shaped their perceptions of their first intercourse experience. That being said, socially constructed gender differences appear to permeate all levels of society and to that extent the findings may well have useful applications for educators and health professionals.

Note

1. We would like to thank Jenn Mitchell, Kim Scott, and Hanna Wajda for their assistance in conducting this study. This research is partially supported by SSHRC funding to the second author.

References

Allgeir, E.R., and B.J.T. Royster. 1991. "New Approaches to Dating and Sexuality," in E. Grauerholz and M.A. Koralewski, eds, *Sexual Coercion: A Sourcebook on Its Nature, Causes, and Prevention*, pp. 133–47. Lexington, MA: Lexington Books.

Burr, J. 2001. "Women Have It. Men Want It. What Is It? Constructions of Sexuality in Rape Discourse," *Psychology, Evolution, & Gender* 3: 103–107.

Carpenter, L.M. 2001. "The Ambiguity of 'Having Sex': The Subjective Experience of Virginity Loss in the United States," *The Journal of Sex Research* 38: 127–39.

Cohen, L.L., and R.L. Shotland. 1996. "Timing of First Sexual Intercourse in a Relationship: Expectations, Experiences, and Perceptions of Others," *The Journal of Sex Research* 33: 291–99.

Darling, C.A., J.K. Davidson, and L.C. Passarello. 1992. "The Mystique of First Intercourse among College Youth: The Role of Partners, Contraceptive Practices, and Psychological Reactions," *Journal of Youth and Adolescence* 21: 97–117.

Fine, M. 1997. "Sexuality, Schooling, and Adolescent Females: The Missing Discourse of Desire," in M.M. Gergen and S.N. Davis, eds., *Toward a New Psychology of Gender*, pp. 375–402. New York, NY: Routledge.

Guggino, J.M., and J.J., Ponzetti, Jr. 1997. "Gender Differences in Affective Reactions to First Coitus," *Journal of Adolescence* 20: 189–200.

Hampton, M.R, P. Smith, B. Jeffery, and B. McWatters. 2001. "Sexual Experience, Contraception, and STI Prevention among High School Students: Results from a Canadian Urban Centre," *The Canadian Journal of Human Sexuality* 10: 111–26.

Holland, J., C. Ramazanoglu, S. Sharpe, and R. Thomson. 2000. "Deconstructing Virginity—Young People's Accounts of First Sex," *Sexual and Relationship Therapy* 15: 221–32.

Quackenbush, D.M., D.S. Strassberg, and C.W. Turner. 1995. "Gender Effects of Romantic Themes in Erotica," *Archives of Sexual Behavior* 24: 21–35.

Appendix A: Survey items and response categories

Questions	Response Categories
Relationship to Partner	
Were you a couple at the time?	Yes/No
Did you consider yourself to be "in love" with this person at the time when you had intercourse?	Yes/No/Not Sure
Looking back, do you think you were actually "in love" with this person when you had intercourse, regardless of your answer to the last question?	Yes/No/Not Sure
How long had you known this person in total, regardless of changes in your relationship to this person?	____ months and____ years

Appendix A (*Continued*)

Questions	Response Categories
Were you the first person with whom your partner has had intercourse?	Yes/No
What is your relationship to this person now?	Partner or Spouse/Friend/Acquaintance/No relationship/Other

Preparations Prior to Intercourse

Questions	Response Categories
Did you and your partner talk about having intercourse beforehand?	Yes/No/Not Sure
Did you and your partner discuss condom use before having first intercourse?	Yes/No/Not Sure
Did you and your partner discuss other methods of birth control before having first intercourse?	Yes/No/Not Sure
Did you and your partner discuss STIs before having first intercourse?	Yes/No/Not Sure
Did you and your partner discuss what to do if you/your partner became pregnant before having first intercourse?	Yes/No/Not Sure
Did you and your partner discuss the emotional implications of having intercourse before having first intercourse?	Yes/No/Not Sure
Do you think that you and your partner decided to have intercourse together, or did one of you take the lead?	Decided together/You took the initiative/Partner took the initiative

Circumstances of First Intercourse

Questions	Response Categories
Did first intercourse occur when you expected it to?	Yes/No/Not Sure
Where did you have intercourse for the first time?	Your home/Partner's home/Hotel or motel/Vehicle/Other
Did you/your partner use a condom?	Yes/No
Did you/your partner use any other form of contraceptive?	Yes/No
At the time you had intercourse, was there alcohol in your system?	Yes/No/Don't remember or know
Was there alcohol in your partner's system?	Yes/No/Don't remember or know
Were you on any drugs?	Yes/No/Don't remember or know
Was your partner on any drugs?	Yes/No/Don't remember or know
Did you find your first intercourse experience to be physically painful in any way?	Yes/No/Not Sure
Did you achieve orgasm?	Yes/Not/Not Sure/Don't Remember
Did your partner achieve orgasm?	Yes/Not/Not Sure/Don't Remember

Feelings/Outcomes Subsequent to First Intercourse

Questions	Response Categories
Did you feel physically satisfied with your first intercourse experience?	Yes/No/Not Sure
Did you feel emotionally satisfied with your first intercourse experience?	Yes/No/Not Sure

(Continued)

Appendix A (*Continued*)

Questions	Response Categories
Did you and this particular partner ever have sex again?	Yes/No/Don't Remember
Did you and this partner stay together as a couple, or, if you were not a couple at the time you had intercourse, did you and this partner become a couple?	Yes/No
Do you regret having shared your first intercourse experience with this person?	Yes/No/Don't Remember
Looking back, what do you think about the timing of your first intercourse experience?	I was about the right age/I was too young/ I was too old/Not Sure
Did you or your partner become pregnant as a result of your first intercourse experience?	Yes/No/I don't know
Did you or your partner get an STI as a result of your first intercourse experience?	Yes, I caught something from him or her/Yes, s/he caught something from me/No/Not Sure
Overall, how would you rate your first intercourse experience?	Perfect, wouldn't change a thing/Very Good/Good/ Neither Good or Bad/Bad/Very Bad

Expectations About First Intercourse by Respondents who had not had Intercourse

Questions	Response Categories
Will it be important to you that the person with whom you have intercourse for the first time is also having intercourse for the first time?	Yes/Maybe/No/Don't Know
Do you think you and your future partner will talk about having intercourse beforehand?	Yes/Maybe/No/Don't Know
Do you think you and your future partner will discuss condom use before having first intercourse?	Yes/Maybe/No/Don't Know
Do you think you and your future partner will discuss other methods of birth control before having first intercourse?	Yes/Maybe/No/Don't Know
Do you think you and your future partner will discuss STIs before having first intercourse?	Yes/Maybe/No/Don't Know
Do you think you and your future partner will discuss what to do if you/your partner became pregnant after having first intercourse?	Yes/Maybe/No/Don't Know
Do you think you and your future partner will discuss the emotional implications of having first intercourse before having first intercourse?	Yes/Maybe/No/Don't Know
Do you think your first intercourse experience will be physically painful in any way?	Yes/Maybe/No/Don't Know
Do you think you will achieve orgasm at first intercourse?	Yes/Maybe/No/Don't Know
Do you think your future partner will achieve orgasm at first intercourse?	Yes/Maybe/No/Don't Know

Chapter 15

Overview

Melanie Beres takes a detailed and perhaps eye-opening look at the micropolitics of sexual negotiation. Her account complements Tsui and Nikoladis's broad-brush picture of heterosexuality among Canadian young people, as she gets up close and personal, asking how people identify a potential sexual partner and communicate their intentions and desires through both verbal and nonverbal means.

Beres goes beyond moralizing about "hookup culture" to reveal how this culture actually works. She identifies four distinct "discourses," or powerful beliefs, about sexuality that men and women use to understand and describe their experiences. These discourses are highly gendered—in contrast to the more gender-neutral patterns described by Tsui and Nikoladis—as men and women are described as having different kinds of sexual drives, orientations to relationships, and sexual agency.

"It Just Happens"
Negotiating Casual Heterosexual Sex
Melanie Beres

In the summer of 2005, Melanie Beres spent several months in Jasper, Alberta, interviewing young people who had come to Jasper for seasonal work in the tourist industry. Her intent was to understand the negotiating of sexual consent in short-term heterosexual encounters ("hooking up" or "one night stands"). Beres chose Jasper because of the dense population of transients and seasonal workers. The youth culture that grew up around this population perceived recreational sex as a common activity. In this chapter, Beres discusses the different ways in which men and women in Jasper talk about casual sex, and how they depict the process of consenting to a sexual encounter.

I begin this chapter by highlighting ways that the negotiation of casual sex in Jasper is dominated by discourses that privilege male sexual desire. I discuss the three discourses of heterosexuality as outlined by Hollway (1984) and I argue for a fourth discourse within casual sex; I label it the "it just happens" discourse. Through this discourse, casual sex is constructed as something that "just happens" and is beyond the control of the partners. I end with an analysis of the ways that women find spaces of power and agency within these discourses. Women do this by placing limits on casual sex, disrupting the "coital imperative" and taking the typically "male" position within the discourse and actively seeking casual sex.

The (Male) Models of Heterosexual Casual Sex in Jasper

"It Just Happens" Discourse

When I approached young adults in Jasper (YAJs) and told them about my study I explained that I was interested in learning about how

Beres, Melanie. "'It Just Happens': Negotiating Casual Heterosexual Sex". This chapter originally appeared in Beres, M.A. (2006). From *Sexual Consent to Heterosexual Casual Sex among Young Adults Living in Jasper.* Unpublished Doctoral Dissertation, University of Alberta, Edmonton, Alberta, Canada. Reprinted by permission of the author.

casual sex happens in Jasper, and how partners communicate their willingness to participate in casual sex. I began interviews by asking them about their lives in Jasper and about their past dating and sexual experiences. At some point during the interview I inevitably asked some version of the question "How does casual sex happen?" or "How do two people come to the understanding that they are going to have sex?" At this point many of the participants stopped and stared at me with perplexed looks on their faces. I interpreted their reactions as saying "Have you never had sex?" The presumption seemed to be that if I had sex at some point, then I would have known how it happened. The answer would have been obvious. The answer (of course) is that "it just happens." Almost all of the women and a few of the men responded with some version of this statement.

Samantha: So you're like kind of like making eye contact, smiling at each other, and then all of a sudden we're like standing by each other talking. And just like . . . I don't know how it happened but we like; all of a sudden we were . . . (laughs) . . . we were just like talking and we were talking about that and like he started kissing me and we went back to my house. And it wasn't even a question of "would you like to come to my house?" You know what I mean? It was just like that. That's what happened. (laughs) And then in the middle of it, it was just like, oh my God!

Anne: He, he just kissed me. Like he just, we were holding hands and dancing then he kissed me and I kissed him back and then it just. . . . Yeah, we were hugging and kissing. I was, it was not . . . I don't know, it just happened.

James: That's a really interesting question, because you don't really, I don't really analyze how it happens really, it just kind of happens.

This discourse of "it just happens" reflects a sense that there is a force greater than and external to the two people involved in casual sex that is ultimately responsible for instigating sex. . . . Gwen provides a particularly poignant example.

Yeah. And then so, yeah, and then he just kept talking. Like we didn't dance or anything. We just sat by the bar and talked for like two hours and he just kept feeding me drinks. (laughs) But he was just drinking just as much as I was so it wasn't that big of a deal. So every time I'd get a drink, he would get a drink. And um . . . yeah, and then. . . . And then I went to the washroom and then when I came out, he wasn't there. It was like okay, I'm just going to go home. And then I was walking outside and he like got a cab and stuff. And he was like do you need a ride? Like I'll give you a cab and I'll give you a ride home. And then like sure, whatever. It was raining. It was ugly out. And then um . . . his friend was with him too and he said well why don't you just come over for a couple of beer? And I was like okay, I don't have to work until 3:30 the next day. I can do that. And um . . . so I went over. We had some beer. And then I was like okay, I'm going to go home. And he was like well no, let's just talk for a bit. And I was like okay, and then one thing led to another. . . .

The way that Gwen tells the story, she sees it as a series of events that took place, finishing with "and one thing led to another." She does not see the man's behaviour as orchestrating her going home with him for casual sex. She dismisses his buying her lots of drinks, because he too is drinking. She does not think anything of him arranging a cab for her, or asking her home. She does not say anything to imply that his actions may have been planned—that he may be buying her alcohol to get her drunk so she would be more likely to go home with him. She ends the story with "and one thing led to another" implying that neither one of them was in control of what was happening.

. . . James is one of the few men who also expresses this sense of "it just happens."

It's just something that happens, and you don't really know how it happened, but it happened. And ah, I've never had an experience where it's happened and then she's been like "I really didn't want that to happen" which

I'm very thankful for. But you know, you go to an after party or something, right like you're already just hard-core making out on the dance floor let's say, right and you're doing dry humping and bumping and grinding and hanging off each other as you leave the bar. You get to the guy's party house or wherever you're at right, you're sitting around. The next thing you know, nobody's in the room and you're lying on each other and one thing leads to another. Right like, that's really the only way to put it, you start making out that leads to nakedness that leads to sex.

James was thankful that no woman has ever told him afterwards that she did not want to have sex. He said this as though he cannot control the situation or outcome—as though he has no access to the woman's comfort levels, interests, or desires. If sex can just happen, and he has no control over what happens, he then has no control over any potential consequences of the interaction. This use of the "it just happens" discourse assumes that they are not responsible for negotiating casual sex. This results in a failure for men to take responsibility for their actions and the potential for these actions to create harm.

Agnes, among others, connected the "it just happens" discourse with alcohol. "Alcohol is a huge key, like huge, and it really makes you, it really limits you, your ability to make good, clear, conscious decisions." I spoke with only one person who said that most often his casual sex hook-ups occur in the absence of alcohol, often with people he meets in coffee shops or on the street. All other participants mentioned that alcohol plays an important part in their casual sex experiences. When I asked Susan how casual sex happens, alcohol was the first thing she mentioned.

Go to the bar. Start buying other people drinks and start drinking yourself. It's really really. . . it's all related to alcohol, I think. And for a lot of other people drugs, but I don't see that side of it because I've never been a part of that side of it. Um, but yeah, well it depends, well as a girl if that's what you're looking for

when you come to Jasper. You dress really skanky and you get out on the dance floor and you drink lots. And there's gonna be a guy there. Guaranteed. . . .

. . .

Male Sexual Drive Discourse

While most women and a few men began talking about casual sex through the "it just happens" discourse, this was not the only way that hookups were conceptualized.

Many men said they went out to parties or bars with an intention of hooking up, and they pay particular attention to what types of things women may want in men, or particular things to do to get women interested in them. For these men, casual sex does not just happen; it is something that they have to work for, and something they practise. Robert, a bouncer in one of the local bars said that he often sees men going from one group of women to another until they find someone willing to talk with them. Don said that he approaches a lot of women when he's looking for sex and that he knows he will get turned down frequently.

This fits in with what Hollway (1984) describes as the male sexual drive discourse in which men's sex drive is insatiable and that women's role in sexual activity is to be passive and go along with men's desires. Within this discourse men are sexual subjects acting in ways to fulfill their desire for sex. Through this discourse men also secure their masculinity, by reinforcing their ever-present sex drive. Conversely, women are positioned as sexual objects, necessary for men to satiate their desire for sex without any desires of their own. Men reported many strategies that they used in order to find a sexual partner. For instance, some men said that they will often approach many women, with the idea that the more women they approach, the greater the likelihood that they will find one who will have sex with them.

Even once men were in conversation, or dancing with a particular woman, it was important for them to continue to monitor women's behaviours in ways that would increase the chance of "getting laid." For instance, it was important that women should feel as though the situation was not threatening, and to feel comfortable and cared for.

Don: You just give her a sense of security like, making them the focal point, and just looking out for them like, just simple sayings like, like obviously getting the door for them, like putting on their jacket but like actually pulling their hair back so it doesn't go under their jacket, like little things like that, and just looking out for them, even if it's just like creating some space for them, like in a crowded club or something like that just little things like that seemed to go a long way. . . . You have to really play it by ear because it can be overdone. . . . You have to give her her space and be relaxed then the same time just be conscientious and make her feel comfortable, you know offer them like something to drink, right. I'm not saying offering them a shot or something like that, but like can I get you a drink, would you like my jacket, are you cold, and something like that.

Don is very deliberate in his approach with women; he sees himself in pursuit of sex and sees it as challenging to get women to have sex with him. He is quite aware of his actions and how they may help him reach his goal. While on the surface he seems concerned about women's comfort level, this is a means to an end, a way to get women to go to bed with him. . . .

In order to satiate his "natural" sexual desires, Don learned and implemented specific strategies that enabled him to have casual sex. In this version of the male sexual drive discourse Don positioned himself in a way that relinquishes both partners from responsibility. Here, Don accepts that he is responsible for learning how to quench his ever-present desire. His drive is "natural" and thus it is "inevitable" that he must have casual sex throughout the summer; however, by becoming skilled at the "arts" of "courting" he increases the likelihood and frequency that he will be able to satisfy these desires.

He talked in detail about monitoring women's behaviour to gauge their comfort level and willingness to have sex. In particular, a woman's breathing was very important.

It is all about the girl's breathing, and that's like, a lot of guys don't realize that, but that's like, that's your like light signal that's your red, yellow, green, right there it's her breathing and just playing that off and so you just gradually sort of progress things forward to taking off clothes.

For Don, it was important that he maintain control over the situation and over casual sex. He talked positively about situations where women initiated casual sex, as long as the woman was not too direct.

The odd time that I get approached by a girl it works, like it's nice to see a girl of confidence and stuff like that but you can't be too direct because then it's just too easy, it kills it, like you know unless I was just slumming it you know, and going for raunchy sex.

Several other men talked in similar ways about women who are actively seeking sex.

Colin: If they come on too strong, then you can kind of tell that they're kinda skanky. But if they come on sort of in a shy manner, then, then it's a good thing. Good cause it gives you room to open them up. You know what I mean? Like you've got to make them feel comfortable obviously or else it's just going to be stupid and suck. . . . If they're really aggressive, it's just like no; I don't want to do this. Cause it's not really giving you a challenge. Cause if they're really aggressive, it's just like well okay, I'll just take my shorts off and let's go.

Thus, the chase becomes a "natural" part of casual sex, and courtship and seduction becomes the property of men. . . .

Women were far less likely to articulate ways that casual sex happens. Even in cases where the women were interested in particular men, women waited for men to initiate contact.

Samantha: It's usually the guy who makes the first move I guess, towards me if they can see I'm attracted to them or whatever.

Even when women initiate sex, they still take up the male sexual drive discourse by assuming that the men will be willing to engage in sex.

Agnes: And I think it's more the girl to . . . be the one that decides whether or not it's going to happen because from my experiences, there's not very many times when a guy won't have sex. In fact, more often than not, that's all they're in it for is and not like looking for a relationship or just somebody to snuggle with.

Men also articulated this aspect of the male sexual drive discourse. When I asked men how they indicated their willingness for sex to their partners, many responded by saying that they do not have to demonstrate willingness.

Colin: I just like I'm, I'm a guy. I'm ready, willing and able anywhere anytime.
Gary: I think it's probably pretty rare that the guy says stop. I mean, I don't know with other guys for sure but . . . from, from what I know, then I say that the guy's not going to say stop. Unless there's something else like he has a girlfriend or something like that.

This male sexual drive discourse was the discourse most frequently referred to by both women and men as they talked about casual sex. The male sexual drive discourse is different from the "it just happens" discourse in that both men and women who take up this discourse recognize that men actively pursue casual sex. This is viewed as the "normal" and "natural" way to engage in casual sex. It remained unquestioned by all but one female participant.

Stacy: It's, it's so unfair that it's really assumed in our society that it's the guy's job to [initiate sex]. You know what I mean. It's the guy's job to invite the girl out on a date. It's the guy's job to initiate this. It's the guy's

job to initiate that. Yeah, it's the guy's job to initiate sex. It's the guy's job to do everything. The girl's kind of the passive like you know? Passive partner who goes along with everything or doesn't. But is always like you know, things happen to her, she doesn't, you know what I mean? . . . Like don't treat me like some idiot! Like some damsel in fucking distress. So I think that that goes a long way into the bedroom too where like I don't expect him, you know what I mean? Like I'm willing to go out on a limb and face rejection, you know what I mean?

Have/Hold Discourse

While the male sexual drive discourse was the most frequently taken up, other discourses described by Hollway (1984) were alluded to by participants. Many women and a few men took up the have/hold discourse, which Hollway describes as the belief that sex comes with a committed and ongoing relationship. In this discourse women are positioned as the sexual subjects who were trying to establish a committed relationship with a man. Men are positioned as the objects of this discourse. Thus, the have/hold discourse works with the male sexual drive discourse; men are attempting to satiate their sexual desires, and women participate in sex to build and maintain a committed relationship.

It was surprising to see this discourse taken up when women and men were talking about casual sex. Although both women and men were aware that many casual sex experiences do not lead to lasting and committed relationships, some women reported that one reason they engage in casual sex is because they may be interested in a relationship. Samantha and Agnes both said that some of the partners they chose were people they were interested in developing a relationship with. Most of these casual sex experiences did not lead to a relationship. Agnes said that she learnt that if she wanted a relationship that she should not sleep with a man the first night they are together because she found that after she slept with a man on the first "date," he would no longer speak to her.

We ended up sleeping together and woke up the next morning, and we slept together again and then he like, never talked to me after that. And we were supposed to hang out on New Year's Eve together, cuz it was like two nights after that and umm, I phoned him on New Year's Eve, and asked him what he was doing, and he was like "oh I think I'm just going to stay home." He totally blew me off.

. . . Agnes told stories about hooking up with people for casual sex, and said "I'm totally, like, fine to have casual sex with people, but like if they're under one impression and I'm under another and it's not the same then that kind of makes me mad." In Agnes's version of this discourse, she is looking for more than just one night of sex. This commitment does not have to be in the form of an exclusive and romantic relationship. It could also be a casual affair that lasts several weeks.

Agnes is not the only woman who spoke of similar ideas. Jane recounts a story where she met a man she was interested in. At first she thinks he is a real "gentleman" because he does not try to sleep with her the first night they are together. They did, however, have sex the second night they were together. Afterwards she was angry because he is no longer speaking to her. She called him a "really big slut" and a liar. She sees his actions as being dishonest because, for her, having sex with someone is a sign that there is at least some interest and some commitment.

Even for some women who actively sought out one-night-stands, their subject position was at least partially constructed through the have/hold discourse. After seeking out casual sex with a particular man Anne turned off her answering machine and purposely spent a lot of time out of the house for the following few days. She did not want to know if he had called or not.

So it was not like I was expecting anything out of it, but I still, I do have like, like, I had like little fantasies about him, like staying or something like that, or like us continuing the relationship, so there must be, and I went into it totally like chasing him. I just wanted to

have, to basically have casual sex, but I still have the future flashes.

Anne has purposely tried to disregard and shed the have/hold discourse and went out looking for a one-night-stand. Yet she still finds that she has what she calls "future flashes" and that she fantasizes about a possible future with the man. She also mentioned a few times that she saw no reason why they could not be friends, or at least talk with one another after having casual sex.

I had one one-night-stand. . . and I just, I thought, like okay, well, you have sex with someone, and to me it doesn't matter, like sex . . . ok, I never felt like a slut when I do it, so I don't see other people . . . like I can never imagine other people thinking of me as a slut, but like, so I thought that we could just hang out with these guys afterwards and be friends, but it's weird, like once you've done the act, it's, there's like very like a lack of interest. . . . How are you supposed to meet anybody in this stupid town to hang out with, you know what I mean?

Here Anne takes up a different form of the have/hold discourse. She is not concerned with creating or maintaining a sexual or romantic relationship. However, she expects that she should be able to maintain a friendly relationship with men with whom she has had sex. She views the men as potential people to hang out with and party with, people who can be part of her larger social network. She resents that most often after she has sex with them, she is excluded from their social network.

Men do not take up this discourse as it relates to casual sex. Almost all the men expected not to engage in any sort of relationship with someone after they had sex, unless there was a relationship established before they had sex. A few men mentioned that they would delay having sex with a woman if they wanted to have a relationship with her.

Colin: Well if you have a connection with this person and you're super attracted to them and you can see yourself being with them, then you won't fuck them the first date. Like if you really want a relationship with them, you're not going to spoil it by screwing them.

Don: Like a really good one is going home to smoke pot or to do blow but like I've cut blow out of my life, that was like a high school thing. But like blow's really good because it shows that you really wanna talk to them because when you do a lot of blow your dick is like a limp spaghetti, and it's just like useless for sex and so shows that you care about conversation and bullshit like that.

For men, the have/hold discourse comes into play only when they want to develop a relationship with a woman, whereas for women, they often take it up whenever they are engaging in casual sex.

This discourse operates along with the male sexual drive discourse to enable casual sex among YAJs. Men engage in casual sex because of their "natural" and insatiable drive for sexual gratification. Conversely, women participate in casual sex with the hope of developing a lasting and committed relationship.

Sexual Permissiveness Discourse

Both men and women deployed the sexual permissiveness discourse, according to which casual sexual activity is considered normal and expected. Many of the men and women I spoke with were surprised at how many women in Jasper initiate and seek out casual sex. Robert said, "When I lived in [another province], it was the guys. But like here, it's anybody who's you know, guys or girls making the first move for sure." . . .

Casual sex for women is accepted, rather than stigmatized, in Jasper (although if they are "too" assertive or aggressive they risk being labelled a slut). Without this discourse, and the feeling that it is acceptable for women to have casual sex, it would be much more difficult for men to find willing partners. This discourse, which on the surface seems to support women's sexual desires, is necessary for men to engage in a lot of casual sex. This discourse can also obscure sexual double

standards. It appears as though it is acceptable for both women and men to engage in casual sex. However, this is only acceptable if they are engaging in a "masculine" version of casual sex and if women are adhering to normative constructions of femininity created through the male sexual drive discourse.

Women's Sexual Agency

The discourses discussed above create depictions of casual sex that benefit male sexual desires and needs and are subject to male initiation. However, within these discourses women carve out spaces to exercise agency over their own sexuality and engage in heterosexual casual sex. Women create different degrees of agency during their casual sex experiences. First, women take advantage of the perception that more men are interested in casual sex than women, and therefore women have more choice about with whom they have sex. Second, women exercise agency by interrupting sexual activity before they engage in casual sex. Third, they actively seek out and orchestrate casual sex to satisfy their own sexual desires.

Women exercise agency by taking advantage of the perception that there are a lot more men seeking casual sex than there are women, creating a situation where women have a lot of choice regarding with whom they go home.

Teresa: There's so many men looking for sex that, you know, women really have their pick and choose of the litter. If they're just looking for a one-night-stand [the men I've talked to] said that you really have to stick out like a sore thumb or like be right there.

Men and women sometimes argue that women have more power than men when it comes to casual sex, because they have the power of choice. Jane says that "girls have a lot of power in whether they go home with a man or not. Guys just kind of take their chance and hope they get lucky." If women are looking for casual sex, it is much easier for them to find someone with whom to go home. In a sense they are taking advantage of the male sexual drive discourse and using it to their advantage to have casual sex when they desire it.

Additionally, women exercise agency within and around the male sexual drive discourse by placing limits on the sexual activity—getting what they want out of it and stopping the interaction when they are satisfied. Agnes says that "I think too because the girl ultimately usually decides on . . . if there's going to be sex or not." Thus, while casual sex operates on the presumption of a male model of sexuality, women and men perceive that women act as the "gatekeepers" and determine whether or not casual sex will happen.

Men, as well as women, reported that women often act as limit-setters. Tim mentioned that sometimes women will be totally "into making out," but they will not let him take off their pants. He reads this as an indication that they are menstruating; he suggests that many women get particularly "horny" while they are menstruating. Regardless of whether or not these women are menstruating, taking up this strategy, or going along with his suggestion that they are menstruating gives them a chance to engage in casual sexual activity that does not lead to penetration. James mentioned similar strategies used by a few women.

> Like, you'll be with the girl and you'll be making out and she'll stop and be like, you know, "I really like you but I don't wanna go all the way because of this reason." Right, like, there are still virgins out there, believe it or not, who are like, saving themselves for marriage, it's a really romantic concept that I really still enjoy, but you . . . it's a rarity I'll say . . . but they'll still have tonnes and tonnes of fun, but they just won't go all the way.

By being up front and telling men their limits, these women are opening up possibilities for casual sexual activity that do not include penetration. James mentioned that often they would engage in oral sex or genital touching. When men mentioned these strategies, they did not mind that the women were placing limits on sexual activity. James mentioned later on that "realistically again, you

know, a lot of them are tourists they're not gonna be around the next day, so you have bad luck that night you always go out a couple nights later and maybe your luck's changed." If one woman is not willing to participate fully in a male model of casual sex that includes sexual penetration, then another one will be later on.

Thus, these women are able to negotiate the "coital imperative" (Jackson, 1984) of heterosexual sex by placing boundaries and limits around the sexual activity. This way, women are able to indirectly satisfy their own sexual desires while operating within normative heterosexual discourses. They do this without completely rejecting the coital imperative. By saying that they want to wait until marriage to have sex or that they are having their period, they imply that they would otherwise be willing to engage in intercourse and are recognizing the central role that intercourse plays in heterosexual relations.

While the women I interviewed did not talk about strategies that included claiming they were menstruating or that they wanted to remain virgins, many of them mentioned setting limits as a way to ensure control over their casual sex.

Agnes: I just don't let it happen. I say no, like when they try to go that direction, I'm like "no, I don't sleep with guys on the first date."

Many women have a sense that they are in control of placing limits on sexual activity. Of course they do have to be careful about how they approach setting these limits.

Laurie: Well I guess, I would just, I don't know, I guess I would try to keep it kind of light and stuff, cause I don't want to piss them off right? Some guys could be weird and psycho (laughs) and so, I don't know I'd probably try to keep it light, put clothes on or whatever if I took my clothes off, and be like, "oh, can you go?" or "I'm gonna go home" or whatever.

While women exercised agency by setting limits and interrupting sexual activity prior to penetration, the reaction of the men they were with varied.

In the examples discussed above, the women's excuses were considered "legitimate" by the men. However, if a man did not consider the excuses "legitimate" he often became frustrated and women were labelled "teases." These consequences acted as constraints and the men attempted to limit women's access to these strategies to create their own agency.

While many women set sexual limits, others reported orchestrating their own casual sex experiences focused on their own pleasure. Anne's story is a good example of this type of agency and of the tension between a male-oriented discursive construction of heterosexual casual sex and women's space for agency within that discourse. Anne carefully sought out and chose a man to have casual sex with.

> He's not young young, he's 19, but like I haven't been with a 19-year-old guy since I was 17, so it was really weird, but um it's so sad but it seems to be safer to me, to go for someone who wasn't like, living in Jasper for so long, than for someone new and innocent, it sounds so dirty! (laughs)... but it's that attitude. Like he was a really good-looking boy, but he probably didn't know how good-looking quite yet you know what I mean... and I knew when I met him that he was like, how old he was and I knew he was leaving in August.

Anne carefully chose a man whose social position enabled her more control over the situation. She liked the idea that Jack was young and new to Jasper. To her, this meant that he was likely not very experienced and that he had not yet developed an attitude like many other men she met in Jasper. This gave her greater control over the situation. She went out with Jack and a few friends one night to go partying. Both of them got quite drunk, but the whole night she was focused on getting him to go home with her. At one point they tried to go to a different bar, but Jack was so drunk that the bouncers would not let him in; he said that he would just go home.

> I was like, no, the whole point of going out with you guys is because of you, you can't go home,

so, but I didn't say that, I'm like oh no no no, we can't leave one person out that's so wrong. And I asked the bouncer if we take him to the park and he sobers up can we come back in an hour, and they said as long as he can walk straight or something like that then we'll let him in. So that, so we ended up doing that.

Anne ensured that Jack would stay with the rest of the group until the end of the night so she could take him home with her. They did end up back at that bar. Anne and Jack were dancing and kissing on the dance floor. One of Jack's friends was leaving the bar and came up and shook Jack's hand to congratulate him on successfully picking up Anne.

> Like when the guy shook the guy's hand and like I don't care cause like, congratulations to me too, you know what I mean, that was my goal for the night, to go home with him. So like, and then we did, and he is so much fun.

Anne felt that she too should be congratulated; she was taking up the typically male role in casual sex. She took up the active role seeking sex, and he took on the more passive role by going along with it. When they did end up back at her place she was concerned about him, and his willingness to participate in sex.

> I know I wanted to have sex, like that was something that was going to happen for me. But I did ask him because I kinda felt . . . just because I was so forward with it all the time, I just wanted to make sure he was along for the, like was there as well. . . . Cause yeah, cause a lot of times I probably haven't been with the guy, and it just happened anyways, you just kind of follow along with the progression of things. . . . Like I asked him before we had sex, are you sure you're okay with this? And he was like, yeah! Like what the fuck, like why are you asking that question?

She knew that she was not always really into the casual sex that took place previously, and she did not like the feeling that gave her. Therefore, she made a point of ensuring that Jack was a willing participant. Jack almost took offence to her question. Her question subverts the male sexual drive discourse by questioning his desire. He took this as also questioning his masculinity as framed within the male sexual drive discourse.

Throughout the sexual activity, Anne ensured that her desires would be met.

> I don't mind like, like helping myself get off when I'm having sex cause some guys are good at it, some guys know how to do it and you don't have to worry about it, but some guys are totally clueless, especially, maybe not so experienced guys and so I don't have an issue at all with for me it's for me and I know that I don't have a problem with I want to do this I want to do that. . . . Like when I was with Jack I did say it. I have no problem saying certain things like, like just stuff like getting on top, different positions and like can you move over here can you move over there.

Anne had no problem taking control over her sexual pleasure. During casual sex, she will pleasure herself if she is not getting what she wants from sex. She is also comfortable enough to ask for what she wants, a switch in position, or for Jack to shift to a different position. Anne uses her sense of agency to get what she wants; at the same time she recognizes that the model of casual sex is a male model and so she has learned how to temporarily manipulate the model to fit her desires.

> Like guys are assholes, I had no idea, no one told me, and it's not that I'm not angry at them, because I just see it, as that's the way they are, you just have to know that. I think girls should be given that knowledge, so that and then they can make their own decisions and what they want. If they want to participate in it or not, because sometimes I do, sometimes I'm like, I want to, and I'm up for it but you have to be really aware of what you're getting into, because you can get really hurt like otherwise.

She feels that now that she knows more about what casual sex is all about, she can choose when and how she participates in it. For Anne, casual sex is deliberately engaged in, which contrasts with many other women's experiences of casual sex as something that "just happens."

Women who take up sexual agency in this way move beyond the permissiveness discourse because they are not just giving themselves permission to participate in sex. They are creating experiences and situations to satisfy their own sexual desires. They do this not by changing the dominant discourses that govern heterosexual casual sex, but by creating spaces within those discourses and subtly challenging them to allow them to cater to their own needs.

The negotiation of heterosexual casual sex is a nuanced process laden with hegemonic and often contradictory discourses. Often, there is the sense that casual sex is not really negotiated at all, that it just happens when two people are together at the bar drinking. Running parallel to this discourse are the male sexual drive discourse and the sexual permissiveness discourse. The male sexual drive discourse is used to create a model of casual sex governed by notions of male sexual desire as being ever-present and never satisfied. This discourse simultaneously silences women's sexual desires and assumes that women play a passive role in sexual relations. For casual sex to take place, the sexual permissiveness discourse is deployed, allowing women to desire and participate in sex as long as it is the version of sex in the male sexual drive discourse—that is, penetrative sex with "no strings attached." A few women however, position themselves within the have/hold discourse and expect that after casual sex the possibility for a friendship or relationship still exists.

Within these discourses that privilege male desire, women have been able to carve out ways to negotiate casual sex that takes into consideration their own desires. Women will place limits on the sexual activity or leave after their needs have been met. Sometimes women will take an even more active role in designing and orchestrating their own casual sex experiences that satisfy their desires. Women are adapting by recognizing that casual sex is often controlled by male sexual desire, then choosing when and how they participate in casual sex to get their own desires met.

Conclusion

When discussing issues of casual sex, YAJs first turn to a discourse of "it just happens" and suggest that casual sex is a serendipitous event. However, through their stories the male sexual drive discourse is the dominant discourse operating in this environment. Casual sex is driven by the assumption that men are perpetually in search of sex. Perhaps surprisingly, the women deploy the have/hold discourse and report that one reason they engage in casual sex is for the possibility of developing a relationship with their casual partner. Finally, casual sex is dependent on the sexual permissiveness discourse that suggests that casual sex is permissible for both women and men (at least within the confines of the male sexual drive discourse). Finally, within these discourses women exert power through their choice in partners, by setting limits and by taking what may be considered a typically masculine role and actively pursuing casual sex.

References

Hollway, W. 1984. "Gender Difference and the Production of Subjectivity," in J. Henriques, W. Hollway, C. Urwin, C. Venn, and V. Walkerdine, eds., *Changing the Subject: Psychology, Social Regulation and Subjectivity*, pp. 227–63. New York: Routledge.

Jackson, M. 1984. "Sex Research and the Construction of Sexuality: A Tool of Male Supremacy?" *Women's Studies International Forum* 7, 43–51.

Chapter 16

Overview

Is love a revolutionary force? And can the conventional expressions of romantic love, such as weddings and marriage, be engines of social change? Elise Chenier argues for the importance of "love-politics," using the example of lesbian weddings in decades past, as a means of transforming gender norms. In doing so, she pushes against a tendency in present-day queer writing to regard same-sex weddings as inherently conservative in their simulation of heterosexual institutions. She finds that the history of same-sex weddings between women in North America extends far back beyond the marriage equality movements of the late twentieth and early twenty-first centuries and includes women who held private and discreet weddings as well as those who publicly announced their desire to marry as a political action. Chenier focuses on the "genderqueerness" of lesbians of colour, who navigated the liberation politics of their own communities as well as emerging feminist critiques of heterosexual marriage in the 1960s and 1970s. Their insistence on the right to marry amounts to a radical challenge to a patriarchal and male-dominated private sphere as well as a powerful link between love and justice.

Love-Politics

Lesbian Wedding Practices in Canada and the United States from the 1920s to the 1970s

Elise Chenier

In 1972 the Brooklyn-based lesbian feminist periodical Echo of Sappho profiled Sandy and June, a white butch and femme couple, on the occasion of their recent wedding ceremony. Sandy and June were one among hundreds of same-sex couples who had exchanged vows at Father Robert Mary Clement's Church of the Beloved Disciple, which opened in 1970 to cater to the spiritual needs of lesbians and gays. When asked how they felt about their wedding "in relationship to the women's movement," Sandy and June did not respond directly, describing instead what their marriage meant to them: it was "a holy union and very beautiful," they said. "This church makes you feel as normal as anyone could be."

Sandy and June's embrace of normal seems to anticipate the queer Left critique of the marriage equality movement that dominated American lesbian and gay politics in the late twentieth and early twenty-first centuries. . . . Lisa Duggan argues, the modern marriage equality movement "upholds, sustains, and seeks inclusion within . . . heterosexist institutions . . . while promising the possibility of a demobilized gay constituency and a privatized, depoliticized gay culture anchored in domesticity and consumption."[1] . . .

. . . When Sandy and June wed, they followed a decades-old practice of transforming romantic, illicit love into a theory of justice. They practiced "love-politics."[2]

. . .

Love was embedded in the political imaginary of some of the earliest women's and gay liberation texts. American radical Left activist Carl Wittman's 1969 "A Gay Manifesto" declared: "Where once there was frustration, alienation, and cynicism . . . we are [now] full of love for each other and are showing it."[3] New York's Gay Liberation Front described itself as "a revolutionary homosexual group . . . creating new social forms and relations . . . based upon brotherhood, cooperation, human love and uninhibited sexuality," and in 1973 radical feminist Robin Morgan claimed, "We have a right, each of us, to a Great Love . . . a committed, secure, nurturing, sensual, aesthetic, revolutionary, holy, ecstatic love. That need, that right, is the heart of our revolution."[4] When lesbian political activist Madeline Davis addressed the Democratic National Convention in 1972, she emphasized the right of gays and lesbians to love.[5]

It was black feminists, however, who developed and theorized love as political praxis, chief among them lesbian poets and writers June Jordan (who had a wedding ceremony in the 1970s) and Audre Lorde, along with writers and intellectuals Alice Walker and Patricia Hill Collins.[6] According to Collins, in the context of America's intense hatred of blacks, loving black people "constitutes a highly rebellious act."[7] Political love, which June Jordan defines as "a steady-state deep caring and respect for every other human being, a love that can only derive from a secure and positive self-love," claims, embraces, and restores the wounded black female self; it "stakes out a radical conception of the public sphere . . . based in a collective 'public feeling' of love."[8] . . .

In this article, I argue that wedding practices, by which I mean the enactment of a conventional wedding ritual by a same-sex couple, is love-politics in action.

. . .

Critics of the late twentieth- and early twenty-first-century marriage equality movement have rightfully argued that advocacy for same-sex marriage privatizes sexuality, something that gay and feminist liberationists fought so hard against. They have convincingly demonstrated how it fosters a new "homonormativity" and shifts queer politics toward neoliberalism. Yet hundreds of thousands of lesbians and gays embraced the opportunity to marry, even when the state did not recognize it, because wedding ceremonies and marriage rituals also serve as a powerful way to affirm queer love and desire. They are semipublic acts that claim, embrace, and restore the wounded self and radically reconceive the public sphere to include genderqueerness and same-sex desire and intimacies. Wedding practices contributed to the formation of social, sexual, and political communities based on a radical ethic of care rather than a shared injury or wounded identity.[9] When black, Latina, and white women like Sandy and June organized wedding ceremonies, they "imagine[d] a world ordered by love, by a radical embrace of difference." Same-sex wedding practices were therefore part of a distinct political tradition that drew on conventional romantic forms to affirm queer life.[10]

Historians have traced female same-sex marriage as far back as 1778, when Sarah Ponsonby and Eleanor Butler established a household together in Wales.[11] Evidence of women who considered themselves married—none had a state license, of course—grows richer in the 1800s and richer still at the beginning of the twentieth century when Boston marriages, a term used in America to describe long-term domestic relationships between two women who were financially independent and usually university educated, became common.[12] These examples concern white women, and no wonder. A stable source of income was essential to establish a household, and literate middle- and upper-class women were more able to produce and preserve records of their lives together.[13] The expansion of employment opportunities during and after World War II meant that many more women could live together and support themselves into old age, and while many of them considered themselves married, a combination of conventional mores that placed a high value on discretion, middle-class sensibilities that held that one did not make a spectacle of oneself (unless of course one was marrying a person of the opposite sex), and the need to avoid exposure in order to maintain one's social and professional position meant that they would never have considered having a ceremony. Of course, in all social and economic classes, one also found women who regarded marriage as oppressive, outdated, and generally something to be avoided, regardless of the sexes involved.

Another type of marriage often framed as same-sex marriage was that between two biological females, one who lived as a man/was a man and the other who was a cisgender woman. Many of these couples applied for and received a marriage license because they presented themselves as female and male, either because the male partner was trans or because presenting as male was a survival strategy for living a lesbian life.[14] This article, however, focuses on women who made a public declaration of commitment as genderqueer women, in the style of a conventional wedding and in the presence of an officiant, and usually other lesbians. . . .

Since at least the 1950s, weddings—by which I mean ceremonies involving two women who declared a commitment to each other before an officiant and that may or may not have included friends—were . . . "carried out with all the seriousness, ceremony and celebration of a natural nuptial proceedings between a male and a female [sic]" in cities across Canada and the United States.[15] Weddings were entirely conventional affairs conducted according to the customs of the time and shaped by the same constraints faced by any other couple; money and resources determined the scope and size of the event, but the wedding involved many of the standard trappings: invitations, rings, bridesmaids, a certificate of marriage, a cake complete with topper, and lots of drinking and dancing. Ivy, a Toronto femme and sex worker, described a wedding she attended in the mid-1950s as "a real wing-ding" complete with fancy clothes, a limousine, and a hired band, all extravagant luxuries for her social group. Some weddings were so big, she explained, that "even the cops would go." She meant as guests, of course. In 1957 Hush, a local tabloid, reported a police raid of the wedding of "little Marlene B., the blushing bride, and Lillian 'Butch' O., the she-male groom who was attired for the occasion," indicating that police attendance was at least as likely to be unfriendly.[16] In 1953 Philadelphians Naomi Garry and Elsie Holmes, an African American couple, sent out embossed invitations for their marriage celebration. Local police raided the event, reportedly on the suspicion that the couple had taken out a marriage license. Garry and Holmes were charged with the illegal sale of alcohol. Neither woman attempted to conceal the gathering's purpose: they defended themselves against the charge on the grounds that they were entertaining wedding guests. The ten-pound turkey, large bowl of eggnog, and five-tier wedding cake served as corroborating evidence.[17]

Hush, February 23, 1957, 1.

Figure 16.1 Toronto tabloid Hush provided regular coverage of goings-on among local butch and femme lesbians, including this wedding ceremony.

Given that . . . lesbians rejected heterosexuality and insisted on making themselves publicly visible as queers, why did they embrace heterosexuality's most defining public ritual? For two principal reasons: first, asserting a right to give expression to same-sex desire extended to the right to make a public declaration of one's love for another; and second, while later critics would see conventional marriage as anathema to queer life, . . . "bride" and "groom" fit with their queer identities and the logic through which they organized their relationships. When Daisy de Jesus married couples in the Broadway Central Hotel lobby in New York City, she would ask the femme if she was willing to take her partner to be her "butch." By reworking its normative conventions, the wedding ceremony gave form and expression to romantic love. Neither ironic nor an appropriation, it was a radical assertion of self-love and queer dignity.

Even though they were released from the social pressures and legal constraints imposed on married heterosexuals, butches and femmes . . . overwhelmingly sought long-term stability in their romantic relationships. . . . "The striking similarity between lesbian and heterosexual relationships of this period is the centrality of the gendered couple to the emotional and affectional life of both communities."[18] Narrators described some relationships as "being like that of husband and wife," even when they had not had a wedding ceremony.[19] Sue Prosin's 1961 study of twenty lesbian couples' attitudes toward role relationship and self-image shows that attitudes on the West Coast were much the same: "In areas related to marriage, the values were no different [from those in heterosexual culture]. They were, in many respects, more strongly projected. The very emphasis on 'togetherness,' the marked emphasis on fidelity, and the consistent expression of the concept of obligation and responsibility would seem to indicate that a great deal of the value system of the dominant culture has been retained." She also noted greater identification with "the cultural concept of marriage among those who expressed an identification with masculine and feminine roles."[20] . . .

A 1951 investigation at the Women's Army Corp (WAC) training camp in Fort Myer, Virginia, reveals how lesbians used wedding ceremonies and marital conventions to identify and define sexual and affective relationships, a practice that stands in stark contrast to the attitudes of military investigators, who identified lesbians solely by sexual activity.[21] On 5 January 1951 Private Shirley Bowdon purportedly confessed to her commanding officer, Major Merrill, that she was a homosexual. The following day Bowdon was interviewed by two male officers of the military's Criminal Investigation Division and admitted to having "performed acts of cunnilingus," an act that in the eyes of the investigators confirmed that she was a true lesbian. The officers asked her to identify other lesbians in the ranks. Bowdon gave them eleven names. Within three months, the list of suspected lesbians had grown to eighty-two and included personnel stationed at Fort Lee, a WAC training camp 133 miles south.

The most common evidence that investigators used to identify homosexuals was eyewitness accounts of acts of physical touching such as kissing, embracing, mutual masturbation, and cunnilingus. Members of the Women's Army Corps, however, were more likely to identify weddings and marriages as proof. At Fort Myer, for example, WACs identified five married couples among their peers. Private First Class Norma Jordan was "married to a girl prior to entering the service and they had a license." Private Breita Burch was married to twenty-year-old Private Alice Grover, and they wore wedding rings they had given to each other. In a love letter Private E. C. McHale had sent to Private Virginia Page, McHale "declared that she was deeply in love with PAGE and that as soon as they could avail themselves of leave, they would go on a 'honeymoon'; buy wedding rings; and after leaving the service, purchase a home together 'a million miles from anyone else' and just live by themselves." One informant told investigators that two women who worked in a local tobacco factory supplied couples with marriage licenses.

. . .

Gay and women's liberationists had plenty of reasons why lesbians and gays should not get married. Martha Shelley characterized marriage as a "form of Uncle Tomism" intended to "reassure the straight society that we are respectable."[22] In his enormously influential text "A Gay Manifesto,"

Carl Wittman embraced love but characterized traditional marriage as "a rotten, oppressive institution." The marriage contract "smothers both people, denies needs, and places impossible demands on both people. . . . Gay people must stop gauging their self-respect by how well they mimic straight marriages. Gay marriages will have the same problems as straight ones except in burlesque. . . . To accept that happiness comes through finding a groovy spouse and settling down, showing the world that 'we're just the same as you' is avoiding the real issues, and is an expression of self-hatred."[23] Many gay and women's liberationists viewed the church, the family, and the state as the key institutions that produced the conditions of their oppression, and they did so by imposing gender roles that reinforced men's authority over women and heterosexuality as natural. This criticism extended to butch and femme culture. Lesbian feminists regarded masculinity and femininity, even among women, as oppressive.

. . .

. . . [However, other lesbian feminists disagreed. Rita] Laporte argued that radicals who denied "the beauty and authenticity of such lifelong, monogamous Lesbian marriages" overlooked a deeply meaningful aspect of queer women's experience.[24] Just as butch and femme reworked conventional sex and gender norms, lesbian weddings reworked conventional heteronormative rituals.

Lesbian wedding practices of the 1950s and 1960s, performed in semiprivate settings, were in the 1970s used in a very public manner to challenge homophobic attitudes, to insist on the dignity of same-sex couples' intimate relationships, and to protest lesbian and gay men's exclusion from the rights and benefits of citizenship. Following on the heels of Troy Perry, on 18 May 1970, second-year law student Jack Baker and librarian Michael McConnell of Minneapolis visited a local county clerk's office to apply for a marriage license. Baker and McConnell had been dating for four years, but their application was about more than romantic attachment and tax benefits; it was a planned political action that aimed "to provoke a heterosexual backlash by rhetorical and psychological confrontation, [and to] make our presence felt by the straight society, make them face the issue."[25] Further, they believed that by integrating gay cultural practices like nonmonogamy and liberationist values that rejected patriarchal gender roles and the legal subordination of one partner, gays would liberate heterosexuals from marriage's oppressive aspects. Conventionally attractive, middle class, and white, Baker and McConnell made great copy, and their story was picked up by mainstream news outlets across America.

Many more women than men, however, undertook similar actions. Significantly, the majority were women of color, and none were middle class.[26] . . .

That all people should be free to love and that gays and lesbians deserved equal rights, including the right to marry, were not two sides of the same coin, although it was easy to see them that way. In a 1973 appearance on David Susskind's enormously popular television talk show, Bernice Goodman, a fierce advocate for lesbian mothers and gay and lesbian youth and the first psychotherapist in America to come out publicly, said that she used to view marriage as a legal institution that oppressed women but that lately she and her long-time partner, Sandy Churnik, had come to feel that marriage validated loving, committed relationships.[27] "There is nothing that makes valid in our society . . . the homosexual way of life, or any part of our lifestyle," Goodman began.

Goodman: We have to validate ourselves . . . [and] realize our importance, and our lifestyle, that it's very respectable, very worthwhile, but we've never had enough images, we've never given ourselves back to ourselves. . . . We like living together and we want to be able to share this with everyone, even down to the corner grocer and shoemaker, as corny and trite as that may sound.

Churnik: I want total recognition of the degree of commitment we share in comparison to the degree of commitment that any man and woman are permitted to share in our society. We're entitled to it equally.[28]

Both supported same-sex marriage, but for different reasons. For Churnik, it was a matter of equal civil rights. For Goodman, the social recognition and legitimization marriage brings would make lesbian life more livable.

As Goodman herself acknowledged, lesbians interested in social and state recognition of their intimate relationship were "a minority in the gay minority." Imagine, then, what it was like for African American and Latina women, who were even more of a minority within the gay minority. Yet five of the lesbian couples who in the early 1970s made their wedding ceremonies an opportunity to publicly demand their love be recognized as on par with that shared by opposite-sex couples were women of color. Like white women and men, they demanded a license and insisted that they had the right to love anyone they wanted. For women of color, these actions put them in a minority within the African American and Latino communities, as well as within lesbian and gay political circles. . . .

The most significant difference between the views held by adherents to gay and women's liberationist ideology and those of African American

Jet, November 1971, p. 20.

Figure 16.2 Donna Burkett and Manonia Evans.

and Latina women was their relationship to the church and the traditional family, institutions viewed by liberationists as the primary source of oppression and exclusion for women and queers. Furthermore, for many people of color, liberationist groups did not provide the network of support needed for everyday survival, and the heterosexual nuclear family remained a valued refuge, as well as an important site for political organizing.[29] Horacio N. Roque Ramírez's research on San Francisco's Gay Latino Alliance (GALA) found that part of the cultural alienation Latina and Latino lesbians and gays felt in mainstream gay culture was the result of that culture's "alienation from one's family, from one's community, from one's self." One of his lesbian narrators reported: "The hardest and most rewarding experience I felt in dealing with my Gayness is the acceptance of familia. It's a very sensitive subject, especially in the Latino culture when the daughter, who is expected to leave only after her wedding, decides to leave because of her Gayness. . . . My gayness is very important to me, but my Raza consciousness tends to come first."[30] Gay liberationists, GALA explained, "suggest our second ailment [after the

Catholic Church] is the family; on the contrary, it is our source of strength. At the core of GALA's philosophy is not to alienate our selves from our families and community but to help them come to understand our gayness in a latino context."[31] . . .

The assertion that love—if "let be"—is the pathway to justice was an argument that many lesbians embraced through their participation in conventional marriage rituals. Wedding practices reinscribed lesbians as capaciously loving and in so doing created—even if only for a brief moment—a radical conception of the public sphere based in a public feeling of love.[32] . . . Just as masculinity did not belong to men nor femininity to women, wedding ceremonies did not belong to heterosexuals. From their perspective, the wedding was a cultural ritual that celebrated and validated loving sexual relationships between two people. It liberated queer love from the shackles of antihomosexual sentiment.[33] When rooted in love-politics, wedding practices assert a radical conception of the public sphere based not on the wounded subject or group rights but on an affirmation of queer life.

Notes

1. Lisa Duggan, *The Twilight of Equality? Neoliberalism, Cultural Politics, and the Attack on Democracy* (Boston: Beacon Press, 2003), 179. See also Gust A. Yepa, Karen E. Lovaasa, and John P. Eliaa, "A Critical Appraisal of Assimilationist and Radical Ideologies Underlying Same-Sex Marriage in LGBT Communities in the United States," *Journal of Homosexuality* 45, no. 1 (2008): 45–64.
2. Jennifer C. Nash, "Practicing Love: Black Feminism, Love-Politics, and Post Intersectionality," *Meridians: Feminism, Race, Transnationalism* 11, no. 2 (2013): 20.
3. Carl Wittman, *Refugees from America: A Gay Manifesto* (San Francisco: Council on Religion and the Homosexual, 1970).
4. Robin Morgan, "Lesbianism and Feminism: Synonyms or Contradictions?," in *Speaking for Our Lives: Historic Speeches and Rhetoric for Gay and Lesbian Rights (1892–2000),* ed. Robert B. Marks Rindiger (New York: Harrington Park Press, 2004), 210. Recently, scholars working in a Western European philosophical tradition have taken up love as a political practice. See Michael Hardt and Antonio Negri, *Commonwealth* (Cambridge, MA: Belknap Press, 2009); and Martha

C. Nussbaum, *Political Emotions: Why Love Matters for Justice* (Cambridge, MA: Harvard University Press, 2013). The analysis presented here, however, draws on four decades of black feminist theorizing that has been overlooked and remains unacknowledged by these scholars.
5. Madeline Davis, "Address to the Democratic National Convention," in Rindiger, *Speaking for Our Lives,* 179–80. Davis would later coauthor with Elizabeth Lapovsky Kennedy *Boots of Leather, Slippers of Gold: The History of a Lesbian Community* (New York: Routledge, 1993).
6. References to these feminists' views on love can be found in Patricia Hill Collins, *Black Feminist Thought* (New York: Routledge, 2000), 161–86; Patricia Hill Collins, *Black Sexual Politics: African Americans, Gender, and the New Racism* (New York: Routledge, 2004), 295–300; June Jordan, "Where Is the Love?," in *Some of Us Did Not Die: New and Selected Essays* (New York: Basic Books, 2002), 268–74; Audre Lorde, *In Search of Our Mother's Garden* (San Diego: Harcourt Brace Jovanovich, 1983), xi–xii; and Lorde, "Uses of the Erotic" and "Eye to Eye: Black Women, Hatred,

and Anger," in *Sister Outsider: Essays and Speeches* (Berkeley: Crossing Press, 1984; repr., 2007), 53–59, 145–75. In her examination of African American feminists' articulation of love as political praxis, Nash coins the term "love-politics." See Nash, "Practicing Love," 2–3.

7. Collins, *Black Sexual Politics*, 3.

8. June Jordan, *Some of Us Did Not Die* (New York: Basic Books, 2003), 272, cited in Nash, "Practicing Love," 13.

9. Cathy Cohen, "Punks, Bulldaggers, and Welfare Queens: The Ratical Potential of Queer Politics?" *GLQ: A Journal of Lesbian and Gay Studies* 3, no. 4 (1997), 14. On the limits of identity politics and its corollary, the politics of recognition in the context of same-sex marriage in the United States, see Tom Boellstorff, "When Marriage Falls: Queer Coincidences in Straight Time," *GLQ: A Journal of Lesbian and Gay Studies* 13, no. 2–3 (2007): 227–48.

10. People participate in ceremonies, rituals, and even political protests for diverse reasons. For example, some women likely wanted to marry because they had spent their youth fantasizing about wearing a white wedding gown and did not want to be robbed of the opportunity. Oral interview evidence suggests that some women married to signal to other women that their partners were "taken" and that flirting with them would not be tolerated. Yet, just as the fact that some people attend LGBTQ rallies in hope of meeting a sexual partner does not diminish the political significance of participating in a march or the march itself, the diverse motivations that led women to hold a semipublic wedding do not diminish the fact that such ceremonies affirmed queer life.

11. Lillian Faderman, *Surpassing the Love of Men: Romantic Friendship and Love between Women from the Renaissance to the Present* (New York: William Morrow and Company, 1998), 120–25.

12. Lillian Faderman, *Surpassing the Love of Men: Romantic Friendship and Love between Women from the Renaissance to the Present* (New York: William Morrow and Company, 1998), 190–230.

13. There are early traces of women of color forming such unions. Addie Brown, a working-class African American servant from Maryland, "longed to call her lover, Rebecca Primus, a Reconstruction-era teacher from a prominent black, Connecticut family 'my husband.'" "'If either Addie or Rebecca were a gent,' commented Primus's mother, 'then they would marry.'" Steven J. Niven, "Blues Singer Gladys Bentley Broke Ground with Marriage to a Woman in 1931," The Root, accessed August 21, 2015, http://www.theroot.com/articles/history/2015/02/gladys_bentley_a_lesbian_icon_and_blues_singer_of_the_harlem_renaissance.html.

14. Alison Owram, *Her Husband Was a Woman! Women's Gender-Crossing in Modern British Popular Culture* (New York: Routledge, 2007), 146–48. For an example

of such a marriage, see "Girl Who 'Wed' Another Girl: Pre-1950 Gay, Lesbian and Transgender Marriages in the U.S.," San Francisco Public Library, accessed August 21, 2015, http://pre-1950sgaymarriage.org/index.php (site discontinued).

15. "She-Male Queer Colony Celebrate 'Do-It-Yourself' Marriage," *Hush*, August 17, 1957.

16. "She-Male Queer Colony Celebrate 'Do-It-Yourself' Marriage," *Hush*, August 17, 1957. The relationship between the Toronto Police Force and gay women is explored in greater detail in Elise Chenier, "Rethinking Class in Lesbian Bar Culture: Living 'the Gay Life' in Toronto, 1955–1965," *Left History* 9, no. 2 (2004): 85–118.

17. "'Wedding' of Two Women Interrupted by Police," *JET*, April 16, 1953. See also Marc Stein, *City of Sisterly and Brotherly Loves: Lesbian and Gay Philadelphia, 1945-1972* (Chicago: University of Chicago Press, 2000), 30, 136.

18. Kennedy and Davis, *Boots of Leather*, 232.

19. Kennedy and Davis, *Boots of Leather*, 280, 286–87.

20. Sue Prosin, "The Lesbian: A Study in Self-Image and Role Playing Patterns," Sue Prosin Papers (Collection 2225), Charles E. Young Research Library, University of California, Los Angeles (UCLA).

21. Testimony of Peggy J. Davis, March 25, 1951, Office of the Provost Marshal, Fort Myer, VA, p. 6, decimal 220.8, box 3778, classified decimal file, 1950–51, Records of the Adjutant General's Office, 1917, Record Group 407, National Archives at College Park, MD.

22. Martha Shelley, "On Marriage," *Ladder*, October/November 1968, 46–47.

23. Carl Wittman, "A Gay Manifesto," in Karla Jay and Allen Young, *Out of the Closets: Voices of Gay Liberation* (New York: Douglas Books, 1972), 330–41. The manifesto was initially distributed by the radical gay liberation group Red Butterfly and by the Council on Religion and the Homosexual. Its appearance in Karla Jay and Allen Young's anthology ensured it the largest possible audience and established it as a foundational text.

24. Rita Laporte, "The Butch/Femme Question," *Ladder*, June/July 1971, 10.

25. Michael Boucai, "Glorious Precedents: When Gay Marriage Was Radical," *Yale Journal of Law and the Humanities* 27, no. 1 (2015): 140.

26. This finding is based on an extensive review of American mainstream and lesbian and gay print media and is part of ongoing research for a book-length manuscript.

27. *The David Susskind Show,* February 11, 1973, Miscellaneous Sound Recordings 0274, Rudy Grillo sound recordings, 1970–89, New York Public Library Manuscripts and Archives Division; Bernice Goodman, *The Lesbian Mother* (New York: Institute for Human Identity, 1973). Interestingly, Goodman appeared on the Susskind show anonymously but then revealed the

name of a book she had just written. For more about
Goodman's activism, see "In Memoriam," *Journal of
Gay and Lesbian Social Services* 17, no. 1 (2004):
xix–xxii.

28. *The David Susskind Show*, February 11, 1973.

29. Hazel V. Carby, "White Woman Listen! Black
Feminism and the Boundaries of Sisterhood," in
Black British Cultural Studies: A Reader, ed. Houston
A. Baker, Manthia Diawara, and Ruth H. Lindeborg
(Chicago: University of Chicago Press, 1996), 63–64.

30. Horacio N. Roque Ramírez, "'That's My Place!':
Negotiating Racial, Sexual, and Gender Politics in San
Francisco's Gay Latino Alliance, 1975–1983," *Journal of
the History of Sexuality* 12, no. 2 (2003): 242.

31. Horacio N. Roque Ramírez, "'That's My Place!':
Negotiating Racial, Sexual, and Gender Politics in San
Francisco's Gay Latino Alliance, 1975–1983," *Journal of
the History of Sexuality* 12, no. 2 (2003): 250–51

32. Nash, "Practicing Love," 13.

33. Heather Love's advocacy for a queer ordinary suggests
a similar effort to create a space for subjectivity
that is not rigidly defined as either normative or
antinormative, as is the tendency in queer theory.
See her "Doing Being Deviant: Deviance Studies,
Description, and the Queer Ordinary," in *differences* 26,
no. 1 (2015): 74–95.

Chapter 17

Overview

Where do we look for love and sex? Because gender is so closely bound up with sexuality, the search can get complicated for people who do not identify as the sex category to which they were assigned at birth or whose desires do not conform to heterosexual norms. Ayden Scheim and colleagues investigate the experiences of transgender men seeking partners among other men in what they term the "queer sexual field." Their participants expressed important distinctions between gay environments and queer ones and were more comfortable in the latter. They associated gay sexual fields with an older style of sexual interaction, in which gender fluidity or gender-transition was not valued and trans men were at risk of being perceived as lesbians or heterosexual women. Online spaces such as Craigslist and physical spaces such as gay bars presented their own distinct challenges and opportunities for finding partners.

Gay, Bisexual, and Queer Trans Men Navigating Sexual Fields

Ayden I. Scheim, Barry D. Adam, and Zack Marshall

Introduction

In this article, we analyze the ways in which transgender (trans) men who are attracted to other men navigate the sexual fields available to them.

Scheim, Ayden I., Barry D. Adam, and Zack Marshall. "Gay, Bisexual, and Queer Trans Men Navigating Sexual Fields." *Sexualities*, 2019, 22(4), pp. 566–586. Reprinted by Permission of SAGE Publications, Ltd.

Trans men are individuals assigned a female sex at birth but who identify as male or masculine. Survey data show that majorities of Canadian and American trans men do not identify as heterosexual, with one-quarter to one-half identifying as bisexual or gay, and higher proportions as queer, which may or may not index attraction to cisgender (non-trans) men (Bauer et al., 2013; James et al., 2016; Iantaffi and Bockting, 2011).

. . .

For many trans men, the process of transitioning across genders and sexes leads to questioning the sexual orientation trichotomy of gay, bisexual, and straight—categories that "presume a congruence between ascribed sex and gender and a permanence of sex and gender" (Gagne and Tewksbury, 1998: 78). Some, but by no means all, trans men relish the opportunity to participate in "queering sexuality" (Vidal-Ortiz, 2002) by either rejecting these categories or radically redefining them, for instance by insisting on a gay male identity while continuing to partner with cisgender women. Sanger (2010) argues that by virtue of their experiences, trans people may embrace a notion of sexuality as alterable, potentially fluid, and relational, rather than a reflection of a "true", authentic self. . . .

Green's (2008a, 2008b, 2014) sexual fields framework provides a sociological model for understanding "collective sexual life" (Green, 2014: 25) by extending the Bourdieusian triad of habitus, field, and capital (Bourdieu, 1977, 1980) to account for the social contribution to sexual ideation, practice, and opportunity. A field is a hierarchical arena in which practice is shaped by the aggregation of individual dispositions (habitus), field-specific rules, and various forms of capital that are mobilized in struggles for position. Thus, sexual fields are "[c]onceived [of] as socially structured contexts composed of situated agents, institutionalized practices and one (or more) logic of desirability . . . " (Adam and Green, 2014: 123) which take form in sites of sexual sociality (Green, 2008a). Key sensitizing concepts of sexual field theory include erotic habitus, structures of desire, and sexual or erotic capital. Erotic habitus is constituted by individual erotic tastes and sensibilities that are subject to change in response to the field (e.g. through processes of sexual socialization). Structures of desire are "transpersonal valuations of attractiveness" (Green, 2014: 14) produced from the aggregation of erotic habitus within a field. An individual's sexual capital is then determined by field-specific structures of desire, and is somewhat convertible, but not entirely reducible to other forms (e.g. social, economic).

Trans men's engagement with extant sexual fields has received little empirical attention. Sociologists have tended to explore questions of sexual identity and micro-level practice in relation to gender transition and shifting embodiment (Devor, 1993; Dozier, 2005; Rubin, 2003; Schleifer, 2006; Vidal-Ortiz, 2002; Williams et al., 2013). In contrast, public health literature has addressed trans men's negotiation of sexual fields in the context of concerns about their risk for HIV and other sexually transmitted infections as they enter gay men's socio-sexual milieus and thus a heightened HIV risk environment (Rowniak et al., 2011). . . .

[T]his article describes trans men's understandings of, and strategies for affective and behavioral negotiation within, virtual and physical sexual fields in which they might find male sexual partners. We draw on qualitative data from a community-based research study on the sexual health of trans men who have sex with men in Ontario, Canada.

Method

These data come from a larger community-based research project led by a team, a majority of whom were gay, bisexual, or queer trans men. . . . Study participants had to identify as trans men or with another transmasculine (female-to-male spectrum) gender identity and live in Ontario, Canada. . . . Forty study participants were recruited through social media, LGBT and HIV organizations, and LGBT venues. . . .

Study participants ranged from 18 to 50 years old, with half being between 25 and 34 and 28% between 18 and 24 years. This reflects the young age distribution of trans men in Ontario (Bauer et al., 2012). Proportions of participants who were Indigenous or people of color, and of those living in the Greater Toronto Area (Canada's largest urban center with the highest concentration of trans resources), were predetermined by quota sampling goals. One-third were non-Indigenous people of color, 10% were Aboriginal or Indigenous (First Nations, Inuit, or Métis), and 57% were white. For comparison, an estimated 72% of Ontario residents in

2011 were white (Statistics Canada, 2013). Most (70%) lived in the Greater Toronto Area. They described their sexual orientation identities as queer (68%), gay (33%), bisexual (25%), Two Spirit (5%),[1] and straight (5%), with 16 participants (40%) selecting multiple categories.

Relationship statuses were diverse: while 38% were single, others were partnered with cisgender men (28%), trans men (23%), cisgender women (23%), and trans women (3%). Some indicated more than one type of partner. The vast majority (90%) reported sex with cisgender men in the past six months (note that we specifically sought to recruit men meeting this criterion, given the study aims). Half said that their preferred sex partners included both male- and female-identified partners. Of the one-third of participants who preferred male-identified partners, most were open to cisgender or trans men, while three were interested in cisgender men only. . . .

Findings

The primary distinction drawn by trans men in interviews was between gay and queer sexual fields, with some describing and participating in subfields inside these two broad arenas. Consistent with previous research (Reisner et al., 2010; Sevelius, 2009), trans men met most of their cisgender male partners online, as an intentional strategy to retain control over the disclosure process and to bypass in-person disclosure of trans status. Specific websites for seeking sex, and Craigslist in particular, also emerged as important fields with their own internal logics and sexual opportunity structures for trans men.

. . .

Queer versus Gay

Many of the trans men we interviewed drew sharp distinctions between *gay* and *queer* communities, socio-sexual venues, and individual cisgender men. For some participants who were queer-identified and described their sexual field preference as queer, their queerness was characterized by a disidentification with (cisgender) gay

men attributed to the perceived apolitical and oppressive nature of gay men's communities:

> I separate them into cis queer dudes and cis gay dudes. And I don't really think of cis gay dudes as being really political or doing any work around anti-oppression. (20s; queer; trans man; racialized; completed transition)

Participants tended to speak of queer or gay fields, with bisexual more often invoked as a property of individuals rather than socio-sexual spheres. However, as an identifier, bisexual could be quite strategically useful for finding male partners open to trans men:

> When I do an OkCupid [mixed-orientation dating website] search, I search bisexual, but really what I'm looking for is non-transphobic people. (40s; queer; male, trans man; white; in process of transitioning)

This did not appear to extend beyond the internet; trans men did not refer to specific physical sites in which they could meet bisexual or queer men. One participant (20s; gay, bisexual, queer; trans man; white) contrasted the queer, predominantly women's community organized around specific venues with "groups of [queer] guys" who feel alienated from gay sexual fields. In Toronto, the boundary between gay and queer mapped onto a geographic distinction between the gay village and the alternative "Queer West" neighborhood west of downtown Toronto. Like the boundaries described by Nash (2013) in her research with queer women, trans men understood the west-end scene as "more queer-ish than gay and so there's a lot more trans and genderqueer people that hang out there" (30s; gay, queer; male, trans man, genderqueer; white; completed transition).

. . .

Queer women's spaces were generally described as sites in which trans men were socially valued and erotically desired. . . .

Since most participants were not exclusively attracted to men, queer spaces were where they met female sexual and romantic partners. They were also spaces in which some participants, who were not consistently read as male, felt more welcome and even celebrated. Yet, for those who wanted to have sex with cisgender men, the queer sexual field proved challenging:

> Meeting other guys is definitely a challenge for me in terms of sexual partners. I find it easier to meet women. Because the spaces that I feel awesome in are "women and trans and gender nonconforming people." . . . I love going to spaces and knowing that people are going to respect my pronouns. (20s; queer; trans man; white; in process of transitioning)

. . .

For those partnered with women, engagement in queer sexual fields was supplemented by seeking sex with men online, often surreptitiously:

> We realize it's kind of like a secret world [of trans men who have sex with men]. . . . Because for the most part, we engage in relationships with women and are part of queer women's circles. And then, so it's just finding out and being like, "Oh, you go on Craigslist too? What?! That's awesome!" (20s; queer; male, trans man, transmasculine, masculine of center; racialized; completed transition)

Gay Sexual Fields

In general, there was a great deal of consensus in our sample about the existence of a specifically *gay* sexual field, and what types of sexual sites (physical and virtual) it comprises: bars, bathhouses, and gay-specific cruising apps. For some trans men, gay sexual field(s) were perceived as largely homogenous and problematic:

> Interviewer: And when you say "gay men's culture", can you give me an example of what you're referring to? Participant: Like, [well-known bar in gay village]. [It's] a good example because . . . you can see the pockets of people, like people of colour over here and older white men are over there. (20s; queer; male; white; completed transition)

This reduction of gay sexual fields to their most visible and mainstream manifestations is not unique to trans men, but may be magnified for trans men with less experience of gay venues. Participants with more experience of gay male sexual fields commented on their heterogeneity. One participant explained that while he certainly did not feel welcome in every gay venue as a racialized trans man, this was not a universal experience across venues:

> Yeah, I mean of course the gay men's community is not homogenous, so I don't feel comfortable in like, bear spaces for example, cause I find them to be oriented towards a certain body type and hairiness and whiteness. (30s; queer; male, trans man; racialized; completed transition)

. . .

Yet others, particularly trans men who had not completed a medical transition, felt entirely outside the realm of desirability within gay sexual fields, based on their interactions with cisgender men and reading of "sign vehicles" (Green, 2011) that relay which types of men are sexually valued:

> I just didn't see any other trans men there. I didn't see any images of trans men. It just seemed like everything is focused on guys with muscley chests and big dicks and that's what everyone wants, and I don't have that. (20s; queer, Two Spirit; male, trans man; Aboriginal; in process of transition)

Barriers to Gay Sexual Spaces

For trans men who had not medically transitioned, were early into a medical transition, and/ or who were not consistently read as men, gay sexual spaces were generally viewed as inaccessible:

> When I try to talk to gay men at bars, they just think I'm a dyke. . . . I just find it so challenging as someone who's not on hormones. (20s; queer; trans man; white; in process of transition)

However, medically transitioning did not in itself result in easier access to bars and bathhouses. Having a female sex designation on identification cards posed a barrier to accessing spaces requiring proof of age. Some trans men who were read as cisgender men still feared being formally excluded from such spaces and were not prepared to face the risk of being barred:

> I've always imagined that trans men are not treated very well there [bathhouses] and I've heard that they're not allowed. . . . Being told that I'm not allowed in gay men's space happens to me in a non-official kind of way often and the idea of it happening in an official way is heartbreaking. (20s; gay; male; white; completed transition)

Perceptions of the degree of transition required to be welcome in gay men's sexual spaces varied; bodily acceptance was feared always to be just out of reach. Trans men who had not undergone "top surgery" (double mastectomy and chest reconstruction) explained that they could not enter these spaces until after surgery, but for some men who had completed top surgery, genital surgery was seen as the final step required.

. . .

In addition to perceived exclusion from gay sexual spaces, fears concerning gender identity disclosure complicated engagement in gay men's sexual spaces. Disclosure in sexualized environments was considered impossible for many participants, which they attributed to social anxiety, the potential for sexual rejection to invalidate gender identity, and the threat of undermining hard-won acceptance or ability to be read as cisgender:

> They're viewing me exactly how I want them to view me . . . so, it's always a difficult thing for me to be like, oh, should I tell them? Should I not? Always. Always. It's constant, constant. (20s; queer; male; racialized; completed transition)

. . .

Virtual Gay Spaces

With few exceptions, the internet and smartphone apps were the primary sources of sexual partners for participants. The collective coming out and proliferation of trans-masculine identities since the mid-2000s has coincided with the online revolution in gay male connection (Gudelunas, 2012), and trans men have taken full advantage of this technology. The most popular site for partner-seeking, Craigslist, appears to constitute a field unto itself, not anchored to the usual categories of sexual orientation (Grov et al., 2014). Some trans men did use men-only sites or apps oriented toward gay men. A participant who was on hormones but had not otherwise medically transitioned explained:

> I'm on Grindr [the most popular geosocial sexual networking application for gay and bisexual men]. . . . Nothing's ever come by it. . . . Most of the messages are people messaging me like, "Are you a guy or a girl?" (20s; gay; trans man; white; in process of transitioning)

For trans men who are read as male, gay cruising websites and apps allowed them to bypass in-person disclosure, otherwise the most challenging aspect of navigating gay sexual fields:

> The most effective way for me [to meet men] has been through Scruff [a gay/bisexual geosocial application associated with the "bear" scene]. . . . The biggest thing probably is that I can just say right on my profile that I'm trans. (30s; gay, queer; male, trans man, genderqueer; white; completed transition)

Craigslist

The online classifieds page, Craigslist, was undoubtedly the most common site for finding sexual partners for study participants. For some, Craigslist was the only partner-seeking venue they accessed, while for others, it complemented their participation in other fields. As with other web- and app-based venues, the primary advantage of seeking sex on Craigslist is the ease with which disclosure can occur in advance of meeting someone in person:

> [At a party for gay men] I was getting approached by lots of men. I almost had an anxiety attack or something. . . . Lots of guys were talking to me but I didn't want to come out to them. . . . Because of that, I prefer to meet people through Scruff or Grindr, or Craigslist just 'cause I can pretty much always out myself before I meet them. (20s; bisexual, queer; trans man; white; completed transition)

Similarly, Craigslist was perceived as providing a non-threatening environment in which to set boundaries around safer sex. Such boundaries might otherwise be difficult to enforce with cisgender men, particularly for those with less confidence negotiating sex with men:

> I don't really hang out in spaces where there's a lot of guys. So I have to kind of turn to Craigslist. . . . I can literally post what I want and what I don't want, and like, you know, I'm fearful of doing that in person. Cause I mean, with queer women I'm learning to do that and it feels okay, but with men I don't. . . . I don't know, I still carry a lot of fear. I don't know if I'd be able to do it. (20s; queer; male, trans man, transmasculine, masculine of center; racialized; completed transition)

Craigslist is unique in that it cuts across sexual orientation and gender binaries that tend to structure other personal ad sites. With search options including open text boxes, and the ability to classify one's ad as "m4m", "t4m", etc., Craigslist allows trans men to find sexual partners who are explicitly interested in trans men (Farr, 2010). On other sites, indicating trans status is not so straightforward:

> I noticed that like, with any other site, it's kind of weird because there's no reliable way to represent that I'm a trans guy. I can write it but people don't read. (20s; bisexual; male, trans man; racialized; in process of transitioning)

. . .

Craigslist was seen as particularly convenient for those in primary relationships with women who were seeking sex outside their relationship, including those who were not in mutually non-monogamous relationships:

> I find that's just the easiest 'cause . . . I want a situation where we hook up and then we leave. I don't want conversation, I'm seeking no kind of intimacy, I don't want a relationship, I don't want dates, I don't want to be your friend. (20s; bisexual, queer; male, trans man; white; completed transition)

. . .

Discussion

This research collaboration of trans and non-trans gay, bisexual, and queer-identified men was particularly interested in documenting the engagement of trans men who have sex with men with the social and sexual fields available to them. The result is a snapshot of people in motion in two senses: (1) at the personal level as they transition into increasing embodiment and comfort with masculinization, and (2) at the historical level as transgender people increasingly claim social space and validation in a world that has long denied or suppressed their existence. . . . These changes include the rise of the internet which has opened new virtual spaces for the social connection of transgender people with each other and with cisgender people who recognize and affirm them, but they also include increasing awareness and acceptance of trans men among cisgender gay and bisexual men and a changing socio-legal environment in Canada that includes human rights protections for trans people in many jurisdictions, as well as relationship and marriage rights regardless of gender.

. . . The participants in this study tended to sort themselves into queer and gay sexual fields, at least in part related to self-assessments of gender presentation combined with perceptions of the norms and hierarchies associated with each field. In general, trans men are unexpected and sometimes unwelcome players in gay sexual fields, and thus issues of "passing" as male and negotiating disclosure are most salient for trans men trying to navigate them. . . . Websites like Craigslist were perceived as alternative sexual fields which provide a specific niche for openly trans-identified individuals seeking cisgender male sex partners, and are populated by men thought to be less bound by the sexual field demands of either gay or heterosexual expectations.

. . .

What trans men seek in pursuing sexual and romantic relationships can be variable—it may be sex, validation, or community—and different social and sexual fields may be accessed in the pursuit of these interests. How they pursue these relationships may involve the balancing of potential pleasure against perceived risk. For participants, medical gender transition, resulting in the acquisition of male-typical secondary sex characteristics that Kessler and McKenna (1978) called "cultural genitalia", was usually a prerequisite for playing the gay sexual field (though the threat of "reality enforcement" (Bettcher, 2014: 392) through genital revelation was ever-present, particularly in sexualized environments). This did not necessarily overlap with identification as a "gay trans man". Indeed, sexual field choice and sexual orientation identity were often unaligned, potentially reflecting, in part, the limited options for those unable (or unwilling) to be read as male and to assimilate to the behavioral expectations and cultural norms they associate with gay male fields.

Unlike queer fields in which gender nonconformity or fluidity are more often celebrated, success in navigating gay male fields required trans men to learn how to navigate social interaction as men, despite varying degrees of female socialization. Schilt (2010: 52) describes the interactive process of "achieving social maleness" through a form of lay ethnomethodology, employing knowledge of male behavioral norms accumulated over the lifetime to develop "gender literacy" and the ability to flexibly apply gendered rules for behavior. . . .

Trans men were inventive and resourceful in making their sex lives "work" in pre-existing sexual fields organized around cisgender bodies, and creatively prospected for men who would accept (or ignore) their trans embodiment. This was often accomplished through some degree of compromise or satisficing: from limiting themselves to performing oral sex to avoid disclosure to potentially "lowering their standards" in the context of meeting men on Craigslist. Depending on a trans man's transition stage and willingness to accept emotional and physical risks, shaping a workable sex life could mean accessing sexual fields not aligned with his ideal preference and/or sexual orientation identity. As trans men continue to move into new socio-sexual spaces and to progress toward greater acceptance in some settings (particularly urban gay, bisexual, and queer communities), we anticipate that their strategies and options for navigating sexual fields will continue to evolve. It remains to be seen whether the growing presence of trans men within gay sexual fields will pose a lasting challenge to their boundaries and erotic capital hierarchies, particularly regarding inclusion of trans men with more gender-diverse or non-binary identities and embodiments.

Note

1. A term used by many North American Indigenous peoples to refer to a range of culturally-specific traditional gender and sexual identities.

References

Adam BD and Green AI (2014) Circuits and the social organization of sexual fields. In: Green AI (ed.) *Sexual Fields: Toward a Sociology of Collective Sexual Life.* Chicago, Ill: University of Chicago Press, pp. 123–42.

Bauer GR, Redman N, Bradley K, et al. (2013) Sexual health of trans men who are gay, bisexual, or who have sex with men: Results from Ontario, Canada. *International Journal of Transgenderism* 14(2): 66–74.

Bauer GR, Travers R, Scanlon K, et al. (2012) High heterogeneity of HIV-related sexual risk among transgender people in Ontario, Canada: A province-wide respondent-driven sampling survey. *BMC Public Health* 12: 292.

Bettcher TM (2014) Trapped in the wrong theory: Rethinking trans oppression and resistance. *Signs* 39(2): 383–406.

Bourdieu P (1977) *Outline of a Theory of Practice*. Cambridge: Cambridge University Press.

Bourdieu P (1980) *The Logic of Practice*. Stanford, Calif: University of Stanford Press.

Devor H (1993) Sexual orientation identities, attractions, and practices of female-to-male transsexuals. *The Journal of Sex Research* 30(4): 303–15.

Dozier R (2005) Beards, breasts, and bodies doing sex in a gendered world. *Gender and Society* 19(3): 297–316.

Farr D (2010) A very personal world: Advertisement and identity of trans-persons on Craigslist. In: Pulen C and Cooper M (eds) *LGBT Identity and Online New Media*. New York, NY: Routledge, pp. 87–99.

Gagne P and Tewksbury R (1998) Rethinking binary conceptions and social constructions: Transgender experiences of gender and sexuality. In: Segal MT and Demos V (eds) *Advances in Gender Research*. Vol 3. Stanford, Conn: Advances in Gender Research, pp. 73–102.

Green AI (2008a) The social organization of desire: The sexual fields approach. *Sociological Theory* 26(1): 25–50.

Green AI (2008b) Erotic habitus: Toward a sociology of desire. *Theory and Society* 37(6): 597–626.

Green AI (2011) Playing the (sexual) field: The interactional basis of systems of sexual stratification. *Social Psychology Quarterly* 74(3): 244–66.

Green AI (ed.) (2014) *Sexual Fields: Toward a Sociology of Collective Sexual Life*. Chicago, Ill: University of Chicago Press.

Grov C, Rendina HJ and Parsons JT (2014) Comparing three cohorts of MSM sampled via sex parties, bars/clubs, and craigslist.org: Implications for researchers and providers. *AIDS Education and Prevention* 26(4): 362–82.

Gudelunas D (2012) There's an app for that: The uses and gratifications of online social networks for gay men. *Sexuality & Culture* 16(4): 347–65.

Iantaffi A and Bockting WO (2011) Views from both sides of the bridge? Gender, sexual legitimacy and transgender people's experiences of relationships. *Culture, Health & Sexuality* 13(3): 355–70.

James SE, Herman JL, Rankin S, et al. (2016) *The Report of the 2015 U.S. Transgender Survey*. Washington, DC: National Center for Transgender Equality.

Kessler SJ and McKenna W (1978) *Gender: An Ethnomethodological Approach*. Chicago, Ill: University of Chicago Press.

Nash CJ (2013) Queering neighbourhoods: Politics and practice in Toronto. *ACME: An International E-Journal for Critical Geographies* 12(2): 193–219.

Reisner SL, Perkovich B and Mimiaga MJ (2010) A mixed methods study of the sexual health needs of New England transmen who have sex with nontransgender men. *AIDS Patient Care and STDs* 24(8): 501–13.

Rowniak S, Chesla C, Rose CD, et al. (2011) Transmen: The HIV risk of gay identity. *AIDS Education & Prevention* 23(6): 508–20.

Rubin H (2003) *Self-Made Men: Identity and Embodiment and Transsexual Men*. Nashville, Tenn: Vanderbilt University Press.

Sanger T (2010) *Trans People's Partnerships: Towards an Ethics of Intimacy*. New York, N.Y: Palgrave Macmillan.

Schilt K (2010) *Just One of the Guys?* Chicago, Ill: University of Chicago Press.

Schleifer D (2006) Make me feel mighty real: Gay female-to-male transgenderists negotiating sex, gender, and sexuality. *Sexualities* 9(1): 57–75.

Sevelius J (2009) "There's no pamphlet for the kind of sex I have": HIV-related risk factors and protective behaviors among transgender men who have sex with nontransgender men. *Journal of the Association of Nurses in AIDS Care* 20(5): 398–410.

Statistics Canada (2013) Ontario (Code 35) (table). 2011 National Household Survey (NHS) Profile. Available at: http://www12.statcan.gc.ca/nhs-enm/2011/dp-pd/prof/index.cfm?Lang¼E (accessed 28 April 2017).

Vidal-Ortiz S (2002) Queering sexuality and doing gender: Transgender men's identification with gender and sexuality. In: Gagne P and Tewksbury R (eds) *Gendered Sexualities (Advances in Gender Research, Vol 6)*. Bingley: Emerald, pp. 181–233.

Williams CJ, Weinberg MS and Rosenberger JG (2013) Trans men: Embodiments, identities, and sexualities. *Sociological Forum* 28(4): 719–41.

Chapter 18

Overview

Who was Jennifer Murphy? If you were watching the news in the early 2000s, you would have come away with the impression of a dangerous predator who played Russian roulette with men's lives by having sex allegedly without informing her male partners that she had HIV, the viral infection that leads to AIDS. Jenny Roth and Chris Sanders investigated the media coverage Murphy received and found that Roth's gender—the fact that she was a woman who was having unprotected sex, rather than a man—strongly inflected the way the criminal case against her was reported. Murphy was depicted as a "hard-luck" case who habitually cursed, dressed in revealing clothing, was overweight, and propositioned men. None of these are crimes, yet they were highlighted in reporting on her case, such as in the writing of the columnist Rosie DiManno, who described her as an "incorrigible slag." Roth and Sanders argue that this kind of reporting constructs Murphy as a person whose alleged crimes are violations of gender norms of demure and quiet femininity as much as crimes against the people who were exposed to HIV by having sex with her. This construction is not just about gender: Roth and Sanders make the claim that Murphy was "coded" as a particular stereotype of a low-income or economically marginalized woman whose very presence in public spaces is considered an affront to proper order.

"Incorrigible Slag," the Case of Jennifer Murphy's HIV Non-disclosure

Gender Norm Policing and the Production of Gender-Class-Race Categories in Canadian News Coverage

Jenny Roth and Chris Sanders

Introduction

In "'Callous, Cold and Deliberately Duplicitous:' Racialization, Immigration and the Representation of HIV Criminalization in Canadian Mainstream Newspapers," Mykhalovskiy, Hastings, Sanders, Hayman, and Bisaillon (2016) explored the institutionalization of racism in news surrounding criminal cases of HIV non-disclosure in Canada. They found that the long-standing discursive "connections between race, crime, and immigration" lead to the overrepresentation of racialized men, generally, and recent immigrant men, in particular, in HIV non-disclosure coverage. Their study found that media reports of the men often reflected historically-bound racist stereotypes of "hypersexual" black men who pose a public health threat to individual (white) women and, more broadly, to the imagined Canadian nation (Mykhalovskiy et al., 2016: 8–9). . . .

There is another layer to the discourse of HIV reporting that appears briefly in their report, and which this paper pursues further: news coverage of Jennifer Murphy, a non-racialized HIV-positive woman who was also over-determined in Canadian news coverage. . . . Murphy's case stands out because of the volume of media coverage she received. The fact that she is one of the few women who have been charged in Canada, and yet one of the most-reported transgressors shows that alongside racialized men, white women who transgress are also easily represented as a threat. This stands in contrast to racialized women, who, when charged, rarely appear at all.

. . . [W]e want to reflect on the Imperial relationship between the gender norm policing of Murphy in news coverage alongside the over-representation of racialized men, and the comparative absence of racialized women and non-racialized men.

. . . [A]lthough we do not mean to suggest that the representations today directly mirror the language and stories that were circulated in the British

Imperial period, we do want to consider how the historical continuum of dominant discourses produces narratives that echo colonial constructions of the sexual licentiousness of poor women and racialized men, while relegating racialized women to a position of relative discursive non-existence. . . .

Methods

Methods—News Articles

Jennifer Murphy first came to media attention in the early 2000s (Kilty, 2014; Mykhalovskiy et al., 2016). To develop our dataset of newspaper articles about Murphy, we conducted an English-language search of Canadian Major Dailies (CMD). The CMD database provides full-text format, archival access to the top national and regional newspapers in Canada. We searched keywords "Jennifer Murphy" and "HIV" or "AIDS" between 2000 and 2018, which yielded 239 hits. Next, we reviewed each article to omit erroneous hits and duplicate articles. This left 103 relevant newspaper articles published between 2005 and 2013.[1] . . .

Our analytic approach uses the method of critical discourse analysis of narrative discourses (e.g., van Dijk, 1987b, 1990). Mass media newspaper articles about criminal cases of HIV non-disclosure are more than just reportage of events from the perspectives of different social actors. The ways by which these stories make both explicit and implicit connections between HIV, gender, crime, sexual relationships, and immoral and salacious behaviour are cause for concern. While there is no single approach by which audiences interpret and respond to news media (Kitzinger, 1998), many researchers agree that mainstream media play a critical role in shaping public perceptions about HIV/AIDS (see, for example, Lupton, 1994; Swain, 2005), and although different readers may come from different social locations, there are dominant gender schema that are socially and culturally fairly consistent, through which the articles are narrated and received.

. . .

Although news is ostensibly socially situated as discourse that serves a "referential function . . . that conveys information," when read through the critical discourse paradigm, it is not "objective, or even 'true' . . . for all given perspectives," particularly because of the dominant cultural narratives that produce the "reality" about women, men, sex, "degeneracy," and dangerous bodies (Georgakopoulou & Goutsos, 2004: 15; see also Reddick 1986: 33–5, 41). These schema, the "structures which represent generalised concepts stored in our memory: concepts which underlie objects, situations, events, actions and sequences of events or actions" are, in the case of Jennifer Murphy rooted in the generalized concepts of gender norms that are used to police bodies and sexuality (Georgakopoulou & Goutsos, 2004: 32; see also, broadly, the early work of Johnson-Laird, 1983, and van Dijk, 1987a). . . .

Gender norms are "ideology inscribed on the body . . . circumscribed by social expectations" which define "appropriate" feminine- and masculine-linked traits and behaviours (Cousineau & Roth, 2012: 423; see also Butler, 1990; Ridgeway, 1991; Butler, 1997; Ridgeway, 2009). . . .

Feminists have long identified the ways in which gender norms operate "to the detriment of all those women who are neither white nor middle class nor heterosexual," and, further, how "[n]onnormative femininity became associated with perversion, marginality and nonreproductive sex" (Grewal and Kaplan 2006: 3). . . . These norms have produced an ordering system wherein "[g]ender is not simply a question of sexuality but also a question of subdued labor and imperial plunder; race is not simply a question of skin color but also a question of labor power, cross-hatched by gender." . . . The gender policing accomplished by the news stories' narratives about Murphy upholds a matrix of femininity that is not only gendered but also classed, and, in Murphy's over-representation alongside the overrepresentation of the "dangerous" bodies of racialized men, is linked with reciprocally constituting constructions of a lack of control and the potential for sexual excesses that are shared discursively by white women and racialized men. For racialized women, the effects of this reciprocal construction are doubled (see, for example, Hooks, 1989; Lorde, 1984; and Hill Collins, 1993).

The analysis, here, is not to whitewash the experiences of racialized women, or to ignore the often-sexualized and violent narratives their bodies are subject to; it is to reflect on how, in the dominant construction of "appropriate" femininity that is leveled specifically against Murphy in reporters' accounts (and which is also leveled against racialized women, differently), there is a relationship between the constitution of gender and race that produces ambiguity in Murphy's position as a "deviant" white woman, the over-criminalization of racialized men, the invisibility of white men, and the symbolic annihilation of racialized women who, when charged with HIV non-disclosure are relatively rarely reported (see Mykhalovskiy et al. 2016: 25). . . .

Jennifer Murphy and the Policing of (Raced and Classed) Gender Norms

. . .

Between 2005 and 2012, Murphy was charged with HIV non-disclosure on three separate occasions: 2005 at CFB Borden in Ontario; 2007 in Newfoundland (but charges were quickly dropped); and 2012 in Barrie, Ontario. Though this may partially explain why so many articles are written about Murphy over time, it does not explain the qualitative or substantive content of the narratives used in the expository sections of the reports. Media reporting on Murphy began in 2005. Then, readers were told that she was a single mother, originally from Newfoundland, who was infected with HIV by an ex-boyfriend in the early 1990s (Verma, 2005a). Eventually, she relocated to Ontario, married a Canadian Armed Forces serviceman and settled in the Kingston area, where her husband was stationed at Canadian Forces Base (CFB) Borden. In 2004, the couple transferred to another CFB base in New Brunswick, where they began to experience marital turmoil which ended in divorce (Verma & Teotonio, 2005). In early 2005, Murphy returned to the CFB Borden area for an extended vacation and to visit friends. During this respite, newspapers reported, she frequently went out to local pubs, where she met various servicemen and had sex with some of them. Coverage

reported that she quickly developed a "reputation" among the servicemen as a "party" girl (Verma, 2005b). Then, rumors began to circulate that she was HIV-positive, and at least one of the servicemen complained to the base command that Murphy was having unprotected sex. She was quickly charged by the local police with HIV non-disclosure (Canadian Press, 2005).

There are multiple narrative turns evident in these early reports. Describing Murphy as a "party" girl who often frequents bars that she rarely leaves alone condemns women for entering the public sphere, and for being sexually active. The description links Murphy with a lack of control, a lack of passivity, and excess. Murphy's social and sexual behaviour is positioned as transgressing gender norms: instead of being sexually passive, she has a "reputation" as a "party" girl. The structure of the article places the "party" girl narrative before the factual pieces, conveying to readers that Murphy's criminality is in part produced by her gender transgressions. Similarly, *Toronto Star* reporter, Isabel Teotonio, after CFB Borden in 2005, opened her article with no reference to the law, but instead with a one-sentence paragraph: "Jennifer Murphy was known for her promiscuity." Teotonio described Murphy as a "hard-luck survivor, who grew up poor in subsidized housing with her mother and two siblings," and whose behaviour, after she returned to the CFB Borden area (where she had met her husband, before they had moved to CFB Gagetown, New Brunswick), was a stunning "transformation . . . like 'night and day,'" as a friend reported. Further, "[w]hen [the friend] confronted Murphy on her erratic behaviour, she explained she'd forgotten her medication in Newfoundland" (Teotonio, 2005). What occurred between Murphy and her husband is left unreported.

Teotonio's narrative relies on dominant gender norm schema to first charge Murphy with licentious female sexuality, foregrounding gender norm transgressions, and then goes on to invoke a number of narrative turns that produce Murphy as inherently dangerous within a gendered and classed system of social order. Murphy, a working-class "hard-luck survivor," is positioned outside of the middle-class gender norms that define "appropriate" feminine-linked behaviour.

She is described as a "survivor," despite "growing up poor in subsidized housing" and being a "single mother," suggesting that a lack of feminine-linked passivity has allowed her to "make it." She is produced as a "dangerous class" outside of patriarchal control and influence: for example, one of the reasons Murphy is a "hard-luck" case is that she grew up "poor," with only "her mother and two siblings," and is herself a "single mother." The gender-class narrative that blames poor, single, mothers for social ills is well-known, and Murphy is produced as part of the "story" about women's vulnerability and transgressions when not safely contained within the private sphere of a heteronormative, middle-class life with a clear patriarchal presence (either as a child or as a mother).

Murphy's inability to participate as a healthy (controlled) member of society is further underscored by Teotino's reporting on Murphy's "medication." This is one of the early instances in the news in which Murphy's medicalized body is categorized as "dangerous" and unruly beyond her HIV status. The problems engendered, according to Teotino's explanation, by Murphy's poverty and single-parent upbringing (and status), can be controlled medically but Murphy has "forgotten" the medicine that will control her impulses in another Province. The gender-class connection between social irresponsibility, working-class status, and the lack of a patriarchal figure coalesces with Murphy's "partying" in the reports to suggest that Murphy's "crime" is as much her poverty, medicalization, and inability to adhere to gender norms as it is her HIV non-disclosure.

Journalist Tracy McLaughlin, who covered both the CFB Borden (2005) and Barrie (2012) trials, similarly uses narrative turns that suggest Murphy's real crime is her transgression of appropriately "feminine-linked" norms and spaces. Transgression and blurring of boundaries is a theme that runs through the reports of both trials. Reflecting back on the Borden case, McLaughlin (2011) writes that "[a] 22-year-old soldier wept as he testified that he slept with her without knowing her HIV status," after "he and another soldier found Murphy wandering through the barracks approaching soldiers to have sex with her." McLaughlin (2013) relates that "Murphy wandered the halls [of the barracks] wearing a pink thong and asking the soldiers to party." In this, Murphy is produced through narrative to be the sexual aggressor: the "young" (22-year-old) soldier who weeps is rendered youthful and vulnerable. In contrast, when Murphy weeps during an appearance at the Barrie trial, McLaughlin describes her as "hot-tempered," "weeping, angry and cussing . . . 'F—, f— and triple f—.'"

Similarly, a *Washington Times* (2005) headline reporting on the Borden incident proclaims "Party girl throws big HIV scare into the military," and the article notes that "[v]arious soldiers . . . said Murphy was a fun-loving woman from Newfoundland, a fixture at parties on the base, a regular at the bars in town, and one who seldom left parties on her own." A female soldier testified against Murphy that, "During her time here she went through all the shacks," and that she had seen "Murphy wandering through the halls of one of the quarters, going from room to room dressed in only a pink G-string and knee-high boots" (Teotonio, 2005). The insertion of a pink-thonged, wandering, partier into a militarized and arguably masculinized space, illustrates a dangerous permeability of boundaries, not only of the Base itself, but also of the nationally-important construction of the soldier as a heroic (male) defender of the nation. Here, the soldier and Canada's international military efforts are discursively undone by one woman: either individually transformed into weeping and vulnerable young men, or collectively put on international alert.

The narratives that are used to condemn Murphy on the basis of gender norm transgression, as opposed to her actual crime, become even more damning during the later Barrie trial, perhaps because, by then, Murphy had appeared three times in court charged with HIV nondisclosure. Reporting for The Star after a court appearance in Barrie, Rosie DiManno (2013) opened her article with the (unattributed) definitions for "Nymphomania," "Sex Addiction," and "Incorrigible slag," the last of which she defines simply as "Jennifer Murphy." In her narrative explanation, DiManno notes that although "[t]he 40-year-old . . . has defined herself as . . . simply, a sexy woman," Murphy does not, in DiManno's assessment, "appear remotely sexy" "[i]n the prisoner's dock of the Barrie Courthouse." DiManno describes Murphy as "[a]shen, blowsy, maybe 30 pounds heavier" than the last time she appeared in the dock. Murphy is associated with ill-health—her not-just-pale, but "ashen" complexion conjures up shock, or even death; she is a course, rustic, dishevelled, frowzy slattern, as the term "blowsy" relates, who, on top of it all, is now fat. DiManno's words, consciously or not, reveal the dominant discourse's fixation on the intersection of sexually-active women with lower-class status and a lack of self-control, similar tropes assigned to the racialized men who receive so much reporting. Murphy's hair is "dishevelled" and unkempt, and the weight gain suggests an impulsive appetite and inability to control her body's urges (see, as just a few examples, Chrisler, 2012; Heyes, 2006; Smith, 2012; van Amsterdam, 2013; Younger, 2003).

The reporters use narratives time and again not to explain Murphy's actual crime, but rather, to provide salaciously-described details of her, and her sex life. Instead of focusing on the complexities of why an HIV-positive woman has unprotected sex without disclosing, who, at the time of the Barrie events, was on HIV antiretroviral medication that reduced her viral count to an undetectable level (see R. v Murphy, 2013), and who did not, therefore, meet the tests set by the Supreme Court of Canada of "significant risk" or a "realistic possibility" of transmission to have to disclose her HIV-positive serostatus (R. v Cuerrier, 1998; R. v Mabior, 2012), reporters' narratives suggested that her real crime was to be an "incorrigible slag;" a working-class woman who did not conform to the dominant gender norms that define "appropriate" middle-class and raced feminine-linked sexual behaviour. In 2013, again reporting on the Barrie case, before DiManno even began to recount the HIV-related portion of the news story, she wrote in her introduction: "That Murphy had sex with three men in one week is not relevant." However, if not relevant, why use rhetorical irony to focus readers' attention on the fact that Murphy had sex

with three men in one week? The "bad woman" narrative DiManno uses provides a context for the gender norm schema in which Murphy's multiple sexual partners are quite relevant to the context of the case, at least in the court of public opinion and the construction of gender norms. DiManno's narrative explanation of the Barrie incidents are damning: Murphy "approached" a man while "he sat drinking beer on the stoop of his boarding house." DiManno writes that Murphy "got flirty," and shared beer and marijuana with the man before going inside to have sex. In DiManno's story, Murphy is the aggressor: she approaches the man, who is minding his business and having a beer, and she instigates flirting. DiManno does not relate whether the Claimant testified he reciprocated her flirtation, although the ensuing intercourse and two nights spent together suggests that he did.

The Public-Private Divide: Gender Norms and Policing "Matter Out of Place"

While Murphy's sexual practices are condemned as gender transgressions, and linked with her working-class status, there is another narrative the reports rely on to condemn Murphy's behaviour, and that is the public-private gendered divide. This is, as we noted earlier, historically linked to the domestic femininity of middle-class, usually white women, so again Murphy's transgressions of the gender norms that police the public-private divide is constituted in relation to her working-class and white status. Of the Borden incident, McLaughlin (2011) reports that the soldier was approached by an indiscriminate, "wandering," Murphy, suggesting that she is aimless, lacking purpose, and, to riff on the work of anthropologist Mary Douglas (1966), matter out of place. The wrongness of her presence is driven home two short paragraphs later, when McLaughlin relates that "Murphy wandered the halls [of the barracks] wearing a pink thong and asking the soldiers to party." There is a discursive clash between the rugged and masculinized military and a wandering, pink-thonged presence that throws the gendered public-private narratives into disarray and erodes their boundaries.

. . .

Narratives about Murphy's spatial transgressions span the cases. Reporting what happened to Murphy between the trials, DiManno (2013) informs the readers that Murphy disappeared: she "has twice gone AWOL on strict bail conditions and was a no-show at her trial last year, eventually picked up by cops at a Toronto squat." Again, the narrative that links "inappropriate" gender behaviour with poverty, and an unmarried, non-middle-class, unhoused, life is apparent. We argue that someone with no fixed address, living at a squat in the large Canadian city of Toronto may be suffering from significant socio-economic barriers while also enduring, as Murphy herself put it, the public humiliation (*CBC News*, 2007), of being "slandered, degraded and discriminated against" (DiManno, 2013).

The gendered "matter out of place" narrative continued in coverage of the Barrie trial. There, McLaughlin (2011) bookended one of her reports with reference to the fact that Murphy had "sex with a man in a wooded area," and that "Barrie police, fearing for public safety, sent out a media advisory with her photograph." The "wooded area" was not important to the case, so the fact that it appears in McLaughlin's explanatory narrative is significant: wooded areas appear often in the stories used to police gendered behaviour. Young women are taught about the dangers of entering the woods and leaving the path in popular children's stories such as *Little Red Riding Hood*, and *Hansel and Gretel*, and woods often appear in horror films as settings where women are taken, chased, killed, or abused. . . .

Conclusion: Discursive Fractures and the Production of Gender-Class-Race

There are glimpses of the discursive fractures that are inevitable when media stories try to transform complex humans into easily-recognizable narrative myths and archetypes. . . . Feminists have long argued that the construction of women as either "good" (and "normal") when they conform to dominant patriarchal social norms of safely-sexually-contained heterosexual wives and mothers, or "bad" when they transgress those norms, is a tool used to control women. The implications of the competing "good" woman/"bad" woman narratives in the reports are clear: women who wear pink thongs and go looking for a "party" are not "normal," "polite," or "well-behaved," and there is not a dominant extant narrative that allows them to exist, simultaneously, as sexually active, HIV-positive, and a good mother, friend, and neighbour. Murphy has to be split into two: the "two faces" that belong to different people which so confound the military investigators.

The narrative tension comes from the historical construction of sexually-active white women as neither safely contained nor safe. Murphy "wanders," uncontained; she crosses discursive boundaries between masculinity and femininity, as in the alleged purchase of oral sex in Barrie when the man who was allegedly paid was also the one who "drove her to a remote area" to perform the act, thus producing a confusing blurring of roles and power dynamics; her pink-thonged intrusion into the masculinized space of military barracks; and her reported marriage to "her female partner in Logy Bay" years prior to the CFB Borden incident at a time when gay marriage was not legal in Canada. All suggest a complex woman. However, reductive gender norm schema invoked by the reporters' narratives, and the construction of "appropriate" hetero-normative, middle-class, white, feminine-linked norms is foundational to Murphy's criminalization.

. . .

We argue that when news reports of HIV non-reporting in Canada focus on the "dangerous" bodies of racialized men and one white woman, a further reality produced is that white men and racialized women are erased, but for different reasons. The suggestion, and power relations behind both absences, is that white men are supported by a patriarchal system in which their bodies have "the right" to others' bodies, sexually, and it is therefore difficult to discursively position them as sexually dangerous[2]; racialized women, in the gender-class-race matrix, have been discursively constructed as sexually "degenerate" for so long within the colonial discursive paradigm, that their transgressions are not "news." The comparative invisibility of both these bodies in the popular news reports of HIV non-reporting, continues a situation in which white men's bodies are assumed to be sexually autonomous in ways that women's and racialized men's bodies are not: white men's relative absence from the news literature occurs despite the fact that they make up over half of the cases in which the race of the defendant can be determined (Mykhalovskiy et al., 2016). This invisibility of the white male body as sexually dangerous upholds the historical "rights" of colonizing men to the bodies of others, and the privilege to have their own sexual transgressions left unfounded. Thus, sexual bodies that appear in the reports, or are conspicuously absent from them, are "a trope for other power relations," specifically the ongoing "invisibilization" of dangerous whiteness and masculinity, in contrast to the uncontrolled sexuality of "dangerous classes." Within the paradigm that connects Murphy with the over-reported racialized men, the discourse remains historically true to form: racialized men are reminded that they and their sexuality are under surveillance; white woman Jennifer Murphy was subjected to gender-policing narratives that remind white women to perform their "appropriately" submissive, reproductively heterosexual, sensitive, amiable, role; white men are protected from censure by the invisibility of whiteness and maleness; and racialized women are relegated to the bottom of the power relations—symbolically annihilated by their absence in reports about HIV non-disclosure.

Notes

1. Most of the reportage clusters around three periods in 2005, 2007, and 2011, when Murphy was charged with non-disclosure. We reason that there is relatively little reportage of the 2007 case as it was dropped early on, whereas the cases in 2005 and 2011 went to trial and were drawn out over a longer time period thus providing greater opportunity for media coverage.
2. Movements such as #metoo may be changing this discourse, but the responses to women who come forward suggest that the discourse of the "innocent" white man is still culturally ingrained.

References

Butler, J. (1990). *Gender trouble: Feminism and the subversion of identity.* New York: Routledge.

Butler, J. (1997). *Excitable speech: A politics of the performative.* New York: Routledge.

Canadian Press (2005, March 24). HIV-infected woman charged in military sex scare. Retrieved from *The Hamilton Spectator*, http://www.cbc.ca/news/canada/hivinfected-woman-charged-in-military-sex-scare-1.549320, Accessed date: 29 August 2017.

CBC News (2007, May 14). Charge withdrawn in St. John's HIV case. CBC News Newfoundland & Labrador. Retrieved from http://www.cbc.ca/news/canada/newfoundland-labrador/charge-withdrawn-in-st-john-s-hiv-case-1.634732, Accessed date: 29 August 2017.

Chrisler, J. (2012). 'Why can't you control yourself?' Fat should be a feminist issue. *Sex Roles*, 66(9/10), 608–16.

Cousineau, L., & Roth, J. (2012). Pervasive patriarchal leadership ideology in seasonal residential summer camp staff. *Leadership*, 8(4), 421–44.

DiManno, R. (2013, August 21). What to do with HIV-positive Jennifer Murphy and the Russian roulette she plays with her sex partners? *Toronto Star*. Retrieved from https://www.thestar.com/news/gta/2013/08/21/dimanno_sentencing_postponed_for_hivpositive_woman_guilty_of_sex_assault.html (accessed 29 August 2017).

Douglas, M. (1966). *Purity and danger: An analysis of the concepts of pollution and taboo.* London: Ark Paperbacks.

Georgakopoulou, A., & Goutsos, D. (2004). *Discourse analysis* (2nd ed). Edinburgh: Edinburgh University Press.

Grewal, I., & Kaplan, C. (2006). Social and historical constructions of gender. In I. Grewal, & C. Kaplan (Eds.). *An introduction to women's studies: Gender in a transnational world* (2nd ed). New York: McGraw Hill.

Heyes, C. (2006). Foucault goes to weight watchers. *Hypatia*, 21(2), 126–49.

Hill Collins, P. (1993). Toward a new vision: Race, class, and gender as categories of analysis and connection. *Race, Sex & Class*, 1(1), 25–45.

Hooks, B. (1989). Travelling theories: Travelling theorists. *Inscriptions*, 5, 159–64.

Johnson-Laird, P. (1983). *Mental models: Towards a cognitive science of language, inference and consciousness*. Cambridge, MA: Harvard University Press.

Kilty, J. M. (2014). Dangerous liaisons, a tale of two cases: Constructing women accused of HIV/AIDS nondisclosure as threats to the (inter)national body politic. In J. M. Kilty (Ed.). *Within the confines: Women and the law in Canada* (pp. 271–292). Toronto: Women's Press.

Kitzinger, J. (1998). Media impact on public beliefs about AIDS. In D. Miller, J. Kitzinger, & P. Beharrell (Eds.). *The circuit of mass communication* (pp. 168–191). London: Sage Publications.

Lorde, A. (1984). Age, race, class, and sex: Women redefining difference. In A. Lorde (Ed.). *Sister outsider: Essays and speeches* (pp. 114–123). Freedom, CA: Crossing Press.

Lupton, D. (1994). *Moral threats and dangerous desires: AIDS in the news media*. London: Taylor & Francis.

McLaughlin, T. (2011, September 14). HIV-infected woman faces new charges. Retrieved from *Toronto Sun* http://www.torontosun.com/2011/09/14/hiv-infected-woman-faces-new-charges, Accessed date: 29 August 2017.

McLaughlin, T. (2013, July 12). HIV-positive Jennifer Murphy denied soliciting herself, trial hears. Retrieved from *Toronto Sun* http://www.torontosun.com/2013/07/12/hiv-positive-jennifer-murphy-denied-soliciting-herself-trial-hears, Accessed date: 29 August 2017.

Mykhalovskiy, E., Hastings, C., Sanders, C., Hayman, M., & Bisaillon, L. (2016). "Callous, cold and deliberately duplicitous": Racialization, immigration and the representation of criminalization in Canadian mainstream newspapers. Toronto: A report funded by a grant from the Canadian Institute of Health Research Centre for Social Research in HIV Prevention. Retrieved from https://papers.ssrn.com/sol3/papers.cfm?abstract_id=2874409, Accessed date: 29 August 2017.

Reddick, R. (1986). Textlinguistics, text theory, and language users. *Word*, 37(1–2), 31–43.

Ridgeway, C. (1991). The social construction of status value: Gender and other nominal characteristics. *Social Forces*, 70(2), 367–386.

Ridgeway, C. (2009). Framed before we know it: How gender shapes social relations. *Gender and Society*, 23(2), 145–160.

Smith, C. (2012). The confounding of fat, control, and physical attractiveness for women. *Sex Roles*, 66(9/10), 628–631.

Swain, K. A. (2005). Approaching the quarter-century mark: AIDS coverage and research decline as infection spreads. *Critical Studies in Media Communication*, 22(3), 258–262.

Teotonio, I. (2005, March 27). Military warns all bases of HIV case: Canadian soldiers around the world told to seek medical advice. *Toronto Star*. Retrieved from www.freerepublic.com/focus/news/1371553/posts (accessed 29 August 2017).

van Amsterdam, N. (2013). Big fat inequalities, thin privilege: An intersectional perspective on "body size". *European Journal of Women's Studies*, 20(2), 155–169.

van Dijk, T. (1987a). Episodic models in discourse processing. In R. Horowitz, & S. Samuels (Eds.). *Comprehending oral and written language* (pp. 161–196). New York: Academic Press.

van Dijk, T. (1987b). *News as discourse*. Hillsdale, NJ: Erlbaum.

van Dijk, T. (1990). The future of the field: Discourse analysis in the 1990s. *Text*, 10(1–2) (133-a56).

Verma, S. (2005a). Jennifer Murphy describes her life. *Toronto Star*.

Verma, S. (2005b). "Party-goer" accused in HIV assault of CFB border soldier. *Toronto Star*, A01.

Verma, S., & Teotonio, I. (2005, March 25). Accused predator once a victim. *Toronto Star*, A01.

Washington Times (2005, March 23). Party girl throws big HIV scare into military. *Washington Times*. Retrieved from http://www.dslreports.com/forum/r12984774-Party-girl-throws-big-HIV-scare-into-military, Accessed date: 29 August 2017 (The original article is no longer available at the *Times* website).

Younger, B. (2003). Pleasure, pain, and the power of being thin: Female sexuality in young adult literature. *NWSA Journal*, 15(2), 45–56.

Part V
Gendered Families

Family—whether you love it or hate it or a mix of both—everybody's got (at least) one. Families are also of the utmost importance in the construction and transformation of gender. Families are not only where some of life's most important relationships are forged, they are also sites of work. This work is rarely compensated and may not even be recognized as "work," even by the people who do it. Labour and caring are bound together in the everyday lives of people in families—the very idea of a "labour of love" shows the emotional connotations of the work that is done in homes to take care of family members. The gendering of this care work has proven to be extraordinarily persistent, even as gender divisions in other arenas of life are gradually breaking down. While men are increasing their share of unpaid work in the home, women still do the lion's share of child care and housekeeping, and this disjuncture creates challenges, and sometimes distress, for people of all genders.

Horne and Breitkreuz examine one form of this distress by looking at the ways in which women who have stepped back from the paid workforce to do child care talk about this shift in their lives. The language of "sacrifice" dominates their stories, underscoring the idea that for these women at least, caregiving and earning are at odds and it can be all but impossible to devote oneself to both. Sacrificing oneself for one's family turns out to take specifically gendered forms.

The women in Man and Chou's study might agree with Horne and Breitkreuz. They are highly educated immigrants from China whose families are not gathered together in one place but dispersed across two continents. Adding physical distance to the challenges of caring for a family results in a double burden for many of these women. Managing the dual roles of parent and professional involves significant sacrifices or deferral of their own happiness, especially within the context of heterosexual marriages where their male partners may not make similar sacrifices.

Mothers, of course, are not the only ones who struggle with the contradictions and tensions of parenthood. The fathers in Dominelli and colleagues' study face a different set of challenges. They are struggling to establish themselves as responsible, credible parents despite having children who are in the public child welfare system. The spectre of the "bad dad" haunts these men as they attempt to sustain relationships with their children. They work against the "bad dad" image to reinvent themselves as a different kind of father—attentive, loving, and devoted to their children.

Similarly, the men studied by Giesbrecht and colleagues struggle to care for dependent loved ones, even though the family members they care for are mainly wives who are physically debilitated or frail. Like the men in Dominelli and colleagues' study, these caregiving men experience the combination of being male and being a caregiver in diverse ways—for some, their gender puts up a wall between them and the rest of the world; for others, providing constant daily care serves to bring them closer to their spouse and other family members.

Questions for Critical Thought

1. What is your vision of ideal family life? Would your parents, siblings, and peers share that vision?

2. Think about a parent (yours or another parent you know) with whom you share a gender. In what ways do you think your life will be different from theirs? In what ways would you like your life to be different from theirs?

3. How is space "gendered" in the homes of your family (or families) of origin?

4. The domestic division of labour still favours men with more leisure time than women, despite significant changes in recent decades. Why don't men do more around the house? What are the costs and rewards—for both men and women—of a lopsided distribution of household work?

5. We may think of caregiving mainly in connection with children, but demographic changes in Canada suggest that elder care may become an even greater challenge in the coming decades. How is the work of caring for elders different from caring for dependent children?

6. What sacrifices do you think a parent should be willing to make for their children? What do you think should not be sacrificed?

7. What do you think might be the gendered consequences if the state took on the responsibility of providing universal and financially accessible child care for all children? Would you support such a policy?

8. Do you know of families in which some members are physically at a great remove from others? How does physical distance affect family dynamics?

9. What makes someone a bad or unfit parent? Do these criteria differ according to the gender of the parent?

Chapter 19

Overview

Raising children is often described as a sacrifice—a series of altruistic decisions to forgo one's own wishes and desires in order to give as much as possible to one's children. Rebecca Horne and Rhonda Breitkreuz argue that this sacrifice has a particularly gendered character as it is experienced by women who became mothers. They argue that mothers are cued or "prompted" by their workplaces and significant others to cut back their paid work to spend more time doing unpaid work caring for their children. These mothers understood themselves to be sacrificing their careers and professional advancement, not so much because they deliberately chose to step back from paid work but because they saw no alternative given that satisfactory out-of-home child care was hard to find and often incompatible with the demands of their jobs. The women in the study believed they had sacrificed not only in terms of professional advancement but had also given up time for themselves and time for their partners so that the "maternal sacrifice" had many unexpected dimensions. Horne and Breitkreuz argue that the disproportionate sacrifices borne by mothers call for changes in the way that child care is organized in Canada in order to support parents of all genders.

The Motherhood Sacrifice

Maternal Experiences of Child Care in the Canadian Context

Rebecca M. Horne and Rhonda S. Breitkreuz

The act of self-sacrifice, or the voluntary restriction of one's self-interest for a purpose of greater perceived value, is a behaviour commonly observed in the family (Bahr & Bahr, 2001). Sacrificial behaviours are particularly prevalent in the mother–child dyad, given that mothers continue to be primarily responsible for the care of children (Bianchi, 2000; Sperling, 2013). Mothers often surrender the activities they enjoy doing or may need to do to promote the physical, cognitive, and emotional development of their child in a safe environment. Often, mothers make these sacrifices due to a personal sense of duty to honour their familial obligations (Corso & Lanz, 2013) or because of societal expectations of persistent and selfless care that is associated with the mothering role (Weaver & Ussher, 1997). Demographic shifts in women's labour force participation, however, have made this situation more complex; as more mothers are undertaking paid employment, more are struggling to integrate paid work and unpaid care work (Wattis, Standing, & Yerkes, 2011) and may have to sacrifice one for the other. This situation may be intensified in Canada, as the increasing need for non-parental care because of mothers' labour force participation is not matched with regulated, affordable, or flexible child care spaces (Beach, Friendly, Ferns, Prabhu, & Forer, 2009; Huff & Cotte, 2013; Stone & Lovejoy, 2004; UNICEF, 2008). These competing paid work and care systems may prompt Canadian mothers to make an unprecedented number of sacrifices to access the limited child care options available. Work-life conflict becomes amplified for these mothers, as they are expected to make "choices

Horne, Rebecca M. and Breitkreuz, Rhonda S. "The Motherhood Sacrifice: Maternal Experiences of Child Care in the Canadian Context." *Journal of Family Studies*, 2018, 24:2, pp. 126–145. Reprinted by permission of Taylor & Francis Ltd. www.tandfonline.com

between a range of possible non-preferred [child care] options" (Barnes, Leach, Sylva, Stein, & Malmberg, 2006, p. 554) within a cultural context that also expects them to be intensive caregivers and devoted employees (Hays, 1996).

[W]e propose that decision-making regarding child care within such constrained contexts is an important, but often overlooked, element of family life that prompts mothers to make numerous and substantial sacrifices in their own lives to achieve the best outcome for their children. . . . This study explores the question: what messages of sacrifice are embedded in Canadian mothers' stories about their experiences with navigating child care? Set within a feminist theoretical framework, we utilize data from focus groups with mothers to understand the complexities surrounding how they organize child care arrangements, what types of sacrifices they make, and the impact this has on their subjective well-being and family functioning. We also explicate the broader practical and conceptual implications this research has for understanding the complexity of sacrifice, work-life integration, and mothers' child care experiences. . . .

Maternal Sacrifice

According to Bahr and Bahr (2001), the definition of sacrifice is "to give up, destroy, permit injury to, or forgo (a valued thing) for the sake of something of greater value or having a more pressing claim" (p. 1232). Although sacrifice and altruism are closely related, sacrifice is distinctive because it involves a perceived loss for the giver who is forfeiting something of personal value. While research is lacking on detailed accounts of the sacrifices mothers make to arrange adequate child care in particular, various explanations and theoretical frameworks have been offered for why mothers engage in sacrificial behaviours more broadly. Within this body of literature, there are two prominent ways of making sense of maternal sacrifice: one is primarily psychological, and the other socio-cultural. According to the first perspective, and influenced by the philosophy of Emmanuel Levinas, Bahr and Bahr (2001) suggested sacrifice is a natural human response that allows us to meet

our overarching purpose of being responsible to others by giving ourselves, which in turn gives form to our core sense of self. In addition to ontological explanations, "cognitive-perceptual" (Bahr & Bahr, 2001, p. 1253) models of sacrifice suggest mothers engage in these behaviours to reciprocate the attachment and love they receive from their children and fulfil their own moral aspirations, empathic needs, and sense of self.

In contrast, the second and more predominant perspective on maternal sacrifice in the literature explores maternal sacrifice through a socio-cultural, feminist lens. Meyering (2013) describes how many second-wave feminists, and arguably some present-day feminists, critique maternal sacrifice because such acts conform to expectations normalized by a patriarchal society that required mothers to intensively care for their families at the cost of their own personal goals, needs, and independence. These sacrifices made for one's children and partner were believed to perpetuate oppressive gender norms that burdened women and further relinquished their liberty (Badinter, 2010; Chorvat, 1995; Hochschild, 1997; Patterson, 1986). In the particular context of Western societies, Hays (1996) hypothesizes that intensive mothering and continual self-sacrifice for one's children may also be behavioural responses to the ambiguity felt from cultural norms that idealize hedonism, individualism, and competitiveness. Abiding by feminist principles of praxis, these writers and scholars draw attention to maternal sacrifices to mobilize advocacy and policy reform around the structural issues responsible for women's struggles with integrating paid and unpaid labour (Randall, 1996).

The psychological and socio-cultural explanations for why mothers sacrifice for their children also provide insight into what mothers perceive as a sacrifice. A key debate in the literature on work–life integration is whether giving up one's career to care for children should be conceptualized as a sacrifice or if the sacrifice is the need to engage in paid work instead of staying at home. We utilize Blair-Loy's (2003) research on work–life integration for employed mothers to introduce and dissect the nuances in this debate. Blair-Loy (2003) devised two theoretical models to explain the primary domains in which these women receive fulfilment, referred to as the cultural "schemas of work devotion and family devotion" (p. 2). The work devotion cultural script states that women's purpose and passion in life comes from having a stable, full-time career. The devoted employed mother, however, is viewed as egocentric due to sacrificing her family life in order to focus on her own career, yet also an inspiring "supermom" (Dillaway & Pare, 2008, p. 445) who somehow navigates obligations in the private and public sphere with relative ease. Although some mothers in the labour force are proud of their ability to delegate child care responsibilities while maintaining full-time careers (Christopher, 2012), others truly want to be their child's primary caregiver and sacrifice this desirable role to (re)enter the workforce out of financial necessity or to protect their job (Gorman & Fritzche, 2002).

On the other hand, the family devotion cultural script posits that women gain the upmost fulfilment from being a nurturer who provides consistent care and stability for their children and partners in the home. Often viewed as more caring, selfless, and committed to family life than employed mothers (Gorman & Fritzche, 2002), stay-at-home mothers are seen as "ideal mothers" because they do not have paid work to distract them from their duties of fostering children's development (Boyd, 2002; Dillaway & Pare, 2008). Yet not all mothers make the autonomous, preference-based decision to stay home, as inflexible workplace policies all but push mothers out of their jobs when they are unable to balance them with child care (Stone & Lovejoy, 2004). Moreover, some mothers indicated that the all-consuming motherhood role deprives them of their previous identities and common modes of self-expression (Weaver & Ussher, 1997), sacrificing their emotional and social health to meet their children's needs (Holmes, Erickson, & Hill, 2012).

. . .

Method

The analysis for this article was nested within a larger study of child care in the Province of Alberta, Canada (Breitkreuz, Collins, Cook, & Gokiert, 2013). The purpose of the broader study was to capture the child care experiences of families with pre-school children in Alberta, given that there was a notable shortage of regulated child care: only 20% of children under the age of five in the province had access to a regulated child care space (CCRU, 2014). Within this context, we wanted to understand how parents managed child care needs. To understand family experiences with child care, we asked questions in focus group settings about the strategies parents utilized to integrate paid work and child care, the kinds of child care arrangements parents made, and the facilitators and barriers to accessing and maintaining child care. Upon conducting the analysis we began to see the notion of sacrifice emerge as a major theme, serving as the basis for this paper.

. . . [W]e employed a focus group method to capture a broad range of experiences from various locations across the province: urban, rural, agricultural, and geographical areas in Alberta in which the oil and gas sector is the key employer. . . .

Eight of the focus groups were conducted in major urban centres, and five were conducted in rural communities. There was a total of 96[1] participants from 13 focus groups conducted between 2012 and 2014. . . .

Results

. . . [D]etailed demographic characteristics of [the] sample are presented in Table 19.1.

As noted in Table 19.2, of the 86 participants who completed their demographic sheets, the most common type of child care utilized was grandparent care (36%), followed by parent turn-taking (29%), day care (22%), day homes (20%), other relatives (18%), and friends and neighbours (18%). Some parents used multiple kinds of child care arrangements, particularly if they were reliant on care from family or friends.

When describing their child care experiences, our participants' stories were filled with references to sacrificial behaviours they have made for child care. In the next section, these stories are divided into three overall themes that

Table 19.1 Demographics of Participants

Number of Participants (*n*=95*)

Age of participants	16–19	7
	20–29	21
	30–39	37
	40–49	18
	50 and above	1
	Not reported	11
Number of children	Expecting	4
	One	31
	Two	31
	Three	10
	Four	6
	Five or more	3
	No reported	11
Family income	Under $20,000	8
	$20,000–29,999	1
	$30,000–49,999	15
	$50,000–69,999	6
	$70,000–89,999	7
	$90,000–109,999	14
	$110,000 and above	24
	Not reported	15
Employment status	Employed	59
	Not employed	27
	Not reported	9
Parenting situation	Single parents	12
	Co-parent with husband or common-law spouse	59
	Ex-spouse	1
	Not reported	18
Age of children	Under 1	29
	1–3	54
	4–5	31
	Not reported	6

* Completing the demographic profile sheet for participants was optional in this study, and some participants chose not to answer all the questions. In addition, there were six other participants who did not complete the demographic profile sheets at all. We excluded the one father in this analysis because of our focus on mothers.

represent the various types of sacrifices mothers made, including sacrificing employment, personal goals, and interpersonal relationships. All individual quotes and stories used are illustrative of broader themes discussed by the collective focus groups.

Table 19.2   Types and Hours of Child Care Arrangements

Number of participants (*n*=95)		
Types of child care arrangements*	Day care	19
	Day home	17
	Parents take turns	25
	Grandparents	31
	Other relatives	15
	Babysitter	11
	Friends and neighbours	15
	Nanny/au pair	1
	Pre-school	5
	Not reported	10
Hours per week in child care arrangements	Day care	7–55 hours
	Day home	5–60 hours
	Parents turn-taking	4–32 hours
	Grandparents	1–30 hours
	Other relatives	1–10 hours
	Babysitter	2–16 hours
	Friends and neighbours	2–16 hours
	Nanny/au pair	25–35 hours
	Pre-school	2–4 hours
	Not reported	6

* More than one type of child care was used by some parents and all of these were included in this table

Employment Sacrifices

Restricted Job Advancement and Taking Time off Work for Child Care

Well over three-quarters of the discussions in the focus groups were centred on the employment sacrifices mothers made in order to access adequate child care, summed up eloquently by one mother who posited that mothers are faced with the decision of having to "sacrifice their career or their children" (FG2). Some women forfeited job advancement opportunities because they could not put in overtime at their workplace or because they took leave from work to raise their children. When a fellow participant asked Kelly[2] (FG2) if she ever worried about her job, she indicated that having a child hindered her career progression:

Always . . . not just [job] security but job advancement. You know, like I can't stay 'til eight o'clock at night, like all the other consultants. So I have to go home. At four thirty I have to leave and it's just . . . I'm never going to be like a senior person until he's maybe in school or graduated.

. . . Other participants worried that their absence from the paid labour market to care for their children may have cost them their marketability for gaining future employment. Jessica (FG9), for instance, left her job for a number of years because she valued being the primary caregiver of her children. She feared she would not get hired again because she lacked sufficient paid work experience and was not familiar with new technological advancements in the workplace, concluding: "you're not actually hirable now because you're a mother". . . . As a whole, the participants felt angered by the fact that employers did not seem to acknowledge or respect the work sacrifices they had to make for child care and felt "sick and tired of being penalized for being a mom" (FG9).

Altering Work Schedule or Type to Adapt to Child Care Needs

Many participants also discussed how they had to alter their work schedules or find an entirely new position because of child care. . . . Gina (FG2) shared the complexity behind this decision to change her job:

> My job has quite a lot of flexibility and so I thought I could, you know, go in early and you know, that sort of thing, but it's been a train wreck, like just crazy [laughingly]. So, you know, my husband, I mean, he's available when he is, but then, you know, like I have to be back at a certain time so he can leave and so, my work is the one that gets sacrificed . . . [sigh] it's silly, it gets really silly and so I'm actually, I'm changing. I'm leaving my job and I'm going to start a day home, which I never thought I'd do.

Some mothers talked about how they adjusted their work schedules to better accommodate their children's care situations. These experiences ranged from skipping lunch breaks to skipping whole days of work in order to pick their children up on time from day care. Even Sarah (FG14), a mother who framed her situation quite positively, still raised the fact that making work sacrifices to accommodate child care is constraining in that it "kind of limits me in when I can do my work". Other participants described how strongly child care regimens influenced their paid work; many noted that the only way they would be able to care for their children would be to quit their job to stay home or to get a different position within their current company that is more flexible. . . . Natalie (FG6) stated that she took her position as a relief carrier for a

postal company solely because of the flexibility it provided, which allowed her to be at home more with her children. One mother even admitted that had she known the difficulties in accessing child care, she would have taken a completely different career path based on something that could be done from home, such as "nails or cutting hair or accounting" (FG7). . . . Jessica (FG5) expanded on the role high child care costs play in employment decisions for mothers:

> It becomes a luxury for people who have to make that decision whether or not I want to go back to work because I enjoy it, but I can't because I can't afford it and I think that's a very common struggle. . . . So it has nothing to do with how great or how close or how wonderful, it's purely the dollars.

Feeling Nostalgic for Work as a New Stay-at-Home Mother

Stay-at-home mothers revealed how strongly they missed their careers that were sacrificed to care for their children. . . . Jane (FG13) was one of them and felt grief-stricken after sacrificing her job working with individuals with developmental disabilities because she described work as her "safe place" where she felt "free" to socialize with other adults. Similarly, Cassidy (FG9) thoroughly discussed the elements she missed about the career she surrendered to care for her children:

> When I was in a position where when I lived in [another country] I was the breadwinner. I had the powerful job, I was a senior manager . . . and I really miss that. I really do. I miss the interaction with people, I miss the line management, the being able to develop people in their roles, I miss the relationship I had with my boss . . . and then I came here and I had this opportunity to take that full year off and then took a decision not to return because really, in all honesty, child care was just too hard to figure out . . . but I see jobs come and go, every few months and I'm like, oh, I really would love to do that, and I just feel I can't.

Other participants revealed similar experiences where their well-being was compromised due to their roles as stay-at-home mothers who "cater" to their children's every need, with apparent messages of isolation, being overwhelmed and under recognized, lacking support, and no longer feeling "accomplished", which perpetuated their longing to return to work. . . .

Personal Sacrifices

Child Care Impeding Educational Attainment

Numerous immigrant women in the sample mentioned forgoing their educational attainment because the unavailability of child care put them in a position where they had to stay at home to care for their children, which was difficult to do because, as one mother noted, "it's your personal goals" (FG9) that are being put aside. These participants viewed their roles as stay-at-home mothers as "temporary" and would "love to go back to school" if they were given the opportunity (FG10). Anita (FG10), for example, came to Canada with her family and wanted to further her education, yet immigration policies prevented her from achieving this because she was not able to attain financial assistance from anywhere other than her husband's earnings. On top of that, she did not have anyone else to help her look after her children if she were to go to college or obtain employment, so her only feasible option was to stay at home as the primary caregiver. Similarly, Nora (FG10) discussed how she "wanted to go to school and learn something", but did not "have a chance to go" because she was expected to stay at home with the children while her husband worked.

Child Care Limiting Personal Time

Participants expanded on other personal sacrifices they have made for their children, such as giving up all of their free time and individual identities outside of their motherhood roles. Some described how badly they needed occasional "mommy moments" where they could leave their child with a trusted care provider with little notice and take a break from motherhood for a few hours to have

some time alone. Jane (FG13), for instance, missed having time for herself and felt like she could no longer identify as a unique individual outside of her roles as a mother and wife. Although she left her job to care for her children for a few years, she looked forward to going back to work to regain that independence:

> I don't mind being a mom. I mean everybody's got to love being a mom, but sometimes you just want something for yourself, just not to be a mom, to be who you are. Like, I want to be that, not "this is my mom", and you know, "this is my wife".

Leslie (FG14) also regarded her paid employment as her "break" from her mother role and believed that taking this personal time was necessary to become a better mother, as she insisted that "you're not doing your best for your child 'cause you're not doing the best for you". . . .

Interpersonal Sacrifices

In addition to sacrificing their own personal time for child care, many participants also spoke of the relational sacrifices they have made. Participants frequently mentioned how they had to sacrifice time with their partner for reasons related to child care. Given that child care options were extremely limited or too expensive, it was common for participants to resort to alternating care shifts with their husbands. Christine (FG13) mentioned that she and her husband "barely get to see each other" because she works as a restaurant server during the evenings and her husband works during the daytime, with the parent who is at home being responsible for watching the kids. . . . Kelsey (FG13) worked as a nurse and was fortunate to have a flexible enough employer to allow her to match her husband's hours. Although she was happy to have matching schedules with her spouse, she reflected on how her marriage would be affected if they had opposite work schedules in order to alternate care:

> Short term it sounds like a really great solution. Yay we don't have a day-care bill! Long term, you never have family time, you never

have couple time, you never have that opportunity to connect as a family, to connect with your partner and to be first and foremost a strong unit, the two of you.

. . . Christine (FG13) described stay-at-home mothers whose husbands work out of town as "single parents with a pay cheque", as she witnessed the strain on many of these marriages because "you don't get a chance to be a family". Some participants also spoke of how they sacrificed their relationships with other family members or friends by consistently asking them to watch their children. For instance, Penelope (FG9) feared she may be "overusing" her familial care arrangements:

I feel really guilty when I ask [my mother] to watch them for things that we want to do, like a date night on a Friday night or, you know, a sanity break every once and a while . . . you feel like you can only ask for the must, must, must do's.

Discussion

. . . The three main themes that emerged from the data represented the types of sacrifices mothers typically made for child care, including sacrificing employment; personal goals, identity, and time; and interpersonal relationships. Some sacrifices are to be expected with the transition to parenthood. . . . Yet these experiences are often overlooked because socially constructed ideals of motherhood conceptualize sacrifice as normal and natural behaviours for mothers to engage in (Weaver & Ussher, 1997). Normalizing intensive maternal sacrifices may impede efforts by policymakers, researchers, or other public figures to critically recognize and analyse the constrained child care contexts that contribute to these behaviours.

The participants in our study tend to experience work-life conflict when organizing child care, as their scenarios are filled with acts of sacrifice where one of these elements essentially overrides the other. Our findings show that mothers were primarily responsible for finding or providing care for their child even if they were in the paid labour force, indicating continued gendered norms of female responsibility in the private sphere (Bianchi, 2000; Sperling, 2013). Moreover, our participants' concerns with taking a break from employment were on par with the recurring wage penalties and discrimination in hiring procedures encountered by mothers in the workforce (Budig & England, 2001; Waldfogel, 1997), which suggests that mothers are aware of the economic repercussions of sacrificing their paid labour for child care, yet do so anyway. . . .

To mitigate . . . tension between individual feelings of strain and romanticized depictions of motherhood, mothers often use particular discursive techniques to conceptualize personal sacrifices as worthwhile for their children (Weaver & Ussher, 1997). For instance, our participants often counterbalanced their descriptions of feeling isolated and stressed by pointing out their unquestionable love for their child and their role as a mother or describing their need for a break as necessary for their children's development, not their own well-being. . . . [S]ome of our participants reconciled rival family and work devotion schemas by describing the former as a temporary necessity to achieve the latter; staying at home to care for their children was required for their families' present needs, but they looked forward to the day where they could further their education and pursue their personal vocations. . . .

Participants also spoke of the relational sacrifices they made for child care. . . . [G]randparents, other relatives, and friends were among the most common care providers for participants' children in our study. Many participants felt guilty asking these individuals to watch their children and thought doing so would sacrifice the quality of these relationships. While many friends and relatives may be happy to help out, the fears participants had with informal care arrangements were not irrational; focus group data from Drake, Greenspoon, Unti, Fawcett, and Neville-Morgan (2006) revealed family members and friends felt as though their close relationship to the parent was being exploited for the use of care, were unsure of their precise role in the care arrangement, and found it difficult to communicate such concerns. Participants in our study also described how they sacrificed their relationship with their spouse by taking turns watching their children to secure two sources of income for their household and avoid the costs of paying for day care. Although the parental turn-taking method may prevent spouses from spending quality time together and reduce relationship satisfaction, this child care routine is common for many couples (Medved, 2004). . . .

Our research has shown that arranging child care is a complex, multi-faceted experience that prompts mothers to make many sacrifices in their lives. Regardless of whether a mother is employed or stays at home, sacrifices are abundant in both scenarios and may be best understood through qualitative inquiries that empower mothers to collectively discuss child care while carefully noting how they frame their child care struggles and navigate the competing cultural schemas of work and family devotion (Blair-Loy, 2003). Acknowledging the sacrifices mothers make for child care equips us with a more comprehensive and direct understanding of how child care contexts can be improved to better facilitate the needs of families. . . . [. . .]

Notes

1. We had 96 participants, but one of them was a father. For the purposes of this analysis, we excluded the data from the father, as our focus here was on mothers.

2. All participant names mentioned in this paper are pseudonyms.

References

Badinter, E. (2010). *Le conflit: La femme et la mere [Conflict: The woman and the mother]*. Montréal, QC: Flammarion Lettres.

Bahr, H., & Bahr, K. (2001). Families and self-sacrifice: Alternative models and meanings for family theory. *Social Forces*, 79(4), 1231–58. doi:10.1353/sof.2001.0030

Barnes, J., Leach, P., Sylva, K., Stein, A., Malmberg, L., & Families, Children and Child Care Team. (2006). Infant care in England: Mothers' aspirations, experiences, satisfaction and caregiver relationships. *Early Child Development and Care*, 176(5), 553–73. doi:10.1080/03004430500317408

Beach, J., Friendly, M., Ferns, C., Prabhu, N., & Forer, B. (2009). *Early childhood education and care in Canada 2008* (8th ed.). Toronto, ON: Child Care Research and Resource Unit.

Bianchi, S. M. (2000). Maternal employment and time with children: Dramatic change or surprising continuity? *Demography*, 37(4), 401–14. doi:10.1353/dem.2000.0001

Blair-Loy, M. (2003). *Competing devotions: Career and family among women executives*. Cambridge, Mass: Harvard University Press.

Boyd, E. R. (2002). "Being there": Mothers who stay at home, gender, and time. *Women's Studies International Forum*, 25(4), 463–70. doi:10.1016/S0277-5395(02)00283-2

Breitkreuz, R. Collins, D. Cook, K. & Gokiert, R. (2013). *Child care policy and the experiences of employed Albertan families with preschool children: Final report*. Edmonton, AB: Alberta Centre for Child, Family, and Community Research.

Budig, M. J., & England, P. (2001). The wage penalty for motherhood. *American Sociological Review*, 66, 204–25. Retrieved from http://www.jstor.org/stable/2657415

Child Care Research Unit (CCRU). (2014). Finding quality child care. Retrieved from http://findingqualitychildcare.ca/index.php/alberta

Chorvat, I. (1995). Women's movement and family: A story of the western feminism. *Sociologia*, 27 (5–6), 337–46.

Christopher, K. (2012). Extensive mothering: Employed mothers' constructions of the good mother. *Gender & Society*, 26(1), 73–96. doi:10.1177/0891243211427700

Corso, A. R. D., & Lanz, M. (2013). Felt obligation and the family life cycle: A study on intergenerational relationships. *International Journal of Psychology*, 48(6), 1196–200. doi:10.1080/00207594.2012.725131

Dillaway, H., & Pare, E. (2008). Locating mothers: How cultural debates about stay-at-home versus working mothers define women and home. *Journal of Family Issues*, 29(4), 437–64. doi:10.1177/0192513X07310309

Drake, P. M., Greenspoon, B., Unti, L., Fawcett, L. K., & Neville-Morgan, S. (2006). Family, friend, and neighbor child caregivers: Results of a statewide study to determine needs and desires for support. *Early Childhood Education Journal*, 33(4), 239–44. doi:10.1007/s10643-006-0071-5

Gorman, K. A., & Fritzche, B. (2002). The good-mother stereotype: Stay at home (or wish that you did!). *Journal of Applied Social Psychology*, 32, 2190–201. doi:10.1111/j.15591816.2002.tb02069.x

Hays, S. (1996). *The cultural contradictions of motherhood*. New Haven, Conn: Yale University Press.

Hochschild, A. R. (1997). *The time bind: When work becomes home and home becomes work*. New York, NY: Metropolitan Books.

Holmes, E. K., Erickson, J. J., & Hill, E. J. (2012). Doing what she thinks is best: Maternal psychological wellbeing and attaining desired work situations. *Human Relations*, 65(4), 501–22. doi:10.1177/0018726711431351

Huff, A. D., & Cotte, J. (2013). Complexities of consumption: The case of child care. *Journal of Consumer Affairs*, 47(1), 72–97. doi:10.1111/joca.12004

Medved, C. E. (2004). The everyday accomplishment of work and family: Exploring practical actions in daily routines. *Communication Studies*, 55(1), 128–45. doi: 10.1080/10510970409388609

Meyering, I. B. (2013). "There must be a better way": Motherhood and the dilemmas of feminist lifestyle change. Outskirts Online Journal: *Feminisms Along the Edge*, 28. Retrieved from http://www.outskirts.arts.uwa.edu.au/volumes/volume-28/isobelle-barrett-meyering

Patterson, Y. A. (1986). Simone de Beauvoir and the demystification of motherhood. *Yale French Studies*, 72, 87–105. Retrieved from http://www.jstor.org/stable/2930228

Randall, V. (1996). Feminism and child daycare. *Journal of Social Policy*, 25, 485–505. doi:10.1017/S0047279400023916

Sperling, J. H. (2013). Reframing the work-family conflict debate by rejecting the ideal parent norm. *Journal of Gender, Social Policy, & The Law*, 22(1), 47–90. Retrieved from http://digitalcommons.wcl.american.edu/jgspl/vol22/iss1/9

Stone, P., & Lovejoy, M. (2004). Fast-track women and the "choice" to stay home. *The ANNALS of the American Academy of Political and Social Science*, 596, 62–83. doi:10.1177/0002716204268552

UNICEF. (2008). *The child care transition: A league table of early childhood education and care in economically advanced countries*. Florence, Italy: Innocenti Research Centre.

Waldfogel, J. (1997). The effect of children on women's wages. *American Sociological Review*, 62, 209–17. Retrieved from http://www.jstor.org/stable/2657300

Wattis, L., Standing, K., & Yerkes, M. A. (2011). Mothers and work-life balance: Exploring the contradictions and complexities involved in work-family negotiation. *Community, Work, & Family*, 16(1), 1–19. doi:10.1080/13668803.2012.722008

Weaver, J. J., & Ussher, J. M. (1997). How motherhood changes life: A discourse analytic study with mothers of young children. *Journal of Reproductive and Infant Psychology*, 15(1), 51–68. doi:10.1080/02646839708404533

Chapter 20

Overview

Men and women all over the world leave their home countries to seek rewarding work in Canada. But even though men and women cross the same spaces, their journeys are quite different. Guida Man and Elena Chou interviewed highly educated female immigrants from mainland China who lived in "astronaut families," with different family members in different countries, which often necessitates a lot of travel back and forth between China and Canada. While the women emigrated with their husbands, at the time of the research the men had given up hope of finding good jobs in Canada and returned to China, leading to pressures within the family for the wives and mothers to do the same. Chou and Man's participants saw the possibility of a return to China in a different light—they believed that as women, they would not have as good prospects as their husbands, so remaining in Canada was a gendered strategy for economic improvement for the family (and for the educational betterment of the children). The women struggled to come up with strategies for meeting gendered familial responsibilities, such as elder care, from a distance but were firm in the belief that remaining in Canada for work was in the best interests of the whole family, even if their husbands might disagree.

Transnational Familial Strategies, Social Reproduction, and Migration

Chinese Immigrant Women Professionals in Canada

Guida Man and Elena Chou

Introduction

The feminization of international migration has been escalating in the last few decades.... Women, particularly those in the developing world, increasingly have to leave their own families to seek work in another country. But transmigrant women may vary in race, class, and abilities; are legal or illegalized....

In the context of the current climate of globalization and neoliberalism, some immigrant families experience unemployment and underemployment, and downward mobility. The difficulties in procuring affordable childcare services and in juggling the contradictory demands of paid work, household work have prompted some immigrant families to resolve to transnational strategies to accomplish the work of social reproduction, such as sending children back to their home country to be cared for by family members.

Social Reproduction and Transnational Migration

... [T]his paper is informed by the theoretical debates on social reproduction....

Feminist political economists generally refer to family as the "social relationships that people create to care for children and other dependents on a daily basis, and also to ensure that the needs of the adults are met" (Fox & Luxton, 2014, p. 6). They also refer to the work of childcare and

the caring of adult family members as "social reproduction" (Bezanson & Luxton, 2006; Gill & Bakker, 2003). Social reproduction refers to the maintenance of life on a daily and generational basis, and includes "how food, clothing, and shelter are made available for immediate consumption, the ways in which the care and socialization of children are provided, the care of the infirm and elderly, and the social organization of sexuality" (Laslett & Brenner, 1989, pp. 382–383). Thus, social reproduction encompasses various physical, mental, and emotional labour that people do to maintain life and to reproduce the next generation. This work is typically carried out by women in the private sphere of their homes....

Social reproductive work that is done in the private sphere of the home, in fact, supports and often substitutes/replaces/supplants work that is done in the public sphere (e.g. the caring of children by family members vis a vis state-subsidized childcare; or the caring of the sick and infirmed at home rather than procuring extended health care in hospitals provided by the state). Much of this work is feminized, but often it is not recognized as work, but as a "labour of love" (Luxton, 1980)....

In the last few decades ... the previously held notion of migration processes as being static has been contested and re-conceptualized to recognize their fluid, dynamic, and transformational characters. Similarly, the im/migrant's country of origin and the country of settlement are not being treated as dichotomized, separate entities, but are conceptualized as interconnected spaces, where transmigrants have continuous interactions in both places. And while scholars may differ in their

Man, Guida, and Elena Chou. "Transnational Familial Strategies, Social Reproduction, and Migration: Chinese Immigrant Women Professionals in Canada," *Journal of Family Studies*, 2017, 26:3, pp. 345–361. Reprinted by permission of Taylor & Francis Ltd. www.tandfonline.com

conceptualization of transnational migration in a narrower interpretation (e.g. Portes, 2003) vis a vis a more expanded approach (e.g. Levitt, 2001); they recognize the emergence and proliferation of transnational communities whereby transmigrants engage in everyday activities; and develop, form, and transform relationships, networks, and identities with their home countries, while at the same time maintain meaningful engagements in their places of settlement. . . .

[A]s structural processes in the larger social, economic, political, and cultural spheres which impact their experiences. Identity differences and structural processes may facilitate or hamper individual immigrant in building cross-border networks and linkages. At the same time, unequal power relations are not being interrogated in this formulation.

Transnational migration occurs among wealthy entrepreneurs (Ley, 2010; Ong, 1999); middle-class professionals (see, e.g. Man, 1995; Preston, Kobayashi, & Man, 2006; Salaff & Greve, 2004); as well as poor racialized men and women, including both documented and undocumented workers from the Philippines, the Caribbean, and other countries in the Global South, and "temporary foreign workers" (see, e.g. Bakan & Stasiulis, 1997; Brigham, 2015; Francisco, 2015). Chinese immigrants have been utilizing transnational practices to maintain family relationships and to accomplish social reproduction. This is observed in the wave of Chinese immigrants who came from Hong Kong to Canada in the 1980s and 1990s (Kobayashi & Preston, 2007; Man, 1995, 1997, 2004b), and more recently with the new immigrants from Mainland China to Canada in the 1990s and continued until today (Man, 2012; Mujahid, Kim, & Man, 2011), but also in historical periods (Chan, 1983; Man, 1995).

. . . [T]his paper explores how middle-class immigrant women professionals from Mainland China navigate transnational familial arrangements, and utilize their agency to devise transnational strategies for social reproduction. Furthermore, the paper examines these practices from the standpoint of the Chinese immigrant women, and investigates how the social, economic, political, and cultural processes in society shape these women's experiences, and at the same

time, how the women's experiences may in turn shape policies and practices.

Based on empirical data from a SSHRC funded research project entitled "Transnational Migration Trajectories of Immigrant Women Professionals in Canada: Strategies of Work and Family" (TTWF), this paper examines the migration experience of highly educated Mainland Chinese women professionals who immigrated to Canada with their husbands and children. . . . In particular, the paper addresses the following questions: What are the social, economic, political, and cultural processes which prompted these women to engage in social reproductive work across national boundaries? How do they accomplish social reproduction transnationally in an era of global economic restructuring and transnational migration?

Our research begins with the Chinese immigrant women's individual experiences by employing the life history method (Cole & Knowles, 2001). . . . Our analysis is centred on three particular strategies of social reproduction employed by the families: migration for better employment opportunities in Canada, migration to facilitate their children's education in Canada, and the transnational strategies of carework.

The Research Study

. . . Adopting a feminist approach, this study puts the Chinese immigrant women as subjects (see Smith, 1987, 2005) and we focus our analysis on the intersections of gender, race/ethnicity, class, migration, transnationalism, and social reproduction. While the study centers on the individual immigrant women's experiences, at the same time, we investigate how the women's lived experiences shape and are shaped by the larger social, economic, cultural, and political processes in the societies in which their experiences are embedded.

Of the 16 Chinese immigrant women interviewed, 9 lived in a transnational familial arrangement at the time of interview. The interview data from these women will form the basis for the analysis of this paper. The 9 women were between the ages of 35 and 46 at the time of the interviews and arrived in Canada between 2003 and 2009. Seven of them were the principal applicants of their family through the Federal Skilled Worker immigration stream, while two arrived as dependents of their husbands who were the main applicants. All were married, and had at least one child, while two women had two children. Almost all the children resided in Canada with their mother except for two families where the children returned to China to live with their fathers. Most arrived with few existing social networks already in place; none had any close family or extended family members in Toronto while a few had some friends they could rely on for help after landing in Canada.

In terms of their career trajectories before and after immigrating to Canada, the women were from middle-class backgrounds and were highly educated. All had obtained at least one university degree, while five had Master's degrees and one had a PhD. Their degrees ranged in fields such as medicine, textile engineering, biochemistry, IT, business administration, accounting, and English literature. Prior to coming to Canada, two women had worked as physicians; two as college or university teachers; two in accounting; two in sales; and one as an operations manager in the IT field. After immigrating to Canada, at the time of interview, none were employed in fields comparable to their preimmigration employment. The two former physicians from China remained in the medical field, but retrained and were employed at the time of interview as a registered practical nurse (RPN), a position somewhat better than that of a nurse's aid; and a medical technician/doctor's assistant. The IT operations manager retrained in social service work was employed in that field, albeit in a position which garners a much lower monetary remuneration and status than her previous position. A woman formerly employed in sales was involved in a transnational import/export business with her husband in China. Three women were taking English language classes and were not employed.

. . .

Employment Opportunities in Canada and Social Mobility

. . .

Since the late 1980s, Canada was an especially popular destination country for immigrants from Hong Kong and Taiwan, although by the 2000s Mainland China had surpassed both to become one of the top source countries for immigrants to Canada. Since 1967 Canadian immigration policy has focused on a point system which favours the admission of economic immigrants and their families who have high levels of human capital, such as advanced education and specialized skills that will benefit the Canadian economy. Canada has also enjoyed a worldwide reputation for being a desirable place to live with high standards of living and good quality of life, a stable government and economy, relative lack of conflict and social strife, and a clean environment. For the middle-class Chinese, Canada is an attractive destination for immigration due to its positive perception as well as its active recruitment of highly skilled workers.

The prospect of better employment opportunities and increased social mobility was one of the driving factors in the initial decision to come to Canada. Some of the women, as well as some of their husbands, had wanted a change of pace in the workplace and everyday life in China and had a desire to challenge themselves, and felt that Canada could provide this opportunity. An example is Tina and her husband, who thought that they would try living in Canada for a while and see what their prospects might be in terms of future educational and employment opportunities. Tina was the principal applicant as she had stronger language skills compared to her husband.

In 2001, my husband and I both worked in a state-owned enterprise. We felt our life was quite dull. Our careers were steadily running into the "bottleneck," so we wanted to seek for a change. Before applying for immigration, I had wanted to study in a MBA program, which was very popular during those years, especially if the degree was obtained from abroad. My husband suggested that we apply for immigration to Canada so that my study abroad would be cheaper. So we started it in the first half year of 2001, submitted our application in Sep. 2001 and passed IELTS. However, my plan changed during the whole application process till Aug. 2002 [when] we were approved. After I prepared for IELTS[1] for a couple of months, I found [that] I was not good at studying any more. Some friends who already landed and studied in Canada told me that it's very hard to study here. So when I received the visa in August, I have completely given up the idea of studying. In 2003, when we landed here, we just wanted to come and see. At that time, the state-owned enterprises in China were closed, merged or transformed. In such a situation, we came here with a come-and-see attitude. If it's not good, we would go back. (TTFW, CH14)

The desire by middle-class families to migrate to Canada can be contextualized within the increasingly neoliberal economic reforms undertaken by the Chinese government since 1980. These reforms have centred on the restructuring of the planned economy model previously employed by the Chinese state in favour of deeper integration with the world economy through the sale of state-owned enterprises and the pursuit of direct foreign investment (Boyd, 2006; Liu, 2007; Zhang, 2006). These have had immense consequences on the welfare and social supports provided by the state: state enterprises, aside from providing guaranteed lifelong employment, also provided their workers with housing, healthcare, and pensions (Liu, 2007; Zhang, 2006). Many of these supports such as maternity leave and childcare directly benefitted women workers, and helped to facilitate their (re)entry into the workforce and eased some of their care work duties (Liu, 2007). . . .

However, upon arrival in Canada, due to discriminatory policies and practices, both the Chinese women and their spouses had difficulties finding work commensurate with their education and experience. . . . [A]lthough recent immigrants tend to have higher levels of education than native-born Canadians, internationally educated professionals are less likely to successfully find employment in their field. This is the case especially for regulated professions such as medical doctors, engineers, and teachers. . . .

In our analysis, the women's spouses returned to China due to their underemployment and unemployment in Canada, resulting in transnational

split familial arrangements known as "astronaut families" where a parent, usually the father, returns to their home country for employment and provides financial support to the rest of the family while the other parent, usually the mother, remains in the destination country with the children (Kobayashi & Preston, 2007; Man, 1995, 1997; Waters, 2002, 2015). In our study, most families had intended to migrate together to Canada as a family unit with the intention of remaining together in Canada. Economic circumstances in Canada as well as difficulties adapting into Canadian society, however, forced the husband in all cases to return to China to resume previous employment or to find employment commensurate with their education and experience. Hence, with the exception of a couple of the families, the astronaut family arrangement emerged out of economic necessity rather than as a predetermined economic strategy.

Laurie's husband is one example. An engineer who owns a business in China, he returned to China within a year of immigrating to Canada as he was not successful in procuring employment in Toronto. Laurie tried to convince her husband to stay in Canada, but he felt that a career in Canada was not possible, partially due to his lack of fluency with English, and believed that he would be better off career-wise in China instead. Laurie remained in Canada with their son. Since the process to recertify in her former profession as a medical doctor (she has an MA in medicine, and another MA in microbiology from China) was very long and arduous, she has since enrolled in a two year course to be retrained to become an RPN, a very low position in nursing which is poorly paid, and requires quite a bit of physical labour. Laurie's husband would like for her and their son to return to China, but she has no plans to do so at the moment. Laurie also does not want to return to China as she is reluctant to start all over again in terms of her career.

> If I go back to China I told my husband I won't work because here [in Canada] you work hard and you get a job and you lose everything in China . . . you go back and you have to do everything again. I said I won't work, I am tired. (TTFW, CH01)

...

For other women, the decision to transition into a transnational family was a deliberate choice. An example is Lee, who had immigrated to Canada alone against the wishes of her husband, a teacher at a university in China. He had no desire to move to Canada and insisted that their son remains in China with him. She could not successfully persuade him to migrate, as she does "not have influence in the family" and that "[what her] husband says, we follow." Her reasons for wanting to immigrate to Canada revolved around her personal life and educational goals.

I wanted to learn the English language. [...] I want to stay if I get a good opportunity. But if I don't see any progress, I'll go back. [...] I don't really have a career goal. People tell me that Toronto doesn't have as much opportunity as in China anyway. [...] I don't really have a long term plan. (TTFW, CH11)

After taking English classes, Lee has been mostly unsuccessful in her job search, but will not return to China as she does not see any benefit to her career in returning to China. Nevertheless, she remains optimistic about her future in Canada and would still like to eventually reunite with her family on a permanent basis whether in Canada or China.

...

The gendered economic implications of migration are evident for the women in our analysis, as the men who returned to China were able to resume their previous job or found new jobs in similar fields, while their wives struggled with reeducation and retraining for new careers in Canada and received financial support from their husbands and families abroad.... For some of the women, the decision to return to China is based on the degree to which they are able to obtain gainful employment in Canada. When asked if she would still like to eventually return to China, Kelly replied that she had a three-year plan after which she would make her decision.

Three years later because now I'm doing different kind of various preparations, three years later if I can get a job in social service, full time job, then I would say [Canada is] my home. But if I can't find ... because I know actually I'm doing my best and I put all my effort for that job three years later and if I still can't find it because of language barrier or discrimination or culture shock, anything related to this thing, then after my children grow up, maybe I would choose to leave the country. But anyway, I already experienced a different life. (TTFW, CH13)

Education Migration as a Strategy of Social Reproduction

The phenomenon of education migration to the West is a well-established and documented practice for social reproduction (see, for example, Heckert, 2015; Ryan & Sales, 2013), particularly amongst middle class and elite East Asian families.... For 6 of the 9 women in our study education migration as a specific and deliberate strategy of social reproduction was cited as one of the key factors in the family's decision to immigrate to Canada.

Maximizing their children's future social capital (Bourdieu, 1986) was a frequently cited reason for education migration, due to the social prestige attached with a Western education (Igarashi & Saito, 2014; Tsang, 2013; Waters, 2005). Many of the women felt that the Chinese education system was too rigid and academically competitive for their children and preferred the more relaxed system in Canada for their children's wellbeing and social development....

Mei and her husband had originally planned to immigrate to Canada to further their own education and then return to China upon completion of their studies. However, after having their daughter they felt that stability for their family was of more importance. Mei's husband had already put into an immigration application and it was accepted, and the family moved to Canada. However, her husband returned to China as he did not want to start from scratch in Canada and give up his job and all the social capital that he had already accrued. He brought back their daughter with him as he felt that China provided a better educational environment for her. While Mei agrees with this decision, she would eventually like their daughter to finish her schooling in Canada.

> I also think the elementary school education in China helps to set a good foundation for my child, so I want my daughter to finish the elementary school in China. It's good for her. If I can stay here till she finishes the elementary school, and our family decides to come, we'll have her continue her study here at that time. (TTFW, CH09)

In Mei's case, their daughter's education is of utmost importance, and Mei is willing to stay in Canada in order to facilitate this regardless of whether or not her husband will join them.

. . .

> Similarly for Min, education migration was a goal both for herself and her daughter:

> At that time, as a visiting scholar, I lived in Toronto for a year and got familiar with the environments here. I felt it's nice for my daughter and me to study here, so I decided to apply for immigration. As a visiting scholar, I had a work permit and it's easier to go through the immigration process. (TTFW, CH15)

However, while initially she felt that her family would be together she soon realized that this might not happen. Her husband never planned to live in Canada as he already has a job back in China, and so he visits Min and their daughter once or twice a year. Min sometimes regrets coming to Canada because her quality of life is lower and she misses her parents. However, she does not regret coming to advance her daughter's education.

In these narratives, we see the gendered effects of education migration in which these mothers are deemed to be willing to "sacrifice"[2] their careers and endure living in a transnational family for their children's education. [. . .] Jing, for example, was concerned about the competitiveness of the Chinese university system and had former colleagues who had sent their children abroad for their education. Her family all arrived together in Toronto, but her husband returned to China after a month and does not want to return to Canada due to his poor English and difficulties with finding employment.

She asserts that her son's education was "the only reason" she immigrated to Canada. Similarly, when Mei was asked about why she would contemplate starting over in Canada again, she simply stated that "I did this for our family and our kid."

Strategies of Transnational Family Care

A recurring trend amongst the women was the degree to which they remained responsible for the bulk of the social reproductive labour in Canada with regards to childcare and daily household duties, as well as the emotional labour in supporting their husbands and maintaining transnational emotional ties. These were exacerbated by the transnational familial arrangements. In China, as middle-class professionals, the women were able to outsource much of their care and household duties either to family members or paid domestic labour. However, as the head of the household in Canada, responsibility for childcare and household tasks fell directly onto women, who had to juggle daily household and family activities along with paid employment. A typical example is described by Kelly.

> For example, in China, [. . .] the labour was very very cheap. Normally less than one Canadian dollar an hour. So I hired somebody to do some kind of job. [. . .] For example, cleaning. Also in China, I have a very big family. I have parents, my parents in law, siblings and whenever I need help, they are always there. [. . .] [in] China, none of us will do house work. But after we came here, and we know we have to share the responsibility, and also we need to support each other so that we can balance the life. (TTFW, CH13)

. . .

Feminist analyses of migration and social reproduction have pointed out the ways in which migration may simultaneously increase female migrants' independence and relieving them of traditional gender roles, but also reinforce gendered divisions of labour in the household (Man, 1997, 2012; Phan, Banerjee, Deacon, & Taraky, 2015). Migration, therefore, affects men and women differently in gender-specific ways. Because of normalized gender roles men have been able to avoid the social reproductive labour necessary for maintaining the household, resulted in a "triple shift" for women in juggling domestic, formal, and informal labour to sustain the family (Spike Petersen, 2010, p. 277). As such, women are usually held to higher standards of family responsibility than men (Ho, 2006).

. . . With regards to return migration, these decisions are largely determined by the stage in the life cycle of the women as well as the family. The women's individual decisions regarding returning to China or remaining in Canada are linked to and shaped by intergenerational familial considerations: eldercare is a primary reason for eventually wanting to return to China while their children's education is frequently cited as a motivation for remaining in Canada. As the family moves through the life course, the carework demands shift, which in turn affect the women's return migration decisions. This is what Min says about eldercare responsibilities and how this is affected by the transnational family:

> Luckily, my parents are in good health condition. My father has minor Parkinson's disease symptom, his right hand shakes, but he has no other health issues and lives quite actively. They retired long time ago and paid much attention to keeping themselves healthy. Luckily, we have no problems until now. Sometimes I feel quite worried that there would be nobody around helping them in case something happens, which is also a reason that I feel I will have to go back and live in China. My parents are there. (TTFW, CH15)

Eldercare concerns do not remain the sole purview of the women, as filial piety is also expected from sons. As Kelly highlights, one of the reasons why her husband returned to China was to help provide care for his aging parents, and this has an effect on the ability of her family to reunite on a longer term basis.

> . . . For the parents, actually. For example, that is another reason why my husband chose to go back to China in recent years. Because my in-laws passed away, one by one, in recent

years. And actually before that, they fell sick and after, as a child you will say it's your responsibility even though you have siblings there, but it's a shared responsibility and you can't . . . it's hard for you to explain to your parents, so you feel guilty when they need your support, you are not there and you feel guilty. . . . That's one of the reasons; so we think maybe he, he can go back in about less than five years, let's say five years. Because now we, our first plan is five years, so I think maybe, maybe he [husband] can spend some times with the family there. It's hard because of the different kind of commitment involved in our lives. (TTFW, CH13)

In our study, although the women were in regular contact with spouses and family members back home, facilitated by relatively low cost communication technologies such as email, telephone and Skype, they were also instrumental in performing the bulk of the emotional labour in comforting husbands abroad and maintaining emotional ties and bonds across distances. Along with carework, emotional labour is also gendered as it is disproportionately taken on by women and often invisible (Eichler, 2008; Liu, 2011). . . .

Conclusion

. . .

The family migration strategies employed by the women and their families reveal how transnational familial migration patterns are not necessarily linear, rooted in migration and then return migration. Rather, they are dynamic and fluid, involving multiple patterns of migration for varying lengths of time which may not eventually result in permanent family reunification. Our study underscores how the notion of the family retains primacy despite geographic and temporal differences, and the mobilization of transnational migration strategies to accomplish the work of social reproduction.

. . . As demonstrated in this paper, these middle-class Chinese immigrant women professionals are not merely dupes who blindly follow the gender and cultural script, despite living in an environment which is often hostile and discriminatory. As betrayed by some of the women's narratives, their decision to migrate to Canada is as much an aspiration to fulfil their desire to live or study in a Western, industrialized and democratic country as for their motivation to obtain better educational opportunities for their children. . . . For the most part, the women were successful in accomplishing the work of social reproduction through their hard work and ingenuity in the home and in the paid labour market, providing materially and emotionally for children and adult members of the family (husbands, aging parents, and in-laws, etc.), whether locally or transnationally. Nonetheless, it is recommended that changes in future policies and practices such as employment practices; regulatory measures in professional associations; and the provision of professional orientated English language classes be put in place to facilitate these families' settlement and integration in their transition into the new country.

Notes

1. The International English language Testing System (IELTS) is an English language proficiency test for higher education.

2. As demonstrated in this study, such "sacrifice" is often not devoid of some degree of agency and self-interest.

Acknowledgement

Guida Man, the principal investigator of SSHRC Research Grant No. 410-2009-2453, would like to extend her deepest gratitude to the Chinese immigrant women participants in this study. Guida would also like to thanks all the project research assistants for their contribution to the research study. In particular, special appreciation is extended to Elena Chou, Ian Hussey, and Willa Liu for their assistance at different stages of the research on the Chinese immigrant women. Tania Das Gupta, Roxana Ng (deceased), and Kiran Mirchandani were the co-investigators of this project.

Funding

The research project "Transnational Migration Trajectories of Immigrant Women Professionals in Canada: Strategies of Work and Family" was supported by Social Sciences and Humanities Research Council of Canada (SSHRC) [grant number 410-2009-2453].

References

Bakan, A.B., & Stasiulis, D. (1997). *Not one of the family: Foreign domestic workers in Canada.* Toronto, ON: University of Toronto Press.

Bezanson, K., & Luxton, M. (Eds.) (2006). *Social reproduction: Feminist political economy challenges neo-liberalism.* Montreal, QC: McGill-Queen's University Press.

Bourdieu, P. (1986). The forms of capital. In J. G. Richardson (Ed.), *Handbook of theory and research for the sociology of education* (pp. 241–58). New York, NY: Greenwood Press.

Boyd, R. (2006). Labour's response to the informalization of work in the current restructuring of global capitalism: China, South Korea, and South Africa. *Canadian Journal of Development Studies, 27,* 487–502.

Brigham, S. M. (2015). Mothering has no borders: The transnational kinship networks of undocumented Jamaican domestic workers in Canada. In G. C. Man & R. Cohen (Eds.), *Engendering transnational voices: Studies in family, work, and identity* (pp. 135–53). Waterloo, ON: Wilfrid Laurier Press.

Chan, A. (1983). *Gold Mountain: The Chinese in the new world.* Vancouver, BC: New Star Books.

Cole, A. L., & Knowles, J. G. (Eds.) (2001). *Lives in context: The art of life history research.* Walnut Creek, Calif: AltaMira Press.

Eichler, M. (2008). Integrating carework and housework into household work: A conceptual clarification. *Journal of the Association for Research on Mothering, 10*(1), 9–17. Retrieved from http://jarm.journals.yorku.ca.ezproxy.library.yorku.ca/index.php/jarm/article/view/16326/15185

Fox, B., & Luxton, M. (2014). Analyzing the familiar: Definitions, approaches and issues at the heart of studying families. In B. Fox (Ed.), *Family patterns, gender relations* (pp. 2–30). Don Mills: Oxford University Press.

Francisco, V. (2015). Multidirectional care in Filipino transnational families. In G. C. Man & R. Cohen (Eds.), *Engendering transnational voices: Studies in family, work, and identity* (pp. 99–116). Waterloo, ON: Wilfrid Laurier University Press.

Gill, S., & Bakker, I. (2003). *Power, production and social reproduction: Human In/security in the global political economy.* Houndmills: Palgrave Macmillan.

Heckert, J. (2015). New perspective on youth migration: Motives and family investment patterns. *Demographic Research*, 33, 765–800.

Ho, C. (2006). Migration as feminisation? Chinese women's experiences of work and family in Australia. *Journal of Ethnic and Migration Studies*, 32(3), 497–514. doi:10.1080/13691830600555053

Igarashi, H., & Saito, H. (2014). Cosmopolitanism as cultural capital: Exploring the intersection of globalization, education and stratification. *Cultural Sociology*, 8, 222–39.

Kobayashi, A., & Preston, V. (2007). Transnationalism through the life course: Hong Kong immigrants in Canada. *Asia Pacific Viewpoint*, 48(2), 151–67. doi:10.1111/j.1467-8373.2007.00338.x

Laslett, B., & Brenner, J. (1989). Gender and social reproduction: Historical perspectives. *Annual Review of Sociology*, 15, 381–404.

Levitt, P. (2001). *The transnational villagers.* Berkeley, Calif: University of California Press.

Ley, D. (2010). *Millionaire migrants: Trans-Pacific life lines.* Oxford: Blackwell-Wiley.

Liu, J. (2007). Gender dynamics and redundancy in urban China. *Feminist Economics*, 13(3–4), 125–58. doi:10.1080/13545700701445322

Liu, L. W. (2011). Emotion work among recent Chinese immigrants to Canada. *Women and Environments International Magazine*, 86–87, 24–26. Retrieved from http://ezproxy.library.yorku.ca/login?url=http://search .proquest.com/docview/897388930?accountid=15182

Luxton, M. (1980). *More than a labour of love: Three generations of women's work in the home.* Toronto, ON: The Women's Press.

Man, G. (1995). The experience of women in recent middle-class Chinese immigrant women from Hong Kong: An inquiry into institutional and organizational processes. *Asian and Pacific Migration Journal*, 4, 303–26.

Man, G. (1997). Women's work is never done: Social organization of work and the experience of women in middle-class Hong Kong Chinese immigrant families in Canada. In V. Demos & M. Texler Segal (Eds.), *Advances in gender research*, Vol. 2 (pp. 183–226). Greenwich: JAI Press.

Man, G. (2004b). Chinese immigrant women in Canada: Examining local and transnational networks. In K. E. Kuah-Pearce (Ed.), *Chinese women and their network capital, Asian women and society series* (pp. 44–69). Singapore: Marshall Cavendish International.

Man, G. (2012). Working and caring: Examining the transnational familial practices of work and family of recent Chinese immigrant women in Canada. *The International Journal of Interdisciplinary Social Sciences*, 6, 199–212.

Mujahid, G., Kim, A. H., & Man, G. (2011). Transnational intergenerational support: Implications of population aging in China for the Chinese in Canada. In H. Cao & V. Poy (Eds.), *Canadian foreign policy in the 21st century: The China challenge* (pp. 177–98). Ottawa, ON: University of Ottawa Press.

Ong, A. (1999). *Flexible citizenship: The cultural logics of transnationality.* Durham, NC: Duke University Press.

Phan, M., Banerjee, R., Deacon, L., & Taraky, H. (2015). Family dynamics and the integration of professional immigrants in Canada. *Journal of Ethnic and Migration Studies*, 41(13), 2061–80. doi.org/10.1080/136918 3X.2015.1045461

Portes, A. (2003). Theoretical convergencies and empirical evidence in the study of immigrant transnationalism. *International Migration Review*, 37(3), 874–92. doi:10.1111/j.1747-7379.2003.tb00161.x

Preston, V., Kobayashi, A., & Man, G. (2006). Transnationalism, gender, and civic participation: Canadian case studies of Hong Kong immigrants. *Environment and Planning A*, 38, 1633–51. doi:abs/10.1068/a37410

Ryan, L., & Sales, R. (2013). Family migration: The role of children and education in family decision-making strategies of polish migrants in London. *International Migration*, 51(2), 90–103. doi:10.1111/j.1468-2435.2010.00652.x

Salaff, J., & Greve, A. (2004). Can women's social networks migrate? *Women's Studies International Forum*, 27, 149–62. doi:10.1016/j.wsif.2004.06.005

Smith, D. (1987). *The everyday world as problematic. A feminist sociology.* Toronto, ON: University of Toronto Press.

Smith, D. (2005). *Institutional ethnography: A sociology for people.* Toronto, ON: Altamira Press.

Spike Petersen, V. (2010). Global householding amid global crises. *Politics & Gender*, 6(2), 271–81. doi:10.1017/ S1743923X10000073

Tsang, E. (2013). The quest for higher education by the Chinese middle class: Retrenching social mobility? *Higher Education*, 66, 653–68. doi:10.1007/ s10734-013-9627-7

Waters, J. L. (2002). Flexible families? "Astronaut" households and the experiences of lone mothers in Vancouver, British Columbia. *Social & Cultural Geography*, 3(2), 117–34. doi:10.1080/14649360220133907

Waters, J. L. (2005). Transnational family strategies and education in the contemporary Chinese diaspora. *Global Networks*, 5, 359–77.

Waters, J. L. (2015). Educational imperatives and the compulsion for credentials: Family migration and children's education in East Asia. *Children's Geographies*, 13(3), 280–93. doi:10.1080/14733285.2015.972646

Zhang, M. (2006). The social marginalization of workers in China's state-owned enterprises. *Social Research*, 73(1), 159–84. Retrieved from http://ezproxy.library .yorku.ca/login?url=http://search.proquest.com/ docview/209671937?accountid=15182

Chapter 21

Overview

Lena Dominelli and colleagues interviewed a group of fathers whose children are in the care of the family welfare system without making judgments as to the merits of their cases or the reasons why their children were "in the system." These fathers believe that they are either invisible as parents in a system that regards mothers as the primary caregivers, or hypervisible in that they are regarded as the source of the family's problems. These fathers adopt different narratives to explain their situations, ranging from the "survivor dad" to the "misrepresented dad."

The fathers also maintain often tense and complex relationships with the social workers who function as gatekeepers and overseers of their relationship with their children. While the dads acknowledge that the social workers are right to be wary of them, given their checkered histories, the dads insist they are using all the resources available to them to build strong relationships with their children.

Of particular interest from the perspective of gender analysis are the dads who define themselves in relation to mothers, seeing themselves as "better than moms." Women's parenting activities become the standard against which these men judge themselves or against which they believe they are being judged by others.

"Here's My Story"

Fathers of "Looked After" Children Recount Their Experiences in the Canadian Child Welfare System

Lena Dominelli, Susan Strega, Chris Walmsley, Marilyn Callahan, and Leslie Brown

Introduction

Fathers of "looked after" children occupy problematic terrain in the child welfare system (Scourfield, 2003) while practitioners configure their status around the "good dad"–"bad dad" binary articulated by Pleck (2004). . . . We investigated how fathers of "looked after" children described their experiences of being fathers within the child welfare system of a middle-sized city in western Canada.

Dominelli, Lena, Susan Strega, Chris Walmsley, Marilyn Callahan, and Leslie Brown. "'Here's My Story': Fathers of 'Looked After' Children Recount Their Experiences in the Canadian Child Welfare System," *British Journal of Social Work*, 2011, 41, 351–67, by permission of Oxford University Press.

Their stories were moving and complex. Fathers described their experiences of being fathers and highlighted the strategies they used to convince (not always effectively) child welfare practitioners that they were "good enough" fathers who could be trusted to care for children. . . . Hearing directly from fathers interacting with child protection systems is unusual. To break this invisibility, the fathers we interviewed speak for themselves without us passing judgment on their stories.

The research took place in Canada, a federated state that gives each province constitutional authority for social services provision. Indigenous peoples are a federal responsibility. . . . This study included indigenous and mainstream agencies. Fathers, aware of their different mandates and services, engaged with those they felt best met their families' needs. . . .

Indigenous or First Nations peoples have complex relationships with non-indigenous Canadians, especially those of British and French origins. A history of racism, colonization, poverty, abuse in residential schools has undermined their well-being, traditional languages, cultures, and resilience and brought forth stereotypes based on violence and substance misuse. As one in three of those in care, First Nations' children are over-represented in Canada's child welfare system (Blackstock et al., 2004; Walmsley, 2005).

Research Method

. . . Our earlier narrative analyses revealed that the theme of fathers' resistance to being configured as "bad dads" was significant (Rutman et al., 2002; Dominelli et al., 2008). For this article, we revisited interview transcripts to examine how fathers configured themselves as worthy of caring for children and challenged child welfare stories of them as "bad dads." The typologies and stories describing fathers' interactions with social workers emerged from this subsequent analysis.

It showed that fathers employed a range of strategies to get social workers to accept that they were responsible enough to play significant roles in children's lives, whether biologically theirs or not (Flood, 2005). They configured their accounts around resistance to social workers' depiction of them as "risky" fathers and sought recognition for being "good enough dads" within trying circumstances. There were many storylines in the fathers' narratives grouped around: "I'm a hero, but you don't see me"; "I'm a survivor"; "I denied my identity to get by"; "I was the mother"; and "I'm a role model dad." From these, we developed the typologies of the "misrepresented dad," "survivor dad," "mothering dad," "denied identity dad," and "citizen dad." . . . We suspect that child welfare professionals might question these accounts or their relevance to decision-making processes.

However, we think they can use fathers' claim that becoming a father is a life-changing event to work with them and make caring for children a more equally shared responsibility between men and women.

Qualitative In-Depth Interviews

We interviewed 11 fathers who volunteered following publicity about the project in child care agencies and/or being told about it by child welfare workers. We used narrative approaches to analyse detailed in-depth interviews of fathers and subjected the transcripts to comprehensive and lengthy processes of analysis to unearth different stories recounted by diverse actors (Reissman, 2002). Narrative approaches to these data are apt because they allow subjugated stories told by "ordinary people" (Fraser, 2004) to become part of public discourses and turn their invisible experiences into visible ones (Devault, 1999). Narrative analyses also enable researchers to uncover the layered contexts of "race," class, and gender (Reissman, 2002). We recognize that as researchers, we become involved in the story-telling process by interpreting what was said and through our commitment to improving child welfare policy and practice (Fraser, 2004).

We sought a purposive sample. To be interviewed, fathers had to have children who either were or had been in the child protection system. The fathers ranged between 24 and 50 years of age at the time of interview. All had cared for the children who either had been or were being processed by the child welfare system. The fathers were either First Nations (six) or white European (five) in origin. All First Nations fathers and three white European-origined ones had problems with substance misuse, either currently or in the past. Five fathers had served time in prison. Nine fathers had quit school early, having achieved grade eight (the level reached at age 13) or less. Most were on benefit, a few in low-paid work. Four fathers had full-time care and custody of children; seven were actively seeking this, jointly with the mother or on their own. We use fictitious names—Tony, Todd, Ben, Peter, Trevor, Darren, Alex, Tom, Gerald, Darryl, Mark—to retain anonymity and enable readers to track their stories. We quote their own words. . . .

Discourses about Fathers

There is a considerable literature on fathers in general written from sociological, psychological, social policy, and legal perspectives. . . . The literature, seldom based on fathers' own voices when discussing their experiences of child protection (Walmsley et al., forthcoming), leaves an important gap for researchers to tackle. We contribute towards filling this by interviewing one excluded group—fathers of "looked after" children—to hear their stories, better understand their situations, and improve practice with them.

We do not examine the validity of the views fathers expressed when interviewed or compare their stories to those of social workers. These fathers were aware that practitioners sought to lower risks for children, but complained that they showed "no respect" for them in the process. Our findings contradicted discourses around the range of roles that fathers occupy in wider society to reveal that the "good dad"–"bad dad" binary (Pleck, 2004) framed practice. The fathers might accept, challenge, or contradict it. But they knew they had to overcome being seen as "bad" dads if they were to convince social workers they were "good dads" who could relate effectively and safely to children. . . .

None of the fathers interviewed wanted sympathy for his "hard luck" story. Some wanted others to know of their successes in surviving the system and strategies for coping with it. Several offered this as a reason for giving interviews. Fathers were aware of the system's concern to protect children and problems faced by overloaded workers (Scourfield and Welsh, 2003). Sympathy with their plight failed to prevent their being fearful of the enormous amount of power that practitioners exerted over their lives (Strega et al., 2008). Mark, for example, states: "You're never free. Once you're in the system, you stay

in the system your whole life. They take your children. They take your grandchildren." This fear motivates fathers to fight to care for children. Confronting powerful welfare workers for the system's failure to meet children's needs is "scary," says Alex.

Most fathers acknowledged the aptness of social workers' scepticism. Their past behaviours included violence, substance misuse, and, for some, a history of being in care. Their realism about their position within child protection meant they relied on lawyers or other professionals to uphold their fathering roles (Strega et al., 2002). They insisted that they be given a chance to look after children based on their current capacity to adapt, change, and act in accordance with practitioners' demands. These fathers often cast social workers as "the enemy"—professionals to stay away from—a finding replicated in Ashley et al. (2006).

Fathers were critical of the constant pressures to which social workers subjected them and the hurdles they encountered to "look promising" (Callahan et al., 2005), behave appropriately by eschewing drugs, alcohol, or violence, and prove they could be trusted with caring for children. Their stories conveyed a complex graduated picture because they maintained that social workers also supported fathers with an array of programmes and insights into their progress—as suggested by Tony, whose performance improves through agency inputs. However, Tony wants daycare to be publicly funded to reduce the pressures of combining work, going to college, and looking after children. . . .

Fathers' Typologies When Recounting Narratives of Fathering in the Child Welfare System

Fathers' self-profiles indicate that they lead complicated lives (Milner, 2004). Those we interviewed disclosed complex, constantly changing existences as they engaged in a perpetual dance to challenge social workers' depiction of them as "bad dads." Persistence in becoming accepted as "good dads" figured strongly in their narratives, as did resilience and coping strategies in confronting a system they perceived as distant, invisible, and dis-empowering. They identified the key stories defining their lives as:

- "misrepresented dad"—*I'm a good dad, but not seen as such*;
- "survivor dad"—*I was expected to fail, but I didn't*;
- "mothering father"—*I act as a (good) mother would*;
- "denied my identity dad"—*I had to play the game of being someone other than myself*; and
- "good role model" or "citizen dad"—*I am a good citizen . . . I join community groups . . . and look after my children.*

We explore how fathers use these descriptions as they struggle to prove their worthiness as fathers, although Pleck's (2004) "good dad"–"bad dad" binary remained embedded in fathers' complex and nuanced understandings of their actual interactions with social workers. They described specific experiences ranging from "I'm a ghost" to "I didn't want to be an aboriginal."

Those who admitted they had problems that needed sorting out rejected social workers' views of them as "bad" dads, thereby highlighting different objectives between social workers and fathers. Practitioners were rightly concerned with minimizing potential risks to children while fathers focused on the hardship and suffering they endured in the child welfare system and skated hurriedly over their limitations and contributions to environments not conducive to raising children. Even problematic fathers amplified resilience and strengths in developing relationships with children, as Todd indicates below. Some stories did not have "happy endings," as child welfare workers had valid reasons for being sceptical of their intentions.

Misrepresented Dad

. . . Fathers saw becoming a father as a life-changing event, a source of identity and pride. The "misrepresented father" was configured when practitioners did not acknowledge men's skills as "good fathers." Mark highlighted how social workers do not appreciate fathers' strengths as carers, focusing instead on making fathers work to pay for meeting children's needs when "it's not in the budget." Mark found practitioners' behaviour unhelpful and arbitrary: "She wasn't returning my calls. . . . When she did talk to me, her attitude sucked because she was telling me . . . if the mom is involved in drugs . . . the other parent is too." Whether social workers cast them as misusing drugs and alcohol or economic providers, fathers had difficulty being heard as "good dads" and felt "misrepresented."

Ben felt mistreated by being denied contact with his child when told to "hang in there" and misrepresented when falsely accused of violence and his drinking was "blown way out of proportion." His unsuccessful attempts to gain custody make him conclude that fathers are hurt when treated as "bad dads" because "they are probably good fathers and all they are doing is trying to see their kids." Ben worries that he will be unable to build a relationship with the child and asks, "how long can people hide her from me?"

Darren and Gerald were "misrepresented" dads because their willingness to change was misbelieved. Darren's partner used his violent history to falsely accuse him of violence to "get him out of the picture." Gerald, a First Nations man, had a restraining order imposed when his partner called the police and alleged he assaulted her brother while planning her father's funeral. He was imprisoned for a few days and their five-week-old baby taken into care. Gerald thought he was a "good dad" and fought a system that assumed allegations of assault were true. He minimized his violence, blaming his ex-partner and social workers for exaggerating his contributions to his predicament.

Victimhood and blaming others featured in misrepresented fathers' stories. For Gerald, this encompassed difficulties in controlling his temper and drinking. Gerald justifies feeling the victim with:

> I didn't want her to go party . . . she called the cops. It was my house. I paid the rent. All of the bills and everything were in my name, but I went to jail.

Child welfare professionals configured misrepresented dads around rigorous assessments that allayed mistrust of their behaviour. Gerald knew that risk assessments could jeopardize his chances of gaining custody of "the baby":

> I had to prove they were wrong now . . . assault with a weapon. That makes me a high risk father right off the bat.

Gerald describes social workers' surveillance practice over misrepresented dads as:

> I had to do all my visits under a glass. They had a two way mirror and a speaker. . . . No matter what I said, it's all being recorded. I had somebody watching me at [sic.] all the times.

Becoming a father, a life-changing event, motivated Gerald, like others, to change. He claims to be "the happiest man alive." Having a baby and looking after it "makes it all worthwhile. It gives you reason to get up. It makes you ten feet tall." Gerald turned his life around after being supported by an indigenous voluntary agency, attending anger management groups and parenting classes, and rejecting alcohol. He demonstrates that supportive interventions are effective in altering behaviour and earns custody of the child by strategizing how to escape the "invisible" category; getting child welfare workers to transcend the "misrepresented dad" label, listen to his views, and see his strengths; and learning from the groups he attended. His decision to "fight me" by not drinking and acquire skills that engaged his worker gave him confidence in getting the practitioner onside. Gerald explains:

> I changed the focus of the whole thing. Instead of . . . taking the full force and running me through the wringer, I switched it so that the focus was now on baby.

By creating a defining moment that began when visiting his child and asking the worker why "baby had a diaper rash," Gerald demonstrated that he could place the baby's interests and well-being above his own. This led the child welfare worker to listen to him, eventually becoming convinced that he was "fit enough" to have custody. Gerald encourages workers to accept "good enough" parenting rather than overwhelm fathers with endless demands and programs for becoming better fathers when they cannot quite meet the white middle-class, heterosexual standards. . . .

Survivor Dad

Todd exemplifies the "survivor dad" who is resilient, overcomes adversity, and becomes a "good" father. He was a "struggler and survivor"; "miracle" baby who should have died at birth; sexually abused child who survived; survivor of a serious motor vehicle accident; and survivor of a suicide attempt. Todd presented himself as a caring provider who made sure children in his relationship (one being his biological child) followed a "nightly routine"; worked; and paid bills. Since he split up with his partner, he has struggled to gain access to the children and be heard as a father who has contributed to their well-being and still can. He feels *entitled* to be with them, but social workers remain unconvinced.

Social workers thought Todd was "a boyfriend" who came and went. His relationship with practitioners was mediated by his ex-partner, a gatekeeper with the power to deny his presence.

She configured him as invisible by ensuring that practitioners remained unaware of his involvement with the children. They had an "open" file on the oldest child (not biologically his) under the mother's name. She had not declared income obtained from renting to Todd and others. Todd thought the system encouraged this invisibility because otherwise she would lose "money." He acknowledges being "suicidal and . . . end[ing] up in the rubber room," but downplays her exclusion of him for being risky by recounting her saying:

> I am keeping you out of the picture for the safety of the children because of [your] emotional state.

He survives invisibility by contacting practitioners with concerns about the oldest child's welfare and demanding access. Social workers did not engage directly with Todd, speak to or interview him about his child or demands for access. Practitioners relied on the mother for information and presumed its accuracy. Without a formal gate-keeping contract, she was expected to report Todd's presence in her life. . . . Social workers did not assess Todd as "looking promising" and the biological father got custody. The mother refused contact when he requested it. His nine-month-old biological child remained with her, with social workers "coming in and checking up on how things were." As the invisible man fighting for custody, Todd said:

> This is so out of whack . . . me not being able to see the children . . . so off the wall.

Darren, asked if he wanted "to be the father," replied "I am the father." He rose to the challenge, saying he could take care of his daughter better than her substance-misusing mother. Social workers helped him become "survivor dad" by configuring him as a deserving father and giving him extensive support. They brought the baby to visit him in prison. Once out, practitioners supported him to get custody, form a good bond with his daughter, become a better father, and stop smoking. His narrative reveals he is not fully trusted, and surveillance systems monitor his performance. He knows that if he "screws up," the child will be removed. He feels the system is "working with me, working at me" and is constantly on guard. Workers also watch how he behaves with a second child, although he was not given information about her medical condition. He constantly feels "spied on" while claiming foster-parents retain their privacy by not discussing the child's allergy with him. Despite expectations of failure, he is "going to prove them wrong." He succeeds as "survivor dad" and social workers are preparing him to receive another child currently in care. Darren thinks he has become "a better person" by becoming a father. He survived by becoming a "good dad" in contrast to the "bad mom" who wanted him to do all the parenting tasks.

Alex can gain custody "as long as we have our support in place and . . . don't drink." His plan to become "survivor dad" fails when a promising working relationship slips as his worker is replaced by one who is unsupportive. Staff turnover can produce decisions that fathers experience as arbitrary in the child welfare dance of surveillance and support that enmeshes them when caring for children.

Mothering Father

A "mothering father" is a better parent than the mother. Scourfield (2003) found this category, too. This role is expressed in diverse ways. Practitioners tell Darren "he is better than most women." Gerald comments on the inadequate mother that allows him to become the "mothering father." He says: "[S]he stood back and wasn't doing anything . . . knowing that if it wasn't for me, baby would have nobody." He reprimands the social worker for inadequate parenting—not knowing about a diaper rash:

> You're going to tell me how to be a mother. You're going to tell me how to be a father and you don't know enough to check if she's got a . . . diaper rash.

Peter would "come home from work, . . . bathe and feed [the child]." He thought he was doing better than the mother, who left the baby "with a bottle propped up and . . . ignored most of the day." As a lone father providing through waged work, looking after a sick child was tough. He lacked "the extra person to fall back on when she's sick at the daycare." His parenting work remained unrecognized: child-care workers did not return his calls, were rude, or hung up.

Trevor cannot establish his right to care for the children. His proof that he is a better mother than the mother—that the children no longer want to stay with her—is not accepted by practitioners. He states: "They have a child-friendly home and everything I do is for them." This includes controlling their behaviour and disciplining them if they do wrong. A key aim of his relationship with his son was to help him acquire self-esteem and self-pride. When chastising his son for getting into the wrong crowd, he goes over the top and assaults him. He calls child welfare to tell them before someone reports him and uses this to request further assistance.

Tony and partner were HIV-positive. As "mothering dad," Tony explains:

> . . . a regular routine day would be for me to get up . . . in the . . . night to make the bottles, heat them up . . . because we're HIV positive there's no breastfeeding . . . I was doing that . . . as well as trying to attend college and . . . keep up my studies.

He feels the system excluded him by removing the children because his "wife pass[ed] out on the lawn" and his mothering efforts are discounted. When refused custody, he attributes it to discrimination for being HIV-positive:

> I had [social workers] that didn't like the fact that I'm HIV positive. . . . They tried to screw with my cheque because they don't think I should have a kid.

The system configured *this* family as problematic because the mother, a First Nations woman,

had been under its gaze earlier; both parents had been in care, were HIV-positive, and thought to be abusing alcohol. Social workers' initial reactions labelled both "unfit" parents:

> You know when that doorbell rang you became scared. Is that the Ministry at the door even though your house is clean and there is nothing you have to worry about?

Tony configures his story within an "all-powerful and unaccountable" system:

> I remember crying like a baby because I never knew they had so much power to seize my child.

He believes cautious workers concluded that an HIV-positive father who looks tired is "on drugs" and takes tests to refute this. Tony was upset by the lack of apology for this mistreatment and lack of respect for him and his family. He feels pushed to succeed as a "father with all the odds against me."

Tony finds the system capricious. Continuing to fight for his child, Tony regrets that his words were twisted by a worker when he gave a life history:

> . . . just for the records so that they could better handle the case, . . . better understand my family dynamics and situations we're coping with. I [was] honest about . . . being an ex-junkie . . . fighting with the police. You think once you fly straight, . . . go to college, they're never going to screw you around, so you tell them the truth.

Sometimes, Tony thought the tricks were more obvious:

> They'd ask me the same questions four or five different ways to try to trip me up. . . . It was just basically undermining.

Tony interprets child welfare workers' queries about reconciliation with his wife as tricks because "had I answered the wrong way, my daughter would have been seized . . . nor was I planning to reconcile." Tony was prepared to "jump through the hoops" to get his daughter back. He finally succeeds and reports his wife for hitting her. He threw his wife out, saying "my daughter is not going to end up in care because you choose not to do anything." When the child is returned, he is under constant surveillance. Anonymous tip-offs lead to his being checked for alcohol and drug misuse, even when tests clear him. Being a mothering father is hard.

Denied My Identity Dad

Proving an identity as a "good enough father" was problematic and required men to behave according to white, middle-class, heterosexual norms consistent with being a Canadian citizen. Tony thought that racism underpinned workers' perceptions of his wife as a First Nations woman who misused substances. Like other First Nations peoples, Daryl resists racist configurations of his family by hiding the impact of residential schools, fights, and substance misuse, and denying his aboriginal identity:

> I was so ashamed of my family . . . of what I was . . . I didn't want to be an aboriginal. My best friends were not aboriginal. . . . Everybody thought we weren't aboriginal. So I pretended I wasn't till I messed up one time.

He had eight children. Most were taken into care, some permanently. Daryl's story gives readers insights into why this is so. At one point, Daryl encountered friendly social workers who supported him to change, find "a different way," and become a "fit" parent. His wife, initially involved, dropped out. Daryl persevered by changing himself, becoming comfortable with asking professionals for help. As "mothering father," he does what was necessary to keep the children. His main strategy was to become "citizen dad," "look promising," continue caring for six children and ensure they did not get into trouble. He controls their

behaviour by getting them to school, keeping them out of gangs, and being a good role model. As Daryl explains:

> . . . my children see me . . . at the school working, at home sleeping, getting up, making . . . breakfast . . . putting a movie on for them, being there for them, not being drunk, not being violent, not hanging around with gang members.

His progress was not straightforward. He got into difficulty when relatives stayed overnight because social workers constructed them as stereotypical aboriginals and potential risks, involved in alcohol, drugs, and violence. Living in an indigenous neighbourhood increased these risks despite his lifestyle being at odds with that of many around him. People jumped to conclusions about his parenting abilities, raising questions for social workers to investigate. Constantly under surveillance (Beck, 1992), his ex-wife creates problems by repeatedly phoning, promising to visit the children, then not showing up. As citizen dad, he lives with the constant fear of not "looking promising" if he steps out of line (Callahan et al., 2005).

Daryl learns to defend himself when challenged. He gives his ex-wife $20 to stay away from the children for a month so she is not "around them when she's high." Nor does he allow her to stay overnight. He draws tight boundaries around the children's "best interests" and keeps to these. These include leaving a "bad" neighbourhood; being proactive about his children's behaviour at school; and acting the "good citizen" through membership of community boards like the Parents Council. He wants his children to know "that I'll be there for them no matter what. I want them to find different avenues than what I did." They have to move out of an "aboriginal identity" and become well behaved, decent kids. He configures himself as the "good dad" who is "involved with them." Helping his disabled son exceed the system's expectations is another crucial parenting ambition. He protects him from "rough kids" and equips him for a "good job." As model dad complying with society's norms, Daryl is:

> . . very proud of him. . . . I don't want to give up on him. . . . I want my son to be able to do something when he goes to grade seven.

Daryl experiences the system's capriciousness: "I always seem to run into a worker that wants to make it hard." He attends different programs, has a part-time job that fits in with the children's schooling, and social assistance workers want him to get a night-time job! This devalues his work in looking after children, as the system does for women, and ignores the extra childcare costs entailed in someone being home to keep children safe at night. Although a support worker proclaims, "He's got all his kids back and he's doing wonderful," Daryl is aware that he cannot stop having to prove himself as a "good" father within a framework dominated by a white child welfare system, even if indigenous agencies in the locality support him. At times, he challenges representatives of this structure as he does police officers who question his caring potential by saying his son is hanging around with gang members. He asks them:

> Why don't you go see the parents? . . . If you're definitely sure that they're gang members why can't you do something about it?

For Daryl, their reply—"it's not our job"—depicts a racialized system of justice that endangers First Nations children "already in the system." He does not complain in case they place his children for "adoption" and jeopardize his fathering role.

Mistrust exists on both sides, with power struggles between the child welfare system and fathers. Alex thinks his family is labelled as "nothing but trouble" because:

> They just want to keep my children. . . . I don't understand why they gave us a hard time. . . . I've been fighting with them over the years. . . . I won't back down . . . but it's taking a toll on me.

Alex's hopes of getting his children back are arbitrarily raised and dashed by workers who constantly undervalue his identity as a father. He says: "They keep giving promises and . . . back out of them." He assumes he has been set up to fail to "start drinking again," thereby proving lack of fitness to parent. . . .

Conclusions

Stories uncovered by this study reveal that although the "good dad"–"bad dad" binary frames fathers' relationships with social workers, these are difficult and complicated because social workers do not completely trust fathers to care for children. The typologies of "misrepresented dad," "survivor dad," "denied my identity dad," "mothering father," or "citizen dad" represent fathers' views of this interaction. The categories overlap and have positive dimensions in exposing fathers' struggles to become "good dads" despite being trapped by social workers' expectations about safeguarding children; scepticism about their endeavours to change their behaviours; and constant demands to "look promising." Fathers, under surveillance, have to act as white heterosexual "citizen dad" to prove they are "good enough" to be entrusted with caring for children.

Practitioner responses to fathers of "looked after" children require sensitivity, courage, and approaches that do not undermine the rights of mothers and children. Fathers argued that the system can better support them in taking a full share of responsibilities in an equal partnership (not necessarily a live-in one) with mothers if social workers:

- listened actively to their views and trusted that they, too, have the best interests of their children at heart;
- had appropriate training, especially for children with fetal alcohol syndrome; and

- provided more continuity and stability in client–worker relationships.

"Trust," flexibility, and sound professional judgments are important ingredients in relationships that promote children's interests and enable practitioners to support fathers. Workers need training for effective intervention in fetal alcohol syndrome cases to enable fathers to change their behaviour and look after such children. Fathers suggested that practitioners learn how to handle problematic, assertive fathers and work with their strengths to help them become better fathers. Their stories indicate that workers can both control and support them. . . .

Acknowledgement

The study on which this article is based was funded by the Social Sciences and Humanities Research Council of Canada.

References

Ashley, C., B. Featherstone, M. Ryan, C. Roskill, and S. White, 2006. *Fathers Matter: Research Findings on Fathers and their Involvement with Social Care Services.* London: Family Rights Group.

Beck, U. 1992. *Risk Society: Towards a New Modernity.* London: Sage.

Blackstock, C., N. Trocmé, and M. Bennett. 2004. "Child Maltreatment Investigations among Aboriginal and Non-Aboriginal Families in Canada: A Comparative Analysis," *Violence Against Women* 10(8): 901–16.

Callahan, M., L. Dominelli, D. Rutman, and S. Strega. 2005. "Looking Promising: Contradictions and Challenges for Young Mothers in Child Welfare," in D.L. Gustafson, ed., *Unbecoming Mothers: The Social Production of Maternal Absences.* New York: Haworth Press.

Devault, M. 1999. "Talking and Listening from Women's Standpoint: Feminist Strategies for Interviewing and Analysis," in M. Devault, ed., *Liberating Method: Feminism and Social Research.* Philadelphia: Temple University Press.

Dominelli, L., L. Brown, M. Callahan, S. Strega, and C. Walmsley. 2008. "Reconfiguring the Fathers," *Trabajo Social* 74: 107–16.

Flood, M. 2005. "Fathers' Rights and the Defense of Paternal Authority in Australia," *Violence against Women* 16(3): 328–47.

Fraser, H. 2004. "Doing Narrative Research: Analysing Person Stories Line-by-Line," *Qualitative Social Work* 3(2): 179–201.

Milner, J. 2004. "From 'Disappearing' to 'Demonised': The Effects on Men and Women of Professional Interventions Based on Men Who Are Violent," *Critical Social Policy* 24(1): 79–101.

Pleck, E. 2004. "Two Dimensions of Fatherhood: A History of the Good Dad–Bad Dad Complex," in M. Lamb, ed., *The Role of the Father in Child Development*, 4th edn. New York: Wiley and Sons, first published in 1997.

Reissman, C. 2002. "Narrative Analysis," in M. Huberman and M.B. Miles, eds., *Qualitative Researcher's Companion.* Thousand Oaks: Sage.

Rutman, D., S. Strega, M. Callahan, and L. Dominelli. 2002. "'Undeserving' Mothers? Practitioners' Experiences Working with Young Mothers in/from Care," *Child and Family Social Work* 7(3): 149–60.

Scourfield, J. 2003. *Gender and Child Protection.* London: Palgrave.

Scourfield, J., and I. Welsh. 2003. "Risk, Reflexivity and Social Control in Child Protection: New Times or Same Old Story?," *Critical Social Policy* 23(3): 398–420.

Strega, S., M. Callahan, L. Dominelli, and D. Rutman. 2002. "Undeserving Mothers: Social Policy and Disadvantaged Mothers," *Canadian Review of Social Policy/Revue Canadienne de Politique Sociale* 40(5): 175–94.

Strega, S., C. Fleet, L. Brown, M. Callahan, L. Dominelli, and C. Walmsley. 2008. "Connecting Father Absence and Mother Blame in Child Welfare Policies and Practice," *Children and Youth Services Review* 30: 705–16.

Walmsley, C. 2005. *Protecting Aboriginal Children.* Vancouver: University of British Columbia Press.

Walmsley, C., L. Brown, L. Dominelli, S. Strega, and M. Callahan. Forthcoming. "Where's Waldo? Fathering in Social Work Education," submitted to the *Canadian Social Work Review.*

Chapter 22

Overview

Who cares? Women have traditionally been positioned as the "caring, nurturing" gender, supposedly because of their connection to motherhood. Men are more often stereotyped as independent, autonomous individuals who don't often tend to the bodily needs of others. But as Melissa Giesbrecht and her collaborators point out, men also do the work of caring for dependent family members and experience an enormous range of emotions associated with caring. They use metaphors of geography and space to describe the emotional tenor of care work in their research with 194 men who provided in-home care for family members with chronic medical conditions, primarily but not exclusively wives. Their participants talked about their caregiving in terms of "nearness" and "distance," with respect to themselves, their immediate network of significant others, and the broader community. Some men said they felt they had "lost" themselves in the gruelling work of looking after someone else, and others believed that their caregiving role had distanced them from their family members and friends. Some felt out of place as a male caregiver in their communities, while others found that their caregiving had actually brought them closer to people around them. Their stories illustrate the wide range of emotions associated with caregiving among men, and also show how metaphors of space and place can be useful for giving words to personal experience.

Feelings of Distance and Proximity

Exploring the Emotional Geographies of Men Caregiving for Family Members with Multiple Chronic Conditions

Melissa Giesbrecht, Allison Williams, Wendy Duggleby, Bharthi Sethi, Jenny Ploeg, and Maureen Markle-Reid

. . . Emotions do not fit neatly into categorical boxes, but rather are incredibly complex, difficult to identify, define and untangle, not only for those who are researching them, but also those experiencing them (Parr, 2005). Yet, there is no doubt that emotions are significantly relevant to place-based experiences and thus, to geography research. In fact, emotions infuse and inform every aspect of our lived realities. . . .

Men, Masculinity and Family Caregiving in Canada

For decades, feminist scholars have been critical of the various structures that forge women into caregiving roles, including their assumed "natural" fit for various forms of emotional work and their

Giesbrecht, Melissa, Allison Williams, Wendy Duggleby, Bharthi Sethi, Jenny Ploeg, and Maureen Markle-Reid. "Feelings of Distance and Proximity: Exploring the Emotional Geographies of Men Caregiving for Family Members with Multiple Chronic Conditions," *Social & Cultural Geography*, 2019, 20:1, pp. 109–129. Reprinted by permission of Taylor & Francis Ltd.

assumed "natural" association with the highly feminized space of the home, the setting where the majority of informal care occurs (Armstrong, Armstrong, & Scott-Dixon, 2008; Bondi, 2008). For example, Graham (1983) describes that: "Caring is 'given' to women: it becomes the defining characteristic of their self-identity and their life-work. At the same time, caring is taken away from men: not caring becomes a defining characteristic of manhood" (p. 18). This points to an infused tension that exists between hegemonic masculinity (the most honoured way of being a man (Connell & Messerschmidt, 2005)) and the traditional feminized role of family caregiving. Within North America, hegemonic masculinity traditionally embodies qualities such as being strong, stoic, capable, reliable and in control, and within the gender hierarchy, is deemed greater than "subordinated masculinities" and defined as the opposite of femininity (Latshaw, 2015). . . . As a result, men's emotions tend to be overlooked, with little known regarding the gendered emotional experiences of men who have become strongly invested in family caregiving, one of the most femininely defined areas of social life (Doucet, 2006; Milligan & Morbey, 2013).

Today, almost half of Canada's 8 million family caregivers (46%) are men and this proportion is only expected to rise (Statistics Canada, 2014). . . . Although it is important to acknowledge that women still provide the majority of this work, shifting demographics, such as smaller family sizes, families that are increasingly dispersed and diverse, increased rates of Alzheimer's Disease (which disproportionally affects women) and both men and women having full-time employment are leading to more men assuming family caregiving roles (McNabb, 2015; Scott, 2015). These men and women informal, or family, caregivers have become the backbone of health systems across much of the global north, including Canada (Canadian Caregiver Coalition, 2009; Lilly, Robinson, Holtzman, & Bottorff, 2012), as they provide care to family members or friends with long-term health conditions, disabilities or ageing needs (Statistics Canada, 2014). . . . Although caregiving can be a rewarding experience, it is often demanding work

with the commonly referred to "caregiver burdens" frequently producing high levels of physical, mental and emotional stress (Bialon & Coke, 2012; Grunfeld, 2004). For some, these caregiver burdens become all-consuming, leading to complete burnout, whereby they become so physically, mentally and emotionally depleted that they are no longer able to provide care, leaving the caregiver in great distress and the care recipient at risk of institutionalization (Bialon & Coke, 2012; Canadian Institute for Health Information, 2012; Lilly et al., 2012; Melin-Johansson, Axelsson, & Danielson, 2007).

Despite the number of studies conducted on caregiving over the past decades, the experiences of men have often been overlooked (Kramer, 2002; McNabb, 2015; Milligan & Morbey, 2013; Scott, 2015). . . . [L]ittle is known regarding how men manage their own emotions in caregiving contexts. In the present analysis, we attempt to take a first step towards addressing this gap by . . . exploring the emotion discourse of a diverse group of men who are primary caregivers for family members with multiple chronic conditions. . . .

Data Collection

Survey interviews were conducted, both over the phone and in person, at two different points in time (six months apart) with 194 participants. A third qualitative semi-structured interviews was conducted in person with a sub-set of 40 participants ($n = 20$ in Alberta; $n = 20$ in Ontario) who were purposively selected to represent the social and demographic diversity of the 194 participant group. . . .
. . .

Emotional Experiences of Distance and Proximity

During the interviews, the participants shared experiences of caregiving which tended to evoke in them numerous emotions, ranging from frustration, anger, guilt, fear, sorrow, anxiety, loneliness, disempowerment and hopelessness to feelings of expressed acceptance, pride, satisfaction, enjoyment, devotion and love. Closer analysis of these findings revealed that many participants implicitly and explicitly articulated their emotional experiences relationally, in a manner reflective of geographic notions of distance (e.g. feeling far, isolated) and proximity (e.g. feeling close, connected). Furthermore, these emotion discourses of "proximity" and "distance" were found to occur in the space between particular interactions, namely in relation to (1) one's own self; (2) the self and others; and (3) the self and the wider community. . . .

Sense of Self

The demands of caregiving for an individual with multiple chronic conditions were expressed by the men to often be demanding, stressful, consuming and draining. . . . Although not explicitly articulated as such, these participants shared, more implicitly, how their caregiving role generated a disjuncture between their previous sense of self and the person felt they had become. Many participants expressed this by sharing how, over time, they felt they had "lost" themselves in the process, where the person they once were, and life they once had, now belonged to the distant past. In other words, caregiving had led to a temporal feeling of distance from their sense of self, with many articulating how they felt transformed as a result of their new role. For some, this translated into expressions of resentment, for example, by John, who is married and caring for his wife:

> I don't feel anger at this because you know, you have no choice, but it does totally screw up your life. You have no life. Your own life gets put on hold and the demands of this person get more and more as time goes by and so you have less and less to be yourself and that's the biggest thing I'm most working on is to retain me in all this.

. . . Worried about not knowing how many years he had left to live, John shared how he hoped to be able to one day be able to "create a life with myself again."

Being a primary caregiver involves incredibly onerous work and it was found that for many, it was very important to find brief moments of respite in their days. It was during these moments that participants created the space to reconnect with themselves, reaffirm their sense of personal identity and provide self-care, which in turn, facilitated caregiver resiliency. For the majority of the men, but particularly those in the younger age groups, these moments involved physical exercise (e.g. going to a gym) or playing sports (e.g. golf with friends). For Luka, when speaking about the demands of caregiving for his mother, he explains that what brings him pleasure, the feeling of control and a sense of self is: ". . . exercise and working out. It is the most, by far the best drug for me to stay on top of things, and then I don't mind challenges." Other participants, like Aditya, articulated how he enjoyed and valued the moments when he could simply be alone to reconnect with his sense of self: "I try to get out myself . . . some time for myself to enjoy quiet time or be able to go out on my own . . . I do that, go for a walk." Intersecting with culture and spirituality, other participants mentioned doing Tai Chi, yoga and meditating, like Amit, who said that he enjoyed those moments when he was able to "sit down and just take a break and meditate a little bit." Here, caregivers' social connectedness with the community (e.g. access to respite services and supports) and the care recipient's physical and/or mental capacity shaped their emotional responses and the opportunity to take some time for themselves, while their gender and cultural/spiritual background tended to influence how these moments of respite were enjoyed. . . .

Relation to Others

Feelings of distance, or growing apart, between caregivers and their care recipients were commonly expressed, often explicitly, by the participants. This was especially the case for husbands caring for wives/life partners with cognitive impairments and who felt alone, while they clung onto fragments of their pre-existing romantic relationships and attempted to reassemble them in the new context of caregiving. This was found to be incredibly distressing for some participants, like David. When asked about the difficulties he faced as a caregiver, David replied "I think it's sort of the growing apart bit. It's not as warm as what it used to be. She's not the warm person she used to be." David's wife is living with dementia, among other chronic conditions, which has resulted in a dramatic reconfiguration of their marital relationship over time. David continued to express his grief, stating that what he missed most was "the closeness. I don't feel close, that's how I feel. It hurts. [crying] Excuse me, but it hurts. It hurts."[1] David clearly expressed his grief and sense of loss while articulating these emotions in a very spatial manner. Here, relationship to the care recipient (e.g. spousal) and a shared emotional history, as well as the diagnosis of their wives/life partners greatly affected their emotional responses.

On the other hand, the ability to find peace and accept the current caregiving context required some men to emotionally distance themselves from their previous intimate, romantic and in some cases more reciprocal relationships with their wives/life partners who had now become care recipients. . . .

I think that there is an important personality change that has to occur if you're going to be the best caregiver and that is to become a servant instead of a partner. There's a big difference. Some people want to call us care partners and I don't think that's right because caregiving involves 100% giving with little expectation of return, and if you can't approach it with that attitude, it's going to be really difficult.

. . . As such, Walter feels distant from what was once a more mutual relationship, where they were able to more equally give to each other what they desired or felt they needed. Not only has this participants' role and identity changed, but so too has the role and identity of their loved one.

Among the participants, caregivers who were sons commonly shared experiences of arguing and fighting with their siblings, resulting in feelings of expanding distance between family members. This anger or frustration with siblings was largely due to the emotionally tense and stressful context of providing care for a parent, which often includes time sensitive critical decisions regarding how to provide the best care, who should provide the care, where the care should take place, or as their parents become increasingly frail, what to do with (or who will get) their residence and/or belongings. At the same time, some caregivers felt that their siblings simply did not recognize the amount of work they do and felt that their role as a caregiver was taken for granted. For example, Matthew states: "What have I disliked? Well again, it's pretty much in relation to my other family members and them not really appreciating what it really takes to do what needs to be done." Matthew continues to share his sense of a growing distance between himself and his brothers:

In a sense I am sort of becoming divorced from my brothers, that there isn't really this thing that's keeping us together and maybe it's actually a growing thing for me . . . in my heart, I would have liked to have seen our family just kind of really remain strong and stick together and so I just don't think I can really control it or influence it all that much.

. . .

While some participants shared feelings of distance expanding between themselves and the care recipient or other family members due to the caregiving context, others explained how they felt the experience brought them closer and deepened their love. For example, James, who provides care for his wife, expressed "in a way it brings us a little bit closer I think. I guess I feel more for her. I feel sorry for her. I know what she is going through and it just brings me a little closer."

Some participants described how love was one of the most important components that influenced the quality of care provided. For example, Jeremy stated that:

> When you have, sometimes, an outside person [formal care provider], they're not as responsible or, how should I say it? Loveable to the person that needs the care. It's just a job to them. . . . It's my wife, like, I love her and so that love gives, if you know what I mean?

Jeremy felt that because of his loving connection to his wife, he was the one best suited to provide her with the highest quality of care. Describing the positive experience of caregiving, Jeremy went on to say that what gives him the greatest pleasure with regard to his caregiving role is that he is able give back to his spouse something that she needs. Many participants echoed this sentiment, expressing how their caregiving role allowed them the opportunity to demonstrate their love and give back to those who provided care for them in the past. Adam, for example, shared that "you love your parents, you want them to be safe, you look after them. They looked after me, now it's my turn to look after them." . . .

Relation to the Wider Community

Feelings of being distant, far, isolated or excluded from the wider community were frequently expressed by participants, particularly those caring for wives/life partners who were living with cognitive impairments. For example, Francis, who is caring for his wife living with Alzheimer's disease, shared his experiences of social excursions into the community. Francis commented that:

> People don't know what to say or what to do and it's not uncommon for people to back off, and they're very uncomfortable. I mean [Laughter] in varying degrees I've seen it. I used to take my wife to a church supper once a month and I was told I shouldn't do it because it makes people feel uncomfortable.

. . . [T]hese findings point to the social stigma that exists towards cognitive impairment and the repercussions this has not only for the care recipient, but the caregiver as well. . . .

Cultural differences were also found to impact feelings of social isolation. For example, Aditya, who self-identified as South-East Asian, shared his perception that in western Canadian culture, people will often not offer to help a stranger, stating "that's the culture here. So people, if you are a stranger, nobody helps, you know?" Aditya cares for both his mother and father largely on his own and expressed feelings of anxiety and loneliness due to the limited social support he had access to. He expressed that, "everybody has their own lives . . . I don't have anyone, you know, in mind that I can, you know, count on." Luka, who is caring for his mother, also described how cultural differences made him feel further removed from the society in which he lives: "I sort of feel isolated coming from another culture. . . . Europeans, kind of feel that sort of European feeling of liking the same things that kind of keep us together." [. . .]

While some participants experienced feelings of isolation and distance from the wider community, others in more socially connected positions experienced feelings of belonging, comfort and support. For example, Walter expressed that what gives him comfort, hope and strength is seeing how his community "cares" for him and provides him with the spiritual and emotional support that he needs. Walter states:

> It's not so much that it's physical support, although my two sons do help me a lot, it's the spiritual support of knowing that people are caring and praying and not just brushing me off and that has been absolutely marvellous. . . . We're a fairly close-knit community and there's my congregation community who support me in spiritual ways, and then there's the community of caregivers who support in a very different way, but nonetheless essential.

. . .

Discussion

. . .

Although the men collectively shared the same identified gender (i.e. being a man) and the experience of being a primary caregiver for one with multiple chronic conditions, the emotional experiences shared varied depending upon the participant's differing situated "place-in-the-world." In other words, the men had different views, feelings and emotions about their caregiving role depending upon their social positionality and biographical relation to the situation, which was shaped by their own prior emotional stances as well as whether or not, or in what way, they chose to express these emotions during their interview.... As such, our findings contribute a nuanced understanding regarding how feeling and emotions, as patterns of relationships, are intersected by and interwoven with one's personal biography and physical and social positionality (Burkitt, 2014). By considering diverse lived contexts and their associated emotional experiences, a more nuanced understanding regarding the complex factors that may contribute to caregiver burden and resilience emerge....

More broadly, our findings challenge the common emphases regarding how emotional work tends to exclusively be given to women (Bondi, 2008; Herron & Skinner, 2013) and diverges from prevailing assumptions that women are emotionally expert, while men lack the emotional capacity required to be "good" caregivers (Holmes, 2015). Of the little emotional literature that applies a gendered lens, much of it tends to focus on men's experiences of anger, aggression or lust, and the implications these emotions have for enactments of risky behaviour or violence, particularly violence against women (Hanlon, 2009; Holmes, 2015). It is well documented that socially, men and women will understand, experience, express and articulate different emotions in differing ways (Chappell et al., 2015; Connell & Messerschmidt, 2005; Lin et al., 2012; Montgomery & Datwyler, 1990). We have found here, that despite men's tendencies to suppress emotions

(Lin et al., 2012; Milligan & Morbey, 2013), many willingly and openly expressed and articulated them during their interviews. The emotions expressed ranged dramatically, falling along a spectrum of positive and distressing feelings, with some men experiencing both at different or even the same times. For example, feeling love and a deep connection to a care recipient, but also feeling far and disconnected from the romantic and reciprocal relationship once shared. As such, our findings uncover some of the multiple, complex, dynamic and relational emotions men may be experiencing as family caregivers and, more specifically, how they draw upon spatial metaphors of proximity and distance to articulate these emotions.

. . . In North America, prevailing images of masculinity are equated with "not caring," and qualities such as stoicism, physical strength and toughness (Doucet, 2006; Hanlon, 2012a). At the same time, prevailing images of femininity are associated with sensitivity, compassion and care (Hanlon, 2012a). As such, masculinity and care are deemed as antithetical. Such binary representations have extensive implications for the way gender is constructed as oppositional, and overlooks the spectrum of ways in which gender varies across social life (Hanlon, 2012b). Our findings disrupt these binary representations and gendered oppositions as many of the men clearly expressed highly emotive (and traditionally labelled as feminine) experiences of love, compassion, sensitivity and vulnerability. Therefore, our analytic findings highlight the need to consider the differing ways in which men "do" masculinity in their roles as family caregivers and the various emotions they feel while assuming such roles (Campbell & Carroll, 2007; Doucet, 2006; Holmes, 2015; Latshaw, 2015; Lorentzen, 2007).
. . .

Conclusion

. . .

[T]his analysis uniquely contributes a geographic "lens" to uncover the emotional and gendered experiences of family caregiving. We believe this lens is easily transferable to various other domains of health and social care that may occur in diverse geographical settings. As care and caregiving is inherently based on social relations, notions of proximity and distance within relations of care is a useful point for analysis. As Bondi (Bondi, 2008) describes, the connections people hold in caring relationships are fragile and delicate, yet produce imaginative and subjective geographies that help to shape people's experiences of giving or receiving care. Building from this analysis, there is still much to do for geography of care researchers to incorporate more fully an understanding of the "doing" of family care work through lived experiences of emotions, as well as how such emotions are shaped by the social locations of its providers.

References

Armstrong, P., Armstrong, H., & Scott-Dixon, K. (2008). *Critical to care: The invisible women in health services.* Toronto: University of Toronto Press.

Bialon, L. N., & Coke, S. (2012). A study on caregiver burden: Stressors, challenges, and possible solutions. *American Journal of Hospice and Palliative Medicine*, 29, 210–18.

Bondi, L. (2008). On the relational dynamics of caring: A psychotherapeutic approach to emotional and power dimensions of women's care work. *Gender, Place & Culture*, 15, 249–65.

Burkitt, I. (2014). *Emotions and social relations.* Thousand Oaks, Calif: Sage Publications.

Canadian Caregiver Coalition. (2009). The Canadian caregiver strategy—Consultation. Retrieved November 11, 2010, from https://www.ccc-ccan.ca/content .php?doc=43

Campbell, L.D., & Carroll, M.P. (2007). The incomplete revolution: Theorizing gender when studying men who provide care to aging parents. *Men & Masculinities*, 9, 491–508.

Canadian Institute for Health Information. (2011). Seniors and the health care system: What is the impact of multiple chronic conditions? Retrieved November 20, 2015, from https://secure.cihi.ca/free_products/ air-chronic_disease_aib_en.pdf

Canadian Institute for Health Information (2012). Supporting informal caregivers—The heart of home care, health system performance series. Ottawa: CIHI.

Chappell, N. L., Dujela, C., & Smith, A. (2015). Caregiver well-being: Intersections of relationship and gender. *Research on Aging*, 37, 623–45.

Connell, R. W., & Messerschmidt, J. W. (2005). Hegemonic masculinity: Rethinking the concept. *Gender and Society*, 19, 829–59.

Doucet, A. (2006). *Do men mother? Fathering, care, and domestic responsibility.* Toronto: University of Toronto Press.

Graham, H. (1983). Caring: A labour of love. In J. Finch & D. Groves (Eds.), *A labour of love: Women, work and caring* (pp. 13–30). London: Routledge and Kegan Paul.

Grunfeld, E. (2004). Family caregiver burden: Results of a longitudinal study of breast cancer patients and their principal caregivers. *Canadian Medical Association Journal*, 170, 1795–801.

Hanlon, N. (2009). Caregiving masculinities: An exploratory analysis. In J. Lynch, J. Baker, & M. Lyons (Eds.), *Affective equality: Love, care and injustice* (pp. 180–98). New York, NY: Palgrave Macmillian.

Hanlon, N. (2012a). *Care in masculinities studies, masculinities, care, and equality: Identity and nurture in men's lives.* New York, NY: Palgrave Macmillan.

Hanlon, N. (2012b). *Masculinities and emotions, masculinities, care, and equality: Identity and nuture in men's lives.* New York, NY: Palgrave Macmillan.

Herron, R., & Skinner, M. W. (2013). The emotional overlay: Older person and carer perspectives on negotiating aging and care in rural Ontario. *Social Science & Medicine*, 91, 186–93.

Holmes, M. (2015). Men's emotions: Heteromasculinity, emotional reflexivity, and intimate relationships. *Men & Masculinities*, 18, 176–92.

Kramer, B. J. (2002). Men caregivers: An overview. In B. J. Kramer & E. H. Thompson (Eds.), *Men as caregivers: Theory, research and service implications* (pp. 3–19). New York, NY: Springer Publishing Company.

Latshaw, B. A. (2015). From mopping to mowing: Masculinity and housework in stay-at-home father households. *The Journal of Men's Studies*, 23, 252–70.

Lilly, M. B., Robinson, C. A., Holtzman, S., & Bottorff, J. L. (2012). Can we move beyond burden and burnout to support the health and wellness of family caregivers to persons with dementia? Evidence from British Columbia, Canada *Health Soc Care Community*, 20, 103–12.

Lin, I. F., Fee, H. R., & Wu, H.-S. (2012). Negative and positive caregiving experiences: A closer look at the intersection of gender and relationship. *Family Relations*, 61, 343–358.

Lorentzen, J. (2007). Love and intimacy in men's lives. *NORA — Nordic Journal of Feminist and Gender Research*, 15, 190–198.

McNabb, S. (2015). Men who care: Unique challenges, unique solutions. Retrieved November 26, 2015, from https://www.caregiversolutions.ca/caregiving/caregiving-advice/

Melin-Johansson, C., Axelsson, B., & Danielson, E. (2007). Caregivers' perceptions about terminally ill family members' quality of life. *European Journal of Cancer Care*, 16, 338–45.

Milligan, C., & Morbey, H. (2013). *Older men who care: Understanding their support and support needs*. Lancaster: Lancaster University Centre for Ageing Research.

Montgomery, R. J. V., & Datwyler, M. M. (1990). Women and men in the caregiving role. *Generations*, 14, 34–38.

Parr, H. (2005). Emotional geographies. In P. Cloke, P. Crang, & M. Goodwin (Eds.), *Introducing human geographies*. London: Arnold.

Scott, P. S. (2015). Caregiver stress syndrome: What's different for men. Retrieved November 26, 2011, from https://www.caring.com/articles/caregiver-stress-syndrome-different-for-men

Statistics Canada. (2014). Portrait of caregivers, 2012. Statistics Canada. Retrieved November 26, 2015, from https://www.statcan.gc.ca/pub/89-652-x/89-652-x2013001-eng.htm

Part VI
The Gendered Classroom

Schools are where people go to learn how to read, write, do math, and (much later) study German philosophy or quantum mechanics. But educational institutions are much more than systems for delivering content to students. They're also powerfully gendered environments for everyone from the youngest kindergarteners to tenured professors. Learners and teachers alike are engaged in constructing gender (and sometimes in deconstructing and reconstructing it).

Kearns and co-authors combine the perspectives of students by studying students who *are* teachers—education students doing their practicums in public schools. Their participants want to make schools a better place for gender-nonconforming students but grapple with institutional pressures from other teachers, parents, and children toward traditional expressions of femininity and masculinity. Even when schools have an explicit and overt commitment to equity, in practice teachers and students fall back on unreflective ways of doing gender.

Meyer offers some insight into why teachers might be reluctant to intervene actively when it comes to gender. Teachers in her study speak candidly about the challenges and costs of responding to gender-based harassment in their schools, including the different pressures from differing institutional layers of the school administration. Schools are one element in a larger social ecosystem of education and public service.

Similarly, Herriot, Burns, and Yeung examine the ways that schools work to sustain gender binaries, not just as sites of learning but as public resources whose use is contested. Different interest groups among parents, teachers, community members, and other stakeholders all have an interest in shaping what goes on in schools. Herriot and colleagues examine the records of debates at the school board level about gender-neutral washrooms and which students may use them as a way of underlining the importance of schools as microcosms of the larger society. Adults with diverging visions of what the ideal society should look like when it comes to gender use educational institutions as terrains of struggle.

Schools are microcosms of society in less positive ways as well. Henry and co-authors interviewed faculty members who identified as racialized minorities about their experience in another public educational institution—the university. Although we might want to think otherwise, "old boys' networks" still dominate much of the decision making in universities, to the detriment of those who are not among the "old boys." With the rise of neoliberal management styles in universities, changes such as budget cutbacks do not affect all faculty the same way. Institutional policies to promote equity and level the playing field do not always make the difference they are supposed to make.

Questions for Critical Thought

1. Educational institutions include not only classrooms and curriculums but also locker rooms, cliques, playgrounds, and other sites of informal education about what gender means. What did you learn about gender at school outside the classroom?

2. One proposed solution to the problem of gender polarization in education is same-sex schools. Would you send your child to a same-sex school? What would be some of the advantages? What about disadvantages?

3. If young children's play reinforces gender stereotypes, should parents or educators be concerned? Should we try to explicitly "teach" gender equality?

4. Did you have any teachers or professors who influenced the way you see gender? If so, how did they achieve this?

5. What do you think are the most effective means of challenging gender biases in school? How do these means differ at different levels of schooling—from elementary through university?

6. What role do you think parents and other community members should have in determining what goes on in schools? What should happen when parents object to the way their children's schools are dealing with gender issues?

7. As you progressed from high school to postsecondary school, did your experiences of gender change?

8. Should universities promote social change or should they be mainly focused on preparing students for jobs?

9. How might your educational experiences have been different if you were born into a different gender category?

Chapter 23

Overview

When it comes to gender, schools are very different places from even 10 years ago. The increasing visibility and representation of students who identify as transgender challenges the assumptions of teachers and educators that the school world can be divided neatly into boys and girls. Laura-Lee Kearns and her colleagues examine how new teachers and teachers-to-be navigate the gendered landscape of schools during the placements that form part of their teacher education. They use "critical incidents" of exclusion or silencing of nonbinary gender, as reported by teachers in training, as a way to examine the ways in which educators can advance or hold back progress toward equal and affirming schools. Their participants observed that teachers, parents, and students all engaged in behaviour that subtly or not-so-subtly reinforced the idea of a restrictive gender binary. Teachers in training recognized that unlearning or relearning gender was important, and also that disrupting rigid gender binaries would call for a major investment of their time and professional skills. Nonetheless, they believed that doing so was an ethical obligation for educators in the twenty-first century.

Transphobia and Cisgender Privilege

Pre-Service Teachers Recognizing and Challenging Gender Rigidity in Schools

Laura-Lee Kearns, Jennifer Mitton-Kükner, and Joanne Tompkins

Introduction

The opportunity for teacher candidates to understand how to incorporate anti-discrimination work in their teaching practice is a key component of school and education reform. Social justice policies and procedures exist in many school settings, but unless new teachers have the opportunity to explore and apply knowledge learned from professional development, these well-meaning policies are often neglected or ignored. Building upon our ongoing longitudinal

Kearns, Laura-Lee, Jennifer Mitton-Kukner, and Joanne Tompkins. "Transphobia and Cisgender Privilege: Pre-Service Teachers Recognizing and Challenging Gender Rigidity in Schools." *Canadian Journal of Education/Revue canadienne de l'éducation*, Vol. 40, No. 1, Special Capsule Issue on Historical Consciousness (2017), pp. 1–27.

study, which investigates the impact of an integrated Lesbian, Gay, Bi-sexual, Transgendered, Two-Spirited, Queering and/or Questioning (LGBTQ) awareness program (Kearns, Mitton-Kukner, & Tompkins 2014a, 2014b; Mitton-Kukner, Kearns, & Tompkins, 2015), we focus on five pre-service teachers who identified critical incidents related to transphobia and gender construction. These incidents, which happened during their first practicum, caused great concern over the enduring gender binary that presents itself in schools. Their experiences highlight the ways in which gender surveillance, both overtly and covertly, reinscribes heteronormativity, and contributes to genderism, homophobia, and transphobia.

LGBTQ and Gender in Schools and Society

Shaped by heteronormativity and rigid gender expectations, LGBTQ youth in schools and society have been vulnerable to harassment (Taylor et al., 2011). In such hostile climates, LGBTQ youth are unlikely to learn and may avoid schools (Palmer, Kosciw, & Bartkiewicz, 2012). Indeed, many learn that discrimination against the LGBTQ community is acceptable (Gender Public Advocacy Coalition, 2006; Haskell & Burtch, 2010), as transgender and gender non-conforming students experience ongoing acts of aggression in schools with little adult intervention (Guasp, 2012; Reis & Saewyc, 1999; Taylor et al., 2011, Wright-Maley, David, Gozalez, & Colwell, 2016). In the midst of increasing recognition that more supports are needed to fully include LGBTQ youth and their families in schools, is the topic of gender. Schools often serve as contexts where students come to narrowly understand gender roles and expectations, which limits the gender expression of all youth, since those who do not conform or perform their gender roles are vulnerable to harassment and bullying (Rands, 2009; Ryan, Patraw, & Bednar, 2013).

With this as the backdrop of teacher education in North America, teacher educators need to prepare pre-service teachers to understand their role in the development of inclusive spaces for sexual minority, transgender, and gender non-conforming youth in schools. Anti-oppressive work (Kumashiro, 2002) in teacher education that aims to support learners who challenge prevailing gender norms in school is complex and necessary (Clark, 2010; Goldstein, Russell, & Daley, 2007; Stiegler, 2008), yet largely under-researched in terms of how programs might proceed. For example, scholars note the lack of explicit LGBTQ education in teacher education programs (Grace & Wells, 2006; Kitchen & Bellini, 2012; Macgillivray & Jennings, 2008; Schneider & Dimito, 2008), as well as the resistance demonstrated by pre-service teachers to LGBTQ education as part of diversity work and curricular inclusion (Jennings & Sherwin, 2008; Robinson & Ferfolja, 2002, 2008; Wright-Maley et al., 2016).

. . .

Gender, Transgender, and LGBTQ in Teacher Education

In a review of social justice literature, Airton (2014) identifies the predominant "hope" that anti-homophobia teacher education (AHTE) can "prepare teachers to contribute to the well-being of gender and sexual minority students" (p. 388). In our work, we have come to see LGBTQ issues and trans issues, in particular, through the lens of gender. The gender binary continues to enforce the identities of all youth in school, with the prescription of rigid gender roles. Men and women are also divided into highly gendered cultural, social, economic, and political roles. In schools, boys and girls are equally divided with little room for fluidity or a range of behaviours on a spectrum of socially constructed roles and behaviours. There is often resistance, and constraints are often imposed on each categorical binary. Trans identities do not easily fit boy or girl categories; trans stories are diverse and require a separation of gender and sexual orientation (Wright-Maley et al., 2016, p. 5). DePalma (2013) notes that trans itself is used as an umbrella term that "encompass[es] discomfort with role expectations, being queer, occasional or more frequent cross-dressing, permanent cross-dressing and cross-gender living, through to accessing major health interventions such as hormone therapy and surgical reassignment procedures" (p. 2, quoting Whittle, 2006).

. . .

There are several challenges associated with thwarting genderism, homophobia, and transphobia. Savage and Harley (2009) note that obstacles impeding safe and inclusive school environments and queer positive curricula in the United States range from fear, laissez-faire attitudes, and a feeling that negative attitudes are challenging to disrupt. In two different universities, one in the United States and the other in Canada, Wright-Maley and colleagues (2016) found that a large majority of Catholic elementary teachers affirmed the principle of inclusive school spaces for trans and LGBTQ youth; however, many were fearful of students, parents, and administrators, and not sure if they would include such topics in their curricula. Keddie, Mills, and Mills (2008) noted that one teacher in their study had to "tread cautiously" (p. 203) because she was trying to "change familiar, comfortable and very deep-seated ways of being" (p. 203).

Some teachers simply do not see the complicity that schools play in supporting the gender binary system. These teachers have accepted "the naturalness of the gendered status quo" (Keddie et al., 2008, p.198). Early schooling, too, often accepts the family and com munity gender expectations that are imposed upon children. While many teachers do see how genderism and sexism manifest themselves in school, they are unsure about what can be done to challenge this. Webb, Schirato, and Danaher (2002) suggest that "we become complicit with gender injustice or "dominant vision[s] of the world not because we nec es sarily agree with [them], or because [they are] in our interests, but because there does not seem to be any alternative" (p. 92). In response to such conditions, scholars suggest new teachers require education if they are to challenge the gender status quo (Bellini, 2012).

...

Although there are challenges to this work, narratives that show a large variety of experiences around not only adversity, but support for LGBTQ youth and families offer hope. Certainly, some successful gender and trans education projects exist. Having seen the power of the *No Outsiders Project*, DePalma (2013) calls for gender work at the elemen tary and secondary levels, and agrees with McQueen (2006), who affirms that "transgen der awareness can work to break down those rigid [gender] stereotypes" (McQueen, as cited in De-Palma, 2013, p. 11).

Situating the Positive Space Program within Our Bachelor of Education

. . . As seen below, the program is woven into each campus term. Levels 1 and 2 are situated in mandatory courses, and Levels 3 and 4 are optional. The course Sociology of Education in term one explicitly and intentionally aims to build a safe and democratic learning space focusing on discussions about power, privilege, equity, social justice, race, class, gender, and sexuality. We believe that nesting the LGBTQ awareness program in core mandatory courses in Year 1 contributes to the positive uptake we have by the pre-service teachers in Year 2 to attend workshops for Levels 3 and 4. Our students' enthusiasm for this training led us to develop Levels 3 and 4 as further professional learning. Table 23.1 provides a visual of how the training is embedded across the two years.

Bridging Sociology and Inclusion: The Critical Incident Paper

. . . As pre-service teachers prepare to leave EDUC 433 Sociology of Education to head into their first field placement they are asked to look for a student or groups of students who are placed on the margins of the classroom or the school. They are simply to observe what is happening around these students. When they return from the field their experiences are unpacked as a class. They also read the article "Teacher Research as a Way of Knowing" (Lytle & Cochran-Smith, 1992), in which Lytle and Cochran-Smith discuss how a researcher stance can both inform and sustain social justice teaching. The pre-service teachers

Table 23.1 Positive Space Training over the Two-Year BEd Program

Year 1 Term Compulsory	Year 1 Term 2 Compulsory	Year 2 Term 1 Optional	Year 2, Term 2 Optional
EDUC 433 Sociology of Education	*EDUC 435 Inclusion 1*	*Students take a range of courses*	*Students take a range of courses*
Positive Space 1 (2.5 hours)	*Positive Space 2 (2.5 hours)*	*Positive Space 3 Exploring Curricular Possibilities (2.5 hours)*	*Positive Space 4 Train the Trainer (4 hours)*
Field Experience (5 weeks)	*Field Experience (6 Weeks)*	*Field Experience (5 weeks)*	*Field Experience (6 weeks)*

then research the subject, issue, experience, and/or exclusion they witnessed during their teaching practicum to see what is known about this phenomenon in the literature so as to deepen their understanding.

. . . In response to this endeavour, we have observed that pre-service teachers tend to notice the many different ways that students become placed on the margins of schooling and what might be done to address such situations. In this way we bring forward a key concept that we have attempted to develop in Sociology of Education—that of teacher agency. We hope to show that educators who are critically conscious, working alone, but more often in collaboration with others, can and do make a difference in classrooms. . . .

Methodology

. . . Since implementing the critical inquiry assignment, there have been over 600 papers written on a variety of topics, but this was actually the first year that five pre-service teachers identified critical incidents in schools related to transphobia and gender construction. . . .

Reading the critical incident papers piqued our interest; in response, we invited all five students to participate in a focus group with us once course work and evaluations had been completed. The five pre-service teachers accepted. The participants reflect the rural university's demographic, as they identified as white, female, heterosexual, and middle class. The participants' ages ranged from the early twenties to early thirties. Of the five, one was a parent. Ethics had been previously obtained as part of the larger ongoing longitudinal study on the impact of the positive space program interwoven in our program, for which we have the approval to use focus groups and documents generated by participants to understand the program's impact. Students were formally invited to participate with letters of invitation and informed consent was obtained. Data consisted of the five critical incident papers (1,200–1,500 words in length) submitted to the research team and the follow-up focus group interview. During the focus group interview, we engaged the participants about the ways in which

gender presented itself in schools during their first practicum. The focus group interview enabled us to hear the opinions of a smaller group with the understanding that the opinions expressed by the focus group might resonate with others from the same community (Merriam & Tisdell, 2016). The focus group conversation was approximately 90 minutes in length. It was recorded and transcribed by a research assistant. The focus group was held in January 2016, when these pre-service teachers were in Year 2 of their program. At the time of the focus group, the pre-service teachers had completed Levels 1, 2, and 3 of the LGBTQ awareness program.
. . .

Findings

Pre-Service Teachers Identifying and Problematizing Gender in Schools

Our study provides practical examples of how critical curricula and social justice education can be brought together to inform teacher education. By embedding Positive Space training into the formal curriculum of two compulsory foundations courses, we are able to model to pre-service teachers how to disrupt, disturb, and de-privilege heteronormativity, and trouble gender. The critical incident paper provided a deep way for our pre-service teachers to reflect upon their experiences. They identified that writing the paper was important, as it gave them permission to critically inquire into what they felt was not present in schools in the form of gender education. Additionally, through the research literature, their feelings were validated that more can be done to create safe and inclusive spaces for transgender students, beginning with gender education for all students. The focus group conversation provided an additional layer to unpack the complexity of social justice work and its ongoing tensions. As the nature of social justice teaching is often complex for beginning teachers, our participants appreciated the opportunities provided by our program to critically reflect upon and share their experiences, learning, and possibilities for their future practice.

Theme One: Policing Gender and Responding

Schools, like society, find ways to police gender overtly and covertly. Although many have rallied against the notion of "sex as destiny" or some "essence" prescribing fixed gender roles to males and females (like de Beauvoir [1989], who wrote *The Second Sex* in 1949), the gender binary persists. Our pre-service teachers were deeply troubled by gender regulation and policing at the schools. Foucault (1979) explored how various levels of surveillance regulate people's behaviours; people are expected to perform a variety of roles, and people perform them due to external and internal regulation for fear of social sanctions or other consequences. The regulation of gender may be similarly seen by the social sanctions and conflicts that can arise when people do not perform and conform to gender roles and expectations. Concerns around the policing of gender by educators, peers, and parents were touched upon by several participants; here, we highlight all three levels of regulation. We also note that our pre-service teachers did try to support youth who were expressing aspects of themselves outside of gender norms. However, the complexity of resisting the pressure to conform to gender stereotypes and the expectations around gender performativity are real, and the tension between resistance and regulation is ongoing. These tensions can often be challenging to navigate, as pre-service teachers themselves are situated in different power positions in the education system in which they seek employment.

Educators Policing Gender

In Janice's school experience, she was encouraged and discouraged by how her two cooperating teachers (CTs) interacted with a particular youth. Janice explained during the focus group interview how her CTs responded in very different ways to a transgender male student:

> So I walked into my first practicum . . . and somebody's female name was scratched out with the new male name he wanted to go by and my first CT was phenomenal. It wasn't a big

deal, this is what you call him [the student]; end of story . . . down to another classroom . . . the teacher [CT 2] wouldn't even acknowledge the existence of this human being . . . it just like suck[ed] the air right out of the whole classroom . . . (Janice, Focus Group Interview, January 8, 2016)

Janice initially wrote about this incident in her paper, and explained that the first CT treated the youth and the change of this person's identity and name as normal. In contrast, the second CT would not even call this youth by name, and simply called the youth "you." In the critical incident paper, Janice shared her first interaction with the second CT and her discomfort in what she witnessed. In one instance, the second CT had asked all the other students in the class by name to read aloud, and when it came time to call upon the transgender student, all the CT could muster was "OK, YOU, your turn!" Janice watched as the student "trembled through the reading and when he was finished he put the book away, head down and continued to doodle on his sheet" (Janice, Critical Incident Paper). What struck Janice was how powerful educators are in their ability to affirm or belittle the existence of youth in their classrooms.

In witnessing such dramatically different responses to gender and name changes, Janice reportedly had the confidence and insight to affirm the child. In our classes and Positive Space training, we talk about power at the individual, institutional, and systemic level. While different strategies are needed to challenge power at different levels and in different ways, it is possible to act. Janice shared how she responded and tried to support this youth:

> So after having some training . . . [I was assured that I could] just to go up to the student afterwards, [so I said,] "Hi Jamie, how are you? I see you're drawing, you are really good at drawing," just to acknowledge their existence. That's all it took, like it wasn't a big thing, but to see [a teacher] say "you" and then watch Jamie have to read out loud in a second language and just crumble . . . it still shakes

me . . . then to just go afterwards [to the student] and say, "Wow, you are a really good drawer Jamie, how did you learn to do this?" . . . [you could] just see a weight lift. (Janice, Focus Group Interview, January 8, 2016)

While the pre-service teacher is mindful of the power imbalance that exists between herself and the CT, she, reportedly, was able to affirm the youth. Her efforts did not challenge the teacher's attitude, the power imbalance, or gender performativity and regulation, but it did affirm the child.

Another student teacher reported how she was horrified by the lack of compassion and the negative comments and judgements made against the children of a trans parent. Susan explained:

In my practicum experience, there was a little boy in my school (in Grade 2), who enjoyed wearing pink, carried a purse, wore necklaces and most of all, loved wearing his sister's clothes. I, personally, thought nothing of it— my CT on the other hand had much to say on the topic. When his sister, who was in my primary classroom would "act out," my CT would say things to me like "She's just doing it because Dad recently became Mom," and "This family will do anything for attention." (Susan, Focus Group Interview, January 8, 2016)

While Susan did feel empowered by researching this incident and was committed to being an ally, she was visibly troubled in class during the talking circle in 2015, and still noticeably shaken in the focus group discussion in 2016. Social justice work is heartfelt work and sometimes there is no easy resolution. Time and opportunities to shape different attitudes is the hope that lingers.

Students Policing Gender

In a different school, another pre-service teacher, Rena, had an encounter in the classroom with students policing gender. She explains:

Well my first practicum I did encounter a trans student, she [was] identified as a female, but she was in the process, I believe, of identifying as

male. But she never told me "call me this or do this" . . . the other students in the classroom, were kind of negative about it. [For example, students would say,] "I don't want to work with her"; stuff like that . . . (Rena, Focus Group Interview, January 8, 2016)

The power of peers in school and their ability to regulate the behaviour of many is not new. In this case, though, students identified a gender difference as a reason and justification to not only be uncomfortable, but a reason to not work with another classmate. This was said overtly and publicly.

Yet, in response to the expectation of gender performativity as a norm governing social and classroom behaviours, Rena was able to act. When confronted by this situation, she explained:

That's when you have to become the ally, that's when the Positive Space training did kick in and you're like why, why is she any different than you? . . . I think it boosted my confidence a bit just to be able to speak about it and talk to the kids and tell them the right way to think of things in that sense. (Rena, Focus Group Interview, January 8, 2016)

Rena did not let the regulation of another student go unchallenged. In anti-bullying train ng, and other social justice work, we are learning that to not challenge, to remain silent, especially if one has some power in the situation, is to covertly affirm the overt negative remarks. By interrupting the narrative around gender rigidity and trying to reteach gender to the peers of the emerging trans student, the pre-service teacher tried to change the unsettling conversation to a teachable moment. It is these moments that educators often encounter. The unplanned, unrehearsed, but often powerful moments and opportunities to help youth be critical and potentially open their ideas to different possibilities, especially in regard to gender and identity.

Parents Policing Gender

The multiple levels on which youth receive messages about gender are profound. The gender messages young children received are shaped from a very early age. This is how the gender binary continues to hold so much power; there is fear of not conforming and performing due to the censure of others. In this exam ple, Susan explains:

> I had a kid in my class and we were in the playroom . . . he was in the house centre, he was assigned to go play house . . . and he said, "Well I can't go [to the] play house" and I said, "Well, why not?" And he said, "Well if my mom finds out that I played with dolls I will get in trouble." (Susan, Critical Incident Paper)

A young male was afraid to get into trouble for playing house. He is already aware of stereotypical gender roles. These are so deeply engrained that even generations of women and men performing different gender roles cannot alleviate his fear of being in trouble. The student teacher tried to affirm his ability to play in a space he worried about going into. In the focus groups, Susan described telling the student:

> "Your mom is not going to find out, go play with the dolls!" And he was so happy, he came up to me after and was like "Thanks Ms. for letting me play with the dolls today" and I was like "You are welcome, you can play with them whenever you want" and that was all it took, right? But just the confirmation that I wasn't going to go tell his mom he played with dolls because he was so scared of getting in trouble. (Susan, Focus Group Interview, January 8, 2016)

Whether or not the fear remains concerning what a child can or cannot do when a parental or other authority figure is watching her or his gender performance is not clear, but in the classroom, the freedom the child had to play was certainly appreciated. Again, gender is complicated and messy, and our "in the moment" reactions to situations that arise can be complicated and messy as well. All in all, the policing of gender presently continues in our classrooms, school, and society. Whether or not the incident is explicitly trans or gender, these are all powerful examples that enable us to see the regulation of gender and the gender binary at play in social dynamics.

. . .

Theme Three: Identifying the Challenges Associated with Re-Teaching Gender

Of all the human diversities, gender is the one we encounter earliest in our lives. At birth, most of us are assigned a gender identity based on a biological sex, and from that moment, gender expectations are placed upon us. Families and communities articulate and enforce those expectations, and schools and teachers often assume an uncritical stance supporting the rigid gender binary system that declares there are only two "opposite" genders. Beginning in early childhood learning centers, many educators, often unconsciously, have failed to see the social construction of gender and the need to critically examine it. Similarly, the idea of "rethinking" gender in a critical way is not on the radar of many in-service teachers. Our pre-service teachers have begun to examine genderism and sexism in their foundations of education courses, and Positive Space Levels 1 and 2 communicate the need to re-teach gender in schools and some of the barriers that prevent that.

Fear of Parents Intersecting with Societal Norms

Rena, during the focus group interview, described her understanding of gender identity as something that is socially-constructed and that the norms around it and the gender binary can be opened up, troubled, and retaught at every grade level. Rena noted that things had changed but challenges remain in schools:

> It's not as bad as it was 20 years ago, but there is still the societal norms and this is how this should be and this is how this should be. . . . And again, the parents . . . I find that's a big, big issue because the parents, that's the wrath, that's who schools get now . . . if you . . . say something to a kid the wrong way, you are going to get a whole lot of crap from someone. Either admin or the parents who contacted the admin . . . it is also like dealing with a lot of different views and beliefs. (Rena, Focus Group Interview, January 8, 2016)

Rena understands that, while schools officially espouse the development of critical thinking, challenging societal norms in schools is not easily done. Rena believes that troubling family and community norms can have consequences for teachers. The overall effect on teachers means that many will avoid any efforts to re-teach gender in schools.

Interrupting the Gender Binary

Schools have traditionally been constructed with the gender binary in mind. This assumes that there are only two possible genders, they are opposite to each other, and they are defined by biological sex. In older school buildings, we can still see evidence of separate entrances for boys and girls. Separate sex washrooms continue to exist in most schools, necessitating the need for separate lines—one for girls and one for boys. Thea noticed,

> In elementary we are always dividing them as boys and girls. What if they are gender neutral? Or they don't know where they fit in, then what do you do? So then I started going if you have brown hair, go line up. . . . That was just something I really noticed in my last practicum especially [teachers] saying . . . "all the boys do this" and "all the girls do this." . . . (Thea, Focus Group Interview, January 8, 2016)

Right from the first day of school, the physical structure of a school further imposes the gender binary on students. Added to this are the ways in which the adults in the building organize the everyday rituals, practices, and language around what is involved in constructing gender identity. Re-teaching gender means breaking apart the gender binary systems and seeing gender as a fluid continuum of identity possibilities. It means that if educators are conscious of the myriad of ways gender presents itself, they can interrupt genderism and sexism on a daily basis. To do so, however, involves a critical re-examining of everything, from taken-for-granted organization of the classrooms, hallways, bathrooms, and change rooms, to curriculum materials and offerings for students in the form of literature choices and LGBTQ representation in books.

Lack of Resources

Educators who are aware of the need to re-teach gender in schools do need classroom resources to support their teaching. In an elementary classroom, this could be finding and having the funds to purchase children's books with diverse representations of gender fluidity. Gina provides an example of how the lack of teacher resources can be problematic. As a French immersion teacher outside of Quebec, she found resources that trouble the gender binary system hard to find. She explains:

> I found it hard to find books . . . this year in French immersion, it's really hard to find French resources . . . I know personally I have been trying to start collecting books that have a really good story you can just use for a read aloud. Because we are reading all the time for our students and it's so easy to kind of fit [the topic] in lessons without making it an official lesson . . . just like teaching them right away that it [gender as fluid] is okay. (Gina, Focus Group Interview, January 8, 2016)

On a hopeful note, Gina shows determination to not let the lack of resources stop her from engaging in social justice teaching. She sees the informal curriculum as a powerful place of challenging social norms. However, we know that not all teachers will have this level of commitment. If we are to re-teach gender in schools, we need to not only change attitudes but also provide the systemic supports necessary for teachers to do so.

Discussion: Challenging Genderism in Schools

The discrimination trans and gender nonconforming youth and their families experience overtly and covertly in schools, staffrooms, classrooms, and hallways is witnessed by our preservice teachers. . . . Rands (2009) suggests that at its very foundation, teacher education must consider the importance of a "gender-complex perspective," one that "question[s] the ways in which gender is operating and what the consequences are" with considerations of "the complex sets of privilege and oppression that students and teachers experience based on their gen der categories, gender expressions, and the gender attributions others make of them" (p. 426).

[W]e found pre-service teachers overwhelmingly noticed the lack of gender education in schools, particularly within the elementary school contexts in which some of them were situated for their first field placement. We acknowledge that preparing pre-service teachers for the kinds of gender rigidity that may be found in elementary schools is challenging in the sense that their own assumptions about what can be taught to elementary-age children must be disrupted first. It takes considerable effort to remain awake to a force as pervasive and as normalized as genderism. Butler, Osborne, and Segal (1994) remind us "it is a collective struggle to rethink a dominant norm" (p. 5). In their struggles, our pre-service teachers referred to the lack of gender education and the need for more awareness of trans and LGBTQ issues in school as problematic, as it limits the gender expression of all youth and creates heteronormative, homophobic, and transphobic school climates.

. . .

We acknowledge that preparing pre-service teachers to disrupt gender rigidity in schools is challenging. Our own study is limited in that the sample size is small and specific to our education and training program. However, there is much to be shared from the experience of recognizing interlocking forms of oppression and explicitly creating a space to train and increase the awareness of pre-service teachers. In sharing what our students have encountered in classrooms, we see there is hope for agency, and the need to

support and help future teachers create change. Teacher research is also about cultivating agency for our pre-service teachers. Encouraging pre-service teachers to investigate issues of concern and have a critical practice does help them commit to systemic changes and challenge inequities in the educational system. In recognizing and sharing practices we can all create better classrooms and schools for all our youth. In interviewing elementary and secondary pre-service teachers, we recognize there is a need to help future educators question and recognize how and when the gender binary inserts itself in schools.
. . .

Concluding Thoughts

The power to been *seen* in the world is intricately linked to one's sense of possibilities. Educators who can interrupt the gender binary can allow spaces for a diversity of genders to be seen. Overall, social justice, anti-homophobia, anti-transphobia, and gender work need to continue to evolve and respond to the complexity of the human condition. At a school and society level, so long as debate around LGBTQ identities persist, and the gender binary is reinscribed and policed, it will be hard for all youth to thrive, in particular trans youth, who embody gender complexity and resist a simple identity-labelling system. In our study, trans identities require the highly nuanced and complicated school, gender, and social justice advocacy discussions that embody social change. We hope the experiences of our pre-service teachers, as they journeyed to being educators capable of research and social justice advocacy, helped to further inform the field in this critical area of teacher-education.

References

Airton, L. (2014). Hatred haunting hallways: Teacher education and the badness of homophobia(s). *Gender and sexualities in education: A reader* (pp. 387–99). New York, NY: Peter Lang.

Bellini, C. (2012). The pink lesson plan: Addressing the emotional needs of gay and lesbian students in teacher education. *Journal of LGBT Youth, 9*(4), 373–96.

Butler, J., Osborne, P., & Segal, L. (1994). Gender as performance: An interview with Judith Butler. *Radical Philosophy, 67,* 32–39.

Clark, C. T. (2010). Preparing LGBTQ-allies and combating homophobia in a US teacher education program. *Teaching and Teacher Education, 26,* 704–13. doi:10.1016/j.tate.2009.10.006

de Beauvoir, Simone. (1989). *The second sex*. New York, NY: Vintage Books. (Originally published in French in 1949)

DePalma, R. (2013). Choosing to lose our gender expertise: Queering sex/gender in school settings. *Sex Education: Sexuality, Society and Learning, 13*(1), 1–15. 10.1080/14681811.2011.634145

Foucault, M. (1979). *Discipline and punish: The birth of the prison*. New York, NY: Vintage Books.

Gender Public Advocacy Coalition. (2006). *50 under 30: Masculinity and the war on America's youth*. Washington, DC: GPAC. https://iambecauseweare.files .wordpress.com/2007/05/50u30.pdf

Goldstein, T., Russell, V., & Daley, A. (2007). Safe positive and queering moments in teaching education and schooling: A conceptual framework. *Teaching Education, 18*(3), 183–99. doi:10.1080/10476210701533035

Grace, A. P., & Wells, K. (2006). The quest for a queer inclusive cultural ethics: Setting directions for teachers' pre-service and continued professional development. In R. J. Hill (Ed.), *New directions for adult and continuing education* (pp. 51–61). San Francisco, CA: Jossey-Bass.

Guasp, A. (2012). *The school report: The experience of gay young people in Britain's schools in 2012*. London, England: Stonewall. Retrieved from Stonewall website: http://www.stonewall.org.uk/at_school/education_for_ all/quick_links/education_ resources/7956.asp

Haskell, R., & Burtch, B. (2010). *Get that freak! Homophobia and transphobia in high school*. Halifax, NS: Fernwood Press.

Jennings, T., & Sherwin, G. (2008). Sexual orientation topics in elementary teacher preparation programs in the USA. *Teaching Education, 19*(4), 261–78.

Kearns, L., Mitton-Kukner, J., & Tompkins, J. (2014a). LGBTQ awareness and allies: Building capacity in a teacher education program. *Canadian Journal of Education, 37*(4). Retrieved from CJE website: http://journals.sfu.ca/ cje/index.php/cje-rce/article/viewFile/1628/1714

Kearns, L., Mitton-Kukner, J., & Tompkins, J. (2014b). Building LGBTQ awareness and allies in our teacher education community and beyond. *CELT: Collected Essays on Learning and Teaching, 7*(1). Retrieved from CELT website: http://celt.uwindsor.ca/ojs/leddy/index .php/CELT/article/view/3980

Keddie, A., Mills, C., & Mills, M. (2008). Struggles to subvert the gendered field: Issues of masculinity, rurality and class. *Pedagogy, Culture & Society, 16*(2), 193–205.

Kitchen, J., & Bellini, C. (2012). Addressing Lesbian, Gay, Bisexual, Transgender, and Queer (LGBTQ) issues in teacher education: Teacher candidate perceptions. *Alberta Journal of Educational Research, 58*(3), 444–60.

Kumashiro, K. (2002). *Troubling education: Queer activism and anti-oppressive pedagogy*. New York, NY: Routledge-Falmer.

Lytle, S., & Cochran-Smith, M. (1992). Teacher research as a way of knowing. *Harvard Educational Review, 62*(4), 447–73.

Macgillivray, I., & Jennings, T. (2008). A content analysis exploring lesbian, gay, bisexual, and transgender topics in foundations of education textbooks. *Journal of Teacher Education, 59*(2), 170–88. doi:10.1177/0022487107313160

McQueen, K. (2006). Breaking the gender dichotomy: The case for transgender education in school curriculum. *Teachers College Record* (August 14). Available with membership at: https://www.tcrecord.org/content .asp?contentid=12663

Merriam, S. B., & Tisdell, E. J. (2016). *Qualitative research: A guide to design and implementation* (4th ed.). San Francisco, Calif: Jossey-Bass.

Mitton Kukner, J., Kearns, L., & Tompkins, J. (2015). Pre-service educators and anti-oppressive pedagogy: Interrupting and challenging LGBTQ oppression in schools. *Asia-Pacific Journal of Teacher Education, 44*(1), 20–34. http://www.tandfonline.com/doi/full/10.1 080/1359866X.2015.1020047

Palmer, N. A., Kosciw, J. G., & Bartkiewicz, M. J. (2012). *Strengths and silences: The experiences of lesbian, gay, bisexual and transgender students in rural and small town schools*. New York, NY: Gay, Lesbian, and Straight Education Network.

Rands, K. (2009). Considering transgender people in education: A gender complex approach. *Journal of Teacher Education, 60*(4), 419–31.

Reis, B., & Saewyc, E. (1999). *Eighty-three thousand youth: Selected findings of eight population based studies as they pertain to anti-gay harassment and the safety and well-being of sexual minority students*. Seattle, WA: Safe Schools Coalition.

Robinson, K. H., & Ferfolja, T. (2002). A reflection of resistance: Discourses of heterosexism and homophobia in teacher training classrooms. *Journal of Gay Lesbian Social Services, 14*(2), 55–64.

Robinson, K. H., & Ferfolja, T. (2008). Playing it up, playing it down, playing it safe: Queering teacher education. *Teaching and Teacher Education, 24*, 846–58. doi:10.1016/j.tate.2007.11.004

Ryan, C. L., Patraw, J. M., & Bednar, M. (2013). Discussing princess boys and pregnant men: Teaching about gender diversity and transgender experiences within an elementary school curriculum. *Journal of LGBT Youth, 10*(1–2), 83–105. doi: 10.1080/19361653.2012.718540

Savage, T., & Harley, D. (2009). A place at the blackboard: Including lesbian, gay, bisexual, transgender, intersex, and queer/questioning issues in the education process. *Multicultural Education, 16*(4), 2–9. Retrieved from ERIC website: http://eric.ed.gov/?id=EJ858582

Schneider, M. S., & Dimito, A. (2008). Educators' beliefs about raising lesbian, gay, bisexual, and transgender issues in the schools: The experience in Ontario, Canada. *Journal of LGBT Youth, 5*(4), 49–71. doi:10.1080/19361650802223003

Stiegler, S. (2008). Queer youth as teachers: Dismantling silence of queer issues in a teacher preparation program committed to social justice. *Journal of LGBTQ Youth*, 5(4), 116–23. doi:10.1080/19361650802223227

Taylor, C., Peter, T., McMinn, T. L., Elliott, T., Beldom, S., Ferry, A., Gross, Z., Paquin, S., & Schachter, K. (2011). *Every class in every school: The first national climate survey on homophobia, biphobia, and transphobia in Canadian schools. Final report*. Toronto, ON: EGALE Canada Human Rights Trust.

Webb, J., Schirato, T., & Danaher, G. (2002). *Understanding Bourdieu*. Crows Nest, Australia: Allen & Unwin.

Wright-Maley, C., David, T., Gonzalez, E., & Colwell, R. (2016). Considering perspectives on transgender inclusion in Canadian Catholic elementary schools: Perspectives, challenges, and opportunities. *The Journal of Social Studies Research*, 40(3), 187–204. 10.1016/j.jssr.2015.12.001

Chapter 24

Overview

What do teachers do when confronted with unacceptable behaviour by students—or worse, by fellow educators? Elizabeth Meyer interviewed secondary school teachers to learn about their reactions to gender-based harassment and their strategies for stopping it. She takes a broad definition of gendered harassment, encompassing harassment directed at LGBTQ+ students as well as harassment between heterosexual boys and girls. The teachers' responses to harassment they witnessed were conditioned by the environment of their schools, both the official institutional constraints, such as the school's formal policies about harassment and the limits of the teachers' roles, and the informal social norms of their workplace, including the degree of tolerance for homophobia or sexism among their fellow teachers. They were particularly discouraged by administrators whom they perceived as not taking gendered harassment seriously enough. Meyer's participants drew on their own internal resources, including their own experiences of harassment or discrimination, to empower them to intervene when they witnessed gendered harassment. For most of the participants, unfortunately, the barriers to intervention proved to be stronger than the resources they were able to draw on to support intervention, making it difficult for them to put into practice their personal commitments to equity and safety in schools.

Gendered Harassment in Secondary Schools

Understanding Teachers' (Non) Interventions

Elizabeth J. Meyer

Introduction

The problem of sexual and homophobic harassment in schools has been the subject of scholarly investigation since the early 1990s. . . . These

Meyer, Elizabeth J. "Gendered Harassment in Secondary Schools: Understanding Teachers' (Non) Interventions," *Gender and Education*, 20:6, pp. 555–570, (2008). Reprinted by permission Taylor & Francis. www.tandfonline.com

studies have shown that sexual and homophobic harassment are accepted parts of school culture where faculty and staff rarely or never intervene to stop this harassment. Students report that teachers stand by and allow biased and hurtful behaviours to go unchallenged. Why teachers do not intervene consistently is the central question for the research presented in this article. Six secondary school teachers in one urban public school district in Canada were interviewed to understand the phenomenon from their point of view.

This article will start by defining gendered harassment and the behaviours that are examined together under this term. This is followed by a description of the methods used for data collection and analysis. The third section presents the findings of this study which indicate that there are *external* and *internal* influences that shape how teachers respond to gendered harassment in their schools. The *external* influences are divided into *institutional* (formal) and *social* (informal) factors which interact with teachers' *internal* influences to shape their experience of their school culture. The interaction of these three influences is explained with specific regard to how it shapes teachers' *perceptions of* and *responses to* student behaviours. After presenting a diagram that summarises the *barriers* and *motivators* that shape how teachers respond to gendered harassment in school, I will conclude with a discussion of how the use of this model can assist educators working to create more inclusive school climates.

What Is Gendered Harassment?

Gendered harassment is defined as any behaviour, verbal, physical, or psychological, that polices the boundaries of traditional heterosexual gender norms and includes (hetero)sexual harassment, homophobic harassment, and harassment for gender non-conformity. Common examples of such behaviours include name-calling, jokes and gestures, as well as physical and sexual assaults that are sexist, homophobic or transphobic in nature (Meyer 2006)....

Queer theorists and other scholars of gender and sexuality have argued effectively that sex, gender and sexual orientation are three distinct aspects of an individual's identity and experience (Butler 1990; Sedgwick 1990/1993; Bem 1993; Connell 1995; Jagose 1996; Sullivan 2003). I share the perspectives advanced by these theorists that it is the hegemony of heteronormative

patriarchy that constructs dominant notions of sex, gender and sexual orientation in very oppressive ways. It is this social construction of opposing binaries (i.e. male/female or gay/straight) (Butler 1990; Bem 1993) combined with the dominance of hegemonic (heterosexual) masculinity (Connell 1995; Mills 2001) that is at the root of gendered harassment. The fact that many individuals conflate these ideas often results in forms of sexual harassment, homophobic harassment and harassment for gender non-conformity. Such conflation can result in gender non-conforming individuals being attacked with anti-gay language (such as a men who are artistic being called "faggot"; or athletic, short-haired women being called "dyke"), and gay men and lesbians being sexually harassed (gay men due to their perceived femininity; or lesbians because women are viewed primarily as objects of male desire)....

...

The ways that teachers understand and perceive these forms of gendered harassment will impact how and when they choose to intervene in incidents that they witness at school. It is important to explore the teachers' perspectives in order to understand the barriers and motivators that shape how and when they choose to intervene....

Methods

This study is based on in-depth interviews with six Canadian teachers working in secondary schools in one urban public school board (Van Manen 1997; Patton 2002). Participants were recruited using both snowball and maximum variation sampling methods (Maykut and Morehouse 1994) to ensure a broad range of experiences and perspectives.... It is important to note that of the teachers who volunteered to participate in this study, none identified as Euro-Canadian heterosexual males....

Findings

In developing an understanding of how teachers perceive and respond to incidents of gendered harassment in secondary schools, a theoretical model emerged from the interview process. There are four elements in this model that demonstrate the relationship between the main factors that influence how teachers respond to gendered harassment in school: *external influences, internal influences, perceptions* and *responses*. The interaction of the *external* and *internal* influences shapes how a teacher *perceives* student behaviors and then decides to *respond* to them. A detailed description of the different external and internal influences is presented in the following sections to demonstrate how they influence perceptions and responses of teachers. These descriptions are supplemented with excerpts from the data to show how teachers talk about these factors and how they shape their practice.

External Influences

Multiple outside forces exert influences over teachers' perceptions and behaviours in school. These external influences are described as the school culture, or the "significant perceptions, thoughts, and beliefs held by individuals associated with the school" (Maehr and Buck 1993, 42). School culture is created by many factors that fall into two categories: *institutional* and *social* influences. In this section, I present the sub-themes in these categories to illustrate how teachers experienced their schools' cultures.

Institutional Influences

The formal structures that impact how participants perceive their school culture include four main aspects of the organization, including: a) administrative structures and responses; b) provincial curriculum demands and teacher workloads; c) teacher education and training; and d) written policies. Through the course of the interviews it became clear that these formal aspects of the school interacted with the informal aspects of the school culture to shape teachers' experiences and interactions with their students.

The first sub-theme in this category, administrative structures and responses, elicited discussion about not feeling supported by their administrators and believing that oftentimes the discipline meted out for instances of sexual or homophobic harassment was not sufficient:

> If there's an incident in my classroom I have to seek out the administration to get the follow-up on it. You just have to get to know the system and know what the expectations are 'cause they're stretched. They don't have any time . . . I personally had a few issues during the year with discipline and the VP wasn't there, and the principal dealt with it, and I always felt the same, the he just wasn't firm enough. (FT03)
>
> As far as discipline, how it's handled, I had to push for action when another kid called a kid "faggot." However, I know that in my school a racist comment was certainly not tolerated and it was dealt with immediately. (MT05)

These comments show a trend of teachers not trusting their administrators to support their actions and the feeling that they have to handle most non-violent discipline issues alone. . . .

The second theme brought up by all the teachers was the challenge they faced meeting the curricular and workload demands of their jobs. This was one of the most common obstacles that teachers talked about that prevented them from acting as consistently as they would like towards various forms of verbal harassment. Many teachers felt great pressure from their administration to cover the required amounts of curricular material and the stresses placed on them by large classes and demanding course loads caused them to ignore certain behaviours.

> [I don't stop name-calling] if I'm too tired, if there are set things I need to get through in a lesson. I know my lesson is going to take 60 minutes, I've only got 70 minutes to deliver it, I've got 10 minutes to waste. Right now my job is being a teacher and I have to get through the math before the end of the year. It's not on my priority list. (MT01)
>
> . . .

You're running all the time, you're pretty well tired constantly and you don't sit. You let stuff slide sometimes. (MT05)

These teachers are exhausted and overwhelmed with the professional demands placed on them and do not feel as if they are given the necessary support or resources to deal with everything that they are expected to address. They expressed frustration when talking about the limitations they felt, but very few of them offered any critique of the formal structures that caused them to feel overwhelmed. By only acting within the micro-structures of their classroom when dealing with behaviour issues rather than addressing the macro structures of the school, they are extremely limited in what they can do to improve student safety and school climate.

Education and training was the third theme. Most teachers felt that their teacher education programmes did not sufficiently prepare them to address incidents of harassment or bullying, particularly related to gender and sexual orientation. . . .

I've had no training [on how to address bullying]. . . . The educational degree was really worthless. I felt that we didn't really get that kind of necessary education. How to deal with certain issues like [bullying]. We were just told, "avoid this and this." . . . We're constantly being told how to protect ourselves. We're not constantly being told how to protect these young people from other young people. (MT06)

[I never got any] training in school [on] bullying. I do not think that we ever studied anything related to that . . . I don't know if I was really attuned to [sexual harassment]—to be quite honest.

. . .

The teachers who did get some education in this area are ones who took it upon themselves to seek out these opportunities. These decisions were shaped by their intrapersonal influences such as their personal identities and educational biography. . . .

The final theme under institutional influences was that of written policies and how teachers'

knowledge of their school's and school board's policies influenced how they addressed various forms of bullying and harassment. One teacher did voice a belief that his school's policy on bullying was clear, yet he spoke at other points in the interview about his frustration with colleagues for their lack of awareness of and attention to the issues of racism, sexism, and homophobia in his school (MT06). The rest of the participants did not share the belief that they had a clear understanding of their school's policies. The perceptions that teachers shared about their experiences with the formal structures of their schools present a clear description of some of the structural obstacles that exist and prevent educators from responding consistently and effectively to incidents of gendered harassment.

Social Influences

It quickly became apparent that the informal structures of the school, or the social norms and values, exerted the most powerful influence over teachers' behaviours. The three most prevalent themes were: a) perceptions of administration; b) interpersonal relationships; and c) community values. These will be addressed in this order to explore how these factors impacted teachers' experiences in their schools.

The first area is teachers' perceptions of their school's administrators. Under this theme, participants spoke of issues such as leadership style, personal values, professional priorities, and policy implementation. . . .

Our administrator who dealt with disciplinary problems was a real jock and the real "man's man" and he'd sit the boys down and say, "what the hell do you think you're doing?" I think that he gave them the old football huddle, sit down and I'm gonna tell you how to act in the classroom. And I think that's as far as it went . . . I feel that the administration didn't want to get involved because they were these [southern European ethnicity] men and, if they were to come into a staff meeting and say, "we need to address some of the homophobic attitudes," I could never hear them talking about something like that.

So maybe that's part of the problem; even the administrators had that [southern European ethnicity] kind of mentality. (FT02)

I always find that when I'm working with principals and vice principals that it's their own morals and their own beliefs that come through and if it's something that they don't really think's a big issue, then why are they going to be proactive about it? Or just the gender of the administrator, I think that plays into it as well. (FT03)

. . . Teachers get messages from their school leaders about what they personally value and what issues they feel are important to address. In the above statements, the teachers are talking about the lack of leadership in addressing sexual and homophobic harassment in their schools. By choosing not to address these issues, administrators teach their staff that these behaviours are not viewed as problematic, and reinforce the primacy of heterosexual masculinity in schools. . . .

The kids are astute enough to see that when they use the word faggot they won't get sent to the office and when they use a racial slur, they get sent to the office. It's a very quick connection to make . . . I had one kid call another a faggot. I hauled him to the principal; I asked for a suspension, the principal didn't want to suspend him. It was one of the vice-principals and they saw that I was about to blow my top so they suspended the kid. But I really had to push for it. (MT05)

. . . Any type of physical harassment would get a strong response. They just don't tolerate any type of fighting or anything in the school, so if that goes on, there's definitely a response to that. But in things where people are just kind of saying things to one another—no, those are not responded to in the same way. And it would be difficult to respond to them because they occur so much—it's almost like they're a part of the school culture. (FT02)

The lack of consistency or clear guidelines for responding to forms of gendered harassment left teachers feeling isolated and unsupported in their efforts to address incidents of non-physical harassment. Conversely, participants reported that any act of physical violence, regardless of its motivation, was handled quickly and uniformly due to zero-tolerance policies regarding such behaviour in schools.

. . .

The working and personal relationships with colleagues also had an impact on their experiences in their schools. The participants in this study spoke regularly about their struggles and alliances with other members of the school staff. They also complained about a lack of consistency in enforcing certain school rules and policies. Many felt that they could not defend taking certain actions against students if other teachers were not also addressing those same issues.

I spent the first couple months enforcing all of this [uniform policy, swearing, and name-calling] and there are some teachers that just never enforce it and so you realize that out of 20 teachers, we have about five who do all the enforcing and you just can't anymore. You can't do it . . . I just feel like some teachers just don't really have a clue. It's scary. It's really scary. (FT03)

In my classroom I can deal with it and give my students a thousand detentions, but if they go into another classroom and they're allowed to bully then they'll come back into my classroom the next day and I'll be dealing with the exact same issues. (FT02)

. . .

Teachers' interactions with and perceptions of their colleagues are also factors that shape how they will act in various situations. Participants in this study spoke of racist, sexist and homophobic comments from other staff and a lack of awareness of these issues from more experienced teachers. The stories that these teachers shared about the frustration they felt and the difficulties they faced due to colleagues who acted in irresponsible or oppressive ways were troubling. One female teacher spoke of students telling her about a fellow male teacher who was sexually harassing them. When she reported it to her department head, he informed her that he was aware of the situation; however, the teacher was never punished and continued to teach at that school (FT02). Several teachers told stories of hearing homophobic jokes and comments among the staff (FT03, FT04, MT01, MT05), as well as of being harassed themselves (MT01, MT05) and getting little or no support from their administration. It is not surprising to see how challenging it is to work against various forms of bias and harassment in students when professional educators and employees of the school are modeling the exact behaviours these teachers are trying to prevent.

. . .

Each of the three schools in this study were in the same school board, but were situated in very different communities. It was clear in the conversations with these teachers that the values and expectations of the community were significant factors that shaped what could and could not happen in their school. Their interpersonal relationships with colleagues and families are created in this context and are often actively transmitting the values of the broader school community. These, in turn, influenced the school culture.

. . .

As other scholars have found, school culture is much more likely to determine and support what it is that students, teachers, and others say and do than is the formal management system. This means that teachers are more inclined to act in ways that reflect shared norms and values of other teachers than in ways defined by school policy (Stader and Garca 2006, 16). The way teachers choose to navigate the culture of their school is shaped by several internal factors that they spoke of in their interviews. The next section offers an explanation of these influences.

Internal Influences

Each individual brought a specific set of identities and experiences to his/her teaching as well as the research process. What quickly became evident in the interviews was the significant influence of their personal identities and their own experiences in school (educational biography) on shaping how they perceived and acted in the culture of their current school. All of the participants talked about their experiences of having felt marginalized in society due to their identities as gay, bisexual, women, or people of colour. These experiences in their own schooling and professional life acted as very strong motivators to act out against discriminatory behaviour that they witnessed as teachers. At times, these factors also acted as barriers to consistent intervention because they felt vulnerable as minorities in their schools. This vulnerability and the tensions it caused for the teachers was a major source of struggle for the participants. . . .

. . . This is an interesting finding as there was not a single volunteer in this study who identified as a white, heterosexual male in spite of repeated attempts to locate one. This is not meant to imply that there are not white straight male allies who are engaged in this work, only that they were more difficult to recruit than I had anticipated. They can be important partners in such transformation efforts in schools and should not be overlooked. As several teachers pointed out, it is their personal experiences with discrimination and marginalisation that made them particularly sensitive to these issues in schools. The challenge that this finding presents is how to raise the awareness of educators who have not personally felt the impacts of discrimination or exclusion from dominant culture.

Conclusion

What became clear through the course of the three interviews was that these teachers did not feel that they could put a stop to gendered harassment in their schools. The presence of so many external barriers challenged their ability and eventually even their willingness to consistently interrupt sexist, homophobic and transphobic language and behaviours. A similar study in the United Kingdom concluded that the prevailing rhetoric of liberal individualism acted as a barrier to teachers' responding to misogynistic bullying by obscuring "structurally reproduced relations of gender domination" (Chambers, van Loon, and Tincknell 2004). As other researchers have pointed out, sexual and homophobic harassment have been normalized as aspects of everyday school culture and are often not questioned or approached by educators from a critical or feminist perspective (Larkin 1994; Hepburn 1997; Chambers, Tincknell, and Van Loon 2004).

. . .

The findings in this research offer us a deeper understanding of how various forms of bullying and harassment are perceived and acted on by teachers in secondary schools. These data offer scholars, educators, and school leaders a clearer picture of some of the challenges that exist when trying to confront such forms of harassment between students in schools. . . .

References

Bem, S. 1993. *The lenses of gender: Transforming the debate on sexual inequality.* New Haven, Conn: Yale University Press.

Butler, J. 1990. *Gender trouble.* New York: Routledge Falmer.

Chambers, D., E. Tincknell, and J. van Loon. 2004. Peer regulation of teenage sexual identities. *Gender and Education* 16, no. 3: 397–415.

Chambers, D., J. van Loon, and E. Tincknell. 2004. Teachers' views of teenage sexual morality. *British Journal of Sociology of Education* 25, no. 5: 563–76.

Connell, R.W. 1995. *Masculinities.* Sydney: Allen and Unwin.

Hepburn, A. 1997. Teachers and secondary school bullying—a postmodern discourse analysis. *Discourse & Society* 8, no. 1: 27–48.

Jagose, A. 1996. *Queer theory: An introduction.* New York: New York University Press.

Larkin, J. 1994. Walking through walls: The sexual harassment of high school girls. *Gender and Education* 6, no. 3: 263–80.

Maehr, M., and R. Buck. 1993. Transforming school culture. In *Education leadership and school culture,* ed. M. Sashkin and H.J. Wahlberg, 40–57. Berkeley, Calif: McCutchan Publishing.

Maykut, P., and R. Morehouse. 1994. *Beginning qualitative research: A philosophic and practical guide.* Philadelphia: Routledge.

Meyer, E.J. 2006. Gendered harassment in North America: School-based interventions for reducing homophobia and heterosexism. In *Combating gender violence in and around schools,* ed. C. Mitchell and F. Leach, 43–50. Stoke-on-Trent: Trentham Books.

Mills, M. 2001. *Challenging violence in schools: An issue of masculinities.* Buckingham: Open University Press.

Patton, M.Q. 2002. *Qualitative research and evaluation methods.* Thousand Oaks, Calif: Sage.

Sedgwick, E.K. 1990/1993. Epistemology of the closet. In *The lesbian and gay studies reader,* ed. H. Abelove, M.A. Barale, and D.M. Halperin, 45–61. New York: Routledge.

Stader, D., and T.J. Garca. 2006. Sexual minority youth and school culture: A study of educational leadership candidates' perceptions of Dallas–Fort Worth area secondary schools. Paper presented at the American Educational Research Association, 7–11 April, in San Francisco, CA. Stein, N. 1992. Bitter lessons for all: Sexual harassment in schools. In *Sexuality and the Curriculum,* ed. J.T. Sears, 10–123. New York: Teachers College Press.

Sullivan, N. 2003. *A critical introduction to queer theory.* New York: New York University Press.

Van Manen, M. 1997. *Human science for an action sensitive pedagogy.* Loudon, ON: Althouse Press.

Chapter 25

Overview

Public schools are meant for kids, but which group of adults—parents or teachers—has the authority to say what kids will learn? Learning about gender is a particularly hot topic. Even when gender is not the explicit subject of classroom lessons, school organization and practices can convey powerful messages about what is or is not acceptable in terms of gender expression. Lindsay Herriot and her colleagues explore the public consultations carried out by the Vancouver School Board on the subject of whether and how schools should affirm students' self-identified gender, which in practice meant a focus on who can use which washroom. While teachers framed the issue in terms of making life better for queer and trans students, many of the parents who spoke at the consultation framed it as an overreach by the school system, conveying messages about gender nonconformity that might conflict with what parents taught their children at home. The idea that trans girls might pose a threat to other girls in the washroom was prominent, which the authors identify as a form of "transmisogyny." The authors explore the dimensions of trans inclusion policies in schools, what they do or don't stand for, and what function schools fulfill in teaching about gender, even through such everyday practices as using the washroom.

Contested Spaces

Trans-Inclusive School Policies and Parental Sovereignty in Canada

Lindsay Herriot, David P. Burns, and Betty Yeung

Introduction

In the spring of 2014, the Vancouver School Board (VSB) held five well-attended public meetings on unceded Coast Salish territory to discuss and debate revisions to *Policy ACB: Sexual Orientation and Gender Identities* (hereafter referred to as Policy ACB), the board's policy on LGBTQ issues. Among other provisions, this policy advanced two salient principles. First, that students' self-identified genders be affirmed in all features of school life, and, second, that teachers and counsellors should be prohibited from "outing" LGBTQ students to their parents without explicit permission from the students themselves. The public controversy (see CBC News 2014; Wente 2014) surrounding Policy ACB centred, in large part, on one particular provision, that "trans*[1] students shall have access to the washroom and change room that corresponds to their gender identity" (Vancouver School Board 2014, 6).

. . .

The Policy ACB deliberations were a poignant example of how school buildings, despite the beliefs of our pre-service and practising teachers' that they are sex-neutral, in fact prescribe and reinforce particular presumptions about sex, gender, and bodies (Grosz 2001). Or as Binnie (1997) puts it, "space is not naturally authentically 'straight,' but rather actively produced and (hetero)sexualized" (223),

and as we found, gendered. The public consultations functioned as a live case study of Rasmussen's (2009) theoretical analysis of the gendered school washroom, wherein, "symbols on toilet doors take for granted that bodies fit into two neat categories, and then proceed to sort them based on this presumption—a presumption rarely questioned in the production of toilet signage" (440). . . .

We . . . situate the VSB's five public consultations regarding Policy ACB as an interpretive case study of how multiple competing and contradictory visions of educational and parental authority can be manifested in the context of a single policy process. By focusing our analysis on these five public meetings, we demonstrate how pieces of educational policy can come to represent social and political disagreement of a much more fundamental sort. We begin by explicating how we approach both policy and policy consultation meetings as multi-layered discursive performance. Shifting focus, we synthesize some of the theoretical perspectives on public and school washrooms as highly gendered spaces, before narrowing our focus to review recent instances of gender regulation in British Columbian K-12 schooling. We then move to discuss the ACB consultations, beginning first with an overview of speakers who supported the policy revisions. The analysis then covers the three substantive (parental) objections to Policy ACB; namely, (1) a refusal to recognize, much less affirm trans identities, (2) deep-seated adherence to transmisogynistic rape myths, and

Herriot, Lindsay, David P. Burns, & Betty Yeung. "Contested spaces: trans-inclusive school policies and parental sovereignty in Canada." *Gender and Education*, 30:6, pp. 695–714 (2018). Reprinted by permission of Taylor & Francis. www.tandfonline.com

(3) an absolutist conception of parental rights. We conclude by rejecting the public square as the most appropriate forum through which to meaningfully address these issues, and offer suggestions for how a more supportive dialogue could have been achieved by including personnel such as school counsellors in leadership and liaison roles during policy revisions.

. . .

Theorizing the School Washroom

. . . School washrooms have long functioned to categorize students and staff alike based on a number of identity markers such as ethnicity, ability, and of relevance to this paper, gender. In particular, ". . . the institution of the public toilet is designed to discipline gender" (Cavanaugh 2010, 5). . . .

Policy ACB both extended the norm of sex-segregated washrooms, by stating that "trans students shall have access to the washroom . . . that corresponds to their gender identity," and began to transgress it by "striv[ing] to make available single stall gender-neutral washrooms at all schools . . ." (6). Critical queer geographers would describe the first part as assimilating trans students into the washroom gender binary, and the latter as a tentative step towards challenging that binary, rather than merely slotting trans students into it (Oswin 2008). True transgression, we argue, would go a step further and advocate multi-stall all gender washrooms.

Conceptualizing gender in segregated washrooms is necessarily contingent on conceptualizing (compulsory) heterosexuality, which relies on a strictly enforced male/female dualism of hegemonic masculinity and emphasized femininity (Butler 1990). . . .

While gender identity and sexual orientation are typically understood as naturally and universally cisgender and heterosexual, schools nonetheless invest considerable effort in teaching and enforcing gender conformity, which begs the question: Why would a student need to be taught something that is both natural and universal? Rules are typically established because someone is behaving contrary to the norm, not to regulate an already-regulated,

natural phenomenon. The investment of time and resources indicates that rather than being a stable, fixed identity, cisgender heterosexuality is seen as somewhat fragile, or at least in need of protection from corrupting influences. . . .

Much of the opposition to the proposed policy revisions stemmed from the belief that transgender women are a form of corruption, that they are not real women, but rather dangerous men who want to access female-only washrooms in order to sexually harass or assault cisgender VSB schoolgirls. Such refusal to legitimize the gender identities of trans women is part of "transmisogyny," "[a] term coined by Juliana Serano (2007), to denote the unique oppression experienced by people on the trans female/feminine spectrum (such as transsexual women) due to both transphobia and the societal devaluation of women and femininity" (Airton and Meyer 2014, 224). Where masculinity is consistently privileged over the feminine, it becomes inconceivable, or un-readable, that those assigned a male gender at birth would eschew masculine supremacy and instead express a feminized gender.

. . .

Background: Heteronormativity, Heterosexism, and British Columbia School Policy

Although a spate of LGBTQ-affirming policies have been adopted across educational jurisdictions over the past 15 years, schooling in Canada continues to be inordinately influenced by heterosexism as defined above, gender policing, and the erasure or pathologization of both queerness and queer bodies (see Taylor et al. 2011; Airton 2013; Short 2013; Meyer and Pullen-Sansfaçon 2014; Morrison et al. 2014; Rayside 2014). . . .

The findings from most research on LGBTQ youth indicates that trans youth experience disproportionately more negative outcomes than their LGBQ counterparts (see Mallon and De-Crescenzo 2006; Ryan 2010; Greytak, Kosciw, and Boesen 2013; Jones and Hillier 2013). Returning to Taylor et al.'s (2011) nationwide survey, not only are trans youth much more likely than their LGB or straight peers to find school, and particularly washrooms and change rooms, unsafe, they unsurprisingly have far lower levels of school attachment (80–88). More than half (55.5%) of Taylor et al.'s trans participants disagreed with the statement "I feel like a real part of my school," as compared to 24.5% of straight respondents in the same survey (94), making school attachment an area of particular importance for trans youth.

. . .

Methodology

. . .

Data were collected from the five public consultation meetings at the VSB's main office in the spring of 2014. Each meeting lasted between four and five hours, and was attended by 200–300 members of the public. . . .

There were a total of 91 speakers spread across the 5 meetings, with 51% of speakers supporting the policy revisions, and 49% opposing them. Table 25.1 provides a breakdown of the speakers.

Educational professionals such as teachers, principals, and school counsellors were notably absent during these consultations as a simultaneous job action prohibited their presence on VSB property after school hours. Parents of openly queer children, current VSB students (half of which identified as queer in their speeches), and legal and mental health professionals all unanimously supported the policy revisions. All objections were voiced from parents of non-queer, or not openly queer students, and community members, and these objections are the primary focus of

our analysis. Policy ACB was eventually adopted with the support of seven VSB trustees and the non-voting student trustee, while two trustees voted against it.

Analysis

Making It Better for Trans Youth

. . .

Many of these public statements concerned the strictly enforced gender requirements for safe bathroom and change room access. Both current and former trans students spoke of frequent, sometimes incessant, gender-based bullying (such as being called "tranny," or other slurs) when using the gender-segregated school washrooms. One youth reported going to extreme lengths to avoid being "caught" by their peers:

> I can tell you how I spent months using only the washroom in the basement of my school where no one ever goes, how I would sneak into it just so no one sees me or would yell at me for using the wrong washroom. (14 May 2014)

Furthermore, several parents spoke of how their trans children minimized or refused eating and drinking while at school in order to avoid such verbal harassment. Besides the obvious health concerns, such as students having repeated urinary tract infections because of refraining from washroom use throughout the school day, these parents also questioned how much their children were actually learning at school when they were struggling to have their basic bodily needs met.

Table 25.1   Speaker's Roles and Position on Policy ACB Revisions

Speaker	Percentage of total speakers	Position on Policy
Parent of a queer child	5% (*n* = 5)	Support: 100%
Parent of a non-queer child	45% (*n* = 41)	Support: 13.3% Opposed: 85.3%
Professional (i.e. physician, lawyer, psychologist, etc.)	24% (*n* = 22)	Support: 100%
Current VSB student	6% (*n* = 6)	100%
Other (VSB alumni, pastor, Vancouver resident, etc.)	21% (*n* = 20)	Support: 50% Opposed: 50%

Statements from healthcare providers corroborated these experiences. A registered psychologist at the University of British Columbia summed up the general consensus among health practitioners who spoke at the public meetings thusly: ". . . in my practice I have seen too many young people who have opted out. [They] stay home from school on every PE day, who avoid going to the bathrooms for fear . . . [they] drop out, [they] change schools" (14 May 2014). . . . The adoption and implementation of the policy revisions were described as urgent. Importantly, not a single trans person, relative of an openly trans VSB student, or educational, psychological, or medical scholar or practitioner, voiced opposition to the proposed revisions. . . .

Our data revealed that school washrooms had dual roles. While they were normatively understood as merely spaces for bodily needs to be privately attended to, it was only when a gendered body was categorized as being in the "wrong" washroom that their role as a regulating structure of ability, gender, sexuality, ethnicity, age, and class become apparent.

. . .

As will become evident in the following three sections, the hostility that trans students reported experiencing in their school's gender-segregated washrooms seemed to stem from deep resistance to the existence of trans conceptions of gender, as well as scepticism and mistrust towards those who identify as trans.

Parental vs. Professional Understandings

Although 16 parents spoke in favour of the policy, most of the objections came from concerned parents, none of whom themselves had an openly queer child. Of the 41 parents without a queer child who spoke at the consultations, a full 85% (n = 35) were against the policy revisions. . . . Many of these parents demonstrated expressed a steadfast commitment to hetero—and cissexist culture by affirming two related positions: (1) the maintenance of the heterosexual nuclear family and (2) the denial of gender variance and gender as a spectrum.

Parents opposing the revisions often opened their remarks by avowing the legitimacy of hetero—and cissexist views. For example, one parent explained, "gender exists in a binary [as opposed to a spectrum] . . . [and] we want to retain these views for lots of religious and cultural reasons, without being called outdated" (29 May 2014). As another speaker put it,

> my role as an educator and teacher of the Bible is to support the home and the role of the school is to support the education of the child—it's being taken down by the Gay Lobby and the indoctrination of the gay lifestyle. (29 May 2014)

. . .

Hetero- and cissexism were further manifested by the denial of gender variance and spectra, with many parents denying the existence of a trans gender identity. One parent understood gender variance as the idea that "children can choose gender based on their feelings" allowing "people [to] think that gender is in their mind," which she likened to a "theory . . . like a religion" (22 May 2014). These parents used the label "gender confusion," rather than gender variance to describe trans identities. . . . Describing gender variance as confusion, and positioning it as a problem for science to "solve" delegitimizes trans identities. As Cavanaugh (2010) argues, "cissexist cultures . . . are predicated upon the idea that transsexual identities are inauthentic or inferior copies of those gender identities had by non-trans folk" (8).

This opposition first demanded and then resisted professional opinions on trans identities. During the first meeting, for example, multiple parents voiced a concern about the lack of research and professional opinion on these topics, and called for more time for this research to be conducted:

> The policy grants the school teacher the right to decide who might be a gender nonconforming child. This should be in the hands of professionals, not teachers. (14 May 2014)

[I'm] here to ask for more time for parents and professionals. . . . Professionals from medicine, psychology, education, and sex studies, should be involved. (14 May 2014)

[I see] this as a political war and [I'm] appalled. And [I want] health care and mental health professionals involved. This policy keeps out doctors, not teachers who are biased and have an agenda—you are using our children in a social experiment. (14 May 2014)

With 100% of the 20 professionals who spoke publicly supporting the policy revisions, these arguments quickly changed. In later meetings, parental demand for professional opinions shifted to complaints of biases in those opinions:

Those who drafted this revised policy, are they unbiased medical and scientific professionals? More presentations and more research is needed to come up with a better and wiser policy. (29 May 2014)

Professionals who build their careers on this. Facts aren't in on this. Why are these policies being rushed through when there are no facts and no consensus? Let's have meaningful consultation and conversation. Board. Please. We're all adults here. The medical and mental health people are, by their own definition, biased. (22 May 2014)

. . .

The demand for, and then rejection of professional or research-based opinions on Policy ACB indicates a fatal flaw in the pervasive assumption that with the right information, or the right education, people will adjust their views accordingly. . . .

Transmisogyny and Rape Myths

Besides being highly resistant to contradictory evidence, we argue that some of the most vociferous opposition to Policy ACB's amendments was deeply rooted in transmisogyny and rape culture. Indeed, many of the arguments against Policy ACB were less pertinent to the actual policy revisions at hand, and had far more to do with maintaining dominant, or toxic masculinity and the rape myths that support it. . . .

What if students pretend to be transgendered for other purposes? In Toronto, a man pretended to be a transwoman to get access to a women's shelter and sexually assaulted two women, one who was blind and homeless. . . . Are we going to wait until these things happen to our daughters? Don't use my kids for social experiments that aren't working in other jurisdictions. (22 May 2014)

There is much to be troubled by in this statement. We first note the faulty assumption that trans women are in fact males who would masquerade as women for any purpose, nefarious or otherwise. Dubbed the "deceptive transsexual" trope (Serano 2007, 36), this deliberate misgendering sees all trans women as "deceivers in an appearance-reality contrast between gender presentation and sexed body" (Bettcher 2007, 48). In this view, gender identity and presentation are construed as a hostile trick being played on unwitting cisgender people, with biological sex or genital configuration privileged as a person's "real" identity. . . .

At a later VSB meeting, a different parent reiterated this diminishment of transwomen's gender identities in favour of anatomical determinism, noting, "I am concerned for my little daughter—what's going to prevent a physical male from going into girl's washrooms?" (29 May 2014). . . . This second parent's concern about a "physical male" being in a female washroom is further laden with assumptions and meanings about masculinity, particularly in public spaces. In private homes, for instance, it is not seen as dangerous that males and females might, and often do, share a single washroom facility. . . . When moved into a public space such as a school, however, dominant masculinity's insistent entitlement to sexual gratification through women's bodies necessarily means that men are read as potential, or even probable, sex offenders, from whom unsuspecting women and girls need protection. Within this line of reasoning, although based on an ultimately demeaning conception of masculinity, the parent's moral panic becomes understandable, though still unacceptable.

. . .

Despite parental objections' linking of trans-women with paedophilia, there was nonetheless faint evidence that public attitudes towards trans people were shifting, however, slightly. In their response to the many statements detailing the verbal, sexual, and physical harassment of trans youth within VSB schools, a significant minority of opposing parents opened their remarks by stating unequivocally that they were not homophobic or transphobic. Statements such as "I believe this trans issue requires medical research . . . [I'm] concerned about children taking hormonal blockers because they are very damaging. We want more time for more consultation. We are not homophobic" (22 May 2014); "I have genuine love and concern for the LGBTQ community: I am opposed to some of the policy, not opposed to you" (29 May 2014); and "we love the trans children" (29 May 2014) were common expressions of this purported non-homophobia and non-transphobia. This sort of prefacing marks a significant shift in tone from even just a few years ago. While these perfunctory opening statements were sometimes followed by what the Chair of these meetings deemed "hate speech" (29 May 2014), they nonetheless indicate a modest form of progress in that it is less socially acceptable to be seen as homophobic or anti-trans.

Parents, Rights, and the State

If one were to accept our argument that the aforementioned parental anxieties are unfounded, a parent might still reasonably object to the policy on the ground that it might infringe on some parental prerogative. From this perspective, policies like ACB are objectionable not because they endanger children (which they do not), but rather because they represent some form of pernicious state or activist control over the moral education of children. This concern sometimes refers to the "gay agenda" or "social experiments."

We suggest that this objection reflects two commonly held misconceptions about parental rights. First, some parents seem to consider these rights absolute, which they are not. Second, some parents assume that their children's being presented with alternative beliefs and lifestyles in schools is a limitation on their cultural or religious rights. If such presentation is a limitation, which it is not clear that it is, it is defended by the Supreme Court of Canada. We address each of these misconceptions using examples from the current case study.

A. Why does the school intervene on such things such as transgender? Why should the parents not know of these things? Nobody can remove my rights as the father of my daughter. (29 May 2014)

B. You are not the parents, if the child has difficulty, I will take care of my child. (29 May 2014)

C. Parents send children to school to be educated not indoctrinated. Parents are first educators, especially on moral education. (29 May 2014)

The above quotes each refer to the same concern—that Policy ACB represents the infringing of parental rights by the school board. This concern, as seen in example C, is particularly acute in moral educational contexts like this one. . . .

The objection to the gender-neutral washroom provision, on this more general reading, seems to revolve around two possible concerns.

First, it refers to the concern that the school is imposing upon religious families by conducting a kind of "social experiment" (from the statement, previously quoted, of 22 May 2014). Since the children of these parents are not asked to take any positive action as a result of this policy (they are merely asked to tolerate a small number of persons in a facility that were not there before), it must be inferred that part of the parental objection is to the idea that these values are being manifested in the school in the first place—that their children are, in other words, merely exposed to a different way of interacting with trans persons. This is, presumably, what the parent in example C is referring to when noting "indoctrination," and

is an argument not without precedent in scholarly analysis of these issues (see especially Burtt 1994).
. . .

There is no suggestion in Policy ACB of encouraging children to have any one identity or another—the policy merely seeks to make safe the learning environment of those who have marginalized identities. Parental objectors, therefore, seem to be asserting that the public reality of being confronted with other person's identities is itself corrupting or dangerous. Given that large Canadian cities already include visible LGBTQ communities, often with clearly defined spaces or neighbourhoods, this is implausible.

Second, even if a transgender-inclusive washroom somehow did encourage gender confusion among children (which, it must be said again, is not true), the presentation of such diversity in school life is explicitly protected by the Canadian Supreme Court.

Children encounter it every day in the public school system as members of a diverse student body. They see their classmates, and perhaps also their teachers, eating foods at lunch that they themselves are not permitted to eat, whether because of their parents' religious strictures or because of other moral beliefs. They see their classmates wearing clothing with features or brand labels which their parents have forbidden them to wear.

And they see their classmates engaging in behaviour on the playground that their parents have told them not to engage in. The cognitive dissonance that results from such encounters is simply a part of living in a diverse society. It is also a part of growing up. Through such experiences, children come to realize that not all of their values are shared by others. (Chamberlain v. Surrey, 2002)

School, in other words, is not just a place that necessarily reflects normal human diversity—it is also a place that ought, to some degree, to prepare children to handle such diversity in adulthood. . . . Each citizen has an interest in the education of children because the tolerance and mutual respect those children learn in school is part of the basic preparation they require to peacefully coexist in a pluralistic society. This role certainly does not negate parental influence, but it does mean that teaching children to coexist with different kinds of people (particularly when the form of identity in question is constitutionally protected, as it is in this case), is a clear and necessary limitation on the rights of parents. . . .

Change, however slow, can be daunting and concerning for parents. While more dubious arguments made by some parental activists need to be confronted, as we have in this paper, it is also important to ensure that non-combative opportunities for public education are provided.

Note

1. "Trans*: an umbrella term that can be used to describe people whose gender identity and/or gender expression differs from what they were assigned at birth" (Vancouver School Board 2014, 13). While recognizing the inherent tensions of collapsing a plurality of identities into a single term, in the interests of readability and cohesion, we will be using trans, without an asterisk in this paper to refer to a broad array of gender non-conforming identities including but not limited to, gender fluid, gender queer, gender non-conforming, pangender, bigender, all gender, agender, transgender, transsexual, etc. Following Gabriel (2014), we eschew the asterisk because it adds caveats and qualifications to "trans," which is itself the umbrella term.

References

Airton, L. 2013. "Leave 'Those Kids' Alone: On the Conflation of School Homophobia and Suffering Queers". *Curriculum Inquiry* 43 (5): 532–62. doi:10.1111/curi.12031.

Airton, L., and E. Meyer. 2014. "Glossary of Terms". In *Supporting Transgender & Gender Creative Youth: Schools, Families, and Communities in Action*, edited by E. Meyer and A. P. Sansfaçon, 217–24. New York: Peter Lang.

Bettcher, T. M. 2007. "Evil Deceivers and Make-believers: On Transphobic Violence and the Politics of Illusion". *Hypatia* 22 (3): 43–65.

Binnie, J. 1997. "Coming Out of Geography: Towards a Queer Epistemology?" *Environment and Planning D: Society and Space* 15 (3): 223–37.

Burtt, S. 1994. "Religious Parents, Secular Schools: A Liberal Defense of an Illiberal Education". *The Review of Politics* 56 (1): 51–70.

Butler, J. 1990. *Gender Trouble*. New York: Routledge.

Cavanaugh, S. 2010. *Queering Bathrooms: Gender, Sexuality, and the Hygienic Imagination*. Toronto: University of Toronto Press.

CBC News. 2014. "Transgender Policy Prompts Mother's Plea to Vancouver School Board". CBC, June 4. http://www.cbc.ca/news/canada/british-columbia/transgender-policy-prompts-mother-s-plea-tovancouver-school-board-1.2662410.

Chamberlain v. Surrey School Board N. 36 volume 86, Case Number 28654, Supreme Court of Canada. 2002. http://scc-csc.lexum.com/scc-csc/scc-csc/en/item/2030/index.do.

Gabriel. 2014. "The Trans Asterisk and Why We Need to Stop Using It". The Pulp Zine Silt, August 25. http://www.thepulpzine.com/the-trans-asterisk-and-why-we-need-to-stop-using-it/.

Greytak, E. A., J. G. Kosciw, and M. J. Boesen. 2013. "Putting the 'T' in 'Resource': The Benefits of LGBT-related School Resources for Transgender Youth". *Journal of LGBT Youth* 10 (1–2): 45–63. doi:10.1080/19361653.2012.718522.

Grosz, E. 2001. *Architecture from the Outside: Essays on Virtual and Real Space*. Cambridge, Mass: MIT Press.

Jones, T., and L. Hillier. 2013. "Comparing Trans-spectrum and Same-sex-attracted Youth in Australia: Increased Risks, Increased Activisms". *Journal of LGBT Youth* 10 (4): 287–307. doi:0.1080/19361653.2013.825197.

Mallon, G. P., and T. DeCrescenzo. 2006. "Transgender Children and Youth: A Child Welfare Practice Perspective". *Child Welfare* 85 (2): 215–41.

Meyer, E. J., and A. Pullen-Sansfaçon. 2014. *Supporting Transgender & Gender Creative Youth: Schools, Families, and Communities in Action*. New York: Peter Lang.

Morrison, M. A., L. M. Jewell, J. M. McCutcheon, and D. B. Cochrane. 2014. "In the Face of Anti-LGBQ Behaviour: Saskatchewan High School Students' Perceptions of School Climate and Consequential Impact". *Canadian Journal of Education* 37 (2): 1–29.

Oswin, N. 2008. "Critical Geographies and the Uses of Sexuality: Deconstructing Queer Space". *Progress in Human Geography* 32 (1): 89–103. doi:10.1177/0309132507085213.

Rasmussen, M. L. 2009. "Beyond Gender Identity?" *Gender and Education* 21 (4): 431–47.

Rayside, D. 2014. "The Inadequate Recognition of Sexual Diversity by Canadian Schools: LGBT Advocacy and Its Impact". *Journal of Canadian Studies* 48 (1): 190–225.

Ryan, C. 2010. "Engaging Families to Support Lesbian, Gay, Bisexual, and Transgender Youth: The Family Acceptance Project". *Prevention Researcher* 17 (4): 11–13.

Serano, J. 2007. *Whipping Girl: A Transsexual Woman on Sexism and the Scapegoating of Femininity*. Emeryville, Calif: Seal Press.

Short, D. 2013. "Don't Be So Gay!" *Queers, Bullying, and Making School Safe*. Vancouver: UBC Press.

Taylor, C., T. Peter, T. L. McMinn, T. Elliott, S. Beldom, A. Ferry, and K. Schachter. 2011. *Every Class in Every School: The First National Climate Survey on Homophobia, Biphobia, and Transphobia in Canadian Schools (Final Report)*. Toronto: Egale Canada Human Rights Trust.

Vancouver School Board. 2014. "Sexual Orientation and Gender Identities Policy ACB – R – 1." http://www.vsb.bc.ca/district-policy/acb-sexual-orientation-and-gender-identities.

Wente, M. 2014. "Welcome to Vancouver's Gender-neutral Pronoun Wars". *The Globe and Mail*, June 19. http://www.theglobeandmail.com/globe-debate/welcome-to-vancouvers-pronoun-wars/article19234644/.

Chapter 26

Overview

Universities should be a place of equality and opportunity for everyone—but they aren't. Frances Henry and colleagues explore the experiences of those who spend most of their adult lives in universities—faculty members and administrators. They interviewed 89 people who identified as racialized (Black, Indigenous, or a person of colour) at 12 Canadian universities. Despite years of rhetoric about multiculturalism and diversity, most of their participants still experienced universities as an extremely white space, especially those who worked in the social sciences and humanities. The authors use the ideas of critical race theory, which connects the dominance of white people to the workings of capitalism, to explore their participants' experiences of being marginalized or otherwise made to feel out of place.

They argue that the rise of neoliberalism within universities, with its emphasis on everything that can be measured or quantified, has been especially arduous for faculty of colour, whose achievements do not always fit the standard metrics, such as the number of books published. Racialized faculty perceive that getting ahead in their professions is more dependent on who knows whom—the "old boys' network"—than on actual accomplishments in scholarship and teaching, placing them at a disadvantage compared to their white male peers. While universities have developed plans for equity and diversity, these plans are often not implemented, and the dominance of whiteness in the upper echelons of the university hierarchy persists.

Race, Racialization, and Indigeneity in Canadian Universities

Frances Henry, Enakshi Dua, Audrey Kobayashi, Carl James, Peter Li, Howard Ramos, and Malinda S. Smith

Introduction

Over the past several decades, Canada has become increasingly ethnically and racially diverse and the Canadian Indigenous population has grown significantly, yet racialized and Indigenous peoples are underrepresented in major institutions. A significant body of research and scholarship on equity and diversity in higher education has documented the persistence of systemic barriers and implicit biases faced by members of equity seeking groups—women, racialized minorities, Aboriginal[1] peoples, and persons with disabilities (Carty 1991; Mukherjee 1994; Monture-Angus 1995, 1998; Razack 1998; Dua and Lawrence 2000; Prentice 2000; Dua 2009; Henry and Tator 2009; Smith 2010). Despite the expanding research on equity and higher education, analyses of racism, racialization, and Indigeneity in the academy are notable by their absence. No major scholarly body—whether representing universities, presidents, deans, or university teachers—has given priority to the implications of the cultural heterogeneity in higher education, and none has undertaken a study of the status and everyday lived experiences of racialized scholars and scholarship in the academy. Despite many efforts, which most often amount to no more than well-worded mission statements and cosmetic changes, inequality, indifference, and reliance on outmoded conservative traditions characterize the modern neoliberal university.

Using data from our recent nationwide study *Race, Racialization and the University* which foregrounds *racism* as a critical variable shaping peoples' lives and experiences, we examine what universities have done, and question the effectiveness of their equity programs. We also set out the experiences of racialized faculty members across Canada for whom strong claims of equal opportunity have not really changed their everyday working conditions.

Henry, Frances, Enakshi Dua, Audrey Kobayashi, Carl James, Peter Li, Howard Ramos, & Malinda S. Smith. "Race, racialization and Indigeneity in Canadian universities." *Race Ethnicity and Education*, 20:3, pp. 300–314, (2017). Reprinted by permission of Taylor & Francis. www.tandfonline.com

Methodology

We employed a multileveled and mixed methods approach—census data (statistical analysis using Public Use Micro Files as well as Research Data Center original data), surveys, interviews, textural, and policy analyses. Our methodology utilized the strength of qualitative and quantitative approaches. To gain an overall picture of the university faculty population as well as their earnings, a questionnaire survey administered in eight universities,[2] and interviews with 89 racialized and Indigenous faculty, equity directors, and administrators were conducted in 12 universities selected on the basis of size, region, and interest in the subject matter. Interviewees were secured through personal contacts and snowballing techniques increased our sample size. Interviews were guided by pre-constructed questions and conducted informally ensuring confidentiality. Faculty members were generally eager to speak of their experiences; for many, this was cathartic since they rarely discussed racism.

. . .

This study is the first national study to address the status of racialized and Indigenous scholars in Canadian universities. . . . We supplemented our national analysis with more detailed study of a sample of 12 Canadian universities which represents a diversity of regions and institutions. . . .

The Context

From the perspective of racialized and Indigenous faculty members, we examine whether institutions seem ready to accommodate not only their presence but also their scholarship, pedagogy, service inclinations, and cultural and social capital shaped by their communities. We ask, what life is like for racialized and Indigenous faculty members in universities shaped by neoliberal individualism, merit, competition, and entrepreneurship (Kurasawa 2002; Luther, Whitmore, and Moreau 2003; Mahtani 2004; Newson 2012; Thornton 2012; Griffin, Bennett, and Harris 2013; Giroux 2014; James and Valluvan 2014).

Drawing on qualitative data of the experiences and perceptions of racialized and Indigenous faculty, we use the prisms of critical race theory (CRT) and whiteness, employment equity, and neoliberalism to examine how the social, political, and cultural climates of their institutions have enabled or limited their role as agents of change, and what their presence has meant in helping to advance equity in their universities. Scholars suggest that the seeming shift over the last four decades toward more accessible and inclusive universities corresponds to the neoliberal shift in society as a whole—which has operated not only to demoralize faculty members, but also to obfuscate the university's shared responsibility (Kurasawa 2002; Luther, Whitmore, and Moreau 2003; Ahmed 2012; Newson 2012; Thornton 2012; Giroux 2014). In a context in which the ideologies of neoliberalism and whiteness structure the articulation and evaluation of merit, democracy, and diversity (in both membership and scholarship), racialized and Indigenous faculty members tend to experience work situations where they have limited control over their working conditions, institutional barriers to their scholarly potential and productivity, and challenges to their professional judgements and entitlements—factors that are typically associated with a precarious work situation (see Braedley and Luxton 2010; Thomas 2010; Law Commission of Ontario 2012).

Disciplines and the departments or programs that host them often function as gateways to the academy. They may open doors but they may also put up walls and police boundaries in ways that limit access and change and, thereby, conserve the prevailing order. In order to advance equity, diversity, and complexity in the university, more attention needs to be focused on disciplines as a unit of analysis and the ways they reflect and represent historical and social realities such as diversity and decolonization. Canadian society is undergoing a fundamental demographic transformation. Despite decades of talking about equity, diversity, and inclusion in society and the academy, this demographic transformation is not reflected in the academy and the absence is especially notable in the composition of faculty and leadership, which remain overwhelming white and primarily male. The invisibility of broader representation of diversity also remains evident despite almost three decades of self-studies, which until recently have narrowly focused on the status of women. Where disciplinary diversity is evident, in hiring or teaching and research, it is primarily in the area of women, gender, and sexuality studies. This means Indigenous and racially and ethnically diverse students in many social science and humanities disciplines, in particular, never or rarely experience someone like themselves as university professors, mentors, and leaders, and as researchers and knowledge producers.

In proceeding, we discuss how the tenets of neoliberalism and whiteness structure how universities respond to perceived needs for equity programs. We first examine the policies that frame "equity" and "representation," noting the results of those programs in terms of measurable aspects, that is: increases/decreases in representation, and variation in salaries. We then address the precariousness of racialized and Indigenous faculty members' work situation using their own assessments from surveys and in-depth interviews. We discuss their perceptions of and experiences in terms of how they are positioned in the university, and the extent to which the climate in which they work opens up or limits scholarly research, teaching, and service opportunities. Finally, we address the process of racialization itself, examining the ways in which everyday events in the university create racial difference and oppression. Three main concepts underlie our research: CRT and whiteness, employment equity, and neoliberalism.

CRT and Whiteness

The project is informed by CRT (Crenshaw et al. 1995; Delgado and Stefancic 2012), including whiteness studies and intersectional thinking. Bell (1980) stressed that the systemic oppression of African Americans, and by extension Black and racialized people in many areas of the world, cannot be understood without reference to how capitalism, the free market economy, the political status quo, and other conservative institutions

maintain white privilege. Institutions of white privilege must be acknowledged if the rights and interests of non-whites are to be fully recognized. . . .

Whiteness Studies is closely aligned to CRT. It focuses on how white skin confers privilege systemically and structurally while excluding racialized people from the benefits of society. The category "white" is socially constructed, and operates in relation to "whiteness," which "refers to a set of assumptions, beliefs, and practices that place the interests and perspectives of white people at the center of what is considered normal and everyday" (Gillborn 2015, 278). Both whiteness and blackness are racialized. Whiteness studies racialize the white race and uncovers the ways in which white privilege is unconsciously acquired and exercised. White privilege is transnational and comes from the history of European imperial and colonial expansion and its continuing legacies globally. Some of the commonly held discourses labeled "discourses of domination" by Henry and Tator (2009) include the myth of color-blindness, in which people are assumed not to recognize skin color as a racial differentiating trait in making decisions. Gotanda (1991; cited in Vaught 2011) criticizes the assumption that people do not "recognize" constructs of race in making decisions and argues that such non-recognition "fosters the systematic denial of racial subordination and the psychological repression of an individual's recognition of that subordination, thereby allowing such subordination to continue." In other words, non-recognition of race permits the continued opacity of white privilege and domination.

Another analytical concept that has relevance to the present study is "intersectionality," as there are many forms of inequality that interact with one another, and individuals and groups have multiple, interacting identities. Race intersects with gender, class, disability, and other social and demographic characteristics to shape social and economic experiences. The concept, originally proposed by legal scholar Crenshaw (2002), is one that "goes beyond conventional analysis in order to focus our attention on injuries we might otherwise not recognize . . . to (1) analyze social problems more fully; (2) shape more effective interventions; and (3) promote more inclusive coalitional advocacy." In our research, we gave attention to gender and its intersectional relationship with differences in income, ethnicity, and daily lived experiences in the lives of racialized faculty. With respect to social class, Solomos has recently reiterated that class hierarchy is still fairly evident in the United Kingdom. The persistence of inequalities is primarily a function of the failure of the state to ease the erosion of the working class (BSC Conference 2015). Class and increasingly immigration have become substitutes for what he calls "color coded" racism. These factors underlie the role of racism and become the major focus of government intervention.[3]

. . .

Employment Equity

It is now more than three decades since the "Abella Commission" ([Abella] 1984) introduced the concept of Employment Equity, a made-in-Canada term intended to address barriers to entering the workplace and conditions in the workplace. Abella named four groups—women, persons with disabilities, Indigenous peoples, and members of visible (or racialized) minorities—that would be designated under Employment Equity legislation. Her recommendations were largely responsible for the 1986 adoption of an Employment Equity Act that initially applied to all federally regulated employers of a certain size. A decade later, the legislation was amended to incorporate the federal government itself and federally regulated employers under one Act, and to strengthen the planning and reporting dimensions of the policy. Within that rubric, universities fall under the Federal Contractors Program, which ties eligibility for contracts to a requirement to file reports and to set targets on equity hiring. Employment Equity programs were established in most Canadian universities in the 1990s, aimed at removing structural barriers and biases that hindered the recruitment, hiring, tenure, and promotion of racialized faculty (Dua 2009).

. . .

Neoliberalism

Our third major concept, neoliberalism, refers to the instrumental governmentality of the late 20th and early 21st Centuries. The term is rooted in monetarist policy of the Thatcher-Reagan era, with their emphasis on shrinking the state, the freedom of the market, the privileging of (certain) entrepreneurial ideas, and the rollback of government spending on social programs and policies. Neoliberal approaches include the withdrawal of governmental support for programs such as accessible education or social housing, as well as the underfunding and de-funding of grassroots and nongovernmental organizations. At the same time, we have stronger governmental intervention through an emphasis on audit culture, narrow notions of accountability and fiscal oversight, and stronger support for private business.

In Canadian universities, the rise of neoliberalism and audit culture have led to the adoption of managerialism, and widespread use of performance indicators and benchmarking. It has meant shifting funding to research projects that have the support of private businesses, and shifting university resources from supporting faculty to creating larger accounting departments with ever stronger audit requirements. All of these developments profoundly affect who gets hired and what they do, how many students they teach, how their time is apportioned, and what kinds of support and respect they receive for their research. More and more of the curriculum is taught by contract faculty rather than those in tenure-track positions. There is substantial evidence that members of the equity-seeking groups are disproportionately affected by neoliberalism.

Our Findings

Representation, Income Differentials: The Survey Results

Our analysis of census data reveals that racialized and Indigenous professors are not only under-represented in universities (a situation which worsened over time);[4] they also earn lower wages than do their white counterparts, even after controlling for variables such as years of service and academic level. These earning differentials points to a number of questions: If racialized and Indigenous professors have the qualification and human capital needed to become professors, why are they not hired at the same rate as white professors? Some people have argued that they might earn a degree but underperform in other criteria evaluated in hiring, such as publication record, lack of success in funding, and providing appropriate service to the university and community. But the onus is on those who use this argument to present convincing data. Differences in income can also be justified according to similar criteria. If racialized and Indigenous professors are less productive than their white counterparts, then this is used as justification for lower remuneration. For such an argument to hold, however, convincing data that indicate their systematic underperformance in productivity compared to white professors at all age levels are needed. At the very least, our data clearly suggest that racial inequality in representation and earnings cannot be easily dismissed by productivity differences alone.

In our national questionnaire survey of eight universities in English Canada, we found a higher number of men than women among racialized and Indigenous faculty, with the vast majority of racialized faculty (two-thirds) identifying as immigrants.[5] They disproportionately worked in Medicine/Dentistry, Engineering, and Science/Computer Science and not the Arts and Humanities; and they have worked fewer years in the academy. This pattern points to evidence of a racialized-segmented-academic-labor market in Canadian universities. While there were only eight universities enumerated in our sample, it is likely that the trend extends more widely. It is clear that far more needs to be done to diversify the entire university and not just a small number of faculties. Canadian universities and their students need more racialized professors who teach in the Social Sciences and Humanities in addition to those already teaching in Engineering, Medicine/Dentistry, and Science/Computer Science. Their perspectives can help change the social and cultural narrative of Canada to one that better reflects an increasingly multi-racial/cultural/ethnic population.

With regard to the productivity of racialized faculty across various disciplines, we found that they are "playing the game." Racialized faculty outperform their non-racialized counterparts in winning research grants and publishing articles but have few book chapters and books. It is worth noting, as heard through our interviews, that these faculty members kept up this publication record even as many were told that their research was too political, too ideological, or too rhetorical. Further, an examination of these faculty members' tenure and promotion found that racialized faculty were less likely to be awarded these benchmarks, but if they do manage to earn them, there is marginal difference in how long it took them. The survey also showed that racialized faculty members perceive tenure and promotion to be influenced as much by "soft" metrics such as personality, civility and collegiality, as by "hard" metrics like publication and winning grants. The opposite pattern is largely found with perceptions about administrative and committee appointments and hiring. Few racialized faculty agreed that equity considerations were factors affecting hiring, tenure, and promotion, as well as appointment to administrative and committee appointments. As other aspects of our study found, these findings suggest that equity policies are not working and racialized faculty are aware of this failure. We further analyzed the perceptions of work load, to find marginal differences in perceptions between racialized and non-racialized faculty.

When asked about perceptions of tenure and promotion, "hard" metrics of performance appear to be undervalued by racialized faculty. This could be because of the tensions between high rates of output and lower rates of reward for them. This is also illustrated by the higher rates of agreement by racialized faculty on the importance of "soft" metrics of performance, those that are least quantifiable and observable empirically. It appears that racialized faculty recognize that their academic output or production might matter less than affinity and network biases, such as who they know and how they get along with them. This pattern might reflect a pragmatic outlook on the devaluing of their labor and skills. Differences between racialized and non-racialized faculty members' perceptions of the role of "hard" and "soft" metrics are also seen in administrative and committee appointments. For the former, racialized faculty appear to prize "hard" metrics more than do non-racialized faculty, which may mean they have confidence in the academy once they have broken barriers into it. This suggestion is in line with the findings on the differential pathways of those who achieved tenure and promotion. . . .

As a whole we find that racialized faculty understand the Canadian academic system and "play the game." That is, they have the human capital and demonstrate a high level of performance on outcomes that should be rewarded by universities; however, their perceptions of how to best navigate that system are clearly different from those of their non-racialized colleagues. Such differences in perception are very much in line with previous research on perception of discrimination in the Canadian academy (Nakhaie 2004, 2007; Henry and Tator 2012). We believe that differences found among racialized faculty generally reflect a pragmatic and skeptical outlook on the Canadian academic system, which shows that some racialized faculty successfully navigate the system, but perhaps through a solitude of experiences that their colleagues fail to see.

University Responses to Inequities: Anti-Racist Initiatives

Our study illustrated that equity initiatives are unevenly developed. Universities vary substantially in the kinds of policies available to address inequities and racism, the mandates of the office responsible for dealing with discrimination, reporting structure, and number of staff.

We found that three dominant frameworks are deployed to address inequity—human rights, equity, and diversity frameworks. These frameworks differ in how they address racism. Human rights frameworks focus on implementing government requirements that employers have anti-harassment and anti—discrimination policies. Equity frameworks employ a broader mandate to address systemic discrimination, while diversity frameworks, emerging as a backlash against equity frameworks, are seen as less conflict ridden. Most universities have some infrastructure in place to implement policies. Thirty-five of forty-nine universities had developed dedicated offices that are directed to address harassment in the workplaces, and enhance equity. These offices often focus on faculty and staff concerns, leaving student issues to be dealt with by Ombudspersons, Student Services, or Deans. These offices vary substantially in the number of staff, and in the reporting structures. Finally, we found a proliferation of equity services, particularly in the larger universities, where senior administration appointments mandated to address equity have emerged, in addition to faculty equity offices.

In dealing with the effectiveness of equity policies in Canadian Universities, we found a broad range of mechanisms that addressed harassment, discrimination, and inequities to some extent, but all were assessed as ineffective in addressing racism. Formal processes for anti-harassment and anti-discrimination polices were riddled with ineffective procedures and resulted in conflict-ridden and unsatisfactory results. In addition, this mechanism was least able to address situations of racial harassment, bullying and discrimination. As a result, most universities attempted to resolve incidents informally. Informal mechanisms were also reported to be ineffective, however, in dealing with racism, racial harassment, and bullying. Educational workshops, despite their inability to reach most members of the university community, were assessed to be effective in shifting some aspects of institutional culture—but changing the influence of "whiteness" was still seen as a challenge. Equity committees were effective in raising concerns about inequities and proposing remedies, but as these committees did not have mandates to ensure implementation, often their efforts were for naught. Equity plans were often put forward with little consultation, and not always enforced. As a result of the ineffectiveness of these mechanisms, in many universities, senior administrators are being mandated to oversee equity. This strategy was assessed to be the most effective in furthering equity, as well as ensuring a systemic approach in which different constituencies are accountable for equity; however, senior administrators reported that resistance to their efforts limited their success.

The ineffectiveness of human rights and equity mechanisms to address racism raises serious questions. Given the expansion of efforts to address equity, why are such efforts not more effective? This question is particularly pertinent as changes that could allow these mechanisms to be more effective were identified including procedural rules and mandates, more resources, greater input from equity activists, greater monitoring, and more administrative support. Why are these mechanisms that seem to be effective in addressing other inequities so ineffective in addressing racism?

. . .

What Our Respondents Said: Interview Findings

The overall picture is of a significant group of faculty across many Canadian universities with deep-seated and profound criticisms of the academy, its structures, and its governance. The university is largely perceived to be a traditional white and male-dominated institution that is taking only minimal steps to provide an inclusive welcoming environment for its racialized and Indigenous faculty.

In reflecting on current hiring practices one faculty member commented that someone like him "would never be hired these days." For the most part, this comment sums up the sentiments of many racialized and Indigenous faculty members we interviewed about their experiences in the academy. Given their experiences, they reckoned that the "good intentions" of universities that brought them onto campuses in the 1980s were mere "rhetoric" without substance—without the necessary institutional policies and practices that created an environment where the

different knowledge and perspectives of Indigenous and racialized scholars were accommodated and incorporated. On this basis, they reasoned that universities were "starting to become less progressive," in that they were reluctant to have more racialized and Indigenous scholars on their campuses. As Giroux (2014, 17) argues, today's universities operate within a culture in which the academics best able to survive its challenges are those most comfortable with "the corporatization of the university and the new regimes of neoliberal governance" where they are "beholden to corporate interests, career building and the insular discourses that accompany specialized scholarship." Many racialized respondents argued that only specific types of knowledge are recognized as legitimate, and Indigenous faculty members talked of their decolonial struggles to re-center Aboriginal history, philosophy, and culture and to incorporate anti-racist models of knowledge. In doing so, they are often met with deep resistance from white students, colleagues, and administration. Racialized faculty commonly experience demands from minority students wishing to have mentors and role models whom they believe can relate to them and their lived experiences.

The Indigenous and racialized faculty members also told us about sitting in hiring committee meetings and being part of conversations where they observed affinity, network and accent biases such that who one knew (or her/his network of friends) and accent (having a "foreign" accent was considered a problem because students will not be able to understand the speaker) operated as invisible barriers to faculty appointments. And there were also the questions about these scholars' "foreign" credentials if not obtained in Europe or North America, their ability to secure research and program funding, and their capacity to live up to expectations and images as representatives of their ethno-racial groups. These demands, questions, and expectations, combined with the absence of mentorship, the problematic relationships with their white colleagues and students, the insecurity generated by the tenure and promotion processes, and their struggles to be taken seriously and gain respect, contribute to precarious working situations and social relationships in which Indigenous and racialized faculty members found themselves, as well as the psychological state of ambivalence, skepticism, uncertainty, low self-esteem, hopelessness, and anguish they felt in their job.[6]

The presence of some Indigenous and racialized faculty disguises the fact that there has been little or no change in the ways institutions operate. Some faculty members increasingly feel marginalized in university environments that appear to be reverting to a traditional, white, homogeneous character, even as the university advertisements declare commitment to having an ethnically and racially diverse faculty body and affirmative action appointment committees are charged with implementing equity policies. Racialized and Indigenous scholars are often called upon to mentor a diverse student population, but such work taxes their time, and it is clear that their numbers are insufficient to address the needs of a future generation. Further, conscious of the fact that universities insist on having "academic stars," many racialized and Indigenous scholars are working diligently to prove themselves worthy of their tenured appointments and, in some cases, to prevent the demands of teaching and service (including that to their own communities) from interfering with their scholarship and limiting their productivity. But the reality is: the sometimes new, emerging, and different scholarship in which many racialized and Indigenous scholars engage has yet to earn the recognition and credibility. Conceding that they tend to be viewed as "representatives" of their communities and as narrowly concerned with issues of equity, these faculty members acknowledged that how their behaviors and scholarly output are read have implications for the future of equity policies and practices, particularly with regard to hiring faculty members from their communities. Theirs is a precarious work situation where they constantly struggle against marginalization, racialization, tokenization, ghettoization, and alienation expressed in the demands that they conform, fit in, be star scholars, and meet an "academic standard" that devalues the critical and transformative knowledge they bring to scholarship and the institution.

Conclusion

> If universities can't figure out how to deal constructively with our differences then you just have to give up hope generally. If we can't do it in universities then what hope does the rest of our society have? (interviewee)

Four decades of equity policies have failed to transform the academy significantly to make it more diverse and reflective of the broader society and student body. In part, this is because of structural barriers and discriminatory practices that have functioned to exclude and stall transformation. It is also a result of the inadequately examined preference for sameness that leads to practices of replication. Change has also eluded universities because of the subtle workings of unacknowledged biases that privilege affinity and the needs of dominant insider groups. Unconscious biases have a significant impact on the career trajectories of racialized and Indigenous scholars and women in the contemporary academy. The cumulative biases and structural barriers mapped along a spectrum or pipeline make visible the challenge for racialized and Indigenous faculty not only at the point of entry but, potentially, at every major stage of their academic careers. The biases tell a story about a potential obstacle to career mobility that many racialized and Indigenous scholars face. The complex dynamics of subtle biases and structural barriers also make visible how much harder they have to work in order to thrive and succeed in the academy. The findings suggest that biases and assumptions of whiteness have exacted an incalculable cost for many racialized and Indigenous scholars. They rob the academy and the broader society of a wealth of talent and the invaluable heterogeneity of people, their knowledge, and the perspectives that could make universities more equitable, diverse and excellent.

. . .

Despite talk about an inclusive curriculum, and demands from Indigenous movements aimed at indigenizing, decolonizing, and internationalizing the curriculum in the westernized university, the scholarship on race/ethnicity, Indigeneity and, to a lesser extent, gender, remain on the margins of teaching and learning. Many students can graduate from a degree program and never grapple with issues of racism and decoloniality. This issue is particularly true of graduate programs engaged in training the next generation of scholars It also means that graduate programs are not providing new scholars the tools they need to grapple with colonial history, its relationship to power and the hegemony of imperial and colonial narratives that have established the terms of, and tools for, conversation in the westernized university.

If universities are places into which racialized and Indigenous people will gain access, fully participate, attain tenure and promotion, and have their scholarship recognized, then critical attention must be given to how the existing diversity discourse sustains color-coded power relations, inculcates expectations, and conveys reminders (e.g. "you know why you were hired"—to represent "your" communities and take care of marginalized students' and communities' concerns) that racialized and Indigenous faculty are not recognized or accepted as legitimate members of the academy with all the earned rights and privileges. What is clear, despite their increasing presence on university campuses, is that racialized and Indigenous faculty continue to struggle against their historical exclusion, and to justify the special measures, however limited, that have been implemented to make their presence in the academy possible. Frequent reminders of the reasons for their presence in the academy mean that they will constantly have to struggle against not only their own erasure, but also that of the faculty members they mentor, the students they teach, the research they conduct, and the scholarship they produce. That silence about race and racial issues remains the norm and does nothing to address the reality that race and racism have shaped and continue to shape the experiences, opportunities, and perceptions of racialized and Indigenous scholars. If the challenges that these faculty members face are to be effectively addressed, then, an institutional commitment to equity is integral to creating a welcoming and supportive academic culture.

Notes

1. Federal Government documents use the term "Aboriginal." We, however, prefer to describe this population as "Indigenous."

2. It should be noted that while the census data were sufficient to allow us to disaggregate Indigenous from racialized faculty (reference to in the census as "visible minority"), for our survey data, the numbers were too small for us to do the same. Hence, our reference here to racialized faculty is a combination of Indigenous and racialized respondents.

3. Due to limited resources and using an analytic framework that foregrounds race and racism, we were only able to get at social class in relation to tenured versus non-tenured faculty. For basically the same reasons, we were unable to include disability because that data are even more unavailable than for race.

4. Interestingly, the situation has remained about the same and slightly improved for Indigenous faculty.

5. Many of these respondents could have been graduates of a Canadian university, but many were likely foreign hires. This raises concerns about what is happening to Canadian-born racialized doctorates who appear not to be transitioning into the academic labor market. It is a problem seen in other job sectors, and one that is raising concern over potential inequality and alienation from Canadian society (Reitz and Bannerjee 2007).

6. In their study of Black male faculty in white university campuses, Griffin, Ward, and Phillips (2014: 1369) found that their everyday routine experiences not only led to "microaggressions," but also to psychological states such as "imposter syndrome and racial battle fatigue. . . . Imposter syndrome refers to strong feelings of self-doubt despite one's intelligence and credentials . . . while racial battle fatigue marks the physical, mental, and emotional stress that racialized oppression brings forth."

References

Abella, R. 1984. *Equality in Employment: A Royal Commission Report*. Ottawa: Minister of Supply and Services.

Ahmed, S. 2012. *On Being Included: Racism and Diversity in Institutional Life*. Durham: Duke University Press.

Bell Jr., D. A. 1980. "Brown V. Board of Education and the Interest-convergence Dilemma". *Harvard Law Review* 93: 518–33.

Braedley, S., and M. Luxton. 2010. "Competing Philosophies: Neoliberalism and the Challenges of Everyday Life". In *Neoliberalism and Everyday Life*, edited by S. Braedley and M. Luxton, 3–21. Montreal: McGill-Queen's University Press.

British Sociological Association Annual Conference. 2015. *Societies in Transition: Progression or Regression*. Glasgow: Caledonian University.

Carty, L. 1991. "Black Women in Academia". In *Unsettling Relations*, edited by Himani Bannerji, Linda Carty, Karl Dehli, Susan Heald, and Kate McKenna, 13–44. Toronto: Women's Press.

Crenshaw, K. 2002. "The First Decade: Critical Reflections, or 'a Foot in the Closing Door'". *UCLA Law Review* 49: 1343–72.

Crenshaw, K., N. Gotanda, G. Peller, and K. Thomas. 1995. *Critical Race Theory: Key Writings That Formed the Movement*. New York: New Press.

Delgado, R., and J. Stefancic. 2012. *Critical Race Theory: An Introduction*. 2nd ed. New York: New York University Press.

Dua, Enakshi. 2009. "Evaluation of the Effectiveness of Anti-racist Policies in Canadian Universities: Issues of Implementation of Policies by Senior Administration". In *Racism in the Academy*, edited by Frances Henry and Carol Tator, 49–74. Calgary: University of Toronto Press.

Dua, Enakshi, and Bonita Lawrence. 2000. "Whose Canada Is It? White Hegemony in University Classrooms, with Bonita Lawrence". *Atlantis* 25 (2). Spring.

Gillborn, D. 2015. "Intersectionality, Critical Race Theory, and the Primacy of Racism: Race, Class, Gender, and Disability in Education". *Qualitative Inquiry* 21 (3): 277–87.

Giroux, H. A. 2014. *Neoliberalism's War on Higher Education*. Toronto: Between the Lines.

Gotanda, N. 1991. Cited in: S. F. Vaught Racism. *Public Schooling and the Entrenchment of White Supremacy*. Albany, N.Y: State University of New York Press, p. 16.

Griffin, K. A., J. C. Bennett, and J. Harris. 2013. "Marginalizing Merit?: Gender Differences in Black Faculty D/Discourses on Tenure, Advancement, and Professional Success". *The Review of Higher Education* 36 (4): 489–512.

Griffin, R. A., L. Ward, and A. R. Phillips. 2014. "Still Flies in Buttermilk: Black Male Faculty, Critical Race Theory, and Composite Counter Story telling". *International Journal of Qualitative Studies in* 27 (10): 1354–75.

Henry, F., and C. Tator, eds. 2009. *Racism in the Canadian University: Demanding Social Justice, Inclusion, and Equity*. Toronto: University of Toronto Press.

Henry, F., and C. Tator. 2012. "Interviews with Racialized Faculty Members in Canadian Universities". *Canadian Ethnic Studies* 44 (1): 75–99.

James, M., and S. Valluvan. 2014. "Higher Education: A Market for Racism?" *Darkmatter in the Ruins of Imperial Culture*. Accessed April. http://www.darkmatter101.org/site/2014/04/25/highereducation-a-market-for-racism/

Kurasawa, F. 2002. "Which Barbarians at the Gates? From the Culture Wars to Market Orthodoxy in the North American Academy". *Canadian Review of Sociology and Anthropology* 39 (3): 323–47.

Law Commission of Ontario. 2012. *Vulnerable Workers and Precarious Work: Final Report*. Accessed December 2014. http://www.lco-cdo.org/en/vulnerable-workers-final-report

Luther, R. E., E. Whitmore, and B. Moreau, eds. 2003. *Seen but Not Heard: Aboriginal Women and Women of Colour in the Academy. Feminist Voices #11*. Ottawa: Canadian Research Institute for the Advancement of Women.

Mahtani, M. 2004. "Mapping Race and Gender in the Academy: The Experiences of Women of Colour Faculty and Graduate Students in Britain, the US and Canada". *Journal of Geography in Higher Education* 28 (1): 91–99.

Monture-Angus, P. 1995. *Thunder in My Soul: A Mohawk Woman Speaks*. Halifax: Fernwood.

Monture-Angus, P. 1998. "Standing against Canadian Law: Naming Omissions of Race, Culture and Gender". *Yearbook of New Zealand Jurisprudence* 2: 7–29.

Mukherjee, A. P. 1994. *Oppositional Aesthetics: Readings from a Hyphenated Space*. Toronto: TSAR Publications.

Nakhaie, M. R. 2004. "Who Controls Canadian Universities? Ethnoracial Origins of Canadian University Administrators and Faculty's Perception of Mistreatment". *Canadian Ethnic Studies* 26 (1): 19–46.

Nakhaie, M. R. 2007. "Universalism, Ascription and Academic Rank: Canadian Professors, 1987–2000". *Canadian Review of Sociology and Anthropology* 44 (3): 361–86.

Newson, J. 2012. "University-on-the-Ground: Reflections on the Canadian Experience". In *Reconsidering Knowledge: Feminism and the Academy*, edited by M. Luxton and M. J. Mossman, 96–127. Halifax: Fernwood Publishing.

Prentice, S. 2000. "The Conceptual Politics of Chilly Climate Controversies". *Gender and Education* 12: 195–207.

Razack, S. 1998. *Looking White People in the Eye: Gender, Race and Culture in Courtrooms and Classrooms.* Toronto: University of Toronto Press.

Reitz, J., and R. Bannerjee. 2007. "Psychosocial Integration of Second and Third Generation Racialized Youth in Canada". *Canadian Diversity/Diversité Canadienne* 6 (2): 54–57.

Smith, M. S. 2010. "Gender, Whiteness, and 'Other Others' in the Academy". In *States of Race: Critical Race Feminism for the 21st Century*, edited by S. Razack, S. Thobani, and M. Smith. Toronto: Between the Lines Press.

Thomas, M. 2010. "Neoliberalism, Racialization, and the Regulation of Employment Standards". In *Neoliberalism and Everyday Life*, edited by S. Braedley and M. Luxton, 68–89. Montreal: McGill-Queen's University Press.

Thornton, M. 2012. "Universities Upside Down: The Impact of the New Knowledge Economy". In *Reconsidering Knowledge: Feminism and the Academy*, edited by M. Luxton and M. J. Mossman, 76–95. Fernwood: Halifax.

Part VII

The Gendered Workplace

Arguably the biggest social shift in high-income countries in the twentieth century has been the mass entry of women with children into the paid workforce. Yet they are not there on equal terms, as gender disparities between men and women are stubbornly persistent. These disparities are least evident at the beginning of men's and women's working lives, widening slowly as time goes by and as other life events (particularly child-bearing) exert different pressures on women and on men. This section, thus, should be read in conjunction with the section on the gendered family to appreciate the double impact of work life and family life in shaping differences and inequalities. Men and women are distributed non-randomly throughout the workforce, with different genders clustered in different sectors and different types of jobs. This clustering leads to certain jobs and sectors acquiring gendered reputations as "men's work" or "women's work."

In the last four decades women have made significant inroads into career areas that were formerly bastions of masculinity, such as medicine or law. Men, however, have been much less likely to "desegregate" women-dominated occupations such as nursery-school teaching or cosmetology. For those men who do enter women-dominated fields, negotiating the pitfalls of being the "wrong" sex for the job means finding one's professional way through a minefield of gender and sexuality, as Ranson shows.

At the other end of the spectrum, the firefighters interviewed by Pacholok inhabit an occupational world characterized by the hallmarks of stereotypical masculinity—risk, danger, strength, and protecting others. However, as Pacholok demonstrates, masculinity is not embedded in the work itself but is constructed through discourse and representations as the different groups of firefighters talk about their work and rank themselves against their peers.

Although paid work is a necessity for economic survival, and can be a source of great satisfaction, it can also be a site of danger and gendered oppression. Robillard and co-authors consider the plight of women who are temporary foreign workers, both in agriculture and as domestic workers. Far from the high-status firefighters and engineers studied by Pacholok and Ranson, these migrant workers are rendered invisible because of where they work, behind the doors of family homes or in out-of-the-way rural areas. Robillard and colleagues use the concept of "structural violence" to describe the intersections of gender, class, and nationality that work against these women.

O'Donnell and MacIntosh take on a different form of gendered stress in their study of men who experience workplace bullying. Acknowledging that one has been the victim of bullying is at odds with the hegemonic version of masculinity that holds men should be strong, tough, and, if all else fails, silent. Identifying oneself as a victim of bullying carries a stigma, which these men must navigate even as they seek out relief from the harassment they endure. O'Donnell and MacIntosh examine help-seeking behaviour and the negotiations of masculinity that accompany it.

Questions for Critical Thought

1. Are you currently training for a particular type of work, or do you have a particular career in mind? Do you expect that your gender will influence your success in this career?

2. If you work with people of different genders, whether in a part-time or full-time job, how do you think gender affects workplace experiences? If your workplace is dominated by one gender, why is that the case?

3. Why do you think women still make less money in their paid jobs then men? Is it because of individual choices or systemic barriers? Or both? Or neither?

4. What workplaces have you encountered as a worker, customer, or visitor that are dominated by one sex or the other? What workplaces have you encountered that are more equally divided between the sexes?

5. How would you react if you encountered a man doing a "feminized" job such as nursing? Would you react differently if you encountered a woman doing a "masculinized" job such as firefighting?

6. Many of the readings in this section emphasize relations and interactions among co-workers in the workplace. How important are these relations or interactions to your own job satisfaction? How do ideas about gender get reinforced or resisted through these connections between co-workers?

7. Paid work is important because it provides income, but the studies here suggest that paid work also contributes to individuals' sense of identity and selfhood. Do you think your identity is the same as what you do for money? What are the impacts on identity and selfhood of not working for pay?

Chapter 27

Overview

Engineering is one of the last bastions of male dominance in the professional world. Women who enter this profession, however, do not necessarily face isolation or discrimination—until family life enters the picture. Gillian Ranson argues that women enter the profession as "conceptual men" who fit easily into the engineering mainstream. However, when this illusion of being conceptual men can no longer be sustained—when pregnancy, childbirth, and child-rearing enter the picture—women find that they can no longer be "one of the boys." Women without children believe that if they were to become parents their career options would be narrowed, and they are right, judging by the experiences of their peers who did go on to become mothers.

The women in Ranson's study understand their circumstances as the result of choices that they made as individuals—to pursue engineering as a career, to move into part-time or consulting work, or to seek out more time at home with their children. Their experiences contrast with the experiences of fathers who are engineers, whom Ranson interviewed in an earlier study. These men were able to hew out their own compromises and work schedules with the assistance of a partner who either worked part time or was not in paid employment.

The experiences of the women in this study call into question the very organization of engineering as a profession. It is predicated on the existence of a workforce made up of individuals with no pressing commitment or family priorities that might interfere with the job. Parenthood—more specifically, motherhood—disrupts the presumption that all workers can and should fit into this mould. However, gendered divisions of unpaid labour, such as those discussed in other articles in this section, mean that the brunt of this disruption is borne by women.

No Longer "One of the Boys"

Negotiations with Motherhood, as Prospect or Reality, among Women in Engineering

Gillian Ranson[1]

Women who train and work as professional engineers in Canada and other industrialized countries are women operating on male turf. Unlike professions such as medicine and law, both of which are much closer to gender parity, engineering remains "archetypically masculine" (Wajcman, 1991: 145).

Ranson, Gillian. "No Longer 'One of the Boys': Negotiations with Motherhood, as Prospect or Reality, among Women in Engineering," *Canadian Review of Sociology & Anthropology* 42(2) (2005): 145–66. Reprinted by permission of John Wiley & Sons, Inc.

In spite of nearly two decades of "women into engineering" campaigns supported by government and industry, the numbers of women entering engineering have been described as "derisory in most countries" (Faulkner, 2000: 92). The Canadian Council of Professional Engineers (CCPE) notes that, though the proportion of women in Canadian engineering schools increased annually after 1972, in the last few years it has levelled off at about 20 per cent (CCPE, 2003). While hardly derisory, these numbers fall far short of gender parity.

Retention of women in engineering over the long haul is also likely to be a problem given that the growth in numbers of those actually practising the profession is among women in their late twenties and early thirties (CCPE, 1998). These women are also at the age where family formation becomes salient. The arrival of children seems to be one critical point at which women, but not men, leave the profession, move to part-time work, and in many other ways put their careers "on the back burner" (Ranson, 1998, 2000).

Motherhood, it seems clear, is a significant watershed, and one that policy-makers and others concerned about retaining women in engineering should take seriously. But the reasons why it is such a watershed—and hence what needs to be done to compensate for its effects—may be more complicated than the conventional explanations about work and family balance suggest. A more elaborated explanation is that motherhood, as embodied and as material experience, exposes a major fallacy inherent in the liberal discourses of equality and gender neutrality, which establish the terms for women's entry into male-dominated occupations and workplaces in the first place. These terms allow women to enter, not as women, but as conceptual men (Snitow, 1990: 26). This conceptual cover is blown when they become, or think about becoming, mothers. For many women (especially those who themselves internalize the gender neutrality discourse), actual or prospective motherhood compels them to confront identities as "engineer" and "mother" that may be "mutually incongruous" (Jorgenson, 2000: 7) and require complex negotiation and management.

In this paper I examine this more nuanced explanation, and explore its implications for all women in male-dominated occupations and workplaces who face the challenges of being "travellers in a male world" (Marshall, 1984; Gherardi, 1996).

Women in a Man's World

Recent women entrants to male-dominated occupations have had more legal, and, increasingly, cultural support for their presence on male turf. But while the terms of their participation have changed somewhat, difficulties persist. A 1992 report by the Canadian Committee on Women in Engineering cited many stories of sexism, systemic discrimination and workplace inequality, and a series of "common and difficult" barriers faced by women engineers (Canadian Committee on Women in Engineering, 1992: 60).

Why should such barriers persist, especially in a discursive climate of gender equality and "family-friendly" workplaces? Acker (1990) contends that organizations are not gender-neutral spaces that women may enter on the same footing as men; neither can a "job" be defined as abstract and gender-neutral, performed by an abstract and disembodied "worker" who exists only in relation to the job. Acker's widely cited argument is that in the real world of actual workers, the closest approximation to the disembodied worker who exists only for the job is "the male worker whose life centers on his full-time, life-long job, while his wife or another woman takes care of his personal needs and his children" (Acker, 1990: 149).

Acker's description was, until recently, a good fit for most engineers. Recent initiatives to get women into engineering have usually been predicated on the assumption that "women must be modified to fit into engineering, not the other way round" (Faulkner, 2000: 93). In ethnographic research on engineering women in a variety of educational and work settings, Eisenhart and Finkel (1998) found that organizational expectations regarding commitment to workplace activities and the worker identity favoured people who were able to put work demands first. At the same time, these expectations were perceived by everyone concerned, women and men alike, as gender-neutral. The researchers came to view gender neutrality as a socially and culturally constructed discourse that "confers legitimacy on women's professional contribution only when they act like men" and "makes discussion of women's distinctive issues virtually impossible" (Eisenhart and Finkel, 1998: 181).

Mothers in a Man's World

Motherhood as a barrier to women's career progress in engineering is demonstrated in much research through the 1990s. Studies in the United States (McIlwee and Robinson,

1992), Britain (Devine, 1992; Evetts, 1994, 1996; Corcoran-Nantes and Roberts, 1995; Wajcman, 1998) and Canada (Ranson, 1998, 2000) all point to the challenges for women in combining "masculine" professional work and motherhood. They may find themselves, as noted earlier, in workplaces in which a discourse of gender neutrality masks clearly masculinist expectations about work performance and career progress. At the same time, they confront cultural expectations about mothers, framed around a dominant ideology of "intensive mothering" (Hays, 1996; Arendell, 2000) that directly contradicts workplace expectations.

In contrast, the men with whom these women work are not subject to the same expectations regarding their family involvement. These men are much more likely than their women colleagues to have partners who can take on the bulk of family responsibilities (Wajcman, 1998; Ranson, 2000).[2] For most men, the prevailing cultural expectation is that they will be responsible for their family's financial provision, whether or not their contribution is supplemented by working partners, and whether or not they are also involved caregivers (Christiansen and Palkovitz, 2001; Ranson, 2001).

Organizational responses in the form of "family-friendly" policies and programs would seem to be the way to overcome this under-resourcing. But research evidence suggests they are not helping nearly as much as company rhetoric and popular discourse would suggest. While policies like parental leave or flexible work schedules are generally couched in gender-neutral terms, and are purported to be directed to both women and men, in practice their take-up by men has been minimal (Andrews and Bailyn, 1993; Pleck, 1993; Rapoport and Bailyn, 1996; Hochschild, 1997). This constitutes women as the prime beneficiaries of such policies, and further entrenches the idea that they are special concessions or benefits for women (Jones and Causer, 1995; Lewis, 1997) rather than rights to which all workers are entitled.

Managing Gender

If women's entry to male occupational turf is largely based on liberal assumptions that women are for practical purposes the same as men, it

follows that women themselves will need to "manage gender" in order to fit themselves into existing organizational cultures and structures (Rubin, 1997: 31). Whatever their standing as "conceptual men," real-life embodied women must negotiate feminine subjectivity as well.[3] This is neatly illustrated by one of Miller's (2004) interviewees, a woman engineer working in the same city as the women in this study:

> When you go to the field, you don't take a purse because you're really rubbing that female helplessness thing in, and you put all your junk—the female hygiene stuff—in your little pockets. Another thing you do when you work downtown is you always wear wide skirts because sometimes you're going to be going to the field in the afternoon. And you can wear high heels to the office but keep a pair of flat loafers there. . . . (Miller, 2004: 54)

While some of the women engineers in a 1999 study by Kvande [1999] did indeed, as noted above, strive to be "one of the boys," others drew on other discourses (or, in Kvande's terms, constructed other femininities) that corresponded to a view of themselves as *different from*, not the same as, their male colleagues. Kvande found that the women who saw themselves in this way were invariably women with children. Jorgenson, whose research (2000, 2002) focused particularly on the ways women engineers with children managed the potentially contradictory discourses of motherhood and engineering, found similar complexity. Sometimes the women positioned themselves as competent career-oriented professionals, sometimes as caring mothers, but usually with an awareness of the incompatibility of the mother–engineer identities. As one of her interviewees commented, "I didn't want to try to be the perfect engineer because I knew I wanted a family" (Jorgenson, 2002: 370).

Jorgenson's work summarizes the position outlined at the start of the paper, that women enter engineering work as "conceptual men," and that motherhood is, in many cases, a "defining moment," separating mothers from others.

"Conceptual Men," Alternative Subjectivities, and Motherhood in Engineering

Women without Children

Sally, who was 41 and childless, provides a good example of the sort of long-term engineering careers available to competent and highly motivated women able to be single-minded about their professional work. This was not the case for the younger women, who still needed to confront the possibility of motherhood. Among these women, particular understandings both of motherhood and of engineering work framed talk that was also significantly shaped by age and family or relationship circumstance.

The experience of Sally—a senior manager in a major oil company—provides a link to the issue of motherhood because she attributed her career success to the fact that—not from choice—she didn't have children. Sally noted that despite her company's public claims to being "family-friendly," the "day-to-day business environment" included the perception that to get ahead "you've got to put in the long hours" and be "willing to sacrifice." Asked if she thought more women in the organization would make a difference, she said: "I think that may be the sort of thing that *keeps* women from making a difference." She was explicit about the difference it had made to her career: "Because I don't have the child connection . . . I have been able to, if need be, go the extra mile, every time they've asked."

The single women's responses to the prospect of motherhood were provisional and speculative, since all saw a permanent relationship as a prerequisite. For example, Rosemary, four years post-graduation, commented:

> I'm probably indifferent either way, you know. I think it would depend on my spouse. Like, if I met somebody and they wanted kids, then I would be open to having one, maybe two. And hopefully maybe they would like

to adopt children rather than (laughter) . . . I just can't see myself just, just staying home and being a mom. . . . So, but if, hey, my previous boyfriend, he was more than happy to be a stay-at-home dad. So that, that's a fit for me as well.

In this way, at the hypothetical level at least, she constructed a family scenario that would allow her to remain "one of the boys." This scenario did not challenge the "intensive" version of mothering that would remove her from the workplace. Instead, Rosemary discursively nominated her hypothetical partner as the full-time caregiver, and gave herself a family role similar to those of her male colleagues. In other words, she positioned herself as a conceptual "father."

Like Rosemary, Julia was also 27 and four years past graduation. Though she did not self-identify as "one of the boys" in the way Rosemary did, she was relishing the hands-on, technical, outdoor nature of her fieldwork job. But she also saw this way of working as contingent:

> [N]ow I don't have the five-year to ten-year plan. I mean, between you and I, I would love to be a stay-at-home mom. . . . But, I'm not married. And I don't have any kids. So *until then*, I'm going to do the best job that I can, and follow my career, and if it happens, it happens. If it doesn't, it doesn't (emphasis added).

Julia's vision of motherhood included the view that "if you have children . . . somebody should be at home"—and she was clear that, in her family, unlike Rosemary's, she would be that somebody. She presented this version of mothering as incompatible with engineering work: "If I could work from home, or if I could work part-time, then that would be my ideal. But in engineering, you don't seem to be able to do that. . . ."

Other single, childless women, with more work experience than Julia, took her story to another level: children needed care that mothers should provide and that they, as mothers, would potentially be willing to provide; in the absence of these family obligations, they were devoting their energies to engineering work; this engineering work was getting to be of a kind and at a level that would not easily accommodate maternal responsibilities. Thus, for example, Sarah—a 34-year-old engineer who had recently been promoted to manage a major energy project for her company—expressed excitement that this project could be "a stepping stone" to "a lot more exciting projects." Asked if she thought she would be able to combine her present job with children and family responsibilities, Sarah said:

> I think I would. I know women that do do that here but they have to have a very understanding spouse that's more flexible. It's very difficult to do this job and have a spouse that's doing exactly the same thing with exactly the same sort of aspirations, I think.

Sarah's immediate qualification of the possibility of a work–family balance in her current job (by positioning herself, like Rosemary, as a father) was qualified still further by her comment later that she "couldn't go on maternity leave in the next two years" even if she wanted to, and that she had "sort of accepted the fact that [having children] might not happen." Sarah had recognized, in Wajcman's (1996) terms, the "domestic basis for the managerial career."

Different versions of the engineering—motherhood balance came from women who were in permanent relationships with men, and who were all anticipating having children sooner or later. These women were in two groups. When interviewed, four were recent graduates, within six years of graduation, and all were in their twenties. Three were a little older and more experienced (all were 34 and had 12 years of engineering experience behind them).

Among the younger four, the ideology of intensive mothering appeared in comments rejecting nannies or daycare as strategies enabling full-time work while having young children. But they also rejected the stay-at-home mother option; all planned to work part-time when their children were young. They all assumed that part-time work would be viable, even when—as in Sheila's

case—there was some evidence from a colleague working an 80 per cent schedule that it might be hard to manage. (Sheila commented, "I honestly think that she's a little bit less organized and that I could probably handle it a little better.") These women also expressed a strong sense of entitlement with respect to what their employer ought to do for them. And they were united in their conviction that their partners—all of whom were also engineers—would share the childcare responsibilities, likely also moving to part-time work to do so. This conviction was striking, given their collective experience of working in resoundingly masculinist workplace cultures where men, for the most part, were able to delegate their family responsibilities, and where male engineers working less than full-time were almost unheard of.

The three older women were characteristic of many women in male-dominated occupations in having deferred childbearing (see Ranson, 1998). All three spoke about their work, and their current workplaces, in terms that clearly indicated career success: a raise or stock options whenever she thought about leaving (Marcie); promotion from a junior position to the same grade as her male colleagues (Helen); a senior management position in a company she had helped to grow (Shelley). All three intended to keep working after having children, and all three, in different ways, planned to make their experience and seniority work for them as they thought about accommodating their jobs to family responsibilities. As Shelley said:

> I've been with the company for a long time and I've always been a very good employee. As a result I'm paid well now, and I have a lot of responsibility and respect [within] the company. And, you know, that's my money to cash in when I need to negotiate a deal. . . . A position of strength to bargain from is always a good thing.

What seems to be the case is that this position of strength is achieved by proof of successful career performance according to male standards—in other words, by women paying their dues as "conceptual men." This is not to suggest that these women achieved their success by aligning themselves with men. For example, some of the experience that earned Helen her current job was gained in an overtly sexist work environment that she was "not ever going to be a part of." It is also not to suggest that "male standards" are uniform. For example, most of Shelley's male colleagues and superiors were about her age; she suggested that their relative youth made them less conventional. But in every case, the standards in place were standards established by men. Having met those standards, women felt freer to negotiate as women for changes they needed to accommodate their family responsibilities.

To summarize, the women without children produced a number of different scenarios for the way motherhood might combine with engineering: motherhood viewed as incompatible with engineering, and chosen as its alternative; motherhood refused, delegated, or privatized to enable the continuation of the engineering career; motherhood and engineering combined by means of modified work arrangements (earned by male-defined career success), and the equal participation of husbands and partners. Of these scenarios, only the first assumed that motherhood and engineering were truly "mutually incongruous," and this was not a common position. But the "strong" view of intensive mothering it implied appeared in more diluted form in all the accounts. This, in turn, shaped how women thought they would need to accommodate their work. Unless (as in Rosemary's case) they planned to become "fathers," motherhood was seen as putting an end to business as usual.

Women with Children

The choices and accommodations anticipated by the childless women turned out to be a generally accurate summary of the routes the mothers took. As with the mothers in Kvande's study, though, they were generally more likely to position themselves as women, differently situated from their current or former male colleagues.

Five of the women gave up full-time engineering work at or shortly after the arrival of their children. At the time they were interviewed, two were not in paid employment at all, and spoke as if a return to engineering was unlikely. Holly commented: "As soon as I had a baby, my total perspective changed." For Jenny, the other stay-at-home mother, her first baby's arrival signalled not so much a change of perspective as the opportunity to retreat gratefully from a world she had never wholeheartedly embraced. Jenny's choice was motherhood over engineering:

> It's not a door that I've closed and I don't have bad memories. Although what I hear about engineering now . . . I think, oh, man, I don't want to get into that any more. I really don't.

The others had had longer and more conventionally successful careers as engineers before having children. All undertook intermittent consulting contracts, but at the time they were interviewed, none were working more than a day or so a week. Kate, at home with her first child, (aged nine months at the time of the interview) framed her stay-at-home-mom status as "a wonderful break" after having worked in engineering for 15 years. The baby was long-awaited. She commented: "I didn't sort of have huge expectations of it but when we finally did [have] him, I just thought, oh, why wouldn't I just kind of stay and enjoy him?" Kate had worked long enough, and recently enough, that the engineer identity was still strong ("even though I'm not working I'll always be an engineer"). But asked whether she would be an engineer 10 years down the road, she replied, "Probably not."

Lisa's work history was similar to Kate's. She had worked full-time for 10 years for one company, then switched to part-time with the birth of her first child. But half-time work with a second child heightened the tension between work and family responsibilities:

> I wasn't doing a good job with anything. . . . If it had gone on any longer I would have regretted it and you can't live your life like that. You've just got to do what you know you can.

Like Julia, cited earlier, Lisa had broader aspirations about family and motherhood, to which this decision conformed:

> I really wanted to be the one with the babies. I wanted to nurse them, I wanted to raise them. . . . It would have been a sacrifice to not be home with them, to me. I really wanted to do that. It was the life experience I wanted to have.

While for all four women, the commitment to motherhood rather than engineering could be construed as voluntary, for Ellie, the fifth woman in the group, it was not. At the time she was interviewed she was recovering from two very difficult pregnancies, residual physical problems following childbirth, and an extremely demanding second baby. ("I think I literally lost my mind," she commented.) In Rothman's (1994) terms, she was experiencing the "embodied challenges" to working like a man—challenges she resisted as much as she could. Echoes of the energetic and driven women engineers described by Kate appeared in her talk of working while pregnant and sick, or doing from her hospital bed the work her (female) replacement was supposed to be doing. Ellie spoke optimistically about returning to work: "I do want to work. I really enjoy working. I never wanted really to be a stay-at-home." The clear implication was that when she was physically able, she would pick up her working life.

Six of the women with children continued to work full-time, or close to full-time, in engineering jobs. But the conscious downplaying of career goals in order to accommodate family responsibilities expressed by Lisa was evident in the talk of these women as well. It was also reflected in their practices—a shift in the kind of work being done to something perceived to be less stressful (Linda), a refusal of promotion in order to remain in a familiar and manageable work environment (Joanne), a move from permanent employment to consulting as a means to achieve flexibility (Kelly), the use of a pregnancy to signal a shifting of gears after a successful corporate career (Hilary), cutting back to four instead of five days a week (Shauna). These work arrangements were accompanied by talk that linked them to family benefits.

The third group of mothers is those whose careers appeared on the surface to have been less affected by motherhood. Given the way these women were working, and the jobs they were doing, they could be described as mothers in careers more often associated with men. The nine women in this group had all reached senior levels of management and/or technical specialty. But in this group also, the balance of motherhood and career was complicated and fluid. It was also in this group that the most vivid images of "conceptual men" becoming mothers emerged. Cassie was one example. As a woman who had always been able to work as "one of the boys," Cassie downplayed issues of gender in the workplace, noting that she had never experienced "discrimination, or anything like that," and was "not a supporter of affirmative action–type programs." She said she thought "opportunities go to those people who are willing to work for them." But this perspective was challenged by an unplanned pregnancy at a time when she was making dramatic career progress.

Carla's case is worth noting because it is such a good example of the discursive positioning of the "professional engineer" and the (very much embodied) mother. When Carla returned to work after her first maternity leave, she tried to breast-feed her baby during her lunch break as a way to continue nursing. She said:

> Well, I tried it for two weeks, but then my milk supply was so big, it was just like . . . you know, here I am a professional engineer and my boobs are leaking all over the place and I just couldn't, couldn't do that.

Asked if those around her at work were supportive, she replied, "Well, I didn't really talk about it with anybody. It was kind of a private thing." Carla's acknowledgment of the incongruity of "professional engineers" breast-feeding, and of breast-feeding itself as belonging in the private domain, hinted at the subjective shifts she also negotiated. Carla's career choices were constrained by her family's need for her income. Like many men also, she was the family breadwinner, in a position to delegate family work to her partner. Unlike most men, however, she expressed unease about this arrangement. Her interview was interspersed with comments that clearly indicated what Smith (1987) would call a bifurcated consciousness, divided between a focus on her work (which she enjoyed), and preoccupation with a domestic life over which she had reluctantly surrendered control. "There are really times that I long to be the stay-at-home parent," she commented.

For other women, there was a more conscious crossing over from a family focus to a more explicit career orientation. Zoe responded to an appeal by a friend to leave her flexible consulting arrangement and lead a small company; Ingrid's long-time male mentor asked her to return to work part-time, two months after her second child was born. Ingrid spoke of having planned not to return to work until the children were in school. But the part-time work quickly turned to full-time, then a partnership. Her account combined expressions of her enjoyment of her job with regrets about its costs.

> I think once a woman works, it's hard not to work. It's hard to stay home and not have that challenge. . . . Knowing that other people are advancing, advancing, advancing. . . . The downside is the time. You don't know (if you raised) your kids yourself. I don't consider, myself, that I've raised my kids . . . I consider that they spend more time with their babysitter than they do with me, right? I consider that and now it's more time at school than with me, right? So I consider myself kind of the secondary raiser, kind of in their lives, my husband and I.

But in this group of mothers there were also those whose accounts were much less conflicted. For example, Denise had her first and only child, at 35. She took 20 weeks of maternity leave, the maximum her company allowed—"and honestly, I was dying to get back to work." She commented:

> It didn't change much in my life. I still worked the same hours. I was still the same person at work as I was before. Just because I have a full-time nanny during the day, I was pretty uninterrupted, having a child, compared to what it could be.

To summarize, the 20 women with children followed fairly closely the paths anticipated by the childless women engineers described earlier with respect to the combination of engineering and motherhood. A very few voluntarily "chose" motherhood. All the others negotiated a balance between being an engineer and being a mother that was both discursive and practical. For some of these negotiators, the balance was achieved by a conscious gearing down on the work side—but usually only after careers had been established and dues paid. For the others, it was achieved (as just noted) by means of privatizing and delegating family responsibilities in order to maintain career progress.

Conclusion

This study has proceeded from the assumption that motherhood is a watershed for women in engineering, and has explored what was described at the start of the paper as a more nuanced explanation for why this might be the case: that women enter engineering jobs as "conceptual men," and that problems arise because mothers can't *be* conceptual men.

What it means to work as a "conceptual man" is not self-evident. In this paper I chose to see women engineers working in this way if they were doing the same kind of work, in the same conditions, for the same hours, and with the same general expectations about quality of performance as their male colleagues. Another part of the definition was that this work was done in workplaces dominated by men—a condition that was more than met in every case. I also tried to distinguish between *working as* a conceptual man, and *aligning oneself*, or *discursively positioning oneself*, with men. On the basis of this definition, all of the women without children were working as conceptual men. Often, though not invariably, they also positioned themselves as "one of the boys"—though this positioning was seldom sustained and consistent. Nine of the 20 women with children were also working as conceptual men—though they were much less likely to position themselves with "the boys."

In my discussion of these nine, and in comments about the plans of some of the childless women also proposing to delegate to partners or otherwise privatize their family responsibilities, I have suggested that these women were or would become "fathers." This proposition is not entirely theoretical. In a separate study (Ranson, 2001) I explored the ways the men with children interviewed for the same engineering project balanced work and family responsibilities. Serious accommodation to family responsibilities generally took two forms: a choice of work (generally office, rather that field-based, with predictable hours); or downshifting from an intensive work focus to a more relaxed pace—usually the choice of men who had achieved considerable career success first. But for all of these men, the balance of work and family still typically involved working days of 8–10 hours, and in almost every case, also involved a partner working part-time or not in paid employment, and available to pick up the slack. Access to this private infrastructure of support

characterized almost all the fathers. For those mothers who have access to something similar, the "father" analogy has some merit.

For the mothers, "downshifting" to accommodate children went much further: an opting out of engineering, temporarily or permanently, or a reduction in work hours. Fathers never employed these strategies; indeed, men with young families working less than full-time never emerged in the larger study. This is why such strategies come to be identified with women, and why so-called "family-friendly" organizational policies purporting to help employees balance work and family responsibilities come to be perceived as helping women fit in to men's workplaces. As noted by researchers cited earlier (Jones and Causer, 1995; Lewis, 1997; Rubin, 1997; Liff and Ward, 2001), these policies may become another organizational device for differentiating women from "the boys"—and mothers from fathers.

Notes

1. The author would like to thank Marilyn Porter and the CRSA reviewers for very helpful comments on an earlier version of the paper. This manuscript was first submitted in September 2003 and accepted in March 2005.

2. In the larger project from which the present study is drawn, only 25 per cent of fathers in engineering jobs had partners who also worked full-time, compared to 92 per cent of the engineering mothers.

3. I am grateful to the anonymous reviewer who urged that this point be made more explicit.

References

Acker, J. 1990. "Hierarchies, Jobs, Bodies: A Theory of Gendered Organizations," *Gender & Society* 4(2): 139–58.

Andrews, A., and L. Bailyn. 1993. "Segmentation and Synergy: Two Models of Linking Work and Family," in J. Hood, ed., *Men, Work and Family*, pp. 262–75. Newbury Park, Calif: Sage.

Arendell, T. 2000. "Conceiving and Investigating Motherhood: The Decade's Scholarship," *Journal of Marriage and Family* 62(4): 1192–207.

Canadian Committee on Women and Engineering. 1992. *More Than Just Numbers.* Fredericton: University of New Brunswick.

Canadian Council of Professional Engineers. 1998. *National Survey of the Canadian Engineering Profession in 1997.* Ottawa: Canadian Council of Professional Engineers.

Canadian Council of Professional Engineers. 2003. "Women in Engineering." Available at www.ccpe.ca/e/prog_women_1.cfm.

Christiansen, S., and R. Palkovitz. 2001. "Why the 'Good Provider' Role Still Matters: Providing as a Form of Paternal Involvement," *Journal of Family Issues* 22(1): 84–106.

Corcoran-Nantes, Y., and K. Roberts. 1995. "'We've got one of those': The Peripheral Status of Women in Male-dominated Industries," *Gender, Work and Organization* 2(1): 21–33.

Devine, F. 1992. "Gender Segregation in the Engineering and Science Professions: A Case of Continuity and Change," *Work, Employment and Society* 6(4): 557–75.

Eisenhart, M., and E. Finkel. 1998. *Women's Science.* Chicago, Ill: University of Chicago Press.

Evetts, J. 1994. "Women and Career in Engineering: Continuity and Change in the Organisation," *Work, Employment and Society* 8(1): 101–12.

Evetts, J. 1996. *Gender and Career in Science and Engineering.* London: Taylor & Francis Ltd.

Faulkner, W. 2000. "The Power *and* the Pleasure? A Research Agenda for 'Making Gender Stick' to Engineers," *Science, Technology, & Human Values* 25(1): 87–119.

Gherardi, S. 1996. "Gendered Organizational Cultures: Narratives of Women Travellers in a Male World," *Gender, Work and Organization* 3(4): 187–201.

Hays, S. 1996. *The Cultural Contradictions of Motherhood.* New Haven, Conn: Yale University Press.

Hochschild, A. 1997. *The Time Bind.* New York: Metropolitan Books.

Jones, C., and G. Causer. 1995. "'Men Don't Have Families': Equality and Motherhood in Technical Employment," *Gender, Work and Organization* 2(2): 51–62.

Jorgenson, J. 2000. "Interpreting the Intersections of Work and Family: Frame Conflicts in Women's Work," *The Electronic Journal of Communication* 10: 3–4.

Jorgenson, J. 2002. "Engineering Selves: Negotiating Gender and Identity in Technical Work," *Management Communication Quarterly* 15(3): 350–80.

Kvande, E. 1999. "'In the Belly of the Beast': Constructing Femininities in Engineering Organizations," *European Journal of Women's Studies* 6(3): 305–28.

Lewis, S. 1997. "'Family-friendly' Employment Policies: A Route to Changing Organizational Culture or Playing About at the Margins?," *Gender, Work and Organization* 4(1): 13–23.

Liff, S., and K. Ward. 2001. "Distorted Views through the Glass Ceiling: The Construction of Women's Understandings of Promotion and Senior Management Positions," *Gender, Work and Organization* 8(1): 19–36.

Marshall, J. 1984. *Women Managers: Travellers in a Male World.* Chichester: John Wiley and Sons.

McIlwee, J., and J. Robinson. 1992. *Women in Engineering.* Albany, NY: SUNY Press.

Miller, G. 2004. "Frontier Masculinity in the Oil Industry: The Experience of Women Engineers," *Gender, Work and Organization* 11(1): 47–73.

Pleck, J. 1993. "Are 'Family-supportive' Employer Policies Relevant to Men?," in J. Hood, ed., *Men, Work and Family*, pp. 217–37. Newbury Park, Calif: Sage.

Ranson, G. 1998. "Education, Work and Family Decision Making: Finding the 'Right Time' to Have a Baby," *Canadian Review of Sociology and Anthropology* 35(4): 517–33.

Ranson, G. 2000. "The Best of Both Worlds? Work, Family Life and the Retention of Women in Engineering." Paper presented at the 8th annual conference of the Canadian Coalition of Women in Engineering, Science, Trades and Technology, St. John's, Newfoundland, 6–8 July.

Ranson, G. 2001. "Men at Work: Change—or No Change?—in the Era of the 'New Father'," *Men and Masculinities* 4(1): 3–26.

Rapoport, R., and L. Bailyn. 1996. *Relinking Life and Work: Toward a Better Future.* New York: Ford Foundation.

Rothman, B. 1994. "Beyond Mothers and Fathers: Ideology in a Patriarchal Society," in E.N. Glenn, G. Chang, and L.R. Forcie, eds., *Mothering: Ideology, Experience and Agency*, pp. 139–57. New York: Routledge.

Rubin, J. 1997. "Gender, Equality and the Culture of Organizational Assessment," *Gender, Work and Organization* 4(1): 24–34.

Smith, D. 1987. *The Everyday World as Problematic: A Feminist Sociology.* Toronto: University of Toronto Press.

Snitow, A. 1990. "A Gender Diary," in M. Hirsch and E.F. Keller, eds., *Conflicts in Feminism.* New York: Routledge.

Wajcman, J. 1991. *Feminism Confronts Technology.* Cambridge: Polity Press.

Wajcman, J. 1996. "The Domestic Basis for the Managerial Career," *Sociological Review* 44(4): 609–29.

Wajcman, J. 1998. *Managing Like a Man.* University Park, PA: Pennsylvania State University Press.

Chapter 28

Overview

The wildfires that nearly destroyed the city of Kelowna, BC, in 2003 form the dramatic backdrop to Shelley Pacholok's investigation of how work intersects with gender to produce particular accounts of oneself. The firefighters interviewed by Pacholok hold jobs that are perhaps the epitome of hegemonic masculinity, involving physical bravery, protection, danger, and strength. Nonetheless, even within this group Pacholok finds evidence of different strategies of masculine self-presentation. Pacholok argues that even though the firefighters do not explicitly invoke the concept of masculinity, the qualities they ascribe to themselves and to other firefighters are related to dominant cultural narratives about gender.

Pacholok draws on the concept of multiple masculinities to examine the differentiation between groups of firefighters, as structural firefighters (who work in towns protecting buildings and populated areas) are more able to partake in the myth of the hero than their counterparts in wildland firefighting, whose work takes place far from admiring observers and media. The structural firefighters, who are most visible in their hegemonically masculine work, reap both symbolic and material rewards from being hailed as heroes. The wildland firefighters define themselves in contrast to their urban counterparts, seeing themselves as superior in the exercise of qualities such as risk-taking, aggression, and control of the situation.

Pacholok reminds us that while we may typically think of masculinity as something that is opposed to femininity, in fact masculinity may be constructed through contrasts men draw between themselves and other men. Masculinity is not simply the difference between men and women.

Gendered Strategies of the Self

Navigating Hierarchy and Contesting Masculinities

Shelley Pacholok

In the summer and autumn of 2003 wildfires in British Columbia, Canada, caused widespread damage to forests, wildlife, animal habitat, homes, suburban neighbourhoods, and tribal lands, the likes of which were unparalleled in recent decades. From a monetary and safety perspective the costs were enormous. The cost of battling with fires in British Columbia was $6 million per day in August 2003 (CTV, 2003). Also, tragically, one air tanker and one helicopter crashed, killing three firefighters. . . .

During this natural disaster firefighters were forced to contend with two challenging situations. First, by and large they felt that they lost the battle against the fire, something that they stressed they were not accustomed to. The occupational culture of firefighting values winning—defined as controlling or exterminating fire and preventing losses to property and other valued resources. Because millions of dollars of property and resources were destroyed, the firefighters' occupational identities

Pacholok, Shelley. "Gendered Strategies of the Self: Navigating Hierarchy and Contesting Masculinities," *Gender, Work, and Organization*, Vol. 16, No. 4 (July 2009), 471–500. Journal compilation © 2009 Blackwell Publishing Ltd.

were threatened by the losses. They were also faced with a social hierarchy in which some firefighting groups were granted more prestige, rewards and status than other groups. . . .

Theorizing Masculinities

Contemporary theoretical approaches to gender relations, and masculinity in particular, provide a number of pertinent insights. Firstly, differences among men shape the ways they experience and enact gender. Masculinity is profoundly influenced by social structures such as race, class, age, and sexuality, and these structures affect men in different ways. In addition, masculinity is historically and culturally contingent. So there is not one pattern of masculinity found everywhere, rather there are masculinities (Connell, 1995; Kimmel, 1994). In addition, some masculinities are deemed culturally superior to others; hegemonic masculinity is the most honoured or desired at a particular time and in a particular setting. Hegemonic masculinity cannot exist unless there are subordinated Others (that is, women and marginalized men) who are constructed as deficient in some way. As a result, hegemonic masculinity upholds power and status inequalities both between men and women, and among men (Connell, 1995, 2000).

The main patterns of contemporary hegemonic masculinity in Western societies include the connection of masculinity with toughness and competitiveness, the subordination of women, and the marginalization of gay men (Connell, 1995). In addition, appropriately masculine men are supposed to (a) remain calm and reliable in a crisis, and hold their emotions in check, (b) be aggressive and take risks, (c) repudiate anything even remotely related to femininity, and (d) strive for power, success and wealth (for example, see Brannon, 1976; Goffman, 1963; Kimmel, 1994). While few men actually meet all these normative standards, hegemonic masculinity is the benchmark against which all men are measured. Moreover, according to Kimmel (1994), it is other men who do the evaluating:

> We are under the constant careful scrutiny of other men. Other men watch us, rank us, grant our acceptance into the realm of manhood. Manhood is demonstrated for other men's approval. It is other men who evaluate the performance. (p. 130)

A further theoretical insight is that hegemonic masculinity cannot be reduced to a simple model of cultural control, as the notion of hegemony implies an active struggle for dominance (Connell and Messerschmidt, 2005). Therefore, while hegemonic masculinity is the standard against which all other masculinities are measured, the position at the top of the hierarchy is never secure and is always contestable (Connell, 1995). . . . Herein lies the key to understanding why firefighters with high status construct superior selves: ascendancy is never guaranteed; therefore, they must continually work to maintain their status vis-à-vis other men and prove that they are, in fact, appropriately masculine and therefore superior. . . .

. . . Because hegemonic masculinity is relational it requires actors to draw boundaries and create superior selves that delineate "us" (superior men) from "them" (marginalized Others). . . .

Method

Sample

. . . [K]ey informants were identified through newspaper accounts of the fires. These informants were located and contacted by phone or e-mail. They were asked to participate in the study and also asked to provide the names of additional firefighters who were then contacted for interviews. I used this snowball technique to generate the remainder of the interview contacts.

Because the Okanagan Mountain Park fire was an interface fire, a number of different groups of firefighters were involved in the firefighting efforts. Four groups of firefighters fought on the front lines of the fire: (a) structural firefighters, (b) wildland firefighters, (c) pilots, and (d) heavy equipment operators.

Data Collection

Between June and December 2004 I travelled to Kelowna to do fieldwork on three separate occasions. I conducted informal observations at a number of sites including four City of Kelowna fire halls, three branch offices of the forestry department, two air tanker centres, and one helicopter base.

I also completed in-depth interviews with firefighters and informal interviews with a number of other people involved in the firefighting efforts (for example, fire centre dispatchers). . . .

. . . [I]nterviews took place in a wide variety of settings including coffee shops, outdoor parks, workplaces, and homes. However, most interviews were conducted at the participant's place of work. The interviews lasted from just over 30 minutes to two and a half hours, with the typical interview lasting from one to one and a half hours. . . .

To document the newspaper coverage of the fire I conducted archival work at the Kelowna library. I examined all the fire-related articles in the two major local newspapers, *The Kelowna Daily Courier* and *Capital News* from 20 August to 25 September 2003. I also retrieved articles from electronic news sources. The newspaper accounts revealed that a number of people in administrative positions played key roles in the event. For example, it became clear that relations with the media had implications for the ways in which the hierarchy emerged. . . .

Findings

Over the course of the fire and in the weeks and months that followed, a social hierarchy became apparent—one in which City of Kelowna firefighters received more recognition, rewards, and status from the media and the public than other firefighting groups.[1] This generated a great deal of animosity between the firefighters. While these were largely unsolicited, I heard numerous disparaging comments that were often, although not exclusively, directed at the City of Kelowna firefighters, especially the fire chief, who was a favourite target.

In addition, firefighters from all groups made a concerted effort to frame their own work group as superior (that is, the ones who put themselves in the most danger, worked the hardest under the most difficult conditions and were the most skilled, did the best job, and so on), while simultaneously positioning the other groups as inferior. The following quote from Greg,[2] a veteran forestry firefighter who was a supervisor during the fire, is representative of comments I heard from many of his colleagues. Greg revealed his frustration at what he felt was unfair recognition of the City of Kelowna firefighters and the lack of praise for forestry firefighters and equipment operators who were "really" the ones who took on the most important and dangerous firefighting tasks:

> I think the role, and what was accomplished by our people, on the ground, doesn't get the attention that it deserves. And I think that has a real psychological impact on our firefighters, and our equipment operators. I think that the glory all goes to the [structural]

fire departments. . . . Our guys are out there, and I'm not just saying this, this isn't biased, this is my personal observation from the first 10, 12 days of the Okanagan fire. . . . Our staff, our crews, the forest service crews, were the last people out, after the fire department had left. Our guys were the ones who held and maintained that fire guard on the south side. It wasn't the [Kelowna] fire department who did that. . . . It was our front line folks and equipment operators that put in that [fire] guard, that worked through the heat and the dust and the hot and the dry. It's our people who do all of that. Those equipment operators chug away, day and night sometimes, 24 hours a day, and they get very little recognition. The glory all goes to the [Kelowna] fire department. And that in itself has a huge impact to the morale. And somehow the credit has to go where it rightfully belongs. . . .

The Making of Heroes

Based on newspaper accounts, it appears that structural firefighters (especially the fire chief) did receive considerably more print media coverage than any other groups or individuals who were involved in the firefighting efforts. . . .

. . . [M]ost of the firefighter personal interest stories were about structural firefighters and, most often, the Kelowna fire chief. While there were several articles about wildland firefighters, equipment operators and pilots, for the most part they appeared near the end of the fire. For example, over two weeks after the fire started one headline in the *Kelowna Daily Courier* exclaimed, "Unsung heroes: heavy equipment operators have put their lives on the line fighting the Okanagan Mountain blaze, but respect has been hard to find" (Poulsen, 2003b). Even the army, brought in to provide support services to the front line firefighters, such as putting out hot spots and performing mop-up duties, received a relatively large share of media coverage.

Chris, . . . a crew leader employed by a wildland firefighting contract company, . . . noted that, as a result of the unequal coverage, the public gave more credit to the structural firefighters than the wildland firefighters. . . .

According to Chris structural firefighters not only fared better than wildland firefighters in terms of media coverage, they won another important battle—the recognition, support, and adoration of the public. Chris was not alone in his sentiments: numerous other wildland firefighters were also critical of the coverage provided by the media. . . .

The Media as Reputational Entrepreneurs: Firefighters and Heroic Masculinity

. . . Both during the fire and in the weeks that followed, the print media covered numerous human interest stories about firefighters. Both of the local newspapers drew on dominant cultural discourses and symbols of heroism in these stories.

Many framed firefighters as heroes, either explicitly (through the use of the word hero), or implicitly (by referring to firefighters as courageous, selfless, and so on). In addition, the *Daily Courier* printed pull-out posters that read, "Thanks for being our heroes!" and urged readers to "show your gratitude and display this poster in your window." The media have been involved in the business of hero-making for more than two centuries (Houchin Winfield, 2003), and this event was no exception.

Again, many of these stories involved the Kelowna fire chief and, to a lesser degree, the structural firefighters who worked for him. Perhaps, in light of the valorization of structural firefighters as heroes in the wake of 9/11 (Langewiesche, 2002; Lorber, 2002), which occurred only two years before the fire, it was strategic for the media to portray structural firefighters as heroes. They want to generate and retain interest and are successful only to the extent that their readers identify with the principal characters and settings (Fine and White, 2002) . . . .

Embedded in the heroism rhetoric were hegemonic constructions of masculinity. It is no secret that media representations enforce and reproduce culturally dominant gender norms, symbols, ideologies, and stereotypes (Dworkin and Wachs, 2000; Howard and Prividera, 2004). Since the use of conventional categories and familiar roles conveys stability, this may be especially true during times of crisis (Lorber, 2002). In addition, the media have a vested interest in supporting culturally dominant conceptions of manliness because they want readers to connect with the characters in their stories, as noted above.

Following are several examples that illustrate the ways in which the media implicitly championed hegemonic masculinity in their coverage of the fire. Two days after Black Friday one headline declared, "Hard fought battle: for every home lost, firefighters saved two, says weary fire chief" (Plant, 2003). The body of the article was punctuated by references to the danger that firefighters placed themselves in ("the fire prompted fierce firefighting that could have turned deadly"), including injuries sustained. It also relayed an incident where firefighters were trapped by the flames; however, the reporter was quick to note that "once [the] flames died down, the men fought their way back in and put out spot fires." Several days later, *Capital News*, reporting on the story of the trapped firefighters, printed the following headline, "Training and experience kept trapped firefighters calm" (Watters, 2003). Another headline in the *Daily Courier* exclaimed, "Hot stuff: studly forest fire point men are not just a couple of hosers" (Seymour, 2003).

These are only several examples among many in which the media implicitly referenced culturally dominant ideals of masculinity such as strength, aggression, courage in the face of danger, heterosexuality, and stoicism. As in other tragedies, the media used this event to protect and articulate dominant gender narratives (Projansky, 1998). The media . . . evoked and perpetuated the parameters of manhood that ultimately provided a context of support for the dynamic reproduction of hegemonic masculinity.[3] Here we can see how the collective actions of the media worked to (re)-inscribe symbolic boundaries around hegemonic masculinity, which ultimately allowed the gendered strategies of self invoked by structural firefighters to take hold. I elaborate on this process in the following section.

On the whole the public appeared to embrace the new heroes. They enthusiastically participated in a yellow ribbon campaign, posted signs of gratitude around the city, attended public events to honour firefighters, supported a number of fundraising causes, and donated a generous amount of time and money to the firefighting efforts.

Wildland firefighters, on the other hand, often expressed mixed emotions about the hero atmosphere that permeated the town, as they did not feel that the praise was necessarily directed at them (despite the fact that there were some signs and media stories that targeted non-structural firefighters). When asked how he felt about seeing the signs, Josh, a 22-year-old wildland firefighter in his third season as a crew member, remarked:

Um, yeah, we saw [the signs] every time we drove in. And, like here at the [forestry] base there's somewhat, there's some animosity between us and the KFD, the Kelowna fire department. . . . Like, because they stopped the fire when it was all in the houses, they kind of got the glory. And it's, like, we all know, we couldn't do anything when it's in that kind of [forest conditions]. . . . So it was, kind of, like, well we did all this work and, despite our efforts, this is going to happen and you can't stop it. You know, we had posters and stuff but as it started kind of slowing down we were kind of, you know, we were back to doing our job and those guys are still kind of in the glory.

So, according to Josh, not only did the structural firefighters receive more credit because they were battling with house fires, they stayed in the limelight when the wildland firefighters went off to fight forest fires in other areas. . . .

In contrast, most of the structural firefighters seemed to recognize that the heroism narrative was directed at them. One newly recruited firefighter, Jeff, maintained that being called a hero was a great "morale booster"; however, he quickly added, "I don't think there's anyone who wants to be called a hero or anything, like it's just, you know that's what we're paid to do." All the structural firefighters denied being heroes and gave the trite answer that what they did was just "part of the job." . . .

If somebody goes in to save a child or a mother or a grandmother, then I that's the risk that we run. We pull people out of burning buildings. We did it the other day, where we pulled a guy out, maybe 5 months ago, out of a burning building, right. Risking their [sic] lives, it's what we do, right? . . .

It's nice to be recognized, but I don't know what the definition of hero is. We, the guys out here, do really dangerous, successful, heroic deeds nearly every day.

So while the structural firefighters claimed to reject the hero label, a hero-like narrative was woven into many of their accounts of their regular duties. The heroism rhetoric that was disseminated through the local media exacerbated the hierarchy among firefighters, as it favoured the fire chief and other structural firefighters. In addition, the hierarchy was perpetuated by the perceptions of the firefighters themselves. Many wildland firefighters seemed to believe that the media praise was directed solely at the structural firefighters and their chief. The structural firefighters, while denying that they were heroes, viewed their job as one that requires selfless acts on a regular basis.

Contesting Credibility

In navigating the status hierarchy that was exacerbated by the organization of the firefighting efforts and the media coverage of the fire, the firefighters constructed boundaries in an attempt to distinguish their group from the others. . . .

They accomplished this by adopting a measuring stick of firefighting competence that was variously deemed to include remaining calm in a crisis, using aggressive tactics, controlling emotions, and exterminating fire (the latter two criteria falling under the more general category of "repudiating the feminine" below). The firefighters drew on these criteria to demonstrate that their group was superior to other firefighting groups. Because these standards are analogous to culturally dominant ideals of masculinity, undermining firefighting competence simultaneously undermined the masculine integrity of the targeted group. These strategies are indicative of the importance of hegemonic masculinity to firefighters, as workers often judge members of other groups to be deficient in respect to the criteria they value most (Lamont, 2000).

The firefighters' gendered strategies of self not only reinforced occupational boundaries but created boundaries that delineated the difference between "us" (the competent firefighters and "real" men) and "them" (inferior firefighters and subordinate men). Ultimately, these tactics were attempts to erode the credibility of the firefighting group to which they were directed. . . .

Calm and Reliable in Crisis

According to Josh, the young wildland firefighter who remarked earlier that the structural firefighters "got all the glory," the wildland crew leaders were calm under pressure, while the structural firefighters fell apart:

> We had some [crew leaders] . . . who have both seen huge fire. But nothing like this. And they were just rock solid. They said, "No worries, get in [the vehicles], we'll get you all through." Everybody else was panicked. Like the Kelowna Fire department was just wiggy.

One of the crew leaders that Josh was referring to, Chris, explained that there were two occasions when he instructed structural firefighters to leave an area for safety reasons and, due to their ignorance of forest fire behaviour, they resisted. However, according to Chris, there were other times when they "took off" when it was safe, which resulted in the loss of houses:

There were times when the structure guys again . . . the times they would leave an area when it was safe, and then homes would go. And you'd say, "Well, where the hell did they go?" So then you get on the radio and you start telling them, "No, you guys, it is safe there. I know what the fire is doing, I know where it is, and I know what it's going to do. If you're there right now you can save a couple." But no, of course they weren't.

Structural firefighters used similar tactics to portray wildland firefighters in an unflattering manner. For example, this structural firefighter seemed to genuinely delight in relaying a story where wildland firefighters apparently pulled back from the front line of the fire while the structural firefighters stayed:

> And I remember we were up in the Rimrock area when the fire broke through. . . . So we're sitting there, and we know it's coming because you can hear it, the heat, the wind, the smoke, the dust, everything. The forestry guys you know, they're all in there. And then all of the sudden we heard these whistles. And that's an emergency signal for the forestry to get the hell out. So all of these whistles, you can just hear them going right across the mountain side, and we're kind of listening and then we're like, "What the hell is that?" And it looked like rats jumping off a burning ship [chuckles]. These guys were running as hard as they could out of the forest, by us, and down the hill and they're gone. . . .

Mark's narrative positions his group as the competent firefighters—the real men who stayed to fight the fire. In contrast, according to Mark, the wildland firefighters ran away when things got bad. . . . Structural firefighters, rational, fearless, and calm under pressure, were ready to take on the fire, and ultimately, as Mark noted later in the interview, it was these men who put it out. . . .

. . . [C]laiming that wildland firefighters ran away, as Mark did, is a serious insult that directly undermines their credibility, both as firefighters and as men.

Aggression and Risk Taking

Greg, the wildland supervisor who earlier criticized the media coverage of the fire, explained that it was actually his people who put themselves in harm's way:

> While the fire department did a great job on the structure side of it, and I don't want to take anything away from anyone, anywhere on the structural side, but when it came to the actual front line of those fires and the people who put themselves at risk, it was our people under there.

In this passage Greg discursively positions his crew (and himself, by association) as the real firefighters—the men who put themselves at risk and got the job done. One wildland firefighter went public with this claim, stating that structural firefighters disappeared when the blaze was burning near his property: "I hate to be cynical, but I don't have a good word to say about them. You need passion and adrenaline to fight a fire. Their tolerance of risk was minimal" (Poulsen, 2003a). . . .

Many structural firefighters also talked about the perils associated with their job, but they tended to view risk and danger as an everyday part of their job, as their discourse about heroism indicated. In both cases the implication is that firefighting competence requires taking risks, and (implicitly) those who are willing to take those risks are the most masculine.

Repudiating the Feminine

Firefighters also accomplished competence negatively; that is, they inferred that other firefighters were incompetent by associating them with characteristics stereotypically associated with femininity. Undermining masculinity is often achieved by implying that the person in question has qualities associated with femininity (for example, see Iacuone, 2005). This tactic is apparent in all the following narratives, although the

discourse varied by occupational group. It is well established that masculinity construction is intertwined with the occupational settings in which men labour (Cheng, 1996; Collinson and Hearn, 1996; Meyer, 1999; Pierce, 1995; Prokos and Padavic, 2002). Since each group of firefighters worked in different occupations, they sometimes used disparate discourses to distance themselves from femininity or liken others to women.

One veteran firefighter, Richard, who had recently moved into an administrative position, explained the differences between structural and wildland firefighters in the following way:

> [The wildland firefighters'] job is more containment. Structural firefighters are aggressive, we don't take loss very well. Forestry firefighters are more tactical, they're more like army guys. They're willing to take some losses to get some gains, if that makes sense to you? I mean, they're willing to give up 100 acres of wildland and burn it themselves to stop the fire. Where we would never burn the house down to save another house. We would try and save that house and we would try and save the other house. That's the mental make-up of a structural firefighter versus a forestry guy, right? Forestry guys are like, okay, we'll build a guard here of dirt, and then we'll burn all this off so it doesn't come here, right. So we'll sacrifice some, to get some. Where structural firefighters are not about sacrificing anything.

Here structural firefighters are portrayed as aggressive, uncompromising, and unwilling to lose, and forestry firefighters as less aggressive (maybe even passive) and prepared to lose (at least some of the time). Clearly this rhetoric positions structural firefighters as better firefighters, while equating the mental make-up of wildland firefighters with characteristics typically associated with femininity, such as passivity (Adler et al., 1992; Gonick, 2006). Richard points to firefighting tactics specific to each occupation and uses these as resources to construct the competence and masculinity of structural firefighters as superior to that of wildland firefighters. . . .

Several forestry firefighters' accounts pointed to the mental state of structural firefighters and an emotional display by the fire chief, in a way that challenged their masculinity. In a well-publicized statement to the media the fire chief broke down in tears while relaying the events of Black Friday. . . .

In a similar vein one of the heavy equipment operators ridiculed structural firefighters who took stress leave or were otherwise having difficulty dealing with the fire. As emotions (except perhaps anger) are equated with femininity (Bird, 1996; Rubin, 2004), they are something to be disparaged. Wildland firefighters' accounts revealed disdain for public displays of emotion and their caustic remarks called into question the fire chief's masculinity.

Discussion

These findings indicate that the status hierarchy that became evident over the course of the Okanagan Mountain Park fire was due, at least in part, to the structural organization of the firefighting efforts and the ways in which the media covered the fire. The central location of the main fire hall and the fact that structural firefighters fought the fire within the city limits meant that they were more accessible to the media and, in turn, received more favourable media coverage. The media cultivated narratives consistent with hegemonic masculinity and heroism. Heroism did not appear to resonate with wildland or structural firefighters but the narratives of structural firefighters were often saturated with hero-like imagery.

In an effort to maintain their place at the top of the hierarchy structural firefighters reinforced the boundary between themselves and other groups by discursively positioning others, especially wildland firefighters, as less competent and implicitly as less manly. Wildland firefighters, equipment operators, and pilots attempted to secure their place at the top of the hierarchy using similar tactics. These strategies were attempts to diminish the credibility of the out-group in question. . . .

What was most notable in my study was that the structural firefighters, who had a relatively high social status, also employed strategies of the superior self. The fact that the structural firefighters used these strategies at all provides evidence to support Connell's (1995) claim that hegemonic masculinity is not statically reproduced, but rather, is always contested. If hegemonic masculinity is a given these tactics would not be required for those with the most power and status.

However, because the positions at the top of the gender hierarchy are never secure, even those with power (in this case, structural firefighters) are compelled to engage in practices that refute the integrity of those they perceive as Other. It is only by theorizing gender—masculinity dynamics that involve active struggles for dominance and the constant need to prove one's masculinity—that we can explain why the firefighters responded to the status hierarchy in the ways that they did.

We also saw that gendered strategies of self are not only used individually to construct superior selves, they are collective efforts that serve a collective end: defining and imposing boundaries between groups. The boundary work of the media, which bounded the parameters of heroism and manhood, enabled the structural firefighters' claims to competence and hegemonic masculinity to take hold. If it appears that groups are essentialized as a result of strategies of self and boundary work, it is because that is precisely their intent. Essentializing is "the making of doctrinal claims that certain good or bad traits inhere in all who share an identity" (Schwalbe and Mason-Schrock, 1996, p. 124). Each group of firefighters attempted to demonstrate that their group was populated by exemplars of masculinity and firefighting competence because they wanted to show that their group members were all of a certain character and quality, while others were not. . . .

Such symbolic "credibility contests" (Lamont and Molnar, 2002, p. 179) involving claims to hegemonic masculinity have symbolic and material implications for inequality. Symbolically, men who embody hegemonic masculinity are given honour, prestige, and authority (Connell, 1995). Materially, men who best exemplify this ideal are granted political and material resources. For example, men at the top of the gender hierarchy earn, on average, higher salaries than women and marginalized men, and are more likely to have political power; resources that can then be used to further their own agendas.

In other words, there are material rewards for those who win symbolic battles. Groups that can claim hegemonic masculinity are able to use their status to gain material resources. In this case, structural firefighters were able to convert their collective social capital into material rewards. With the help of their union representative, the fire chief, and the media, the structural firefighters successfully rallied the public and city hall and secured a pay raise less than one year after the fire.[4] The firefighters deliberately referred to the fire and their status as heroes to argue that they deserved a salary increase.[5] The fire chief, who became a local and national celebrity, also reaped many rewards. He was featured on the cover of a prominent national magazine, received an honorary degree and numerous gifts and awards, was invited to do public speaking engagements all over the country, and was asked to run for political office (which he declined).

Importantly, there were also costs associated with being on, or striving for, the top. Research indicates that hegemonic masculinity comes at a personal cost to men who wholeheartedly embrace it. For example, impoverished emotional relationships (Kaufman, 2001; Rubin, 2004), dysfunctional sexual relations (Gerschick and Miller, 2001), risk-taking (Courtenay, 2000; Iacuone, 2005), and negative health outcomes (Sabo, 2004) have been linked to hegemonic masculinity construction. . . .

Consistent with these findings, many firefighters noted that the fire and its aftermath was a difficult experience. In addition, there were long-term consequences for some. Several were on stress leave at the time of the interviews, at least one firefighter resigned, one senior member retired shortly after the fire, the fire chief retired two years later (at the age of 56), some were having marital difficulties, a number were on medication to reduce stress, and a least two senior firefighters were diagnosed with post-traumatic stress disorder. There were also a handful of firefighters who chose to leave their jobs a year or more after the fire, citing the fire as one reason for their decision. . . .

Acknowledgements

I would like to thank Steve Lopez, Tim Curry, Townsand Price-Spratlen, Liana Sayer, numerous other colleagues at the Ohio State University, and three anonymous reviewers for comments and suggestions that helped further develop the ideas in this article. This research was supported by the Social Sciences and Humanities Research Council of Canada.

Notes

1. There were also divisions in these groups. However, due to space limitations these intra-group divisions are not discussed here.
2. All names are pseudonyms.
3. I am indebted to an anonymous reviewer for this idea.
4. The wildland firefighters' organization also received some resources (such as more crew positions) as a result of the fire. However, I was told by a number of people that these were primarily resources that had been cut in recent years and had simply been reinstated.
5. Some firefighters expressed discomfort with this strategy, but it was one that the group utilized nonetheless.

References

Adler, P., S. Kless, and P. Adler. 1992. "Socialization to Gender Roles: Popularity among Elementary School Boys and Girls," *Sociology of Education* 65(3): 169–87.

Bird, S. 1996. "Welcome to the Men's Club: Homosociality and the Maintenance of Hegemonic Masculinity," *Gender & Society* 10(2): 120–32.

Brannon, R. 1976. "The Male Sex Role—and What It's Done for Us Lately," in R. Brannon and D. David, eds., *The Forty-nine Percent Majority*, pp. 1–40. Reading, Mass: Addison-Wesley.

Cheng, C. 1996. *Masculinities in Organizations*. Thousand Oaks, Calif: Sage.

Collinson, D., and J. Hearn. 1996. *Men as Managers, Managers as Men*. London: Sage.

Connell, R.W. 1995. *Masculinities*. Berkeley, Calif: University of California Press.

Connell, R.W. 2000. *The Men and the Boys*. Berkeley, Calif: University of California Press.

Connell, R.W., and J.W. Messerschmidt. 2005. "Hegemonic Masculinity: Rethinking the Concept," *Gender & Society* 19(6): 829–59.

Courtenay, W. 2000. "Constructions of Masculinity and Their Influence on Men's Well-being: A Theory of Gender and Health," *Social Science and Medicine* 50(10): 1385–401.

CTV. 2003. "Support from Public Keeps B.C. Fire Crews Going." Available online at www.ctv.ca/servlet/ ArticleNews/print?brand=genericandarchive= CTVNewsanddate=2. Last consulted 15 February 2004.

Dworkin, S., and F. Wachs. 2000. "The Morality/Manhood Paradox," in J. McKay, M.A. Messner, and D.F. Sabo, eds., *Masculinities, Gender Relations, and Sport*, pp. 47–66. Thousand Oaks, Calif: Sage Publications.

Fine, G.A., and R. White. 2002. "Creating Collective Attention in the Public Domain: Human Interest Narratives and the Rescue of Floyd Collins," *Social Forces* 81(1): 57–85.

Gerschick, T., and A.S. Miller. 2001. "Coming to Terms: Masculinity and Physical Disability," in M.S. Kimmel and M.A. Messner, eds., *Men's Lives*, pp. 392–406. Boston, Mass: Allyn and Bacon.

Goffman, B. 1963. *Stigma; Notes on the Management of Spoiled Identity*. Englewood Cliffs, N.J: Prentice-Hall.

Gonick, M. 2006. "Between 'Girl Power' and 'Reviving Ophelia': Constituting the Neoliberal Girl Subject," *NWSA Journal* 18(2): 1–23.

Houchin Winfield, B. 2003. "The Press Response to the Corps of Discovery: The Making of Heroes in an Egalitarian Age," *Journalism and Mass Communication Quarterly* 80(4): 866–83.

Howard, J.W., and L. Prividera. 2004. "Rescuing Patriarchy or Saving 'Jessica Lynch': The Rhetorical Construction of the American Woman Soldier," *Women and Language* 27(2): 89–97.

Iacuone, D. 2005. "'Real Men Are Rough Guys': Hegemonic Masculinity and Safety in the Construction Industry," *The Journal of Men's Studies* 13(2): 247–66.

Kaufman, M. 2001. "The Construction of Masculinity and the Triad of Men's Violence," in M.S. Kimmel and M.A.

Messner, eds., *Men's Lives*, 5th edn, pp. 4–18. Needham Heights, Mass: Allyn and Bacon.

Kimmel, M.S. 1994. "Masculinities as Homophobia: Fear, Shame, and Silence in the Construction of Gender Identity," in H. Brod and M. Kaufman, eds., *Theorizing Masculinities*, pp. 119–41. Thousand Oaks, Calif: Sage.

Lamont, M. 2000. *The Dignity of Working Men: Morality and the Boundaries of Race, Class, and Immigration*. Cambridge, Mass: Harvard University Press.

Lamont, M., and V. Molnar. 2002, "The Study of Boundaries in the Social Sciences," *Annual Review of Sociology*, 28: 167–95.

Langewiesche, W. 2002. *American Ground: Unbuilding the World Trade Center*. New York: North Point Press.

Lorber, J. 2002. "Heroes, Warriors, and Burqas: A Feminist Sociologist's Reflections on September 11," *Sociological Forum* 17(3): 377–96.

Meyer, S. 1999. "Work, Play, and Power: Masculine Culture on the Shop Floor; 1930–1960," *Men and Masculinities* 2(2): 115–34.

Pierce, J. 1995. *Gender Trials: Emotional Lives in Contemporary Law Firms*. Berkeley, Calif: University of California Press.

Plant, D. 2003. "Hard Fought Battle," *Okanagan Sunday*, Kelowna.

Poulsen, C. 2003a. "Fire Actions under Scope," *The Daily Courier*, Kelowna.

Poulsen, C. 2003b. "Unsung Heroes: Heavy Equipment Operators Put Their Lives on the Line Fighting the Okanagan Mountain Blaze, But Respect Has Been Hard to Find," *The Daily Courier*, Kelowna.

Projansky, S. 1998. "Girls Who Act Like Women Who Fly: Jessica Dubroff as Cultural Troublemaker," *Signs: Journal of Women in Culture and Society* 23(3): 771–808.

Prokos, A., and I. Padavic. 2002. "'There Oughtta Be a Law against Bitches': Masculinity Lessons in Police Academy Training," *Gender, Work & Organization* 9(4): 439–59.

Rubin, L. 2004. "The Approach–Avoidance Dance: Men, Women, and Intimacy," in M.S. Kimmel and M.A. Messner, eds., *Men's Lives*, 5th edn, pp. 409–15. Boston, Mass: Allyn and Bacon.

Sabo, D.F. 2004. "Masculinities and Men's Health: Moving Toward Post-Superman Era Prevention," in M.S. Kimmel and M.A. Messner, eds., *Men's Lives*, 5th edn, pp. 347–61. Boston, Mass: Allyn and Bacon.

Schwalbe, M., and D. Mason-Schrock. 1996. "Identity Work as Group Process," in B. Markovsky, M. Lovaglia, and R. Simon, eds., *Advances in Group Processes*, pp. 115–49. Greenwich, Conn: JAI Press.

Seymour, R. 2003 "Hot Stuff," *The Daily Courier*, Kelowna.

Watters, A. 2003. "Training and Experience Kept Trapped Firefighters Calm," *Capital News*, Kelowna.

Chapter 29

Overview

Violence isn't always physical. Chantal Robillard and colleagues argue that structural violence—conditions that prevent people from acting to protect their own well-being or that disempower them—can be as destructive as physical harm. They interviewed professionals who provide support services to temporary foreign workers in Ontario and Quebec, including live-in caregivers and agricultural workers. They argue that while temporary foreign workers provide "just-in-time" labour and flexibility to Canadian employers, and while the wages sent home by these workers help to support families abroad, the conditions of labour migration are harsh for women. Compared to their Canadian counterparts, female temporary workers have fewer options as to where they will live or whom they will live with, and they have less recourse if they have problems with an employer or if things go badly. They are "captives to the contract" and are vulnerable to being sent back to their home country if they protest violence or intolerable living or working conditions. Their positions as wives and mothers, and often as the main source of income for their families, makes their position especially precarious. For caregivers in particular, their work is privatized within homes, limiting their access to outside information or support, especially when language barriers come into play.

"Caught in the Same Webs"

Service Providers' Insights on Gender-Based and Structural Violence among Female Temporary Foreign Workers in Canada

Chantal Robillard, Janet McLaughlin, Donald C. Cole,
Biljana Vasilevska, and Richard Gendron

Introduction

Female migrants from the global south are positioned in a structural framework that reproduces colonial domination while restricting their rights. Such a position exposes them to a combination of gender, sexual, class, and/or racial discrimination (Altman and Pannell 2012; Preibisch and Encalada Grez 2010). The resultant inequities are deeply rooted in the larger formal and informal structures regulating the migratory work processes exemplifying a form of "structural violence." The latter is exerted systematically, and at times unintentionally, by privileged groups striving to maintain a certain social order, thus rendering those facing oppression to a greater risk of assault and

Robillard, Chantal, Janet McLaughlin, Donald C. Cole, Biljana Vasilevska, and Richard Gendron. "'Caught in the Same Webs'— Service Providers' Insights on Gender-Based and Structural Violence Among Female Temporary Foreign Workers in Canada." *Journal of International Migration and Integration*, Springer, vol. 19(3), pages 583–606, (August 2018). Reprinted by permission of Springer Nature.

harm (Farmer 2004). Many migrant women experience structural violence at multiple levels: first, through the global inequities which leave them without adequate resources to support their families in their countries of origin, and propel them to migrate; second, in the discriminatory policies within countries of work, which exclude them from many of the rights and protections associated with citizenship; and third, in the gender- and race-based discrimination that they regularly encounter both at work and in their social and domestic lives. . . .

Canada's regulation of the Temporary Foreign Worker Program (TFWP) provides an apposite example of the manifestation of such structurally violent processes. . . . Our objective is to analyze how migration and labor policies and practices around TFW programs set the conditions for structural violence among female temporary foreign workers. More specifically, we articulate how policies and practices foster a power imbalance that contributes to silence surrounding violence and abuse of female temporary foreign workers, with consequent gaps and limitations in access to services.

Our data are drawn from the experiences of service providers supporting live-in caregivers and migrant agricultural workers in two Canadian provinces (Ontario and Quebec). . . .

Canadian Context: The Temporary Foreign Worker Program

The Canadian government facilitates access by employers to foreign applicants for jobs in occupations requiring lower levels of formal training—those considered "low-skilled"—through several streams of its TFWP, including the Seasonal Agricultural Worker Program (SAWP), the Agricultural Stream, and the stream for Low-Wage Positions. Prior to the program restructuring in 2014 (after the time of the research conducted for this study), a separate stream for caregivers, the Live-In Caregiver Program (LICP), was also in place. In November 2014, the Canadian government scrapped the LICP and replaced it with two pathways within a general in-home Caregiver Program: the Caring for Children Pathway and the Caring for People with High Medical Needs Pathway. The live-in requirement for both categories was dropped (CIC 2016).

Compared to the SAWP, which generally recruits candidates with lower levels of education (McLaughlin 2010), candidates in the LICP were required to have a diploma equivalent to a Canadian high school degree; one year of full-time experience in a similar position or six-month training within the last three years; and mastery of one of the two official Canadian language. Current caregivers face even stricter language and education requirements, with a recognized post-secondary degree or diploma required (CIC 2017 a, b). In addition, the Quebec provincial government has its own requirements, similar to the Canadian ones, with the exception of demonstrated advanced intermediate knowledge of oral French.

In 2014, 177,704 unique individuals were reported to hold TFWP permits (CIC 2015): 23,174 were live-in caregivers, 45,281 were agricultural workers, and 109,847 were other kinds of workers. Given the increasing complexity of the streams, these are likely under-estimates (Faraday 2016, see pp. 13–17). The majority of caregivers came from the Philippines while agricultural workers through the SAWP, which is governed through bilateral agreements, originate only from Mexico and Commonwealth Caribbean countries. Agricultural workers through other streams may come from any country, with popular choices include the SAWP countries as well as Guatemala, Indonesia, Thailand, and the Philippines, among others. Workers involved in caregiving are mostly young women while migrant agricultural workers are predominantly men, despite a growing proportion of women among the latter.

. . .

Canada benefits from the TFWP by having "just-in-time" flexible labor to fulfill local needs, as well as collects taxes and benefits on income earned, in addition to the workers' locally purchased goods and services. In some cases, workers contribute to benefit programs, such as Employment Insurance, which they cannot access (UFCW 2014). Contravening domestic employment standards legislation, both the gender and national origin of workforces are driven by employer preferences and stereotyping (McLaughlin 2010).

. . . According to Özden and Schiff (2006), remittances from migrants to their relatives in countries of origin surpass foreign aid as the largest source of foreign capital for many countries. These remittances come from both "high-skilled" and "low-skilled" workers, but in countries like the Philippines and Mexico, the latter clearly outnumbers the former. While remittances have helped many workers to support their families, the dependency on foreign jobs has its drawbacks. . . . [N]ot only must workers endure painful family separations and cultural dislocations, but they are also more likely to tolerate abuse in order to maintain their coveted foreign positions (Binford 2009; McLaughlin et al. 2017; Wells et al. 2014).

The Production of Second-Class Workers: Limitations on Labor Rights and Access to Citizenship

. . .

Live-in caregivers were expected to live in their employer's home, while agricultural workers are provided accommodations close to or on the farm. Domestic work differs from other labor because it occurs within the private sphere and is thus subject to little or no surveillance from regulatory authorities. Furthermore, in situations where workers live with employers, this arrangement can lead to the expectation of long unpaid overtime working hours, given that workers are viewed as physically available at any moment. . . .

The production of "second-class" workers within the TFWP in Canada sets the stage for "precarious migratory status," conceptualized by Oxman-Martinez et al. (2005) as the absence of rights, and/or the dependence on someone else for existing rights. . . . Such precarity can be further associated with the absence of social citizenship rights, such as access to public education and public health coverage, which are available to permanent residents and some legal migrant groups (Bhuyan and Smith-Carrier 2010; Goldring et al.

2009; Goldring and Landolt 2013). Canada actively contributes to the production of unfree and precarious migrant workers—the vast majority of whom are racialized individuals from the global south—through its policies that differentiate rights between citizens and those deemed "temporary migrants," irrespective of how many years they have lived in and contributed to the county (see Choudry and Smith 2014; Sharma 2006). . . .

Methodology

. . .

In the southwestern regions of Quebec and Ontario, we identified potential participating organizations providing services to temporary foreign workers by a number of means, including their affiliation with different forms of precarious migrants; with anti-violence against women coalitions; and with migrant worker advocacy groups. Participants were recruited directly through email and telephone invitations. Semi-structured interviews were conducted in person, in either English or French according to the interviewee's preference, with 47 service providers and decision makers: 23 from Quebec and 24 from Ontario. In Ontario, interviews occurred in the cities of Toronto ($n = 12$) and Hamilton ($n = 7$) and the agricultural Niagara region ($n = 5$). In Quebec, the majority were in the greater region of Montreal ($n = 22$) with one in the agricultural region of St. Remi. . . .

The interviews were conducted between 2011 and 2012. They focused on circumstances of women in lower-skilled occupations in the SAWP and other agricultural streams of the TFWP, as well as in the LICP. . . .

. . .

Results

Service providers shared their opinions about structural violence shaping the precarious conditions of female temporary foreign workers. They expressed how the transnational social pressure to maintain employment, the captivity of the employment contract, and the limitations in unionization, as well as the isolation and lack of privacy, act together to create an unbalanced relationship between the employer and female worker, leading to precarious migration and work conditions that foster a vulnerability to violence and abuse. . . .

The Gendered Context of Female Temporary Foreign Work

The proportion of women who worked in LICP is higher than in the SAWP, and more explicitly determined. For caregivers originating primarily from the Philippines, the gendered criteria for the program were explicit, be it through broader social policy or the specific criteria for applicants, as defined by the sending countries. According to an advocate for Filipina-Canadian women, "many millions of Filipinos now are actually being exported by the Philippines through a government sanctioned program, which is the labour export policy" (Ontario Service Provider). . . . Meanwhile, service providers highlighted how women who have participated in the SAWP in Ontario and Quebec are often single mothers.

> I've worked primarily with Mexican women, so I guess I'll speak specifically to that context because that's the one I know the best. But women are a minority in the program and there aren't a lot of spots available to women, and the ones that do get accepted to the program seem to . . . represent the most vulnerable of the vulnerable, the neediest women. I mean, they have to come from a rural background and be single I guess it's [an] informal criteria that women be single mothers and so it seems to be a lot of single mothers come and women who have really pretty severe financial need. (Ontario Service Provider)

Whether single mothers or not, the foreign work became for these women an important source of income in support of family members back home. . . . Reporting violence could jeopardize their continued employment and remittances, or in the case of caregivers, in particular, their immigration aspirations for themselves and

their families. Service providers reported that female migrant workers may fear not being recalled the following year or being deported if they ever report abuse. . . .

Major financial debts for women's consultations with recruitment agencies, particularly for caregivers, further push women to remain silent and endure difficult working conditions and forms of violence they would otherwise not accept, in order to reimburse such expenses. . . .

> Most of the time, because of the desperation of the Filipinos that they don't have jobs, they will take anything or hold the sharp edge of the knife. It's a double sharp edge [sic], they will hold it just to be able to get the job and find money to support their family. They will go to some agency who will find them a job somewhere in Canada for example, then they will be asking for a $4000 for all the so-called services by finding them an employer and facilitating the process of the paper. It's you don't have the money they have to sell everything that they can, including their soul, also they will get a loan from [a] loan shark just to be able to leave, that's how desperate we are with the Philippines. (. . .) It's the person that's leaving that has the burden of the debts because if she gets here then they have the money to pay back by instalment plus the money that they have to [provide] support. (Quebec Service Provider)

Transnational Social Pressure to Remain Silent

. . . [W]omen would only make a claim for more severe situations, whereas psychological abuse would remain hidden. Speaking of live-in caregivers, one service provider explained:

> Some of them have not disclosed fully what they have experienced and I know that some of them are really affected by it, but don't want to come forward to press charges against the employer because they're saying they're trying to rationalize to themselves that they

already have their landed immigrant [status], that it doesn't matter now. . . . And usually they always compare themselves when the time they were working in Singapore or Hong Kong or Middle East and they were saying that, "Oh, we suffered worse there than here," . . . (Ontario Service Provider)

. . .

In addition, service providers reported that family back home would even put pressure on the temporary foreign workers to remain quiet in cases of abuse or violence:

Just about all of the women that I've met under the temp foreign worker program have been single mothers and it continues to amaze me how families are dealing with the family separation issue specifically when you're a single mother, and how the extended family becomes even more critical and the communication and the link to that extended family has to be even more secure . . . There's a lot of insecurity and [it is] a destabilized situation that you're dealing with. (Ontario Service Provider)

. . .

"Doing Time": Captivity to the Employment Contract

Service providers raised concerns in regard to migrant workers' captivity to their employment contracts contributing to a disproportionate power imbalance between employers and workers, and in the particular case of live-in caregivers, overarching dependency on their employment status in order to access citizenship:

They came [to Canada] already structurally disadvantaged. I mean, they are living with their employer, their employer's name is on their passport, on their visa. It sets the tone of their relationship with the employer, an unequal relationship. They know the fact that the employer is going to be important in obtaining their landed immigrant status,

because Immigration required them to have a letter of employment . . . That's why sometimes they would stay with an abusive employer, so that they can comply with that need from the Live-in Caregiver Program. (Ontario Service Provider)

. . .

These conditions create tensions where workers "police" themselves and their colleagues, strive to stay under the radar, without causing problems, for fear that their future employment opportunities may be jeopardized. Workers choose to remain silent about their abuse, "doing their time" or "toughing it out," not wishing to attract attention to themselves:

In the underground community, it's keep your head low, keep quiet, don't make any waves, don't report anybody if something happens. Just try and move on and never talk about it. (Ontario Service Provider)

. . .

Unionization: Second-Class Workers

. . .

Despite the efforts of community organizations and unions, our respondents had common concerns that labor standards were not being enforced in temporary foreign workers' workplaces. Indeed, in both provinces, active attempts on the part of workers and their advocates to push for such enforcement could result in negative consequences for the workers. The labor and employment standards and benefits to which Canadian workers had access were seen as in conflict with the migration conditions under which temporary foreign workers have been granted the opportunity to work legally in Canada. In other words, service providers insisted that temporary foreign workers are generally more concerned with keeping their jobs than reporting workplace abuses or violations of their rights.

In addition, because temporary foreign workers are not often made aware of their rights when they come to Canada, and have little or no knowledge of what is available to them in the host country, they are vulnerable to exploitation on the employer's part and severely restricted in their ability to challenge this exploitation, be it through legal means or through access to services. Although some migrant workers, such as caregivers, receive an information session or work-related training prior to departure, this session tends to highlight workers' obligations to employers and facilitate assimilation of Canada's cultural norms, rather than their rights (McLaughlin 2009; Polanco and Zell 2017). One service provider in an Ontario farming region explained what he considered to be the main difference between foreign and Canadian workers:

> [Employers are] not going to treat the Canadians the way they treat the Mexicans. (. . .) They [the latter] have no vacation. They have no right to be sick, no right to leave in case they have an accident or anything. They have to work within the next day. If [there's no work] they don't get paid. They have no rights to unionize. (. . .) In that information session that they have in Mexico, and before coming [to Canada], all the remarks are about their duties and responsibilities and obligations here, but they don't say anything about any rights they have, about what they can do. (. . .) if they call the consulate, the consulate is the one who starts arguing with them. Like, "why did you do this, you have to obey your supervisor, you shouldn't leave because you were sick." (Ontario Service Provider)

. . .

Beyond the Call of Duty: Isolation and Lack of Privacy

The co-location of the worker's home and workplace was a major concern of respondents, across both provinces and programs. Since many temporary foreign workers live on or in close proximity to their employer's property, they typically do not control their home as renters do, with employers often putting conditions on visitors, curfews, etc. These restrictions are especially pronounced for women workers, whose sexuality is more closely policed (McLaughlin 2009) in a male-centered labor environment which hyper-sexualizes their bodies (Preibisch and Encalada Grez 2013). A service provider in Quebec explained this legal issue:

> When your housing is part of your employment contract, it's as if you are renting your own home. (. . .) It's your home because you rent it even if you do not see it come out of your wages. Then in this case, you have the right to access your housing as if you rented it. When I rent an apartment, the landlord cannot prevent me from inviting over whomever I want, even if it is the landlord's private property. Yes, it is a question of private property. . . . These people rent their home. We ought to permit them to have guests just like anybody else. (Quebec Service Provider)

In addition, temporary foreign workers find themselves in places where they have very little control and what could or should be considered their private "home" space, instead of being a place of reprieve, ultimately adds to their feelings of powerlessness. Not only are the women often prevented from having guests, but they are sometimes confined. Urban live-in caregivers not only live on their employer's property, but also often in their employer's home. A number of employers deny their caregiver the privacy (including a door which locks), which is written into the employment contract. This blurring of boundaries between work and private spaces often bleeds work into leisure time, whereby the employer feels empowered to place increased work demands on the caregiver, who in turn feels disempowered to refuse those demands.

> You live with the employer. Can you imagine living with your employer 24 hours? Or it's not 24 hours because it's five days. Can you imagine? Would you feel comfortable walking around in the middle of the night thinking that they can just open the door anytime they want? You could be taking the shower and they could just walk in. You just don't feel like this is your home. (Ontario Service Provider)

Agricultural workers may live in dormitories or extra rooms on the farms, and safety violations of these dwellings have been well documented (UFCW 2011). Farm workers are isolated on rural farms and often cannot leave the farm to travel to the closest town unless their employer or a supervisor drives them. Such physical isolation was reported by our participants as an aggravating factor for abuse and an obstacle to its denunciation:

> [There tends to be] a real lack of consideration about confidentiality and a lot of breaches of confidentiality in interactions with hospitals, doctors, nurses, medical services in general. (Ontario Service Provider)

. . .

Discussion

The results of this study corroborate the claim that women migrating for work in Canada, across various streams of the TFWP, face structurally embedded forms of social inequities based on their gender, origins, migratory status, and economic class (Altman and Pannell 2012; Preibisch and Encalada Grez 2010). . . . These women have tended to come from lower socioeconomic status, and in many cases, they are single mothers with the economic burden of supporting a family. Such transnational pressures, in addition to their precarious migration status, their captivity to the employment contract, isolation, and limitations in their capacity to unionize, create conditions of vulnerability to violence or abuse. The intersection of these social, economic, and political inequities provides employers with disproportionate power over them, silencing violence, abuse, or exploitation, as well as limiting access to services. . . .

The structural violence faced by female temporary foreign workers may not be unique to their gender, but service providers' testimonies illustrated how the conditions in which women migrated for work were nonetheless colored by it (Preibisch 2005). Silencing the violence appears to be reinforced by the symbolic violence defining female temporary foreign workers' femininity (Barber 2000). Indeed, with respect to caregivers, the recruitment process may vary based on sending countries' policies and regulations, but they remain governed by the shared criterion of an "ideal maid" who conforms to the requirements of inferiority, submission, discipline, and docility (Liang 2011; Pratt 2009). Female temporary foreign workers are negatively positioned in a global structure that reproduces colonial domination, which is representative of an uneven distribution of global economic and political forces; their vulnerability to abuse is compounded by their racialized status, their gender, and their positioning as "third-world women." Consequently, female temporary foreign workers face disproportionately heightened risks for sexual abuse and violence.

. . . [M]any employers do not treat the work performed as real work, and caregivers are not viewed as "real workers" who are entitled to working rights. Service providers highlighted concerns in regard to the living conditions of workers in both program streams, which inherently blur the boundaries between work and home, and work and leisure time, further entrenching employers' unbalanced power over their employees and enhancing the workers' isolation or even invisibility. The ties that bound migrant workers to their contractual employment provide employers with a disproportionate decisional power over workers' migration and working conditions, leaving workers and service providers with limited possibilities to react to violence and abuse. Moreover, service providers expressed difficulties in providing proof of such abuse and bemoaned the absence of appeal over the contract loss. Temporary foreign workers therefore "do their time" by keeping quiet and enduring adverse work and living conditions.

. . .

In the end, temporary foreign workers have an impact on and contribute to Canadian society (Preibisch 2005), making it incumbent upon the Canadian state to ensure the respect of their universal human rights while living and working on Canadian soil. Such is the least those serving temporary foreign workers would expect.

References

Altman, M., & Pannell, K. (2012). Policy gaps and theory gaps: women and migrant domestic labor. *Feminist Economics*, 18(2), 291–315.

Barber, P. G. (2000). Agency in Philippine women's labour migration and provisional diaspora. *Women's Studies International Forum*, 23(4), 399–411.

Bhuyan, R., & Smith-Carrier, T. (2010). Precarious migratory status in Canada: implications for social work and social service delivery. *Canadian Social Work Journal*, 12(1), 51–60.

Binford, L. (2009). From fields of power to fields of seat: The dual process of constructing temporary migrant labour in Mexico and Canada. *Third World Quarterly*, 30(3), 503–17.

Choudry, A., & Smith, A.A. (2014). Unfree labour?: struggles of migrant and immigrant workers in Canada. https://secure.pmpress.org/index.php?l=product_detail&p=781. Accessed 28 January 2018.

Citizenship and Immigration Canada (CIC) (2016). What are the improvements to the caregiver program. Government of Canada. http://www.cic.gc.ca/English/helpcentre/answer.asp?qnum=912&top=28. Accessed 28 January 2018.

Citizenship and Immigration Canada (CIC). (2017a). Find out if you can apply for permanent residence as a caregiver for children. Government of Canada. https://www.canada.ca/en/immigration-refugees-citizenship/services/immigrate-canada/caregivers/children/eligibility.html. Accessed 28 January 2018.

Citizenship and Immigration Canada (CIC). (2017b). Find out if you're eligible to apply for permanent residence—caring for people with high medical needs. Government of Canada. https://www.canada.ca/en/immigration-refugees-citizenship/services/immigrate-canada/caregivers/people-high-medical-needs/eligibility.html. Accessed 28 January 2018.

Citizenship and Immigration Canada—Research and Evaluation Branch (CIC) (2015). Canada facts and figures immigrant overview temporary residents. Table 2.3 and 2.4, 2005 to 2014. www.cic.gc.ca/english/pdf/2014-Facts-Figures-Temporary.pdf. Accessed 14 September 2016.

Faraday, F. (2016). Canada's choice decent work or entrenched exploitation for Canada's migrant workers? Report prepared for Metcalf Foundation. Toronto, ON. Retrieved from http://metcalffoundation.com/wp-content/uploads/2016/06/Canadas-Choice-2.pdf. Accessed 14 September 2016.

Farmer, P. (2004). An anthropology of structural violence. *Current Anthropology*, 45(3), 305–25.

Goldring, L., Berinstein, C., & Bernhard, J. (2009). Institutionalizing precarious migratory status in Canada. *Citizenship Studies*, 13(3), 239.

Goldring, L., & Landolt, P. (Eds.). (2013). *Producing and negotiating non-citizenship: precarious legal status in Canada*. Toronto: University of Toronto Press.

Liang, L. (2011). The making of an "ideal" live-in migrant care worker: recruiting, training, matching and disciplining. *Ethnic and Racial Studies*, 34(11), 1815–34.

McLaughlin, J. (2009). Migration and health: implications for development. A case study of Mexican and Jamaican migrants in Canada's Seasonal Agricultural Workers Program. Policy paper. Canadian Foundation for the Americas (FOCAL). http://www.focal.ca/pdf/Migrant%20Health%20McLaughlin%202009.pdf. Accessed 23 August 2016.

McLaughlin, J. (2010). Classifying "ideal migrant workers": Mexican and Jamaican transnational farmworkers in Canada. *Focaal–Journal of Global and Historical Anthropology*, 2010(57), 79–94.

McLaughlin, J., Don Wells, A. L., & Diaz, A. (2017). "Temporary workers", temporary fathers: transnational family impacts of Canada's Seasonal Agricultural Workers' Program. *Relations Industrielles*, 72(4), 682–709.

Oxman-Martinez, J., Hanley, J., Lach, L., Khanlou, N., Weerasinghe, S., & Agnew, V. (2005). Intersection of Canadian policy parameters affecting women with precarious immigration status: a baseline for understanding barriers to health. *Journal of Immigrant Health*, 7(4), 247–58.

Özden, C., & Schiff, M. (2006). *International migration, remittances and the brain drain*. Washington: World Bank and Palgrave Macmillan.

Polanco, G., & Zell, S. (2017). English as a border-drawing matter: language and the regulation of migrant service worker mobility in international labor markets. *Journal of International Migration and Integration*, 18(1), 267–289.

Pratt, G. (2009). Circulating sadness: witnessing Filipina mothers' stories of family separation. *Gender, Place and Culture*, 16(1), 3–22.

Preibisch, K. (2005). Gender transformation odysseys: tracing the experiences of transnational migrant women in rural Canada. *Canadian Women Studies*, 24(4), 91–97.

Preibisch, K. L., & Encalada Grez, E. (2010). The other side of el otro lado: Mexican migrant women and labor flexibility in Canadian agriculture. *Signs*, 35(2), 289–316.

Preibisch, K. L., & Encalada Grez, E. (2013). Between hearts and pockets: locating the outcomes of transnational homemaking practices among Mexican women in Canada's temporary migration programmes. *Citizenship Studies*, 17(6–7), 785–802.

Sharma, N. R. (2006). *Home economics: nationalism and the making of "migrant workers" in Canada.* Toronto: University of Toronto Press.

UFCW Canada and the Agricultural Workers Alliance. (2011). UFCW Canada report on the status of migrant farm workers in Canada, 2010–2011. http://s3.amazonaws.com/migrants_heroku_production/datas/487/UFCW-Status_of_MF_Workers_2010-2011_EN_original.pdf?1358374318. Accessed 23 August 2016.

UFCW Canada and the Agriculture Workers' Alliance (2014). The great Canadian rip-off! An economic case

for restoring full EI special benefits access to SAWP workers. http://www.ufcw.ca/templates/ufcwcanada/images/directions14/march/1420/The-Great-Canadian-Rip-Off-An-Economic-Case-for-Restoring-Full-EI-Special-Benefits-Access-to-SAWP-Workers.pdf. Accessed 28 January 2018.

Wells, D., McLaughlin, J., Lyn, A., & Diaz, A. (2014). Sustaining North-South migrant precarity: remittances and transnational families in Canada's seasonal agricultural program. *Just Labour, 22.*

Chapter 30

Overview

Who gets bullied at work? When it comes to gender, we might at first assume that women are the ones getting victimized. However, Sue O'Donnell and Judith MacIntosh argue that men too are exposed to harassment, belittling, and sometimes outright abuse, often because they don't conform to narrow ideas about what a man should do or be. Based on interviews with 20 men in Atlantic Canada, O'Donnell and MacIntosh documented the cost of workplace bullying to men's emotional and physical health, as well as the deficient response by authorities, which the authors call the "abandonment" of bullied employees. Men sought ways to take care of themselves to withstand the toxic effects of bullying but were sometimes constrained by the belief that as men they should be strong and not "wimpy." They also experienced a sense of inadequacy when they were unable to live up to the masculine ideal of the successful breadwinner and all-around tough guy. The authors establish that workplace bullying can have distinctly gendered components when directed against men, and that dominant definitions of masculinity can infect workplaces, making them toxic for men who can't or won't embody those definitions.

Gender and Workplace Bullying

Men's Experiences of Surviving Bullying at Work

Sue M. O'Donnell and Judith A. MacIntosh

Even though both women and men are targets of workplace bullying (WPB), to date, there has been very little research aimed at understanding men's experiences (Salin & Hoel, 2013). Furthermore,

O'Donnell, Sue M., and Judith A. MacIntosh, "Gender and Workplace Bullying: Men's Experiences of Surviving Bullying at Work," *Qualitative Health Research.* 2016; 26 (3): pp. 351–366, © 2016. Reprinted by Permission of SAGE Publications, Ltd.

understanding of men's experiences has been based primarily on combined samples of men and women; an approach that reinforces the prevailing assumption that all men face similar experiences and challenges when they are bullied. Men might face different challenges when they are bullied for a number of reasons. For example, constructions and expressions of gender could influence vulnerability and exposure to experiences of WPB as well as the nature and severity of those experiences. Health consequences of WPB and subsequent management might also vary according to gender.

. . .

Overall, sex difference and initial gender research has indicated that some men can be targeted for displaying non-masculine behaviors (Berdahl, Magley, & Waldo, 1996; Lee, 2002) or working in non-traditional roles (Eriksen & Einarsen, 2004; Henson & Krasas-Rogers, 2001; Richman et al., 1999). When it comes to recognizing and naming the problem of WPB, Salin (2003) suggested that, in general, men might be more hesitant than women to identify themselves as targets. . . .

Because understanding of men's experiences of WPB has mainly been limited to comparisons between women and men, variation in men's experiences has been largely unaccounted for. To understand and address the problem of WPB among men, it is important to examine and focus on those cases, for example, where men do seek help. Furthermore, it is critical to learn about varying conditions, including gender, that influence men's experiences of WPB. To address these gaps we used a qualitative grounded theory method to explore and explain men's experiences of and responses to WPB, and to examine whether gender or other qualities of difference influenced these experiences.

Method

. . .

Sample

We recruited 20 men from the Atlantic Canadian provinces of New Brunswick (17), Nova Scotia (2), and Newfoundland (1) using computer, newspaper, and radio advertising. . . .

Men in the study ranged in age from 35 to 75 years (average 56 years) and all identified themselves as White. . . . Men were bullied most often by other men (60%) but were also targeted by women (20%) and groups of men and women (20%); a phenomenon known as mobbing (Leymann, 1996). Most men were bullied by superiors

(75%). These findings are consistent with other research reports where it has been noted that men were bullied most often by other men (Jones, 2006; Namie, 2003; Zapf, Einarsen, Hoel, & Vartia, 2003) and in 70% to 80% of cases persons who bullied were in positions of power (Namie, 2003; Workplace Bullying Institute, 2007).

. . .

To situate the theory of surviving within the broader context of WPB, we first describe men's experiences of WPB. We then provide a theoretical overview of the central problem of abandonment, the process of surviving, and contextual influences (which have emerged from and have been defined in terms of the data). Next, we present the process of surviving that involved processes of addressing health and seeking relief. Contextual influences are woven throughout the description of the theory to explain differences in how men survive.

Results

Men's Experiences of WPB

Men in this study were targets of persistent bullying that involved a repeated pattern of harmful behaviors that included things such as manipulation, intimidation, humiliation, teasing, belittling, name-calling, criticism, blame, exclusion, isolation, punishment, oppression, withholding of information and resources, undermining work, credibility, and reputation, removing work roles and responsibilities, altering work expectations, hampering or denying advancement, dismissal and threats of dismissal, yelling, and physical threats. One participant noted, "The belittling, insulting, exclusion. The demeaning and downright ignoring. My boss would call a staff meeting, and I would not be invited, would find out later." Another described, "I was required to post my whereabouts whenever I left the office while the other employees were free to come and go as they saw fit." . . . Some men described bullying behavior as subtle and insidious (e.g., occurring in private or behind closed doors), whereas others described it as more overt (threats or humiliating jokes made in front of others).

Health Consequences

Emotional consequences were most commonly described and included stress, anxiety, panic attacks, depression, self-doubt and blame, lowered self-confidence and esteem, humiliation, fear, anger, frustration, irritability, powerlessness, hopelessness, decreased concentration, and memory changes. Some men described post-traumatic stress symptoms and disorder, self-harm, and suicidal thoughts. One man expressed, "I developed panic attacks and depression from this, and I still deal with it today. I still take medication." Another described struggling with thoughts of suicide, "I am not proud to say, but there were four occasions where I had had enough. I didn't attempt it, but everything was set up. The last time it happened I wrote the note."

Physical consequences, which were sometimes physical manifestations of stress, included headaches, sleep disturbances, decreased energy and fatigue, weight changes, gastrointestinal problems, cardiac problems, and exacerbation of chronic illness. One individual noted, "I was grinding my teeth so much from the stress that I was beating out my teeth, and I was getting these wicked headaches and stuff"; "I started not being able to sleep, and my memory was starting to become a problem"; "My cholesterol went up, stomach problems. I'm on pills for all of that stuff since this happened."

Bullying influenced personal, professional, and financial well-being and resulted in social consequences such as changes in relationships, withdrawal and isolation at work and at home, unemployment, loss of pension or reduced pension, reduced pay (disability, over qualified for jobs), career reputation changes, and health care costs. One man described, "I became testy with people including my loved ones." Some other men described the financial impact: "Disability was nothing compared to what I was getting and with that comes your credit, trying to survive, you know what I mean."

Responses to Bullying

In response to experiencing WPB, most men took some action (formal or informal) to address and resolve the problem. This involved seeking information and help from workplace professionals, including managers, bosses, human resource personnel, and union representatives. Although men perceived some of these sources as supportive, others were described as adding to the problem. There were no cases where seeking help from these sources resulted in workplace organizations taking appropriate steps to resolve the bullying. . . . Some men, for example, were offered opportunities to alter schedules or work from home as a means of dealing with the bullying. Such responses resulted in feelings of frustration and isolation as workplace organizations were seen as avoiding responsibility and perpetuating the problem: "I have a job to do. I don't just sit in a corner and do it myself. I oversee 14 people. Why don't you deal with the problem and tell that man to back off, that is the problem."

Among those men who chose not to seek formal help, there was often a perception that seeking help and bringing attention to the bullying would make the problem worse or would not result in positive or lasting change. . . . Although choosing not to take action might be seen as a passive or ineffective strategy, in some circumstances it was a useful approach as a number of men described experiencing negative consequences as a result of speaking up to try resolve the bullying. After having confronted the bully one man described, "Well he [*bully*] realized he was called out. He didn't say anything. But then after that, it just got worse." Based on her qualitative study of quitting and other forms of resistance to WPB, Lutgen-Sandvik (2006) reported that speaking up resulted in negative consequences for targets, including having their integrity, reputation, and mental health questioned.

The stress and energy required to go through the process of formal reporting (particularly when unsuccessful) was devastating for some targets. After having gone through a lengthy investigation process, one man described how the investigator (who he perceived as having written a clear and fair report) was terminated, the report was deemed biased, and a new investigation was ordered. When administration presented this news the participant described, "I stood up and said,

'I understand why people jump off the bridge,' and I walked out the door. I cried and cried and cried. It was just unbelievable, we had put so much into it."

Overview of Problem, Process, and Contextual Influences

Problem of Abandonment

Even though in some cases men were not surprised by the lack of support available to address WPB, all described feelings of distress and injustice associated with the desire for support and beliefs that WPB should not be allowed to persist in workplace organizations. In this context of divergent support, the central problem identified in these data is abandonment. Despite the need for support, men described feelings of being abandoned again and again: "I would go to the bosses that were involved and tell them what is being done to me and they wouldn't do anything"; "I got no support from HR [*human resources*], they left me, did not contact me. I told EFAP [*employee and family assistance program counselor*] my story. I still couldn't get any support from the company, they just abandoned me"; "I've got no closure with the whole thing because it was never addressed, it was just dropped." Another man expressed similar feelings based on the reaction from his employer: "The lack of response from the company, I felt like I was being abandoned."

. . .

Contextual Influences

Support

In the context of this study, men described support as the nature and availability of help and resources from a range of sources, including formal help from workplace, business, and community, and health care professionals and informal help from friends, family, and coworkers. . . . The mere presence of support and support mechanisms (e.g., human resources, policies to address WPB) was not sufficient for addressing the problem and, thus, the nature and availability of support refer to whether support was available, accessible, appropriate, helpful, and so on. Likewise, support was affected by men's ability and willingness to reach out and seek help, a factor influenced by perceived benefits and risks and ideas about when and how men ought to seek help.

Severity of Health Problems

Even though all participants experienced health consequences as a result of abandonment and ongoing WPB, health symptoms and problems varied. Less severe health problems were characterized by symptoms of stress and anxiety and continued ability to manage work and day-to-day activities and more severe health problems were characterized by acute depression and lack of motivation, withdrawal and isolation, post-traumatic stress symptoms and disorder, suicidal thoughts, and/or being hospitalized or admitted to treatment facilities. Strategies applied throughout the process were contingent on the severity of health symptoms, for example, when health was very poor some men expressed feeling that they had little choice but to leave the workplace as a means of surviving.

Financial Circumstances

Financial considerations and resources influenced surviving by constraining or enhancing perceived options for addressing health and seeking relief. Employment benefits including health insurance and sick leave and disability benefits, for example, limited or enhanced options for addressing health. As one man described, "Well I quit seeing the psychiatrist because I just can't afford to keep paying for it." Consideration of job opportunities and employability, family responsibilities, number of years to retirement, and pension benefits also influenced perceived choices for addressing abandonment.

Gender

In the context of this study, we used the term gender to describe how societal, familial, and personal beliefs about how men ought to behave influenced men's day-to-day lives and interactions with others. Social influences, including upbringing and role socialization, cause different men to act and respond to experiences of WPB and the associated health consequences in different ways. . . . For example, when seeking help to manage problems was limited by men's thoughts that they ought to be strong and tough or manage challenges independently, surviving was more difficult. On the contrary, when seeking help was a usual approach to handling problems, surviving was easier.

Theory of Surviving

Addressing Health

. . .

Caring for Self

Caring for self was a process of dealing with daily stressors and symptoms associated with abandonment and ongoing WPB and involved the use of personal coping strategies; strategies that varied according to individual coping styles and skills and contextual influences. Helpful strategies aimed at caring for self include the following: reading, writing, exercising, focusing on hobbies and spirituality, and talking to and spending time with family, friends, and others. Neglectful or potentially harmful ways of caring for self include the following: lashing out, over and undereating, increasing or initiating substance use (including cigarettes, alcohol, and drugs), isolating and keeping to self, and suicidal thoughts and self-harm.

Writing about experiences as a way of documenting the bullying and demonstrating evidence of this significant life event was a useful approach to coping. This took many forms, including keeping track of events in ledgers, letters, reflective documents, and poetry. Even though the process of writing and recalling details of experiences sometimes invoked stress, important benefits included sorting through thoughts and feelings, legitimizing and providing proof of the experience, and providing an outlet for reprieve. One man described turning to writing as a form of release: "I do a fair bit of writing and I write a lot of poetry, so I get a chance to get back at people in my poems." In

many cases, these documents were not shared with others, rather kept private. Some men who felt that the problem needed to be addressed or exposed as a matter of principle did submit their writing to employers and others considered it: "I have a letter for [company president], the head guy with the company, and I want him to read it."

. . .

Hobbies including exercise and recreation activities provided an outlet for distraction, relieving stress, and lifting spirits. As one man described, "I went out biking. I played tennis that was another release." Another noted, "Tai-chi has really helped me get my physical health in order and relieve mental tension." The nature and severity of health symptoms influenced health promotion and recreation activities, for example, depressive symptoms left some men feeling less motivated and interested in participating in activities: "I mean I love to golf, at least I did, [I] couldn't care less [now]." Social support also influenced self-care, including health promotion activities, despite ongoing depression and a lack of interest in activity one man described: "I bike when she [girlfriend] wants to go, that's the driving force. Once I'm out, I'm fine. But to come up with something fun, [I] just [have] no sense of joy."

. . .

For some men, reaching out and seeking support from others was difficult. Role socialization including beliefs about appropriate coping and help-seeking behaviors influenced ways of caring: "Kept it bottled in, did my job. I had to be tough. I think it started pretty damn young. Dad was an alcoholic. If he wasn't beating me it was mom. I bottled a lot of it up." Others found it difficult to admit vulnerabilities and were embarrassed by having been targeted: "Even my closest friends don't know because that's the other thing about being a man, it's embarrassing. It's hard to admit I'm being harassed at work because, no offense, that's something that I would anticipate a woman experiencing." Fear of being a burden or upsetting others also influenced support seeking: "I didn't want to go too far into it with her [wife] because I didn't want to worry her too much. I was just thinking I can handle this, it will be alright."

Fear of admitting vulnerabilities and the desire to be self-reliant and manage problems independently are responses to addressing problems among men that have been described by others (Addis & Mahalik, 2003; Connell, 1995; O'Brien, Hunt, & Hart, 2005).

As a result of abandonment and the associated consequences, relationships with others including typical sources of support were sometimes interrupted or fractured. One man described his coworkers as being hesitant to provide support because of fear of being bullied: "They [*coworkers*] all knew what was going on, but nobody would ever watch my back. Because if they [*bullies*] would do it to me, they would do it to them." Others described how abandonment and the associated consequences interrupted personal relationships: "I lost a lot of good friends. A lot of people have misconceptions about mental illness. And I mean it's treatable, a lot of it. And ah, they just stay away." When support was limited, or reaching out to others was met with reluctance, surviving was more difficult and feelings of abandonment were magnified.

. . .

Substance use as a way of coping with ongoing stress and caring for self was described by four participants. When asked about strategies to manage daily stressors and persistent WPB one man responded, "Beer, marijuana." Another described, "I tried to John Wayne my way through it. Just try to cope, endure, you know, drinking and partying. I was doing my best to forget." Smoking, over- and undereating, and excessive spending were other strategies used to cope with abandonment: "I started buying things to kind of fill that . . . to feel good. I also put on about 45 pounds, I would just eat and eat and eat."

. . .

Seeking Care

[. . .] In comparison with caring for self, which had a more short-term focus aimed at coping with immediate health symptoms, seeking care was directed at understanding and managing underlying health problems and diagnoses. Typical help-seeking practices and perceptions of health,

including ideas about if and when it was appropriate to seek help influenced seeking care. Social support, including encouragement or urging from others, and the perceived nature and helpfulness of health care providers influenced actions to seek care. Gender ideals were also influential and seeking care was sometimes avoided as a means of maintaining masculine identity and image.

For most men, changes in health occurred gradually over time and symptoms were often poorly understood. As one man described, "It [*depression*] kind of crept up on me, I didn't really see it coming. It's like all of a sudden I said, 'What the hell is going on?'" Another compared the gradual change in health to hearing loss: "If you subject yourself to loud noises over time, it's a cumulative effect, and all of a sudden you realize you're deaf. It's the same. You have no idea what it's doing until suddenly everything goes for a poop." Changes in health altered men's self-perceptions and sense of stability: "It wasn't something I was expecting. I always considered myself strong until this happened."

When health problems were new and unexpected, identifying and managing symptoms was difficult for some men and thus seeking necessary services was sometimes delayed. For example, although more than half of the participants did in fact seek help from health care professionals, it was often when health problems were quite serious and could no longer be avoided:

That morning I got up, showered, shaved, and packed a lunch and I just started shaking and couldn't stop. I called my drive and [*I called my*] work and told them I wouldn't be making it. Then I called my doctor.

Another man described, "Finally, I booked an appointment with the doctor and [he/she] thought, being stressed, I should go to counseling. Then, we find out, I [am experiencing] moderate to high depression." Although some researchers have reported that men might avoid or delay seeking help for fear of seeking services prematurely or without sufficient reason (Mahalik, Burns, & Syzdek, 2007; O'Brien et al., 2005), our previous research (O'Donnell et al., 2010) revealed that uncertainty surrounding experiences of WPB and associated health symptoms also influenced the nature and timing of help seeking among women.

. . .

Perceptions of health symptoms including what types of services were appropriate varied and influenced strategies to seek care. In considering sickness absence, for example, one man described, "I couldn't imagine going on stress leave. I thought about it enough to realize it wasn't really for me. I don't think I was ever bad enough. Cause to me, stress leave, you're on tranquilizers, you know?" Some others recognized the need for sickness absence more readily, particularly when health problems made it difficult to continue working: "That's why I went off work. I just couldn't function any more." Likewise, there were several examples where men were actively involved in seeking services: "[My] first connection with mental health was through the doctor. I asked him to set up an appointment." When reaching out and seeking care was a usual approach to handling health problems, addressing health was easier. As evident from some examples in this research, being socialized and encouraged to seek help and participate in regular health promotion activities early on influenced health behaviors among men in adulthood.

For some men, the desire to remain strong and maintain emotional control also limited seeking care. Despite suffering from anxiety, panic attacks, and suicidal thoughts, one man disclosed that he never discussed these consequences with his doctor or wife: "Well hindsight being the way it is, maybe it would have been better to go and talk to a doctor, but in my way of thinking, what the hell can a doctor do." Another man described, "Stress was really bad. I was going to go to the doctor, and I hate doctors. I hate to go to doctors. But it was bothering me bad. I'm not sleeping, tired, and just not right." When asked to reflect on the decision not to seek care the same individual replied, "I think it's a man thing, I really do. Like, I just didn't want to be a wimp [*laugh*]. And that's not right either. Things bother men as much as they do women I suppose." Other researchers

have reported that some men view not being able to handle problems on their own as a sign of weakness (O'Brien et al., 2005; Royster, Richmond, Eng, & Margolis, 2006).

. . .

Seeking Relief

Seeking relief was a process of taking action to limit and/or address persistent WPB and the associated consequences as a means of dealing with abandonment. Men sought relief by protecting and seeking resolution, processes that were instinctive and reactive or more measured and deliberate, and were influenced by support, severity of health symptoms, financial considerations, and the nature and context of the workplace and experiences of WPB. An important consequence of seeking relief was that targets found reprieve by temporarily or permanently putting a stop to the bullying.

Protecting

Protecting was a process of minimizing the bullying and its impact that involved avoiding and limiting contact with persons who were bullying. Protective strategies were often reactive and included things such as skipping meetings, monitoring and avoiding correspondence (e.g., phone calls, email), closing the office door, taking more frequent breaks, keeping to oneself, seeking opportunities to work from home or offsite, and avoiding work and work-related functions. Keeping track of WPB by documenting details of bullying incidents and saving correspondence (e.g., email, memos) were other forms of protecting.

. . . Avoiding bullying often required considerable planning and effort. For example, one man described plans to limit meetings with the persons who were bullying: "I am hoping to discuss if they [*supervisors*] would take a conscious look at when they're calling a meeting and whether or not they really need me there." Another man, who regularly worked offsite, ignored phone calls to avoid persistent bullying from his boss: "Caller ID is a wonderful thing." . . .

Withdrawing by creating physical distance from the workplace and experiences of bullying also provided relief. As one man described, "I started to take a break each morning and afternoon for 20 minutes. Something really foreign to me." Another noted, "I used to go to coffee breaks or lunch with these people often I just go myself now 'cause often it turns to some form of picking on me." Even though withdrawing provided short-term relief, it could also contribute to isolation by limiting support from others, including coworkers. Other researchers have described withdrawing and distancing as responses to WPB (Hallberg & Strandmark, 2006; Lutgen-Sandvik, 2006; O'Donnell et al., 2010).

. . .

Although protecting did provide relief, when faced with continued abandonment and WPB, potential benefits were difficult to sustain. Men who faced persistent WPB approached work with a sense of dread, "I hated to go in every day wondering what on earth is going to happen today," and found it difficult to go about their day as usual: "The areas that I had to go to day-to-day included his areas. I avoided these as much as possible. I found I could not do my job effectively and was constantly looking over my shoulder." When protecting was not effective in providing relief, many participants considered and enacted more lasting solutions to address abandonment.

Seeking Resolution

Seeking resolution was a process of putting a stop to WPB and occurred in the context of a lack of workplace support to address and resolve bullying. . . .

Seeking legal assistance to explore and enact options for resolving bullying was one approach to seeking resolution. After being threatened with dismissal, one man explained, "I took it to a labor relations lawyer, drafted a letter and had a defense all worked out, but it cost me 1,200 dollars." Even though legal action resulted in the letter of dismissal being withdrawn, the bullying persisted and the man eventually left for another job. To avoid legal battles, some targets were offered

settlements by workplace organizations. When settlements or payouts were not sufficient for covering basic expenses, including medications, they were not an effective or realistic solution for targets: "But right now, there's not enough money. We make ends meet, but it's horrible."

Seeking assistance from advocacy organizations such as Human Rights and Occupational Health and Safety was another approach to seeking resolution: "I talked to Human Rights and I talked to Occupational Health and Safety and they couldn't get any cooperation [*from workplace*] whatsoever. They just dropped it." Perhaps because at present, Human Rights and Occupational Health and Safety legislation in the Canadian provinces where the study took place does not specifically address WPB (or psychological harassment as it is often referred to in legal terms), it has not been a helpful approach for dealing with WPB. . . .

Leaving was aimed at putting a stop to WPB and involved separating from the bullying environment using strategies of transferring, retiring, and resigning. In some circumstances, transferring to another department or workplace location was considered a suitable option for ending the bullying: "Unless I can find something on a lateral and get out of there, it would be great." Opportunities for transfer were sometimes limited, however, and typically depended on whether job postings were available. Because transferring could require moving and would result in additional consequences, including disrupted relationships and social support, it was not preferred: "There may be potential in [*location*]. Could do that, really don't want to, my kids are here."

Because of employment and financial considerations, some targets perceived having little choice but to stay and endure bullying. A number of men, for example, described retirement and retirement benefits as influencing the decision to stay.

. . .

Factors including education, employment experience and opportunity, and wages influence decisions and actions around leaving. Even when job opportunities or offers were present, for some men, reduced wages made it difficult to leave: "You have to have schooling to make my kind of money. I've been around so long, they paid me just enough." Financial commitments including providing for family also influenced decision to stay: "I dreaded going to work but I had a wife and two kids and I needed to work." In comparison, work opportunities that offer improved working conditions and wages made it easier to leave. Greater financial stability and emotional and financial support from a spouse or partner also made leaving easier.

At the time of the study, 10 (50%) participants had left their jobs as a means of seeking relief, some others were contemplating it. Even though this was not a preferred choice, most of these men felt that they had little choice but to leave. . . .

Unemployment and difficulty finding employment, reduced pay, and career changes were other consequences of leaving: "We had to refinance twice. I am still in the hole and I'm 60 years old." Similar consequences associated with leaving or being terminated as a result of WPB have been described by other researchers (Hallberg & Strandmark, 2006; Lutgen-Sandvik, 2006; O'Donnell et al., 2010). As a result of abandonment and negative feelings toward work in general, some targets placed less importance on work. After leaving a senior management position, one man described that he was no longer interested in working in a supervisory role, a decision his wife had difficulty accepting: "My wife was ashamed of me when I worked in a junior position. She said, 'You should be doing consulting for 400 dollars a day,' I said, 'That's the last thing I want to do, it's too much responsibility.'" Although we often think of men as trying to live up to dominant masculine ideals, other people also position men in relation to these ideals (Connell, 1995; Willott & Griffin, 1997, 2004). . . .

On the whole, leaving made it easier to focus on and improve health. When targets chose to stay, conditions that changed or removed the bullying, such as the bully retiring or leaving, made it easier. When targets choose to stay despite persistent abandonment, continued efforts to survive WPB and the associated health consequences were

required. This was significant, given that a number of men chose to stay and endure the bullying and possibility of continued declines in health. Although the sustainability of enduring the bullying in the context of abandonment is poorly understood, it is not without challenges. When asked what was most difficult about dealing with ongoing abandonment, one man replied, "Coming in every day until then [*retirement*] and dealing with the asshole who screwed you."

Discussion

Findings from this research establish WPB as a serious and legitimate problem for men. The theory of surviving extends our understanding of men's experiences by providing a detailed and contextual understanding of the challenges faced by men who are bullied. . . .

This research establishes a connection between gender and health in the context of WPB and extends existing sex difference research by offering a gender perspective. Findings demonstrate that not all men conform to dominant norms, and there is a considerable range in men's behaviors when it comes to managing bullying and the associated health consequences. That more than half of the men sought help from workplace and organizational (13) and health care (11) professionals suggests that men can and do seek help. In addition, the fact that the central concern described by men was a lack of workplace support to address and resolve WPB demonstrates a desire for support among men.

Demonstrating evidence of variation among men (and the influence of dominant masculine ideals), some men have difficulties seeking help. Fear of being seen as weak, wimpy, or unable to handle work and WPB were described as barriers to seeking help. In many cases, it was only when health was poor and symptoms could no longer be avoided that men sought help. Whether this response is related to men's desires to be tough and live up to dominant masculine norms by avoiding or delaying help seeking (Mahalik et al., 2007; O'Brien et al., 2005) or the gradual and cumulative nature of health effects associated with bullying is difficult to determine. That women who were bullied also reported delaying treatment because of the gradual emergence of health symptoms (O'Donnell et al., 2010) suggests that delayed help seeking might be a common response among targets of bullying in general.

. . .

Although relating more to the research process, given reports that some men are hesitant to seek help and discuss problems including emotional health problems, it is significant to note that the men who participated in this study discussed a range of topics, including substance use, sexual function, mental illness, thoughts of suicide, and feelings of hurt and sadness. Some were teary during interviews. Gast and Peak (2011) also noted that men in their qualitative study health beliefs were very willing to talk about health. Although it could be argued that the group of men who responded to advertising and agreed to participate might also be those men who are more willing to talk about problems, some participants had never discussed details of the experience with anyone. Because gender is recognized as an important determinant of health, and WPB is a significant workplace health issue, incorporating gender analysis into studies of WPB is important.

. . .

References

Addis, M., & Mahalik, J. (2003). Men, masculinity, and the contexts of help seeking. *American Psychologist, 58*, 5–14. doi:10.1037/0003-066X.58.1.5

Berdahl, J., Magley, V., & Waldo, C. (1996). The sexual harassment of men? Exploring the concept with theory and data. *Psychology of Women Quarterly, 20*, 527–47. doi:10.1111/j.1471-6402.1996.tb00320.x

Connell, R. (1995). *Masculinities*. Los Angeles: University of California Press.

Eriksen, W., & Einarsen, S. (2004). Gender minority as a risk factor for exposure to bullying at work. *European Journal of Work & Organizational Psychology, 13*, 473–92. doi:10.1080/13594320444000173

Gast, J., & Peak, T. (2011). "It used to be that if it weren't broken and bleeding profusely, I would never go to the doctor": Men, masculinity, and health. *American Journal of Men's Health, 5*, 318–31. doi:10.1177/1557988310377926

Hallberg, L., & Strandmark, K. (2006). Health consequences of workplace bullying: Experiences from the perspective of employees in the public service sector. *International Journal of Qualitative Studies on Health and Well Being, 1*, 109–19. doi:10.1080/17482620600555664

Henson, K., & Krasas-Rogers, J. (2001). "Why Marcia you've changed!" Male clerical temporary workers doing masculinity in feminized occupations. *Gender & Society, 15*, 218–38. doi:10.1177/089124301015002004

Jones, C. (2006). Drawing boundaries: Exploring the relationship between sexual harassment, gender and bullying. *Women's Studies International Forum, 29*, 147–58. doi:10.1016/j.wsif.2006.03.001

Lee, D. (2002). Gendered workplace bullying in the restructured UK civil service. *Personnel Review, 31*, 205–27. doi:10.1108/00483480210416874

Leymann, H. (1996). The content and development of mobbing at work. *European Journal of Work and Organizational Psychology, 5*, 165–84. doi:10.1080/13594329608414853

Lutgen-Sandvik, P. (2006). Take this job and . . . : Quitting and other forms of resistance to workplace bullying. *Communication Monographs, 73*, 406–33. doi:10.1080/03637750601024156

Mahalik, J., Burns, S., & Syzdek, M. (2007). Masculinity and perceived normative health behaviors as predictors of men's health behaviors. *Social Science & Medicine, 64*, 2201–209. doi:10.1016/j.socscimed.2007.02.035

Namie, G. (2003). Workplace bullying: Escalated incivility. *Ivey Business Journal, 68*(2), 1–6.

O'Brien, R., Hunt, K., & Hart, G. (2005). "It's caveman stuff, but that is to a certain extent how guys still operate": Men's accounts of masculinity and help seeking. *Social Science & Medicine, 61*, 501–16. doi:10.1016/j.socscimed.2004.12.008

O'Donnell, S., MacIntosh, J., & Wuest, J. (2010). A theoretical understanding of sickness absence among women who have experienced workplace bullying. *Qualitative Health Research, 20*, 439–52. doi:10.1177/1049732310361242

Richman, J., Rospenda, K., Nawyn, S., Flaherty, J., Fendrich, M., Drum, M., & Johnson, T. (1999). Sexual harassment and generalized workplace abuse among university employees: Prevalence and mental health correlates. *American Journal of Public Health, 89*, 358–363. doi:10.2105/AJPH.89.3.358

Royster, M., Richmond, A., Eng, E., & Margolis, L. (2006). Hey brother how's your health? A focus group analysis of the health and health related concerns of African American men in a southern city in the United States. *Men and Masculinities, 8*, 389–404. doi:10.1177/1097184X04268798

Salin, D. (2003). The significance of gender in the prevalence, forms and perceptions of workplace bullying. *Nordiske Organisasjjonsstudier, 5*(3), 30–50.

Salin, D., & Hoel, H. (2013). Workplace bullying as a gendered phenomenon. *Journal of Managerial Psychology, 28*, 235–51. doi:10.1108/02683941311321187

Willott, S., & Griffin, C. (1997). "Wham bam, am I a man?" Unemployed men talk about masculinities. *Feminism & Psychology, 7*, 107–28. doi:10.1177/0959353597071012

Willott, S., & Griffin, C. (2004). Redundant men: Constraints on identity change. *Journal of Community & Applied Social Psychology, 14*, 53–69. doi:10.1002/casp.762

Workplace Bullying Institute. (2007). *U.S. Workplace Bullying Survey.* Retrieved from http://www .workplacebullying.org/wbiresearch/wbi-2007/

Zapf, D., Einarsen, S., Hoel, H., & Vartia, M. (2003). Empirical findings of bullying in the workplace. In S. Einarsen, H. Hoel, D. Zapf, & C. Cooper (Eds.), *Bullying and emotional abuse in the workplace: International perspectives in research and practice* (pp. 102–26). London: Taylor & Francis.

Part VIII
Gender and Media

The notion that Canadian society is saturated by media has become a cliché. Pop psychology and sociology abound with accounts of how media shape our beliefs and behaviours concerning gender. According to the most simplistic of these accounts, men and women mindlessly imitate the images of masculinity and femininity shown on their screens and pages, so that young women strive to be sexually provocative and skinny, while young men obsess over the macho trappings of violence.

The authors in this section go beyond this monkey-see-monkey-do approach to media and gender to examine how gender is constituted, represented, and differentiated in media products. There is much more to gender and media than simple imitation. Ideas about gender appear in ways that are not obvious or overt, and the "gendering" of media texts is often more complex than it appears at first.

Jackson addresses masculinized representations of Canada, but he does so through a rather different set of texts—beer advertisements. These will probably be familiar to everyone reading this text, but you may never before have thought of them as templates for masculinity. Jackson argues that these ads are not just offering up a "guidebook" for being masculine, they are offering a particularly *Canadian* vision of masculinity. In a globalizing world, in which much national distinctiveness is being erased, the creation of a distinct and self-conscious Canadian identity through gendered metaphors is noteworthy. This Canadian masculinity is not simply a way of being; it is also, inevitably, a commodity that is bought and sold through buying and selling beer.

Moving from the depiction of normative masculinity to the depiction of deviant femininity, Collins examines how female criminals have been represented in print and television media in Canada. Women who commit violent crimes are judged not just as lawbreakers but as failures at femininity, and Collins shows how selective use of words conveys the impression that these women are beyond the bounds of normalcy. While

Jackson's work focuses on how certain behaviours (like drinking beer) are gendered as masculine and praiseworthy, Collins shows how behaviour that stands in sharp contrast to gendered norms of femininity are treated as especially horrifying when not treated as laughable.

Media is a lot more than paper and TV screens, and Bivens and MacLeod and McArthur explore the world of internet-based social media. These media are noteworthy because users interact with them as creators, not just consumers. We don't just watch things on the internet, we create content, and in so doing we create ourselves (or at least the image of ourselves we want others to see). But how much freedom do users have when it comes to gender? Not much, it appears. Bivens demonstrates how deeply buried algorithms in Facebook constrain gender identity to a male/female binary, despite Facebook's public pronouncement that nonbinary identities are accommodated. Bivens argues that this is a technique of governance which produces regulated identities while purporting to allow free expression.

Similarly, MacLeod and McArthur find that the most popular dating apps also apply subtle pressure to conform to gendered binaries and presumptions of heterosexuality. If users are highly motivated they can subvert these pressures, but the default of these social media is toward a sex/gender binary. Nonbinary gender identity is still the "alternative" or "exception" rather than being one possibility in a palette of gender identities and sexual orientations.

Questions for Critical Thought

1. Do you consider yourself a critical consumer of media? What have you learned about gender from TV, the internet, social media, or print media?

2. Ads are often critiqued for their promotion of gender stereotypes, but Jackson argues that these gender stereotypes are also laden with connotations of other social categories, such as nationality. Are there any other media products you can think of that promote visions of "Canadianness" (or of any other national identity)?

3. Why is beer advertising so strongly gendered, compared to (for example) ads for fast food or cleaning products?

4. Can you recall media products you consumed as a child? How is children's media different from media targeted at adults, in terms of gender?

5. Should media be regulated in terms of the representation of gender? Should certain images or texts be censored or prohibited, or should anything be allowed?

6. If you have lived in different communities over the course of your life, have you noticed any difference in terms of the "mediascapes" and how gender is represented in different media products?

7. Have you or anyone you know used an online dating app? What sorts of gendered performances or expressions were made possible through the app?

8. Do you think people use Facebook or other social networking sites to perform or express their gender identity?

9. Do you consider yourself a content creator or primarily a consumer of content on the internet?

Chapter 31

Overview

Steven Jackson argues that beer, sports, and masculinity form a "holy trinity" of Canadian identity and that these three concepts become welded together through media and advertising. Focusing on iconic Molson ads, Jackson demonstrates how beer companies use sports to sell a version of masculinity that involves physical activity, outdoor recreation, camaraderie, and lots of beer. However, this is not simply any masculinity—this is a specifically *Canadian* articulation of masculinity. Two running ad campaigns, "The Rant" and "The Code," Jackson argues, are texts of gendered nationalism, selling a vision of masculinity in which any Canadian man can partake simply by buying beer. These advertising texts define hockey and beer-drinking as male spheres of action, in which an idealized form of Canadianness can be enacted.

Globalization, Corporate Nationalism, and Masculinity in Canada

Sport, Molson Beer Advertising, and Consumer Citizenship

Steven Jackson

Introduction

Within the context of globalization, nations have increasingly become the object of both production and consumption. Simply stated: "nation-branding has been incorporated into the project of nation building."[1] On one hand nations are being produced as branded tourist destinations or as sites of valuable material resources for either development or investment by international capital. On the other hand, nations, and their symbolic value, are increasingly being used by both global and local corporations as a means of aligning brands with national identity. . . . This is often achieved through a carefully orchestrated practice that involves corporations using the currency of "the nation," that is, its symbols, images, stereotypes, collective identities, and memories

Jackson, S. J. "Globalisation, Corporate Nationalism and Masculinity in Canada: Sport, Molson Beer Advertising and Consumer Citizenship." Sport in Society, 17(7) 901–16. (2014). Reprinted by permission of Taylor & Francis Ltd. www.tandfonline.com

as part of their overall branding strategy.[2] To this extent, advertising, marketing, and the creative promotional industries more generally play a key role in producing and representing particular visions of the nation that link brands and commodities with aspects of contemporary social life, ultimately influencing individual and group identity formation. This paper examines the relationship between one global commodity (beer) as it is located within one particular national context (Canada) through one particular brand (Molson) in order to explore how the process of corporate nationalism engages with and shapes other identities including masculinity. Specifically, this paper seeks to advance our understanding of how the circuit of culture[3]—that is, the production, symbolic representation, and consumption of commodities—plays a key role in contemporary identity formation and citizenship.

The relationship between sport, alcohol, and masculinity has arguably achieved holy trinity status[4] offering us unique insights into the nature of the contemporary consumer citizen. This point has become particularly evident in the context of professional and corporatized sport where various organizations have become dependent on breweries that serve as either team owners and investors, direct team sponsors, or sponsors via the purchase of various forms of attendant advertising time and space.[5] Historically, the basis of the relationship between beer and masculinity (and herein it is also argued sport) was structured around and through assumptions about what men do, where they do it, when they do it, why they do it, and with whom they do it.[6] In short, sport and beer have been consumed by a male audience sharing the experience of watching male athletes perform hypermasculine activities as a means of confirming and defining their own maleness. . . . Beer advertising provides an ideal site of analysis because of the intense pressure on breweries and their allied advertising agencies to continually accommodate and nurture new, often marginalized, target markets while simultaneously reaffirming a dominant form of masculinity that is steeped in nationalism and offered through a nostalgic lens all within the context of a highly competitive marketplace. . . .

The Holy Trinity

Historically, sport has long been celebrated as a man's world based largely on its links with the military and nationhood.[7] However, amidst a wide range of social changes and the advancement of women's rights, including their access to education, employment, and the political sphere, sport has gained renewed prominence and significance at particular junctures.[8] Indeed, within the context of contemporary gender relations, we might consider sport to be one of the last frontiers of masculinity. There are few cultural institutions and practices outside of sport that are as clearly defined in terms of gender and accepted as exclusive male spaces. Consider, for example, that sport (1) provides the opportunity to perform sanctioned physical aggression; (2) provides a context for the demonstration of courage, commitment, and sacrifice; (3) helps reaffirm historical links

with war and the military largely through popular discourse; (4) offers an exclusive space for men away from work and family; (5) provides a context where groups of men can engage in regular body contact without the fear of being labelled gay; and (6) offers a legitimated setting for male bonding and the consumption of alcohol and in particular beer. These factors reinforce sports' centrality in the holy trinity, a historically based, unique configuration of social institutions and practices, social identities and power relations that collectively form part of "a remarkably resilient bastion of hegemonic masculinity."[9] What role then do the production, representation, and consumption of beer play in articulating the holy trinity and corporate nationalism? To begin to address this question and its wider cultural implications, it is necessary to outline the social significance of beer and its promotional, symbolic representation via advertising.

Despite its seeming universality, the real power of beer (its production, representation, and its consumption) may lie in its taken-for-granted nature. It is this "naturalness" that enables beer to articulate with a range of other powerful social institutions, commodities, and social relations, thus reinforcing its elevated position. . . .

. . . The sheer economics of the industry point to the commodity's importance. For example, in the US, the alcohol industry spent $8.2 billion to air approximately 2.6 million commercials on television between 2001 and 2009; and expenditures increased 27% over this period, leading to a 30% increase in alcohol ad exposure.[10] Furthermore, highlighting both the significance of sport and its highly gendered consumer base, it is worth noting that almost three-fifths of television spending are typically allocated to sports programming.[11] Overall this confirms that:

[s]port offers a unique avenue for the drinks industry to reach its most lucrative target audience of males aged between 16 and 35. The increasingly global nature of sports brands, whether belonging to competitions or clubs, makes them even more attractive to an industry which itself is consolidating across national boundaries into "super-breweries."[12]

This quote reveals the more contemporary configuration and manifestation of the holy trinity by emphasizing the relationship between media, advertising, sport, and male consumers. How and why then do advertisers seek to reach men through beer advertising, and what are the possible consequences for society, gender relations, and contemporary forms of citizenship?

According to Strate,[13] there are five basic questions that can guide explorations of what it means to be a man in contemporary society: What kinds of things do men do? What kinds of settings do men prefer? How do men relate to each other? How do boys become men? How do men relate to women? Further, Strate asserts that beer advertisements may provide valuable insights into these questions given that "no other industry's commercials focus so exclusively and so exhaustively on images of the man's man."[14] To this end, Strate suggests that the power and pervasiveness of beer advertising's representations are such that they serve as a virtual "manual on masculinity":

> The manifest function of beer advertising is to promote a particular brand, but collectively the commercials provide a clear and consistent image of the masculine role; in a sense, they constitute a guide for becoming a man, a rulebook for appropriate male behavior, in short, a manual on masculinity.[15]

Confirming Strate's sentiments and referring to some of the wider socializing effects of beer and its promotion, McCracken[16] asserts that:

> Beer is no mere incident of masculinity . . . beer is crucial to the way in which young men present themselves to other males. Beer is not just one of the things that happens to be invested with maleness in our culture; it is at the very heart of the way maleness is constructed and experienced.

Clearly, beer is not just a commodity that is symbolically used and consumed to perform and confirm masculinity. Rather, its extensive promotional representations through advertising may also serve as both mirrors and systems of surveillance where men evaluate themselves and other men. The next section explores one particular beer brand, *Molson Canadian*, as perhaps the quintessential example of the articulation between the holy trinity and corporate nationalism in Canada. At this point, the paper explores how Molson brewery has endeavoured to link beer consumption with both national and masculine identities in Canada highlighting a particular manifestation of how spheres of consumption and citizenship are increasingly intertwined.

Molson Beer Advertisements: Manuals of Masculinity for Canadian Males

Founded in 1786, Molson is the oldest brewery in North America and, after merging with Coors (US) in 2005, is now part of the world's fifth largest "super-brewery." Through careful management of the family-owned trademark, including links with a wide range of sport leagues, teams, venues, and events, Molson emerged as "one of the few brands in Canada with the heritage and ubiquity needed to become an icon."[17] In 1994, Molson created one of the most definitive examples of corporate nationalism with the launch of their "I am Canadian" slogan and campaign that was tagged to their "Canadian" brand of beer. This marketing strategy gave Molson the advantage they needed to retain their market share over their number one rival in Canada, Labatt's.[18] However, Molson's next marketing campaign entitled "This is where we get Canadian" resulted in a loss of market share and was eventually abandoned. Undertaking what is best described as a brand soul search, Molson carefully reviewed its position using a range of market research techniques including surveys, qualitative observation, and focus groups to gain insight into what young people, and young men in particular, felt about Canada, nationalism, and national identity.[19]

With the market research completed on Sunday, March 26, 2000, Molson purchased a single television advertising spot during the Academy Awards. What quickly became an advertising phenomenon both within and outside Canada, "The Rant" (see narrative below) seemed to capture people's imaginations. Of particular note with respect to this analysis is the fact that sport played a key role in the campaign during the spring of 2000. Although Labatt's Breweries held the sponsorship rights to one of the longest running and highest rating sporting programmes on television, *Hockey Night In Canada*, Molson strategically maintained team sponsorships with all six Canadian franchises of the National Hockey League (NHL) and was thus able to gain brand exposure via signage and other promotions. Perhaps most significant was the live performance of "Joe" Canadian (played by actor Jeff Douglas) who performed "The Rant" live at NHL games in both Toronto and Ottawa during the playoffs. Although the "The Rant" campaign has been described and analyzed by others,[20] it is included here briefly as it serves as an important point of departure for understanding future Molson advertising campaigns.

Molson's "The Rant" Campaign

I am not a lumberjack or a fur trader. I don't live in an igloo or eat blubber or own a dogsled. And I don't know Jimmy, Sally, or Susie from Canada although I'm certain they're really, really nice. I have a Prime Minister, not a President. I speak English and French, not American. I pronounce it about, not "aboot." I can proudly sew my country's flag on my backpack. I believe in peacekeeping not policing, diversity not assimilation, that the beaver is a truly proud and noble animal. A toque is a hat, a chesterfield is a couch, and it is pronounced "Zed," not "Zee," "Zed." Canada is the second largest land mass, the first nation of hockey, and the best part of North America. My name is Joe and I AM CANADIAN! Thank You.[21]

Drawing upon a wide range of stereotypes, the commercial is a humble salute to many self-proclaimed positive features of being Canadian: friendly, polite, bilingual, multicultural,

champions at ice hockey, and advocates of peace. Of equal importance the entire advertisement is an illustration of how identity is defined out of difference, in this case to Canada's southern neighbour the US. The advertisement was widely celebrated both for its humour and its ability to capture/articulate a piece of the Canadian popular imagination. However, it did have its critics. According to Millard, Riegel, and Wright,[22] "The Rant" was both antagonistic and paradoxical for a nation that espouses modesty:

> The rant was an overtly, even belligerently, patriotic message that struck a chord in a country that . . . is supposed to be distinguished . . . by its absence of overt patriotism. . . . The rant was . . . the most spectacular manifestation of the wider trend towards loud nationalism in Canada. Canadians are now in effect, shouting about how quiet they are . . . in paradoxical contrast to the "loud American."[23]

"The Rant" was created by Glen Hunt of the advertising firm Ben Simon Ben Darcy.[24] Strikingly, while much of advertising is about storytelling, "The Rant" is partly autobiographical. Hunt had worked in New York and fell victim to many jokes about Canada and being Canadian, which included stereotypes about toques, beavers, and how certain words are pronounced. Hence, the ad was based, in part, on his own experience and taken in this context: it can be seen as both Canadian pride and a critique of America. Notably, and in keeping with the expectations of Canadian generosity, Hunt signed over the rights to "The Rant" to Molson for $2.

Despite the number of Molson campaigns that have been created and aired since 2000, "I am Canadian" remains the brand's signature tagline. Just under a decade after "The Rant," Molson launched a multi-platform campaign titled "The Code" mirroring, in many ways, various aspects of "The Rant." At this juncture, it is worth reiterating a key point about the social significance of beer to reinforce the multiple ways in which it shapes human interaction, social relations, and national identity and citizenship. As such, the production, representation, and consumption of Molson, like any other beer and its associated brand, are important because:

> drinking is a historical and contemporary process of identity formation, maintenance, and reproduction and transformation. Its importance to scholars of national identity and ethnicity is not principally in its role in grand state policies and the loftier ideals of the nation (although there too alcohol has played a role). Rather, drinking is the stuff of everyday life, quotidian culture which at the end of the day may be as important to the lifeblood of the nation as are its origin myths, heroes, and grand narratives.[25]

Molson's "The Code" Campaign

In 2008, Molson returned to the link between their brand and national identity with a series of advertisements referred to as "The Code." Similar to the "The Rant," "The Code" campaign draws upon a pastiche of Canadian stereotypes, involves a bit of national self-mocking, and is male dominated. The focus on men and masculinity in "The Code" campaign, however, is much more explicit. Moreover, central to "The Code" campaign is a commitment to linking the Molson brand to both masculinity and nationalism. Throughout the campaign, this occurs rather effortlessly given that it makes repeated reference to the sport of ice hockey—a gendered cultural institution and practice in Canada that conspicuously articulates nationalism and masculinity.[26] From this, it is suggested that masculinity itself emerges from and is performed within particular national contexts just as national identity may emerge from and be performed within particular contexts of masculinity. Hence, the way in which *masculine nationalisms*—where masculinity is socially constructed in and through different types of national spaces and practices (ice hockey in Canada, football/soccer in Europe, the UK, and South America, and rugby in New Zealand and South Africa)—and *national masculinisms*—where

particular characteristics or significations of nationality define masculinity (e.g., military, drinking cultures)—are produced, represented, and consumed within beer advertising and, arguably, corporate nationalism is paramount to this analysis.

Four television advertisements were produced for "The Code," series and these were strategically released to air during the 2008 NHL playoffs. The appeal to men is fully acknowledged by Molson, as brand director Michael Shekter explains:

> The strategy for [Molson] Canadian has not changed in years. The purpose of these ads is to reflect the role that Molson Canadian plays in the Canadian beer environment. It stands up for what it means to be a Canadian guy.[27]

In each advertisement, the audience hears dramatic music and a strong, serious, deep male voiceover accompanied by a series of fast-paced images corresponding to the dialogue. The narratives for all four advertisements (along with website links for viewing) are given below. To achieve consistency of brand communication, they all begin with "There is an unwritten code in Canada" and they all end with "This is our beer, Molson Canadian."

"The Code 1"[28]
There's an unwritten code in Canada. If you live by it, chances are: You've left your coat on some pile, and knew it wouldn't get stolen. You've never made a move on your buddy's girlfriend. You know that on a road trip the strongest bladder determines the pit stops. You've kept all your hockey trophies. You've replaced someone's pint if you've knocked theirs over. If your buddy's in trouble, you've got his back. You've clapped for a dancer even though she shouldn't be a dancer. You've used a blow torch to curve your stick. You've used your arm as an ice-scraper, and, you've grown a beard in the post-season. This is our beer, Molson Canadian.

"The Code 2"[29]
There's an unwritten code in Canada. If you live by it, chances are: You have a hockey scar

somewhere. You've gone on a road trip with a car that had no business going on a road trip. You're proud to know a girl who got jiggy with a pro hockey player. You feel kinda bad reclining your seat in an airplane. You've used a cheesy pick-up line because your buddy dared you. You fill your friend's pint before your own. You think hockey tape can fix anything. You've gotten kicked out of somewhere, and, you've turned down a booty call in the post-season. This is our beer, Molson Canadian.

"The Code 3"[30]

There's an unwritten code in Canada. If you live by it, chances are: You've driven an hour for 19 minutes of ice time. You've been to a bar that starts with Mc or ends in Annigan's. You appreciate a woman who's into sports. You'll call anyone with goalie equipment, a friend. You know what a J-stroke is. And sometimes, figure skating is worth watching. You know the sippy cup lid isn't as dumb as it sounds. You've worn a canoe as a hat. You've assembled a barbecue, and, they're not dents, they're goals. This is our beer, Molson Canadian.

"The Code 4"[31]

There's an unwritten code in Canada. If you live by it, chances are: You've overcome bad directions to find your friend's cottage. You know what happens on the ice stays on the ice. You've come face to face with some type of freaky bird. You hold a pint with all five fingers. And, it's never okay to rub another man's rhubarb. You know the last box in is the first to get unpacked. Your soap smells like soap. You've guess-timated a phone number. You've cooked with a flashlight and you recycle. This is our beer, Molson Canadian.

Throughout the ads, a range of fleeting signifiers are used to communicate the rules or "codes" of Canadian masculinity. Yet, despite their diversity, there are some common themes throughout the ads including Canadian politeness and demonstrations of male strength and courage. Furthermore, there are two key signifiers of masculinity in each advertisement: relationships with women

and dedication to sport. Here, women occupy marginal, sexually infused, positions as strippers, desperate amorous girlfriends, and prospective one-night stands, although humour or Canadian courtesy is used to neutralize any insult or offence that might be taken. References to sport are evident throughout the series, not only with respect to the context of the NHL playoffs within which the ads were aired but also in regard to the demarcated meaning of hockey to Canadian males whether it be through long-standing traditions (growing a beard during the playoffs, using a blowtorch to curve your hockey stick, driving long distances just to play a game) or the nonchalant parading of real or metaphorical badges of competition (keeping old hockey trophies, displaying a hockey scar).

Reminiscent of Strate's[32] "manual of masculinity" mentioned earlier, "The Code" certainly provides a series of defining characteristics and/or guidelines for Canadian men.

However, the opening catchphrase "There's an unwritten code in Canada" suggests that these rules are not formal and explicit; rather there is a subtle expectation that they are known. To this extent, the codes infer hegemony, whereby they are the widely represented, accepted, and reproduced commonsense, modus operandi for many Canadian males. As Williams[33] notes:

> Because the code is unwritten, and hence lost, the advertisement goes on to list not what the code states, but what the effects of following it look like; this allows you to know you're doing your job as a Canadian man without memorizing a bunch of rules and stuff.

According to Aaron Starkman, creative director at Zig Advertising, the agency credited with developing the campaign, "We wanted to continue to exemplify the values of the young Canadian guy in a heroic way.... This year's commercials are more honed in on beer occasions."[34] Thus, according to this cultural intermediary, it was not simply about representing both masculinity and national identity but celebrating it and articulating it with particular "beer moments," which are often highly gendered or exclusive male spaces or zones. And, in light of various discussions and debates about a contemporary crisis of masculinity,[35] these exclusive male spaces and zones serve as the means to enable the construction, negotiation, and even the evaluation of masculinities.[36] . . .

Conclusion

The holy trinity and its particular nation-based manifestations offer—for a number of reasons—a unique site through which the complexities and contradictions of contemporary identity formation can be explored. First, both masculinity and national identity have been commodified, that is, while they may operate as subjectivities that we embody, they are increasingly available through various forms of consumption thus confirming the articulation of the citizen-consumer. For example, with respect to masculinity specifically, Edwards[37] asserts that: "masculinities now are not so much something possessed as an identity as something marketed, bought—and sold . . . across the world of visual media culture more generally." Evidence of this reveals that men are investing more of their identity into consumption. According to Holt and Thompson's[38]

compensatory consumption thesis, "Men use the plasticity of consumer identity construction to forge atavistic masculine identities based upon an imagined life of self-reliant, pre-modern men who lived outside the confines of cities, families, and work bureaucracies." Yet, an exploration of the observation that males are increasingly seeking to find or express their masculinity through consumption warrants attention. . . .

. . . This paper has examined the power of both beer and sport as commodities steeped in masculinity and nationalism as illustrated through two of Molson's "I am Canadian" campaigns. In addition, the paper has highlighted potential implications for the reproduction of a particular form of national hegemonic masculinity through the articulation of the holy trinity (sport, beer, and masculinity) and national identity. Future cross-cultural research examining the articulation of the holy trinity in other national contexts will provide further insights into the similarities and differences in how local/national cultures embrace or resist particular global campaigns including those that reproduce inequities with respect to citizenship, identity, and human rights.

Acknowledgements

The author would like to thank the guest editor and Sarah Gee for their helpful feedback on this paper and the anonymous reviewers of earlier versions of this paper.

Notes

1. Huang, "Nation-Branding and Transnational Consumption," 3.
2. Jackson, "Reading New Zealand."
3. See du Gay et al., *Doing Cultural Studies.*
4. Wenner and Jackson, *Sport, Beer, and Gender.*
5. Collins and Vamplew, *Mud, Sweat and Beers.*
6. Strate, "Beer Commercials."
7. Burstyn, *Rites of Men.*
8. Messner, *Sport, Men and Gender.*
9. Sabo and Jansen, "Prometheus Unbound," 211.
10. Center on Alcohol Marketing and Youth, *Youth Exposure to Television Advertising.*
11. Center on Alcohol Marketing and Youth, *Youth Exposure to Television Advertising.*
12. Collins and Vamplew, *Mud, Sweat and Beers*, 123–4.
13. Strate, "Beer Commercials."
14. Strate, "Beer Commercials," 78.

15. Strate, "Beer Commercials," 78.
16. McCracken, "Value of the Brand," 131.
17. "Molson Canadian," 2.
18. Labatt's Breweries belongs to Anheuser-Busch InBev, "one of the world's top-5 consumer products companies, that manages a portfolio of well over 200 beer brands and holds the No. 1 or No. 2 market position in 19 countries."
19. For a range of reasons that may never quite fully be understood, there was a strong sense of Canadian nationalism (re)emerging at the beginning of the new millennium.
20. Cf. MacGregor, "I am Canadian"; and Manning, "I AM CANADIAN Identity."
21. B. Garfield, "Blame Canada and Molson for Brilliant Rant at States," 8 May 2000, www.adage.com/news_ and_features/ad_review/archives/ar20000508.html

22. Millard, Riegel, and Wright, "Here's Where We Get Canadian."
23. Millard, Riegel, and Wright, "Here's Where We Get Canadian," 15.
24. It has been suggested that Molson got the idea for the "I am Canadian" campaign from a song by David Hook titled "I'm Canadian," which can be traced back to at least 1994 and whose lyrics contain many of the references in the beer commercial.
25. Wilson, *Drinking Cultures*, 12.
26. Gee, "Mythical Ice Hockey Hero"; and Whitson and Gruneau, *Artificial Ice*. This is despite the enormous success of the Canadian Women's ice hockey team in the Olympics and World Championships and the massive growth of female ice hockey in Canada.
27. J. Lloyd, "New Molson Canadian Platform Is in the Code," April 15, 2008, www.marketingmag.ca/brands/new-molson-canadian-platform-is-in-code-13820
28. www.youtube.com/watch?v=XAwg71Gg9ek
29. www.youtube.com/watch?v=i4cIDO1w4Bw&NR=1
30. www.youtube.com/watch?v=aQL0Q6EvdH0
31. www.youtube.com/watch?v=TRvwWcUsrE8&NR¼1
32. Strate, "Beer Commercials."
33. "Williams Reviews That New Molson Canadian Advertisement," January 13, 2009, http://maxandwilliams.wordpress.com/2009/01/13/williams-reviews-that-new-molson-canadianadvertisement/
34. Lloyd, "New Molson Canadian Platform."
35. Atkinson, *Deconstructing Men & Masculinities*; Clare, *On Men*; Edwards, *Cultures of Masculinity*; and Gee, "Mythical Ice Hockey Hero."
36. West, "Negotiating Masculinities."
37. Edwards, *Cultures of Masculinity*, 43.
38. Holt and Thompson, "Man-of-Action Heroes," 426.

References

Atkinson, M. 2011. *Deconstructing Men and Masculinities*. Toronto: Oxford University Press.

Burstyn, V. 1999. *The Rites of Men: Manhood, Politics, and the Culture of Sport*. Toronto: University of Toronto Press.

Center on Alcohol Marketing and Youth. 2009. *Youth Exposure to Television Advertising on Television, 2001–2009*. Baltimore, Md: John Hopkins Bloomberg School of Public Health.

Clare, A. 2000. *On Men: Masculinity in Crisis*. London: Chatto & Windus.

Collins, T., and W. Vamplew. 2002. *Mud, Sweat and Beers: A Cultural History of Sport and Alcohol*. Oxford: Berg.

du Gay, P., S. Hall, L. Janes, H. Mackay, and K. Negus. 1997. *Doing Cultural Studies: The Story of the Sony Walkman*. London: Sage in association with The Open University Press.

Edwards, T. 2006. *Cultures of Masculinity*. New York: Routledge.

Gee, S. 2009. "The Mythical Ice Hockey Hero and the Contemporary Crisis of Masculinity: The National Hockey League's 'Inside the Warrior' Advertising Campaign," *Sociology of Sport Journal* 26(4): 578–98.

Holt, D., and C. Thompson. 2004. "Man-of-Action Heroes: The Pursuit of Heroic Masculinity in Everyday Consumption," *Journal of Consumer Research* 31: 425–40.

Huang, S. 2011. "Nation-Branding and Transnational Consumption: Japan-Mania and the Korean Wave in Taiwan," *Media, Culture & Society* 33(1): 3–18.

Jackson, S.J. 2004. "Reading New Zealand Within the New Global Order: Sport and the Visualisation of National Identity," *International Sport Studies* 26(1): 13–29.

Lloyd, J. 2008. "New Molson Canadian platform is in the code," April 15, *Marketing Magazine*. www.marketingmag.ca/brands/new-molson-canadian-platform-is-in-code-13820

MacGregor, R.M. 2003. "I am Canadian: Canadian Identity in Beer Commercials," *Journal of Popular Culture* 37(2): 276–86.

Manning, E. 2000. "I AM CANADIAN Identity, Territory and the Canadian National Landscape," *Theory and Event* 4(4): https://muse.jhu.edu/journals/theory_and_event/v004/4.4manning.html

McCracken, G. 1993. "The Value of the Brand: An Anthropological Perspective," in D.A. Aaker and A.L. Biel, eds., *Brand Equity and Advertising*, pp. 125–42. Hillside, NJ: Lawrence Erlbaum.

Messner, M. 1992. *Sport, Men and Gender: Sports and the Problem of Masculinity*. Boston, Mass: Beacon Press.

Molson Canadian. 2001. *Canadian Advertising Success Stories*. Toronto: Canadian Congress of Advertising.

Millard, G., S. Riegel, and J. Wright. 2002. "Here's Where We Get Canadian: English Canadian Nationalism and Popular Culture," *The American Review of Canadian Studies* 32(1): 11–34.

Sabo, D., and S.C. Jansen. 1998. "Prometheus Unbound: Construction of Masculinity in Sports Media," in L. Wenner, ed., *Mediasport*, pp. 202–20. London: Routledge.

Strate, L. 1992. "Beer Commercials: A Manual on Masculinity," in S. Craig, ed., *Men, Masculinity and the Media*, pp. 78–92. London: Sage.

Wenner, L., and S.J. Jackson. 2009. *Sport, Beer, and Gender: Promotional Culture and Contemporary Social Life*. Zurich: Peter Lang.

West, L.A. 2001. "Negotiating Masculinities in American Drinking Subcultures," *Journal of Men's Studies* 9: 371–92.

Whitson, D., and R. Gruneau. 2006. *Artificial Ice: Hockey, Culture and Commerce*. Peterborough, ON: Broadview Press.

Wilson, T. 2005. *Drinking Cultures*. Oxford: Berg.

Chapter 32

Overview

It used to be the case in criminology that violent offenders were assumed to be men. In the last few decades, however, a series of sensational and high-profile crimes with presumed female criminals have complicated that picture. Rachel Collins sets out to explore whether media coverage of Canadian female criminals takes up or plays off of stereotypes of femininity. Women are frequently figured as victims in crime stories; their positioning as perpetrators requires that this apparent deviance from gender norms be explained to readers.

Through a careful quantitative analysis of major Canadian newspapers, Collins shows that the language used for female perpetrators is generally more extreme and fear-inducing than that used when the perpetrator is male. Female criminals are provided as evidence that crime is indeed rampant and out of control, if even girls and women are engaging in it. Female criminals are also described in terms that suggest mental illness or highly sexualized behaviour, with their sexiness and attractiveness (or lack thereof) played up while the violent details of their crimes are played down. The intersecting oppressions of race, Indigeneity, and gender are also evident, as Indigenous women and women of colour are described in ways that emphasize poverty, marginality, and distance from "mainstream" society.

"Beauty and Bullets"

A Content Analysis of Female Offenders and Victims in Four Canadian Newspapers

Rachael E. Collins

Media sensationalism around female violence and aggression is not a novel phenomenon; women and girls who break the law have long captured the attention of mass audiences (Chesney-Lind and Irwin, 2008). Over the past two decades, however, negative images portraying hyper-violent and bad girls have become pervasive. These images often exaggerate girls' aggression by implying that women are more likely to engage in criminal activity than ever before (Chesney-Lind and Irwin, 2008; Schissel, 2006). Furthermore, the media can sensationalize certain acts of violence through portrayals of female victims. . . .

[M]ixed methods research (MMR) combining content and critical discourse analyses was conducted on four Canadian newspapers (*Vancouver Sun, Saskatoon Star Phoenix, Winnipeg Free Press* and the *Toronto Star*) that constitute a cross-sectional sample based on population size, ethnic diversity, and geographical location. In order to explicate the gendered archetypal portrayals of criminals and victims, the current analysis sets out to determine whether a series of themes relating to fear of crime and marginalization are more prevalent in articles referring to female offenders and victims relative to their male counterparts. These data further our understanding of how media

Collins Rachael E. "'Beauty and bullets': A content analysis of female offenders and victims in four Canadian newspapers." Journal of Sociology: 52(2):296–310 © 2016. Reprinted by Permission of SAGE Publications, Ltd.

portrayals create the "Other" based on gender, race, and social class.

Depictions of Female Offenders

The images and discourse used throughout media outlets provides a framework with which its consumers may construct representations of the world in which they live. This representation becomes flawed, however, when crime coverage is disproportionate to the true risk of victimization (Dowler et al., 2006). Female offenders have a distinct disadvantage in the media as coverage frequently disseminates portrayals of masculinized hyperviolent girls and women (Chesney-Lind and Irwin, 2008). As a result, female offenders can be stigmatized twice—as a criminal and as breaking the societal conventions of female submission. This often results in the media labelling female offenders as *nasty girls* (Barron and Lacombe, 2005), *bad girls* (Chesney-Lind and Irwin, 2008), and *monsters, misfits and manipulators* (Comack, 2006). The perception that women are increasingly entering the world of male-dominated violence is largely a reaction to the shifting of gendered social boundaries and weakening of the traditional spheres of informal control over women (Kruttschnitt and Gartner, 2008; Steffensmeier et al., 2005). For example, Schissel (2006: 71) points to an article in the *Alberta Report* entitled "Killer Girls":

> Girls, it used to be said, were made of sugar and spice. Not anymore. The latest crop of teenage girls can be as violent, malicious, and downright evil as the boys. . . . It's an unexpected by-product of the feminist push for equality.

. . .

Depictions of Female Victims

The archetypal portrayal of the crime victim often depicts personal stories of suffering at the hands of strangers. According to McShane and Williams (1992), the images of victims seen in news media are largely comprised of middle-class symbolism. Adding to this symbolism, Greer (2007) explains how images of victims are located along a continuum between the good victims, who deserve a great deal of sympathy, and the bad/culpable victims who, for one reason or another, deserve relatively little. The good victims are innocent, naive bystanders swept up by a crime that is both fearsome and unexpected. The bad victims, however, are culpable because they are seen as people who jeopardized their own safety through a series of bad decisions. This narrative depicts people who ultimately pay the price for being poor or breaking social norms.

Research suggests the innocent/good victim is designed to evoke a passionate response to the crime by creating empathy. The persistent depiction of innocent victims can elicit fear of our own potential victimization by "identification through shared experience" (McShane and Williams 1992: 267). The news media attempt to connect the consumer with the victim through excessive detail of their victimization and reinforcing that the victims were normal people who did nothing to deserve being victims, stressing that similar events could happen to anyone, anywhere, at any time.

These portrayals are most common in descriptions of what Nils Christie (1986: 19) refers to as the ideal victim—a victim that the public can relate to and thus is most effective at generating fear. According to Christie, the ideal victim is weak, carrying out a respectful chore at the time of victimization (such as Christie's example of caring for a sick relative), and *she* is where *she* cannot be blamed for being. Finally, the victim is violated by an offender that is not known to the victim. Thus, by contrast the ideal victim creates the ideal offender and together they create a powerful discursive tool: the ideal victim creates sympathy because the ideal offender creates fear, and vice versa.

In contrast, the narrative surrounding the bad victim typically portrays a demonized woman who likely has been accused of alcohol and drug abuse, sexual promiscuity, and dressing provocatively (Madriz, 1997: 88–9). Moreover, the bad victim is often portrayed as uneducated and poor.

This portrayal alludes to the victim's character flaws, implying that they have failed to achieve a normal amount of prestige and wealth, and thus lack a moral compass, so victimization is expected as the privileges of good victims do not apply to them (Humphries, 2009).

Methods

Mixed Methods Research

. . .

Four Canadian cities (100,000+) were chosen as a cross-sectional sample based on population size, ethnic diversity and geographical location. . . . Crime articles were collected from the *Vancouver Sun* (*VS*), *Saskatoon Star Phoenix* (*SSP*), *Winnipeg Free Press* (*WFP*), and the *Toronto Star* (*TS*) using a retrospective longitudinal design. Two numbers (two and seven) were randomly selected, yielding 1982, 1987, 1992, 1997, 2002, and 2007 as the sampled years. Twenty dates were then selected by a pseudo-random number generator to determine the issues sampled from each newspaper. In total, 1,190 articles were collected from 480 newspapers.

. . .

Themes for Fear of Crime

The study analyzed how the discourse of difference occurred through a series of themes grounded in existing literature on some of the potential causes of fear of crime and/or marginalization in the media. Language promoting fear of crime was divided into five sub-themes: words that relate to fear; excessive violence; the dehumanization of the crime; crime used as a metaphor; and crime is everywhere. Briefly, each sub-theme is discussed and examples from the newspapers are provided.

(1) *Fear*: The current analysis coded the presence of fear, any of its synonyms (e.g. "panic," "dread," or "terror"), or descriptions over the fear of specific people or groups. . . .

(2) *Excessive violence*: A common axiom in media reports on crime is described in the words

"if it bleeds, it leads" (Lee, 2007: 187). [. . .] It should be noted, however, that this theme is intended to capture the graphic depiction of violence rather than the selection of more extreme violent crimes per se. . . .

(3) *Dehumanization of the crime*: This sub-theme coded the presence of references to crime as an act that is brutal or animalistic (e.g. "savage," "wild"). Accounts were tallied as dehumanizing if the crime was described as mechanistic or devoid of emotion (e.g. "the crime was pure evil," "a calculated killing").

(4) *Crime as a metaphor*: The shocking nature of women committing crimes may lead to a discourse of crime and/or violence being described in metaphors that suggest crime is catastrophic. Example: "firebomb"; "tide"; "cancer"; "volcanic."

(5) *Crime is everywhere*: Coded the use of language (stated or implied) that crime was ubiquitous and rampant. Example: "classic case"; "all too familiar"; "another bloody weekend."

Themes for Marginalization

The second theme, separated into seven subthemes, analyzed the various ways the newspapers may potentially marginalize women. These subthemes were designed to capture what the media might say (or systematically exclude) about the crime itself, the offender, or the victim. The subthemes were: rationalization for why the crime occurred; dehumanization of the offender; offender as crazy or unstable; history of criminal behavior; reference to occupation; mention of poverty; and rationalizations for the offender.

(1) *Rationalizing the crime*: This sub-theme coded descriptions that provided an explanation, typically centering on extraordinary circumstances as to why the crime was committed. Comparing these data against descriptions of the crimes, offenders, and victims may explain why the newspapers choose to rationalize the crimes committed by different groups. Example: "battered wife syndrome";

"diagnosed kleptomaniac"; "it was the governments' fault for not checking the qualifications or psychological background."

(2) *Dehumanization of the offender*: Language that portrays the offender as abnormal or extraordinary. The type of language may mitigate fear by portraying the event as something normal people cannot experience. . . .

(3) *Crazy/unstable*: The section was designed to capture the narratives in which women, especially those who kill, are pathologized and demonized in the media. Example: "psychopath"; "deemed insane"; "mad"; "mental disorder"; "depressive illness that led to crime"; "brain abnormality"; "completely deranged."

(4) *History of crime/violence*: Analyzed the language used to refer to past crimes or violence as this discourse can further the portrayal that women are out of control. Example: "violent in the past"; "career criminal"; "known to police"; "repeat offender."

(5) *Reference to occupation*: Crime reports occasionally focus on stories that are out of the ordinary based on the unbelievable nature of educated people committing crimes. Example: "respected doctor"; "school teacher"; "wealthy, professional woman."

(6) *Poverty*: The notion that poverty begets crime has been a popular discourse in the media for years and single mothers living in poverty have often been blamed for juvenile delinquency. How many articles stated that the offender was poor or lived in a poor neighborhood? Example: "A site known for its low cost single parent housing"; "known prostitute and crack addict"; "collecting mothers' allowance."

(7) *Rationalization of the offender*: This subtheme analyzes how often the newspapers included rationalizations for female offenders. How did these rationalizations differ from those for male offenders? Example: "grew up in a single mother household"; "seduced by Satan"; "killed him because they thought he was a loser"; "drugged her unfaithful husband . . . in a deliberate jealous rage."

. . .

Results

The current data yielded 145 articles with female offenders and 941 articles with male offenders, as well as 458 articles describing female victims and 587 articles describing male victims (for detailed breakdown, see Table 32.1). Tables 32.2 and 32.3 provide the quantitative distribution of themes within the articles.

. . .

Table 32.1 Descriptive Statistics of the Crime Articles Sampled

Category	N
Total articles	1,190
Total crimes mentioned	1,815 (100%)
Total violent crimes	1,325 (73%)
Total articles with male offenders	941 (79%)
Total articles with female offenders	145 (12%)
Total offenders	1,614
Total male offenders	1,418 (88%)
Total female offenders	196 (12%)
Articles that mention race of offender	291 (24%)

(Continued)

Table 32.1 (*Continued*)

Category	N
Total race mentioned in all articles	464
White offender total	228 (49%)
Black offender total	50 (11%)
Aboriginal offender total	92 (20%)
Chinese offender total	28 (6%)
South Asian offender total	57(12%)
Other non-White	9 (2%)
Total local crime articles	558 (47%)
Vancouver	90 out of 257 (35%)
Winnipeg	115 out of 273 (42%)
Toronto	213 out of 348 (61%)
Saskatoon	140 out of 312 (45%)
Total race of victims mentioned	338
White victim total	209 (62%)
Black victim total	47 (14%)
Aboriginal victim total	42 (12%)
Chinese victim total	44 (13%)
South East Asian victim total	24 (7%)

Table 32.2 Prevalence of Sub-themes in Language Referring to the Offender

Theme	Females[1]		Males	
Fear	0.490 ±	0.032	0.431 ±	0.017
Excessive violence	0.211 ±	0.024	0.018 ±	0.013
Crime as a metaphor	0.014 ±	0.007	0.013 ±	0.004
Rationalization of the crime	0.098 ±	0.016	0.071 ±	0.009
Dehumanizing the crime	0.077 ±	0.016	0.069 ±	0.009
Crime is everywhere	0.104 ±	0.015	0.042 ±	0.008*†
Dehumanizing the offender	0.082 ±	0.018	0.088 ±	0.010
Crazy/unstable	0.049 ±	0.017	0.084 ±	0.009
History of crime	0.034 ±	0.019	0.105 ±	0.010*
Occupation	0.056 ±	0.020	0.125 ±	0.011*
Poverty	0.059 ±	0.015	0.060 ±	0.008
Rationalization of the offender	0.050 ±	0.013	0.038 ±	0.007

[1]Estimate of the marginal mean for the prevalence of each theme across 30 years.
*$p < 0.05$ main effect, male vs. female offenders.
†$p < 0.05$ interaction, gender and decade.

Table 32.3 Prevalence of Sub-themes in Language Referring to the Victim

Theme	Females[1]		Males	
Fear	0.442	± 0.024	0.480	± 0.027
Excessive violence	*0.186*	*± 0.018*	*0.200*	*± 0.020†*
Crime as a metaphor	0.008	± 0.005	0.018	± 0.006
Rationalization of the crime	*0.075*	*± 0.012*	*0.093*	*± 0.014†*
Dehumanizing the crime	0.074	± 0.012	0.071	± 0.014
Crime is everywhere	0.076	± 0.011	0.071	± 0.012
Dehumanizing the offender	0.105	± 0.014	0.065	± 0.015
Crazy/unstable	0.071	± 0.013	0.062	± 0.014
History of crime	0.076	± 0.014	0.063	± 0.016
Occupation	0.090	± 0.016	0.092	± 0.017
Poverty	*0.070*	*± 0.012*	*0.049*	*± 0.013†*
Rationalization of the offender	0.045	± 0.010	0.043	± 0.014

[1]Estimate of the marginal mean for the prevalence of each theme across 30 years.
*$p < 0.05$ main effect, male vs. female offenders.
†$p < 0.05$ interaction, gender and decade.

Discussion and Conclusions

The results have shown that significant differences in language exist in Canadian crime reports based on the gender of the offender and victim. Moreover, these differences were consistent: there were no differences between individual newspapers, and in many cases these biases could be seen across 30 years of crime reports. Given these reliable differences in language, qualitative inquiry is needed in order to provide context to these effects and reveal the narrative that they collectively create.

The Offender

The quantitative analysis demonstrated a significant profile for the female offender relative to her male counterpart. . . . The largest and most consistent of these differences, however, was the presence of language describing crime as being rampant and out-of-control in articles describing the crimes of female offenders. Collectively, these differences give rise to a powerful gendered narrative surrounding the female offender that became apparent during subsequent qualitative inquiry. The portrayal of women as less violent and relatively low-risk compared to males is an accurate one: women commit fewer violent crimes than men do (Comack, 2006). Moreover, male offenders were more often described as crazy or unstable. The narrative, however, was often replaced by other (arguably more damaging) discourses for these women—often portraying them as evil, cunning, and methodical, or as sexualized objects. An example from the *WFP* (1987: 8) illustrates a portrayal of a female offender that is highly sexualized and devoid of violence:

> A pair of bombshell-blond bandits pulled a daring daylight hold-up . . . sporting baseball caps, mirrored shades and white leather gloves, the women with the fuchsia lips pulled a sawed off shot gun and stuck up Western Water Works. . . . The shell-shocked salesman has run into beauty and bullets before, "it didn't feel too good, I'll tell you that."

Even though the above article recalled an incident about a violent robbery, the article did not include graphic depictions of violence (as was often the case for comparable offenses committed by males), but instead used terms like "bombshell bandits" and "beauty and bullets" to portray a fantasy depiction of the sexy bad girl with long white gloves and fuchsia lips. This sexualization was strictly reserved for women. In 1,190 crime articles, no single instance could be found that commented on a man's appearance as the primary focus of the article.

Another significant effect observed in the quantitative analysis was decreased rationalization for the crimes of female offenders. When examining the explanations provided for the crimes of men and women, the qualitative inquiry found powerful stereotypes surrounding female offenders. The discourse embedded within the explanations framed female offenders as cunning and methodical. Consider the following portrayal of a woman who killed her spouse as reported in the *WFP* (Janzen, 1997: 5):

> she sadistically bludgeoned her husband to death . . . she is a convincing woman who tried to cover it up . . . this was a vicious, sustained attack on a vulnerable, defenseless old man . . . she stood to gain more than 800,000 dollars . . . the whole scam was orchestrated by her.

The article conveys the portrait of a woman who is cold, calculating, and manipulative, playing to the archetype of the black widow. Similarly, a second article in the *TS* (Easton, 2002: 5) wrote: "Suspecting her husband of having an affair, [the offender] did what wealthy wives can afford to do: hire an investigator . . . then run him over with her silver Mercedes three times." These observations are consistent with those of Menzies and Chunn (2006), who show that mass media often portray women who kill their husbands as the embodiment of intimate danger. The language above stands in stark contrast to the language used when describing men who killed their wives.

The following example was a court report in the *TS* (Tyler, 1987: 5), during which the arresting officer stated the following about the man who killed his wife:

> He was a kind and loving person who did a tragic but very understandable thing . . . what you did was a people crime . . . everyone can experience the feeling of wanting to kill their wife out of anger.

The officer went on to testify that the offender's wife started swearing and lashing out at him after she found out that he was planning a Jamaican holiday with his mistress. "She called him a son of a bitch then slumped to the floor . . . and the screaming stopped" (Tyler, 1987: 5). She was stabbed by her husband eight times in the heart, liver and lungs; the article then went on to say he (the offender) "Was dressed impeccably in a charcoal suit" (Tyler, 1987: 5). The language used in the article simultaneously places blame on the victim for confronting her husband about his affair and rationalizes the behavior of the offender.

. . . Female offenders were sometimes subject to a much more lax treatment in the media. For example, the perception that women are non-threatening (i.e. the example of blond bandits) and sexualized. Alternatively, violent women were also occasionally subjected to labels of double deviance (Copeland, 1997). In short, women are often faced with a societal expectation of purity and goodness. Thus a woman who commits a crime may be stigmatized both for committing that crime and for breaking the societal norm of how a woman should act. This dichotomy is consistent with "the pedestal effect" (Crew, 1991)—women are treated as a gender less capable of crime. Therefore, their attempts at criminal behavior are sexualized and made in some sense playful, up to some ill-defined moral threshold. Female offenders who cross this threshold (by killing their spouse, for instance) are treated more harshly by the media than their male counterparts. They are portrayed as cold and calculating, and their crimes are less likely to be blamed on exceptional circumstances or mental instability. It is perhaps not surprising, in this context, that these portrayals are so often accompanied by text bemoaning the moral decay of western society and proclaiming that crime is everywhere.

. . .

The Victim

The current study recorded several changes in the language used over time. Over the last three decades, descriptions of excessive violence, as well as increases in the mention of poverty and the provision of rationalizations for why the crime occurred have become progressively more frequent within the discourse surrounding female victims. Subsequent qualitative analysis shows that the language differed greatly among female victims. The difference was greatest between those victims who were seen as good and deserving over the victims who were bad or not deserving of our sympathy, similar to the dichotomy observed for female offenders.

The crimes committed against "good" victims used graphic violence throughout the articles. For example: a victim "whose forearms were hacked off by a rapist" (*Vancouver Sun*, 1982: 1) and offenders who "bought a hacksaw and started to dismember the body . . . [then] boiled the woman's head and other body parts, and put the skull and other remains in his freezer" (Mitchell, 2007a: 8). In a similar vein, another article describes an "ex-boyfriend poured a jug of sulfuric acid over her head . . . her son watched as his mother screamed in pain . . . after with scissors he began to cut off her hair" (Shephard, 2002: 3). The heightened reference to excessive violence within the articles, particularly when coupled with the presentation of sympathetic characters, can create a sense of outrage and frustration. This fear can contribute to the politicization of crime and excessive measures of crime deterrence (Garland, 2001).

Portrayals of undeserving victims were predominantly poor and members of visible minority groups. Furthermore, newspapers rationalized the crimes committed against undeserving victims.

The result is consistent with the findings that media depictions can blame some rape victims for their own victimization due to the perception that "the victim wanted it, deserved it or lied about it" (Humphries, 2009: 20). The language provides simplistic and compelling explanations for victimization, creating a discourse that some women are victims due to poor decisions and lifestyle choices.

In the following two examples, the differences in language become obvious when two women with different lifestyles are murdered. The first article relays the murder of a poor Aboriginal woman (Dimmock, 2007: 8):

> the young mother pregnant with another child, was killed over a handful of crack cocaine . . . neighbourhood known for its street prostitution and crack houses. It was her neighbourhood, and on its streets she occasionally sold her body for sex.

The language of the second article, found in the *TS* (Mitchell, 2007b: 4), describing a white, upper-class victim is quite different:

> brutal beating . . . frenzied assault that occurred during a confrontation in a pathway between their upscale Markham homes . . . at the time of her death she was enjoying the summer of her life because she loved her new job and loved her new boyfriend . . . she was being considered for a promotion.

The articles depicted the victims using very different language based predominantly on their socioeconomic status and race. Throughout the articles examined, victims seen as deserving their fate were often portrayed as uneducated, neglectful mothers, who more often than not reside in a poor neighborhood.

. . . The danger, of course, is that the constant mention of poverty and poor lifestyle choices as the cause for victimization among women can become part of our commonsense understanding of why crime happens and who is responsible. In this context, it should be noted that race and gender are intertwined in these representations, as can be seen from the examples provided. In fact, others have pointed to the intersection between race and gender as critical for determining how women are portrayed in media crime reports (e.g. Brennan and Vandenberg, 2009).

. . . [I]t must be noted that the labels attached to both female offenders and victims are not simply assigned by the media, nor do the media create these labels in isolation. The labels are deeply embedded in public discourse and together encourage these dual ideological constructs of women and crime.

References

Barron, C. and D. Lacombe (2005) "Moral Panic and the Nasty Girl", *Canadian Review of Sociology & Anthropology* 42(1): 51–69.

Brennan, P.K. and A.L. Vandenberg (2009) "Depictions of Female Offenders in Front-page Newspaper Stories: The Importance of Race/Ethnicity", *International Journal of Social Inquiry* 2(2): 141–75.

Chesney-Lind, M. and K. Irwin (2008) *Beyond Bad Girls: Gender, Violence and Hype*. New York: Routledge.

Christie, N. (1986) "The Ideal Victim", pp. 17–30 in E. Fattah (ed.) *From Crime Policy to Victim Policy*. New York: St Martin's Press.

Comack, E. (2006) "The Feminist Engagement with Criminology", pp. 22–55 in G. Balfour and E. Comack (eds) *Criminalizing Women: Gender and (In)Justice in Neoliberal Times*. Halifax, NS: Fernwood.

Copeland, J. (1997) "A Qualitative Study of Barriers to Formal Treatment among Women Who Self-managed Change in Addictive Behaviours", *Journal of Substance Abuse Treatment* 14(2): 183–90.

Crew, B.K. (1991) "Sex Differences in Criminal Sentencing: Chivalry or Patriarchy?", *Justice Quarterly* 8(1): 59–83.

Dimmock, G. (2007) "Slaying Suspect Evades Police", *Winnipeg Free Press* 17 March: 8.

Dowler, K., T. Fleming and S.L. Muzzatti (2006) "Constructing Crime: Media, Crime and Popular Culture", *Canadian Journal of Criminology and Criminal Justice* 48(6): 837–50.

Easton, P. (2002) "Death by Car Caught on Camera", *Toronto Star* 6 August: 3.

Garland, D. (2001) *The Culture of Control: Crime and Social Order in Contemporary Society*. Chicago: University of Chicago Press.

Greer, C. (2007) "News Media, Victims and Crime", pp. 1–30 in P. Davies, P. Francis and C. Greer (eds) *Victims, Crime and Society*. London: Sage.

Humphries, D. (2009) "Introduction: Toward a Framework for Integrating Women, Violence, and the Media", pp. 1–17 in D. Humphries (ed.) *Women, Violence and the Media: Readings in Feminist Criminology*. Evanston, Ill: Northwestern University Press.

Janzen, L. (1997) "Professor's Beating Death Was Sadistic, Crown Says", *Winnipeg Free Press* 4 November: 5.

Kruttschnitt, C. and R. Gartner (2008) "Female Violent Offenders: Moral Panics or More Serious Offenders", *Australian and New Zealand Journal of Criminology* 41(1): 9–35.

Lee, M. (2007) *Inventing Fear of Crime: Criminology and the Politics of Anxiety*. London: Willan Publishing.

Madriz, E. (1997) *Nothing Bad Happened to Good Girls: Fear of Crime in Women's Lives*. Berkeley: University of California Press.

McShane, M. and F.P. Williams (1992) "Radical Victimology: A Critique of the Concept of Victim in Traditional Victimology", *Crime & Delinquency* 38(2): 258–71.

Menzies, R. and D.E. Chunn (2006) "The Making of the Black Widow: The Criminal and Psychiatric Control of Women", pp. 174–94 in G. Balfour and E. Comack (eds) *Criminalizing Women: Gender and (In)Justice in Neoliberal Times*. Halifax, NS: Fernwood.

Mitchell, B. (2007a) "Accused Man Is Not a Sociopath, Doctor Testifies", *Toronto Star* 8 June: 8.

Mitchell, B. (2007b) "This Is Not a "Whodunnit" Crown Says", *Toronto Star* 8 May: 4.

Schissel, B. (2006) *Still Blaming Children: Youth Conduct and the Politics of Child Hating*. Halifax, NS: Fernwood.

Shephard, M. (2002) "Ex-boyfriend Guilty of Acid Attack", *Toronto Star* 22 February: 5.

Steffensmeier, D., J. Schwartz, H. Zhong and J. Ackerman (2005) "An Assessment of Recent Trends in Girls' Violence Using Diverse Longitudinal Sources: Is the Gender Gap Closing?", *Criminology* 45(2): 355–405.

Tyler, T. (1987) "Confessed Wife Killer Breaks Down in Court as Officer Testifies", *Toronto Star* 13 June: 5.

Vancouver Sun (1982) "Arms Aid Denied", 17 March: 1.

WFP (*Winnipeg Free Press*) (1987) "Blond Beauties with Shotgun Hold Up Store", 8 June: 8.

Chapter 33

Overview

Facebook's enormously successful business model relies on marketing users to advertisers. What happens when user gender becomes a commodity too—and the gender binary comes along with it? Rena Bivens dives into the code behind Facebook to demonstrate how the social media site appears to incorporate gender diversity when attracting new potential users (following a much-publicized decision to allow users to identify themselves in nonbinary forms), but defaults to male/female (and occasionally "other") deep within the app, where most users never go. Some users who selected a nonbinary identity in the past ("legacy users") are able to retain a nonbinary status within Facebook, but others get recoded or regendered. Drawing on insights from queer theory about the construction and maintenance of gender binaries, Bivens shows how Facebook manufactures a gender regime that may not align with users' own gender identity. Bivens argues that this imposition of "gender authenticity" is a technique of governance.

The Gender Binary Will Not Be Deprogrammed
Ten Years of Coding Gender on Facebook

Rena Bivens

Introduction

On 13 February 2014, mainstream news organizations reported a change to the popular social media site, Facebook. Instead of two options for users to choose from when identifying their gender ("male" and "female"[1]), users were given a third option ("custom") that, if selected, offered 56 additional options. A few examples include agender, gender non-conforming, genderqueer, non-binary, and transgender (Goldman, 2014). These options are dependent on a user's selected language and were initially rolled out only for the English (US) version of the site, which any user can select to gain access.[2] Before confirming a "custom" gender selection, users are required to select a preferred pronoun: "he," "she," or "them." Reactions have ranged from cautious optimism and

joy to surprise, confusion, and mockery (Ferraro, 2014; Jones, 2014). Many lesbian, gay, bisexual, transgender, and queer (LGBTQ) organizations have praised practical implications for non-binary users, while several news anchors and anonymous commenters have instead sought to reassert the hegemony of the gender binary.

. . .

. . . Facebook's software configures, constructs, and attempts to impose a menu of gender identities (Nakamura, 2002) onto the users it interacts with. These users can also resist and hack these configurations. Ultimately, users and software designers mutually shape these programmed configurations of gender, severing and opening up possibilities for gendered life. The litany of other human actors who shape these interactions—programmers who wrote the code, superiors who managed design decisions, advertisers who desire increasingly granular data, and many

Bivens, Rena. "The gender binary will not be deprogrammed: Ten years of coding gender on Facebook." New Media & Society; 19(6):880–898, © 2017. Reprinted by Permission of SAGE Publications, Ltd.

other stakeholders—become specters in this software-user relationship, invisible on the front-stage, graphic user interface displayed by the software.

This analysis is restricted to a 10-year history, beginning with Facebook's original release in 2004 and ending with the 2014 custom gender settings. I demonstrate that the relationship between Facebook's software and its users is deeply structured by the gender binary while simultaneously productive of non-binary possibilities. The binary exists and does not exist at the same time. Considering both surface and deep software levels (the graphic user interface and the database), Facebook's software has always existed somewhere between a rigid gender binary and fluid spectrum.[3]

Methods

To examine Facebook's user interface as a historical artifact, I collected screenshots from different iterations of Facebook ranging from 2004 to 2014. Online image-based search engines were used for this purpose (including Google Images, Yahoo Image Search, and Flickr) since Facebook is inaccessible through archival engines like the Wayback Machine. . . .

. . . The analysis begins with a discussion of how gender is coded, resulting sociotechnical problems, and how programming decisions relate to monetization strategies. The next section, "Designing non-mandatory gender in year zero and custom gender in year 10," compares the non-mandatory gender design in 2004 with the custom gender project released in 2014. I then demonstrate how the binary has dominated design decisions with access to non-binary possibilities increasingly restricted during this 10-year history. Next, I explore how users have resisted Facebook's control by hacking their gender, followed by a discussion of surveillance, authenticity, and interoperability.

Coding Gender, Sociotechnical Problems, and Monetization

Just as there is more than one way to conceptualize gender in society, there is more than one way to code gender in software. . . .

In our non-binary world, choosing to code gender as a binary echoes the societal status quo and is in line with other practices that "code" gender, such as sex or gender identification on surveys and official documents. When restricted to a binary, all of these practices erase nonconforming genders and create sociotechnical problems in the process. It is technically (and legally) impossible for a non-binary user to register for a service that demands mandatory binary gender identification. If the user submits the form with a blank gender field, the software—in this case, Facebook—is programmed to reject the submission, demanding that the user "select either male or female." Having likely encountered similarly frustrating scenarios many times before, the user may resolve the technical error by misrepresenting their gender. . . .

. . . Facebook has been heavy-handed in its search for the "authentic selves" (Associated Press, 2014) and "real names" of its users. . . . When Facebook announced that the estimated 5–6% of fake accounts detailed with the company's initial public offering (IPO) on 18 May 2012 had grown to 8.7% (by 30 June 2012), Facebook's stock dropped to less than $20 (from $38 3 months earlier) and the company faced a lot of criticism (Rushe, 2012; Tavakoli, 2012). . . . Leading up to the IPO, Facebook's (2012) prospectus, filed with the US Securities and Exchange Commission, highlighted "authentic identity" as the first of three elements forming "the foundation of the social web":

> Authentic identity is core to the Facebook experience, and we believe that it is central to the future of the web. Our terms of service require you to use your real name and we encourage you to be your true self online, enabling us and Platform developers to provide you with more personalized experiences. (p. 2)

. . .

In more public-facing spaces, Facebook's rhetoric about authenticity becomes more about morality. Facebook's (former) Chief Privacy Officer, Chris Kelly, once argued that "Trust on the Internet depends on having identity fixed and known" (Kirkpatrick, 2010: 16) and Facebook creater Mark Zuckerberg has said that "Having two identities for yourself is an example of a lack of integrity" (Zimmer, 2010). These attempts at regulating identity erase and delegitimize the many authentic experiences of people who question their identity, people with identities that change over time, and people who depend on aliases for safety.[4] Ultimately, this regulatory regime forecloses everyone's capacity to inhabit fluid identities.

Designing Non-mandatory Gender in Year Zero and Custom Gender in Year 10

This 10-year analysis begins and ends with two important design decisions. In February 2004, Facebook's software was programmed with: a genderless sign-up page, a non-mandatory, binary field on profile pages, and three possible values for storing gender in the database. By February 2014, each of these elements had been modified: a mandatory, binary gender field on the sign-up page; a mandatory, non-binary field on profile pages; and four possible values for storing gender in the database. Both of these snapshots include software layers regulated by the binary and others that generate non-binary possibilities.

The early, 2004 design decision that programmed gender as non-mandatory on Facebook's profile pages created an important fissure for non-binary possibilities. At a deep level of the software, in the database, Facebook's gender field type was originally programmed to accept more than two values: 1 = female, 2 = male, and 0 = undefined. While a zero is inadequate in many ways, it is still a value beyond the binary of ones and twos. From a user's perspective—looking only at the user interface, not the database—the only non-binary option was to leave the field blank. This coding practice grants validity to binary genders while erasing non-binary genders, but it also produces conditions that allow for existence outside of the binary. The material reality of three accepted values in the database transgresses a rigid binary, yet falls short of a fluid spectrum, positioning the database somewhere in-between. . . .

By 2008, gender had been added as a mandatory, binary field on the sign-up page. Even in the February 2014, iteration—when the company finally capitulated to user demands for more gender options by reprogramming profile pages—the mandatory, binary field remained on the sign-up page. Meanwhile, deep in the database, users who select custom gender options are re-coded—without their knowledge—back into a binary/other classification system that is almost identical to the original 2004 database storage programming. The 2014 custom gender project offers the illusion of inclusion since surface changes to profile pages mask the binary regulation that continues underneath, at a deeper level of the software. . . . [C]onditions for gendered existence beyond the binary are activated on the software's surface. Yet, underneath the surface, these conditions are severed in favor of the binary. The design strategy that generates these conditions simultaneously reconfigures gender into data that conforms to the hegemonic regime embraced by marketing and advertising institutions. By actively employing divergent gender schemas within these two software levels, users and clients are satisfied simultaneously. Consequently, Facebook exercises power over its users by invisibly re-inscribing the binary. This technique maintains public-facing progressive politics while bolstering hegemonic regimes of gender control.

To explore this in more detail, consider the updated profile pages. In 2014, it is noteworthy that "custom" appeared as a third option, positioned only in relation to a normalized binary (McNicol, 2013). The binary is inscribed as dominant and "normal" while any "other" genders are positioned somewhere else in the hierarchy, only visible after the user clicks on "custom." . . .

In the database, however, the code forces users back into a binary logic. To explain this finding, I will revisit Facebook's Graph API Explorer. My use of this tool involved navigating to the online website for Graph API Explorer, signing in to my Facebook account, retrieving an access token, and selecting fields to explore (see Figure 33.1). To test how custom gender options are stored, I selected gender, along with identity (ID) and name fields to help determine which user was being tested. I also manipulated a test account. Each selected field became part of a "get" request that

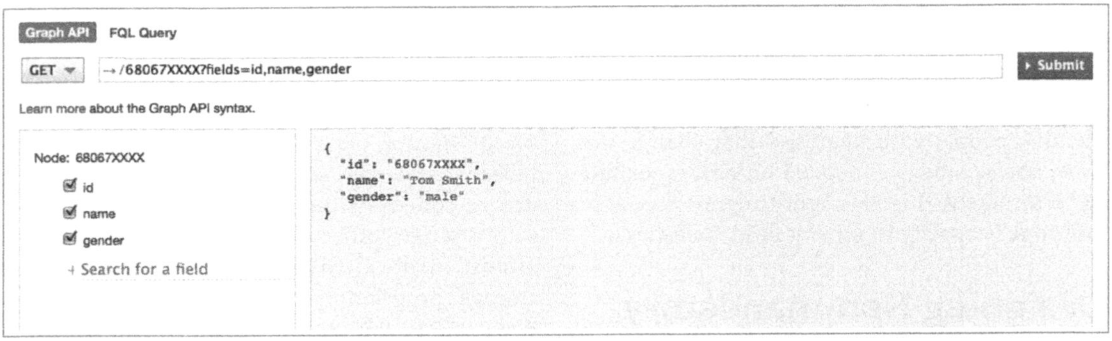

Figure 33.1. Example Query Using Facebook's Graph API Explorer Tool

I submitted to obtain a response to my database query. When I queried the names and genders of my Facebook "friends" and test account, information was returned in the format displayed in Figure 33.1.

Through these queries, it became clear that the database was programmed to store gender based on a user's pronoun, not the gender they selected. For instance, a user who selects "gender questioning" and the pronoun "she," will be coded as "female" in the database despite having selected "gender questioning." A query will identify the user's gender as "female" (see Figure 33.2). The pronouns "he" and "she" equate to male and female, but when querying a user with the pronoun "them," only name and ID are returned without any information about gender—as if the user has no gender at all (see Figure 33.3). The gender field actually turns gray, as seen in Figure 33.3.
. . .

Binary by Design: Restricting Access to Non-binary Possibilities

The original design decision to program gender as a non-mandatory field eventually became a thorny issue. As Facebook grew up—as a social network, a company, and an advertising hub—gender became an increasingly valuable data point. Monetization strategies became more sophisticated and design strategies revolving around gender turned interventionist. . . .

While there have been several changes to Facebook's sign-up page over the past 10 years,[5] the first 4 years were genderless. By 2008, "I am" appeared, followed by a drop-down list populated by male and female (see Figure 33.4). The field was mandatory and it has continued to be mandatory ever since. The only significant modification has

Figure 33.2. Example Query with "She" Pronoun Selected

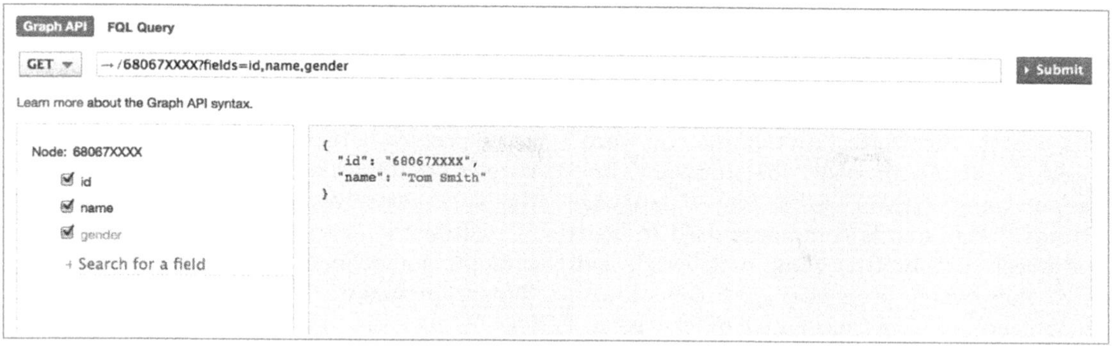

Figure 33.3. Example Query with "Them" Pronoun Selected

been to replace the drop-down list with two radio buttons.

While the persistence of the binary on the sign-up page in 2014 despite the new custom gender options is puzzling, it highlights the continuing tension between the software's production of binary and non-binary conditions for existence. . . .

With the release of the custom gender project, Facebook representatives declared that the company "want[s] you to feel comfortable being your true, authentic self" (Facebook Diversity, 2014). Director of Growth, Alex Shultz, said, "It was simple: not allowing people to express something so fundamental is not really cool so we did something. Hopefully a more open and connected world will,

by extension, make this a more understanding and tolerant world" (Associated Press, 2014). . . .

. . .

Forcing a database into a rigid binary by removing pre-existing (undefined) zero values is not an easy feat. . . . With each new user registration, the database expands while undefined values continue to accumulate in the gender field. Facebook's "solution" involved targeting undefined users and asking them to select a binary pronoun. Yet, the consequences of selecting a binary pronoun were concealed (re-coding gender from 0 to 1 or 2 in the database and obstructing future access to non-binary programmatic possibilities).

This is how it happened. On 27 June 2008, a post on Facebook's company blog noted growth

Year	Sign-Up Page		
	Gender Field	**Description**	**Mandatory**
2004			
2005	No	N/A	N/A
2006			
2007			
2008			
2009		'I am: Select	
2010	Yes	Sex/Male/Female'	Yes
2011		(drop-down list)	
2012			
2013	Yes	'male' & 'female'	Yes
2014		(radio buttons)	

Figure 33.4. Timeline of Gender-Related Changes to Facebook's Sign-up Page

in non-English users and pronoun translation problems. The neutral "them" pronoun was deemed grammatically problematic: "Ever see a story about a friend who tagged 'themselves' in a photo? 'Themselves' isn't even a real word" (Gleit, 2008). As an aside, the singular "they" has an extensive history in the English language (Santos, 2013), and is commonly used in trans and queer communities along with ze, zir, and other non-binary pronouns. . . . Facebook also recognized problems presented by the gender binary:

> We've received pushback in the past from groups that find the male/female distinction too limiting. We have a lot of respect for these communities, which is why it will still be possible to remove gender entirely from your account, including how we refer to you in Mini-Feed. (Gleit, 2008)

Yet, Facebook's design decisions did not extend programmatic possibilities beyond the binary nor move to a genderless design (remove gender as a category altogether). Either of these decisions could have offered a more respectful solution to this sociotechnical problem. "Removing gender entirely" equated to hiding gender from the surface level while retaining a gender value in the database. Even

this binary-driven compromise was incomplete, with leaks occurring in unexpected places. For example, the pre-populated labels "son" or "daughter" appear when familial relationships are expressed between users. Non-binary alternatives are unavailable and users cannot select the label themselves.

Ultimately, Facebook's "solution" involved prompting undefined users to indicate a preferred (binary) pronoun:

> we've decided to request that all Facebook users fill out this information [about their "sex"] on their profile. If you haven't yet selected a sex, you will probably see a prompt to choose whether you want to be referred to as "him" or "her" in the coming weeks. (Gleit, 2008)

Shortly following this announcement, a user posted a screenshot of this prompt, received upon log in (HTTF, 2008), as seen in Figure 33.5.

Targeting users who have previously decided not to offer gender data, requesting that data under vague circumstances (obfuscating the consequences by drawing attention to a "confusing" pronoun), and positioning the binary as the only way forward is ethically suspect, concealing the surveillance and opaque data collection practices that accompany binary selection.
. . .

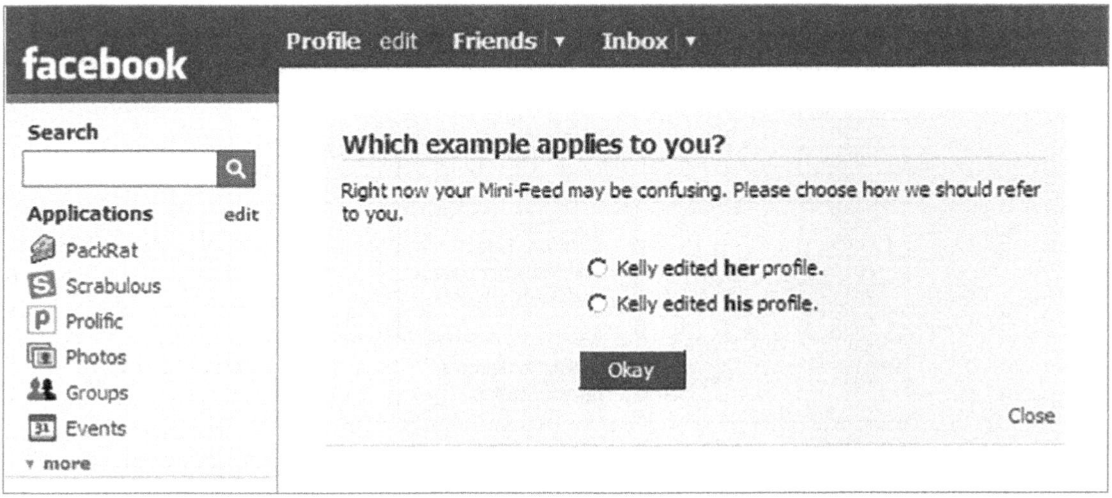

Figure 33.5. Request to Select Gendered Pronoun, 2008

[. . .]

Resisting Control by Hacking Gender

Despite these binary-driven design strategies, there was a loophole that was highly dependent on the early-2004 decision to code gender as a non-mandatory field. In defiance of Facebook's regulatory regime, a hack was developed. . . . The gender hack represented both a challenge and an important resistance to the binary regulation imposed by Facebook's design.

The experience of Facebook user Rae Picher[6] offers a useful illustration of how the gender hack worked. As Picher explains in a public post on 27 April 2011, "I recently lost my carefully preserved genderless status on Facebook due to an April Fools' Day joke where I came out as a heterosexual woman." . . . [W]hen Picher selected "female," the software replaced the 0 associated with Picher's user ID in the database with a value of 1. . . . Picher (2011) explains what happened next:

> When I tried to switch BACK to not having my gender identified, Facebook threw a hissy fit and demanded that I binary-gender ID for them, and proceeded to use gendered pronouns for me on my wall and in my friends' news feeds. Now that's just not cool.

Conclusion

This analysis of the materiality of antagonistic constructions of gender in social media software offers important opportunities for nuanced and dialectic insights into the "invisibly visible," shallow/deep capacities for the production and enactment of power in and through software-user relationships and the regulation of social life through code and design decisions. Despite the addition of 56 gender options in February 2014, the gender binary has not been deprogrammed from Facebook's software. . . . Overall, Facebook's software exists somewhere in-between a rigid binary and fluid spectrum. Yet, within this liminal space, and at a deep level, Facebook's software normalizes a binary logic that regulates the social life of users. . . .

Within this 10-year history, "authentic" representation of a user's gender identity reaches a peak with the 2014 custom gender project. Yet, the conditions for this non-binary existence are restricted to the surface of the software (and continue to be denied on the sign-up page where the binary remains an important regulator in the user verification process). Inauthenticity looms large in the deeper level of the database through the misgendering of custom gender users who select a binary pronoun and, as a result, are produced by the software as "female" or "male" instead of the custom option they selected. Paradoxically, Facebook's rhetoric and business model re-interprets these inauthentic, misgendered users as highly marketable, "authentic," and "real" while rendering the only users who have managed to escape Facebook's binary-driven design interventions—limited in numbers as these legacy users must be—as inauthentic. In the end, authenticity does not have to be authentic to be financially viable, as long as your clients perceive it as authentic.

Given that Facebook continues to dominate the social media industry, at least in the United States (Duggan et al., 2015), the company's design choices, coding practices, and business model are well-positioned to influence new start-up ventures and as such are important sites of critique. While more research is needed that critically examines how gender, race, and other salient social categories are produced within both surface and deep layers of software, it is clear, in this case, that Facebook has actively governed the formation of its users as gendered subjects. . . .

To be clear, the issue at hand is not supplying advertisers and marketers with better data about gender. Since corporate data collection comes with serious risks, including surveillance of marginalized populations, our efforts should not be geared toward creating more "authentic" and "real" data sets by programming more inclusive (and granular) categories on surface or deep software levels. Facebook's attempt to ally with trans and gender non-conforming communities resulted in programming practices that actively misgender them. This misgendering reinforces hegemonic regimes of gender control that perpetuate the violence and discrimination disproportionately faced by these communities. The capacity for software to invisibly enact this symbolic violence by burying it deep in the software's core is the most pressing issue to attend to.

Notes

1. Facebook's software offers no affordance for distinguishing between sex (sexual organs, represented as male, female, and intersex) and gender (feelings and expressions associated with gender identity). Both terms appear interchangeably within the user interface and policy documents over time.

2. Custom gender remains under development and has been incrementally released for other languages with varying sets of gender options. As of June 2014, English (UK) offered over 70 options; English (US) was modified to a free-form text-field in February 2015. Meanwhile, Français (Canada) still offers a mandatory binary as of July 2015

3. A fluid spectrum can be crudely understood as a continuum between masculinity and femininity, including every shade of masculine-femininity and feminine-masculinity, along with genders existing closer to the center (such as genderqueer) and gender-questioning identities. It also represents possibilities not yet fully imagined or embodied.

4. Consider victims of sexual abuse, people who keep their sexual orientation private from family or colleagues, and people who have careers that require anonymity.

5. Originally restricted to Harvard students, Facebook's 2004 sign-up page included name, student status, email address, and password. By September 2006, anyone over the age of 13 with a valid email address could join. In 2007, "birthday" became a mandatory field. By 2008, "status" (previously modified to allow non-students to join) had been removed

6. I obtained permission from Picher to include this experience.

References

Associated Press (2014) Facebook expands gender options: transgender activists hail "big advance." *The Guardian*, 14 February. Available at: http://www.theguardian.com/technology/2014/feb/13/transgender-facebook-expands-gender-options (accessed 14 February 2014).

Duggan M, Ellison NB, Lampe C, et al. (2015) Social media update 2014. *Pew Research Center*, January. Available at: http://www.pewinternet.org/2015/01/09/social-media-update-2014/ (accessed 9 July 2015).

Facebook (2012) Form S-1 registration statement. Available at: https://infodocket.files.wordpress.com/2012/02/facebook_s1-copy.pdf (accessed 6 July 2015).

Facebook Diversity (2014) Timeline photo. *Facebook*, 13 February. Available at: https://www.facebook.com/photo.php?fbid=567587973337709 (accessed 7 July 2015).

Ferraro R (2014) Facebook introduces custom gender field to allow users to more accurately reflect who they are. *GLAAD*, 13 February. Available at: http://www.glaad.org/blog/facebook-introduces-custom-gender-field-allow-users-more-accurately-reflect-who-they-are (accessed 1 July 2015).

Gleit N (2008) He/She/They: grammar and Facebook. *Facebook*, 27 June. Available at: https://www.facebook.com/notes/facebook/heshethey-grammar-and-facebook/21089187130 (accessed 2 March 2014).

Goldman R (2014) Here's a list of 58 gender options for Facebook users. *ABC News Blogs*, 13 February. Available at: http://abcnews.go.com/blogs/headlines/2014/02/heres-a-list-of-58-gender-options-for-facebook-users/ (accessed 25 February 2014).

HTTF (2008) Facebook's gender blunder. *Token Attempt*, 10 July. Available at: http://httf.livejournal.com/43728.html (accessed 25 February 2014).

Jones A (2014) Facebook's new gender options. *Storify*. Available at: https://storify.com/JonesAmberM/facebook-gender-options (accessed 4 July 2015).

Kirkpatrick D (2010) *The Facebook Effect*. New York: Simon & Schuster.

McNicol A (2013) None of your business? Analyzing the legitimacy and effects of gendering social spaces through system design. In: Rasch M and Lovink G (eds) *Unlike Us Reader: Social Media Monopolies and Their Alternatives*. Amsterdam: Institute of Network Cultures, pp. 200–19.

Nakamura L (2002) *Cybertypes: Race, Ethnicity, and Identity on the Internet*. New York: Routledge.

Picher R (2011) Facebook's gender binary got you down? *Facebook User Note*, 27 April. Available at: https://www.facebook.com/notes/rae-picher/updatefacebooks-gender-binary-got-you-downupdate/10150166319923922 (accessed 27 February 2014).

Rushe D (2012) Facebook share price slumps below $20 amid fake account flap. *The Guardian*, 3 August. Available at: http://www.theguardian.com/technology/2012/aug/02/facebook-share-price-slumps-20-dollars (accessed 6 July 2015).

Santos SR (2013) Let's talk about the history of gender pronouns (and gender-neutral pronouns) in English. *SaintRidley*, 22 September. Available at: http://saintridley.kinja.com/

lets-talk-about-the-history-of-gender-and-pronouns-an-1365242291 (accessed 12 January 2014).

Tavakoli J (2012) Facebook's fake numbers: "One billion users" may be less than 500 million. *Huffington Post*, 12 July. Available at: http://www.huffingtonpost.com/janet-tavakoli/facebooks-fake-numbers-on_b_2276515.html (accessed 6 July 2015).

Zimmer M (2010) Facebook's Zuckerbeg: "Having two identities for yourself is an example of a lack of integrity." *Michael Zimmer*, 14 May. Available at: http://www.michaelzimmer.org/2010/05/14/facebooks-zuckerberg-having-two-identities-for-yourself-is-an-example-ofa-lack-of-integrity/ (accessed 20 September 2014).

Chapter 34

Overview

Like Facebook profiles, dating apps are another field in which users consciously construct themselves, including their gender identities. Caitlin MacLeod and Victoria McArthur examine two popular apps (Bumble and Tinder) to determine how they govern their users' gendered presence. They use the concept of "affordances"—the cues and signals that one person can create to attract or dissipate the attention of another person—which take the form of customizable "widgets" on these two apps. Officially, users can identify themselves only by using a pre-set menu of choices, in the identity widgets, but other affordances provide room to complicate the gender picture. However, when indicating what sort of person the user wants to date, the app's functioning based on the presumption of a gender binary comes into play. MacLeod and McArthur argue that with this setup, gender becomes the primary determinant of who the app thinks you might want to date, and gender is treated as a restrictive and finite set of categories. They get into the nitty-gritty of how these apps might be redesigned so that gender is no longer the main driver of matchmaking, consistent with a twenty-first-century social world in which gender is understood by many to be fluid and diverse.

The Construction of Gender in Dating Apps

An Interface Analysis of Tinder and Bumble

Caitlin MacLeod and Victoria McArthur

Introduction

Is your dating profile true to who you are? Social networking technologies present us with tools to create representations of ourselves and to interact

MacLeod, Caitlin, and Victoria McArthur. "The construction of gender in dating apps: an interface analysis of Tinder and Bumble," *Feminist Media Studies*, 19:6, pp. 822–840, (2019). Reprinted by permission of Taylor & Francis Ltd. www.tandfonline.com

with others. These attempts at making our selves intelligible in computer-mediated contexts bring to bear both our lived identities and the structural supports and frictions afforded by the interfaces through which we act. . . .

In this article, we address that second need. Through an interface analysis of two mobile dating applications, Tinder and Bumble, we show how the affordances of these digital communication tools structure their users' identities as they are constructed and performed through the technology. In particular, we address two research questions. First, what options are available for presenting or obscuring one's gender? Second, in what ways do the apps' affordances offer cues through which subjects are made intelligible to strangers? We argue that gender is constructed within the apps both implicitly and explicitly, and while tools that support implicit gender cues allow users to share or obscure their gender with a degree of choice, those that require explicit declarations of gender do not account for a full range of user identities and experiences, and instead reflect the apps' sorting and matching processes.

. . .

About the Apps

. . .

In this article, we examine two . . . location-based mobile dating applications, Tinder and Bumble. These are not taken to be a representative sample, and indeed, this article specifically analyses version 1.10.4 of Bumble and version 6.3.2 of Tinder, as displayed on an iPhone 6 using iOS 10.0.2 on November 2 2016.[1] . . . This tight focus on two objects, without extending to the behaviours and motivations that surround them, is intended not to discount the role of individual agency in computer-mediated interactions, but rather to highlight the effects of design in encouraging and constraining user behaviours in a digital environment.

Tinder is a popular dating app available for iPhone and Android. It was founded by Jonathan Badeen, Justin Mateen, Joe Munoz, Dinesh Mrjani, Chis Gylczynski, and Whitney Wolfe, and launched in September 2012 (Laura Entis 2015). To use the app, users must enable their smartphone's location tracking and grant the app access to that data. Users can then set filters for age, gender, and geographical distance, and are presented with the profiles of prospective partners with the option to swipe left to reject the person or swipe right if they want to be matched with them. If two users swipe right on each other's profiles, they form a match and are able to message one another.

. . .

Bumble resembles Tinder with several key differences. With location tracking enabled, users set age, gender, and distance filters, and are presented with the profiles of prospective partners. Users swipe left to reject them or right to anonymously indicate interest, or "like" them. If both users swipe right, they form a match, and messaging becomes possible. In the case of a man–woman match, only the woman can initiate contact; in the case of same-gender matches, either user can initiate messaging. Bumble has an additional option, "BFF," which creates platonic same-gender matches. As in the case of romantic/sexual same-gender matches, either user in a BFF match can initiate conversation (Bumble 2016a).

Theoretical Framing

Feminist Technoscience

. . . In modern graphical user interfaces (GUIs), users are often limited to the gender binary of male/female, conflating biological sex with gender via interface text. The distinction between sex and gender is made in feminist theory (Judith Butler 1990), but gender is still used as a formal variant for sex even in academic papers today (David Haig 2004). This language is relevant in the context of online identity, where several GUIs use the term gender when they really offer a binary choice between male and female (Victoria McArthur 2014).

. . . Where text allows for an array of gender identities, modern GUIs are designed with pre-packaged options for sexed bodies (Jenny Sundén 2009). Mobilizing the work of Butler (1990), we argue that interfaces that only allow for the production of heteronormative identities act as "regulatory regimes," forcing users to align themselves with a rigid binary system. This is not to say that users do not find creative ways to play with gender in spite of these limitations (Sundén 2009). However, we argue that there is no technological reason for these constraints; rather, they are the product of a hegemonic cycle of heteronormative design practices.

This hetornormativity is present in multiple societal and sociotechnical systems. Thus, we argue that the majority of GUIs typically reify what Butler refers to as a "universal rationality" (Butler 1990, 9), presenting users with a range of choices that exist within a range of options that is deemed acceptable both by the majority of developers and the majority of users. These options are often conflated with gender via interface labels but generally boil down to a binary choice between male or female (Adrienne Shaw 2015). . . .

Identity and Affordances

According to Goffman 1990, 240), we use information "substitutes—cues, tests, hints, expressive gestures, status symbols etc.—as predictive devices" when meeting strangers for the first time. Using the metaphor of a stage production to describe the roles and practices that structure social interaction, Goffman argues that these substitutes for direct access to the performer's underlying self, and other elements of the staging (214–215) and the information conditions of the performance (216), are important for how that performance is received. . . .

Together, these theoretical perspectives begin to suggest the effect that the constraints imposed by the app's self-presentation tools have on users' abilities to present their genders both authentically and intelligibly to other users. The apps' interfaces determine what types of information can and must be shown frontstage (Goffman 1990, 32), and the nature of profile-based communication obscures all information that cannot be included in the performance. . . .

Affordances represent a way of understanding the role of the apps' interface in providing cues through which performances of identity are made intelligible to users of the app and to the apps' algorithms. The concept of affordances, originated by James J. Gibson (1979) in reference to animals in relation to their environment and applied to designed objects by Donald A. Norman ([1988] 2002), refers to the cues provided by an object that suggest its functions and operation. These clues and constraints reduce the number of alternatives from which we must chose, and so reduce the amount of specific knowledge required (Norman [1988] 2002, 55). . . .

Method and Data

We began our data-collection process by documenting every screen visible to the user throughout both apps' Profile and Settings sections using the screenshotting function on an iPhone 6. This included all widgets and menus, not only those relevant to gender, and extended as far as the initial screens of those apps, like Spotify and Instagram, that can be added to users' profiles on one or both dating apps.

. . .

Within the structure of both Tinder and Bumble, the majority of widgets for customizing one's presentation are located within the Profile section of the app. The exceptions are the widget to make one's profile public and the widget to select the gender or genders with which one might be matched, which are located in the Settings sections of both apps. In the following sub-sections, we present individual discussions of the affordances of those widgets that most directly pertain to gender.

Tinder

From within the profile-editing screen, it appears that the main tool Tinder version 6.3.2 gives users to present themselves with a particular gender is the gender widget within the "Edit Info" section of the app. The value selected in this widget, however, does not appear when the profile is displayed. Nevertheless, this widget cannot be left unset. The Own-Gender widget allows users to select one of two gender options, male or female, from a list that appears after tapping on the currently selected gender label. Users must select one option or the other; the widget defaults to the gender pulled from Facebook, but users can switch between the two options. The About widget presents a more public opportunity for gender performance. This could be done implicitly, using language, emoji or references that create a particular gender presentation; or it could be used explicitly, to add nuance to the (perceived) presentation afforded by the Gender widget. For example, a user could add their pronouns, clarify their transgender status or specify that, despite what the Gender widget required, they have a non-binary gender.

Tinder requires users to present themselves using photographs, which are the first thing that is seen when looking at a Tinder profile. The app automatically pulls from Facebook's profile pictures; photos can be reordered, deleted, or replaced with other photos from Facebook or from their phone's memory. The app will not allow a profile created from a photo-less Facebook profile to progress without adding at least one photo, and while it is possible to delete five photos by tapping and confirming, tapping on the sixth and final photo does not bring up the option to delete, only to replace the main photo or add a new one. Tinder does not require that photos be images of the user, only that they respect the intellectual property and privacy rights of others (Tinder 2016a). However, while it is conceivable that an individual could chose to mask their gender by refraining from including an image of their face and/or body, given the primacy of photographs within Tinder, it is unlikely that this would be conducive to successfully using the app. Instead, photos are likely to be used by both performer and audience to construct an understanding of the performer's identity, using visual cues as resources for making their identity intelligible.

Bumble

Bumble's primary tool for establishing gender is the Gender widget within the My Info section of the app, which does not display outside of the profile-editing screen. This widget's use of radio buttons labelled "Male" and "Female" presents the options as a strict binary. The app pre-selects one based on the user's Facebook profile. While it is possible to switch to the other gender option, tapping the button for that option first prompts a confirmation alert warning, "You can only change your gender once, and won't be able to change it back. Are you sure?" In this two-step process, the user must tap "Yes" before the change is made, and the change is not reversible. Every subsequent attempt to select the other gender option prompts an alert reading "You have already changed your gender. Please contact us if it needs to be changed again." Thus, while Bumble was created with the

intention of addressing a particular issue pertaining to gender, this does not necessarily translate into a sophisticated understanding of gender. In fact, the choice to restrict messaging capability based on gender makes stable gender categorization central to Bumble in a way that is not the case with Tinder. Limiting the ability to switch back and forth prevents men frustrated with the app's restriction on their messaging abilities from circumventing the restriction by temporarily adopting the female label. This strategy reifies the assumption that gender is both binary and static. Like Tinder, Bumble's "About Me" text box gives users a means to present a nuanced version of gender using identity labels not available in the Gender widget, pronouns, and evocative language, references and emoji.
. . .

Analysis

In both Tinder and Bumble, the widget to set one's own gender consists of a two-item list from which the user can select one option: either "male" or "female." In Bumble, the widget's structure is a pair of radio buttons presented next to each other on the same line. This is displayed on the main profile-editing screen with the identifier "Gender." In Tinder, the main profile-editing screen has the identifier "Gender" with the currently selected gender option below it. The selected gender option appears in a bar with an arrow at the end indicating a behaviour: the user can tap on it for more options. Doing so opens up a new screen with the heading "I Am." This screen displays both gender options in a menu that uses Tinder's style of white bars against a grey background, with the selected option denoted by a red checkmark. Both Tinder and Bumble import gender from Facebook and use that to preselect one of the binary options supported by the app, although the degree of convergence differs as Tinder, unlike Bumble, does not restrict users' ability to change away from the pre-selected option.

The two Own-Gender widgets differ in the extent to which they communicate that other gender options are possible. Bumble presents the range of choices directly on the Profile screen, whereas on Tinder's profile-editing screen, only the current selection is visible. But within Tinder's gender-section screen, the structure suggests that not only is an alternative to the selected gender possible but so too are genders that are not listed. Bumble's radio buttons are positioned so that there is no space for alternatives, but Tinder's menu of stacked bars leaves plenty of room for more options. Indeed, while Tinder's widget structure is a set of radio buttons with the selection of one option deselecting the other, Bumble's radio button affordances are forestalled by the alert that pops up when the unselected gender is tapped, which limits the behaviour to one action. And so while Tinder's message of mutually exclusive binary options is not communicated visually by the widget and must instead be discovered though experimentation, Bumble's structure does not allow the mutual-exclusivity that is communicated through radio buttons to take full effect. Even with its limited gender options, Tinder's "I Am" heading and the ability to switch back and forth communicate a conception of gender that is less a static fact than a potentially dynamic element of the self and of identity, in contrast to the assumption enforced by Bumble's restrictiveness, that gender is not only binary but static.

In both apps, the other widget specifically having to do with gender is the Show-Gender widget in the Settings section, which has the function of allowing the user to select the gender or genders with which they want the people the app shows them to have identified themselves. Bumble displays the full set of options on the main settings screen, with the indicator "Show." Tinder has a bar labelled "Gender" with the selected setting displayed next to an arrow, which when tapped brings up a new screen with the list of options under the heading "Show Me," a more effective indicator than Tinder's first. In both apps, the default selection is notable in its lack of convergence with Facebook, relative to other widgets that automatically import their value: even if the user's Facebook profile specifies that they are "Interested in" their own gender, both apps default to showing profiles of the so-called opposite gender.[2]

Tinder's and Bumble's Show-Gender widgets are about the genders of other people and not the user making the selection. With the exception of the setting to be shown both men and women, the selections made here constitute an a priori gendering of people yet to be encountered in the app (Goffman 1990, 216). Selecting "Men" in Bumble or "Only Men" in Tinder creates the expectation that all the profiles displayed by the app will have the "Male" Own-Gender option selected and will depict individuals who identify—and are recognizable to the viewer—as men.

. . .

. . . Given that the app does not solicit a public gender declaration nor any declaration of sexual orientation, "gender" within the apps is not about identity as such but rather is a way of sorting users into groups that make matches more likely. For example, a person who has selected "Female" and "Only Women" on Tinder is more likely to match with other users who have selected "Female" and either "Only Women" or "Men and Women" than users who have selected "Male" and/or "Only Men." It may map onto culturally contextual sexual identities, but in terms of the app design, this structuring seems to be pragmatically focused on how the app will be used as opposed to who is using it. Accordingly, the restrictiveness of the Gender widgets may not only be an uncritical replication of assumptions about gender, but also a deliberate data strategy: having users select the gender category from which the app will draw profiles to show them requires that those genders be intelligible not only to other users but to the algorithm that calls up profiles to display.

. . .

Recommendations and Future Research

In light of this analysis, apps like Tinder and Bumble could make certain changes to create an interface that better supports a full range of genders and experiences of gender. Putting the Own-Gender widget in the Settings section alongside the Show-Gender widget would better reflect the role of this information within the app as a sorting mechanism rather than an outward identity cue. The location of these widgets within the Profile sections of both Tinder and Bumble is misleading in that it suggests that these widgets will display gender information in an explicit way rather than by determining a staging of the profile's display within a gendered search. The app design should also include a third gender option in the Own-Gender widget—labelled so as to indicate that this option accommodates non-binary genders and other genders that are both, or neither, male and female—and options in the Show-Gender widget that allow all seven possible groupings of the three gender options. The Own-Gender widget should be labelled to explicitly indicate that this setting determines the set of search results in which one's profile will appear, and the Show-Gender widget's identifier should similarly reflect this distinction between individual gender identity and gender categories within the app. Giving users control over their gender categorization and the gendered stagings of their profiles could be a first step toward striking a balance between neither outing people nor erasing their identities.

. . .

Conclusion

Dating apps like Tinder and Bumble present fruitful objects of study for interrogating how users' identities interact with the design of social networking technologies. After all, facets of identity like gender and sexuality are central to the relationships on which the apps are centred. Drawing on the work of Goffman (1990) and Suchman (2007), in this article we have analysed the affordances of Tinder and Bumble in terms of self-presentation, and in so doing extended the reach of Goffman's theory to include the informational resources presented by the affordances of digital environments.

With gender intrinsic to the technical aspects of the apps, Bumble and Tinder structure it in a way that is useful to their design rather than accommodating of nuanced and varied lived experiences of gender. Indeed, the widget best suited to a nuanced and explicit declaration of gender, the About text field, is not identified as such, and its usefulness is downplayed by the presence of other widgets labelled "Gender." By contrast, the Own-Gender widgets, tools whose design suggest that they afford the most direct presentation of gender, do not display outside of the editing interface. The Own-Gender widgets, unlike the About widgets, are purely functional: necessary for efficiently presenting users with profiles they are likely to find attractive but unconcerned with supporting an accurate public portrayal of one's gender. Inasmuch as the Own-Gender widgets do contribute to the collaborative construction of mutually intelligible gender between performer and audience, they do so indirectly and contextually.

More broadly, this prioritization of convenience as opposed to nuance can be seen in examples of convergence, like Tinder and Bumble's reliance on Facebook as a guarantor of authenticity. When this convergence and the algorithmic needs of platforms' operations intersect in the construction of subjects, one result is that identities become standardized. While this has some benefits, it should not come at the expense of user control over how and why identities, like gender identity, are implicated in the design and function of technologies. Understanding how identities interact with app affordances is a resource for developing apps that are more conscientious and inclusive, and that are accountable to all people who choose to use them.

Notes

1. Tinder announced new gender options on November 15, 2016 (Tinder 2016b). See Section 7 for discussion of this change.

2. Tinder increased the app's gender options in November 2016.

References

Bumble. 2016a. "Bumble - Help." Bumble. Accessed October 16 2016. https://bumble.com/en/faq.

Butler, Judith. 1990. *Gender Trouble: Feminism and the Subversion of Identity.* New York: Routledge.

Entis, Laura. 2015. "5 Things You Didn't Know About Tinder's Sean Rad." Entrepreneur. August 13. https://www.entrepreneur.com/article/247967.

Gibson, James J. 1979. *The Ecological Approach to Visual Perception.* Boston: Houghton Mifflin.

Goffman, Erving. 1990. *The Presentation of Self in Everyday Life (1959).* London: Penguin.

Haig, David. 2004. "The Inexorable Rise of Gender and the Decline of Sex: Social Change in Academic Titles, 1945–2001." *Archives of Sexual Behaviour* 33 (2): 87–96. doi:10.1023/B:ASEB.0000014323.56281.0d.

McArthur, Victoria. (2014). "The Affordances of Gender in the Character Creation Interfaces of Digital Games." Paper presented at the CONSOLE-ING PASSIONS, International Conference on Television, Video, Audio, New Media and Feminism. Columbia, MO, April 10–12.

Norman, Donald A. [1988]. 2002. *The Design of Everyday Things.* New York: Basic Books.

Shaw, Adrienne. 2015. *Gaming at the Edge. Sexuality and Gender at the Margins of Gamer Culture.* Minneapolis: University of Minnesota Press.

Suchman, Lucille Alice. 2007. *Human-Machine Reconfigurations: Plans and Situated Actions.* Cambridge: Cambridge University Press.

Sundén, Jenny. 2009. "Play as Transgression: An Ethnographic Approach to Queer Game Culture." Paper presented at the DiGRA conference, London, September 1–4.

Tinder. 2016a. "Terms of Use." Tinder. September 14. http://tinder.com/terms.

Tinder. 2016b. "Introducing More Genders on Tinder." Tinder Blog. November 15. http://blog.gotinder.com/genders/.

Part IX
Gender and Violence

Perhaps the most notorious form of gendered violence is domestic violence, or intimate partner violence, in which physical and psychological abuse happens between people who are bound to each other by ties of partnership or family. Victimization statistics tell us that although people of all genders can be perpetrators or victims of domestic violence, the prevalent form of this violence involves a male perpetrator using physical strength and a distorted sense of masculinity to exert control over a female partner and/or children.

These violent relationships are never simple, and Sheehy unpacks some of the complexities of gendered domestic violence in her study of one particular case in which years of abuse culminated in murder—of the male perpetrator by the female victim. Sheehy argues that the gendered dynamics of this violent marriage fit a model called "coercive control," and without exonerating the female perpetrator she seeks to show how the homicide was produced by years of abuse.

However, gender alone is not the whole story in domestic violence. As Guruge, Khanlou, and Gastaldo demonstrate, this violence does not arise from the simple fact of maleness. The authors track the important influences that ethnicity and economic class, as well as the stresses and insecurities of international migration and "outsider" status in Canada, have on gendered violence.

Simpson situates gendered violence in a broader context, considering diverse forms of violence inflicted on Indigenous women. For Simpson, this violence is closely connected to time and space—Canada's settler history and the social geography of its towns and provinces. Gendered and racialized bodies, whether white men or Indigenous women, hold different social meanings depending on where those bodies might be located.

Although the bodies of Indigenous women have been subjected to appalling violence, they have also created opportunities for calling attention to and resisting violence against Indigenous Peoples, as Simpson demonstrates in her analysis of Theresa Spence's hunger strike. She suggests parallels between the harms done to the bodies of Indigenous women and harms done to the lands of Indigenous Peoples though unethical extractive industry production. Symbolic violence, bodily violence, and environmental violence are fused together through the thread of gender.

Questions for Critical Thought

1. What do you think it would take to reduce rates of gendered violence in Canada? Are you optimistic or pessimistic about the possibility that Canada could become a "rape-free society"?

2. What defines violence? Are there some acts that are considered violent and unacceptable in some contexts but acceptable in others? Where would you draw the line between acceptable and unacceptable conduct, especially with respect to intimate or domestic relationships?

3. How is racism connected to gendered violence, according to Guruge and colleagues? Can you see any other connections between other forms of violence and gendered violence?

4. Have you known individuals who were subjected to violence because they didn't conform to stereotypical expectations for their gender? How did the people around them react to this violence?

5. Guruge and colleagues argue that domestic violence has to be understood within micro, meso, and macro contexts. Could you apply this micro-meso-macro framework to understanding some of the other violent incidents in this section, such as the murder of Pamela George or the trial of Teresa Craig?

6. Why do you think the Crown in the Teresa Craig trial wanted to exclude the idea of "coercive control"? If you had been on the jury hearing evidence in Craig's trial, how much weight would you have given to this concept?

7. Most of these readings deal with physical violence, yet psychological or emotional violence is arguably equally damaging. How does non-physical violence differ from the physical kind?

Chapter 35

Overview

When Teresa Craig killed her husband in Kemptville, Ontario, in 2006, it wasn't an act of self-defence, in the strictest sense of the word. Teresa acted after years of verbal abuse and "coercive control" from her husband—a pattern of behaviour aimed at subduing and ensuring obedience from her and her son. She feared that the abuse would escalate to result in her own death or her son's death, and her husband's control over every aspect of household resources made it impossible for her to escape. When her case went to trial, her defence counsel attempted to make the argument that Mr. Craig's years of coercing and threatening Ms. Craig created the conditions in which she saw no other way out but to kill him. This created an opportunity to bring forth evidence on the prevalence and severity of coercive control as a form of domestic violence. Elizabeth Sheehy reviews this evidence, presented by experts in psychiatry and criminology, which describes a pattern of abuse that pivots not only on the gender of the victim but also on their racialization and their precarious status in Canada. Domestic violence is not only gendered but is also an intersectional form of violence. Ultimately, Teresa Craig was convicted of manslaughter rather than homicide and sentenced to eight years in prison.

Expert Evidence on Coercive Control in Support of Self-Defence

The Trial of Teresa Craig

Elizabeth Sheehy

Introduction

Teresa Craig stabbed her husband Jack Craig four times while he slept off his intoxication on a couch in their recreational vehicle (RV) on 31 March 2006 in rural Kemptville, Ontario. He screamed and tried to struggle to his feet. Teresa fled to her closest neighbour's, leaving their nine-year-old son Martyn asleep in the bedroom at the back of the RV. Charmaine Crockett got out of bed to find Teresa on her doorstep in her pajamas, crying: "Help me, please help me, call 911, I killed my husband."[1]

Sheehy Elizabeth. "Expert evidence on coercive control in support of self-defence: The trial of Teresa Craig." *Criminology & Criminal Justice*; 18 (1):pp. 100–114 © 2018. Reprinted by Permission of SAGE Publications, Ltd.

What distinguished Teresa from so many other women who kill their abusers is that she maintained that Jack had not assaulted her over their 10-year relationship, beyond minor violence such as elbowing her and shoving her out of his way. Neither had he threatened to harm her or Martyn, or committed sexual assault. A straightforward self-defence claim would be difficult to make out under Canada's Criminal Code, given the paucity of evidence regarding the necessary elements of Teresa's subjective and objectively reasonable perception that she was being "unlawfully assaulted," that she faced serious bodily harm or death and that she could not otherwise preserve herself (Canada, 1985: s. 34).

Jack did, however, subject Martyn to verbal and physical assault and Teresa to his controlling behaviour, verbal abuse and fits of rage, making her very afraid. Teresa's defence lawyer therefore called expert evidence on coercive control—men's use of threats, intimidation and surveillance to achieve control over women—to support the complete defence of self-defence. Her counsel also introduced Battered Women's Syndrome (BWS) and Post Traumatic Stress Disorder (PTSD) evidence to make a secondary argument that Teresa was debilitated from forming the intent to kill Jack, a partial defence that reduces murder to manslaughter.

Teresa's trial, which took place in Ottawa, Ontario over 37 days in 2008, was the first battered woman's[2] murder trial in Canada in which coercive control evidence was called to support self-defence. Her counsel hoped this evidence could give voice to her unarticulated fear of death or serious bodily harm, demonstrate that her fear was "reasonable," even if vaguely expressed and show that Jack's exercise of coercive control left her no other means of escape than to kill him or to leave Martyn to his fate with his father. Evan Stark (1999–2000: 55) calls this "the battered mother's dilemma": "the choice many victims are forced to make between their own safety and the safety of their children."

The defence theory was that Jack had learned his lesson when his first wife—a Canadian—fled his violence 30 years before. This time he advertised for an Asian woman as a "mail order bride" and found Teresa, a shy and passive woman who longed to escape her life in Malaysia and have, according to her trial evidence, "beautiful white babies." Dr Stark as Teresa's expert witness explained that Jack could terrorize her into obedience without using physical violence, control her by harming their son and commandeer her financial resources.

The Crown, however, succeeded in persuading the trial judge that there was no "air of reality"—the legal threshold of sufficiency of evidence for a defence—to self-defence. This defence was therefore not put before the jury, thereby blunting the impact of Stark's evidence. Teresa was convicted

of manslaughter, presumably on the basis that the Crown could not prove the intent to kill required for murder, and sentenced to eight years of incarceration. . . .

This article reflects on the challenges and implications of using coercive control evidence to support self-defence for battered women. Although self-defence was kept from the jury's consideration, Stark's evidence did serve an educative function regarding men's use of coercive control to entrap women (Stark, 2007). It also provided a frame for understanding Teresa's crime and for highlighting details of Jack's abuse, some of which were recognized in the appellate decision. . . .

Teresa Craig's Murder Trial

The evidence against Teresa was overwhelming. She admitted stabbing Jack. To 911 personnel she said "I'm not happy with my life, so I killed my husband." To police she said that she had used Jack's chef's knife—the sharpest in the block. She explained why she had run from the RV: "He know that I trying to kill him." She said to police "I cannot kill Jack when he's awake—he's too strong." When told he had succumbed to his wounds, she said "Good for him [. . .] I hate him. Yeah, enough is enough. I kill him."

The Crown also relied on the fact that Teresa had moved her sleeping son from the couch where Jack had flopped down to the bedroom in the back before she stabbed Jack, and she had pulled from her housecoat a napkin with the phone number of Jack's sister on it, begging her neighbour to make sure her son was safe. When combined with the absence of evidence of violence by Jack towards Teresa and the fact that Teresa exercised independence and resourcefulness in escaping Malaysia, creating a life in Canada and even leaving Jack on two prior occasions, once with custody of Martyn, the Crown could plausibly argue that Teresa had no need to use fatal violence to escape her marriage.

Yet a more complex story was to unfold. When news of a Craig family homicide reached them, Teresa's former neighbours from British

Columbia (BC) spoke to media: "the first reaction of many was that Jack had finally lost it and killed his wife or son—or both" (Clough, 2006). Neighbours described Teresa as a "gentle and devoted mother," a "pleasant and hard-working" employee (Clough, 2006) and "the most forgiving woman ever" (Baron, 2006). Even Jack's mother had good things to say about Teresa (Clough, 2006).

Friends explained that Teresa and her son Martyn faced "day-to-day" abuse by Jack. Mary Langford said that Teresa sought "refuge" at her home; Langford urged her to flee before "something terrible happened," but Teresa was "too afraid" to leave Jack. Co-worker Shirley Rieger told reporters that Jack would storm into their workplace to yell at Teresa, calling her "stupid" and an "idiot." . . .

According to media, "Just about everyone you meet . . . tells a story of their own unique run-in with a man who's been described as a 'bully', a 'powder-keg', 'someone you tiptoed around'" (Clough, 2006). . . .

Confronted by this powerful narrative that portrayed Teresa so sympathetically and Jack as a dangerous abuser, Teresa's prosecutors relied on several strategies that they returned to repeatedly throughout her first-degree murder trial. . . . [T]hey strove to undercut Teresa's victimization by presenting her as a remorseless killer. And third, they attempted to shut out the coercive control evidence by eliminating from the evidentiary record testimony that supported self-defence.

. . .

In pursuing its . . . strategy of portraying Teresa as a cold-blooded killer, the Crown put Teresa's womanhood on trial, painting her as opportunistic, self-centred, a bad mother and an indifferent wife. Teresa's "race" or ethnicity played a less obvious role in the Crown's narrative, but it was never absent. Teresa was variously described by the Crown witnesses as Asian, Oriental, from the Far East, Chinese and Malaysian. Her facility with the English language was asserted, even though Teresa accidentally pled "guilty" upon arraignment and could communicate only in the simplest of sentences, with a limited vocabulary. . . .

Sergeant Tim Hodgins testified that when he informed her that Jack had died Teresa began crying for a few seconds, then said "good for him." He re-informed her of her rights, but she replied: "I don't care what rights are." Sergeant Keith Patrick told jurors that he observed a "smirk" on Teresa's face when she told him she had used Jack's own knife—a sharp one—to stab him and when saying she already said "too much" to police.

Dr Brian Calvin, a doctor who treated Teresa in BC when she was hospitalized for a suicide attempt in 2005, months before Jack moved the family to Ontario, testified that she told him that she had fantasized about poking her nine-year-old son with a knife when he was "pestering" her in the kitchen. He said Teresa told him she planned to return to Malaysia and leave Martyn to be raised by Jack. She wanted to be alone and was "too selfish" to be a mother: she had "no problem" with leaving her son with Jack because he was a "good father." She said Jack "whined and cried a lot" about his chronic pain; she declined to go to a women's shelter; and refused to purchase the anti-depressants Calvin prescribed.

Dr Stephen Hucker, the Crown's forensic psychiatrist, cast Teresa as a woman who entered the relationship with her eyes wide open. He testified that she set out to marry a "Caucasian," have "beautiful babies" and escape her impoverished background, decisions that undercut her vulnerability as a "mail order bride." Teresa was aware of Jack's difficult personality before she married him, but "maybe I want to come back to Canada." Jack verbally abused her and screamed at her, and one time threw a sweeper at her. But, Hucker said, she claimed not to have experienced fear and instead worried Jack had broken the sweeper. According to Hucker, Teresa found Harmony House stressful: she feared she might stab a child in the shelter.

In pursuit of the third strategy, the Crown fought hard to narrowly constrain the defence by objecting to all questions, answers, words and phrases that might support self-defence, including coercive control evidence. The Crown argued that because Teresa told police that Jack was never violent with her—his abuse was verbal—and because she recounted no specific threat or fear that night, self-defence could not possibly be available. . . .

. . . [D]efence witnesses were allowed to testify to some aspects of Jack's abuse and Teresa's endangerment. For example, her friend Gina Lum, with whom she lived in Nanaimo while they were separated, was so terrified of Jack that she barred him from her home with a restraining order. Teresa's testimony mirrored her police statements: she did not mention any acts of serious violence or threat against her by Jack. She described herself as fearful but could not name what she was afraid of. She testified at length about how Jack assaulted, berated and humiliated Martyn. When she tried to intervene, he threw a sweeper at her. Teresa believed she prevented Jack from assaulting her by "walking away" whenever he became agitated: he was a big man, very strong, and she was a small "lady."

. . .

Dr Kunjukrishnan, Teresa's treating psychiatrist in Ottawa, also testified. He diagnosed Teresa with a serious depressive illness and PTSD, both of which he attributed to her relationship with Jack. In her condition, she could not face her husband's intimidation and anger that she knew would follow the morning after a night of heavy drinking. According to him, in Teresa's state of mental suffering she acted impulsively to stab Jack, unable either to plan this assault or even to intend its consequences, a critical element of murder.

Coercive Control Evidence

Although the Crown did not challenge either the expertise or fundamental relevance of Dr Kunjukrishnan's testimony regarding Teresa's state of mind, it launched a full-out assault on Dr Stark's proposed evidence. . . .

. . .

The Crown's fierce opposition to coercive control evidence and Stark's testimony can be explained by its potential to disrupt the murder prosecution and put self-defence at play. Coercive control evidence as a substitute for BWS evidence in battered women's homicide trials was advanced by Stark more than a decade before Teresa's trial. He pointed out that "BWS and PTSD require proof of severe traumatic episodes, proof that may

be impossible in cases characterized by repetitive, but minor acts of abuse embedded in an ongoing pattern of control" (Stark, 1995: 1000).

Most abused women experience chronic but low levels of violence, yet still endure highly crippling sequelae. Battered women report that psychological abuse, sexual humiliation and denigration are more difficult to recover from than physical violence (Stark, 2007: 278). When combined with minor acts of violence, men's "micro-regulation of everyday behaviors associated with stereotypic female roles, such as how women dress, cook, clean, socialize, care for their children, or perform sexually" (Stark, 2007: 5), used to limit their female partners' freedoms, curtail their liberties, exploit their resources and subjugate them, induces fear. Thus, "[e]ven non-violent control tactics take on a violent meaning through their implicit connection with potential physical harm" (Goodman and Epstein, 2008: 9).

Coercive control also puts women at risk of the "slow, homicidal process" of battering described by Ogle and Jacobs (2002: 81–85). Women's efforts to assert themselves or to resist trigger escalated efforts by the abuser to retain control, making "[t]he situation [. . .] constantly potentially homicidal" (Ogle and Jacobs, 2002: 82–83). In fact, as Stark (2007: 276–277) points out, coercive control is a more significant risk factor for lethality than the severity of a man's physical violence, especially when combined with separation or the threat of separation. Furthermore, a US study reports that "[T]he risk of intimate partner femicide [is] increased 9-fold by the combination of a highly controlling abuser and the couple's separation after living together" (Campbell et al., 2003: 1090).

Stark also argues that the BWS narrative fails to capture women's resistance strategies and requires them to play the role of the passive and dependent battered woman—a role that may be impossible for survivors, particularly those who have fought for their lives. He suggests that this narrative "is designed to elicit the court's sense of outrage by imagining the woman who is no longer there" (Stark, 1995: 1009), which can pose a credibility problem if she shows anger or sounds defensive on the witness stand. Coercive control instead focuses jurors on the abuser's calculated course of action: what did it take to make this capable woman afraid and deprive her of her freedom (1995: 1009–1010)? A related advantage is that coercive control theory highlights the abuser's strategies and behaviours rather than focusing on whether the woman suffers from a "syndrome" or is a "real" or deserving victim.

Acknowledging battered women's resistance strategies also allows accused women their dignity, permitting jurors to recognize women's efforts to exercise "control in the context of no control." Thus, even if women feel they can "control individual episodes," such strategies ultimately fail to protect them from an abuser's escalated tactics. A woman's homicidal act can thus be the "culmination of a rational strategy of defense, not an act of insanity or vengeance" (Stark, 1995: 1023).

Coercive control had not, prior to Teresa's trial, been presented in a Canadian court in support of self-defence although it certainly has been in US courts (Stark, 1995, 2007). . . .

Stark described how Jack isolated Teresa from her work mates and friends in BC. He deepened her isolation by unilaterally moving the family to rural Ontario where, after some time spent in his 90-year-old mother's home, he fought with her and they had to live in the RV on a gas station lot in the middle of winter. By the night Teresa stabbed Jack, the family had run out of money, gas and water: she had not bathed in two weeks. Stark explained that although Teresa had at one time secured custody of Martyn, leaving Jack with access rights, she had returned because he expressed contrition, she was lonely and Martyn missed his father. After that Jack prohibited her from leaving with Martyn and swore he would get custody. He withdrew Martyn from public school over Teresa's objection and insisted he would home-school him. He engaged in daily abuse of Martyn in "schooling," hitting on the head, punching him hard on the arm and whipping him with a belt. He demanded that Teresa too use force against Martyn—another source of suffering for Teresa. Stark told the jury that Martyn was the person she loved most in the world; she found it intolerable to be unable to protect him. She could not leave with Martyn and she could not abandon him, although at one point she attempted to do so by flying to Malaysia by herself.

She found her son's grief unbearable and returned home after only a few weeks.

Jack intimidated Teresa, telling her that if she left she would never see Martyn again and uttering other vague threats. He yelled at her and called her abusive names that she did not understand, like whore and c**t, both in their home and in public. He monitored her movements when she left the house, threatened to harm others, shot and killed animals on their property, began to time her in the bathroom and treated her like an "indentured servant"—an object.

. . .

On cross-examination the Crown highlighted aspects of the report that he said were proved inaccurate by the evidence adduced at trial. These included Stark's use of the word "several" to refer to two instances of Teresa attempting to leave Jack; the fact that there was no evidence Jack attempted to "control" Teresa on the night of the homicide; and the failure of Stark to include some of Teresa's damning words in his report. . . .

The prosecutor then warmed to his theme. He accused Stark of being neither a clinician nor a scientist but rather an "advocate," someone who was "manipulating" the facts, and whose conclusions were "unsupported by the evidence." He was using Teresa's trial for his own purpose of "jumpstarting the [battered women's] revolution," a goal articulated by Stark's (2007) book. On this dramatic note he ended.

The Crown then again moved to exclude self-defence, this time succeeding. Although Morris attempted to cobble together bits and pieces from the evidence of Teresa, the witnesses and his experts to meet the evidentiary threshold, arguing that it was unfair to penalize Teresa for her inability to articulate her fear of serious bodily harm or death, the trial judge ruled against him. There was some evidence going to the first element of self-defence, that Teresa subjectively and reasonably believed herself to having been "unlawfully assaulted" on the night of the homicide, but there was no "air of reality" to the other two elements of self-defence:

In this case, there is, at its highest, a marginal amount of evidence of an assault, but by any objective evaluation of the case, including any plausible inferences, the Court cannot find any evidence on the issues of an apprehension of death or harm on the part of the accused, or on the reasonableness of killing being the only option available to the accused at the time. (*R v Craig*, 2008: 3131–3132)

The judge reached the same conclusion with respect to defence of Martyn: Teresa had not articulated fear that he would be seriously injured or killed. Neither self-defence nor defence of others would be available to the jury.

What followed immediately was the judge's ruling that Stark's report, unlike those of the other experts, be withheld from the jury, even after the extensive editing. With self-defence off the table, the judge said, Stark's evidence was of little assistance to the jury, possibly limited to his opinions on BWS. The judge observed that this decision precluded an acquittal, a point that no one commented on, including Teresa's counsel. The judge proceeded to prepare jury instructions on first-degree and second-degree murder and manslaughter.

. . .

It took the jury four long days to return a verdict of not guilty to first- and second-degree murder, but guilty of manslaughter. At Teresa's sentencing hearing a month later, the Crown advocated for imprisonment of seven to nine years even though this meant an automatic deportation order would be issued against Teresa, and her relationship with Martyn would be severed. Morris urged conditional imprisonment—house-arrest—a sentence that would allow Teresa to remain in Canada and parent her son. The judge sentenced Teresa to eight years in prison, emphasizing deterrence and denunciation, calling her crime a "near murder" and thereby tipping his endorsement of the Crown theory that Teresa was a cold-blooded killer.

A new counsel argued Teresa's appeal to the Ontario Court of Appeal against conviction and sentence. On the denial of self-defence the court ruled:

A person who kills another to escape from a miserable life of subservience to that person

does not act in self-defence absent reasonably perceived threats of significant physical harm and reasonably held beliefs that the killing is necessary to preserve one's self from significant physical harm or death. (*R v Craig*, 2011: para. 35)

It is fair to say, based on her evidence and statements, that what she feared was not death or grievous bodily harm, but having to live with the deceased at least until her son was on his own, in the isolated, destitute, loveless and seemingly hopeless environment the deceased had created for them. (*R v Craig*, 2011: para. 38)

. . .

Conclusion: Lessons for Coercive Control

In the end, while self-defence was withheld from her jury, Teresa's trial broke new ground by recognizing coercive control theory in a Canadian murder trial. . . . His sentencing decision accepted some threads of the coercive control analysis, for example referring to Jack as a "domineering, bullying, controlling man who always insisted that 'it was his way or the highway'" (*R v Craig*, 2011: para. 55), even if he did not find them legally relevant for self-defence or sentencing. . . .

One cannot know whether coercive control evidence had any impact on the jury. No doubt Morris saw the manslaughter conviction as a victory—the most positive verdict available to the jury—and the Crown surely saw it as a loss, having offered evidence in support of the planning and deliberation required for first-degree murder and the intent to kill needed for second-degree murder. It is possible that Stark's evidence influenced what must have been the jury finding that Teresa did not possess the intent to kill, although Dr Kunjukrishnan's evidence more squarely addressed this point. Nor can we know whether, had self-defence or the possibility of acquittal been before the jury, the coercive control evidence would have persuaded them to acquit. Yet Teresa's case does show the crucial role coercive control evidence could play in supporting self-defence.

. . .

Will the changes to Canada's self-defence law make it easier for abused women to use coercive control evidence in future? Section 34(1) now requires that the accused or another person have faced an actual or threatened use of force, that the accused have acted with the motive of protecting themselves or another and that their use of force be "reasonable." Thus Teresa would still need to assert that she acted to protect herself or Martyn, but need no longer show either that she reasonably believed she faced death or serious bodily harm, or that she reasonably believed she had no other alternative, in order to get self-defence before the jury. Instead, section 34(2) provides a non-exhaustive list of the factors relevant to assessing reasonableness, such as imminence, proportionality and the parties' relationship history. These considerations are not framed in absolute terms

or as hard limits (MacDonnell, 2013: 304), making it possible for a jury to acquit even someone like Teresa who stabbed a sleeping man.

The changes to self-defence thus seem to have made coercive control evidence more accessible to lawyers defending battered women who kill. It remains to be seen whether juries, even with an expanded self-defence law, will adhere to narrower social interpretations of when homicide is justified by self-defence (MacDonnell, 2013: 323–324). Only through examination of emerging trends in the application and interpretation of the new self-defence law, as well as "cutting edge" defence lawyering on behalf of battered women, will we be able to assess the full potential of coercive control as part of the case for self-defence. However, until men's deprivation of women's liberty through coercive control is cast as criminal behavior, we may wait in vain.

Notes

1. Unless otherwise referenced, all quotations in this article derive from the unpublished trial transcript of *R v Craig* (2008), on file with the author.
2. I acknowledge that some academics and activists have rejected this terminology as both improperly universalizing and stigmatizing (Randall, 2004: 145).

It is, however, terminology that is widely used in the Canadian legal system, particularly in criminal trials, by expert witnesses, lawyers and judges (Sheehy, 2014: 12–13). I also use the terminology "batterers" and "abusers" to refer to perpetrators.

References

Baron E (2006) Death of "bully" not a surprise to many people. *The [British Columbia] Province*, 4 April, A3.

Campbell JC, Webster D, Koziol-McLain J, et al. (2003) Risk factors for femicide in abusive relationships: Results from a multisite case control study. *American Journal of Public Health* 93(7): 1089–97.

Canada (1985) *Criminal Code*. Revised Statutes, c. C-46, s. 34.

Clough P (2006) BC islanders come to aid of accused. *The Ottawa Citizen*, 3 July, C1.

Goodman L and Epstein D (2008) *Listening to Battered Women: A Survivor-Centered Approach to Advocacy, Mental Health, and Justice*. Washington, DC: American Psychological Association.

MacDonnell V (2013) The new self-defence law: Progressive development or status quo? *Canadian Bar Review* 92: 301–26.

Ogle R and Jacobs S (2002) *Self-Defense and Battered Women Who Kill: A New Framework*. Westport, Conn: Praeger.

R v Craig (2008) Trial transcript. Ottawa: Superior Court of Ontario, 14 April–15 June, 37 volumes.

R v Craig (2011) Ontario Court of Appeal Decision No. 142.

Randall M (2004) Domestic violence and the construction of the "ideal victim": Assaulted women's "image problems" in law. *St Louis University Public Law Review* 23: 107–54.

Sheehy E (2014) *Defending Battered Women on Trial: Lessons from the Transcripts*. Vancouver: University of British Columbia Press.

Stark E (1995) Re-presenting woman battering: From Battered Woman Syndrome to coercive control. *Albany Law Review* 58(4): 973–1026.

Stark E (1999–2000) A failure to protect: Unraveling "the battered mother's dilemma". *Wayne State University Law Review* 27: 29–110.

Stark E (2007) *Coercive Control: How Men Entrap Women in Personal Life*. New York: Oxford University Press.

Chapter 36

Overview

Sepali Guruge and colleagues take up the concern of the previous chapter with the contexts of gendered violence. In their research on intimate partner violence in a Tamil immigrant community, they describe their theoretical approach as "feminist post-colonial": While noting the gender imbalance in the violence, they also situate it within global inequalities and asymmetries, such as the civil war that forced Tamil families from their homes, bringing violence into family life. The researchers adopt an ecosystemic approach that examines variables at different levels of social life, from the "micro" world of the couple relationship to the "meso" world of the extended family and community to the "macro" world of global changes and dynamics that disrupted life in Sri Lanka and created the conditions requiring movement to Canada.

The move from one set of circumstances in Sri Lanka to a very different world in Canada is also connected to stressors and pressures that find expression at times in violence against family members. Changes in social networks, different expectations of marriage in Sri Lanka and in Canada, and the everyday racism experienced in Canadian life form the social context within which violence occurs.

Guruge and colleagues do not lay all the blame for intimate partner violence on the experience of immigration and dislocation. As they note, some women experienced this violence even before immigration, while other couples move to Canada and handle the stresses and conflicts that result without resorting to violence. However, they argue that intimate partner violence cannot be understood by simply focusing on incidents of violence; instead the micro, meso, and macro influences must be examined.

Intimate Male Partner Violence in the Migration Process

Intersections of Gender, Race, and Class

Sepali Guruge, Nazilla Khanlou, and Denise Gastaldo

Introduction

Intimate partner violence is the threat of, and/or actual, physical, sexual, psychological, or verbal abuse by a current or former spouse or non-marital partner, as well as coercion, or the arbitrary deprivation of liberty that can occur in public or private life (United Nations [UN] 1993). Intimate male partner violence (IMPV) is widely acknowledged as

Guruge, Sepali, Nazilla Khanlou, and Denise Gastaldo. "Intimate Male Partner Violence in the Migration Process: Intersections of Gender, Race, and Class," *Journal of Advanced Nursing*, Vol. 66, No. 1 (January 2010) 103–13. Reprinted by permission of John Wiley & Sons, Inc.

a critical health issue for women worldwide; however, relatively little is known about its production in diverse settings and contexts. Data compiled by the World Health Organization (WHO) (2000) for IMPV across many countries has suggested that the percentage of women who had ever been physically assaulted by a male intimate partner ranged from 5.1 per cent to 67 per cent. In addition to other limitations, these statistics do not include other forms of abuse such as emotional and sexual abuse, and thus do not accurately demonstrate the prevalence and seriousness of the issue. The recent WHO (2006) study addressing some of these concerns showed that the prevalence of diverse forms of IMPV ranged from 15 per cent to 71 per cent across 10 countries ($n = 24,000$) and rates of lifetime IMPV varied widely, as did women's responses to IMPV, with many factors affecting the production of IMPV. The findings reinforced the need to develop context-specific knowledge about this issue.

Background

IMPV as a Global Health Issue

The IMPV is a significant cause of morbidity and mortality for women worldwide (Heise et al. 1994), the most common physical injuries being multi-site contusions and soft tissue injuries (Muellman et al. 1996). Chronic physical health conditions linked to IMPV include neck and back pain, arthritis, headaches and migraines, hypertension, unexplained dizziness, sexually transmitted infections, chronic pelvic pain, gynecological symptoms, and gastrointestinal problems (Ratner, 1995; Campbell and Lewandowski, 1997; Coker et al., 2000). Mental health problems include depression, acute and chronic symptoms of anxiety, symptoms consistent with post-traumatic stress disorder, substance use/dependence and thoughts of suicide (Eby et al., 1995; Ratner, 1995; Fischbach and Herbert, 1997).

IMPV in the Canadian Context

The 1993 *Violence against Women Survey*, well known in Canada, in which 12,300 randomly selected women were interviewed, showed that 51 per cent had been physically or sexually assaulted at least once since the age of 16 years, 29 per cent had been physically abused, and 8 per cent had been sexually assaulted by a male intimate partner (Rodgers, 1994). According to the more recent (2000) *General Social Survey* (GSS) of over 14,000 women (over 15 years) from 10 provinces, approximately 37 per cent of women who had ever been married or ever had a male live-in intimate partner had experienced IMPV at least once. The attempts to assess IMPV prevalence in immigrant households through secondary analysis of GSS

data (e.g., Hyman, 2002; Ahmad et al., 2005) were constrained by the survey's limitations. Among others, it excluded those who did not speak Canada's two official languages.

Interest in IMPV in the post-migration context has recently increased in Canada. We consider this a positive move, given that more than 200,000 immigrants and refugees arrive annually, women make up about half of this number, and lack of attention to this topic limits the resources and policy attention devoted to it.

Theorizing IMPV

Numerous theories have been offered to explain why IMPV occurs. In general, they can be divided into those focusing on the individual level (e.g., based on biological and psychological explanations) and those emphasizing the relationship at the micro-, meso- or macro-systemic levels (e.g., based on social and gender perspectives). Most theories have not explored the intersectionality of migration, race, culture, gender, and class in understanding IMPV.

To overcome these limitations, we used a post-colonial feminist perspective in this study. A review of some key post-colonial feminist authors' (Memmi, 1967; hooks, 1984; Jayawardena, 1986; Minh-Ha, 1989; Collins, 1990; Mohanty, 1991) work indicates that there is no single post-colonial feminist perspective. However, all these perspectives emphasize the importance of understanding the historical construction of women in and from low- and middle-income countries and its consequences, and the need to recognize, as well as construct, knowledge from their perspective (Spivak, 1988; McClintock, 1995).

An ecosystemic framework was also used in this study. Ecosystemic frameworks help reveal how people and their environments are understood in the context of their continuous and reciprocal relationships (Loue and Faust, 1998; Germain and Bloom, 1999). The factors considered are ontogenic (the individual history of the partners); micro-systemic (the family setting in which the abuse occurs); meso-systemic (the social networks in which the family participates); and macro-systemic (the culture and society-at-large).

Using an ecosystemic framework, situated in a postcolonial feminist perspective, avoids the creation of simplistic views of IMPV as relating to particular groups or to people with particular characteristics. The relevance of the two together in addressing post-migration IMPV has been discussed elsewhere (see Guruge and Khanlou, 2004).

Migration and Displacement of Sri Lankan Tamils

The estimated 188 million people living in Sri Lanka in 1998 (UN, 1999) represented several different ethnic groups. As each group struggled to overcome damage from a colonial past and on-going neo-colonialism, new forms of domination and exploitation evolved within the country. For 25 years, civil war raged between the Sri Lankan government and the Liberation Tigers of Tamil Eelam, a militant/separatist group fighting for full independence and a separate homeland for Tamils. Since 1983, many Tamils have fled the war to countries such as India, Australia, Norway, Germany, England, and the United States of America (USA). Canada is the home to the largest Sri Lankan Tamil community outside Sri Lanka.

The Study

Aim

This paper is a report of a study of Sri Lankan Tamil Canadian immigrants' perspectives on factors that contribute to IMPV in the post-migration context.

Design

An exploratory qualitative descriptive design was used.

Participants

Combining opportunity, snowball, and purposive sampling strategies, we recruited participants from October 2004 to May 2005. The data were collected through individual interviews with 16 community leaders in health and settlement work (Set 1); four focus groups with women (6–12 in each group) and another four with men (4–6 in each group) from the general Tamil community (Set 2); and individual interviews with six women who had experienced IMPV (Set 3). The purpose of selecting these groups was to capture the phenomenon from diverse viewpoints (Schensul et al., 1999). For example, community leaders were better suited to exploring macro-systemic factors, community members had knowledge of meso-factors, and abused women were better qualified to discuss their individual situations. Similarly, we wanted to hear from women and men, and women with an abuse history and those without. The underlying premise was that topics such as male violence against women cannot be understood fully by only hearing abused women's stories; we must also understand the viewpoints of the oppressors (Anderson and Hill Collins, 1995) if we are to challenge the status quo, especially along the lines of multiple sites of oppression.

Data Collection

Interviews and focus groups were, on average, two hours long. The first author conducted all individual interviews (in Sets 1 and 3) ($n = 22$), except for one interview that required an interpreter. The (Set 2) focus groups with women and men were conducted in Tamil, respectively by a female and male community leader. The first author co-facilitated all eight focus group discussions ($n = 41$). The focus groups conducted in Tamil created a space for participants to voice in their own language the concerns of importance to them. According to the post-colonial feminist perspective, the idea of giving voice to those who might not be heard (e.g., due to language differences), guided this study. The individual and group discussions were guided by exploratory, open-ended questions (see Tables 36.1 and 36.2). The interviews were transcribed verbatim, and focus groups were translated and transcribed.

Ethical Considerations

Ethics approval was obtained from the appropriate university. All potential participants were informed, both via consent form and verbally, of their right to refuse to participate or answer any questions or to

Table 36.1   Examples of Individual Interview Questions Posed

What do you think about Tamil men's and women's relationships in Sri Lanka/Canada?

What do you think about wife abuse in the Tamil community? Why do you think it happens in Sri Lanka/Canada? (probe about gender, culture, class)

How do you think what happens at home between a husband and wife is influenced by their friends, family, and neighbours? (probe about gender, culture, class, race)

How are the couples influenced by what is happening in Canadian culture and society? (probe about gender, culture, class, race)

Table 36.2   Examples of Focus Group Questions Asked

Please tell me about your experience about coming to live in Canada.

What was it like to build a new life here?

What would have been helpful to you and your family in getting settled in Canada?

What leads to conflicts among Tamil couples living in Canada?

How do they resolve these conflicts?

Wife abuse happens in every community and culture. Why do you think it happens in the Tamil community?

How does being in Canada shape why/how wife abuse happens?

terminate participation at any time. Focus group participants were also made aware, in advance, of who the facilitators were. At the beginning of focus group sessions, participants were asked to respect each other's information and not to disclose identifying information about themselves. Focus group facilitators and the transcriptionists signed a confidentiality agreement.

Findings

The participants represented the demographics of the Sri Lankan Tamil community in Canada in terms of age (range = 24–70 years), education (range = elementary school to university), length of stay in Canada (range = 1–20 years), and religion (most were Hindu) (see also Tables 36.3, 36.4, 36.5). Their conceptualizations of the production of IMPV are presented under four themes.

Experiences of Violence Pre-migration and during Border-Crossing

Participants in all three sets spoke about their experiences during the civil war. Many lost homes,

businesses, and employment. They spoke about frequent roadside checking, bomb threats, and sounds of sirens and having to run to bunkers. Young men were arrested and tortured; some disappeared and/or died in prison. Participants from Set 1 connected men participating in, witnessing, or being victims of war violence with intolerance, anger, suspicion, and aggression at home:

> Husbands being separated from wives (. . .) have been taken out for interrogation . . . having to always suspect another person, whether he is an enemy or not. (Set 1, Participant 6)

> The children grow up seeing people fighting and killing, you know. Anger and aggression becomes an acceptable way of expressing discontent with something. Which is what you have often when you come to a new place. (Set 1, Participant 10)

The second quote also implies that learned behaviour can affect how a person manages discontent or anger. Overall, participants perceived that psychological stress and trauma from the war influenced men negatively.

Table 36.3   Demographic Characteristics of Community Leaders

Characteristic	
Gender	10 women, 6 men
Age group	6 (in their 30s), 5 (in their 40s), 5 (over 50 years)
Birth city	9 (Jaffna)
Decade left Sri Lanka	1 (1970s), 8 (1980s), 4 (1990s), 3 (2000s)
Lived in a third country	10
Years in Canada	1.5–20: 6 (1–5 years); 2 (6–10 years); 6 (11–15 years); 2 (16–20 years)
Level of education	Grade 10–University
Work type in Canada	Health or settlement sectors ($n = 16$)

Table 36.4   Demographic Characteristics of Focus Group Participants

Focus group	1 (n = 8)	2 (n = 6)	3 (n = 12)	4 (n = 5)	5 (n = 6)	6 (n = 4)
Gender	Women	Men	Women	Men	Women	Men
Age range (years)	30–63	41–50	27–65	25–62	24–69	35–69
Birth city	Jaffna	Jaffna	Jaffna	Jaffna	Jaffna	Jaffna
Years in Canada	1–10	2–12	2–11	1–11	2–11	8–18
Level of education	8–13	8–13	10–13	10–13	<8–Univ.	1.3–Univ.
Arranged marriage	All	3	8	2	4	2
Second session	Yes ($n = 7$)	–	–	–	–	Yes ($n = 4$)

Table 36.5   Demographic Characteristics of Abused Women Participants

Characteristic	
Age	25–70 years
Birth city	Mostly Jaffna ($n = 5$)
Years in Canada	3–12
Level of education	Grade–University
Length of marriage	2–50 years
Arranged marriage	Yes ($n = 5$)
Worked outside home in Sri Lanka	Yes ($n = 5$)
Currently employed	Yes ($n = 3$)
Number of children	0–5

Conflicts and wars increase violence against women, which is the case in Sri Lanka. In all three sets, participants spoke about the vulnerability of girls and women. Parents often feared for their daughters' safety and attempted to send them out of the country:

> Unfortunately a friend of mine . . . disappeared. My family was worried that I was going to disappear. So they proposed [a marriage for] me to (. . .) from (. . .). I didn't want to marry that time. I wanted to study and get a good job, but I didn't feel safe. We hear all kinds of things happening to girls. I was missing my friend and that had a very bad effect on me. My family was scared and started to react. That is how I ended up in this situation. (Set 3, Participant 5)

Because of the country's situation, this participant agreed to marry a man who later became abusive. There had not been enough time to investigate her potential husband's background, the usual procedure in arranged marriages.

Violence was reported to occur also during border-crossing. Although Canada has made considerable efforts to accept refugees, current immigration policies make the process difficult for Tamils. For example, Tamils are unable to register with the United Nations High Commissioner for Refugees (UNHCR) to obtain refugee status while still living in Sri Lanka (Fuglerud 1999), and they cannot apply for a Canadian visa, for example, if they have lost necessary documents during displacement or cannot easily replace them because villages have been destroyed or evacuated. Further, family sponsorship applications in Canada are often delayed. These problems drive Tamils to other ways of reaching safety or reuniting with family members, including hiring agents who bring them to Canada, often breaking international laws. The following illustrates some of the complexity of border-crossing:

> It is because of the civil war we had to leave the country. I came here through the US. Until then, I have never been to a jail. But there, they put me in jail for a month. I was very much affected mentally due to this, as we didn't commit any crime. (Set 2, Participant 2)

Some participants highlighted evidence of violation of people's rights by those in authority in various countries as well as the unacceptable daily life conditions that some Tamils had to endure to reach their final destination. While the hope of a new home and safer place drive people to such travel, uncertainty, fear, anxiety, and stress associated with these steps were identified by participants as having a negative psychological impact on people, both short- and long-term. According to most, these incidents also shaped how people view others, and whether or not they would seek help from others, for example to cope better with post-migration stressors, especially from those in authority, such as health care professionals, settlement workers and child welfare officers.

Gender Inequity in the Marital Institution

Coming from a patriarchal society, participants had learned gender roles in childhood and adulthood from family, neighbours, schools, workplaces, and society-at-large. In Sri Lanka men were the primary breadwinners; they often did not do household work but were responsible for household repairs and physically demanding work, such as lifting and moving. Although gendered responsibilities varied over time, among families, and across socio-economic groups, women were primarily responsible for cooking, cleaning, and child-rearing.

After migration, Tamil men who came alone were forced to assume household tasks. However, according to participants, most men continued to perceive household responsibilities as women's domain. Most single men returned to Sri Lanka to find a suitable wife who would fulfil such expectations:

> As soon as their mother, wife, or sisters come, men expect the women to work for them. There are exceptions. (Set 1, Participant 5)

In the new context, some couples successfully negotiated household responsibilities based on who could do the tasks better/more easily, who was available at a particular time of day, and who enjoyed doing the task. Such change was perceived to be more common among those who immigrated at a younger age:

> He is a young guy . . . very much a short-tempered guy. . . . I saw a change in him. He told me, "I am helping my wife." She has two kids. "I am a truck driver, and she is alone, so I have to come back and clean for her . . . so I decided to take local trips instead of long-distance trips." (Set 1, Participant 4)

Others changed because they had no choice—owing to their work commitments, timing, and so on—allowing for a more equal distribution of work between the couple. In contrast, some husbands held their wives responsible for household work even if they worked outside the home as many hours as he did and contributed equally to the family income.

Participants in Sets 1 and 2 spoke about a general perception in the community that some disciplining of the women was justified, especially to prevent bigger problems. The reasons presented included incomplete household work, suspected or real extramarital affairs, refusing husbands' requests for sex, arguing or complaining, and asking for things such as money or tasks to be completed at "inappropriate times." These were also the justifications used by the abusive husbands of participants in Set 3. These expectations/perceptions/responses were also shaped by the changes in post-migration social networks.

Changes in Social Networks and Supports

The Tamils were used to a social structure and networks that often strongly influenced their lives in Sri Lanka. Such networks often provided instrumental, informational, emotional, and psychological support, especially to new couples, young families, and those who were dealing with life challenges. However, post-migration social networks are usually smaller or non-existent, especially for women who often arrive sponsored by their husbands. According to most participants, even if family members were in Canada, the values that governed the expected/perceived/given support have changed since coming to a more individualistic society:

> Relationships are much tighter back home. It is not the same here. Even when we have relatives here, we would think about interfering or not [in people's personal lives by trying to help them]. (Set 2, Participant 4)

The changes in the quantity and quality of support have also changed due to the extremely busy lives they lived in Canada.

The resulting lack/loss of support has increased the household responsibilities of both spouses and their reliance on each other for support. While the latter has positive effects, such as increased communication and shared decision making between the couple without the influence or interference of family, sole reliance on one person causes tremendous stress. A participant highlighted a possible scenario:

> When there is pregnancy, when there is childbirth, they have no one to care for them, and that is the time when they need family the most. That is when the husband might feel stressed out (. . .) and move out. (Set 1, Participant 7)

Overall, participants emphasized that increases in stress resentment, and arguments about the quantity and quality of household work each spouse did contributed to conflict and abuse. If the woman's family was not in Canada, the husband also had more power over her (especially if his family was living with them or nearby). In some cases, the husband's family was reported to be the instigator or the abuser. Women's family members also were perceived to reinforce patriarchal practices. Participants in Set 2, for example, spoke about the indirect and direct pressure women themselves placed upon other women to adhere to such patriarchal practices. This idea was confirmed by a participant in Set 1:

> My mum tells me, "Your husband is coming, now, you're talking with me, why don't you go greet your husband and serve him food?" My mother-in-law immediately stops whatever she is doing and serves food for her son. But she never told me [directly] "Oh, you are his wife, you have to go and do things." (Set 1, Participant 3)

These changes in social networks and supports were perceived to be particularly negative for women who were not fluent in English or not in paid employment, as they were more isolated and further dependent on their husbands.

Perceptions of Changes in Social Status and Privilege: Gender and Race Lenses

Immigration to a new country is often imbued with changes in socioeconomic status and privileges. A negative change in this regard is more likely for immigrants from low- and medium-income countries who move to high-income nations. According to most of our women participants, their husbands and other men in their community often were stuck in jobs that they began as stepping stones to better jobs that never materialized because of racism in the employment sector in Canada. Their accounts implied that immigrants are being used as a source of cheap labour:

> [Canada] needs people for its economy. They need people to clean their offices, clean toilets, deliver newspapers, and wash dishes in restaurants, because not that many white Canadian people want to do these low-paying, low-status jobs. . . . So there is no real motivation for [the] government to invest in these people [immigrants] in a way that they become successful. Then who will do these types of jobs? (Set 1, Participant 1)

This participant's perception of the new forms of colonization taking place in immigrant-receiving countries in the West was in line with the perceptions of most others in Sets 1 and 2. Tamil men's downward mobility in professional and economic status led to loss of social status at home, and within their extended families, the Tamil community, and larger Canadian society. As can be gleaned from the next excerpt, patriarchal ideological values dictated that men assume the responsibilities of paying off family debts, sponsoring their wives and children for immigration, financially supporting their extended families in Sri Lanka, and paying dowries for their sisters and daughters to be married:

> I borrowed money from an uncle to come here. I was worried if I could give back the loan if I get deported. Also, my siblings were back home. I was the eldest. In our culture, as you know, the girls have to be married off by the boys and we need to give dowry for that and only then we can get married. So these were all pressures on me. I have an elder sister [who needed to be married off] and I was crying about that situation. (Set 2, Participant 6)

Across interviews, participants agreed that, as part of arranged-marriage customs in Sri Lanka, women almost always married men of equal or higher educational and professional status and then enjoyed the associated living standard. One woman commented on the implications of husbands' status change on family dynamics:

> Here a woman lawyer can marry a chef and it is not a problem at home. But our society is set up to say that women should always marry up or someone who is doing a better job or is better than you professionally. So, when we come here, things become upside down. You don't know what it does to the family . . . not just to the man. (Set 1, Participant 15)

Inability to fulfil these responsibilities as well as expectations associated with their previous status demoralized men; some became depressed or turned to alcohol. In some cases, couple conflict ensued.

Discussion

Study Limitations

The study sample was limited to those who, in Canada, belonged to the lower-middle class and working class and were under 65 years of age, and it is possible that those outside these criteria might perceive IMPV differently. To avoid placing them at risk, we did not speak with women who were living with abusive husbands; thus, their voices are absent from this study. The presence of community leaders as focus groups facilitators might have limited the openness with which participants spoke about the issues.

Factors Influencing Post-migration IMPV

Participants' accounts revealed a complex range of factors that influenced IMPV after migration, presented here according to the ecosystemic framework. All were specifically connected to the intersectionality of gender, race, and class, and were congruent with post-colonial thought.

Individual-Level Factors

The individual-level factor that we found to be key to IMPV was pre-migration exposure to war and multiple trauma. Men who experienced or engaged in violence were perceived to have mental health problems, such as low tolerance for stress (e.g., job loss) and various stimuli (e.g., loud noise at home), and symptoms of anxiety and depression. They were perceived to be more suspicious of their wives because they had learned to distrust people in general. Chambion (1989) and Penalosa (1986) noted that immigrant men's previous exposure to violence could be connected to aggressive or violent behaviour towards their wives. In a recent study by Gupta et al. (2009) involving a group of immigrant men to the USA, a statistically significant relationship between pre-migration

exposure to political violence and IMPV perpetration in the post-migration context was found. However, there is limited literature on this topic.

Micro-Level Factors

Key micro-level factor influencing the production of IMPV post-migration included the changes in husband's and wife's socio-economic statuses. These changes contributed to two scenarios of post-migration family power imbalance. In the first, some husbands gained control, authority, and power within their families after migration—for example, by being sole breadwinner or through their wife's isolation and/or lack of English skill. Other researchers have also reported this scenario (e.g., Abraham's 1999, 2000 studies of South-Asian immigrants). In the second scenario, some husbands' power and authority decreased owing to the deskilling and deprofessionalization they experienced. Wives' greater access to paid (albeit low status and low paid) employment post-migration, and their relatively increased earnings, led some husbands to reassert their authority through violence. Other researchers in the USA and Canada (e.g., Krulfeld, 1994; Kulig, 1994; Morrison et al., 1999; Oxman-Martinez et al., 2000; Min, 2001; Tang and Oatley, 2002) have noted similar findings. An important contribution of our study to the literature is the recognition that the two scenarios can co-exist within the same community.

Meso-Level Factors

The most important meso-level factor affecting the post-migration production of IMPV was the change in social networks and supports. In Canada, Tamil couples might have no family members to help with day-to-day life, and thus rely heavily on each other. Under economic and time constraints, this situation leads to stress, resentment, and conflict. Hyman et al. (2004) reported similar findings in their study with Ethiopian-immigrant married couples in Toronto, and in their follow-up study (Hyman et al., 2006) with divorced women and men from the same community. McSpadden and Moussa (1993) also found that loss of extended family support and advice led to marital conflict among Canadian Ethiopian immigrants.

As in other communities, Tamil women are often held as the bearers of the community values and beliefs. As such, even when family members were available in Canada, they often enforced patriarchal norms and practices. Husbands' family involvement (in the absence of women's families) was noted to be particularly negative for the woman when couple conflicts occurred. Women's sole reliance on husbands and their families also increased the likelihood of a woman being abused by her husband's relatives, mainly female in-laws. Similar findings were noted in the USA among "Asian-Americans" (Huisman, 1996), "Asian-Indians" (Mehotra, 1999), and Mexicans (Morash et al., 2000). The Tamil community further enforced, both subtly and overtly, patriarchal rules and practices, even when some such practices were reported to have changed/are changing in Sri-Lanka. Overall, this situation gave men an upper hand over the rest of the family.

What Is Already Known about This Topic

- Numerous factors explain the production of intimate male partner violence, with little consensus on its etiology.
- Etiological theories of violence have included psychological explanations, biological differences, sociological perspectives, and feminist approaches.
- Some etiological theories explain intimate male partner violence at an individual level, while others look to the family for an explanation, and some operate at the societal level.

What This Paper Adds

- Rather than being caused by one or several factors operating within a single level of society, intimate male partner violence is produced by a complex and interrelated set of factors operating at individual, family, community, and societal levels in the pre-migration, border-crossing, and post-migration contexts.

- Production of post-migration intimate male partner violence involved experiences of violence in the pre-migration and border crossing contexts; gender inequity in the marital institution; and post-migration changes in social supports as well as in socioeconomic status and privilege.
- Women who had been married and lived with their husbands in Sri Lanka experienced wife abuse only after coming to Canada; thus, the relevance of the post-migration context in the production of intimate male partner violence should not be underestimated.

Macro-Level Factors

Our findings, along with those of a number of previous studies, show that post-migration factors operating at the macro-level of society, including economic insecurity resulting from non-recognition of professional/educational credentials, workplace deskilling, and racial/ethnic discrimination—added to patriarchal pressure for men to meet family and social responsibilities—pushed men to self- and family destructive behaviours such as alcohol and other addictions, and to infidelity (Perilla et al., 1994; Rhee, 1997; Morash et al., 2000; Tran and Des Jardins, 2000) as well as to engaging in abusive behaviours (George & Ramkissoon, 1998; Perry et al., 1998; Moghissi & Goodman, 1999; Abraham, 2000). In other words, our findings along with these other studies findings illuminate the connection between the social inequities and their impact on individual men and their families (i.e., how gender and class intersected with race to create conflicts and abuse post-migration). Our findings thus can be used to contest uni-factoral explanations of IMPV, such as patriarchy.

Conclusion

Post-colonial feminist perspectives are useful in understanding post-migration IMPV, which is produced by the interaction of multiple forms of inequities that men and women experience before migration, while crossing borders, and after migration that are created in the intersection of several forms of neo-colonial oppressive relations, such as racism, classism, and sexism. While we did not explore the reproduction of IMPV in this study—that is, IMPV that began before migration and continued after couples reunited, it is noteworthy that women in this study who had married and lived with their husbands in Sri-Lanka experienced abuse only after coming to Canada. Thus, we propose that post-migration IMPV can only be explained by such plurality of factors that capture the complexity of immigrants' lives in diaspora and displacement.

Acknowledgements

We acknowledge the contribution of Dr Shahrzad Mojab, thesis committee member, and Dr Ruth Gallop, co-supervisor and thesis committee member, during the project development phase of the study.

Funding

The first author gratefully acknowledges the financial support she received for her work from the Canadian Institutes of Health Research in the form of a Doctoral Fellowship (2003–2006) and a New Investigator Award (2008–2013) in the area of Gender and Health.

Conflict of Interest

No conflict of interest has been declared by the authors.

Author Contributions

SG, NK, and DG were responsible for the study conception and design. SG performed the data collection. SG performed the data analysis. SG was responsible for the drafting of the manuscript. SG, NK, and DG made critical revisions to the paper for important intellectual content. SG and NK obtained funding. NK and DG supervised the study. SG, NK, and DG provided other contributions.

Contribution to the Paper

This paper is based on SG's doctoral dissertation defended in December 2006 at the Faculty of Nursing, University of Toronto. NK and DG supervised SG's thesis. SG drafted the paper, and NK and DG critically revised it.

References

Abraham, M. 1999. "Sexual Abuse in South Asian Immigrant Marriages," *Violence against Women* 5: 591–618.

Abraham, M. 2000. "Isolation as a Form of Marital Violence: The South Asian Immigrant Experience," *Journal of Social Distress and the Homeless* 9: 221–36.

Ahmad, F., M. Ali, and D.E. Stewart. 2005. "Spousal Abuse among Canadian Immigrant Women," *Journal of Immigration Health* 7: 239–46.

Anderson, M.L., and P. Hill Collins. 1995. *Race, Class, and Gender: An Anthology*, 2nd edn. Belmont, Calif: Wadsworth.

Campbell, J., and L. Lewandowski. 1997. "Mental and Psychical Health Effects of Intimate Partner Violence on Women and Children," *Psychiatric Clinics of North America* 20: 353–74.

Chambion, A. 1989. "Refugee Families' Experiences: Three Family Themes—Family Disruption, Violent Trauma, and Acculturation," *Journal of Strategic and Systemic Therapies* 8: 3–13.

Coker, A.L., P.H. Smith, F. Bertea, M.R. King, and R.E. McKeown. 2000. "Physical Health Consequences of Physical and Psychological Intimate Partner Violence," *Archives of Family Medicine* 9: 451–57.

Collins, P.H. 1990. *Black Feminist Thought: Knowledge, Consciousness, and the Politics of Empowerment*. New York: Routledge.

Eby, K., I. Campbell, C. Sullivan, and W. Davidson. 1995. "Health Effects of Experiences of Sexual Violence for Women with Abusive Partners," *Health Care for Women International* 16: 563–76.

Fischbach, R., and B. Herbert. 1997. "Domestic Violence and Mental Health: Correlates and Conundrums within and across Cultures," *Social Science and Medicine* 45: 1161–76.

Fuglerud, O. 1999 *Life on the Outside: The Tamil Diaspora and Long Distance Nationalism*. London: Pluto.

George, U., and S. Ramkissoon. 1998. "Race, Gender and Class: Interlocking Oppressions in the Lives of South Asian Women in Canada," *Affilia* 13: 102–19.

Germain, C.B., and M. Bloom. 1999. *Human Behaviour in the Social Environment*, 2nd edn. New York: Columbia University Press.

Gupta, J., D. Acevedo-Garcia, D. Hemenway, M.R. Decker, A. Raj, and J.G. Silverman. 2009. "Premigration Exposure to Political Violence and Perpetration of Intimate Partner Violence among Immigrant Men in Boston," *American Journal of Public Health* 99: 462–69.

Guruge, S., and N. Khanlou. 2004. "Intersectionalities of Influence: Researching Health of Immigrant and Refugee Women," *Canadian Journal of Nursing Research* 36: 32–47.

Heise, L.L., J. Pitanguy, and A. Germain. 1994. *Violence Against Women: The Hidden Health Burden: World Bank Discussion Papers (No. 255)*. Washington, DC: International Bank for Reconstruction and Development/World Bank.

hooks, b. 1984. *Feminist Theory: From Margin to Center*. Boston: South End.

Huisman, K.A. 1996. "Wife Battering in Asian American Communities: Identifying the Service Needs of an Overlooked Segment of the U.S. Population," *Violence Against Women* 2: 260–83.

Hyman, I. 2002. "Immigrant and Visible Minority Women," in D.E. Stewart, A. Cheung, L.E. Ferris, I. Hyman, M. Cohen, and I.J. Williams, eds., *Ontario Women's Health Status Report*, pp. 338–58. Toronto: Ontario Women's Health Council.

Hyman, I., S. Guruge, R. Mason, N. Stuckless, J. Gould, T. Tang, H. Teffera, and G. Mekonnen. 2004. "Post Migration Changes in Gender Relations among Ethiopian Immigrant Couples in Toronto," *Canadian Journal of Nursing Research* 36(4): 74–89.

Hyman, I., S. Guruge, R. Mason, N. Stuckless, J. Gould, T. Tang, H. Teffera, and G. Mekonnen. 2006. *Post Migration Changes in Gender Relations in the Ethiopian Community in Toronto: Phase II*. Centre of Excellence for Research on Immigration and Settlement, Toronto, Canada. Retrieved from http://ceris.metropolis.net/ Virtual%20Library/RFPReports/Hyman_PhaseII2004 .pdf on 9 June 2006.

Jayawardena, K. 1986. *Feminism and Nationalism in the Third World*. London: Zed Books.

Krulfeld, R.M. 1994. "Changing Concepts of Gender Roles and Identities in Refugee Communities," in L.A. Camino and R.M. Krulfeld, eds., *Reconstructing Lives, Recapturing Memory: Refugee Identity, Gender and Culture Change*, pp. 71–74. Washington, DC: Gordon and Breach.

Kulig, J. 1994. "Old Traditions in a New World: Changing Gender Relations among Cambodian Refugees," in L.A. Camino and R.M. Krulfeld, eds., *Reconstructing Lives, Recapturing Memory: Refugee Identity, Gender and Culture Change*, pp. 129–46. Washington, DC: Gordon and Breach.

Loue, S., and M. Faust. 1998. "Intimate Partner Violence among Immigrants," in S. Loue, ed., *Handbook of Immigrant Health*, pp. 521–44. New York: Plenum Press.

McClintock, A. 1995. *Imperial Leather*. New York: Routledge.

McSpadden, L.A., and H. Moussa. 1993. "I Have a Name: The Gender Dynamics in Asylum and in Resettlement of Ethiopian and Eritrean Refugees in North America," *Journal of Refugee Studies* 6: 203–25.

Mehotra, M. 1999. "The Social Construction of Wife Abuse: Experiences of Asian Indian Women in the United States," *Violence against Women* 5: 619–40.

Memmi, A. 1967. *The Colonizer and the Colonized*. Boston: Beacon Press.

Min, P. 2001. "Changes in Korean Immigrants' Gender Role and Social Status, and Their Marital Conflicts," *Sociological Forum* 16: 301–20.

Minh-Ha, T.T. 1989. *Woman, Native, Other: Postcolonial Feminism*. Indianapolis: Indiana University Press.

Moghissi, H., and M.J. Goodman. 1999. "'Cultures of Violence' and Diaspora: Dislocation and Gendered Conflict in Iranian-Canadian Communities," *Humanity and Society* 23: 291–318.

Mohanty, C.T. 1991. "Under Western Eyes: Feminist Scholarship and Colonial Discourses," in C.T. Mohanty, ed., *Third World Women and the Politics of Feminism*, pp. 51–80. Bloomington: Indiana University Press.

Morash, M., H.N. Bui, and A.M. Santiago. 2000. "Cultural-specific Gender Ideology and Wife Abuse in Mexican-descent Families," *International Review of Victimology* 7: 67–91.

Morrison, F., S. Guruge, and K.A. Snarr. 1999. "Sri Lankan Tamil Immigrants in Toronto: Gender, Marriage Patterns, and Sexuality," in G.A. Kelson and D.L. DeLaet, eds., *Gender and Immigration*, pp. 144–60. New York: New York University Press.

Muellman, R.L., P.A. Lenaghan, and R. A. Pakieser. 1996. "Battered Women: Injury Locations and Types," *Annals of Emergency Medicine* 28: 486–92.

Oxman-Martinez, J., S. Abdool, and M. Loiselle-Leonard. 2000. "Immigration, Women and Health in Canada," *Canadian Journal of Public Health* 91: 394–95.

Penalosa, F. 1986. *Central Americans in Los Angeles: Background, Language and Education* (Occasional Paper 21). Los Angeles: Spanish Speaking Mental Health Research Center.

Perilla, J., R. Bakeman, and K. Norris. 1994. "Culture and Domestic Violence: The Ecology of Abused Latinas," *Violence and Victims* 9: 325–39.

Perry, C.M., M. Shams, and C.C. DeLeon. 1998. "Voices from an Afghan Community," *Journal of Cultural Diversity* 5: 127–31.

Ratner, P. 1995. "Indicators of Exposure to Wife Abuse," *Canadian Journal of Nursing Research* 27: 31–46.

Rhee, S. 1997. "Domestic Violence in the Korean Immigrant Family," *Journal of Sociology and Social Welfare* 24: 63–77.

Rodgers, K. 1994. "Wife Assault in Canada: The Findings of a National Survey," *Juristat Service Bulletin, Canadian Centre for Justice Statistics* 14(9): 1–21.

Schensul, S.L., J.J. Schensul, and M.D. LeCompte. 1999. *Essential Ethnographic Methods*. Walnut Creek, Calif: Altamira Press.

Spivak, G.C. 1988. "Can the Subaltern Speak?," in C. Nelson and L. Grossberg, eds., *Marxism and the Interpretation of Culture*, pp. 271–313. Chicago: University of Illinois Press.

Tang, T.N., and K. Oatley. 2002. *Transition and Engagement of Life Roles among Chinese Immigrant Women*. Paper presented at American Psychological Association Annual Convention, Chicago.

Tran, C.G., and K. Des Jardins. 2000. "Domestic Violence in Vietnamese Refugee and Korean Immigrant Communities," in J.L. Chin, ed., *Relationships among Asian American Women*, pp. 71–96. Washington, DC: American Psychological Association.

United Nations. 1993. *Declaration on the Elimination of Violence against Women*. Canada–USA New York: Women's Health Forum, p. 6. Retrieved from www .hc-sc.gc.ca/canusa/papers/canada/english/violence. htm on 1 February 2005.

United Nations. 1999. *Consideration of Reports Submitted by States Parties under Article 18 of the Convention on the Elimination of All Forms of Discrimination Against Women: Third and Fourth Reports*.

World Health Organization. 2000. *Prevalence of Violence against Women by an Intimate Male Partner*. Retrieved from www.who.int/violence_injury_prevention/vaw/ prevalence.htm on 11 June 2006.

World Health Organization. 2006. *Multi-country Study on Women's Health and Domestic Violence against Women. Summary Report: Initial Results on Prevalence, Health Outcomes and Women's Responses*. Geneva, Switzerland: World Health Organization.

Chapter 37

Overview

Audra Simpson provides a classic and enormously influential analysis of the Canadian state, settler-colonial politics, and the bodies of Indigenous women. Simpson describes the deaths and disappearance of Indigenous women as "sovereign" deaths—deaths that secure the racial hierarchy of Canadian politics—going back to the beginning of white colonialism. She uses the example of Theresa Spence, a former chief of the Attawapiskat First Nation in Ontario, who embarked on a hunger strike in Ottawa to protest the federal government's failings to uphold its treaty obligations to provide clean water and housing to her nation. Simpson shows how the obsessive media focus on Simpson's physical body and on the possibility that she might (or might not) die of hunger parallels the treatment of Indigenous lands as a site for resources to be extracted for the benefit of Canadian and international corporations, without regard for how the land and its people might survive. Simpson also considers the death by homicide of Loretta Saunders, a young Inuk student in Halifax, and compares the erasure of her life to the erasure through murder or disappearance of many other Indigenous women and girls. Simpson is pessimistic about the success of "reconciliation" efforts in the form they currently take, and her assessment is grounded in appreciating and understanding the gendered nature of both colonial violence and resistance to that violence.

The State Is a Man

Theresa Spence, Loretta Saunders, and the Gender of Settler Sovereignty

Audra Simpson

This article makes two very simple arguments: one about settler statecraft, and the other about settler imperative. First: Canada requires the death and so called "disappearance" of Indigenous women in order to secure its sovereignty.[1] Two: that this sovereign death drive then requires that we think about the ways in which we imagine not only nations and states but what counts as governance itself. Underpinning these arguments is a crucial premise: in spite of the innocence of the story that Canada likes to tell about itself, that it is a place of immigrant and settler founding, that in this, it is a place that somehow escapes the ugliness of history, that it is a place that is not like the place below it, across that border. . . . And, in spite of those present-day discourses from Canadian political scientists and policy makers that imagine a process of equality through the space afforded to Indigenous political orders as the "third order of government," the evidence suggests that Canada is quite simply, a settler society whose multicultural, liberal and democratic structure and performance of governance seeks an ongoing "settling" of this land. . . . This settling thus is not innocent—it is dispossession, the taking of Indigenous lands and it is not over, it is ongoing. It is killing Native women[2] in order to do so and has historically done this to do so. It is this killing that allows me to also qualify the governance project as gendered and murderous.

. . .

. . . The state that I seek to name has a character, it has a male character, it is more than likely white, or aspiring to an unmarked center of whiteness, and definitely heteropatriarchal. I say

heteropatriarchal because it serves the interests of what is understood now as "straightness" or heterosexuality and patriarchy, the rule by men.[3] As well, it seeks to destroy what is not. The state does so with a death drive to eliminate, contain, hide and in other ways "disappear" what fundamentally challenges is legitimacy: Indigenous political orders. And here is the rub, Indigenous political orders are quite simply, first, are prior to the project of founding, of settling, and as such continue to point, in their persistence and vigor, to the failure of the settler project to eliminate them,[4] and yet are subjects of dispossession, of removal, but their polities serve as alternative forms of legitimacy and sovereignties to that of the settler state.

Settler states do not narrate themselves in the following manner: "as settler states we are: founded upon Native dispossession, outright and unambiguous enslavement, we are tethered to capitalist modes of production that allow for the deep social and economic differences that takes the shape in the contemporary of "unequal" social relations. We now seek to repair these unequal social relations through invigorated forms of economic liberalism that further dispossess and some would say consensually enslave those who do not own their means of production or opt out or fall out of this form of economic life." More often than not, and here I am thinking of the US (in its cagey political project), Australia and Canada fancy themselves as "multicultural, democratic, economically liberal," and committed to free trade among nations and sometimes, social policies that allow for forms of historical redress that correct or attempt to repair the fundamental and un-narratable violences that bring them into being. Their histories do not live fully within the present, do not enter into a cacophony of discourses, but instead take the form of supposedly good policy and good intentions, liberal, settler governance. . . .

How do the subjects of such states reach for life in the face of this death? How do they not lose themselves in the cacophony? What does this speak of for the future? . . .

Bodies

In December 2012 Theresa Spence announced that she would stop eating until the Prime Minister of Canada and the Governor General of Canada—the official representative of the Crown, met with her to discuss treaties, to discuss the deplorable conditions of life in her community as well as the broader and also deplorable conditions of life in the North. Each of these men, as the embodiments of states, she said, had a hand in suffering, in the failure to meet their historic obligations to the land and the people upon the land who were living in contaminated conditions, were without clean water and proper housing, in legendarily cold and bitter winters. . . .

As with all spectacularized political cases, things were not what they seemed. The Hunger Strike was not a hunger strike in a strict sense of the term, and to be fair, which many were not at the time, a hunger strike under conditions of ongoing death deserve more interpretive flexibility than Theresa Spence or any indigenous or racialized woman in Canada would or could be afforded in those moments. But to continue with my other point, this was not a hunger strike in a "classic" sense—it was rendered a "soft" hunger strike. And as such we read in endless newspaper articles, blog posts, vicious comments sections, in twitter flame wars and heard on TV.[5] . . . Canadians "weighed in" continuously on her insincerity, her avarice, her body, and in particular, her fat. Yet as the hours turned into days and the days turned into weeks, people caravanned to her camp across from Parliament to assemble around her, to offer strength to her, to visit,—to pray with her. They did not care if she drank fish broth twice a day. In fact, they prayed for her continued life, and they celebrated her fortitude. . . .

Out of respect for her action and for her sovereignty, other Indigenous people stopped eating in solidarity, all repeating her "demand" to meet with the PM, to have the Treaties upheld, to make something happen in a governmental storm of complete and total indifference to the life of land and people in Canada. This indifference has a life of its own, of course, and its clearest embodiment and manifestation. . . .

Here I want to gender this argument and move to her body. Theresa Spence's appearance, her fleshy appearance, was itself a site of ire by commentators on-line, in twitter flame wars, and in print journalism. She was too fat! We heard in different ways, over and over again, to be sincere, to be what she was supposed to be, which was a person in starvation. Yet her "excess" flesh, flesh that exceeds the western, normative Body Mass Index (BMI) of under 25, itself defies a logic of genocide and in this, settler domination. Why this link between fat, her fat in particular, and a resistance or refusal of domination? Because what she is required to do, with or without the starvation, is die. In fact, her very life, like the lives of all Indian women in Canada is an anomaly because since the 1870s they have been legally mandated to disappear, in various forms—either through the *Indian Act's* previous instantiation of Victorian marriage rules whereby an Indian woman who married a non-Indian man lost her Indian status (her legal rights based identity) and as such her right to reside on her reserve. With this legal casting out was the casting out as well of the possibility of transmitting that status to her children, a loss as well of governmental power with Indigenous governance itself, the political form that her body and mind signified.

Here I want to use an example to demonstrate this argument about symbolization, Indigenous political orders and settler governance. In the case of Iroquois or Haudenosaunee peoples (the peoples who signal North America's first "new world" democracy) this move to make Indian women white, to remove their status as Indians was a blow to the knees, if not a strangulation of Indigenous governance and political order, as Iroquois women appointed Chiefs, held property, counseled chiefs and de-horned them if necessary (removed them from their position of Chief). They divorced their men by placing their belongings outside of the Longhouse. They were the inverse of the settler colonial woman, they had legally mandated authority and power, and so, they represented an alternative political order to that which was in play or was starting to be in play in the late 19th Century. They embodied and signaled something radically different to Euro Canadian governance and this meant that part of dispossession, and settler possession meant that coercive and modifying sometimes killing power had to target their bodies. Because as with all bodies, these bodies were more than just "flesh"—these were and are sign systems and symbols that could effect and affect political life. So they had to be killed, or, at the very least subjected because what they were signaling or symbolizing was a direct threat to settlement. . . .

It is in this context as well that Theresa Spence, out of what some may say is desperation or deep strategy, stopped declaring states of emergency from the North and, while down south in their nation's capital—Ottawa, for an Assembly of First Nations General Meeting, decided to declare her own body an exception. In this, she declared her own body a space for the pronouncement of need, of sovereignty, the site of the decision *not* to eat. And to *not* eat solid food until the Prime Minister, Stephen Harper would meet with her to talk about the indifference his Conservative government had shown to Attawapiskat, but also to all communities in the North, to the land, to the people on the land. She then started her fast in a traditional dwelling constructed parallel to Parliament and her body, her action became a piece with the "Idle No More" movement—what may be largest, broad based, grass roots social and political movement to unfold in Canadian history.[6] Its goals are literally and directly to (and I quote) "stop the [Stephen] Harper government from passing more laws and legislation that will further erode treaty and indigenous rights and the rights of all Canadians."[7] Further it stated "Idle No More calls on all people to join in a revolution which honors and fulfills Indigenous sovereignty which protects the land and water."[8]

With those objectives the movement has taken the form of "actions": flash mobs and round dances in public spaces that were peopled by at times, hundreds and thousands of participants who drummed and danced peaceably, as well peaceful road blockages. . . .

Flesh and Sovereignty

. . . Spence fasted for six weeks, drinking one cup of fish broth in the morning, one at night. During that time The Sarah Palin of electoral politics in Canada, then Conservative (Algonquin) Senator Patrick Brazeau declared at a fundraising dinner that he had the flu and lost more weight in one week than she did in six weeks. This prompted a heckler to chime in, (and be reported in the Press repeatedly), "I think she gained weight!"[9] Spence's fleshy body was not seen as a sign of resurgent Indigenous life to white Canada, it was not seen as a stubborn, resolute, and sovereign refusal to die, staying alive to *have that conversation* about Crown obligations, about housing and about historical obligations—it was read as a failure to do what it was supposed to do—perish. . . . Feminist scholars have argued that Native women's bodies were to the settler eye, like land, and as such in the settler mind, the Native woman is rendered "unrapeable" (or, "highly rapeable")[10] because she was like land, matter to be extracted from, used, sullied, taken from, over and over again, something that is already violated and violatable in a great march to accumulate surplus, to so called "production."

This helps us to understand the so-called "phenomenon" of the disappeared women, the murdered and missing Native women and girls in Canada. When we account for this way of looking at Indian women it is not a mystery, is not without explanation, their so called "disappearances" are consistent with this ongoing project of dispossession. And we can see that this *is* sociology and this *is* criminal. Sherene Razack (2002), Andrea Smith (2005), Beverly Jacobs and Amnesty International (2004, 2009), the film-makers Christine Welsh (2006) and Sharmeen Chinoy (2006),[11] as well as countless activists and heartbroken, devastated family members who have marched and petitioned who have stayed on the police have all documented, theorized, and written about these deaths, these disappearances, which are explained not only by police ineptitude, by police racism, by gendered indifference, but by

Canada's dispossession of Indian people from land. This dispossession is raced and gendered, and its violence is still born by the living, the dead, and the disappeared corporealities of Native women. The disappearance of Indian women now takes on a sturdy sociological appearance: "missing" in the past decade, gone from their homes, murdered on the now-legendary "Highway of Tears"[12] in Northern British Columbia, off streets or reservations. Indian women "disappear" because they have been deemed killable, rapeable, expendable. Their bodies have *historically* been rendered less valuable because of what they are taken to represent: land, reproduction, Indigenous kinship and governance, an alternative to heteropatriarchal and Victorian rules of descent. As such, they suffer disproportionately to other women. Their lives are shorter, they are poorer, less educated, sicker, raped more frequently, and they "disappear." . . .

Grief

I now want to turn now to a recent death, which was a grief filled, nerve ending in this. Loretta Saunders was a young Inuk woman who was killed in February 2014. I will unpack some of the details of her passing shortly but will say for now that this violent murder, which is actually unexceptional when considered against the larger corpus that I have been talking about: the sociological fact, the crime of "Murdered and Missing Indigenous Women in Canada" is one that was exceptional in that it that actually seemed to matter, it seemed to shock Canada. It was saturated with grievability and managed to rouse the murdered and missing women to settler (and Indigenous) consciousness in ways perhaps that it had not before.[13] . . .

So let me return to this person, the late Loretta Saunders and what her passing means in all of this. For those of you that don't know who Loretta Saunders is, she was a 26-year old Inuk student from Labrador who was studying at St. Mary's University in Halifax, Nova Scotia. She was writing her honor's thesis on the so called "phenomenon" of murdered and missing Native women in Canada, and during the course of her thesis research and writing, in February, 2014 her lifeless body was found in a hockey bag along the Trans-Canada highway in New Brunswick.[14] She was pregnant on multiple levels, pregnant with this thesis that she was researching and writing, and quite literally, three months pregnant. According to all accounts, she was a great student, working hard, looking forward to starting these new chapters in her life, and then was killed shockingly, suddenly by a white couple subletting her apartment when she went to collect the overdue rent from them.[15]

Loretta Saunders' murder really, really upset everyone, registering grievability and forms of action[16] in ways not seen before for reasons that are both predictable and yet, not. One, she was, like all of these Native women, killed in part of what looks like a vaporous crime spree that belongs to not one serial murder, but an entire citizenship. As mentioned earlier 1,060[17] Native women have disappeared or been killed in the past decade—there have been two Amnesty International reports, calls for a national public inquiry, reports into police ineptitude, a municipal inquiry followed by an apology by the Vancouver police chief Jim Chu for years of doddering inaction regarding the murdered and missing women in that city and the specificity and particular heinousness of Robert Pickton's perfectly commodifying site of gendered pain and gendered elimination, the "piggy farm." At the so called "piggy farm" 49 women (he confessed to 49 and was charged for six) were murdered and ground, like meat. Like Saunders' body, found in a hockey bag, a container for the sport that seems to condense meaning, and hope, while sublimating white male violence in a civil form, to stand for Canada itself, Pickton's violence does perfectly disgusting, and unambiguous work to tell us, to scream at us, "Native women will be killed by this country and its people."
. . .

When history and sensibility is "the perp" a lot has to get done. And the Saunders case agitated all that in ways not seen before. So that is the one way in which this fairly recent murder scrapes at whatever iota of patience Indigenous people have with the state of affairs. But I suspect the other reason is that Loretta Saunders looked like a white girl. She had fair skin, blond hair, light eyes, she could have infiltrated a KKK meeting without notice. Perhaps, and we will find more than likely, perhaps not. It isn't white skin privilege that upset people, in that she is more precious than the darker ones among us—it is that her death demonstrates that *no one* is safe. . . . In the numerous YouTube videos on this case you can see her distraught family plead the public for information, you can see her sister Delilah Saunders with tear stained cheeks calmly ask for information from the public about her sister, and then wait and ask and then organize a search for her body. When the news comes to the Saunders family, we see them embrace each other with the relief of knowing simply that her body had been found—frozen, in the hockey bag. They were happy simply that she had been *found* because so many of these women have not. . . .

Pedagogies of Contention

When I first wrote an earlier version of this article I presented it in Austin, Texas for a graduate student conference on "Violence and Indigenous Identity."[18] This was in April of 2014. Like many other people, I was thinking a lot about Loretta Saunders, about the other women, and Leroux's piece made me think about my students,[19] about my job as Professor but specifically as a research Professor that takes teaching very seriously. And as a research Professor, I should not work so hard on my teaching. But nonetheless, I take it seriously and push things to the point of almost total bodily collapse every year

when I get a long, painful and relentless bronchitis. I can barely walk to work, let alone lecture, and I work across the street from my apartment. I say this not to dramatize a point about exertion, we all work very hard, but to talk about what I teach and its crucial capacity to exhaust. What I teach: violence, dispossession, Indigenous political life in the face of death, is high stakes and I know it. *Where* I teach is high stakes and I know it—in the US a site of complete atrophied disavowal of dispossession and ongoing colonialism, disavowal of indigeneity itself. And the courses push up and expose the structures of that dispossession and disavowal to students while providing an historical narrative with analytics to help them along. Repeatedly I hear, and read from them in different ways, "we didn't know this" and from my Indigenous students, of which there are more than I ever expected, "this helps to put it all together." From all, "let's do something!" I don't seek to make a claim of an extraordinary status for native studies alongside other crucial, non-canonical and subaltern histories, all with their own very serious and searing urgencies, but let me make the modest claim that the material serves as a "surprise" that topples things and so I would say, is crucial. But because of its generally non-curricular nature if I don't get it right, if I don't ensnare my students with this information, they may never get it, and they may never get it because they may never even *hear* it. . . .

Acknowledgements

This article is dedicated to the late Loretta Saunders and the MMIWG who have been stolen from their territories and their loved ones.

Notes

1. For the reach of global, imperial and comparative analysis of settler colonialism see Bruno Cornellier and Michael Griffith's volume of *Settler Colonial Studies* (2016) 6: 4. See also Alyosha Alex Lubins edited volume of *South Atlantic Quarterly* (2008): 107 (4).

2. And over-incarcerating Native men. Please see Sherene Razack's (2014) *Dying from Improvement: Inquiries and Inquests into Indigenous Deaths in Custody* (Toronto: University of Toronto Press) for a book length analysis

of the over preponderance of deaths in custody, most are men.

3. This is argued in various ways by Aileen Moreton-Robinson in *The White Possessive: Property Power and Indigenous Sovereignty* (2014). Minneapolis: University of Minnesota Press.

4. See Kevin Bruyneel *The Third Space of Sovereignty* (2007) and Audra Simpson, *Mohawk Interruptus* (2014) for related arguments.

5. For an excellent summary please see http://www. huffingtonpost.ca/2013/01/31/patrick-brazeau-theresa-spence_n_2589799.html [last accessed 4/7/2013]

6. This admittedly a difficult claim to prove as the INM movement was and perhaps still is amorphous and prone to spontaneous public actions and thus difficult to "calculate." Other "to the streets" and protests have been significant in demographic scale, notably the Winnipeg workers strikes of 1919. See Craig Heron, ed. (1998) *The Workers Revolt in Canada 1917-1925*. Toronto: University of Toronto Press and the gendered consumer activism of "the Homemakers" organizations through out the 1930s who organized in vigorous protest against rising milk prices. See Julie Guard (2010) "A Mighty Power Against the Cost of Living: Canadian Housewives organize in the 1930's." *International Labor and Working Class History* 77: 27-47). I am grateful to Jarvis Brownlie for pushing me on this claim.

7. http://www.cbc.ca/news/canada/9-questions-about-idle-no-more-1.1301843 (last accessed 09/20/2015).

8. http://www.idlenomore.ca/vision (last accessed 09/20/2015).

9. The exchange as reported by Huffington Post Canada: "I look at Miss Spence, when she started her hunger strike, and now?" Brazeau asked. A spectator then cried out, "She's fatter," sparking laughter. (http://www. huffingtonpost.ca/2013/01/31/patrick-brazeau-theresa-spence_n_2589799.html) (las accessed 09/20/2015)

10. See Andrea Smith, *Conquest* (2005), Jacki Rand, *Kiowa Humanity and the Invasion of the State*, (2008) specifically chapter 6, which links a degraded status of Kiowa women to settler capitalism. There is reference to sexual violence as well in Ned Blackhawk's *Violence over the Land* (2006) and James Daschuk's *Clearing the Plains* (2014) but they do not make the claim regarding gender and territory that Smith and Rand do.

11. Amnesty International (2004) *No More Stolen Sisters: A Human Rights Response to Discrimination and Violence Against Indigenous Women in Canada*. London: Amnesty International.
Amnesty International (2009) *No More Stolen Sisters: The Need for a Comprehensive Response to Violence Against Indigenous Women in Canada*. London: Amnesty International Publications.
See also Sharmeen Obaid Chinoy (dir.) 2006 *Highway of Tears*. DVD. Al Jazeera International 26 mins., Razack, Sherene (2002) "The Murder of Pamela George" in *Race, Space and the Law: Unmapping a White Settler Society* (Sherene Razack, ed). Toronto: Between the Lines Press. Smith, Andrea (2005) *Conquest: Sexual Violence and Native American Genocide*. Boston: South End Press. Pp: 121–147. Welsh, Christine (dir.) (2006) *Finding Dawn*. Ottawa: National Film Board of Canada.

12. Highway 16 stretches across Northern British Columbia. Eighteen women have been murdered between Prince Rupert and Prince George, rendering that stretch "the Highway of Tears" (Chinoy 2006). On September 12, 2012 it was reported that Bobby Jack Fowler murdered one of these women in British Columbia and died in an Oregan jail in 2006.

13. I will explain some of this shortly but let the attention paid to her death, shocking because of what Doenmez calls a "fatal symmetry" (2015), not override the sustained memorialization and activism of the families and other loved ones of the Indigenous women and girls or the grass roots community activism and documentation. Every February 14 is a day of remembrance for the women and girls which sees memorial marches all throughout Canada. Please consult as well http://www.itstartswithus-mmiw.com/ (last accessed 09/20/2015) for a "No More Silence" database that documents the missing women. This site works in partnership with "Sisters in Spirit" through the Native Women's Association of Canada. Defunded by the Conservative government, the Sister's in Spirit initiative documented the root causes of violence and harm in Native women's lives.

14. In her thesis *Already Disappeared: Interrogating the Right to Life of Indigenous Women in Canada* Caroline Doenmez has called the shock of Saunder's writing about what would befall her as a "fatal symmetry" in her analysis of the Canadian government's "failure to protect" in the case of Saunders (along side of analysis of the treatment Cindy Gladue and Tina Fontaine) (2015: 13).

15. The details of her murder and the sentencing of Blake Legette and Victoria Henneberry, the couple that killed her may be found here http://www.cbc.ca/news/canada/nova-scotia/loretta-saunders-murder-was-despicable-horrifying-and-cowardly-1.3052465 (last accessed 08/31/2016).

16. Hers is the only individual murder that occasioned a march on Parliament http://www.cbc.ca/news/canada/nova-scotia/loretta-saunders-vigil-draws-hundreds-to-parliament-hill-1.2561062 (last accessed 09/30/2015)

17. These numbers are based on Royal Canadian Mounted Police data, which is flawed as it does not include cities where RCMP do not have jurisdiction, like Vancouver and Toronto (Doenmez ibid: 14-15).

18. *Violence Against Native and Indigenous Identities: Unearthing and Healing Our Communities*, University of Texas—Austin, March 28, 2014.

19. It was my former student, Lakota Pochedley who invited to me UT-Austin as she was then a graduate student there and had gone on after completing a thesis under my supervision at Columbia.

Part X
Gendered Activism

By the time you've reached this section in the book, you may be thinking "All of this information and analysis is good, but what do we do about gender in its problematic aspects? How do we change gender relations?" That's where this final section comes in, ending this book on the optimistic note that positive change is possible through collective as well as individual action. When most people think about gender and social activism, they picture suffragists marching for women's right to vote in the 1920s, or perhaps the "women's lib" movement of the 1960s and 1970s (in which, by the way, no bras were ever burned—the torching of lingerie was a media invention). These movements were about redistributing power between the genders through political, economic, domestic, and cultural actions.

Gender is also implicated in social movements that are not explicitly about transforming gender. Labour movements, environmental protection movements, Indigenous rights movements, and more have all produced transformations in gender. Any collective effort to make the world a better place will inevitably involve working on relations between and among gendered people.

In the twenty-first century, new technologies and new collective identities are creating new forms of gendered activism as well as new opportunities to push for social change. The twentysomething baristas that Brickner and Dalton studied bring their diverse and fluid gender identities to their activism—not just because they have experienced bias or discrimination for being gender nonconforming, but also because these identities provide a reservoir of energy and motivation in their fights to organize their workplace. They are transforming the labour movement as they bring their gendered selves to their organizing work.

The baristas of Halifax share common generational experiences with the "digital activists" studied by Mendes and colleagues. These young women who promoted #MeToo and #BeenRapedNeverReported describe how being a feminist on Twitter and the internet in general is fraught with trolls and other pests, but can also generate solidarity and empowerment with other feminist activists in ways that might not have been possible in pre-internet days. They understand activism as a form of "affective labour," which requires emotion as well as time and resources. "Working on gender," for these activists, is a way of processing their own emotions as well as connecting with others in a common purpose.

Similarly, moving off the internet and into the living spaces of migrant Filipino women, Tungohan shows how these women create and sustain organizations to promote their well-being that are independent of both their sending and receiving countries. These organizations engage in transnational activism that not only helps to create real material change in the conditions of life for migrant workers but also helps women to break out of the isolation of being far from home and often at the mercy of a capricious employer or government.

Finally, John's work places intersectionality at the forefront of feminist organizing as she considers the feminist roots and futures of Idle No More, the Indigenous rights movement that swept up youth across Canada in 2013 and 2014. Idle No More activists found that the inherent biases in much of white feminist thought did not speak to their own experiences as Indigenous women, so they crafted their own forms of politics in which both gender and Indigeneity are foundational. Their gendered activism goes far beyond "women's issues" as narrowly defined and shows how intersectional politics can lead to empowerment and transformation for people of all genders, including but not limited to women. Idle No More shows the power and promise of intersectional gender analysis for social change.

Questions for Critical Thought

1.   Have you ever participated in a social movement? (Or perhaps you currently consider yourself a proponent of a particular cause?) If so, what drew you to take part? Was there anything gendered about the movement or about your participation?

2.   If you had unlimited time and resources, are there any social movements or causes that you would like to get involved with? Do these causes have a gendered dimension?

3.   Do you consider yourself a feminist? Why or why not? Have you encountered self-defined feminists in your own life?

4. What do you think the current political climate in your home province is like for gender activism? What are some of the current gender issues where you live?

5. What should the role of the government be in promoting gender equality? Should governments (federal, provincial, municipal) take active roles and advocate for change, or should they mainly just respond to the efforts of grassroots groups?

6. Some observers of social movements claim that internet activism is not "real" activism—that social change only happens when there are boots on the ground or votes in the ballot box. Do you agree? What are the benefits and limitations of internet-based activism?

Chapter 38

Overview

If you're reading this book for a university course, chances are pretty good that you identify as either a millennial or Gen Z—the age cohorts born just before or just after the beginning of the twenty-first century. For many millennials and members of Gen Z, precarious work is their first introduction to employment—unpredictable hours, often part time, with limited job security. Rachel Brickner and Meaghan Dalton examine how gender and sexual identities shape the experience of precarious work for 20 baristas in Halifax—specifically, how these identities shape the workers' efforts to secure better employment conditions. They find that because women and queer workers experienced some of the harshest conditions at work, they were very supportive of union organizing efforts. When workers talked about the broader economic picture within which their work fit, gender identity and sexual orientation informed the way they saw the world. In this respect, they are different from previous cohorts of workers for whom class was the overriding identification. If strategies for labour organizing do not take into account the importance of gendered experiences, the authors argue, they will not improve the working lives of precarious millennial workers.

Organizing Baristas in Halifax Cafes

Precarious Work and Gender and Class Identities in the Millennial Generation

Rachel K. Brickner and Meaghan Dalton

Introduction

In December 2012, a drive to unionize the baristas at the Just Us! cafe on Spring Garden Road in Halifax was the first in a wave of union drives in four other local cafes. The issues prompting baristas to take steps toward unionization were rooted in specific concerns about their individual workplaces—frustrations over the lack of clear processes to voice concerns or grievances, unfair tip distribution, favoritism, as well as a general feeling of a lack of respect from employers. These specific issues were embedded in broader concerns baristas had about the kind of jobs that are available to young workers in a stagnant economy, where a university degree no longer guarantees a ticket out of part-time work in the retail and service sector. Could unionization be a way to make precarious work better work, or even turn it into a career?

. . .

As we explored these questions in interviews with 20 participants in and supporters of the barista union drives that took place in Halifax between 2012–2015, it became clear that issues of gender, sexual orientation, and gender

Brickner, Rachel K., and Meaghan Dalton. "Organizing Baristas in Halifax Cafes: Precarious Work and Gender and Class Identities in the Millennial Generation." *Critical Sociology*;45 (4–5): 485–500. © 2019. Reprinted by Permission of SAGE Publications, Ltd.

identity (hereafter, "gender") informed important aspects of the drives: women and queer baristas experienced gender-based discrimination and marginalization from managers and customers; they were more likely to support the unionization drives; queer baristas were noted leaders in some of the drives and drew on activist networks to rally community support for the unionization effort. Finally, issues of gender and sexuality informed some of the baristas' broader economic analysis. As one former barista noted, "this struggle is more than just about the working class, but about why some people are in the working class" (Kelly, 9 April 2014, author interview). As such, we argue that the barista union drives in Halifax offer a framework for understanding how gender informs unjust experiences in precarious workplaces and strategies for confronting them. A gendered analysis of the barista union drives suggests that there can be a mutually beneficial relationship between labor and young workers and, further, that engaging with workers with attention to intersectionality is an important organizational strategy.

The rest of this article unfolds in five sections. In the next section, we discuss our research methods. In the third section, we explore the relevant literature on young workers, gendered power relations, and sexual politics in the labor movement and work force. The fourth section provides a basic timeline of events that occurred leading up to and during the 2012–2015 barista union drives, while the fifth section draws on our interview data to analyze the events through the lens of gender relations and sexual politics. In the final section, we offer a concluding analysis.

Methods

Our analysis is based on a series of 20 semi-structured interviews conducted between April 2014 and March 2015.[1] Of these, nine interview respondents were current or former baristas at the cafes discussed in the analysis. Six interviews were conducted with organizers from the Service Employees International Union (SEIU) and leaders of other local labor organizations. Two interviews were conducted with members of the organization

Solidarity Halifax, which provided support to the Baristas Rise Up (BRU) movement. Finally, one interview was conducted with a senior manager at one of the cafe chains. . . .

Young Workers, Unions, and Class Identity

Young people have long been employed in low wage service work. As Stuart Tannock has argued, structural changes in the retail and service sectors in the post-war period—for example, the emergence of the fast-food industry, longer hours of service, and increasing levels of automation—combined with an increase in the number of young people pursuing university educations, led to dramatic increases in part-time youth employment (Tannock, 2002: 13–14). It was once the case, and remains a powerful political narrative, that such work was a temporary stop on the road to permanent employment and a place in the middle class, particularly for young workers with a university degree (Bednar et al., 2016; Guastella, 2016; Tannock, 2002). However, studies in both the USA and Canada show that workers of the millennial generation are spending longer in the precarious service sector, even when they are educated (Bednar et al., 2016; Canadian Labour Congress, n.d.; Kroeger et al., 2016). . . .

This new employment reality is reshaping young workers' views of class. In the USA, Guastella argues, "more millennials [60%] self-identify as working class than any generation in recent history." He further notes that they "are in shit shape economically and through no fault of their own . . . many millennials see their stagnant and declining wages, among other signs of economic precarity, and ultimately recognize their class position" (Guastella, 2016).
. . .

Despite these challenges, young people are politically engaged around the issues of economic inequality that shape their lives. Ruth Milkman's (2014, 2017) work on the political activism of American millennials analyzes the ways that young activists synthesize the "old left's" attention to economic inequality with new social movements' focus on gender- and identity-based discrimination and inequity. She also highlights the importance millennial activists give to intersectional organizing and the leadership of women and LGBTQ-identifying activists.[2] The case of baristas' organizing in Halifax reflects much of Milkman's analysis: they were led by women and LGBTQ-identified millennials who understood their experiences as workers in intersectional terms. Importantly, our interviews underscored, labor's efforts to organize young workers ought to recognize and respond to the intersectional dimensions of their experiences as workers, how these experiences are shaped not only by their position in the precarious retail and service sectors, but also by other axes of identity, including race, level of education, citizenship and indigenous status, and, as our interviews demonstrate, gender and gender identity.

Gender Relations and Sexual Politics at Work

. . .

Gendered power dynamics, especially those that reinforce the centrality of "masculine, heteronormative sexualities and identities" and experiences are present at all levels of the global capitalism (Franzway and Fonow, 2009). At a global level, we see gendered power relations in the political economy of caregiving and sexual labor (Ehrenreich and Hochschild, 2004; Sassen, 2000), and in the gendered distribution of labor within global manufacturing networks (Salzinger, 2003). At the national level, we see gendered power relations in regulatory and legal frameworks that continue to organize economies according to a male breadwinner/female caregiver model (Vosko, 2011), and in the persistence of occupational segregation (Branch, 2011; Charles and Grusky, 2005). And we see gender dynamics at work at the individual level, from experiences of sexual harassment (Hughes and Tadic, 1998; MacKinnon, 1979); to the demands of emotional labor (Meier et al., 2006; Wingfield, 2016). The reliance on women, minorities, and other marginalized groups in the precarious service sector

demonstrates just another example of the way that gendered power dynamics are built into the structure of employment relationships (Cranford et al., 2003). As if to illustrate this point, the manager of a Canadian corporate coffee chain franchise suggested that precarious work is "appropriate for women" (Woodhall and Muszynski, 2011).

Sexual politics . . . requires that we broaden our analysis of gendered power relationships to include queer workers as well as straight and cisgender women. Indeed, queer workers may confront a number of particular challenges in the workplace. An over-scrutiny of the appearance of visibly queer and transgender people can prove to be a barrier to being hired at all or invite doubts about the ability of a worker to perform their job well (Enxuga, 2013). Queer workers are subject to expressions and displays of homophobia and transphobia, including threats of violence, from customers, co-workers, and managers. Such displays and threats can lead to the fear of coming out for those who are not already (Balay, 2014; Enxuga, 2013; Franzway and Fonow, 2009; Grant et al., 2011; Sweeney, 1999). Managers are not always effective in helping queer workers remedy workplace harassment and discrimination (Enxuga, 2013). Finally, where legal protections against workplace harassment, discrimination, and dismissal on the grounds of sexual orientation and gender identity are lacking, they increase precarious employment for queer employees (Beaumont, 2014).

. . .

. . . Resisting the gendered power dynamics that marginalize queer workers requires us to be realistic about the historical and contemporary limitations of traditional labor organizing—rates of unionization are in decline, and organizing precarious workers has been a challenge for labor unions—and to draw on existing social movements as sources of solidarity that will be necessary "to revitalize and expand the boundaries of labor by considering new forms of organizing, different workplaces, new issues" (Franzway and Fonow, 2009; see also Chun, 2016). The service and retail sectors may provide a productive opportunity to develop new strategies in labor-LGBTQ collaboration. . . .

Brewing Dissent at Just Us!, Second Cup, and Coburg Coffee

From December 2012 to June 2015 barista union drives developed at several local cafes—two locations of Nova Scotia-based Just Us! Coffee Roasters Co-op, two locations of Second Cup, a national chain, and the single location of family-run Coburg Coffee House. The barista union drives represented a unique phenomenon in local and national labor organizing where organizing in the food and retail service sectors is rare (Jesse and Shawn, 7 May 2014, author interview; Chris, 29 May 2014, author interview).

. . .

Although the baristas tended to highlight working conditions as the motivation to unionize, it became clear in our interviews that gendered power dynamics and sexual politics contributed to baristas experiences at work, their analysis of the political economy for young workers, the decision to pursue unionization, and the specific values and strategies of organizational leaders. It is to this analysis that we now turn.

Gendered Power Dynamics and Sexual Politics in the Barista Union Drives

. . .

Baristas' Experiences of Gendered Power Dynamics in Halifax Cafes

Not all of the baristas interviewed felt that their experiences at work reflected gendered power dynamics, but the baristas who did spoke primarily of favoritism exhibited toward cisgender male employees and the experiences of marginalization faced by queer baristas. Baristas at three different cafes spoke in detail about favoritism. Sydney, a former barista at Just Us-Wolfville, noted that when their cafe manager left the position, senior managers promoted the only male employee at the cafe, even though he had the least experience (Sydney,

25 April 2014, author interview). At Just Us-Spring Garden, Frankie recounted that "the dudes were being cut more slack in terms of their performance, being forgiven more often than women." As they described, a male coworker would fall asleep at the cafe, take longer than scheduled lunch breaks, and call in sick—all without penalty. On the other hand, another coworker was fired after not being able to work shifts that the manager rescheduled (Frankie, 17 April 2014, author interview). . . .

In addition to favoritism towards male employees, baristas described exclusionary, homophobic, and transphobic treatment of queer workers. Alex told us about some basic employment barriers for LGBTQ workers: "it's just hard to find a job . . . if you want to medically transition, or if you . . . [use] the pronoun 'they' . . . it's hard to find a job where your employers will respect that" (Alex, 10 April 2014, author interview). Frankie told us, "we end up being treated, women and trans folk end up getting the shit end of the stick in terms of our working conditions . . . I think it's a lack of self-awareness on the managers' part not to realize that they are doing that. So it's just kind of inherent sexism" (Frankie, 17 April 2014, author interview). Corey highlighted the ways that managers can contribute to an exclusionary workplace by failing to effectively respond to homophobic and transphobic treatment: "Even during the union drive, someone would come to the counter and say, 'Oh another faggot union drive.' And then [an employee related to the owner was] openly laughing in agreement, with [an openly queer barista] standing right behind him" (Corey, 15 June 2014, author interview).

In addition to discussing their personal experiences and observations about how gender, sexual orientation, and gender identity informed work in the cafes, interview respondents focused on how these inform the structure of the workplace more generally. For example, when asked if and how gender played a role in their desire to [. . .], Kelly immediately focused on the gendered nature of the service industry:

> I think [being a barista] is a job that a lot of queer people work in because of historical— and it's the same reason that women work

in the service industry, because it's this idea that it's not that good of a job and, you know, you're going to get paid less and you work really hard. . . . And I think that we're kind of transitioning to the bottom of the working class not being women anymore, necessarily, or people of color, but like trans people or people who are gender-queer people. (Kelly, 9 April 2014, author interview)

. . . The difficulty queer workers have finding and changing jobs leads to a practice called "following," which came up repeatedly. As Alex explained, it is "easier to go to a place where you know that they've already [hired queer workers]. And you don't have any idea of how much work has been done to break down stigma or whatnot, but you know that they've at least been through it once" (Alex, 10 April 2014, author interview). This series of quotations emphasizes the gendered power relations that marginalize queer workers in service sector jobs, as well as at least one practice for navigating such marginalization.
. . .

Pushing Back: How Gender Informed the Baristas' Organizing Campaigns

. . .

Despite a limited knowledge about unions, all the labor organizers we interviewed commented on the fact that queer baristas were leaders of the unionization drives and that they began the process with an understanding of the gendered dynamics at play. Former SEIU organizer Dana's quotation is representative:

> [The baristas] had a very political take on . . . unionizing and their rights at work, and their specific reasons. And it's also, you know, [queer] workers in the service industry also face a particular type of challenge in discrimination with things like dress, with things like how a customer perceives [them]. Like from big to small, issues that . . . really matter. (Dana, 21 May 2014, author interview)

For Corey, it made sense that BRU and the union drives were "a queer-led movement and a women-led movement" because "people are marginalized on two fronts, being working class or having minimum wage jobs, but also it being like it's coming from a place of gender disparity as well" (Corey, 15 June 2014, author interview). Interestingly, the importance of the baristas' unionization drive in pushing back against gendered power dynamics was reflected in who among the baristas supported the drive. One theme in the interviews was that cisgender men were not as supportive of the union drives. Frankie told us that "a lot of straight cis-dudes are just, like they almost think that they have to be macho enough to be able to handle shitty working conditions in terms of like breaks and stuff. Like, 'I don't need a break,' or those sorts of behaviours" (Frankie, 17 April 2014, author interview; Dalton, 2015, field notes).
. . . Drawing on activist networks allowed the baristas to quickly generate media attention, mobilize supporters for rallies, and develop stronger links between queer and labor activists. Alex further recollected that after reaching out to social networks, the Halifax Media Co-op was quick to publish a story about the dismissal of the two baristas who had started the union drive at Just Us-Spring Garden (Alex, 10 April 2014, author interview). SEIU organizer Shawn commented on activist connections that allowed the baristas to mobilize support for various rallies:

> [I]n the case of the baristas, you know, we mentioned that they were connected to different activist networks, not only that, they were connected to the LGBTQ community here. Many of the lead activists were from the queer and trans community. [A local labor leader] here also is a member of the queer community. They're involved with Solidarity Halifax, which encompasses a lot of activists here, so there's a lot of overlapping social networks that occurred with the baristas so that when a Solidarity Rally was called for the baristas, it really spread across many social networks. (Shawn, 7 May 2014, author interview)

. . .

Conclusion: Some Lessons for Intersectional Organizing

Our interviews demonstrate the importance of organized labor forging a stronger relationship with young workers in the precarious service and retail sectors, and, in particular, the importance of integrating into organizational strategies a focus on the ways that multiple forms of oppression shape their experiences as workers. . . .

. . . The importance of this intersectional approach to organizing, or what one barista referred to as "gender-based" labor organizing, was reflected in interviews with both labour organizers and baristas. As Chris from the Canadian Labour Congress noted, "it's very interesting that there was such a high percentage of queer . . . workers who are the forefront of that campaign. And that's an interesting thing for us to figure out . . . as we look at diversity in our labor movement" (Chris, 29 May 2014, author inter- view). Corey reflected that workers themselves have a role to play alongside unions in pushing back against their marginalization in the workforce: "something that just has to happen among us young people, [is that] we have to sort of challenge that in ourselves or educate each other, which is something we can do through gender-based labor organizing" (Corey,

15 June 2014, author interview). Jordan, from the Halifax District Labour Council, noted that queer baristas reaching out to the labor movement was part of a growing trend: "More broadly, I think you're seeing a larger number of young folks, women, young people of color, get involved in the labor movement across the country and actually around the world as folks continue to struggle against various intersecting levels of oppression" (Jordan, 29 May 2014, author interview).

. . .

A third lesson of the barista union drives is the importance of building relationships with and drawing support from activist networks. Interview respondents mentioned the importance of activist networks in generating media attention, mobilizing support at rallies, making statements of support for the union drives, and helping develop a public dialogue about the importance of organized labor in progressive politics, especially for queer workers. In the vein of social movement unionism, it is important for labor organizations to build and maintain connections with other com- munity and activist groups in order to articulate an understanding of why unionization is important for (young) workers in the service sector, and how this can benefit communities as a whole. . . .

Notes

1. This study is part of a larger project, "L'action collective et le travail atypique," which was funded by an Insight Development Grant from the Social Sciences and Humanities Research Council of Canada.
2. The concept of intersectionality was first theorized by Kimberle Crenshaw (1989). It has gone on to

become an important concept for understanding not only intersecting experiences of oppression, but also strategies for building inclusive progressive movements. In addition to the movements Milkman describes, see Women's March (2016).

References

Balay A (2014) *Steel Closets: Voices of Gay, Lesbian, and Transgender Steelworkers.* Durham, NC: University of North Carolina Press.

Beaumont H (2014) Coburg baristas await ruling on union vote. *Halifax Magazine.* Available (accessed 3 October 2014) at: http://halifaxmag.com/cityscape/coburg-baristas-await-ruling-on-union-vote

Bednar V, MacKenzie A, Cameron P, et al. (2016) *Understanding the realities: Interim report of the Expert Panel on Youth Employment.* Report for the

Government of Canada. Available (accessed 5 July 2017) at: https://www.canada.ca/en/employment-social-development/corporate/youth-expert-panel/interim-report.html

Branch E (2011) *Opportunity Denied: Limiting Black Women to Devalued Work.* New Brunswick, NJ: Rutgers University Press.

Canadian Labour Congress (n.d.) Tip sheet: Facts and figures: What is the situation for young workers today? Available (accessed 15 July 2015) at: http://

canadianlabour.ca/sites/default/files/Hand-outs-EngagingYoungWorkers%20-FactsAndFigures-EN.pdf

Charles M and Grusky DB (2005) *Occupational Ghettos: The Worldwide Segregation of Women and Men*. Stanford, Calif: Stanford University Press.

Chun JJ (2016) The affective politics of the precariat: Reconsidering alternative histories of grassroots worker organising. *Global Labour Journal* 7(2). Available (accessed 29 September 2016) at: https://mulpress.mcmaster.ca/globallabour/article/view/2483

Cranford C, Vosko LF and Zukewich N (2003) Precarious employment in the Canadian labour market: A statistical portrait. *Just Labour* 3(Fall): 6–22.

Crenshaw K (1989) Demarginalizing the intersection of race and sex: A black feminist critique of antidiscrimination doctrine, feminist theory and antiracist politics. *University of Chicago Legal Forum* 1989(1): 139–67.

Ehrenreich B and Hochschild AR (2004) *Global Woman: Nannies, Maids, and Sex Workers in the New Economy*. New York, NY: Henry Holt and Company.

Enxuga S (2013) Keep pride political: Queer rights are worker rights. *Halifax Media Co-op*, 27 July. Available (accessed 13 July 2016) at: http://halifax.mediacoop.ca/fr/blog/editor/18402

Franzway S and Fonow MM (2009) Queer activism, feminism and the transnational labor movement. *Scholar and Feminist Online* 7(3). Available (accessed 8 April 2015) at: http://sfonline.barnard.edu/sexecon/ff_01.htm

Grant JM, Mottet LA, Tanis J, et al. (2011) Injustice at every turn: A report of the National Transgender Discrimination Survey. *Report of the National Center for Transgender Equality and National Gay and Lesbian Taskforce*. Available (accessed 14 February 2016) at: http://www.thetaskforce.org/static_html/downloads/reports/reports/ntds_full.pdf

Guastella D (2016) Class is in session. *Jacobin*, 9 July. Available (accessed 9 July 2016) at: https://www.jacobinmag.com/2016/07/millennials-bernie-sanders-working-class-college-education-precarity-wages-jobs

Hughes KD and Tadic V (1998) "Something to deal with": Customer sexual harassment and women's retail service work in Canada. *Gender, Work & Organization* 5(4): 207–19.

Kroeger T, Cooke T and Gould E (2016) The class of 2016: The labor market is still far from ideal for young graduates. Economic Policy Institute. Available (accessed 15 July 2016) at: http://www.epi.org/publication/class-of-2016/

MacKinnon CA (1979) *Sexual Harassment of Working Women: A Case of Sex Discrimination*. New Haven, Conn: Yale University Press.

Meier KJ, Mastracci SH and Wilson K (2006) Gender and emotional labor in public organizations: An empirical examination of the link to performance. *Public Administration Review* 66(6): 899–909.

Milkman R (2014) Millennial movements: Occupy Wall Street and the Dreamers. *Dissent* 61(3): 55–59.

Milkman R (2017) A new political generation: Millennials and the post-2008 wave of protest. *American Sociological Review* 82(1): 1–31.

Salzinger L (2003) *Genders in Production: Making Workers in Mexico's Global Factories*. Berkeley, Calif: University of California Press.

Sassen S (2000) Women's burden: Counter-geographies of globalization and the feminization of survival. *Journal of International Affairs* 53(2): 503–24.

Sweeney JJ (1999) The growing alliance between gay and union activists. *Social Text* 61: 31–38.

Tannock S (2002) Why do working youth work where they do? A report from the young worker project. Report, University of California Berkeley Labor Center, March.

Vosko LF (2011) *Managing the Margins: Gender, Citizenship, and the International Regulation of Precarious Employment*. Oxford: Oxford University Press.

Wingfield AH (2016) How "service with a smile" takes a toll on women. *The Atlantic*. Available (accessed 15 July 2016) at: http://www.theatlantic.com/business/archive/2016/01/gender-emotional-labor/427083/

Women's March (2016) Mission and vision. *Available* (accessed 29 May 2017) at: https://www.womensmarch.com/mission/

Woodhall JR and Muszynski A (2011) Fordism at work in Canadian coffee shops. *Just Labour: A Canadian Journal of Work and Society* 17–18: 56–69.

Chapter 39

Overview

"Digital activism" has emerged as a new form of social movement that looks quite different from the rallies, marches, and protests that have characterized earlier campaigns. It looks simple—invent a hashtag and publicize it—but the authors argue that digital activism exacts its own toll of time and emotional labour. Focusing on two of the most prevalent hashtags about gender relations—#MeToo and #BeenRapedNeverReported—they interview online activists about the emotional and affective work that went into their campaigns. Their participants speak of the toll that the campaigns exact, both the stresses of listening to other people's stories of abuse and mistreatment and their own harassment by misogynist trolls. However, they take exception to the common characterization of social media, especially Twitter, as an innately hostile space for women and nonbinary people. The authors find that their participants adopt a stance of cautious optimism about the possibilities for meaningful social change through digital activism and find social media both empowering and disheartening.

#MeToo and the Promise and Pitfalls of Challenging Rape Culture through Digital Feminist Activism

Kaitlynn Mendes, Jessica Ringrose, and Jessalynn Keller

On 24 October 2017, the #MeToo hashtag began trending on Twitter. Although the phrase was initiated by African American women's rights activists Tarana Burke in 2006, it gained widespread attention when actress Alyssa Milano used it as a Twitter hashtag in response to allegations of sexual assault by Hollywood producer Harvey Weinstein. Through the #MeToo hashtag, Milano encouraged members of the public to join in to showcase the magnitude of the problem of sexual violence. Capturing both public and media attention, the hashtag was used 12 million times in the first 24 hours alone (CBS, 2017).

. . . Although #MeToo is perhaps one of the most high-profile examples of digital feminist activism we have yet encountered, it follows a growing trend of the public's willingness to engage with *resistance* and *challenges to* sexism, patriarchy and other forms of oppression via feminist uptake of digital communication.

. . . Digital feminist activism is far more complex and nuanced than one might initially expect, and a variety of digital platforms are used in a multitude of ways, for many purposes. Furthermore, although it may be *technologically easy* for many groups to engage in digital feminist activism, there *remain emotional, mental* or *practical* barriers which create different experiences, and legitimate some feminist voices, perspectives and experiences over others.

Hashtag Feminism and Social Change

Hashtag feminism is one of the most popular forms of feminist activism and involves using hashtags (the # symbol followed by a thematic word of phrase) to produce communities of conversation among disparate Twitter users (Berridge and Portwood-Stacer, 2015; Dixon, 2014; Horeck, 2014). While hashtag feminism has received substantial attention from mainstream media, we still know very little about what hashtags like #MeToo actually do; or whether and how they can produce social change. We also have scarce research that takes stock of what engaging with hashtags actually looks and feels like. One of our research case studies, the #BeenRapedNeverReported hashtag which trended in 2014 (see Keller et al., 2018 for detailed discussion of this hashtag), functioned

Mendes, Kaitlynn, Jessica Ringrose, and Jessalynn Keller. "#MeToo and the Promise and Pitfalls of Challenging Rape Culture Through Digital Feminist Activism." *European Journal of Women's Studies*;25(2):236–246 © 2018. Reprinted by Permission of SAGE Publications, Ltd.

very similarly to #MeToo in the ways in which it was used by girls and women to share personal stories of sexual violence and why they didn't report them to authorities. . . .

As part of this case study we analysed hundreds of #BeenRapedNeverReported tweets and interviewed several girls and women who used this hashtag to share their experiences of sexual violence. While we understood that the hashtag touched a cultural nerve that propelled it to be circulated millions of times (Teotonio, 2014), our interviews revealed the complex terrain of emotions that sustained the "tsunami" (Teotonio, 2014) of #BeenRapedNeverReported tweets. We discovered that these tweets were not flippant responses, but carefully produced testimonials that were scaffolded after sleepless nights. One participant told us:

> It was very emotional and it was very upsetting to me, this whole thing, being a part of that hashtag, reading other women's little tweets, 140-character tweets. One resonated and it was really a tough couple of weeks. Even though it was positive, it was very, very difficult for me. There were some nights where I didn't sleep.

This comment reflects the ways in which participating in a hashtag like #BeenRapedNeverReported is often both triggering and comforting to participants, a tension that was common among almost all our interviewees, and must be recognized as part of the complexity of doing digital feminist activism.

Yet despite the difficult emotions raised by the hashtag, our participants spoke of the significant support they received from tweeting about their assaults. One woman reported:

> I got an overwhelming awesome response the night I posted. . . . There was one . . . all she said was, "we stand with you, friend." And that one made me cry. I'll admit it, that one made me cry. And then there was one that told me I was incredibly strong and brave for doing what I did . . . there was six or seven comments like that. Which, for me, was

overwhelming because I didn't really think that anyone would say these things, you know, it was just I was helping the hashtag understand why things weren't being reported. And I didn't really expect any response at all. And next thing you know, I got likes and favourites and comments, and I was just, like, oh, my gosh, what is going on here.

. . . Not only did the women we interviewed describe being surprised by public responses to their tweet, but many emphasized how much that support in the form of "favourites," "retweets," or "DMs" (direct messages) from strangers meant to them as a form of solidarity and support. We cannot dismiss the significance of this, because if hashtags like #BeenRapedNeverReported and #MeToo are making survivors feel heard as our participant describes above, then they are doing meaningful and worthwhile work in building networks of solidarity.

We also discovered that this solidarity often transforms into a feminist consciousness amongst hashtag participants, which allows them to understand sexual violence as a structural rather than personal problem. For example, another one of our interviewees told us that she began to identify as a feminist only after sharing her story of sexual assault on social media. This experience allowed her to begin to understand her own history of sexual violence as part of a broader structural social problem, rather than an individual experience that arose from encounters with "bad men." Another young woman we interviewed, who was assaulted on a university campus, told us that sharing her experience online was the first step in reporting her assault to the campus police:

> For me, [sharing my story with the #BeenRapedNeverReported hashtag] was kind of the strength to say I can report this. And so it gave me the option and the power to actually go through to campus security . . . I'm not sure if it was because I finally put my name to it [the assault] or because I had seen so many other stories. There was a solidarity with it where I felt comfortable and ready to.

By reporting her assault to campus police, this young woman is not only overcoming stigma on a personal level, she is also contributing to social change by challenging the stigma of reporting and making campus sexual assault more visible and knowable.

This brief overview of some of our interview findings suggest that hashtags like #BeenRapedNeverReported and #MeToo provide important opportunities for the development of feminist solidarity and consciousness, and even, social change. This is especially true for girls and women who may not be familiar with feminism as a personal and political imperative. . . .

The Labour of Digital Feminist Activism

It is perhaps easy to assume that the labour involved in running a feminist campaign such as #MeToo or #BeenRapedNeverReported is minimal—after all, one only has to coin a hashtag and let the public take over. While to some extent, hashtag feminism is perhaps the "easiest" type of digital feminist campaign to run, this does not mean that it is easy, or that there is no further labour after the initial conceptualization or tweet. Indeed, when hashtags or other digital feminist campaigns gain momentum and are widely used, its founders often become subject to much mainstream attention, scrutiny and follow-on initiatives. The founders of #BeenRapedNeverReported were regularly asked to write about the hashtag and its significance, and take part in media interviews and debates. Our interviews with 18 feminist organizers showcase the often hidden labour involved in maintaining these campaigns, and public interest. In many cases, organizers devoted several hours each day or week to these initiatives with little to no financial compensation or regularly scheduled breaks. . . . Although more often than not such work is undertaken because of the individual's desire and passion for the subject (see also McRobbie, 2016), the fact remains that it is very difficult (and contentious) to seek financial compensation from this type of work. Like other types of "women's work," the labour involved in running these digital feminist campaigns is highly affective, precarious and exploitative—and as such, we raise questions about the sustainability of such unpaid labour in light of online abuse, burnout and other issues around work–life balance in the digital age.

Throughout our interviews, many participants talked about the emotional "tax" they experienced from listening to stories of abuse, harassment, misogyny and sexism. This included the "weightiness" of the work and how at times they had to take breaks, limit what they take on, and in some cases, walk away, even if only for a short time. As one organizer for the Tumblr site Who Needs Feminism? shared, "It does get tiring and it does get . . . it's definitely emotionally taxing and you have to take care of yourself. I did have to take a break from it sometimes" (Ashley Tsai, personal communication, 18 May 2015). Some of our participants talked about the panic attacks they felt as a result of the weight and sheer amount of work needed to run these campaigns. In sharing her experience of quitting Everyday Sexism shortly after taking up her first full-time academic position, Emer O'Toole explained how her exit was abrupt and unexpected:

> I was sitting down to do the volunteer coordination and I was kind of going like, oh, having trouble breathing. And I just wrote to Laura [Bates of the Everyday Sexism Project] and said, "I'm so sorry, I can't do it, I can't even really train someone else up to take over from me. I'm so sorry but here's where everything's at, I just have to bow out right now." (Emer O'Toole, personal communication, 11 May 2015)

Everyday Experiences of Doing Digital Feminist Activism

. . . Our data also included an in-depth online survey targeted at everyday Twitter users who self-defined as "feminist activists." . . . [W]e wanted to extend our analysis to contextualize the experiences of getting involved through social media to ask what happens *after* women and girls begin to participate in digital feminist politics around rape culture and sexual violence by posting on a trending hashtag? How do they sustain and build upon their feminist consciousness through their digital networks online?

Survey participants were recruited through our own Twitter networks, generating 46 responses (including four self-defined feminist men). Albeit a small sample, the responses were richly descriptive regarding participants' experiences of using Twitter for feminist activism, and specifically to combat rape culture. Indeed, all but two of our survey respondents (96%) reported that they had directly challenged sexual violence and "rape culture" in their social media posts. We have three major findings from the survey data we want to highlight in the final sections of this article: the positive potential of Twitter; hostility and trolling on Twitter; and finally, how engaging in feminist debate on Twitter is still understood as easier than discussing feminist views in real life, which further illustrates how important digital platforms are in providing spaces to develop both individual and collective feminist consciousness, and to find and maintain support for feminist views.

Is Twitter a Safe Space for Feminist Activism?

A first significant finding was that respondents identified overwhelmingly positive aspects of using Twitter to communicate their feminist views with much wider audiences than their immediate social circles.

> The first place I heard about feminism was on the internet. Feminism saved my life. The internet has the ability to reach so many people, and if it can change my life, it can change theirs. I definitely see internet feminism as a form of activism with the potential to change society.

The themes of global reach, speed, immediacy, dialogue, visibility, engagement, contact, connection, collectivity and shared understanding all emerged as important for participants. For

example, one respondent said Twitter was critical for sustaining her feminist politics because of:

> . . . the potential to connect with others. I have so many like-minded friends on Twitter now that I sometimes forget not everyone is as sensitive and understanding of issues around feminism, gender and trauma as they are. You can get involved in reacting [to] a huge audience without putting yourself too much as risk too, i.e. retweeting or sharing information.

. . .

The idea of safe spaces to feel comfortable sharing, and connecting with "like-minded" people and "knowing that others feel the same as you" on Twitter was described as particularly important for learning, awareness and consciousness raising:

> Twitter allows a greater number of people to engage in debate, it creates greater awareness, it provides a platform to address many issues relating to feminism and allows us to call people out when they make misogynistic comments. Through exposing them on a public forum, we might encourage one to re-evaluate their views and actions and hopefully encourage change.

We can see that self-defined digital feminist activists feel very strongly that digital "calling out" practices are a critical part of instigating social change. In addition, the issues of raising the visibility of feminism and enabling the voice of marginalized groups were reiterated:

> Visibility is important and Twitter allows feminists to express opinions and share stories that aren't publicised in the mainstream. I'm a believer that the personal is political and if a person can connect to another's story their political views can be changed. Internet activism is also useful for activists with mental or physical disabilities who may not be able to attend protests and meetings.

Historically women have had little to no way to meet up and to discuss and share ideas, which has arguably lead to a narrow and white feminism being dominant, yet now through social media being accessible for many it is so much more easier to share ideas, to discuss and develop feminism, to help others through advice and through petitions, through raising awareness, and through holding others to a higher standard and pointing out others' inexcusable misogyny.

Women's historical exclusion from the public sphere and participation in political debates is explained through reference to accessibility, ability, race and class privilege through what we might term an intersectional lens, typically understood to be a key aspect of "fourth wave" digital feminism (Munro, 2013). Age was also raised several times as a critical aspect of being denied a political voice in many social contexts and structures, with Twitter offering an alternative space for political participation. Thirty-three per cent of the survey respondents were teenagers attending school, who argued Twitter provided knowledge and opportunities for learning and dialogue that school could not. Respondents also felt that they may be able to use social media information and learning to influence their *known peers* at school (see also Kim and Ringrose, 2018; Retallack et al., 2016):

> . . .
>
> I think the biggest benefit of using social media for my feminism is the fact that it helps me feel as if I'm making a difference, and interacting with a community, on a daily basis. In my high school environment, it's easy to forget that there are other people out there with the same progressive beliefs as me; the ability to interact with other feminists reminds me that there's still hope.
>
> I mostly tweet and retweet about what I find to be misogynistic. What I really think makes the most impact from my account, is that there are people from school I know following me that don't share my beliefs. The fact

that they're seeing my opinions, is hopefully making them realize that these things are issues, and we have a responsibility to care about them.

Does Fear, Hostility and Trolling Dominate Twitter?

In recent years, in tandem with the growth in scholarship around the "popularity" of feminism (see Banet-Weiser and Miltner, 2016; Gill, 2016; Keller and Ringrose, 2015), scholars are paying attention to how the rise of digital technologies has enabled the flourishing of much misogynist vitriol against feminism and even specific feminists (see Citron, 2014; Jane, 2014, 2017; Poland, 2016; Powell and Henry, 2017). Within our own study, trolling and online abuse was indeed a common experience, with 72% of our survey respondents experiencing negativity, hostility or trolling in response to their feminist views and challenges to rape culture online. Participants shared their experiences of a wide range of practices—from seemingly mundane, ubiquitous, or "low-level" comments such as "you're fat" or "ugly" to vitriolic, violent and graphic rape and death threats:

> . . .
>
> I get called a bitch and an ugly whore pretty much weekly. I was also told that I deserved to be raped and that that would be the only way I'd ever get laid and that I should be grateful.

Some of these episodes of what participants called "trolling," were recounted as involving persistent and multiple attacks from strangers on their Twitter feeds:

> It tends to be very predictable—anti-feminists popping up in response to a RT/comment/ discussion and quite aggressively belittling the feminist point of view. Very rarely, if ever, do they respectfully challenge—rather they attempt to bully/dominate by demanding evidence/ proof etc, and telling us in no uncertain terms that we are wrong. At best it's

sarcastic and patronizing, at worst it's offensive—for example making reference to those who object to pornography as ugly/jealous/needing to be f**ked.

[P]articipants had developed a range of strategies to cope with these "predictable" forms of anti-feminism. . . . These strategies included purposefully avoiding engaging with aggressive tweets and blocking and muting these accounts. Some engaged in "digilante" (digital vigilante, see Jane, 2017) tactics, for example finding out the school attended by teen boys sexually harassing someone on Twitter and threatening to contact the boys' headteacher to report their activity. In another case one of our participants worked with Twitter headquarters and the police to locate and charge a serial troll who was creating multiple accounts to continue abusive activities. We found that despite threats women and girls encountered, designed to challenge their rights to political participation in the online pubic sphere (Salter, 2016), our participants largely persisted in their digital feminist activities.

Is Doing Feminism Easier in Digital Spaces?

The third and final finding we want to discuss in this short overview of our survey findings is how, despite the risk and hostility on Twitter, the digital sphere was still largely understood as a relatively *safer* and *easier* space to engage in feminist discussions than in participants' offline contexts. Moreover, we found that experiences of engaging with and developing feminist consciousness online actually created a range of clashes in their everyday relationships with colleagues, family and friends. The tension between their online feminist community where they could share views and opinions and get support contrasted strongly with experiences of dismissal by significant others in their everyday lives:

Most of my offline friends wouldn't identify as [feminist]. I have been really surprised and disheartened, when talking to them about feminism, by their reluctance to acknowledge the socially constructed nature of femininity

and the influence of culture on behaviours/practices that they consider entirely free choices. I have found this frustrating, and at times upsetting because I have come away from some conversations feeling *as though the problem lies with me*—as though I'm imagining things, that it's about my personal issues, that I'm over-sensitive and so on. This has encouraged me to get more involved with feminism online, where I have found support and realised that I'm not alone. (emphasis added)

Again, the issue of "feeling alone" in one's feminist views and feeling upset by institutionalized cultures of sexism among friends and family as well as at work, school and university was salient. We are reminded of Sara Ahmed's (2010) figure of the feminist "killjoy" and how discursively and affectively the person practising feminism is positioned as the "problem" and creating trouble and tension for others. Several teens experienced such tension with peers at school when they expressed their feminist views or challenged sexual violence through their uses of social media (see also Ringrose and Renold, 2016a). As one explained, "Most of the negativity I've experienced online has been from people that actually know me from school." Another confirmed, "The worst problems are in school. One person related my feminist tweet to fascism. Others made sarcastic remarks. . . . Some would make 'jokes' that they know are sexist/racist." . . .

Concluding Thoughts

In summary, when thinking about what hashtags such as #MeToo actually do, and what platforms like Twitter can enable for feminist politics, the answer is complicated. Our findings of the lived experiences of posting on anti-rape hashtags, leading and participating in feminist campaigns against sexual violence and developing feminist networks via Twitter reveal a complicated picture defined by contradictions. It is now common knowledge that digital technologies make the distribution of online vitriol easy, persistent and vicious; and a range of feminist research has suggested that Twitter is overwhelmingly a negative and toxic space for women (Jane, 2017; Shaw, 2014). In line with this, most participants experienced anxiety and fear of being attacked for their feminist views. However, in contrast, our findings also reveal how digital feminism can simultaneously be experienced as extremely positive in generating community, connection and support for feminist views, and solidarity in calling out rape culture. Despite widespread fear of attack and experiences of trolling, the participants found strategies to tackle this. Moreover, Twitter and online platforms were viewed by many participants as safer and easier spaces for engaging in feminist activism than offline places such as the street, workplaces, schools and among family and friends. This was particularly true for teenagers who found that practising feminism offline at school was extremely difficult to navigate.

In conclusion, then, our findings lead us to be both optimistic and cautious about the experiences of viral digital movements such as #MeToo, and many more like it (such as #BeenRapedNeverReported and #YesAllWomen). These campaigns are providing important spaces for a wider range of women and girls (in relation to age, ability, race and other factors) to participate in public debates on sexual harassment, sexism and rape culture. These platforms are also making women's and girls' voices and participation *visible* in ways that can generate the type of ripple effect we have witnessed in the aftermath of #MeToo, where many powerful (mainly white) men are being held accountable for historic instances of abuse and harassment. At the same time, our findings clearly demonstrate that it is never *easy* to engage in such activism. Aside from the celebrated statements of defiance valorized by the media with cases such as #MeToo, more hidden are the emotional, mental or practical factors which make engaging in digital feminist activism risky, exhausting, draining and overwhelming, depending on the context. So, while we are confident that conversations around digital feminist activism against rape culture, sexism and harassment will continue, we encourage researchers to continue to explore the experiences of those who are participating in such initiatives, so we can understand the fuller picture and long-term effects and impacts of such feminist activisms.

References

Ahmed S (2010) Happy objects. In: Gregg M and Seigworth GJ (eds) *The Affect Theory Reader*. Durham, NC: Duke University Press, pp. 29–51.

Banet-Weiser S and Miltner KM (2016) #MasculinitySoFragile: Culture, structure, and networked misogyny. *Feminist Media Studies* 16(1): 171–74.

Berridge S and Portwood-Stacer L (2015) Introduction: Feminism, hashtags and violence against women and girls. *Feminist Media Studies* 15(2): 341–44.

CBS (2017) More than 12M "MeToo" Facebook posts, comments, reactions in 24 hours. Available at: www.cbsnews.com/news/metoo-more-than-12-million-facebook-posts-comments-reactions-24-hours/ (accessed 1 December 2017).

Citron D (2014) *Hate Crimes in Cyberspace*. Cambridge, Mass: Harvard University Press.

Dixon K (2014) Feminist online identity: Analyzing the presence of hashtag feminism. *Journal of Arts and Humanities* 3(7): 34.

Gill R (2016) Post-postfeminism? New feminist visibilities in postfeminist times. *Feminist Media Studies* 16(4): 610–30.

Horeck T (2014) #AskThicke: "Blurred lines," rape culture, and the feminist hashtag takeover. *Feminist Media Studies* 14(6): 1105–107.

Jane EJ (2014) "Your a ugly, whorish slut": Understanding e-bile. *Feminist Media Studies* 14(4): 531–46.

Jane EJ (2017) *Misogyny Online: A Short (and Brutish) History*. London, Thousand Oaks, Calif and New Delhi: Sage.

Keller J and Ringrose J (2015) "But then feminism goes out the window!": Exploring teenage girls' critical response to celebrity feminism. *Celebrity Studies* 6(1): 132–35.

Keller J, Mendes K and Ringrose J (2018) Speaking "unspeakable things": Documenting digital feminist responses to rape culture. *Journal of Gender Studies* 27(1): 22–36.

Kim C and Ringrose J (2018) "Stumbling upon feminism": Teenage girls' forays into digital and school-based feminisms. *Girlhood Studies* 11(2).

McRobbie A (2016) *Be Creative: Making a Living in the New Cultural Industries*. Cambridge and Malden, Mass: Polity Press.

Munro E (2013) Feminism: A fourth wave? *Political Insight* 4(2): 22–25.

Poland B (2016) *Cybersexism in the 21st Century*. Lincoln: University of Nebraska Press.

Powell A and Henry N (2017) *Sexual Violence in a Digital Age*. Basingstoke: Palgrave Macmillan.

Retallack H, Ringrose J and Lawrence E (2016) "Fuck your body image": Teen girls' Twitter and Instagram feminism in and around school. In: Coffey J, Budgeon S and Cahill H (eds) *Learning Bodies: The Body in Youth and Childhood Studies*. London: Springer, pp. 85–103.

Ringrose J and Renold E (2016a) Cows, cabins and tweets: Posthuman intra-acting affect and feminist fires in secondary school. In: Taylor C and Hughes C (eds) *Posthuman Research Practices in Education*. London: Palgrave.

Salter M (2016) *Crime, Justice and Social Media*. London: Routledge.

Shaw A (2014) The internet is full of jerks because the world is full of jerks: What feminist theory teaches us about the internet. *Communication and Critical/Cultural Studies* 11(3): 273–77.

Teotonio I (2014) Women find power in #BennRapedNeverReported hashtag. *Toronto Star*, 5 November. Available at: www.thestar .com/life/2014/11/05/women_find_power_in_ beenrapedneverreported_hashtag.html (accessed 17 December 2017).

Chapter 40

Overview

Ethel Tungohan asserts that feminist activism is alive and well in Canada, both on and off the screen. She provides a survey of migrant women's activism today, which demonstrates that the boundaries of "Canada" are not confined to the physical borders of the country. Migrant women move across transnational fields, from the countries of their origin to Canada and back again. Global political and economic forces, as well as gendered expectations of women, shape their trajectories to and from Canada. In the example of the Philippines, women are actively encouraged by their government to go abroad and earn money to send home, yet in Canada they face obstacles to their security and safety at work. Tungohan shows how migrant women's networks provide spaces for women that are not tied to promoting the agendas of sending or receiving countries. By carving out autonomous social and political spaces for migrant women, the significance of the associations goes beyond merely representing migrant women's interests and constitutes a transformative feminist practice.

The Transformative and Radical Feminism of Grassroots Migrant Women's Movement(s) in Canada

Ethel Tungohan

Introduction

Feminism is still alive and well in the 21st century. The millions of people across the United States, Canada and around the world who participated

Tungohan, Ethel. "The Transformative and Radical Feminism of Grassroots Migrant Women's Movement(s) in Canada." *Canadian Journal of Political Science/Revue canadienne de science politique,* 50(2) 2017, pp. 479–494.

in the "Women's March" on January 22, 2017 is testament to the relevance of feminism to people's lives. . . .

The National Domestic Workers Alliance (NDWA), an umbrella organization of different migrant domestic worker organizations in the United States, sent 100 migrant domestic workers to Washington, DC to protest, many asking for an "economy that works for everyone" (National Domestic Workers Alliance 2017). . . .

Migrant domestic workers who were part of Gabriela-Ontario, the Caregivers Action Centre, Migrante-Canada and other organizations were present at the Women's March in Toronto. . . .

This article critically examines some of these grassroots migrant women's organizations in Canada. I argue that for migrant women's organizations to understand the complexities of migrant women's "parallel lives" (Briones 2009: 20) a vision of feminist politics is needed that embraces a multiplicity of perspectives with contradictions in strategies. Hence, a transnational perspective grounded in the use of "counter-topographies" that see how migrant women's lives are lived across different locales and that consequently "links different places analytically and therefore builds oppositional politics in the name of common interests" (Katz 2001: 1230) becomes necessary. Such a perspective shows that gender equality is not only advanced through liberal modes of inclusion but also through structural transformations. These migrant women embody Briones's contention that "agency and rights are not enough" (2009). Instead, as her analysis of the experiences of domestic workers in Paris and in Hong Kong shows, it is crucial that migrant women have the ability to carve out a space of economic security amidst the vagaries of neoliberal economic restructuring.

The arguments are discussed in three sections. First, I discuss the methodology informing this work. Second, I show how migrant domestic work is the byproduct of structural inequalities between migrant-ending and migrant-receiving states. Third, I assess the type of activist politics used by different grassroots migrant domestic worker organizations. In this section, I focus on the ability of these organizations to overturn harmful discourses against migrant domestic work, to provide services and safe spaces for migrant workers, and to safeguard migrant women's well-being amid the economic uncertainties wrought by neoliberalism. I conclude by reflecting on how grassroots migrant women's movements represent the possibilities of a radical and transformative feminism.

Methodology

The ensuing analysis is based on 75 one-on-one interviews I undertook from 2009 until 2012 with representatives of migrant women's organizations across Canada. When analyzing my interviews, I was attentive to how human beings "shape and create their lives in the context of larger societal power relationships" and sought to interpret their narratives in this light. . . .

The organizations I examined varied in scope and in membership. Some grassroots organizations were self-supporting, whereas others were funded by government as settlement agencies and yet others received funding from different sources but otherwise did not have the same reporting requirements as the first set of organizations. These organizations also varied in terms of membership. Some primarily had Filipina members, reflecting the dominance of Filipina women in domestic work in many parts of Canada. Others served migrants from various racial backgrounds and migrant categories in domestic worker programmes. . . .

Neoliberalism, Philippine Labour Export, and Migrant Domestic Work in Canada

Much has been written about migrant export and import policies in sending and receiving states (see, e.g., Romero, Preston and Giles, ed. 2014). This includes analysis of the Philippines' role as the global "supplier" of migrant labour, such as Robyn Rodriguez's (2010) incisive analysis of how the Philippines' role as a "brokerage state" has led the Philippine government to tie its economic well-being to the remittances sent by Filipino migrants, particularly female migrants. . . .

A rich body of work documents Canada's reliance on migrant domestic labour to meet its caregiving needs. Canada's migrant domestic worker programmes have undergone several iterations, including the Caribbean Domestics Scheme in the middle of the 20th century, the Foreign Domestics Movement in 1982 and the Live-in Caregiver Program in 1992, which allowed domestic workers to apply for permanent residency after completing a two-year live-in work requirement (. . . Arat-Koc 1999, 2003, Bakan and Stasiulis 1997, 2005, Pratt 1997, 1999). In 2014, the Caregiver Program eliminated the live-in requirement but severely restricted the numbers of women who could acquire permanent residency after finishing their work contracts by imposing language and workplace licensing requirements and also annual quotas. Despite changes to the programme, migrant domestic workers remain vulnerable to abuse. . . .

Migration researchers have not paid as much attention to the links between neoliberalism, the state, and the various migrant institutions (such as employment and recruitment agencies and social networks) that facilitate the exodus of migrant workers from developing countries into developed countries. Neoliberalism, which holds that "human well-being can best be advanced by liberating individual entrepreneurial freedoms and skills within an institutional framework characterized by . . . free market and free trade," sees the role of the state as one that primarily facilitates these conditions (Harvey 2005:2). In the context of labour migration, it becomes clear that neoliberal states see the "free trade" of people as not only maximizing economic growth but also "liberating" individual freedoms. Migrant institutions are thus geared towards helping the state do both. . . .

The most fruitful approach in unpacking these inter-linkages is Jon Goss and Bruce Lindquist's (1995) application of Anthony Giddens' structuration theory to migration. Like Giddens, they believe that it is important not to see "agency" and "structure" as diametrically opposed concepts for to do so is to assume that only one of these explains the prevalence of international migration (331). . . .

Applying these concepts to migration, Goss and Lindquist state that migrants, as "knowledgeable agents," are aware of the structures of power that make their migration from their home countries necessary and use their knowledge of migrant institutions, including "social networks," to their advantage (335). Individual migrants' decisions and the "complex of international and national institutions that transcend the boundaries of scales and locales [and] link employers in the developed and rapidly developing economies with individuals in the furthest peripheries of the Third World" in turn institutionalizes migration (336). . . . Their decisions bolster and support the very structures that make international migration a reality.

The notion of migrants' agency should, of course, be unpacked further, for agency is not only about believing that human beings knowingly make decisions for their well-being, but is also about "cognitive processes, such as imagination" (Mahler and Pessar 2001: 447). Cognitive processes—"imagining, planning, strategizing"—"must be valued and factored into people's agency" (Mahler and Pessar 2001: 447). In other words, human beings decide to migrate not only because of a rational economic calculation but also because they "live their lives in a transnational cognitive space," where dreams to go abroad, perhaps implanted in childhood, become factors. But how freely agentic can human beings be when colonialist and neoliberal ideas about life abroad take hold? Hence, ideational factors, combined with structures and institutions encouraging labour migration, influence people's decisions to migrate and complicates notions of "agency."

. . .

Migrant Activism

All the organizations in my study represent migrant domestic workers and have at the centre of their mandates putting migrant domestic workers' interests first. All can be classified as "feminist" in that they focus on migrant women's rights, as seen through their mission statements and programming.

During my interviews, the organizations' representatives all referenced "women's rights," "empowerment" and "feminism," identifying themselves as feminist. . . .

While both types of organizations focus on migrant domestic workers' needs, feminist migrant worker organizations' differ in understanding that such women need their own forms of representation that can empower them both as migrant domestic workers and as women. When sending states valorize migrant workers as "heroes of the nation" who can save countries like the Philippines from economic destitution (see, e.g., Rodriguez 2010 and Guevarra 2009) and receiving states claim that they should be grateful for being "allowed" to work in the country, the needs and interests of migrant workers are ignored. As "heroes" who sacrifice for their countries and families, migrant workers are not given the discursive space to assert their needs. Nor are their needs considered in receiving states' rhetoric about how grateful they should be for the opportunity to work, which obscures how crucial migrant domestic workers' labour is in helping receiving states meet their care deficit (Lutz and Palenga-Mollenbeck 2010).

Moreover, migrants' employers and families also see them instrumentally, with employers oftentimes solely seeing migrant domestic workers' as domestic "helpers" or as senders of remittance cheques. This leaves the needs and interests of migrant women domestic workers unaddressed except by those feminist organizations whose affirmation of them is empowering. As one of the women I interviewed disclosed, "in between my employers wanting me to care for them and their kids, and my family wanting me to care for them by sending them money and being available, who is left to care for me?"

. . .

Feminist organizations also strive to represent migrant workers' "parallel lives" in Canada and abroad. Unlike other progressive organizations, feminist migrant organizations understand that their members live physically in Canada but also have virtual lives that they live through Skype and other forms of communications technology that allow them to remain in contact with their families at home. Thus, many organizations' activities are geared towards normalizing transnational families. For example, plays that members have written and performed feature transnational families. Leaders of these groups recognize the loneliness that migrant workers face, particularly during holidays, and thus organize parties for them and assist migrant families. . . .

Furthermore, migrant worker organizations reframe how migrant domestic workers, Filipino community members, and even Canadian society at large see migrant domestic work. As social movement theorists David A. Snow and Robert D. Benford (1992) argue:

> Movement actors and organizations are actively engaged in the production and maintenance of meaning for constituents, antagonists, and bystanders or observers . . . we thus view movements as functioning in part as signifying agents that often are deeply embroiled, along with the media, the government, and the state, in what has aptly been referred to as the "politics of signification" (136).

By taking ownership of such discursive representations, feminist organizations of migrant workers ensure that discussions surrounding migrant work consider their humanity.

Events such as beauty pageants and theatrical productions, which some organizations hold, showcase migrant domestic workers in a different light to members of the Canadian public. Rather than being "only" domestic workers, the women involved in these events become beauty pageant contestants and artists. While not normally part of feminist politics, such "political theatre" is extensively used by migrant communities to give migrants the ability to give voice to their stories, form community, and reach others. As one woman who was part of a migrant beauty pageant told me in the aftermath of the Migrant Mothers of the Year Beauty Pageant, which I attended in 2011, "it's not just about the pageant but about meeting other caregivers and knowing about each other's lives . . . and it is a chance for us to show [to the audience] that we have lives outside our nannying!" . . . In this way, feminist migrant domestic worker organizations are able to reclaim discourses about performing domestic work, reframing these in an empowering way.

Organizations for migrant domestic workers also provide services, such as information on the LCP and resources to mitigate abuse they may face in the programme. "Know your rights" sessions are common across migrant domestic worker organizations, with some providing informational booklets outlining rights. Sessions also include information on changes to the LCP. Some of these meetings feature Members of Parliament and immigration lawyers, who discuss the long-term policy ramifications of these changes and explain how policy changes may affect migrant domestic workers and the family members they hoped to sponsor. Significantly, many of these sessions involve workshops on skills development, financial literacy, educational opportunities, building a resume and running a small business. Migrant worker organizations–even those that take an anti-capitalist approach to their work–see the value of helping migrant workers become more economically secure. . . . All of the migrant worker organizations studied provide some of these services and so meet the needs of an otherwise ignored group.

In addition, for these organizations, providing migrant domestic workers with a safe space to gather is foremost among their activities, because under the terms of the LCP migrant domestic workers have days off and face the problem of where to spend them. They do not feel they can stay in their employers' households on their days off because they are afraid they will be asked to work or seen as "transgressing" their employers' private space. In fact, migrant domestic workers say they never truly feel at home in their employers' houses but see them as spaces of regulation and supervision. Public spaces such as food courts inside shopping malls or public parks make some of the migrant domestic workers I spoke to uncomfortable, evoking Sherene Razack's observation that some spaces are exclusionary, underscoring how "brown and black bodies are relegated to degenerate spaces" (2002: 89). Because these spaces are not "theirs," migrant domestic workers become reluctant to use them. Having access to physical spaces where they can feel at ease during their days off is important for migrant domestic workers.

This also involves having access to a support network of fellow migrant domestic workers which enhances feelings of safety. Even organizations that do not have offices make sure that gatherings are regularly held so migrant domestic workers can have the opportunity to meet and touch base with each other. Participating in social events may not appear political but the act of "being there" for each other is a form of "radical democracy" in that it reframes citizenship such that migrant domestic workers–who otherwise do not normally qualify for services available only to Canadian citizens because of their status as migrant workers–are "given this support as fellow members of the political community" (emphasis mine, Brown 1997: 133). . . .

All migrant domestic organizations have contacts with safe houses that can provide migrant domestic workers with shelter. Certain organizations, such as Migrante-Canada, provide migrant domestic workers needing shelter access to a national and even international network of members with whom they can stay. Migrante-Canada's toll-free 1-800 number allows migrant workers in trouble instantaneous access to this network. Moreover, migrant worker organizations can also provide referrals that may help abused migrant workers find new employers. In drastic situations, organizations can launch rescue missions and dispatch members to help abused migrant workers escape.

Jocelyn Tomas, of the First Ontario Alliance of Caregivers in Canada (FOACC), described her participation in rescue missions as follows:

> Our work is really hands-on. We feel for distressed caregivers. When I do rescues, that's when I feel the fear that they are experiencing, when you're in the middle of it all. When I did that for the first time, my car was running, the caregiver we were rescuing was running to us, I was so afraid because I was by myself, and the caregiver is crying and you start crying too. So our emotions join together.

By providing migrant workers with the ability to "be there" for each other, which involves providing each other with support when facing mundane problems and dangerous situations, migrant worker organizations are therefore forming their own independent networks that are not tied to sending and receiving states and other groups with agendas that do not give priority to migrant workers. Instead of assuming that sending and receiving states and other organizations will be meeting their needs, migrant domestic workers proactively establish their own spaces.

Some migrant worker organizations gear their activities towards opposing structural inequities and link their campaigns to transnational grassroots social justice organizing. Organizations like Gabriela-Ontario, Migrante-Canada, and PWC, were helmed by activists who were previously active in opposing Philippine dictator Ferdinand Marcos, whose authoritarian regime in the 1970s and the 1980s led to the mass persecution of various groups, including students, labour leaders, and other politicians. Some of the activists who Marcos targeted fled to Canada; their experiences with anti-Marcos activism imbued them with an underlying belief in the importance of "true democratic reform." . . . It was Marcos who first instituted the Philippines' "labour export policy," which was initially meant to be "temporary" and which activists now call "permanently temporary" (see, e.g., Rodriguez 2010; Guevarra 2009). . . .

By linking their activities towards larger, structural issues, these organizations continuously educate migrant workers and the Canadian public about the role played by neoliberalism in creating a cycle of economic dependency, forcing workers to seek jobs abroad and fragmenting migrant families. In this, their activities diverge from mainstream feminist organizations that look primarily at liberal modes of inclusion to rectify inequality. . . .

Public artistic performances as forms of individual and collective political expression became an important site of resistance for Gabriela-ON, Migrante-BC, and PWC. The PWC's participation in the play "Nanay" and its sponsorship of political fashion shows, Gabriela-Ontario's "Teatro Lila," Pinay's diverse theatrical endeavors and Migrante-Youth's mural project all poignantly express the pains of migration, as experienced by migrant domestic workers and their children. As Petronila Cleto, one of Gabriela-Ontario's founding members, told me in an interview in May 2011, "it's sometimes hard for women to be direct about their painful experiences. Participating in artistic endeavours, such as being part of a play or a writing group, makes it easier to draw out their emotions." These activities also raise awareness about migration issues among other migrant workers, Filipino community members and the Canadian public. As British playwright John McGrath, who spearheaded "political theatre" in England, observed, these performances "can assert, draw attention to, give voice to threatened communities, [and] can, by allowing [marginalized people to speak] allow them to survive (as quoted in Kershaw, 1992: 11)." This sort of activity can "make a challenge to the values imposed on it by the dominant group–it can help to stop ruling class, or race, or male, or multinational capitalist values being 'universalized' as common sense or self-evident truth" (as quoted in Kershaw, 1992: 11).

These organizations nevertheless diverge on the question of normative solutions to the problems raised by migrant work. Groups like Gabriela-ON and Migrante-Canada take account of these multiple harms and see the short and medium-term solution as lying in the reform of the LCP whereas groups like AAFQ and PWC want the LCP's abolished. In fact, it is the very issue of abolition versus reform that is arguably the biggest source of conflict within Canada's migrant domestic workers' movement (Tungohan 2013).

Conclusion

All of the migrant workers in my study are "knowledgeable agents," to again quote Goss and Lindquist (1995). They respond to challenges by finding ways to express their agency through participation in organizations. They are aware of the structural elements that make their labour migration necessary and are strategic about navigating neoliberal landscapes by both critiquing them and seeking to benefit from them economically.

Consequently, while one could say that they perpetuate the exploitative cycle of labour migration by participating in the migration process, their activism shows that they are also resisting neoliberal power structures. Their activism therefore points to their messy and complex encounters with neoliberalism. The migrant workers I interviewed fought against the harmful effects of immigration policy and migration structures while also ensuring the perpetuation of these policies and structures. The regular remittances they send home, their ability to meet Canadian families' caregiving needs, and their support of migration institutions such as their use of labour brokers and remittance agencies reinforce the idea that migrant domestic work is beneficial. This, then, provides empirical credence to Newman's observations that "it is the contradictions inherent in such struggles which opens up spaces of power" (2013: 215).

What does the vibrancy of the migrant workers' movement tell us about the state of feminism in the 21st century? First, rather than fixating on a single feminism, it is important for activists and scholars to consider that multiple strands of feminism exist. Feminism encompasses multiple individuals and communities, and represents different groups of women, oftentimes with competing beliefs and agendas. Feminism should include the perspectives of different groups of women, such as the migrant domestic workers in this study.

Instead of understanding feminism as occurring in waves, with one "type" of feminism giving way to another, we should see feminism and movements as occurring simultaneously; migrant domestic workers, for example, have been active in resisting their living and working conditions throughout the different "waves" of feminist history. For the migrant activists in my study, activism occurred not so much in distinct waves but rather as a continuous flow from one generation to the next. There were connections forged between different generations of activists, with previous generations of anti-Marcos activists continuing to give ongoing mentorship and support to later generations of activists, whose campaigns grew to encompass not only issues of domestic work but also issues facing migrant youth. Second and more importantly, for migrant women participating in grassroots feminist movements, the struggle for gender justice has never been more important, particularly considering recent political events where anti-migrant sentiments abound. For as long as neoliberal structures that facilitate their departure from their home countries and that fragment their families exist, migrant women's resistance to these structures will concurrently occur. Their participation in the different women's marches discussed in the first part of this article highlight their conviction that organizing within feminist movements is vital to their work. Their activism shows the strengths of their conviction in the possibilities of a transformative feminism that pushes back against neoliberalism.

References

Arat-Koc, Sedef. 1999. "Gender and Race in Non-Discriminatory Immigration Policies in Canada: 1960s to the Present." In *Scratching the Surface: Canadian Anti-Racist Feminist Thought*, eds. Enakshi Dua and Angela Robertson. Toronto: Women's Press, 207–33.

Arat-Koc, Sedef. 2003. "Good Enough to Work but Not Good Enough to Stay: Foreign Domestic Workers and the Law." In *Locating Law: Race, Class, Gender Connections*, ed. Elizabeth Cormack. Halifax: Fernwood Press, 121–51.

Bakan, Abigail and Daiva Stasiulis. 1997. "Foreign Domestic Workers in Canada and the Social Boundaries of Modern Citizenship." In *Not One of the Family: Foreign Domestic Workers in Canada*, eds. Abigail Bakan and Daiva Stasiulis. Toronto: University of Toronto Press, 29–52.

Bakan, Abigail and Daiva Stasiulis. 2005. *Negotiating Citizenship: Migrant Women in Canada and the Global System*. Toronto: University of Toronto Press.

Briones, Leah. 2009. Empowering Migrant Women: Why Rights and Agency Are Not Enough. Burlington, Vt: Ashgate.

Brown, Michael. 1997. *RePlacing Citizenship: AIDS Activism and Radical Democracy*. New York: Guilford Press.

Goss, Jon and Bruce Lindquist. 1995. "Conceptualizing Labour Migration: A Structuration Perspective." *International Migration Review* 29 (2): 317–51.

Guevarra, Anna. 2009. *Marketing Dreams, Manufacturing Heroes: The Transnational Labour Brokering of Filipino Workers*. Rutgers, N.J: Rutgers University Press.

Harvey, David. 2005. *A Brief History of Neoliberalism*. Oxford, UK: OUP.

Katz, Cindy. 2001. "On the Grounds of Globalization: A Topography of Feminist Political Engagement." *Signs* 26 (4): 1213–34.

Kershaw, Baz. 1992. *The Politics of Performance: Radical Theatre as Cultural Intervention*. New York: Routledge.

Lutz, Helma, and Ew Palenga-Mollenbeck. 2010. "Care Work Migration in Germany: Semi-Compliance and Complicity." *Social Policy & Society* 9 (3): 419–30.

Mahler, Sarah and Patricia Pessar. 2001. "Gendered Geographies of Power: Analyzing Gender Across Transnational Spaces." *Identities* 7(4): 441–59.

National Domestic Workers Association. 2017. *Domestic Workers at the Women's March*. https://www. domesticworkers.org/domestic-workers-at-the-womens-march Accessed on 1 February 2017.

Newman, Janet. 2013. "Spaces of Power: Feminism, Neoliberalism, and Gendered Labor." *Social Politics* 20 (2): 200–21.

Pratt, Geraldine. 1997. "Stereotypes and Ambivalence: The Construction of Domestic Workers in Vancouver, BC." *Gender, Space, Culture* 4 (2): 159–77.

Pratt, Geraldine. 1999. "From Registered Nurse to Registered Nanay: Discursive Geographies of Filipina Domestic Workers in Vancouver, BC." *Economic Geographies* 75 (3): 215–36.

Razack, Sherene. 2002. *Race, Space, and the Law: Unmapping White Settler Society*. Toronto: Between the Lines Publishers.

Rodriguez, Robyn. 2010. *Migrants for Export: How the Philippine State Brokers Workers to the World*. Minneapolis: University of Minnesota Press.

Romero, Mary, Valerie Preston and Wenona Giles, ed. 2014. *When Care Work Goes Global: Locating the Social Relations of Domestic Work*. Burlington, Vt: Ashgate.

Snow, David A., and Benford, Robert D. 1992. "Master Frames and Cycles of Protest." In *Frontiers in Social Movement Theory*, eds. Aldon D. Morris & Carol McClurg Mueller. New Haven: Yale University Press, 133–55.

Tungohan, Ethel. 2013. "Reconceptualizing Motherhood, Reconceptualizing Resistance: Migrant Domestic Workers, Transnational Hyper-Maternalism, and Activism." *International Feminist Journal of Politics* 15 (1): 39–57.

Chapter 41

Overview

Idle No More swept across North America in 2013 and 2014. It was a movement to transform Canadian politics led by Indigenous women, but the founders and leaders did not proclaim that Idle No More was *either* an Indigenous movement *or* a women's movement. Instead, they integrated gender and Indigeneity into their intersectional work. Sonja John traces the relations between the Idle No More founders, and Indigenous women theorists more broadly, and the intellectual and political structure within which they must operate. Indigenous women have experienced some of the harshest manifestations of colonialism and patriarchy, but white-dominated feminist theory did not speak to their lives. Protecting land and water was central to Idle No More activism. Inextricably tied to the land were questions of gender and women's sexuality and the politics of the production of knowledge. The Canadian state, which threatens the security of the land, is a patriarchal state as well as a colonial one. Idle No More emphasizes the importance of knowledge and education so that Indigenous and non-Indigenous people in Canada can acquire a more complete understanding of the gendered impacts of colonialism, rather than just accepting the standard history-book accounts that privilege the interests of white people.

Idle No More—Indigenous Activism and Feminism

Sonja John

Introduction

The grassroots movement Idle No More spread over the North American continent like a fire on the prairie. In October 2012 Sheelah McLean, Sylvia McAdam, Nina Wilson and Jessica Gordon, four women from the Canadian province of Saskatchewan, protested the federal omnibus budget bills C-45 and C-31, that would substantially diminish First Nations treaty, sovereignty and land rights. Idle No More locates itself within the framework of Indigenous renaissance, decoloniality and Indigenous[1] activism. Although founded and led by Indigenous women, this group does neither define itself as a women's movement nor as an Indigenous movement. "We are a movement led by Indigenous women" (Sylvia McAdam, June 14, 2013). Nonetheless, Idle No More members contemplate how feminist theory and praxis may have influenced the movement. Indeed, the movement applies strategies that have been theorized within Indigenous feminism for decades. Looking at Idle No More in particular, I will identify possible interleaving and commonalities as well as differences between feminist and Indigenous decolonial concerns. Exemplified by the emancipative character of Idle No More I will show under which circumstances struggles under the flags of resource conflicts and decoloniality can complement Indigenous feminism. Therefore, in the following I will look at the activities and goals of the movement within the frameworks of Indigenous feminism as well as postcolonial feminism.

John, Sonja. (2015). "Idle No More-Indigenous Activism and Feminism." *Theory in Action*, 8(4), 38.

Complicated Subject Positions

Indigenous women, including the Idle No More activists, speak from complicated subject positions; on the one hand they negotiate their individual rights in postindustrial nation states, on the other they demand their collective sovereignty rights as members of First Nations, exercising power over their Indigenous territories. The position of Indigenous women is further complicated and weakened by internal conflicts introduced into First Nations communities by the dominant society. Additionally, even the sentiments of Indigenous women towards feminisms are ambiguous; some do not see themselves included by feminists who are unwilling to understand Indigenous women in their full historical and contemporary contexts, while others view feminist positions as valid and feminist theory as helpful and adequate to articulate critique on unequal social, economic and political conditions (Green 2007, 20f.). However, Indigenous feminists are being accused of colonial attitudes in their own communities (see below).

. . .

In regards to the characteristics of Idle No More I refer to their own statements which I interpret in front of the background of Indigenous feminist epistemologies. Without explicit reference to feminist critique and analyses, Idle No More follows the suggestions of Verna St. Denis, to choose this intersectional approach to not only gain an understanding of the circumstances but also of the practices and justifications of those who are responsible for these circumstances (St. Denis 2007, 43). Although Indigenous women do not share one single, common culture, they share similar experiences of colonization that have changed Indigenous societies considerably.

The special relationship between Indigenous or First Nations and the Canadian government is founded on international treaties with the British Crown and finds recognition in federal law. The recognition of these treaty rights and the perpetuation of this special nation-to-nation relationship have always been at the heart of Indigenous political struggles and form the basic demands of Idle No More. They fight an omnibus budget bill that in its consequences undermines the nation-to-nation relationship in a colonial act in order to appropriate and expropriate Indigenous resources.

Since Idle No More resists current politics of the Canadian government, the context analysis of this paper addresses the situation in contemporary Canada. Under the conservative government—since 2006 led by Prime Minister Stephen Harper—the situation of First Nations has deteriorated to a degree that led Attawapiskat Chief Theresa Spence to declare a state of emergency for her reserve in October 2011. In December 2012, inspired by the actions of Idle No More, she began a six-week lasting hunger strike to pressure the Harper government to fulfill its share of treaty obligations (Van Dusen/Tomas 2013). The analysis could be broadened to include other settler states because the practices of colonization in other regions are similar in application and results.

This article is based on presentations by the Idle No More founders Sylvia McAdam and Sheela McLean as well as the organizers Alexandria Wilson and Erica Lee at the Native American and Indigenous Studies Annual Meeting on June 15, 2013. . . .

Idle No More: The Formation of a Social Movement

Idle No More formed to protest bill C-45 and bill C-31 at the end of the year 2012. This omnibus budget bill, introduced on October 18, 2012, would allow companies access to untapped resources by lifting regulations in those two areas hindering unlimited resource extraction: environmental protection and land and sovereignty rights of First Nations. A considerable amount of desired natural resources—predominantly oil—is located in Indigenous territories. Idle No More drew attention to the crucial points of the budget bill, especially to the proposed changes to the Indian Act and the Navigable Waters Protection Act; these would substantially impact sovereignty rights of First Nations as well as environmental protection policies. Three Indigenous women Sylvia McAdam (Nehiyaw—in English Cree), Nina Wilson (Nakota and Nehiyaw) and Jessica Gordon (Pasqua), first discussed the bill in an internet chat room. When they decided to educate the public outside of the World Wide Web about this scheme, they drew in non-Indigenous political activist Sheelah McLean, well-known in Saskatoon for her anti racist and anti-discrimination work. . . .

The Twitter hashtag IdleNoMore rapidly gained momentum and weight. In December 2012, the movement succeeded in carrying the protest from the internet into the streets of dozens of North American cities. At the second National Day of Action in January 2013 the protests gained global scope with rounddance flashmobs in North American cities and supporting declarations of solidarity in front of numerous Canadian embassies on different continents. The goal of the movement is to, "give the voices of our people a forum," to direct attention to the continuous constraints of fundamental rights and to pressure the Canadian government through collective actions to uphold existing rights and respect treaties as well as protect environmental laws (Idle No More 2012).

Idle No More defends treaties, Indigenous sovereignty and water; it's that simple (Sylvia McAdam, June 14, 2013). Of course, it is not that simple. On different levels Idle No More faces unequal and unfavorable power relations. Although the law has been passed in the meantime, Idle No More continues to educate the public. The movement criticizes not only the amendments themselves but also the social and political contexts in which these changes occur.

I will look at the debates Idle No More intervenes in with the help of Anibal Quijano's (2000) concepts of coloniality.[2] According to Quijano the formation of the colonial power matrix depends on four dimensions: (1) control over authority; (2) appropriation of land; (3) control over gender and sexuality; and (4) control over subjectivity and knowledge. Further, Quijano stresses the effects of the interrelations of these spheres and how they limit access to education, knowledge and capital and how these, in turn, connect to racist discrimination. Along the four spheres defined by Quijano I will now introduce the goals of Idle No More.

Control over Authority

The Indian Act, passed in 1876 . . . regulates who receives the official status *Indian*, how Indigenous societies are to be politically structured and governed, and how the Canadian government administers their land and resources. The traditional leaders and elder councils were replaced by nominated *chiefs*. These *Indian Act chiefs* take upon the role of administrator for the settler state. Canada established male dominated administrative structures within (formerly mainly matrilineal and matriarchal) Indigenous societies. . . . Idle No More criticizes the representation of the chiefs and advocates for a more basic democratic organization of First Nations. In its work Idle No More stresses independence from and keeping a distance to the AFN; it does not intend to copy hierarchical structures within the grassroots movement. Idle No More also criticizes the Canadian state's failure to consult the AFN before introducing the law; this constitutes a violation of the principle of consent. However, Idle No More participants were even more appalled when they learned that some AFN chiefs met in consultations and gave their consent to Bill C-45—without communicating the issue to the Indigenous communities concerned, the very communities they represent (Sylvia McAdam, June 14, 2013). This may indicate that some chiefs are more committed to the Canadian state then to their own communities.

Most First Nations do not have accountability procedures in place to report to their members; they only report to the Canadian government (McAdam, June 15, 2013). The endeavors of Idle No More to pluralize the access to power and to expose the omnibus budget bill as a continuation of colonization did not remain unnoticed by the settler state. In August 2013 the Canadian Security Intelligence Service declared that Idle No More was under observation. The activities of the movement were characterized as a threat to national security. Reports of the observation were passed on to the AFN. Ironically, the chiefs learned from the Canadian Security Intelligence Service of the needs and demands of the very people they officially represent (CBC 2013).

However, the AFN cannot be confined in a black-and-white dichotomy. Several chiefs and major opposition parties in Ottawa have co-signed a joint declaration demanding "a fundamental change in the relationship of First Nations and the Crown" (Christoff 2013). In pre-Idle No More-times this alliance and this outcome was unthinkable. . . .

In order to illustrate political pitfalls, Idle No More points out the problematic changes to the Indian Act and the establishing of an androcentric system of control in Indigenous societies. Foreign control over authority has allowed for the continued dispossession of Indigenous land, resources, and rights.

Appropriation of Land

Idle No More argues that the settler state uses bill C-45 to continue its colonial conquering expedition. . . . With the changes to the Indian Act under bill C-45 (paragraphs 37, 39 and 40) the disposal of Indigenous land is considerably more easily achieved (Parliament of Canada 2012a). These amendments can be seen in a historic continuum; the founding and rise of settler states like the USA and Canada are based on Indigenous dispossession, dislocation and at times extinction. Bill C-45 follows elimination politics (from warfare to assimilation) that intend to separate the Indigenous population of the

Americas from their land. Idle No More intervenes in these concrete resource wars with its rejection of the underlying capitalist exploitation logic as well as the white supremacist attitude of manifest destiny.

> We have never surrendered our land, our water or our resources; they were stolen from us. . . . Decolonization means restitution to First Nations what rightfully belongs to them. Justice means restitution. Justice means that my people not only survive but that they are able to flourish (McAdam, June 14, 2013).

In Native American Studies the term survivance is used to express the resistant aspect of Indigenous survival despite the overarching conditions (Vizenor 2008, 19). The Muscogee-Creek historian Donald Fixico views Native Americans as considerably underestimated underdog champions: "The rest of society should look towards Indian Country and acknowledge the resilience of Native people and the rebuilding of their nations" (Fixico 2013, 226). Idle No More takes part in this self determined Native rebuilding.

. . .

The concept of land is the most fundamental aspect of Indigeneity. Land is a barometer of intact communities, a marker of Native identity, the focal point of land-based creation stories and sacral practices, as well as a resource for cultural and socioeconomic stability. When Sylvia McAdam went into the woods to build a hunting cabin on treaty land and encouraged other Natives to do the same, she challenged the legitimacy of the Indian Act, the very foundation of the administration of First Nations' land, resources and self-government. Idle No More criticizes settler colonialism and resource extraction; however, it does not agitate against settlers but rather against continued colonialism and unleashed capitalism. The movement turns towards settlers because everybody depends on clean water and, as Idle No More stresses, only through combined efforts is change possible.

Control over Gender and Sexuality

In their analysis of contemporary internal political conflicts in First Nations communities the Idle No More women point to the double form of discrimination based on race and gender. They argue that only through the exclusion of women from political roles was the introduction of the omnibus budget bill possible. The term *femicide* is used in the context of Indigenous women when referring to the *missing women* (Troian 2013) and also when referring to the systematic separation of Native women from their home communities and from leadership roles. Andrea Smith (2005) explained how colonization of First Nations became possible through gender-based violence and the forceful imposition of European gender roles upon Indigenous societies. Indigenous feminists stress that in the process of colonization Indigenous cultures internalized gender based discrimination that now continues to oppress women (St. Denis 2007, 45). Andrea Smith argues that decolonization and sovereignty are impossible to recuperate as long as Indigenous societies hold on to patriarchal gender systems introduced by agents of the settler state (Smith 2007, 100). . . .

An example of double discrimination along the categories of gender and race is the case of Jeanette Corbiere Lavall. In 1970 Corbiere Lavall called upon the courts because she saw herself discriminated by Paragraph 12 (1) (b), which spelled out that she would lose her tribal membership—and consequently her status as an Indigenous woman and the contiguous (land) rights—if she were to marry her non-Native partner. She lost the lawsuit. In a discussion of the Lavell-decision author Kathleen Jamieson formulates:

> One thing is clear—that to be born poor, an Indian and a female is to be a member of the most disadvantaged minority in Canada today, a citizen minus. It is to be victimized and utterly powerless and to be by government decree without legal recourse of any kind (Jamieson 1980, 92).

When educating the public about contemporary Indigenous existence in Canada, Idle No More also draws upon the debates held by Indigenous feminists who highlight the harmful consequences of the colonial Indian Act to tribal (USA) respective band (Canada) membership and the status of Native women. Without formal Indian status Natives lose the right of band membership and consequently the right to live on reserves. Before 1985, two-thirds of Indigenous people in Canada had lost their status and their land (Lawrence 2003, 6). In 1985 the Canadian government changed the membership criteria of the Indian Act and *permitted* First Nations to draft their own membership rules. Many of the First Nations voted to keep the externally introduced, yet in the meantime familiarized, discriminatory rules.[3]

The marginal subject position of Native women finds its equivalence in the movement. In the 1960s and 1970s many women were active in the Red Power movement but subordinated themselves under men. . . . During that time women stayed in the background and did not articulate gender cleavage. Lorelei DeCora Means explains:

> We are American Indian women, in that order. We are oppressed, first and foremost, as American Indians, as peoples colonized by the United States of America, not as women (Lorelei DeCora Means, cited in Jaimes/Halsey 1992, 314).

As is true for many *women of color,* Indigenous women are confronted with the expectation that they should be loyal to their own people first, not to their gender. When they criticize oppression within their own communities, they tend to face accusations of betrayal and colonialism. Fan Blaney of the Aboriginal Women's Action Network of Canada states: "Patriarchy is so ingrained in our communities that it is now seen as a 'traditional trait'" (Blaney 2003, 158).

Hence, Blaney sees the main task of Indigenous feminism as addressing the internalized oppression of women within their home communities; otherwise this part of the colonial legacy would further politically weaken Indigenous societies. Bonita Lawrence and Kim Anderson (2005, 3) warn that band leaders should not reduce this debate to women's issues or misrepresent it as a threat to Native self determination. Instead, they declare, attacks against Indigenous women—physically as well as politically—constitute attacks against Indigenous sovereignty. Throughout Indian Country women are referred to as the backbone of the nation. . . . This short insight into Indigenous feminism shows that "Native women's engagement with feminist politics is much more complex than generally depicted" (Smith 2007, 97).

Idle No More does not view women as an independent, separate group that has to fight against men. Instead, it views women as part of a collective that exists to achieve better conditions for everybody. Its members fight not only for women's rights but for group rights "together with all solidary people inside and outside of Canada" (McAdam, June 14, 2013). With this approach Idle No More expresses its intersectional understanding of the conditions of oppression that are interlinked and can only be dealt with satisfactorily if reduced to individual issues.

There is an obvious strong presence of women in the movement. Sylvia McAdam reckons that the call to *defend the children* spoke more to women than to men. In a consultation with the elders' council—the traditional leadership that exists parallel the Indian Act chiefs—about the consequences of the controversial bill C-45 the elders declared the traditional Nehiyaw law *Notawamissouin,* meaning protection of children in a broader sense:

> *Notawamissouin* means to defend for the children. And not just Indigenous children—all children. But it extends beyond that. You also have to defend for the animal children, the tree nation, the winged nation, the earth nation, all their children. And this law is sacred. It's peaceful, it's prayerful, and it's profound because it's not only that you are defending for this generation in

our time but all the seven generations ahead (McAdam, June 14, 2013).

Control over Subjectivity and Knowledge

The movement focuses on educating the public about the ecological consequences of bill C-45 and about the negative effects this law has on Indigenous self-determination . . .

> Even with our resounding "No, you do not have our consent" they still put it through on December 14th. And it's unprecedented in the history of their Canadian Parliament that a bill that huge, a 450-page omnibus bill, to go through their Parliament in such a short time. It was introduced in the middle of October and became law on December14th which is unheard of it. There was no proper debate, no proper consultation, no free prior and informed consent, nothing (McAdam June 14, 2013).

. . .

> The movement also addresses interlinked issues of inequality in Canada. The workshop "Idle? Know More!," held in summer 2013, dealt with the construction of the *Other* in the dominant society over the markers race, class, gender and sexuality. The workshop addressed the question how these practices of inequality and colonial oppression are being justified today (SAFE 2013). Idle No More sparked discussions on the issues raised that led to various conferences, talks, and lectures, many of which were live streamed over the internet. Thus, an internet chat room discussion of four women has evolved into a global revolutionary education movement—a movement that is founded on the principles of non-hierarchy, broad participation, and inclusion.

Idle No More does not only want to voice opposition; its members want to be part of a collective that is non-oppressive. Sheelah McLean expresses the openness of the movement when she invites people to become pro-active:

> You ask us: 'What can you do?' We ask you: 'What do you think needs to be done?' 'How

can we help you to reach your goals?' (Sheelah McLean, June 15, 2013).

Keeping with the grassroots principle McLean stresses that every voice has the same value. People should not wait until things get done for them but should get together and find solutions. With the claim to self presentation Idle No More postulates, they aim to "undo a form of patriarchy" (McLean, June 15, 2013).

Indirectly Idle No More follows Audre Lorde's call to address racist laws by channeling rage constructively to bring about change. Rage and dissatisfaction voiced by the female elements are characterized as the roots of change and development in many Indigenous creation stories (i.e. Walker 1983, 208ff.). . . . The lawyer Sylvia McAdam is not only politically active, she is also personally affected by the developments of increasing resource extraction on Indigenous land without respecting treaty laws; her father's land is subject to massive logging he did not consent to, although the land should be protected from intrusion under Treaty 6. While acting locally and building hunting cabins on treaty land McAdam also uses her legal tools to articulate resistance against the unconstitutional bills and to transport this knowledge. . . . Idle No More aims to democratize access to knowledge and to prioritize Indigenous knowledge.

Educating, Not Accusing

The movement Idle No More was formed to protest an omnibus budget bill. It drew attention to the consequences of bill C-45 and bill C 31—both the end of treaty relations between Canada and Indigenous nations and the harmful ecological consequences the bills held for the continent. Protest by Indigenous groups against laws detrimentally affecting their lives and group rights is not new. What is new is the quality and the approach of this mass movement. While the Red Power movement of past decades defined itself by conflict and used Native identity to keep the movement exclusive, Idle No More stresses commonalities and invites everybody to join. Idle No More shows that Indigenous feminism—as political strategy and political project—can be strengthened through alliances built by engagement, participation and support by Native men and non-Natives working together. The emancipative character of Idle No More shows that feminist agendas and Indigenous struggles for decolonization do not have to contradict each other. Idle No More separates feminist rhetoric from the—in Indigenous contexts—frequently voiced allegation of acting colonial. Although they do share the Indigenous-feminist analysis of sexist and patriarchal power relations, the movement does not identify itself as feminist

per se. Idle No More problematizes the shift in power structures in Native communities not by accusing but by educating. By applying this participative and inclusive approach the emancipative character of Idle No More in the field of resource struggles and decoloniality can complement Indigenous feminism. By setting the anti colonial struggle as central, Idle No More questions the legitimacy of (patriarchal) nation states. Such a political project imagines for colonized—and non-colonized—societies a more desirable, more just, and more sustainably oriented world beyond nation states.

Notes

1. When possible I use the self-referential term of Indigenous nations. When trans-national contexts are concerned I use the terms Indigenous and First Nations that express the unique quality of these groups as first nations and also transports the connectedness with the land.
2. Indigenous scholars generally describe the situation of external control experienced by First Nations as colonial or coloniality and not as postcolonial,

while simultaneously valuing postcolonial theory for providing the language to articulate the conflicts (Wilson 2004, 69f.).

3. The Mi'kmaq lawyer Pamela D. Palmater (2011) argues for the introduction of more inclusive instead of exclusive membership rules; rather than measuring blood-quantum, cultural determinants should have more weight.

Literature

Blaney, Fay, 2003: Aboriginal Women's Action Network. In: Anderson, Kim/Lawrence, Bonita (ed.): *Strong Women Stories. Native Vision and Community Survival.* Toronto: Sumach Press, 156–71.

CBC, 2013: Thoughts on CSIS and Idle No More. Internet (audiofile; August 12, 2013): www.cbc.ca./bluesky/episodes/2013/08/12/thoughts-on-csis-and-idle-no-more (September 23, 2013).

Christoff, Stefan, 2013: Idle No More and Colonial Canada. In: Aljazeera, 30.1.2013. Internet: www.aljazeera.com/indepth/opinion/2013/01/20131289123344980.html (December 14, 2013).

Fixico, Donald L., 2013: *Indian Resilience and Rebuilding. Indigenous Nations in the Modern American West.* Phoenix: University of Arizona Press.

Green, Joyce, 2007: Taking Account of Aboriginal Feminism. In: Green, Joyce, (ed.): *Making Space for Indigenous Feminism.* Winnipeg: Fernwood Publishing, 20–32.

Idle No More, 2012: History of Idle No More Grassroots Movement. (December 10, 2013). Internet: www.idlenomore1.blogspot.ca/p/background-on-idle-no-more.html (April 15, 2013).

Jaimes, M. Annette/Halsey, Theresa, 1992: American Indian Women. At the Center of Indigenous Resistance in North America. In: M. Annette Jaimes (ed.): *State of Native America. Strong Women Stories. Native Vision and Community Survival.* Boston, 311–44.

Jamieson, Kathleen, 1980: *Indian Women and the Law in Canada. Citizen Minus.* Ottawa, Minister of Supply and Services.

Lawrence, Bonita, 2003. Gender, Race, and the Regulation of Native Identity in Canada and the United States. An Overview. In: *Hypatia*, 18 (2), 3–31. http://dx.doi.org/10.1111/j.1527-2001.2003.tb00799.x

Lawrence, Bonita/Anderson, Kim, 2005. Indigenous Women. The State of our Nations. In: *Atlantis*, 29 (2). Internet: http://forms.msvu.ca/atlantis/vol/292pdf/292intro.PDF (September 25, 2013)

McAdam, Sylvia, 2013: Personal Interview held on June 14, 2013.

Mihesuah, Devon Abbot, 2003: *Indigenous American Women. Decolonization, Empowerment, Activism.* Lincoln: University of Nebraska Press.

Palmater, Pamela D., 2011: *Beyond Blood. Rethinking Indigenous Identity.* Saskatoon, SK: Purich Publishing.

Parliament of Canada, 2012a: *Jobs and Growth Act. (Changes of the Indian Act in Bill C-45)* Internet: www.parl.gc.ca/HousePublications/Publication.aspx?Language=E&Mode=1&DocId=5942521&File=194#6 (November 4, 2013).

Quijano, Anibal, 2000: Coloniality of Power, Eurocentrism, and Latin America. In: *Views from the South* 1 (3), 533–80.

SAFE, 2013: Internet: www.safe-2011.blogspot.ca (September 23, 2013).

Schilling, Vincent, 2014: ICTM Exclusive Conversation: 2014 Nobel Peace Prize Nominee James Anaya. (13.2.2014). Internet: http://indiancountrytodaymedianetwork.com/2014/02/13/ictmn exclusive-conversation-2014-nobel-peace-prize-nominee-james anaya-153543 (June 23, 2014).

Smith, Andrea, 2005: *Conquest: Sexual Violence and American Indian Genocide*. Cambridge, Mass: South End Press.

Smith, Andrea, 2007: Native Feminism, Sovereignty and Social Change. In: Green, Joyce, (ed.): *Making Space for Indigenous Feminism*. Winnipeg: Fernwood Publishing, 93–107.

St. Denis, Verna, 2007: Feminism Is for Everybody. Aboriginal Women, Feminism and Diversity. In: Green, Joyce, (ed.): *Making Space for Indigenous Feminism*. Winnipeg: Fernwood Publishing, 33–52.

Troian, Martha, 2013: Taking Control. Indigenous in Canada Compile Own Database on Missing and Murdered Women. (September 25, 2013) Internet: www.indiancountrytodaymedianetwork.com/2013/09/25/taking-control-canadas-aboriginals-compile-own-database-missing-and murdered-women-151417 (November 18, 2013).

Van Dusen, Julie/Thomas, Megan, 2013: Chief Theresa Spence to End Hunger Strike. In: *CBC News*, 23.1.2013. Internet: www.cbc.ca/news/politics/chief-theresa-spence-to-end-hunger-strike-today-1.1341571 (November 3, 2013).

Vizenor, Gerald (ed.), 2008: *Survivance. Narratives of Native Presence*. Lincoln: University of Nebraska Press.

Walker, James R., 1983: *Lakota Myth*. (Edited by Elaine A. Jahner). Lincoln: University of Nebraska Press.

Wilson, Angela Cavender, 2004: Reclaiming Our Humanity. Decolonizing and the Recovery of Indigenous Knowledge. In: Mihesuah, Devon Abbott/Wilson, Angela Cavender (ed.): *Indigenizing the Academy. Transforming Scholarship and Empowering Communities*. Lincoln: University of Nebraska Press, 69–88.